Shopping Center Development Handbook

Third Edition

ULI Development Handbook Series

Urban Land Institute

About ULI–the Urban Land Institute

ULI–the Urban Land Institute is a nonprofit education and research institute that is supported and directed by its members. Its mission is to provide responsible leadership in the use of land to enhance the total environment.

ULI sponsors educational programs and forums to encourage an open international exchange of ideas and sharing of experience; initiates research that anticipates emerging land use trends and issues and proposes creative solutions based on that research; provides advisory services; and publishes a wide variety of materials to disseminate information on land use and development.

Established in 1936, the Institute today has more than 15,000 members and associates from more than 50 countries representing the entire spectrum of the land use and development disciplines. They include developers, builders, property owners, investors, architects, public officials, planners, real estate brokers, appraisers, attorneys, engineers, financiers, academics, students, and librarians. ULI members contribute to higher standards of land use by sharing their knowledge and experience. The Institute has long been recognized as one of America's most respected and widely quoted sources of objective information on urban planning, growth, and development.

Richard M. Rosan
President

For more information about ULI and the resources that it offers related to shopping center development and a variety of other real estate and urban development issues, visit ULI's Web site at www.uli.org.

Cover photo: Phillips Place; Charlotte, North Carolina

Project Staff

Rachelle L. Levitt
Senior Vice President, Policy and Practice
Publisher

Gayle Berens
Vice President, Real Estate Development Practice

Michael D. Beyard
Vice President, Strategic Development
Senior Resident Fellow, Retail
Project Director

Nancy H. Stewart
Director, Book Program

Eileen Hughes
Managing Editor

Barbara M. Fishel/Editech
Manuscript Editor

Helene Redmond/HYR Graphics
Book Design/Layout

Meg Batdorff
Cover Design

Kim Rusch
Graphic Artist

Maria-Rose Cain
Word Processing

Craig Chapman
Director of Publishing Operations

Recommended bibliographic listing:

Beyard, Michael D., W. Paul O'Mara, et al. *Shopping Center Development Handbook.* Third Edition. Washington, D.C.: ULI–the Urban Land Institute, 1999.

ULI Catalog Number: S30
International Standard Book Number: 0-87420-852-1
Library of Congress Catalog Card Number: 99-61546

Copyright ©1999 by ULI–the Urban Land Institute
1025 Thomas Jefferson Street, N.W.
Suite 500 West
Washington, D.C. 20007-5201

Third Printing, 2006

Books in the ULI Development Handbook Series
(formerly Community Builders Handbook Series)
Business and Industrial Park Development Handbook, 1988
Downtown Development Handbook, Second Edition, 1992
Mixed-Use Development Handbook, 1987
Office Development Handbook, Second Edition, 1998
Residential Development Handbook, Second Edition, 1990
Resort Development Handbook, 1997

Acknowledgments

The Urban Land Foundation (ULF), as part of its commitment to support ULI's core research program, is providing major funding for the new and revised editions of the ULI Development Handbook Series being published during the last half of this decade. The *Shopping Center Development Handbook* was funded in part by grants from ULF, for which the Urban Land Institute is very grateful.

Like all Urban Land Institute handbooks, this one is the product of the collective effort of many individuals. Although it is impossible to mention everyone who participated in this project, a number of individuals deserve special acknowledgment and thanks. Since this is the third edition, much of the basic information—including the history of shopping center development, types of shopping centers and tenants, planning, design, and leasing—was drawn from previous editions and updated to reflect current practices. So we would like to thank first the authors of the second edition, John Casazza and Frank Spink, for providing us with such a strong base of knowledge on which to build.

The authors of the case studies—Michael Baker, Steven Fader, Christine Kaufman, Terry Jill Lassar, and David Mulvihill—deserve thanks and special recognition for their thorough research and their commitment to digging for information that often was hard to get. We also would like to thank the shopping center developers, architects, and designers who spent time with the case study authors and provided the written materials, data, and photographs that we needed for each case study. They always were available to answer our questions as we double-checked information, and they were equally accommodating of our sometimes demanding production schedule. We thank the International Council of Shopping Centers for providing the sample shopping center lease and the sample merchants' association bylaws that we have included in the appendices, and we thank the publishers of the periodicals who graciously allowed us to reprint several articles as feature boxes in this handbook. Also, we would like to thank the members of ULI, especially the members of the Commercial, Retail Development, and Entertainment Development councils, for their support.

Finally, we would like to thank the Urban Land Institute staff for its skill and dedication in bringing this book together. A book of this size and complexity requires the help of many individuals, and they all deserve praise for the results. We especially want to thank the editorial staff for ensuring that the information was clearly written and presented in a way that would make it most useful to our many audiences. We would like to thank Eileen Hughes for managing the day-to-day editorial process and doing a great job of making sure that all the pieces came together; Barbara Fishel for doing a wonderful and comprehensive edit of the entire text; Helene Redmond for doing a superb job of designing and laying out the entire book; Diann Stanley-Austin for handling the printing schedule; Meg Batdorff for designing the cover (many covers in fact); and Nancy Stewart for overseeing the entire process and ensuring that every detail was taken care of to her usual high standards. We also would like to thank Michael Baker for selecting and captioning all the photos and feature boxes; Jeff Hinkle for editing the feature boxes; Joan Campbell for searching her databases for obscure information that we needed; and Ronnie Van Alstyne for taking care of so many assignments. Finally, we would like to thank Rachelle Levitt and Gayle Berens for their support throughout the book's lengthy gestation period.

And to all others who had a hand in this work, we extend our sincere appreciation and thanks.

Michael D. Beyard
W. Paul O'Mara

Authors

Principal Authors

Michael D. Beyard
Vice President, Strategic Development, and
    Senior Resident Fellow, Retail
ULI–the Urban Land Institute
Washington, D.C.

W. Paul O'Mara
CMA Management Consultants
Vienna, Virginia

Case Study Authors

Michael Baker
Senior Associate
ULI–the Urban Land Institute
Washington, D.C.

Steven Fader
Steven Fader Architect
Los Angeles, California

Christine Kaufman
Director
American Communities Fund
Fannie Mae
Washington, D.C.

Terry Jill Lassar
Communications Consultant
Portland, Oregon

David Mulvihill
Director, Information Services
ULI–the Urban Land Institute
Washington, D.C.

W. Paul O'Mara
CMA Management Consultants
Vienna, Virginia

Contents

Foreword

This handbook is the third in the completely redesigned ULI Development Handbook Series, a set of volumes on real estate development that traces its roots back to 1947, when ULI published the first edition of the *Community Builders Handbook*. That edition was revised and updated several times over the next 25 years, and in 1975, ULI initiated the Community Builders Handbook Series with the publication of the *Industrial Development Handbook*. A number of titles were published in this series over a period of years, covering industrial (later called business park), residential, shopping center, office, mixed-use, downtown, and recreational development. The publication of the *Resort Development Handbook* in 1997 marked the complete redesign of the handbook series and its renaming as the ULI Development Handbook Series.

This also is the third edition of ULI's *Shopping Center Development Handbook* itself. Chapter 7 includes 15 all-new case studies covering cutting-edge shopping centers that highlight the latest trends in shopping center development, including town center, transit-oriented, inner-city, streetfront, outlet, off-price (power), and entertainment projects as well as the more conventional neighborhood, community, and regional centers. Cases include centers that have been renovated and expanded as well as new centers, and centers found in downtown as well as suburban locations.

A completely new Chapter 8 predicts the future direction of the shopping center industry. All other chapters have been updated to reflect changes in shopping center development practices since the second edition was published in 1985. These chapters cover shopping center types, feasibility, planning and design, renovation and expansion, tenants, and operations and management. All-new feature boxes and photographs round out the new edition, covering projects in Europe, Asia, South America, and Australia, as well as the United States, some of which already have opened and others that are planned for future development.

To succeed in today's rapidly changing and overbuilt retail market, a project must be grounded in an understanding of the complexities and nuances of the changes that are buffeting the shopping center industry and its developer must know where the industry is headed. The objective of this handbook, therefore, as well as of all the handbooks in the series, is to provide a broad overview of the land use and real estate sector under discussion and to guide the development process toward projects that best meet public as well as private goals and that lead to more livable communities. This book therefore presents a comprehensive and lengthy discourse on all aspects of shopping center development and describes what ULI believes to be the best practices of the industry. As with other forms of development, there are many ways to succeed, and ULI reflects that variety in its handbook series.

Michael D. Beyard
Project Director

Shopping Center
Development Handbook

1. Introduction

The shopping center has been perhaps the most successful land use, real estate, and retail business concept of the 20th century, and it has become the most powerful and adaptable machine for consumption that the world has ever seen. Being to the 20th century what the department store was to the 19th century, the modern shopping center is largely a post–World War II concept, although its prototypes were created earlier in the century. Today shopping centers take many forms, from the archetypal suburban shopping malls and neighborhood and community centers to more specialized forms such as power, convenience, entertainment, outlet, town center, resort, transit-oriented, off-price, and vertical specialty centers. The variety of shopping center types and forms continues to expand rapidly, and hybrids are becoming common. Increasingly, the distinctions between shopping center types are blurring to the point that some centers are difficult to categorize as one type or another.

Since the 1950s, shopping centers have played a major role in the economy of the United States. In 1950, according to records kept by the Urban Land Institute, only 100 centers existed, and they were small neighborhood and community centers. By 1953, the number of shopping centers had tripled, and by the end of 1998, according to the National Research Bureau, 43,662 shopping centers existed in this country, containing 5.3 billion square feet of leasable space and having $1.03 trillion total retail sales. Eighty-seven percent of all shopping centers had less than 200,000 square feet of leasable space, however, and these smaller centers accounted for only 54 percent of total shopping center sales. Since 1950, the percent of retail sales occurring in shopping centers has grown rapidly. By 1974, it was estimated that more than 25 percent of all nonautomotive retail sales were made in shopping centers. By 1982, the percentage had risen to almost 42 percent, and, by 1996, it was an estimated 52 percent.[1]

Shopping centers continue to be highly specialized forms of development. In the recent past, the largest shopping centers were developed, owned, and managed by entrepreneurial firms whose primary real estate activity was confined to shopping centers or to a single shopping center. Some of the larger national retailers—Sears, JCPenney, Dayton-Hudson, the May Company, for example—even had development subsidiaries. Today, pension funds, insurance companies, and other institutions tend to dominate the field, and many shopping centers are developed and owned by real estate investment trusts (REITs). Although the dominance of large firms is less common in smaller neighborhood and community shop-

One important element characterizing shopping centers and making them different from other commercial land uses is a unified architectural theme. Pattaya Central Festival Center near Bangkok, Thailand, features an architectural design by RTKL that revolves around Thai festivals and folktales. Fables recounting how the fox freed the lion or the tiger earned its stripes are illlustrated through sculptures, fountains, and paving patterns.

Twenty years after it was first constructed in 1967, Fashion Island in Newport Beach, California, had been upstaged by more freeway-accessible and up-to-date shopping centers. The Irvine Company repositioned the center by creating an animated, open-air seaside "village" that enabled the center to survive in a highly competitive market.

ping centers, numerous examples exist of multiple centers developed and owned by the same company in these categories as well.

The shopping center industry is mature. The great spurt of shopping center construction over the past 50 years that has led to more than 43,000 centers in the United States alone has now slowed as suburban markets have become saturated—but it has by no means come to a halt. Redevelopment, repositioning, retenanting, and reconfiguration are the major forces in the industry today as the immense inventory of retail properties ages. Competition is intense as obsolete centers are eclipsed by newer concepts, designs, retail formats, combinations of tenants, and site plans. Niche markets, such as entertainment, streetfront, inner-city, resort, transit-integrated, and off-price centers and town centers, are emerging strongly. At the same time, shopping centers that have outlived their usefulness and cannot be remade are dying or being converted into other more appropriate land uses.

The shopping center industry is in the midst of a sea change resulting from consumers' changing preferences and behavior and intensified competition, not only from other shopping centers but also from nonstore shopping alternatives such as catalogs, television, and Internet shopping. While the intense competition has created unprecedented risks for many existing properties that have not kept pace with emerging trends, it has also created enormous opportunities that sophisticated shopping center owners and developers are exploiting at the expense of their less nimble competitors.

What Is a "Shopping Center"?

The shopping center is distinct from other forms of commercial retail development. It is a specialized, commercial land use and building type, which today is found throughout the world but until the late 1970s thrived primarily

figure 1-1
Shopping Center Inventory in the United States as of December 31, 1998

Size (Square Feet)	Number of Centers	Total Square Feet Gross Leasable Area (000)	Total Retail Sales (000)	Average Sales per Square Foot
Less than 100,001	27,317	1,340,389	$299,744,066	$223.62
100,001–200,000	10,581	1,457,834	$262,245,650	$179.89
200,001–400,000	3,696	988,317	$157,708,427	$159.57
400,001–800,000	1,354	752,027	$133,674,646	$177.75
800,000–1 million	319	287,346	$65,791,291	$228.96
More than 1 million	395	506,648	$113,221,013	$223.47
Total	43,662	5,332,561	$1,032,385,093	$193.60

Source: *Shopping Center Directions,* no. 25 (Chicago: National Research Bureau, Spring 1999), p. 1.

in American suburbia, occurring only rarely in downtowns or rural areas. Over the years, it has been transformed from a suburban concept to one with much broader and varied applications. While the term "shopping center" is often used rather loosely, its definition and those of related terms have been standardized by the Urban Land Institute. In 1947, ULI defined a shopping center as:

> . . . a group of architecturally unified commercial establishments built on a site that is planned, developed, owned, and managed as an operating unit related by its location, size, and type of shops to the trade area that it serves. The unit provides on-site parking in definite relationship to the types and total size of the stores.[2]

In the decades that followed, ULI has refined this definition so that a shopping center must also have a minimum of three commercial establishments, and, in the case of urban shopping centers, its on-site parking needs may be related not only to the types and sizes of the stores but also to the availability of off-site parking and alternate means of access.

Although the scope of this revised definition still appears broad, it actually is rather restrictive and excludes much retail development. Individual retail stores, even when grouped side by side along streets and highways or owned by a single owner, are excluded if they are not centrally managed. Thus, any number of commercial strips or downtown shopping clusters do not qualify as shopping centers, although they may constitute significant shopping districts. On the other hand, a shopping center can form the nucleus of a shopping district in an existing or emerging commercially zoned area, or it may represent the first project around which other commercial land uses eventually are developed.

The following elements characterize the well-planned shopping center and set it apart from other commercial land uses:

- A unified architectural treatment, concept, or theme for the building or buildings, providing space for tenants that are selected and managed as a unit for the benefit of all tenants. A shopping center is not a miscellaneous or unplanned assemblage of separate or common-wall structures.
- A unified site, suited to the type of center called for by the market. The site may permit expansion of buildings or the parking lot if the trade area and other growth factors are likely to demand them.

The interior courtyard of Centro Oberhausen in Germany includes oval skylights that drape this megamall in natural light.

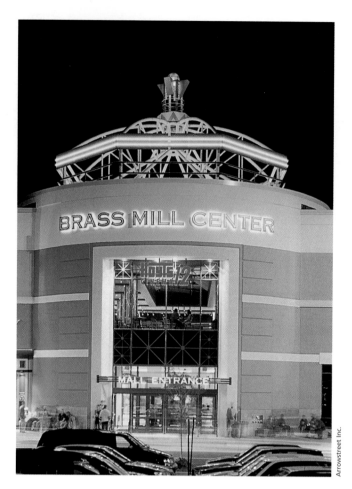

The design of Brass Mill Center, a 1 million-square-foot super regional mall in Waterbury, Connecticut, incorporates the imagery of the brass industry, which was important to this region's early economic development. The history of the site and of Waterbury is recalled through a design theme of stylized mechanical forms, including cogs and gears, watch faces, and buttons (see the case study in Chapter 7).

- An easily accessible location within the trade area with adequate entrances and exits for vehicular and pedestrian traffic as well as transit passengers if necessary.
- Sufficient on-site parking to meet demand generated by the retail uses. Parking should be arranged to enhance pedestrian traffic flow to the maximum advantage for retail shopping and to provide acceptable walking distances from parked cars to center entrances and to all individual stores.
- Service facilities (screened from customers) for the delivery of merchandise.
- Site improvements, such as landscaping, lighting, and signage, that create a desirable, attractive, and safe shopping environment.
- A tenant mix and grouping that provide synergistic merchandising among stores and the widest possible range and depth of merchandise appropriate for the trade area.
- Comfortable surroundings for shopping and related activities that create a strong sense of identity and place.

Although some shopping centers may not exhibit all of these characteristics, the most successful shopping centers project a strong overall image and a clearly identifiable lifestyle orientation for customers and tenants alike. Unified ownership and management and joint promotion by tenants and owners make it possible.

Each element in a shopping center should be adapted to fit the circumstances peculiar to the site, neighborhood, development concept, and market. Innovations and new interpretations of the basic features must always be considered in planning, developing, operating, and remaking a successful shopping center. To succeed, each center must be not only profitable but also an asset to the community where it is located.

Several terms are commonly used in the shopping center development and management industry:

- Gross leasable area (GLA) is the total floor area designed for a tenant's occupancy and exclusive use —including basements, mezzanines, or upper floors— expressed in square feet (or square meters) and measured from the centerline of joint partitions and from outside wall faces. It is the space, including sales areas and integral stock areas, for which tenants pay rent.[3] In the shopping center industry, the size of both shopping centers and tenant spaces within them is expressed in terms of GLA. Gross leasable area, a unit of measure that is universally understood in the industry, is the measurement used for uniform comparison and accurate measurement of physical space within a shopping center.

The difference between gross *leasable* area and gross *building* area (GBA) is that enclosed common areas and spaces occupied by centerwide support services and management offices are not included in GLA because they are not leased to individual tenants. Specifically, GBA includes public or common areas such as public toilets, corridors, stairwells, elevators, machine

Two Rodeo Drive in Beverly Hills, California, caters to premier retailers of haute couture, fine jewelry, and other high-end impulse goods in a neo-traditional storefront setting.

and equipment rooms, lobbies, enclosed mall areas, and other areas integral to the building's function. The enclosed common area is typically less than 1 percent in open centers and 10 to 15 percent in centers developed as enclosed malls. Because the percentage of common area varies with the design of the center, the measurement of GLA was developed.

- The parking index also uses GLA to determine the appropriate number of parking spaces for a shopping center, because it affords a comparison between the shopping area and the parking demand from shoppers. Except for management offices and other spaces for specific uses, the common areas and storage areas in shopping centers do not generate parking demand. In defining the relationship between the demand for parking and the building area of a center, the shopping center industry developed a uniform standard by which to measure parking needs. The standard, known as the "parking index," is the number of parking spaces per 1,000 square feet of GLA.

The currently recommended indices range from 4.0 to 5.0 spaces per 1,000 square feet of GLA, depending on size of the center, with required additions based on the quantitative presence of certain tenant categories and reductions based on the availability of transit and shared parking. These standards were developed from the results of a major survey in 1982 of parking demand conducted and published by ULI and sponsored by the International Council of Shopping Centers (ICSC).[4]

Before 1965, no empirical studies were available on which the industry could base recommendations for parking spaces. In 1963 and 1964, however, ULI conducted a research project sponsored by the Research Foundation of ICSC, and in 1965, it published the first comprehensive study of parking requirements for shopping centers.

By 1980, a series of changing demographic and behavioral factors, along with the findings of some interim studies, suggested that the original standard of 5.5 spaces per 1,000 square feet of GLA needed to be restudied. Findings of another major study at that time led the industry to recommend a range of standards based on center size and modified by the presence of certain tenants, rather than the single index previously recommended.[5]

- Trade area is that geographic area containing people who are likely to purchase a given class of goods or services from a particular shopping center or retail district. The size of the trade area varies based on the shopping center type and size, tenant categories, proximity of competitive centers, population density, and accessibility. The trade area is usually expressed as primary or secondary.

- Shopping goods are those on which shoppers spend the most effort and for which they have the greatest desire to comparison shop. The trade area for shopping goods tends to be governed by the urge among shoppers to compare goods based on selection, service, and price. Therefore, the size of the trade area for shopping goods is affected most by the overall availability of such goods in alternate locations.

- Convenience goods are those that consumers need immediately and frequently and are therefore purchased where it is most convenient for shoppers. Shoppers as a rule find it most convenient to buy such goods near home, near work, or near a temporary residence when traveling.

- Specialty goods are those on which shoppers spend greater effort to purchase. Such merchandise has no clear trade area, because customers will go out of their way to find specialty items wherever they are sold. By definition, comparison shopping for specialty goods is much less significant than for shopping goods.

- Impulse goods are those that shoppers do not actively or consciously seek. Within stores, impulse goods are positioned near entrances or exits or in carefully considered relationships to shopping goods. For example, a table of scarves or other accessories might be located between the entrance and the dress department in a women's clothing store. Within a shopping center as well, certain stores are stocked primarily with impulse goods—costume jewelry, accessories, snack food, for example. Such tenants need positions within a center where they can feed off the traffic generated by stores selling shopping, convenience, and specialty goods. Many of the stores selling impulse goods could not exist outside shopping centers, because they require anchor tenants to attract customers. In highly specialized centers such as urban entertainment centers, most retail tenants sell impulse goods. They rely on anchor tenants such as cineplexes and themed restaurants to draw customers past their stores, which must themselves provide an entertaining environment to draw customers and generate sales.

Types of Shopping Centers

Shopping centers were originally divided into three principal types—neighborhood, community, and regional—each with a clear and distinct function, trade area, and tenant mix. In actual practice, however, the distinction among the three types has not always been crystal clear. Further, as specialized market opportunities have been identified over the years, numerous new types of shopping centers have evolved. These types are usually considered distinct categories of shopping centers, although earlier they were not. In some cases, they share important characteristics with the original three basic categories. The difficulty in distinguishing shopping centers by type is becoming more pronounced as the development of hybrids increases. In all cases, even among variations, the major tenant classifications and to a lesser extent the center size and trade area determine the type of center.

Some segments of the shopping center industry have historically classified centers by size alone or by configuration, for example, enclosed or strip. In its annual surveys, the ICSC uses both factors, while the National Research Bureau and the Institute of Real Estate Management report shopping centers by size alone.[6] ULI believes, however, that size alone, or size and configuration, is inadequate in defining shopping centers, as it implies a direct correlation between size and trade area, tenant characteristics and mix, and functions served in terms of categories of retail goods. This handbook classifies shopping center types by using all these factors.

Figure 1-2 compares the characteristics of the major types of shopping centers. The numbers shown on the table must be regarded only as convenient indicators to define the various types of centers; the basic elements of any center may change if it needs to adapt to the changing characteristics of the trade area, including the nature of the competition, population density, and income. The number of people needed to support a shopping center of any type cannot be fixed, because income, disposable income, competition, and changing tenant mixes, methods of merchandising, and store sizes all enter into these calculations. No rigid standard for size could be realistic; local conditions within a trade area (number of households, income, existing retail outlets) are more important than any standard population data in estimating the purchasing power needed to support a center.

Regional Malls

ULI divides regional malls into two subcategories—regional centers and super regional centers. By definition, a regional center has one or two full-line department stores. It typically contains a GLA of about 450,000 square feet and can range from about 300,000 to 900,000 square feet. From a sample of 49 regional centers, *Dollars & Cents of Shopping Centers: 1998* found that the median total floor space is 435,458 square feet. Early regional centers typically had only one department store, but that is no longer the case. Two department stores are now more common,

figure 1-2

Characteristics of Shopping Centers

Type of Center	Leading Tenant (Basis for Classification)	Typical GLA (Square Feet)	General Range in GLA (Square Feet)	Usual Minimum Site Area (Acres)	Minimum Population Support Required
Neighborhood	Supermarket	50,000	30,000–100,000	3–10	3,000– 40,000
Community	Junior department store; large variety, discount, or department store	150,000	100,000–450,000	10–30	40,000– 150,000
Regional	One or two full-line department stores	450,000	300,000–900,000	10–60	150,000 or more
Super Regional	Three or more full-line department stores	900,000	500,000–2 million	15–100 or more	300,000 or more

Regional centers can range from about 300,000 to 900,000 square feet. The mixed-use Redmond Town Center in Redmond, Washington, includes approximately 500,000 square feet of retail space. It is divided into city-sized blocks along typical urban streets, with street-level retail stores that promote pedestrian-friendly shopping.

More and more, tourists posing for pictures aren't standing in front of the arch in St. Louis or the Golden Gate Bridge in San Francisco. Instead, they're savoring a Kodak moment in front of a Ralph Lauren store. Increasingly, the can't-miss-it event on a vacationer's itinerary is a shopping expedition that goes beyond the souvenir T-shirt and into the realm of Tommy Hilfiger jackets, Coach bags, and Villeroy & Boch fine china.

For several reasons, shopping—and not just for trinkets to take back to friends and relatives—has become an accepted and anticipated part of vacationing.

Many tourists visit the same stores they have at home and buy many of the same things—jeans, stereo speakers, kitchen accessories—sold in their local malls. The malls have taken notice, teaming up with airlines, hotels, and tour operators to offer shopping-themed travel packages. Retailers realize the buying power of vacationers and want space in resort communities.

"The number one thing many vacationers do is shop," says Brian Kendrick, vice chair of upscale retailer Saks Fifth Avenue, which operates eight stores at vacation destinations. "And the resort stores reflect that. They are performing well above the rest."

People lead busy lives, juggling commuting, work, and family obligations. That leaves little time for trips to the mall. But on vacation, they don't have to live by the clock. They can stroll in and out of stores and consider what they want to buy. They have time to try on clothes, a luxury that many harried shoppers skip in their daily lives.

About 77 percent of adults do some shopping on vacation, from buying a simple item at a hotel gift shop to an extravagant purchase at a pricey boutique, according to a survey of 1,500 people nationwide by the Travel Industry Association, a Washington-based trade group. Three percent of those who shop on vacation said it was the primary reason for their trip, the survey found.

Malls are among the top tourist attractions in ten states, including Illinois, Texas, Missouri, Virginia, and Colorado, according to research by McCormick Marketing, a Napa, California–based retail consulting firm.

People visited the Mall of America 43 million times in 1997, more than Disney World, the Grand Canyon, and Graceland combined. In New York, Bloomingdale's says it is the third largest tourist attraction, after the Empire State Building and the Statue of Liberty.

"I get groups all the time that want to go to Michigan or Pennsylvania to shop," says Nanette Ream, who organizes bus tours through her travel agency, Fidelity Tours, in

Arrowstreet, a Massachusetts-based architecture and planning firm, refashioned Plaza Rio Hondo in Bayamon, Puerto Rico, with a river theme in the mid-1990s. The exterior was painted in bright tropical colors and freestanding portals were added in front.

Massillon, Ohio. "This country is saturated with malls and outlet centers, and millions of people want to visit them, no matter where they are. Shopping is the vacation."

Tourists spend four to ten times more than local shoppers and rarely return what they buy, according to McCormick Marketing.

The Taubman Co., one of the nation's largest mall managers and developers, runs World Class Shopping, offering discounts on hotels and airfares to many of the cities where its 27 shopping centers are located. Visitors to Short Hills, New Jersey, can stay at the Hilton, where they receive a tote bag, a discount coupon book for the Mall at Short Hills, and free admission to the hotel spa, where they can soak their weary bones after a long day lapping the mall. The price per night for a weekend stay is $165 —at least $30.00 less than the regular room rate.

Urban Retail Properties Co., which manages malls, is also tapping the tourist market. The Chicago-based company started a toll-free hot line (888-MY-SPREE) that travelers can use to find out about shopping and travel packages in ten U.S. cities.

More promotions are in the works. A new trade group, Shop America, is bringing together representatives from malls, retailers, and travel organizations to work on vacation shopping. "There is an incredible intent to spend on vacation," says Rosemary McCormick, who heads McCormick Marketing and is a Shop America organizer. "Finally, more malls and travel groups are beginning to realize it."

Source: Excerpted from Associated Press, "Many Are Spending Vacations at Malls: Shopping Centers Are Common Tourist Stops," *The [Baltimore] Sun* (August 3, 1998).

although some specialized urban locations still have space to accommodate only one.

Super regional shopping centers share all of the same characteristics as regional centers except that they have three or more department stores and are usually, although not always, larger. A super regional center typically contains a GLA of about 900,000 square feet but can range from 500,000 to 2 million square feet; a few centers exceed 2 million square feet. *Dollars & Cents of Shopping Centers: 1998* reports a median size of 948,632 square feet based on a sample of 76 super regional centers.[7]

Regional and super regional centers generally seek to reproduce all of the shopping facilities once available only in central business districts. They provide primarily a full depth and variety of shopping goods, general merchandise, shoes, clothing and accessories, home furnishings, gifts and specialty items, and electronics. Increasingly, they also provide food, personal services, and entertainment. The main attraction, around which the center is built, has traditionally been the department store, which as a rule has a minimum GLA of 75,000 square feet but ranges from about 40,000 square feet in smaller markets and older centers to more than 200,000 square feet, particularly in super regional centers.

As a result of bankruptcies and consolidation in the department store industry during the late 1980s and early 1990s, a shortage of suitable department store anchors occurred. Consequently, nontraditional anchors that earlier would have been considered inappropriate or unworkable are now becoming commonplace in regional and super regional centers. These new-generation anchors include elaborate food courts, large off-price category killers, megaplex cinemas, and specialized, large-scale entertainment attractions. The range of tenant types also continues to expand in regional and super regional centers, with more than 140 types reported in the latest *Dollars & Cents* survey.

Regional and super regional malls do not differ in function—only in their range and strength in attracting customers. Regional centers typically serve a population in excess of 150,000 people, who will often travel more than 25 to 30 minutes to reach the center. Super regional centers require a larger trade area that typically includes a minimum of 300,000 people. Both regional and super regional centers attract customers through their ability to offer a full range of shopping facilities and goods, thereby extending their trade areas to the fullest extent possible. In some cases, the trade areas of regional and super regional centers may overlap. Customers will sometimes pass a smaller regional mall to shop at a super regional mall to take advantage of greater choice and more diverse tenants. The sites for regional and super regional centers vary dramatically—from ten acres or less for a vertical multilevel urban center to more than 100 acres for a large single-level exurban one.

Community Shopping Centers

Community centers were developed initially around a junior department store or large variety store as anchor tenants in addition to a supermarket. Of all the basic center types, community centers have undergone and continue to undergo the most change. The original typical anchor tenants—a junior department store and a variety store—were largely supplanted in the 1970s and 1980s as principal anchor tenants by discount or off-price department stores such as Kmart or Marshalls or by a strong specialty store such as a hardware, building/home improvement, furniture, or catalog store. In the late 1980s and 1990s, expanded-format stores, often known as category killers and specializing in such items as books, sporting goods, and office supplies, became anchor options. A new form of community center, the power center, appeared. It contains multiple off-price and category killer anchors and few side tenants.

A community shopping center can be defined largely by what it does and does not have. It does not have a full-line department store, which would automatically categorize it as a regional shopping center. It does have a market area larger than a neighborhood center and thus draws customers from a longer distance. It offers greater depth and range of merchandise in shopping and specialty goods than the neighborhood center. It tends also to provide certain categories of goods, particularly commodities, that are less likely to be found in regional centers, such as furniture, hardware, and garden and building supplies. The community center is the "in-between" center, and so it is the most difficult to categorize. Some neighborhood centers have the potential to grow into community centers, just as some community centers can expand into power or regional centers.

The community center typically has a GLA of about 150,000 square feet but can range from 100,000 to 450,000 square feet (and more) in some cases. The median center size, out of a sample of 287 centers reported in *Dollars & Cents of Shopping Centers: 1998,* was 157,298 square feet.[8] The community center needs a site of ten to 30 acres, normally serves a trade area of 40,000 to 150,000 people within a ten- to 20-minute drive, and has a typical parking index of five spaces per 1,000 square feet of GLA, which ranges from four to six spaces.[9]

Because the range for this type of center is so great, a new subcategory was established in the 1980s—the super community center. Super community centers range from 250,000 to more than 500,000 square feet, with a median of 316,795 square feet in a sample of 56 such centers.[10] The top five tenants found in super community centers are women's ready-to-wear, family shoes, men's wear, women's specialty wear, and family wear.

In metropolitan areas, a community center can be quite vulnerable to competition. It is too large to thrive off its immediate neighborhood trade area but too small to make a strong impact on the whole community unless it is located in a smaller city with a population ranging from 50,000 to 100,000. The development of a strong regional center, with the pulling power of one or more department stores, may impinge on a community center's trade area if both centers sell the same types of merchandise. In a typical market area, however, both can succeed even if they are close to each other because of the difference in the types of merchandise offered and because they form a synergistic shopping destination that is stronger than each center would be standing alone.

In cities with populations of 50,000 to 100,000, the community center, although lacking a full-line department store, may actually take on the stature of a regional center because of the center's local dominance and pulling power. An off-price or discount store may function as the leading tenant, substituting for a full-line department store.

Of all the shopping center types, the community shopping center is the most difficult to categorize in terms of its anchors, market size, and drawing power. Because the community center offers increasingly large amounts of shopping goods and, in certain cases, special categories of goods, the market area is less predictable. In the case of major subtypes such as off-price megamalls and power centers, the trade area can be as large as for regional

shopping centers, and instead of traditional anchors such as a grocery store, drugstore, or junior department store, they have multiple anchors, including category killers and other big-box formats.

Neighborhood Shopping Centers

The neighborhood center provides for the sale of convenience goods (food, drugs, and sundries) and personal services (those that meet the daily needs of an immediate neighborhood trade area). A supermarket or superstore that combines grocery shopping with a pharmacy and other convenience goods and services is the principal anchor tenant in most neighborhood centers. Consumer shopping patterns show that geographical convenience is the most important factor in determining a shopper's choice of supermarkets. A wide selection of merchandise and customer service is a secondary consideration. Other principal tenants in neighborhood centers are drugstores and small variety stores. Often, centers without a super-

The community shopping center typically ranges from 100,000 to 450,000 square feet of GLA. The Commons at Calabasas is a 200,000-square-foot community center on a 21-acre site in suburban Los Angeles.

market but similar in GLA to neighborhood centers are also referred to as neighborhood centers; however, unless other food tenants can be aggregated as the equivalent of a supermarket, the center would probably be more appropriately classified as a small community center (because to be successful it would likely have to draw from a larger market area).

The neighborhood center has a typical GLA of about 50,000 square feet but ranges from 30,000 to 100,000 square feet, with a median size of 65,279 square feet based on a sample of 233 centers.[11] Requiring a site of three to ten acres, the neighborhood center normally serves a trade area of 3,000 to 40,000 people within a five- to ten-minute drive. The parking index is about five spaces per 1,000 square feet of GLA, somewhat lower than for larger shopping centers, as customers do not spend as much time on each visit and turnover of vehicles is higher.

Convenience Shopping Centers

The convenience center contains a group of small shops and stores dedicated to providing a limited range of personal services and sundries for customers making a quick stop. The center is commonly anchored by a convenience market (often referred to as a minimart), and its tenants are similar to those found in neighborhood centers. Tenants most frequently found in convenience centers are restaurants and other food services; personal services such as dry cleaners, beauty parlors, and photocopy stores; and professional services such as medical doctors and dentists, and finance, insurance, and real estate offices.[12] Frequently a convenience center is an adjunct to a neighborhood shopping center and as such functions as an integral part of that center, but it may also be a freestanding entity.

Typically, a convenience center is about 20,000 square feet of GLA, but it does not exceed 30,000 square feet.[13] Customers typically live near the center and walk or drive to it on the way to other activities. Sales per customer are typically small and often involve a limited number of items that may have been forgotten on previous shopping trips or single items for which convenience and speed of purchase are more important than price.

Variations of the Major Types

Shopping centers can no longer be neatly confined to the major categories; even early in their development, shopping centers varied somewhat. Over the years, the shopping center industry has invented a variety of additional real estate products to accommodate and advance trends in retailing. Specialization or subcategorization of shopping centers became a widening trend as early as the 1970s, and the trend has accelerated in the 1990s.

Specialty Centers. One of the first subcategories to evolve after the principal types were established was the "specialty shopping center." Initially, the term was applied to any center that failed to meet the traditional definitions. Although the term is widely recognized in the shopping center industry as an appropriate classification for nontraditional shopping centers, the industry never has agreed on a clear definition of it and so it means differ-

The neighborhood shopping center typically consists of 50,000 square feet of GLA and often includes a large supermarket, drugstore, and small variety stores as the principal tenants. Porter Square in Cambridge, Massachusetts, is a neighborhood center anchored by a drugstore/pharmacy.

ent things to different people. One salient characteristic that has often differentiated a specialty center from a conventional center is the absence of a traditional anchor tenant. The role of the anchor tenant might be played by another type of tenant or by a group of tenants that together might function as an anchor tenant or by any number of other variations. In a neighborhood specialty center, for example, a combination of gourmet food shop, delicatessen, meat market, and greengrocery might function in lieu of a supermarket. A food service cluster, several restaurants, and a cinema complex might also serve as anchor tenants. Specialty centers, especially those that have a special architectural character or environmental ambience, have sometimes been referred to as "themed centers" or "themed specialty centers." Since the advent of "urban entertainment" and "lifestyle centers," however, the term "themed center" has fallen into disuse.

In any case, "specialty center" is no longer an adequate description of the numerous disparate shopping center

Rapid changes in the retail industry have made it increasingly difficult to neatly confine shopping centers to the major categories. For example, El Tejar Shopping Center, designed by the Beame Architectural Partnership to open in Bucaramanga, Colombia, in 2000, will feature a wide range of retail uses, including 150 shops, a food court, a special event area, a cineplex, restaurants, and indoor entertainment.

subcategories, and the format needs to be more precisely defined to be meaningful. Today, with shopping center specialization becoming the norm and with market segmentation dividing the retail pie into more complex and overlapping segments, specialty centers need to be characterized as what they are: "entertainment," "fashion," "off-price," "outlet," "megamall," "home improvement," "lifestyle," "power," and other qualifiers that more precisely define their character, focus, and targeted retail segment.

Outlet Centers. One of the most important retail developments in the 1980s was the advent of off-price and outlet centers. An outlet center is an aggregation of factory outlet stores, each owned by a different manufacturer but managed collectively as any other shopping center. With $12 billion in annual retail sales, manufacturers' outlets have ranked as one of the fastest-growing segments of the retail industry in the 1990s. A total of 294 outlet centers with 13,654 stores and 57.2 million square feet were open as of December 31, 1998.[14]

Outlet stores have existed for decades. Mill stores on the East Coast have offered excess and damaged apparel and shoes to employees since the middle to late 19th century. In 1936, Anderson-Little, a men's clothing manufacturer, opened the first "factory direct" stores. Initially, outlet stores served mainly as centers to dispose of overruns and slightly damaged merchandise (seconds). Currently, these categories are often supplemented by merchandise lines not sold in the manufacturers' retail stores.

The outlet center has no specific anchor tenant, although one or more of the largest or most prestigious tenants may perform this role. The trade area for an outlet center is regional or extraregional, and such centers can also enjoy a strong tourist trade. Irregular and damaged merchandise accounts for less than 15 percent of all outlet goods; the majority of the merchandise is first quality and in season.[15] Outlet centers are being built in clusters near resort communities, along major freeways leading to those

communities, and in smaller towns about an hour's drive from major metropolitan areas.

Grove City Factory Shops, north of Pittsburgh, is one of the largest outlet centers in the United States. Opened in 1994, the 533,000-square-foot center is a well-executed example of the genre in a village-like configuration (see the case study in Chapter 7).

Off-Price Centers. The off-price center is a rapidly evolving shopping center type that at one time was termed a discount center. Some off-price centers are oriented toward fashion with a commensurate high-style design image; other off-price centers stock more conventional, middle-range goods. In all cases, off-price centers specialize in name-brand merchandise that is sold significantly below the prices asked in full-line department stores and/or specialty stores. Off-price chain stores such as Marshalls, TJ Maxx, and Filene's Basement that typically might be found in an off-price center are not owned by manufacturers but instead buy overallotments representing a range of designers and manufacturers from department stores.

The size of the market for an off-price center is typically between that of community centers and regional centers, with relatively little tourist orientation. Some off-price centers are beginning to experiment with a mix of discount and full-price tenants at the same time some community and regional centers are beginning to lease space to some off-price tenants in an attempt to broaden and deepen their market penetration.

Power Centers. In the late 1980s and early 1990s, power centers were one of the most talked-about retailing concepts. Power centers entered a retail arena that, for the previous 40 years, had been dominated by enclosed regional shopping centers. Borrowing elements from most other categories of shopping centers, power centers constituted a departure from tradition for both developers and retailers.

Power centers are a type of super community center exhibiting the following characteristics:

- More than 250,000 square feet of GLA and floor space not owned by the center's management;
- At least one super anchor store, such as a discount department store or a home improvement store, containing at least 100,000 square feet of GLA;
- At least four smaller, category-specific anchor tenants, each with 20,000 to 25,000 square feet of GLA or more;
- A minimum number of small shops, each usually less than 10,000 square feet of GLA but collectively totaling no more than 10 to 15 percent of the center's total GLA;
- Generally open air and configured as a strip, "L," or "U";
- Customers from a trade area that is close in size to that of a regional shopping center; and
- Managed as a unified shopping center.[16]

The biggest push for the development of power centers is the result of a combination of social, demographic, economic, and retailing changes. The supply of and demand for shopping center space, consumers' demand for value and retailers' delivery of that value, demographics and patterns of consumption (aging buyers have purchased most of their durable goods and so most future purchases are discretionary), and retail merchandising have all changed.

Off-Price Megamalls. The shift toward value retailing has helped create other types of value-oriented retail centers that make up a small but growing segment of the shopping center industry. The off-price megamalls —Potomac Mills near Washington, D.C., Ontario Mills near Los Angeles, Gurnee Mills near Chicago, and Sawgrass Mills near Fort Lauderdale, for example—combine a variety of outlet, off-price, and other value-oriented retailers. The mix may include factory outlet stores coupled with department store outlets, such as Nordstrom Rack and Off Fifth, category killers such as The Sports Authority, and large specialty retailers such as IKEA and Waccamaw. Increasingly, this form of megamall is now being combined with large-scale entertainment attractions.

Such value-oriented malls are huge, often encompassing 1.5 million to 2.5 million square feet, usually laid out in a linear or circular design, and located along a major freeway on the exurban fringe of a metropolitan area so that their factory outlet tenants will not encroach on the manufacturers' full-price retail clients. Typically, a metropolitan area can support only one or two off-price megamalls, although a megalopolis like New York or Los Angeles may ultimately have several. Customers regularly will drive 25 miles or more to take advantage of the perceived bargains. These centers also rely heavily on tourist trade for their success. Sawgrass Mills, for example, markets itself heavily in South America, and Potomac Mills intercepts a high volume of tourist traffic traveling on I-95 from the Northeast to Florida. Potomac Mills is one of the most popular tourist attractions in the Washington, D.C., area and is routinely included on bus tours for foreign visitors.[17]

Urban Entertainment Centers. One of the hottest concepts in real estate merges elements of entertainment with retailing to form the urban entertainment center. The forerunners of this concept were festival marketplaces such as the Rouse Company's Harborplace in Baltimore. Urban entertainment centers are based on a concept of "trinity of synergy," which combines entertainment, dining, and retailing within a pedestrian-oriented environment. The new generation of cinema megaplexes, often approaching category killer status with 30 or more screens and 100,000 square feet of space, is the most common entertainment attraction, although numerous other retailers such as Gameworks and California Wilderness Experience are typical. Entertainment attractions are often combined with a variety of entertainment/impulse dining attractions such as the Rainforest Cafe and Planet Hollywood, and entertainment-oriented, brand extension retailers such as the Disney Store, product showcase stores such as NikeTown, leisure-oriented category killers such as Barnes & Noble, brand license stores such as the Discovery Store, specialty retailers such as Dapy,

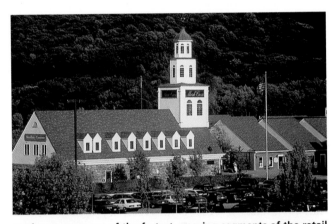

Outlet centers, one of the fastest-growing segments of the retail industry during the 1990s, feature a collection of factory outlet stores. Woodbury Common Factory Outlets in Central Valley, New York, opened in the 1980s and expanded in the early 1990s. Although the primary trade area is New York and New Jersey, the project also attracts domestic and international tourists.

Power centers are usually open air and draw customers from a trade area that is close in size to that of a regional shopping center. The Tustin Marketplace was developed to take advantage of its proximity to a 12-lane freeway in Orange County, California, with more than 200,000 vehicle trips per day.

family entertainment centers, specialty film venues such as IMAX, and fully themed attractions in malls such as Camp Snoopy at the Mall of America in Bloomington, Minnesota.[18]

If this type of retailing involves any formula for success, it may be in creating a powerful sense of place where people can congregate in a safe, sociable, and entertaining environment. For example, the Forum Shops at Caesars Palace in Las Vegas is designed like an ancient Roman villa, complete with oversized statuary, a barrel-vaulted ceiling, and interactive themed shows. Universal City-Walk in Universal City, California, and the Irvine Spectrum Center in Irvine, California, are other such centers that entertain customers at regular intervals (see the case study in Chapter 7).

Fashion Centers. The fashion center, unanchored by a full-line department store, is a concentration of apparel shops, boutiques, and custom quality shops carrying special merchandise, usually of high quality and with high prices. It represents market segmentation by quality, taste, and price. Although not a necessary criterion, a fashion center may include one or more small specialty or "resort" department stores; gourmet food and food service or a "gourmet" supermarket could be included. High-fashion centers can also draw on wide rather than limited trade areas when high-income areas are more broadly scattered. A fashion center could therefore have a market area scaled toward a neighborhood, community, or regional center. When it serves a neighborhood or community, it will comprise small clothing and gift shops, and the traditional supermarket might instead be represented by a gourmet food shop, a butcher, and a greengrocery. When such centers reach community and regional size, they will typically have as an "anchor tenant" a group of small specialty department stores; they also will probably have some tourist trade.

Generally, a fashion center sports distinctive architecture using high-cost finishes and materials. It often has a sophisticated architectural theme (occasionally as an adaptation of a historical structure), special landscaping, or an unusual site configuration because of site restrictions. On average, fashion centers have smaller site areas than more traditional neighborhood, community, or regional centers. Parking requirements for a fashion center are usually below those typically required for similarly sized centers, as the dollar volume per customer at a fashion center is higher than that at a conventional center and customer trips required for the center's success are therefore fewer but longer. A fashion center often provides additional amenities, such as valet parking and reserved parking. The term "fashion center" is now often inaccurately applied in advertising copy to many conventional malls whose management sees its use as an effective marketing tool. As a result, the term's impact has been diluted.

Festival Centers. "Festival centers" were invented by the Rouse Company with the opening of Faneuil Hall Marketplace in Boston. A limited number of festival centers were built in the 1970s and 1980s; because of their heavy

The planned Barra urban entertainment center in Rio de Janeiro, designed by Kaplan McLaughlin Diaz Architects, will include a 16-screen cinema, multimedia game arcade, music stores, themed restaurants, and an IMAX theater.

El Pedregal (place with many stones) in Scottsdale was the first festival marketplace in Arizona when it was completed in 1988. The design firm, Architectonica, created a "vernacular desert oasis" that combines shopping, dining, and entertainment with a festive desert theme.

reliance on tourists, their success was confined to large markets such as Boston, New York, Baltimore, and San Francisco. They are considered among the forerunners of urban entertainment centers, and some of their characteristics have been incorporated into this newer form of shopping center. As its name suggests, this type of shopping center was intended to create a special, festive experience. A high percentage of festival centers' GLA is devoted to specialty restaurants and food vendors. Food vendors typically are concentrated as they are in a conventional food court, but a much greater emphasis is placed on ethnic authenticity and distinctive offerings, and frequently the center includes a blend of on-site food service and specialty food retailing. Retail goods at a festival center tend to emphasize impulse and specialty items. A strong ambient entertainment theme is often present, with regular informal events featuring street mimes, jugglers, dancers, strolling musicians, and other entertainers; until recently, however, no major entertainment anchor such as a cineplex was included to draw customers. The trade area for a festival center must be quite large, as a significant portion of its business activity comes from tourists. Thus, most festival centers are first categorized as regional because of their market and then as festival centers because they do not have department store anchors. Typical of the festival center are its memorable architecture and its relationship to other significant land uses, perhaps a waterfront (or other significant water feature), a historic area, or both.

Retail Uses in Mixed-Use Development. A mixed-use development is a large-scale real estate project with the following characteristics:

- Three or more significant revenue-producing uses (such as retail, office, residential, hotel/motel, and recreation) that in well-planned projects are mutually supporting;
- Significant physical and functional integration of project components (and thus a highly intensive use of land), including uninterrupted pedestrian connections; and
- Development conforming to a coherent plan (which frequently stipulates the type and scale of uses, permitted densities, and related items).[19]

A mixed-use development relies heavily on the synergistically related major uses within the project. The retail component in a mixed-use development may range from convenience retailing to serve the project's major land uses to a regional shopping center configured as a traditional regional shopping center (in terms of tenant mix and anchor tenants) or as a specialty center (most likely a fashion or festival center). The retail component of a mixed-use development often has multiple levels and is always carefully integrated with the other land uses through interconnecting pedestrian pathways, shared parking, and retail stores specifically tailored to the needs of other users in the development.

Consumers' changing habits and an oversupply of shopping centers have caused a shakeout in the retail industry, leaving many leading developers and designers looking for new retail formats and new ways to revitalize old ones. The use of anchors, which was so prevalent over the last three decades, continues to fade, causing both developers and designers to experiment with unorthodox tenant mixes and to focus on new property designs and new uses for existing big boxes.

One option is to group together social and public components such as banks, post offices, science centers, public libraries, and even public elementary schools. Public-oriented tenants may not be great revenue generators by themselves, but they are capable of bringing people back into shopping centers time and again. A set of in-mall surveys conducted jointly by the architectural firm RTKL Associates and Cornell University found that shoppers most frequently expressed a desire for these public/social components in shopping centers.

To capitalize on the symbiotic relationship between film and food, empty big boxes also are being converted into

TrizecHahn Centers's rehabilitation of a department store into restaurants, stores, and theaters at Horton Plaza in San Diego more than doubled annual sales for the space.

"stacked" entertainment zones featuring restaurants, food courts, and multiplex cinemas. At the Promenade in Woodland Hills, California, for example, a former Saks Fifth Avenue store has been converted to a 120,000-square-foot destination anchor that works as an integral part of the upscale shopping center. The three-level entertainment nucleus features an AMC 16-screen theater and a tiered gourmet food court that seats 700. Theatrical lighting, abstractions of film reels, and colorful movie-related graphics create a Hollywood atmosphere that enlivens the interior of the cinema complex. For Westfield America, the mall's owner, and AMC of Kansas City, the proof lies in the numbers. The complex has helped attract new retailers to the mall, sales have increased, and an estimated 90,000 people visit the theater complex each weekend.

Ice arenas, a product that is the hottest it has been since the 1950s, also can be accommodated in big boxes. A standard National Hockey League rink measures 85 by 200 feet, an international rink 100 by 200 feet. Fueling demand for construction of new rinks are the thousands of Olympic hopefuls as well as the lack of such facilities in the United States. Only 2,200 rinks in the United States serve a population of 260 million; in Canada, 30 million people have access to well over 6,000 rinks. The NHL is working with a number of developers to create a new prototype that includes restaurants and gaming and expects to introduce it in selected locations in the near future.

Given that 73 percent of all primary mall shoppers are women, according to the Mass Retail Association, how empty space in shopping centers is filled should be considered carefully. In a 1997 survey conducted by JB Research in Ojai, California, women who were interviewed said that they avoid family entertainment centers, motion simulators, video game arcades, laser tag, and violent virtual reality. What they want is restaurants, movies, art galleries, health and beauty services, live theaters, museums, children's entertainment centers, and bowling. Although many may find it surprising, bowling is big, and several new bowling concepts suitable for shopping centers are now under development. And bowling works well in combination with a billiards/night club format.

As developers continue to focus on alternative anchors, large-format specialty stores, such as Crate & Barrel, Banana Republic, and Eddie Bauer, are being layered or stacked on top of each other to create lifestyle-oriented destination wings. Or they may have several levels above a smaller ground-floor space, thus allowing malls to accommodate more tenants on the ground floor.

Also a hot commodity for empty spaces is the spa, which is popping up in retail centers throughout the United States. Spas enhance a property's drawing power, helping to attract an upscale clientele. They are an antidote to the stress and strain of the fast-paced 1990s and hold appeal for overworked adults looking for a way to relax. Spas are big, according to Indianapolis-based Simon Property Group, which is adding them to many of its properties. For customers looking for a quick "pick-me-up" at the end of a long day, mall spas are convenient and easily accessible. While some spas focus primarily on services, such as facials and a wide variety of massages and wraps, others also include a broad line of hair and beauty products, vitamins, and related items.

U.S. malls traditionally have been fashion oriented; in contrast, those in Europe and the Pacific Rim have long incorporated a more diverse mix of tenants. Supermarkets, fresh-food halls, auto showrooms, and even chapels have proved to have great drawing power. Forward-thinking U.S. developers are just now beginning to explore these alternatives, focusing primarily on blending high-end, specialty, or boutique food stores, restaurants, and perhaps a large-format retailer that specializes in products for the home. These new anchor destinations should be popular with women, who remain the primary purchasing agents in 85 percent of homes for food, clothing, and household products, despite the fact that they constitute approximately 50 percent of the workforce.

Empty big boxes present an opportunity for developers to respond to demand from consumers that shopping centers not only provide shopping but also serve as a focal point for community and leisure activity, fulfilling a dual civic/commercial role.

Source: David Brotman and Norman Garden, "Innovative Approaches Fill Big Boxes," *Urban Land,* July 1998, p. 34.

The majority of mixed-use projects thus far have been developed in urban or suburban downtown locations, although some exceptions have been built, particularly in the West and Southwest. As existing shopping centers are rehabilitated and expanded in urbanizing suburbs, many of them evolve into mixed-use or multiple-use developments. Many shopping centers today already are part of multiuse developments, in that the shopping center developer or other landowners controlling the surrounding parcels have constructed a variety of related land uses, such as office buildings, high-density residential units, restaurants, cinema complexes, and other uses that benefit from the attraction of customers to such a center. Clearly, the advantages of a mixed-use development are to be considered in the development of new centers and in the remodeling and expansion of existing centers.

Circle Centre, an 800,000-square-foot urban mall in downtown Indianapolis, is an example of a regional retail center that pulls together the synergies created by its links with hotels, office buildings, a convention center, and a professional sports venue. It also is designed to fit within the downtown street grid and use the historic building facades where they could be saved and recycled (see the case study in Chapter 7).

Downtown Retailing. While suburban shopping centers boomed from the 1950s through the 1980s, downtown retailing—along with the downtowns themselves—declined. And when the revitalization of many core cities began during that period, it was usually organized around the development of new office space. For many years, revitalization plans failed to include shopping centers, even though developers, planners, and city managers looked with envy upon the success of suburban shopping centers and frequently saw them as a threat to the survival of downtown retailing.

That situation began to change in the late 1970s and early 1980s with the introduction of festival marketplaces in a few cities, the most successful of which were Faneuil Hall Marketplace in Boston, Harborplace in Baltimore, and South Street Seaport in New York. Regional shopping centers began to be built in a few downtown areas —from the Glendale Galleria in Glendale, California, and Hawthorne Plaza in Hawthorne, California, to centers that were more carefully integrated into the fabric of downtown, such as the Gallery at Market East in Philadelphia and Eaton Centre in Toronto. This trend has continued in the 1990s with the development of regional centers like Circle Center in Indianapolis and San Francisco Centre. With the overall decline in the construction of regional centers, however, few such centers are expected to be built downtown in the coming years.

Mixed-use developments that include a significant retail component are another form of downtown retailing that has proved successful, particularly in major cities. The best early examples are Water Tower Place in Chicago and Embarcadero Plaza in San Francisco. North Michigan Avenue in Chicago now has multiple large-scale mixed-use projects, including Chicago Center and 600 North Michigan, that have turned it into one of the world's premier shopping streets. Increasing numbers of such mixed-use projects are being planned in downtowns and suburban downtowns.

The latest generation of downtown centers began with Horton Plaza in San Diego, a regional center that illustrates how shopping centers increasingly have been integrated into the surrounding cultural and historic fabric of the downtown, including, in San Diego's case, the Gaslight District, and have incorporated a focus on the outdoors and entertainment. Rather than isolating themselves from the rest of downtown and sucking the retail vitality from surrounding streets, these new-generation centers form anchors within the downtown retail environment and encourage spillover of retail growth throughout the surrounding neighborhood. Urban entertainment centers are the latest version of downtown retailing. Such centers containing cinemas, themed restaurants, specialized lifestyle and entertainment retailers, and other entertainment attractions are being designed to blend seam-lessly into downtown environments. E-Walk on 42nd Street in New York City and CocoWalk in Coconut Grove, Florida, are among the major examples.

Town Centers. Today, downtown retail and entertainment centers are usually designed as part of larger multiuse development initiatives that include cultural, educational, institutional, and sports facilities as well as housing, hotels, and offices. They are often configured as neotraditional developments, with streetfront retail stores and residential and office uses on the upper floors. This form of development is an attempt to create or re-create the essential elements of downtowns as they once existed. This type of development typically is master planned and developed block by block in line with projections for absorption of space for the various components. Town centers are being created on greenfield sites in the centers of new communities such as Reston, Virginia, and in older downtowns such as Silver Spring, Maryland, West Palm Beach, Florida, and Kansas City, Missouri. This approach

Stephen Simpson

Horton Plaza in San Diego was designed by the Jerde Partnership to blend in with the existing cultural and historic fabric of downtown. The project served as a catalyst in the revitalization of downtown San Diego.

Reston Town Center is a 20-acre mixed-use district that introduces the pedestrian character of a traditional downtown to a suburban setting. The Town Center, developed by the Mobil Land Development Corporation in 1990, includes offices, retail stores, and a 514-room hotel.

to retailing is as much about creating a social environment as it is about providing a commercial center. Some development specialists believe that it is a more promising form of development for the new millennium than a typical suburban shopping center, because it counteracts sprawl, encourages walking rather than driving, and integrates retailing with other daily activities in a more convenient configuration. Other specialists point out its limitations, which include the difficulty of incorporating large-format big-box stores and the types of value retailing that are not conducive to a pedestrian environment and cannot afford the costs associated with downtown locations.

Resort Retailing. Retailing plays a large role in the success of destination resorts and tourist attractions. In a resort community, shopping facilities may be constructed to provide services not only to the tourists and seasonal residents but also to the community at large. Whatever the type of facility, however, it is important to remember that resort residents and guests come there "to find something a little different from what they are used to at home." The design, plan, and tenant mix of the retail facility should therefore reflect this expectation."[20]

Unlike traditional shopping centers, successful resort-based retail stores exhibit several characteristics. In general, they:

- Are geared to visitors and are usually unable to survive on local traffic alone;
- Offer an intimate scale with a distinctive ambience and are strongly oriented toward pedestrian traffic;
- Create an "experience" that increases the resort's appeal;
- Present a distinctive and consistent architectural design and a line of merchandise that convey a unifying theme;
- Offer a variety of restaurants, bars, and other entertainment facilities that function as key tenants and help create a social ambience;
- Lack traditional anchor tenants;

- May have shops offering goods with distinctive logos and, depending on the market profile, higher-end commemorative merchandise; and
- Offer an ongoing program of special events and activities to entertain and inform.

And although there is no set formula for success—each site is different—six key principals of design have been identified:

- Milieu—Capitalizing on the distinctiveness of the setting and other special attributes of the location enhances the center's draw.
- Multiactivity Environments—By investing in multiple activities and making the resort a year-round destination, developers can ensure the feasibility of more diverse retail goods that can appeal to sightseers, local residents, regional residents, resort employees, and/ or corporate, meeting, or conference attendees.
- Town Center Hub—Clustering retail functions in a central area increases their appeal and drawing power.
- Character through Tenant Mix—A carefully selected mix of retail tenants helps to create a distinctive image for the resort.
- The Right Retailers—The tenant mix should carefully capitalize on the attractiveness of good health, wellness, and longevity; small indulgences and outdoor accessories; and entertainment.
- Design and Merchandising—Design and architectural guidelines further strengthen a resort's identity by offering a consistent image.[21]

Transportation-Integrated Retailing. Although retail shops have been part of transportation facilities such as train stations and airports for some time, they usually have been limited and disorganized. They typically were not managed or merchandised in a coordinated way, and retailers usually occupied leftover space that was not needed for the efficient operation of the related transportation

What do you call a shopping center that offers a resort experience? A "retail resort," says TrizecHahn Centers, describing its 1.5 million-square-foot Park Meadows. Located 14 miles south of Denver, this one-of-a-kind project was designed in the style of a grand mountain lodge by Anthony Belluschi Architects of Chicago.

Shoppers at Park Meadows are considered "guests" and are invited to relax in timber-ceilinged "living rooms" furnished with leather sofas, Mission-style chairs, and stone fireplaces. Copper rooftops, oak and maple floors, huge boulders, cascading waterfalls, and a Rocky Mountain backdrop all contribute to the feeling that one is visiting a luxurious resort rather than a super regional shopping center. Interior wildlife murals created by local artists and the integration of lush indigenous landscaping featuring prairie grass, towering pines, aspen trees, and locally quarried stone add to the project's sense of place.

Park Meadows offers five times more seating than a typical shopping center. Instead of a food court, the center features an 800-seat, cathedral-vaulted "grand dining hall" with a two-story stone fireplace. Complimentary hot chocolate is served on cold winter days. Child-care services and family bathrooms also are provided.

Retailers at Park Meadows—30 of which are new to the market—are organized into four districts, each with a distinct theme: family, lifestyle, fashion, and entertainment. Anchor stores include Colorado's first Nordstrom, Denver's only Dillard's, the area's largest Foley's, and a flagship Joslins. Many of the specialty stores are much larger than those typically found in regional malls. Eddie Bauer, for example, has a 35,000-square-foot store that features all of its merchandising concepts as well as a small coffee bar.

The basic idea behind the design is to entice shoppers to stay longer and come more frequently, while making each visit efficient and enjoyable. Retailers have reported sales well above their goals, and total sales also are well above expectations. During its first year of operation, sales (excluding department store sales) totaled $430 per square foot, beating TrizecHahn's goal of $415 per square foot and putting Park Meadows among the top-performing malls in the United States. Sales tax revenues during the same period were more than $2 million.

Located in Douglas County, the fastest-growing county in the United States, Park Meadows has been the catalyst for almost 7 million square feet of new commercial development in the southeast Denver corridor. Project planning, with Douglas County an eager partner, took more than 15 years. The developer and county worked hand in hand to create a place that is sensitive to its outstanding landscape and appreciative of the local lifestyle. The project also added $26 million in infrastructure improvements to the surrounding area. Bonds issued to finance these improvements are being paid off with a 1.4 percent "public improvement fee" that Park Meadows passes on to its retailers. The fee is projected to expire after the bonds are paid off in six to eight years.

Source: Libby Howland, "Park Meadows: An Entertaining Retail Resort," *Urban Land,* April 1998, p. 25.

The unique design, materials, and amenities at Park Meadows all contribute to the ambience of a retail resort.

Cairns Central in Queensland, Australia, is a two-level retail center integrated into an existing railway station. The center includes a 600-seat food court, a six-screen movie theater, and retail stores.

system. In other words, they did not qualify as shopping centers. But the restoration of Union Station in Washington, D.C., in the late 1980s demonstrated the potential for shopping centers in major transit stations, and others have followed on a smaller scale, including 30th Street Station in Philadelphia and Union Station in Los Angeles. The restoration of Grand Central Terminal in New York City has created the opportunity for high-end specialty shopping that will serve commuters, tourists, and office workers in the surrounding Midtown office core. Retail amenities that are desirable in or near a suburban rail station may include newsstands, sit-down restaurants, fast-food outlets, photo-finishing shops, dry cleaners, banking/ATM facilities, video rental stores, and perhaps even daycare facilities.

Mass-transit stations also provide a captive market of commuters and intracity travelers for various types of retail development from convenience centers to regional malls, and they can add significantly to the performance of these centers. Transit authorities are now touting their stations to developers as ideal locations for a variety of retail amenities. Such amenities are community assets with economic benefits to the city, its residents and workers, and visitors. Retail development at transit stops allows transit systems to capture additional revenues through joint development of station property, increase ridership by providing a more efficient and pleasurable experience, increase property and sales taxes to the community where the station is located, and add enough buying power to

a neighborhood's market to provide retailing that otherwise could not be supported. For example, successful urban and suburban transit-integrated retail centers are numerous along the Washington, D.C., heavy-rail system. Pentagon City, Ballston Common, and Mazza Gallerie are regional shopping centers with direct, enclosed access to Metrorail stations, and Crystal City, International Square, Union Station, and Chevy Chase Pavilion are specialty centers with directly connected access to the system.

Airport retailing also has come a long way from the days of a small newsstand, a gift shop, a lack of merchandising, bad food, and inflated prices. At a time when many airports have become "hubs," arriving passengers often must wait an hour or more between incoming and outgoing flights. Portland (Oregon) International Airport expanded its retail facilities in the late 1980s, one of the first airports in this country to do so (see the case study in Chapter 7). Since that time, airport operators have embraced a new philosophy of retailing and have joined with shopping center developers and operators who specialize in airport locations to create carefully integrated and centrally managed shopping centers that capture what otherwise could be downtime, offering a wide range of retail concessions at prices comparable to in-town locations. Typical mall stores such as the Nature Company, Bally, the Body Shop, and Speedo; local specialty retailers, often offering locally made products; or other stores that relate specifically to the local community, such as the Smithsonian Store at Ronald Reagan Washington National

The trend toward a higher level of architectural quality in shopping centers can be seen in the renovation and expansion plans for Plaza Vespucio in Santiago, Chile. Plans call for a vertical expansion of the existing structure and a new building featuring a bold architectural expression that is a dramatic and deliberate departure from the rest of the center and gives it a visually exciting identity from the surrounding neighborhood.

Airport, have found their way successfully into the retail mix in airports in Pittsburgh, London, Amsterdam, San Francisco, and elsewhere.

Strip Commercial Development. Strip commercial development does not constitute a shopping center. Such a development is a string of commercially zoned lots developed independently or a string of retail commercial stores on a single site that has no anchor tenant and no central management and whose mix of tenants results from leasing to available tenants with good credit, not from planning and executing a leasing program. Strip commercial development typically is linear and faces a street or parking lot; planning and design generally are not coordinated. Access, curb cuts, parking, and landscaping often are chaotic, site and building plans do not conform to any unified urban design, and the layout is decidedly pedestrian *un*friendly, making it difficult to walk from store to store. As a result, strip commercial developments are less concerned with customers' con-

venience or being assets to the communities where they are located, and are less likely to succeed over the long term. But this situation need not be the norm. Much of the guidance and experience presented in this handbook could be applied to strip commercial development if the disparate owners and tenants coordinated their operations privately, formed some kind of centralized retail management, or created a partnership with the public sector to create a cohesive shopping district.

Variations in Design. As will be discussed in Chapter 3, "Planning and Design," building design and configurations associated with early shopping centers have changed dramatically. For the most part, shopping centers were designed with single-level buildings for mall shops and multilevel buildings for department store tenants. They were clustered together as one group and surrounded by a large surface parking lot with a few ancillary enterprises like auto accessory stores, service stations, banks, and cinemas on outparcels. Then malls started to become multilevel centers because of site characteristics and, as centers grew larger, the increasing distances between anchors; moreover, single-level malls limited the sales of anchor tenants on the second and third levels.

Over the decades, the diversification of shopping center types has led to considerable variety in the physical responses. Giving a center a theme, in which architectural design and landscape elements are used to differentiate one center from another, has become an important part of the segmentation of shopping center markets. Existing buildings have been adapted for use as shopping centers in downtowns and in the suburbs. The adaptability of shopping centers to changing design and locational criteria, merchandising strategies, and shoppers' preferences seems limitless.

The theme for a shopping center is more clearly understood as a design and merchandising strategy used to position a particular shopping center in the marketplace; it does not necessarily indicate a type of center. A theme aids in the center's identification and enhances market attraction through physical design and architectural character.

A current trend in design is a move toward a higher level of architectural quality, even in off-price and strip centers. New centers are using more contemporary colors, banners, vertical landmark elements, brighter signage and lighting, classier materials, and more specific guidelines for storefronts and storefront displays. Newer centers often have a distinctive profile and varied rooflines, and architects use steeples, towers, canopies, chimneys, exotic landscaping, and large expanses of glass and decorative signs for heightened visual effect.

The answer to the age-old question of whether to build an enclosed or open-air mall is not as cut and dried as it once was. Until the 1990s, regional centers were designed almost exclusively as enclosed malls, except in some warm climates. Community and neighborhood centers, on the other hand, were almost always open air. Today, some regional malls are being created or reconfigured as open-air designs, even in seasonal climates. Some specialty centers and off-price centers are now enclosed, and urban entertainment centers are being created using both configurations, depending on the location. The decision turns on the particular site and neighborhood, the need to differentiate a center from its competitors, and response to consumers' demands for new shopping experiences.

Evolution of the Shopping Center

The creation and evolution of the shopping center have depended and continue to depend largely on the use of automobiles and the continuing growth, maturation, and demographic changes in cities and their suburbs. In the early decades of the 20th century, when cities spread beyond established transportation lines, automobiles came into greater use to meet a variety of transportation needs. In pursuit of the shifting locational pattern of purchasing power, retailing began to decentralize. A variety of shopping centers began to be constructed in suburbs, and the present-day hierarchy of shopping center types was launched. Beginning as early as the 1920s, the provision of parking for vehicles became a necessary adjunct of retail facilities.

As travel patterns and buying habits shifted, new concentrations of stores bloomed away from established downtowns and business corridors. New shopping facilities were built on new kinds of sites: the narrow and shallow strip commercial lots in established downtown business districts and along major streets could not readily accommodate the on-site parking needed. Nor did established retail locations lend themselves to large-scale redevelopment as shopping centers because of multiple owners and high land costs. In many cities, public inertia and regulatory overkill drove businesses away, created a situation encouraging the expansion of blight, and allowed the general quality of life as well as education, public safety, and other essential services to deteriorate. Retailing cannot succeed in this type of environment, and most cities failed to enact policy or form public/private

partnerships that could have prevented the natural and unavoidable mass exodus of retailing from most American downtowns.

Developers and retailers responded to the need for new shopping centers in the suburbs by devising a new form of marketplace with its own built-in customer parking. Through a process of innovative development in response to the shifting nature of the market, early shopping centers were created on undeveloped greenfield sites. They gradually evolved from a coordinated strip of stores fronting on a street into the complex array of shopping center types seen today, identifiable by their efficient planning, carefully structured array of tenants, standardized development procedures, and professional operating practices.

Early Experiments and Patterns
The concept of shopping centers grew out of early free-standing Sears and Montgomery Ward stores and out of the innovative grocery outlets that were first built outside downtowns on plots large enough to accommodate both the store and parking spaces for customers' cars. From these experiments developed the unified row of stores with display windows fronting on traffic streets and with parking for customers at the rear or side of the strip; tenants usually included a food store, a drugstore, and several service shops. Gradually, the concept of grouping stores acquired the sophistication of site design, location, tenant selection, and operation found in today's shopping centers.

The earliest "shopping center" predated even the advent of the large grocery markets that provided some lots for customer parking. In 1907 in Baltimore, Edward H. Bouton, president of the Roland Park Company, constructed an architecturally unified building, set back from the street, to contain several shops. The site also provided space for horse-drawn carriages. Later, that space was converted to parking for automobiles by paving the front grass and the carriage drive. In the 1970s, when the Roland

Themed architecture, unified management policies, and "parking stations" are important components of many modern shopping centers. Country Club Plaza in Kansas City, Missouri, pioneered these concepts in the 1920s.

Park Company filed for a permit to tear down the building, local residents protested the action, viewing the demolition as the destruction of a historic landmark.

Bouton, also the developer of the prestigious residential community Roland Park, pioneered in many other ways. He initiated the use of protective covenants, "zoning" for a specific use, setback requirements, architectural controls, flexible restrictions, wider lots, homeowners' maintenance funds, extensive landscaping, and civic responsibility on the part of developers. He gathered other developers at his Roland Park home to discuss these advances in subdividing land as well as in integrating commercial facilities to serve nearby residential areas. At Bouton's home, community builders such as J.C. Nichols of Kansas City and Hugh Potter of Houston, past presidents of ULI and former chairs of the Community Builders Council, received inspiration and guidance.[22]

In the early 1920s, unified commercial ventures were often identified with high-quality residential communities fostered by forward-looking developers. It was during this period that J.C. Nichols began development of his Country Club Plaza in what was then the outlying area of Kansas City. Nichols inaugurated stylized architecture (the first themed center) and unified management policies, sign control, and landscaping amenities. He provided parking in "parking stations." In the strictest sense, Country Club Plaza is not a shopping center but a shopping district; parking spaces are provided in parking garages and along public streets that cross the district. Still, the

principles of a shopping center exist at Country Club Plaza in such areas as quality of management, tenant mix, and merchandising operations.

In 1931, in Dallas, Hugh Prather developed the first unified commercial project in which stores faced inward, away from the surrounding streets. Highland Park Shopping Village in Dallas can be called the prototype for today's planned shopping center: a site all in one piece unbisected by public streets, individual stores unified under one image, built and managed as a unit under single ownership, and the amount of on-site parking determined by parking demand.

In 1937, Hugh Potter started a shopping center as an adjunct to his renowned Houston residential community, River Oaks. Potter used a then contemporary style of architecture that included cantilevered canopies along the storefronts. Although he violated an important current principle by allowing a major public street to bisect the center, River Oaks initiated many operational practices—for example, percentage leases and a merchants' association—that became standards in the industry. These pioneers of the 1930s, each working to meet the needs of a particular area but without significant precedent to guide them, established the patterns of development that ultimately determined the merchandising concept that became today's shopping center.

After World War II, suburban development boomed, fueled by years of pent-up demand from the war and from the depression that preceded it. A wave of residential and commercial development swept through the country, forming "bedroom" suburbs. Neighborhood shopping centers sprang up to accommodate these residential areas and to become ultimately a part of the new suburban scene.

In 1950, the next great innovation in shopping center development took place. On behalf of the Allied Stores Corporation of New York, James B. Douglas opened Northgate in Seattle—the first suburban regional shopping center built with a major full-line branch department store as the leading tenant. Northgate was also the first center to feature a central pedestrian mall with a service truck tunnel below. The open pedestrian mall and underground truck tunnel became an early building pattern for regional centers, although the truck tunnel soon proved to be too expensive to provide and alternative loading docks were devised. Northgate has since seen several expansions and changes. It was expanded in 1963 and, in 1974, became an enclosed, air-conditioned mall. It now contains more than 1.1 million square feet of GLA, and the original anchor tenant, the Bon, has been joined by JCPenney, Nordstrom, and Lamont.

During the 1950s, the continued spread of the suburbs gradually spurred the construction of shopping centers to serve the new market. That decade produced successful practices and innovations that led to proved procedures for shopping center planning. The shopping center became recognized as a distinct building and land use type, and innovations began to come more quickly. The first regional shopping center to have an enclosed mall was

The development of enclosed shopping centers greatly increased during the booming 1960s. Oglethorpe Mall in Savannah, Georgia is a modern example.

Perhaps the most powerful new concept of land use to emerge in the United States in the 1970s was the mixed-use development, which generally includes a major retail component. Baltimore's Inner Harbor, which began as a mixed-use redevelopment in the 1970s, continues to attract residents and tourists. One of the latest additions to the Inner Harbor is the Power Plant, which involved the rehabilitation of a closed and dilapidated turn-of-the-century power plant into a stunning new entertainment complex.

planned in 1953 and opened in 1956. Southdale, near Minneapolis, instituted weatherproofed shopping on two levels surrounding a "garden court," all enclosed and under one roof. In 1957, the shopping center as an industry came of age. The International Council of Shopping Centers, headquartered in New York City, was founded as a trade association to foster interest in and improve operating practices among shopping center developers, owners, managers, and tenants.

Development of shopping centers greatly increased in the 1960s. Planning and operating principles were tested and refined. Adjustments were made in response to changing conditions in financing, leasing, location, construction, and operational aspects of expanding markets. Variations of standard types began to appear, with the enclosed, heated, and air-conditioned mall emerging as the dominant building form for regional centers. By adding two, three, and four full-line department stores, a regional complex gained strength in attracting customers. Such

a broad range of shopping goods and other retail categories had once been found only in downtowns. By the second half of the 1960s, previously developed open mall centers were being converted to covered malls.

Diversification in the 1970s

While the 1960s experienced a rapid growth of shopping centers and a refinement of the basic concepts, the 1970s saw the emergence of specialization in regional markets and increasing regulatory controls. The fashion center, a regional mall with an upper-end department store or a high-end limited department store as anchor tenant and quality boutiques as mall tenants, came into style. The identification of market segments and differentiation of center types resulted.

A new kind of market area—the middle market—had several meanings, depending on the group of shopping center experts consulted. For some, it was a geographic concept, identifying sites for regional shopping centers that fell between existing major markets. For others, it meant bringing the concept of large regional shopping centers into middle-sized (as opposed to major) cities or clusters of cities in the United States—that is, bringing regional centers to smaller cities and metropolitan areas. It also included siting centers to serve a cluster of these smaller market areas. In some small isolated towns, regional centers also functioned as community centers, and they exhibited characteristics of both—including the presence of small department stores and grocery stores in the same center. In Canada, this mix is still common.

In the 1970s, middle markets were defined as growth opportunities for regional centers. The 1970s also saw the growth of super regional shopping centers. Many regional centers expanded to become super regional, and many new super regionals were developed. At the end of the 1960s, the single-level mall was still the most popular concept, even for a large mall, but by the end of the 1970s, most regional malls were multilevel and many began to include structured parking, primarily in urbanizing locations with high property values.

Diversification of uses occurred during the 1970s. While the typical mall development of the 1960s was simply a shopping center, beginning in the 1970s, the development community began to recognize the opportunities for peripheral development or for land uses on the shopping center site not directly related to retailing. The Galleria at Tysons II in McLean, Virginia, for example, features a Ritz-Carlton Hotel and office towers as part of the shopping center complex. Although office buildings and ancillary commercial activities became part of some shopping center developments, they were generally treated as separate development activities and managed separately.

Up to this point, shopping centers were freestanding, located on sites in rapidly growing areas. As communities began revitalizing downtowns through public policy initiatives, a limited number of shopping centers were constructed downtown. In the western part of the United States, the first downtown centers were often merely suburban mall designs with some modifications—most notably, structured parking—inserted into the downtown of what was already an auto-oriented post–World War II suburban community. The situation was different in cities in the East and Midwest, where the shopping center was modified and reshaped to become a part of the urban downtown.

Perhaps the most significant innovation of the 1970s was that regional centers grew in stature from being simply locations for retail sales to becoming the focus of some community activity. In addition to retail shopping, some regional malls began offering food, cinemas, and other forms of family recreation or leisure activity. The percentage of a center's GLA devoted to food service rose dramatically. Movie theaters were increasingly integrated into the mall, singly or in clusters, usually on freestanding pads or in leftover space in basements and dead-end corridors unsuited for retail tenants. Health spas, game rooms, kiddie rides, and other recreational uses were in-

troduced. The common area mall of the regional shopping center became a new form of downtown Main Street —a place to meet people, a place to see people.

During the 1970s, the community shopping center also began to diversify in various ways—the most obvious being a change in anchor tenants. The original junior department store or large variety store combined with a supermarket was replaced by the discount department store or by the superstore (drugstore, junior department store, and grocery store all under one roof). The community center further specialized by using as anchor tenants stores that had previously been freestanding—lumber, hardware, home improvement, warehouse, furniture, and catalog warehouse stores, as well as off-price women's specialty stores (although in the 1970s that term had not yet been coined), depending on the market.

The minimall was a relatively short-lived concept that tried to capture the characteristics of the enclosed regional mall on a much smaller scale. (This concept was also tried in neighborhood centers in a few cases.) Most minimalls require a market significantly larger than a neighborhood to survive but, because of specialization and the characteristics of the immediate market, do not need a regional market area.

In the 1970s, the neighborhood shopping center, on average, grew larger. Supermarkets expanded, and the drug superstore (a combination of drug, sundry, variety, garden, and automotive supply goods) became popular. In some areas of the country where neighborhood centers were being developed in conjunction with rapidly growing residential areas, builders emphasized a design compatible between the neighborhood center and its adjacent residential areas. Higher densities and some office uses were often planned as transitional land uses between neighborhood centers and the adjoining community. Neighborhood centers also began to specialize as the tenant mix and the characteristics of even the grocery store were more carefully shaped and tailored to the demographics of the market area. Many large supermarket chains began to refine their product to incorporate delicatessens, bakeries, prepared food sections, gourmet wine and cheese shops, and a variety of other sections that could be mixed and matched to meet the demographics of a particular market. The number of different types of tenants finding homes in neighborhood shopping centers grew considerably during the 1970s, which undoubtedly reflected the increasing number of centers and the growing differences of opinion within management as to which tenants were appropriate. Neighborhood shopping centers to a greater degree than either community or regional centers are managed by a more diverse group of owners and managers, who may be less skillful in selecting appropriate tenants than managers of large regional centers, who tend to have permanent leasing and management personnel on site.

Of all the refinement, diversification, and innovation that occurred in the development industry in general in the 1970s, perhaps the most powerful new concept to emerge in the United States during that period was the

Renovation and expansion, rather than new construction, have been the major source of growth in the shopping center industry since 1991. Phipps Plaza, a regional mall in Atlanta, was renovated by Compass Retail in the early 1990s. The renovation introduced 100 new shops and updated and improved finishes to the exterior and interior of the mall.

Phillips Place, a mixed-use project in the South Park area of Charlotte, North Carolina, clusters shops and restaurants with townhouses above along the primary street, creating the impression of an old quarter of a European or Southern city. With 130,000 square feet of retail, restaurant, and theater space—including a multiplex cinema, 402 residential units, and a 124-room, all-suite hotel—Phillips Place represents an investment of $77 million. Its commercial tenants include Dean & Deluca, a gourmet market based in New York City; Via Veneto, an Italian shoe retailer; J. Richards Gallery and Waverly Home, interior design stores; and the Palm restaurant.

The 32-acre site was the last large parcel of undeveloped land with retail potential in the South Park area. The Harris Group of Charlotte, developers of the project, worked closely with the city's planning staff, including zoning director Walter Fields and planning director Martin Crampton, to create a new zoning category that would allow the integration of retail and residential uses. Although designers took new urbanist principles into account during planning, they realized that the type of retail space planned for the project was the exact opposite of the small, neighborhood shops usually included in new urbanist designs. "Phillips Place is retail as entertainment," explains Jim Williams, Charlotte-based TBA[2]

Architects's chief designer for the project. "Nothing is essential here—no supermarkets or drugstores. That's important for the synergy. We've created an environment that is romantic in nature, a destination for people who want to enjoy themselves and who want to return again and again.

"The 402 residential units here are not enough to support Phillips Place retail," he adds. Because retailers needed to draw customers from a much broader geographic area, "we had to deal realistically with the car and other economic realities. We call this approach 'economic urbanism' because it adapts to economic realities.

"The track we took was to create an environment that allowed for adequate parking, but the car is not the overriding visual element," explains Williams. All the retail space opens onto the main thoroughfare, which features limited angled parking (50 spaces) broken up by trees. The bulk of the commercial center's 875 parking spaces are wrapped behind the stores—in one section, below street level—minimizing the visual impact of cars while ensuring convenient parking.

The project features classical building facades, varying roofscapes, and windows reminiscent of old Italy, England,

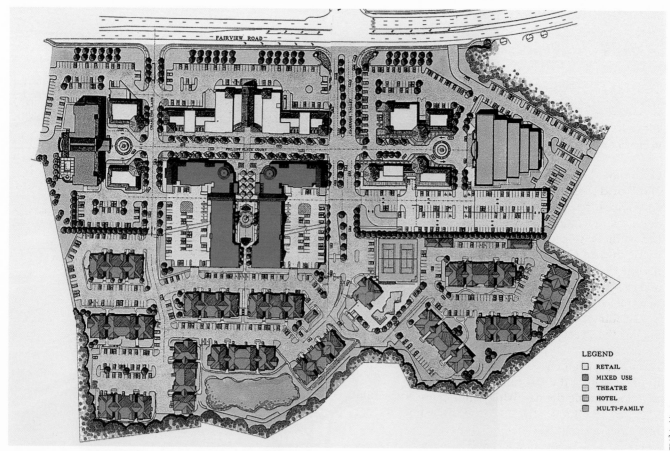

LEGEND
- ☐ RETAIL
- ◩ MIXED USE
- ☐ THEATRE
- ▨ HOTEL
- ▨ MULTI-FAMILY

TBA[2] Architects

An area containing only apartments is located behind the mixed commercial uses that front on the main thoroughfare.

Brick sidewalks, extensive landscaping, outdoor seating, and other amenities encourage strolling and relaxing. The main thoroughfare terminates at the hotel.

Charleston, South Carolina, and Savannah, Georgia. The Old World look of limestone exteriors is simulated by synthetic stucco. Precast concrete panels, more typically associated with industrial buildings, are covered with decorative synthetic stucco details to form the exterior of the movie theater. Colorful awnings inspired by Charleston's historic "Rainbow Row" accent the buildings' beige, taupe, and peach walls. Brick sidewalks, extensive landscaping, outdoor seating, fountains, and other amenities encourage strolling and relaxing. The movie theater and hotel anchor the street's ends.

Atlanta-based lighting consultant Sheila Sullins was brought in to make sure the environment works as well at night as it does during the day. While lighting levels at Phillips Place are less intense than those at most shopping centers, the consistent yet subdued lighting was intended to create a romantic mood as well as a sense of safety for pedestrians.

The Harris Group partnered with Post Properties of Atlanta to construct and manage the over-the-shop apartments as well as a separate all-apartment area nearby. Chris Cassidy, vice president for development for Post Properties, comments that Phillips Place offers "things to do day and night. It's a destination spot." Cassidy believes that "the character of the development will continue to emerge as it matures."

Source: Julie D. Stern, "'Economic Urbanist' Retail: Phillips Place," *Urban Land,* July 1998, pp. 20–21.

mixed-use development, which frequently included a major retail component. First identified and defined by ULI in 1976, the mixed-use development has become a major concept.[23] The intensity of development required to qualify as a mixed-use development is far stronger than that required for a multiuse development, another major concept beginning in the late 1960s that is also associated with the development of suburban shopping centers.

By the middle of the 1970s, the industry faced adjustments to new sets of conditions that continue to this day. Development regulations and restrictions were expanded to protect the environment and to save energy, and they slowed the pace of all land development, including shopping centers. The public was reacting to flagrant abuses generated by uncontrolled urban growth, and measures were taken to legislate national land use policies regarding air and water pollution, infringement on sensitive ecological zones, and uncoordinated sprawl. National and state controls were enacted over sensitive ecological areas, such as wetlands, scenic areas, and coastal zones. The Environmental Protection Agency (EPA) promulgated air quality regulations under the Clean Air Act of 1970, which focused sharply on shopping centers as an "indirect source" of deteriorating air quality. Although shopping centers are not significant sources of air pollution per se, the EPA examined them because they rely almost entirely on automobile traffic for business, which leads to vast on-site concentrations of automobiles in parking lots. Regulations based on evidence that concentrations of parked vehicles induce deteriorated air quality proved to be impractical, however, and in mid-1975, the EPA indefinitely suspended those portions of its regulations governing parking-related facilities.

Energy conservation, spurred initially by the energy crisis of the 1970s, has had a long-term impact on shopping centers, both existing and planned. Centers have been retrofitted by increasing insulation, installing automatic climate controls, and altering heating, ventilating, and air-conditioning (HVAC) systems to make operations more efficient. Operational changes were also made in temperature standards and lighting levels. These techniques—innovative for the 1970s—are now standard development practice.

Another major challenge to the shopping center and its place in the economy occurred at the end of the decade. In 1979, the U.S. Department of Housing and Urban Development released a draft of "A Regional Shopping Center Policy," ultimately called "Community Conservation Guidance." The principal objective of the policy was to control the development of regional shopping centers that would be detrimental to the retail areas of existing communities. The presumption was that objectives for urban revitalization could not be achieved without restraining competition. The basic mechanism for assessing the potential effects of proposed centers was called a "community impact analysis." Only three or four such analyses were ever completed, and they were released to mixed reactions about the possible impacts on existing retail activity from proposed new centers. This policy was discontinued with the change of administrations in 1980, and as a result it had no measurable impact on shopping center development.

Maturation in the 1980s

The construction of shopping centers continued to boom in the first half of the 1980s, but overbuilding and recession brought construction to its lowest point in decades by 1990. The shopping center industry had reached the end of a historic era that transformed the retail landscape of the United States into a decentralized hierarchy of shopping center types and locations. The shopping center industry reached maturity after decades of rapid construction and vigorous efforts to meet the demand for new regional and strip centers not only in rapidly sprawling suburban growth corridors but also in small communities in the most remote locations. Metropolitan areas in particular became overbuilt in terms of market demand. At the same time, the vast quantity of shopping centers built in the previous boom years were beginning to age and needed major renovation, expansion, or repositioning to stay competitive with newer centers. In some cases, demographic market characteristics of older centers in older neighborhoods changed dramatically, leading to the first major signs of decline. Other locations languished as retail destinations as newer centers with better access, newer retail formats, and more sophisticated tenants took away their markets.

Consolidations and bankruptcies among weaker department store chains led to a shortage of powerful anchors. This situation made the construction of regional malls more difficult, because there were fewer anchors to choose from. It also affected the profitability of many malls that were unable to replace lost anchors, and it limited the opportunities for smaller centers to expand. Nontraditional anchors—food courts, off-price department stores, and entertainment centers—began to be considered out of necessity.

Neighborhood centers were particularly affected by the highly competitive nature of the grocery business and the narrow profit margins that have led to the gradually increasing size of individual supermarkets and to the introduction of various forms of discount stores. The design of stores had to be rethought for new centers and ways found to expand stores at existing centers. These changing characteristics put pressure on the economic viability of some chains, causing sellouts and consolidations in the early 1980s.

Remaking the Shopping Center in the 1990s and Beyond

The shopping center industry is at a crossroads. Much of the huge stock of shopping centers built in the 1950s, 1960s, 1970s, and 1980s is now outdated. The great wave of shopping center construction necessitated by the suburbanization of America is largely over. Retailing is now fully decentralized, with few markets unserved by the complete range of shopping center types. Overbuilding in the 1980s, competition from nonstore retail options, and changing consumer interests have greatly reduced the need for new shopping center space, at the same time that new forms of shopping centers are being created. This situation has led to a savage competitive situation, with new shopping centers cannibalizing their older, obsolete neighbors.

Since 1991, the primary vehicle for growth in the shopping center industry has been renovation and expansion, not new construction. For example, the number of large regional malls opened slowed from 27 in 1989 to only eight in 1995. Yet per capita retail square footage continues to grow in the United States. In 1992, almost 18.5 square feet of shopping center space existed for every person. By 1996, this figure had risen to 19.4 square feet. An old rule of thumb had suggested that 12 to 14 square feet per capita was sufficient, which is about how much retail space existed in 1980. Clearly, this rule no longer applies. It takes more than square footage to be competitive, however, and many shopping centers that no longer meet consumers' expectations will go out of business.

To respond to consumers' changing shopping preferences and to compete in an overbuilt market, some owners are trying to extend their trade area penetration by transforming regional shopping malls into entertainment hubs and community social centers. As super regional centers increase their market dominance over smaller centers, most two-anchor and even some three-anchor malls are finding it hard to compete. In fact, some of the worst-performing enclosed malls are being closed or redesigned as power centers. Others are mixing full and off-price tenants, and still others are "de-malling" by opening themselves up with outward-facing stores and creating streetfront or town center retailing. Sycamore Plaza at Kenwood, in Cincinnati, Ohio, is an example of an obsolete 1960s enclosed mall that lost its sole anchor tenant and thus its competitive position. In 1994, following extensive redevelopment, the mall was reopened as an upscale power center with five category killer anchors (see the case study in Chapter 7).

The Mall of America in Minneapolis is the largest enclosed retail mall in the United States. It was developed by a subsidiary of the Simon Property Group, one of the largest national REITs involved in retail development.

Kaleidoscope, in Mission Viejo, California, was designed by Altoon + Porter to be a festive, entertaining, new-generation community center.

Ownership of shopping centers has also been transformed in the 1990s. What was largely an independent, entrepreneurial development activity has been gradually transformed into an activity driven by large public corporations. The industry is increasingly dominated by innovative national giants such as Taubman, Simon Property Group, General Growth, Rouse, and TrizecHahn. Construction is increasingly funded by large institutional investors, including REITs, pension funds, and insurance companies. Although operational standardization is still not the norm, the industry is moving in that direction with increased demands for reliable performance data, public disclosures, and more rapid transference of information as demanded by the market.

In the late 1990s, the overall importance of shopping centers to the U.S. economy is at its apogee, and this situation will not change in the foreseeable future. The sustained ability of shopping centers to respond positively to the challenges of economic recessions, energy shortages,

environmental concerns, changing consumer demands, shifting demographics, and overbuilding are clear measures of their staying power. As in the past, they will continue to adapt to changing market opportunities, although at the beginning of the new millennium, shopping center owners and developers must be more nimble than they have ever had to be to stay on top. In a highly competitive and more sophisticated marketplace, there is less room for error. Important retail niches—streetfront shopping centers, town centers, entertainment centers, transit-integrated centers, and inner-city shopping centers—are still waiting to be filled, and they are just beginning to be filled as the century ends. At the same time, the majority of the existing stock of 43,000+ shopping centers will need to be remade continuously and adapted to meet emerging consumer demands. The basic underlying principles of shopping center development, design, and operations set forth in this handbook are more important than ever in carrying out both these monumental undertakings.

Notes

1. International Council of Shopping Centers, *http://www.icsc.org.*
2. This definition was originated by ULI's Community Builders Council. This council, established in 1944, formulated many planning and development principles and terms for the shopping center that are basic in the industry. In 1947, under the chairmanship of Jesse Clyde Nichols of Kansas City, the Community Builders Council produced its first major publication, *The Community Builders Handbook,* which was divided into two sections—residential development and shopping center development. The original *Community Builders Handbook* and its later editions were the forerunners of the present Community Builders Handbook Series, of which this handbook is a part.
3. This definition has been adopted by the shopping center industry as the standard for statistical comparison. It is both the unit of measure used to establish recommended parking standards and the unit of measure used in ULI's annual study of receipts and expenses in shopping center operations, *Dollars & Cents of Shopping Centers.*
4. *Parking Requirements for Shopping Centers* (Washington, D.C.: ULI–the Urban Land Institute, 1982).
5. Ibid. By the late 1990s, the emergence of new shopping center types required a new parking survey that includes traditional types of shopping centers as well as off-price centers, outlet centers, and entertainment centers. See ULI and ICSC, *Parking Requirements for Shopping Centers,* 2d ed., forthcoming.
6. *Shopping Center World,* Communication Channels, Inc., New York, New York. Since 1973, a census has been conducted every two years and reported in the January issue of the odd-numbered years.
7. *Dollars & Cents of Shopping Centers: 1998* (Washington, D.C.: ULI–the Urban Land Institute, 1998), p. 53.
8. Ibid., p. 74.
9. Ibid., p. 403.
10. *Dollars & Cents of Power Centers: 1997. A Comparison with Super Community and Community Shopping Centers* (Washington, D.C.: ULI–the Urban Land Institute, 1997), p. 47.
11. *Dollars & Cents of Shopping Centers: 1998,* p. 88.
12. Ibid., p. 102.
13. Ibid.
14. *Value Retail News,* May 1999, pp. 15, 16.
15. Prime Retail, *http://www.primeretail.com.*
16. See W. Paul O'Mara et al. *Developing Power Centers* (Washington, D.C.: ULI–the Urban Land Institute, 1996).
17. See Laurence C. Siegel, "The Changing Face of Value Retail," *Urban Land,* May 1996, pp. 29–32.
18. See Michael Beyard et al., *Developing Urban Entertainment Centers* (Washington, D.C.: ULI–the Urban Land Institute, 1998).
19. *Mixed-Use Development Handbook* (Washington, D.C.: ULI–the Urban Land Institute, 1987), p. 3.
20. *Resort Development Handbook* (Washington, D.C.: ULI–the Urban Land Institute, 1997), pp. 170–75.
21. Ibid., pp. 172–73.
22. The following works discuss shopping center development during this period: J.C. Nichols, *Mistakes We Have Made in Developing Shopping Centers,* ULI Technical Bulletin No. 4 (Washington, D.C.: ULI–the Urban Land Institute, 1945); Seward H. Mott and Max S. Wehrly, eds., *Shopping Centers: An Analysis,* ULI Technical Bulletin No. 11 (Washington, D.C.: ULI–the Urban Land Institute, 1949); J. Ross McKeever, *Shopping Centers: Planning Principles and Tested Policies,* ULI Technical Bulletin No. 20 (Washington, D.C.: ULI–the Urban Land Institute, 1953); and *Shopping Centers Restudied: Part 1, Emerging Patterns,* and *Part 2, Practical Experiences,* ULI Technical Bulletin No. 30 (Washington, D.C.: ULI–the Urban Land Institute, 1957).
23. *Mixed-Use Development: New Ways of Land Use* (Washington, D.C.: ULI–the Urban Land Institute, 1976).

2. Project Feasibility

The shopping center, in all its forms, is a commercial land use that is more than a real estate venture. It is also a retail merchandising complex that not only provides many of the basic goods and services that a community requires but also functions to a greater or lesser extent as a social and community center. It supports the development of housing, spawns complementary land uses, including hotels and offices, and positively influences a community's real estate values. By definition, all shopping centers are distinguished by several basic precepts: a coordinated development strategy, a unified spatial arrangement, a carefully planned mix of mutually supportive tenants, and centralized management control.

The development of a shopping center requires certain essential stages and comprises a complex series of economic, financial, merchandising, and design decisions (all of which are described in the following chapters of this handbook). These decisions relate to market analysis, assessment of the political climate, environmental impact evaluation, site planning, traffic planning, selection of tenants, lease negotiations, financial analysis, architectural design, operations and management, and advertising and public relations. In addition, the public approval process in many jurisdictions has become highly complex and may be the most difficult part of the development process. In an era when growth management,

Two Rodeo Drive in Beverly Hills features an open-air, European-style shopping street.

traffic mitigation, environmental protection, zoning and subdivision restrictions, energy conservation, and personalized neighborhood concerns can stop a project in its tracks or require major changes to an original plan, a sophisticated team approach is necessary to coordinate and expedite federal, regional, state, local, and neighborhood approvals. Intense coordination and partnership with the public sector throughout the development process, from inception to completion of a shopping center project, are now standard operating procedures.

A range of technical experts is usually called upon to carry out development. They include a market analyst, land planner, architect, landscape architect, lawyer, engineering and construction specialist, accountant, financial adviser, leasing agent, and shopping center manager. In some cases, several or all of these disciplines are represented on the developer's own staff; in others, the shopping center developer hires specialized consultants. In putting together any shopping center project, whether infill or greenfield, urban or suburban, the development team must conduct a series of feasibility studies to aid in the decision-making process and satisfy public agencies while proceeding toward construction. At key points in this process, the developer typically builds in go or no-go decisions to limit risk or cut losses.

The timetable for completing essential development tasks typically grows longer as the project proceeds. Snags invariably arise because of local conditions and such contingencies as negotiations with key tenants, financing

An innovative public/private partnership led to the redevelopment of a failing downtown mall in Boca Raton, Florida. In addition to becoming a successful retail center, Mizner Park has evolved into an urban village and important community gathering place.

commitments, permit approvals, and clearances. The development process for some major regional shopping centers has taken 15 years or longer. Timetables are usually much shorter for smaller centers whose impact on the community is less.

A feasibility study for construction of a shopping center has several essential parts:

- Market analysis, including an evaluation of the existing competition; the potential future competition; the economic characteristics of the metropolitan area or city; the size, characteristics, and demographics of the trade area; access and visibility; and factors affecting growth of the trade area;
- Financial analysis, including projections of anticipated development costs and operating income and expenses for the project;
- Site selection, evaluation, and control;
- Commitments from key tenants;
- A leasing plan;
- Financial considerations;
- Zoning, subdivision, environmental and traffic impact, and other public approvals.

No precise how-to formula holds, because interlocking preliminary work precedes any final decision. Ultimate site acquisition, for example, depends on zoning approval. In turn, leasing depends on site approvals and on securing key tenants, while financing depends on leasing. Each of these issues is described in the following sections of this handbook.

Market Analysis

Before embarking on the development of a new shopping center or the repositioning of an existing center, a developer must identify and evaluate the retail market—the supply and demand of retail offerings—and calculate the potential patronage for various categories of goods and services.[1] This step should be taken even before looking for suitable sites, because it is the primary consideration on which new shopping center development can be justified. If the population and disposable income of a market have increased, the potential for new construction is readily discernible. If the population has not increased appreciably and disposable incomes have not risen, the existing retail space in the trade area may already be adequate, at least quantitatively. Nevertheless, some markets that are saturated or overbuilt may still need new retail space if the existing space is obsolete, if existing tenants and layout cannot accommodate current consumers' demands, or if some of the existing shopping space is in the wrong location to conveniently serve shifting population and emerging shopping patterns. The market study is not as simple as it once was as a result of new types of shopping centers and retail tenants. What was once primarily a quantitative study of needed retail space has now become heavily qualitative. In all situations, however, the developer must be sure the market can absorb the increase in retail space proposed. To address market needs may require providing a new type of shopping center, a more up-to-date merchandising mix, a better location, a more current design, and/or stronger tenants.

Shepherd Square, a grocery-anchored neighborhood center in Houston, was developed with a second-story retail component because of the relatively high land costs. The proximity to many of Houston's upscale residential neighborhoods made it feasible for the developer, Friendswood Development, to build the additional level of retail space.

Measuring a project's possibilities is the first exploratory step in determining the feasibility of a shopping center. The developer's first aim is to match the location, size, and composition of the center with the needs of the trade area. To do so, the developer usually tries to obtain an accurate economic analysis of the trade area, based on a market survey, that he or she can use to develop a tentative plan for a shopping center.

A specialist in the retail field should conduct the market analysis. Its measurements should show quantitatively whether or not a new center appears to be justified. Strong competition in the retail field, the high cost of land development and building construction, increasingly fickle and more demanding consumers, and communities' strong attitudes about growth management, traffic congestion, and keeping existing concentrations of retail activity leave little room for miscalculation.

The market analysis tells the developer/investor whether a demand exists for new shopping facilities. It also indicates why the new facilities are needed: increased population and purchasing power, unmet demand, or replacements for obsolete, noncompetitive facilities. The market study also provides the information the developer most needs to "sell" his project to major tenants, local governments, and financial institutions. The analysis helps to determine how the project would serve the prospective market and whether it would generate enough sales volume to justify its development. The importance of a market study should not be underestimated, as the development of a large regional shopping center can add as much retail space to the market as that found in a small city.

A shopping center cannot generate new business or create new buying power; it can only attract customers

figure 2-1

Sales Potential for a Retail Center: Analytical Process

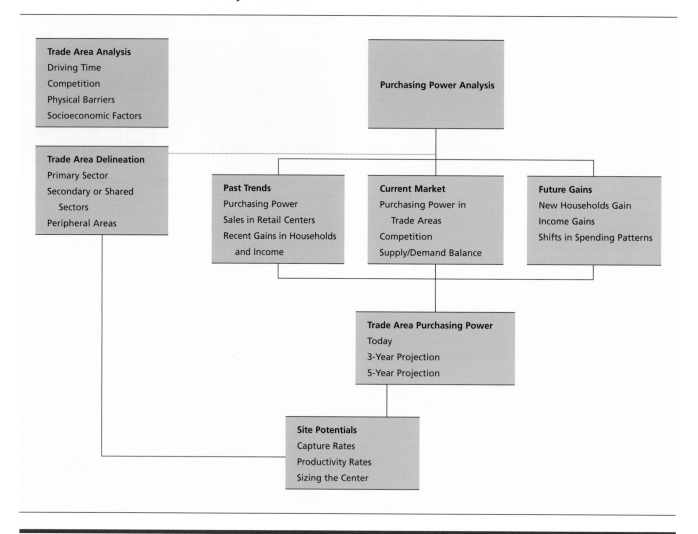

from existing businesses within or beyond the trade area that may be obsolete, fulfill an unmet need in the market area, or capture increased purchasing power that accrues with growth in population, number of households, employment, and/or income. It can cause a redistribution of business outlets and patronage, but it cannot create new customers. It can, however, induce change in consumers' purchasing behavior. Each new center must be justified by gauging the purchasing power available to it in light of competitive offerings.

The following key elements are typically part of a comprehensive market study for a shopping center. The extent to which all these elements are examined depends on the resources available, the complexity of the proposed center, and the level of sophistication desired.

- An analysis of the economic base in the metropolitan area, showing general characteristics of the market such as overall economic trends, employment trends, projections of economic activity, and growth patterns;
- Delineation of primary, secondary, and peripheral trade areas and accessibility to them;

- Population data for each trade area, including existing sizes, historic trends, and future projections;
- Demographic data for each market segment targeted and information about the resident population in the trade areas, including tourists, office workers, and convention and business travelers;
- Population characteristics for each trade area, including the number of households, families and singles, lifestyles, age cohorts, historic trends, and future projections;
- Income characteristics for each trade area, including household, family, and per capita totals, trends in disposable income, purchasing power, and future projections (three years, five years, and ten years);
- Patterns of and trends in expenditures by type of goods and services in the trade areas;
- Location, characteristics, and sales of competitive retail centers, by type of center, in the trade areas;
- Availability and absorption of retail space, and sales trends by retail category in the trade areas;
- Characteristics and status of proposed and planned retail developments in the trade areas;

- Neighborhood and site characteristics if a specific site has already been chosen for the center, or comparisons if multiple sites are under consideration;
- Capture rates, productivity rates, and recommended characteristics/anchors/sizing of the center or centers, depending on the scenarios being considered.

In addition, a retail analyst usually investigates ancillary indices of market area growth, such as land costs for housing, housing absorption rates, sales tax revenues, and bond programs for roads and utility infrastructure.

The territory from which customers will be drawn is indicated by a study of access roads; it is limited by distance, travel time, and competition. A demographic study of the supporting population's income and composition decides the type of retail outlets needed or wanted in the market area. The age groups and other characteristics of the trade area's population strongly influences the composition of tenants. Do major segments of the population consist of families or singles, blue-collar or professional workers, college-educated young people, or retirees? Accurately analyzing population traits and any changes in the composition of the population is of paramount importance in evaluating the feasibility of any retail location. The number, composition, density, growth rate, income, expenditures, buying habits, and lifestyles of the population can be translated into market potential. Much of this information can be extracted from census tract data, including metropolitan area supplements, sales tax reports, Bureau of Labor Statistics consumer expenditures, the Census Bureau's "Survey of Buying Power," and local trade area statistics available at the jurisdiction's planning and economic development offices.

Anchor Tenants

Seasoned developers clearly know characteristics of the trade area that will suit the type of center they want to build. But until they know what anchor tenants they can obtain, they can only surmise the type or size of center that might be feasible. For example, assume a neighborhood center is under consideration. If the most desirable supermarket chain operating in the region does not already have a store in the vicinity of the proposed center, and if the chain seeks to expand its number of outlets, and if its management typically makes reasonable deals with land developers, then the developer can project a certain pattern of success. On the other hand, if major chains have already established the optimal number of stores in the vicinity, leaving only weaker competitors available for the proposed site, the size of the center, its success, and other factors are evaluated differently. Only an astute leasing professional can recognize all these elements in terms of the selection of key tenants. For a proposed regional shopping center, the strength of the anchor tenants interested in the site selected determines the size, character, and success of the center—even the price that can be paid for the land.

A developer must be equipped with hard data to interest prospective tenants, to identify the site, to sketch the proposed plan, to satisfy the community, to obtain zoning approvals, and to secure financing. The result is a match between location, size, and composition of the center and the needs of the trade area. A market study is analogous to the chicken-and-egg conundrum, however. A potential key tenant will not be interested in a center until a market analysis has been completed, but a thorough analysis cannot be completed until it is known what kinds of key tenants the trade area will attract. Thus, two types of analyses must be made simultaneously: one to interest potential key tenants in anchoring a prospective center and one to determine the number and types of customers who might be attracted to the center. The customer draw influences the volume of business that can be expected by other major and supplementary tenants.

Obtaining commitments from major tenants is fundamental in determining the type and size of project, estimating project costs, and framing leasing arrangements with other tenants. Such commitments are key to a proj-

RTKL Associates Inc., LA

The Desert Passage at Aladdin, scheduled to open in Las Vegas in spring 2000, is a 450,000-square-foot mixed-use retail/ entertainment center. Its strategic location at the mid-point of the Las Vegas Strip will provide the center with high visibility and easy access to visitors.

Canal City Hakata, an urban entertainment/retail center that opened in 1996 on a nine-acre site in downtown Fukuoka, Japan, has attracted a diverse mix of international tenants as a result of its prime location and proximity to mass transit.

ect's economic feasibility. Without key tenants, no shopping center—no matter the size—can materialize. Even though specialty centers often do not have traditional anchor tenants, tenanting is still important, as a cluster or group of tenants probably will function as an anchor.

Pursuing and choosing appropriate anchor tenants depends on a clear understanding of the type of store that will benefit the center as well as locations such tenants are looking for and will accept. A good location for one anchor tenant (or other type of retailer) may not be a good location for another. For example, a location in a strip commercial development or a power center for a destination-type tenant such as a home improvement warehouse would not work for a specialty department store, which needs to be in a more centrally located regional center surrounded by other specialty stores, with significant pedestrian traffic leading to the store. The centers' ambience, character, and finishes will also be quite different for these fundamentally different types of tenants. Perhaps most important, the location and type of center have a strong impact on a retailer's drawing power, sales, and rent structure; moreover, anchor tenants very clearly understand the types of locations and shopping centers that will meet their requirements on all these issues. A well-conceived market study will make these distinctions and requirements clear.

A retailer analyzing new or existing markets is likely to ask two questions: how many stores of this type can the market support, and what is the minimum number of stores needed to gain a foothold in the market? The first retailer in a market often captures enough of the market potential to thwart competition until sufficient growth allows a second store, either his or a competitor's. In addition, many major retailers are public companies, and embarking on an aggressive expansion program is the only way to maintain a company's growth, earnings potential, and corporate objectives. Last, a retailer's distribution center may be underused or an investment in some new technology requires spreading out the cost to all existing stores in the chain; thus, the more stores, the lower the cost per store, even though some stores may be marginal performers.

Big-box anchor tenants, which are the anchors in power centers and some community centers, are a special case. Their corporate goal is to drive the competition from a market altogether (hence the name "category killer"). It is not uncommon for such stores to be built in such profusion that they oversaturate a market and eliminate the competition, leaving empty big-box anchors in the least competitive centers. Having won the competition, the winning big-box chains may then close some of their own stores that had been built solely to establish dominance in the market. As a result, it is particularly important to choose the strongest anchors as tenants in developing a power center.[2]

Trade Areas and Market Segments

The character of a prospective trade area and the nature of the competition in it shape the character of a shop-

If your office is like mine, not a day goes by without someone calling to offer what has to be "the best location conceivable" for our use. Sometimes, the caller even knows what it is we do! (With our name, America's Favorite Chicken Company, people are not sure who we are.) We have all heard the pitch: "I have this location that would be great for you. It is located in front of, or beside, or next to the highest-volume XYZ Restaurant in the system. You would do well there." When asked what this judgment is based on, the response is usually "because XYZ is doing such a bang-up job." Unless the corporate real estate group understands its company's business, which includes the targeted customer and business objectives, it will be hard pressed to make an effective argument against this reasoning. It is important to understand that the real estate expansion plan is very closely related to all other corporate business objectives.

Howard L. Green underscores this point in *Guide to Store Location Research*. Although the book was published in 1968, the recommendations in it are still applicable.

Appropriate financial and sales objectives of a retail firm that should be considered in retail site selection include the following:

1. Make enough profit
   a. to grow by renovating, expanding, or relocating an existing store, or building a new store in untapped portions of the market, or by expanding into markets new to the firm.
   b. to invest in new and improved supporting distributive facilities, and to [ensure] an appropriate supply of merchandise as needed.
2. Realize a satisfactory return on investment.
3. Increase the amount of sales and the number of customer transactions.
   a. Retain old customers and attract new ones.
   b. Increase the amount and/or quality of merchandise sold to each customer.

Requirements for attaining these sales objectives include:

1. Direct the overall merchandising effort to a specific market segment.
2. Develop a specific company "personality" or image by appealing to and satisfying consumer desires within the market segment served.
3. Establish specific merchandising practices.

When the objectives of the retail firm and its operating and merchandising policies are known, an analyst is in a position to determine the firm's store location strategy.

Several dozen factors related to analyzing the market, the trade area, and the specific site combine at different levels to generate sales. Their relative importance varies with the use, but all are important to the whole picture. Which factor should have the most impact on the decision to develop a site? In the past, but not so much today, a lot of the strategy on where to locate was to be as close as possible to McDonald's. Everyone knew that this company extensively reviewed and analyzed sites before they selected one. They also tended to draw a tremendous amount of traffic into an area. This fact was accepted by the evidence: McDonald's seemed to have very few failed locations. This kind of thinking and strategy, however, can lead to immediate trouble, because hamburger customers are not necessarily fish or Mexican food or pizza customers. Each potential customer probably likes, and does on occasion eat at, each of these restaurants, but the frequency of visits is very important. And the frequency of visits depends on how target customers are represented in the demographic comparison of the area.

Another approach to site selection is the "field of dreams strategy," also know as "if you build it, they will come." Perhaps early in the emerging restaurant business, it was true. Choices were limited, making the decision about where to shop for food relatively easy. If consumers decided to stop, it was at Joe's or Good Eats or Edna's Home Cooking. Today, if the restaurant is built, the customer may or may not come, depending on many factors. Today, it is not even necessary to go out for restaurant food. Many emerging companies will deliver dinner right to the customer's door. The virtual restaurant is also becoming a fact of life. People are choosing to stay at home, eat in, and not go out.

All of these changes, plus the addition of so many new types of restaurants, have made the entire decision process much more complicated for consumers. If a customer decides to go out for food, will it be to a destination-type restaurant, a specialty restaurant, or a quick-service restaurant? Will it be hamburgers, tacos, chicken, Chinese, or fish? Will it be McDonald's, Burger King, Hardens, Wands, Whataburger, Sonic, or White Castle? Will it be KFC, Kenny Rogers, Chick-fil-A, Bojangles, Popeyes, or Churchs? To facilitate decision making, the restaurant developer must remove as many obstacles as possible from the path of a potential customer.

So what are the basic criteria? Where does it all begin? William Applebaum, in Chapter 7 of *Guide to Store Location Research*, gives an overview of Richard L. Nelson's eight principles of retail location:

1. Adequacy of present area potential—Determine the trade area; count the people; ascertain how much money they have and are willing to spend on the type of goods a proposed store will sell; determine how much . . . the store could capture.
2. Accessibility of the site to the trade area—Secure maximum accessibility . . . from three sources:
   a. generative business—produced by the store itself.

b. shared business—secured by the store as the result of the generative power of neighboring stores.

c. ... business not generated by our own or neighboring stores, but attracted coincidentally.

3. Growth potential—The site should be, so far as possible, in a trade area where population and income are growing.

4. Business interception—Establish the store between where the people live and where they traditionally buy so that customers will be intercepted on their way to the marketplace.

5. Cumulative attraction—Stores together can draw more than stores apart. This applies to both similar and complementary sites.

6. Compatibility—Avoid interruption in shopper traffic and seek maximum customer interchange between stores.

7. Minimum competitive hazard—Select a location where there is a minimum of intercepting competitive sites and consider controlling such sites.

8. Site economies—Choose the most promising site in terms of cost to its productivity and future growth.

The application of these eight principles in a focused site search is a multistep process. Although each step involves a different amount of time and information for the different users, the steps generally can be broken down as follows:

1. Define the objective—If the company's business objectives are not known, an effective location for the best site is not possible.

2. Define the trade area—A site generally has a primary and a secondary trade area, and it might have a tertiary area. The primary trade area should generally supply 70 to 80 percent of the sales generated by the site. These boundaries are set by geographical and psychological obstacles.

3. Collect the demographic information—The information should show where customers live, where they work, their mobility within the market area, their socioeconomic characteristics, and their shopping habits.

4. Consider the market environment—This step includes all aspects of the market area. The market may be very strong and viable today, but what about five or ten years in the future? Does the local employment base bring the profile customer into the area daily? Is the local governing body proactive, or are insurmountable barriers placed in the path? Can active local groups assist in the plans, or will they be vocal opponents?

5. Study the competition—Competition can mean any restaurant that competes directly or indirectly for the same food dollar. Collect information about competitors' locations, available service, product served, cost of product, and sales estimates. Compare it to the other locations the chain might have in the area as well as to the site being developed.

6. Study your company's performance—The trade areas of existing locations and the amount of estimated penetration for existing locations need to be established.

The operating results of existing locations can be used as a barometer of the market.

7. Plan the strategy—Look at underpenetrated areas. Try to determine why the area is not developed. Does this area offer future opportunities? Is it possible that competitors will move into these areas? How does this site fit into current plans? Does it strengthen the market position? Does it fill a void? Does it serve as a stepping stone into new areas that are not yet served?

8. Do a financial analysis—Determine whether the projected financial investment will meet the financial hurdles set by the company.

The strength of any site is based on the combined strength of distinct sets of factors. Specific factors should be considered in a review of the market area, trade area, and specific site. The review of the market area should include demographic information, the potential for lunchtime customers, draw, distribution, and existing restaurants. As the focus is narrowed, some of the trade area factors that should be considered are the quantity and quality of traffic, access, exposure, and competitors.

It is accepted that the type of food from a quick-service restaurant is an impulse item and that the visit is basically a planned impulse purchase. Because of the nature of such visits, certain physical attributes must be considered for each specific use, including visibility, access, and the site's geography.

A final group of factors to be considered includes any that give the area a special advantage and supply additional traffic with additional customers. Very few, if any, quick-service restaurants can survive on this type of traffic alone. Specialty or destination-type locations can usually build a strong business from the traffic generated into regional centers of activity, interstate systems, and schools.

Several variables and factors are involved specifically in the selection of the site for a restaurant. Experience seems to indicate that the most important factors to be considered are those that deal with draw, distribution, site access, visibility, and exposure. Being near a regional center of activity also seems to add the extra push that a successful site needs.

But even with a complete action plan in place and a complete understanding of the concept, errors in judgment can and will be made. With the proper groundwork, however, they should be fewer. Some common errors are made as the direct result of overconfidence, the lack of consistent follow-through, and underpreparation:

- Assuming market share—This error is also known as the "king of the hill syndrome": the thought that no one else can take over a particular market niche.

The Glendale Marketplace replaced 12 blighted buildings in downtown Glendale, California. The project was fully leased upon opening in 1998, because the developer collaborated with tenants to ensure the new space met their needs.

- Miscalculating available spending power—Spending power does not always equal demand. Spending power is basically a mathematical function of the number of people, their income, and the number of competitors. Make certain that any information used about dollars available takes into account disposable income. For example, newer areas tend to have less disposable income even though income may be higher, partly because residents have higher mortgages and other payments. Another factor sometimes overlooked is how much money flows into another area when people who live in one area shop somewhere else.
- Misapplying trade area assumptions—This factor comes into play when the original estimates do not meet the criteria set for the investment. It is very tempting and easy to expand the boundaries of the trade area to create a pool large enough to draw from and substantiate the analysis. The simplest way to establish boundaries for the trade area is with concentric circles set at any chosen diameter. It is also the one area subject to the most error, because it does not take into consideration important aspects that will change the diameter in any given sector of the circle. Drive times may be a better indicator of what a trade area may look and act like. Using them takes more field time, but it is time well spent. The configuration of trade areas is affected by a number of items that could change the driving habits and patterns of customers, including alternative shopping choices, barriers, and pockets of congestion. The actual drive time a customer will spend in a car for a particular objective is the strongest parameter in setting the boundaries of a trade area.
- Failing to do adequate research—Make certain that as much shopping/buying history, current activity, and future plans are researched as possible.
- Using market averages to forecast potential—It is a lot easier to look at averages and make predictions than it is to get out into the field and do the research necessary for a clear decision.
- Ignoring business risks—Take care not to get caught up in the idea that being the biggest is good enough for any situation. Do not ignore the known risks of any business venture.
- Accepting quantity for quality—It seems sometimes that some sites are submitted on the basis of the broker submitting them. Quantity is not a replacement for quality.
- Assuming it's a good deal—It is not a good deal if it does not fit into your company's business plan and if it does not make any money.

Is site selection an art, a science, or black magic? Perhaps it is a combination of all three. One thing is certain: the process is important to the life of a concept. It is easy to see that to select the best possible site, it is imperative that the real estate team understand the business and what drives its success. Some basic requirements are used to build on for specific types of development. It is important that the corporate real estate group understand these differences to best serve the company and to be a vital part of the life of the corporation.

Source: Terry L. Conley, "A Site Savvy Primer for the Retail Sector," *Corporate Real Estate Executive*, June 1996.

figure 2–2

General Guidelines for a Primary Trade Area

Type of Center	Minimum Population Support Required	Radius	Driving Time
Super Regional	300,000 or more	12 miles	30 minutes
Regional	150,000 or more	8 miles	20 minutes
Community	40,000–150,000	3–5 miles	10–20 minutes
Neighborhood	3,000–40,000	1½ miles	5–10 minutes

Note: This table provides only general guidelines, which must be modified according to the characteristics of the specific shopping center being considered.

ping center, including type, quality, and tone. The trade area traditionally is the geographic area that provides the majority of the steady customers necessary to support a shopping center. The delineation of trade areas is more complex than in the past as a result of the proliferation in the variety and volume of shopping centers already present in most trade areas. It is further complicated by the existence of multiple consumer markets attracted to a center by their affinity for the type of goods sold and the environment in which they are sold rather than because the center is located within a prescribed distance of home or office. The boundaries of the trade area are determined by a number of factors, including the type of shopping center, accessibility, physical barriers, the location of competing facilities, and driving time and distance. Other factors may help define the trade area as well: government boundaries, ethnic neighborhoods, employment centers, mass-transit corridors, the density of development, and traffic congestion. A trade area does not lend itself to concentric circles around a potential site.[3]

As new shopping centers do not create buying power, they must attract existing customers from their trade areas and capture a portion of new buying power as those areas grow. Hence, the extent of the area from which a new center can be expected to draw the most significant number of its customers—whether residents, workers, tourists, or business travelers—must first be established. Within a shopping center's trade area, customers closest to the site affect the center most strongly, with their influence diminishing gradually as the distance increases. Trade areas are usually divided into three categories or zones of influence, although the following general guidelines describing these categories vary depending on the type of center and other factors.

- The *primary trade area* is the geographical area from which the center derives its largest share of repeat sales. This area typically extends to one and one-half miles for a neighborhood center, three to five miles for a community center, and eight to 12 miles for a regional mall. Driving time within the primary trade area ranges correspondingly from five to 30 minutes, and 70 to 80 percent of the center's regular customers

are drawn from this area. As market areas become increasingly saturated with shopping options, driving times normally decline, although increasing traffic congestion counteracts this trend. Some newer specialty centers like entertainment centers and off-price megamalls have even larger trade areas and may draw from an entire metropolitan area.

- The *secondary trade area* generates 15 to 20 percent of the total sales of an average shopping center. The extent of the secondary trade area is heavily influenced by the existence of similar centers nearby, and as a result, the extent of secondary trade areas varies widely, depending on the center's type and size, and the competition. For the largest centers, it may extend three to seven miles beyond the primary trade area.

- The *tertiary or fringe trade area* is the broadest area from which customers may be drawn. A small but sometimes significant share of a center's customers—particularly for large specialty centers, downtown centers, off-price centers, and entertainment centers—may be drawn from tourists and other travelers who do not live in the market at all. Although customers in the tertiary trade area must travel greater distances, they may be attracted to a center because it is more accessible or it offers unusual goods, greater parking, more stores, better value, or higher-quality merchandise than closer centers. For the largest centers, driving time from the tertiary market area to the site can be an hour or more, extending 15 miles beyond the primary trade area in major metropolitan markets. In much smaller markets, however, it may extend 50 miles or more.

Geographic distance and travel time must be differentiated. The competitive relationships among retail areas largely control the movement of shoppers in an urban area, and this situation can vary widely. Distance alone is therefore not a reliable criterion for establishing the extent of a trade area. In addition, a shopping center's trade area may extend farther in one direction than in another. Natural barriers such as lakes, rivers, hills, parks, and other open space or undevelopable land, as well as manmade barriers (which may by psychological) such as railroads, freeways, and large institutions, can act as boundaries to the trade area.

The size of a trade area also depends on a site's accessibility from streets, highways, and mass-transit stops (especially for infill sites for the latter). Travel times should be determined by actual trial runs over all access routes, with the runs made during peak and off-peak hours and under weather conditions typical of the area. Driving times, traffic lights, roadside hazards, and barriers such as steep slopes, stream valleys, parks, and railroads are all factors in determining access. And any proposed changes in existing routes must also be considered.

If a factory outlet or off-price megamall is considered, the market analysis generally should survey a larger trade area than if a traditional center of the same size is considered. Similarly, if a downtown entertainment center is proposed, the market analysis should reflect the fact that it will draw from far beyond the population living in the primary trade area. An entertainment center will draw heavily from metropolitan area residents, downtown office workers, business travelers, and tourists. The market

analysis for such a center should also take into account the drawing power of other downtown anchors and attractions, such as museums, sports facilities, historic sites, the overall character of the downtown environment in terms of appearance and safety, and how well the proposed center is integrated with this environment. All these factors can directly affect the center's potential to succeed or fail.

Using GIS (Geographic Information System) imagery and readily available computer software programs, a map of the geographic trade area can easily be plotted. Such a map puts into perspective current and proposed access routes, population density of developed areas, any commercial locations and competitive facilities, and topography and land use. Ordinary route maps, such as those issued by service stations, topographic maps published by the U.S. Geological Survey, and aerial photos available from or specially prepared by commercial air mapping services can also be helpful. The availability of this technology allows a developer to easily test different scenarios,

The primary trade area for a regional shopping center is typically eight to 12 miles; about 70 to 80 percent of the center's regular customers are drawn from this area. The Wolfchase Galleria in Memphis, Tennessee, draws from emerging residential areas on the east side of the metropolitan region.

General References and Market Guides

Bureau of the Census Catalog. Information about census products on housing, business, population, etc. (www.census.gov).

Market Guide (annual). Market data for more than 1,500 U.S. and Canadian cities. Editor and Publisher, 11 West 19th Street, New York, NY 10011-4234 (www.mediainfo.com).

"Surveying of Buying Power," one of four statistical compilations in *Sales & Marketing Management* (16 issues/year). Gives current estimates of U.S. and Canadian geographic variations in population, income, and retail trade. Bill Communications, Inc., 355 Park Avenue South, New York, NY 10010.

Government Data

The following publications may be ordered from the Superintendent of Documents, U.S. Government Printing Office, Washington, D.C. 20402, from field offices maintained by the U.S. Department of Commerce in 48 large cities, or, except where noted, from the Customer Services Branch, Data Users Service Division, Bureau of the Census, Washington, D.C. 20233.

1997 Census of Retail trade. In four parts.

- *Geographic Area Series* reports consist of 52 volumes, one for the United States, each state, and the District of Columbia.
- *ZIP Code Statistics Series* summarizes data for retail employers by five-digit ZIP Code and gives kind-of-business detail for establishments by sales and employment size category. Data are available only on CD-ROMs.
- *Nonemployer Statistics Series* reports include data on the number of establishments and receipts by kind of business, establishments with and without payroll, and number of proprietorships and partnerships.
- *Subject Series* reports consist of four volumes presenting tabulations for the United States with some additional geographic detail.

Current Business Reports. The Government Printing Office offers only the entire series; individual reports

must be ordered from the Bureau of the Census.

- *BR Monthly Retail Trade*—Sales and Inventories with annual cumulation.
- *BW Monthly Wholesale Trade*—Sales and Inventories with annual cumulation.
- *CB Advance Monthly Retail Sales.*

Survey of Current Business. Current business statistics compiled by the Bureau of Economic Analysis, U.S. Department of Commerce, in 12 issues per year.

Selected Construction and Housing Reports
- Housing Starts
- New Residential Construction In Selected Metropolitan Areas
- American Housing Survey for Selected Metropolitan Areas

Selected Population Reports
- Population Projections, States, 1995 to 2025
- Population Estimates: Metropolitan Area Population Estimates; Place and County Subdivision Estimates; County Estimates; and State Estimates

Population Characteristics, Special Studies, and Income
- P-60. *Money Income of Households, Families, and Persons in the United States.*
- *Consumer Expenditures and Income,* published periodically by the U.S. Department of Labor.

ULI Sources

ULI Market Profiles: North America, annual.
Provides insight and data on development activity by sector for 70 metropolitan areas. Profiles also are available for Europe and the Pacific Rim. ULI–Urban Land Institute, 1025 Thomas Jefferson St., N.W., Suite 500 W, Washington, D.C. 20007–5201 (www.uli.org).

ULI Metro Packets, updated annually.
Metro Packets provide a quick education in economic and market conditions in a specific metropolitan area. ULI –Urban Land Institute, 1025 Thomas Jefferson St., N.W., Suite 500 W, Washington, D.C. 20007–5201 (www.uli.org). ∎

---

trade area sizes and configurations, and assumptions to determine the optimum type and size of shopping center to be developed.

Population Data

The trade area's population and projected growth are key determinants of a proposed shopping center's viability. Secondarily, the composition of the population according to age, income levels, and family and household sizes is

helpful in refining the center's characteristics. The U.S. Census of Population and Housing (taken each decade) and the Census of Retail Trade (conducted every five years as part of economic censuses) offer basic statistics (see the accompanying feature box for specific reference works and sources). Projections for the trade area's population are often based on estimates for metropolitan area zones made by various planning agencies. It is important to understand the underlying assumptions in population projections, because they often vary depending on source and methodology used so they can be used to create an independent assessment of the market's potential for growth.

Because the shopping center development industry has become much more complex and centers are being targeted to even more specific market segments and niches, the need for timely, accurate, and sophisticated demographic data has increased significantly. In response to this need, a number of firms specializing in demographic data have emerged over the past ten years. Many of these firms offer sophisticated demographic analyses, including the use of a statistical technique known as "cluster analysis." These demographic groups are based on lifestyle/psychographic information (as well as basic age, sex, and income data) in recognition of the fact that people with different lifestyles shop differently.

Population also can be determined by using information from traffic zone studies, school district studies, building permit data, utility permit/hookup data, aerial photography, newspaper data, and studies performed by commercial demographic companies. For example, if aerial photography is available for a census base year, current photographs will make it possible to identify growth and may even allow a count of housing. Another source is building permit records showing the number of new dwelling units constructed in each census tract since the base census year. Many metropolitan newspapers maintain updated census tract maps and regularly conduct surveys of buyers. Utility companies have information on installation of new meters, which increase in direct proportion to the increase in new dwelling units. Figures can be adjusted to allow for known absorption of vacancies or demolitions. Fairly accurate estimates for population and households can be made in postcensus years by these indirect devices. In addition, in areas of rapid growth, state or local governments often conduct special censuses, as allocation of funds for roads, schools, and health and welfare services may be tied to population or to growth rates.

Demographic information on primary nonresident markets, including office workers, tourists, and business travelers, should be gathered from public agencies and private business and neighborhood associations that track these data. They include local urban planning and economic development departments, business improvement districts, downtown associations, chambers of commerce, hotel associations, convention center authorities, local tourist offices, and transportation management associations.

Purchasing Power

The income level within the trade area is critical to the success of a proposed center, not only in terms of total dollars available but also in relation to disposable income by retail category. Disposable income for households in the trade area can be derived from the census. In addition, the Bureau of Labor Statistics tracks how much families and individuals spend by category of income for each

RTKL Associates Inc., LA

Access to highways, streets, and mass transit helps determine the size of a shopping center's trade area. The renovation of the historic flagship Grace Bros. department store in downtown Sydney by RTKL has benefited from the more than 80,000 people who circulate daily from the nearby mass-transit station.

KMD

The concentration of many households with large disposable incomes in and near Pasadena, California, led to the redevelopment of a historic block of buildings into a successful retail center, One Colorado, that features art galleries, restaurants, and an eight-screen movie theater.

Centro Oberhausen, a mixed-use retail/entertainment center in northwest Germany, was the first megamall in Germany. The mall's trade area includes portions of Germany, France, Belgium, and the Netherlands. The size of the trade area results from the center's offering entertainment and retail options new to the European market.

major category of goods and services—food, food services, general merchandise, clothing and accessories, shoes, home furnishings, home appliances, building materials, hobbies, gifts, jewelry, liquor, drugs, automotive parts and accessories, and a range of personal services. Potential expenditures in each category can be estimated based on per capita purchasing power available in the trade area.

The total number of people multiplied by the average per capita expenditure within each retail category yields an area's total sales potential. A comparison of the total potential retail sales and the total actual sales in existing retail areas shows whether excess purchasing power is available that is not being spent or is leaking to surrounding trade areas. In either case, such a situation clearly indicates unmet potential for new retail development. But even without excess potential, the opportunity for new retail activity may exist if some of the existing retail stock is obsolete. Given the rapidly changing demands of consumers and the large stock of older retail space built in the 1960s, 1970s, and 1980s, obsolete space is becoming increasingly common. Estimating the amount of uncaptured trade potential, the potential trade that can be drawn from obsolete space to the proposed center, and the variation in expenditure patterns by different income groups helps to determine the size, type, and development concept for a proposed center.

In growing trade areas, it is not uncommon for centers to be built that exceed the size needed to meet current demand. Such centers depend on the continued growth of the trade area for success. In these cases, the area's future purchasing power must be carefully estimated and factored into the area's total available purchasing power. The full potential of centers that rely heavily on future growth of the trade area may not be reached for ten years as the market matures around them. Thus, the market study must take into account the center's anticipated underperformance in the early years to reap the benefits when the center and its market reach maturity.

The risk increases if a center is located too far on the leading edge of growth or too aggressive in its projections of purchasing power, as national economic trends and cycles can slow or stop growth for years, throwing carefully made projections out the window. Given the increasingly competitive nature of the shopping center industry, entry into the market more often requires riskier and earlier decisions to secure a location that will benefit from future growth in the trade area and beat the competition to the market.

Developers of new communities at the fringe of metropolitan areas or in more isolated areas may have to provide some initial shopping facilities before the market fully justifies them so they can sell houses and provide limited goods for the first families who move into the area.

In trade areas with low incomes or where income is declining, the proportion of total family income spent in nonfood stores typically is less than that in an area of medium-income or high-income families, while the proportion spent for food is higher. Thus, in a trade area where average family income is lower than the average for the city as a whole, the composition of stores is different from that in a trade area with a large proportion of high-income families. Nonetheless, significant purchasing power exists even in the poorest of neighborhoods, a demand that is rarely met. As a result, most purchasing power in lower-income neighborhoods leaks into surrounding wealthier trade areas, which residents often find are difficult to reach because they do not have automobiles. Developers and retailers are just beginning to understand the significant dimensions of untapped markets in lower-income urban areas (see the case study on New Community Shopping Center in Chapter 7).

Sales Forecasting and Competition

A new shopping center will not attract all the business in its trade area (primary, secondary, or tertiary), but it will draw on three sources: patrons from existing stores in the trade area, customers seeking goods and services currently not offered in the trade area, and, in the future, new residents, workers, tourists, and business travelers. A shopping center cannot, by definition, generate more purchasing power than already exists within the trade area, but it will cause a redistribution of expenditures. For this reason, a comprehensive market analysis should examine the types of retail facilities and stores available in the trade area as well as those that will come to the

market soon. The portion of spendable income that is unsatisfied by current offerings reveals the extent of potential sales leaking to other communities.

The increasing complexity of shopping centers and the multiple overlapping trade areas require the developer of a new shopping center to use several methods to estimate potential sales. Thus, the developer can bracket the range of anticipated sales at the proposed center and plan for different scenarios using expected, lower-than-expected, and higher-than-expected sales. Sales can be estimated using any method discussed in the following paragraphs.

A number of computer programs have been created to help forecast sales volume for individual retail stores. In some cases, they rely on an analog model in which market share for a new addition is compared with existing stores having roughly similar site and trade area characteristics. With the use of a regression model to project sales in new stores, sales in existing stores can be adjusted by factors expected to influence sales at a specific new location. Other simpler methods bracketing estimated potential sales volume can also be used: 1) a comparison of sales per square foot with other stores in the chain, assuming a similar productivity per square foot for a new store adjusted for variations in characteristics of the trade area; 2) an estimate of the volume achieved by competitors in the trade area and then redistributed based on

figure 2-3

Comparison of Performance Expectations

Performance Parameters	Traditional Super Regional Mall	New-Generation Retail Entertainment Destination Development
Scale	800,000 to 1.7 million square feet	250,000 to 600,000 square feet
Sales per Square Foot	$300 to $330	$700 to $1,200
Drawing Radius	Approximately 20 miles	Estimated 35 to 40 miles
Repeat Visitation	Average of three times per month, penetration of 80 to 200 percent	Average of two to four times per month, penetration of 100 to 400 percent
Regional Dominance	Achieved through department store anchors/scale/mix	Achieved through offerings unique to the region
Appeal	Tends to be focused on shopping trips	Broadened through entertainment and dining offerings
Duration of Visit	Approximately 1.24 hours	Estimated 3.5 hours
Demand Period Productivity	Concentrated across number of periods, affected by seasonality	Concentrated over evening and daytime periods, low periods enhanced through tourism and leisure activities
Tourist Draw	Limited	Potentially 20 to 40 percent of visitor base, depending on location

Source: MRA International.

Camden Park, a shopping center completed in the early 1990s in San Jose, California, features more retail shops than typically found in a neighborhood center. Camden Union Partners developed the center with a greater number of retail shops to tap unmet demand for retail and restaurant services in surrounding urban neighborhoods.

the new center's entry into the market; and 3) an estimate of market share based on market shares achieved in comparable locations.

Finally, some retailers have used a "gravity model" that combines store sizes and relationships in geographic distances. Reilly's Law of Retail Gravitation, formulated more than 60 years ago by William J. Reilly at the University of Texas–Austin, states generally that when two cities compete for retail trade, the breaking point for the attraction of such trade is more or less in direct proportion to the population of the two cities and in inverse proportion to the square of the distance from the immediate area of each city. In effect, people will travel to the largest place most easily reached, assuming the places offer the same types of goods and services (except for neighborhood centers, where customers are interested in convenience, not size). The model also assumes that the greater the store's or center's real or potential image or pull (because of the brands it sells), the greater its

market share. This pull, however, depends more and more not just on the size of a center; it also depends on the synergistic effects of the center's multiple stores, services, and entertainment attractions. This phenomenon is "the bundling effect," and the gravity model does not lend itself well to analyzing it. It is very difficult to estimate bundling effects except through past experience with similar concepts, and for this analysis the developer must rely on a sophisticated understanding of how consumers behave, how strongly emerging types of anchors attract customers, and the mix of retailing concepts and specific tenants that have the longest-lived appeal.

The projection of potential sales volume at a new shopping center presupposes a clear understanding of other shopping centers—both existing and those likely to be built—against which a new center will compete. They include suburban shopping centers within and beyond the trade area, retail facilities in the central business district(s), and streetfront retailing throughout the trade area, all of which might exercise a strong though vary-ing influence on residents throughout a metropolitan area. Although in the past tenants were clearly distinct according to shopping center types, in the 1980s and particularly in the 1990s, shopping center types are less distinct from one another and tenants that used to be found only in regional malls are increasingly found in other types of centers and vice versa. Moreover, new types of hybrid shopping centers and others filling newly iden-tified market niches are emerging—even in markets that by traditional standards are saturated with retail space. Sales at these new centers will depend on some existing centers' inability to meet the changing demands of today's consumers, with the result that some of their business will be cannibalized by emerging centers.

Determining what others are likely to build in the near future is a subjective call based on construction starts, announced plans, applications for approvals, and proposals being discussed in the media and among real estate pro-fessionals in the market. Public agencies keep records of building permits for shopping centers and applications for planning approvals and zoning variances. Some staff are likely to track retail construction and the issues it raises. The developer must remember, however, that not all pro-posals and plans will come to fruition; in fact, many projects in the pipeline most likely will never be built.

Shaping the Character of the Center

After the trade area and potential retail sales have been established, the character of the most feasible center begins to take shape. Developers typically specialize in certain types of centers, and the most successful of them develop long-term relationships with favored anchors and other key tenants. The advantages for developers are that they understand how these tenants do business, what kind of deals they seek, what their requirements are for location and amount of business, and under what circum-stances they will perform well. They are somewhat pre-dictable partners, and their presence lessens the risks of development. Developers are also able to leverage key tenants' demand for top center locations with locations that are less desirable, making it easier to fill secondary space. Moreover, retailers benefit from long-term relation-ships with shopping center developers. Their investors demand physical expansion and growing sales, and long-term relationships with key developers create a continu-ous source of new locations as well as the opportunity to strike deals for more flexibility on rents, overages, com-mon area maintenance charges, and other charges.

Shaping a shopping center's character usually begins with a determination of key anchor tenants. For conve-nience centers, anchors typically are minimarts, although as shown in Figure 2-4, numerous other options are avail-able. For neighborhood centers, supermarkets and drug-stores are the most common anchors, as they provide the basic goods and services most people need daily. Community centers have even more varied options for anchors. In traditional community centers, anchors are typically junior and discount department stores, super-markets, and off-price superstores. Power centers include the same types of anchors, but there are more of them and therefore less side space. Regional and super regional shopping centers are anchored by full-line department store and fashion department stores. In some cases, non-traditional anchors are added as department stores go dark. Such new anchors include entertainment centers, megaplexes, elaborate food courts that include sit-down as well as takeout food, and large-format specialty and off-price stores.

Retail analysts prepare lists of probable tenants, in-cluding anchors and key tenants, while the market analy-sis is being conducted. Increasingly, developers strive for a mix of local and national tenants. National tenants, also called "credit tenants," provide the strong credit ratings needed to finance a shopping center, while local tenants provide the offerings that give the center its distinctive character. In most areas, some local merchants are stronger than others, and a merchant's local standing should be

figure 2-4
Typical Shopping Center Anchors

Convenience	Neighborhood	Community	Regional/Super Regional
Minimart	Supermarket	Junior department store	Full-line department store
Restaurant	Drugstore	Discount department store	Fashion department store
Beauty parlor	Discount department store	Supermarket	Megaplex
Dry cleaners	Restaurant	Off-price superstores	Entertainment center
Fast food service	Furniture store	Variety store	Food court
Medical and dental office	Hardware store	Family wear store	Large-format specialty store
	Automotive store	Furniture store	Large-format off-price store
	Liquor/wine store	Sporting goods store	
	Videotape rental store	Drugstore	
	Bank	Office supply store	
		Cinema	

Source: *Dollars & Cents of Shopping Centers: 1997* (Washington, D.C.: ULI–the Urban Land Institute, 1997).

considered. For example, a majority of customers might prefer one supermarket over another. Therefore, popular established merchants are likely to draw more patrons to a new center, strengthening its appeal.

Identified market segments in a trade area, combined with national trends in the shopping center industry, often suggest a special character for the proposed center that would allow it to depart from the traditional tenant mix for a neighborhood, community, or regional center, and special tenant categories to include that could be supported because of their presence, or absence, in the market. For example, conventional wisdom indicates that if an area has few children and the population of children is projected to remain low, the demand for children's shoes, clothing, and toys would be low. If a large population of elderly resides in the market, however, the demand for children's goods could be great, because grandparents are known to buy a large number of gifts for their grandchildren. In a market with a large number of young professional singles, the demand for food-service tenants will likely be greater, because adults without children tend to eat out more often. Additional market analysis could quantify such potential.

Based on the estimated sales volume and the character of the projected sales resulting from the market analysis, the developer/investor and the staff should estimate the types of stores, the physical formats needed to house them, the number of levels, and the approximate square footage of building space that can be supported. Necessary

parking should be estimated based on the type of center planned, its total gross leasable area, and any special uses that require unusual numbers of parking spaces, such as cinemas. Local zoning regulations typically require a certain number of parking spaces per 1,000 square feet of gross leasable space. As reported in *Dollars & Cents of Shopping Centers: 1997,* the median parking index is currently 5.39 spaces per 1,000 square feet for super regional centers, 5.42 for regional centers, 4.98 for community centers, and 5.00 for neighborhood centers, although local regulations for each type of center vary.

The total land area required for a shopping center, including parking and access, can then be measured and the figure compared with requirements for coverage dictated by local zoning on potential sites. If the site is large enough to accommodate the planned center, a schematic layout can be sketched. If the site is not large enough, the developer must choose one of several options: choose another site, apply for rezoning, or reconfigure the center with additional levels.

Assumptions made by the developer in any market study should be conservatively made, clearly understood, and based on realizable goals. The assumptions are critical to the validity of the study, as the primary purpose of a market survey is to find out whether the area can support a new shopping center of the type considered, not to convince prospective tenants that the trade area needs and can support a proposed center. Key tenants will themselves conduct their own market studies, as

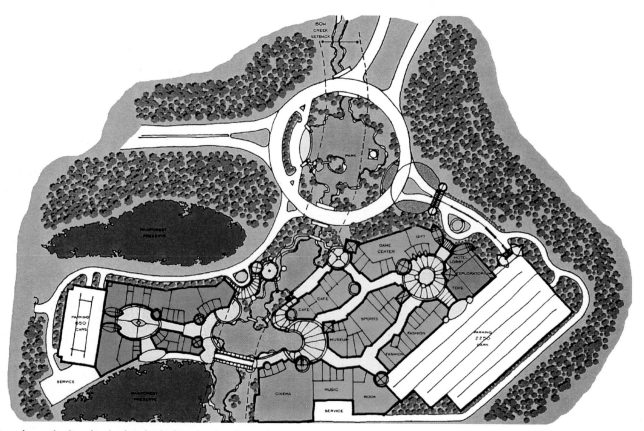

The schematic site plan is sketched after the developer determines that the site is large enough to accommodate the proposed center. The Tambore Entertainment Center in Brazil required a creative site plan because it is surrounded by a protected rain forest and bisected by a river.

The mix of tenants and the amount of space reserved for each type of tenant greatly influence the level of income a shopping center will generate. Arrowstreet's redesign of a failing downtown shopping center in Worcester, Massachusetts, has made the Worcester Common Fashion Outlets a successful upscale outlet mall. Early preleasing commitments from the Saks Clearinghouse, the Sports Authority, and Bed Bath & Beyond helped ensure greater confidence in projected revenue.

Arrowstreet Inc.

Arrowstreet Inc.

Waterfront and highway access make Bridgeport Harbour Place an excellent site for a mixed-use commercial development in Bridgeport, Connecticut.

their criteria and assumptions are likely different from the developer's in some respects.

Financial Feasibility

The economic analysis should follow the market study, because it draws upon and interprets the findings of the market study. It largely determines the proposed center's financial feasibility. The feasibility study reveals more of the kind of center that might be developed by analyzing the total retail space (with space assigned to key tenants and supplementary stores) and by projecting rental income (with minimum rents, annual sales volume, and percentage rents).

Projections should be consolidated in pro forma statements on the estimated cost of development, income and expenses of the center, and the center's projected cash flow in the initial years, in a stabilized year at maturity, and in later years when sales may decline absent additional investment in physical improvements. The pro forma statement on development costs indicates the estimated total investment or capital cost for the project, broken down into several major categories—land and land improvements, buildings and equipment, and overhead and development costs incurred before a center opens (sometimes called "soft costs")—which include several items (see Figure 2-5):

- The basic cost of land plus carrying charges until construction is completed;
- Off-site improvements, such as extending utilities to the site and improving roads or traffic access;
- On-site improvements, such as grading, underground utilities, storm drainage, paving, striping, and lighting the parking lot, and landscaping;
- Building costs for construction of the basic building shell as well as the cost of tenant improvements paid by the landlord;

- Professional fees for lawyers, economic analysts, land planners, architects, interior and graphic designers, engineers, landscape architects, and those who prepare environmental impact statements and applications for zoning approval;
- Commissions and financing fees for permanent financing;
- Leasing costs;
- Carrying charges during construction and until the project reaches the break-even point, including interest and fees for construction financing, taxes and insurance costs incurred during construction, and expenses incurred before opening for publicity, public relations, and the grand opening; and
- Development fees imposed by the local jurisdiction.

The operating statement lists anticipated income and expenses and indicates the projected net operating income and cash flow for the center. Four major items provide income: minimum rents; percentage rents; reimbursements from tenants for operating expenses (including common area maintenance charges), taxes, and insurance; and miscellaneous income. Expenditures include general and administrative costs such as management fees and leasing costs, on-site management costs, common area and building maintenance costs, HVAC, utilities for tenant space, insurance, real estate taxes, advertising and promotion, and other miscellaneous items (see Figure 2-6).

The cash flow statement includes all quantifiable data in relation to time. It can help determine a project's profitability, the amount of debt financing needed, the ability of the project to carry the debt service, and the project's value.[4]

Projections of income included in the pro forma statements are based on a leasing plan that represents the developer's estimate of the amount of space to be rented to specific types of tenants. Thus, the allocation of space to the various types of tenants is a critical com-

figure 2–5
Shopping Center Capital Costs

Land and Land Improvements

Land or Leasehold Acquisition

Cost of land

Good faith deposit

Broker's fee

Escrow

Title guarantee policy

Standby fee

Chattel search

Legal fee

Recording fee

Off-Site and On-Site Land Improvements

Off-site streets and sidewalks

Off-site sewers, utilities, and lights

Relocation of power lines

Traffic controls

Surveys and test borings

Utilities

- Water connection to central system or on-site supply
- Storm sewers
- Sanitary sewer connection to system or on-site disposal
- Gas distribution connection to central system
- Primary electrical distribution
- Telephone distribution

Parking areas

- Curbs and gutters
- Paving and striping
- Pedestrian walkways
- Traffic controls and signs
- Lighting
- Service area screens and fences

Landscaping

- Grading
- Planting

Buildings and Equipment

Shell and Mall Building

Layout

Excavation

Footing and foundations

Structural frame

Exterior walls

Roofing and insulation

Subfloor

Sidewalk canopy

Sidewalks and mall paving

Loading docks and service courts

Truck and service tunnels

Equipment rooms, transformer vaults, cooling towers

Heating and cooling—central plants or units

Incinerator

Community meeting rooms

Offices for center management and merchants' association

Electric wiring—roughed in

Plumbing—roughed in

Fire sprinkler system

Public toilets

Elevators, escalators, stairways

Contractor's overhead and profit

Pylons

Shopping center signs

Mall furniture, fountains, etc.

Maintenance equipment and tools

Office furniture and equipment

Tenant Improvements (if paid for by developer)

Tenant finish allowance

Storefronts

Window backs and fronts

Finished ceiling and acoustical tile

Finished walls

Interior painting

Floor coverings

Interior partitioning

Lighting fixtures

Plumbing fixtures

Doors, frames, and hardware

Storefront signs

Store fixtures

Overhead and Development

Architecture and Engineering

Site planning

Buildings and improvements

Internal and Financing

Interest during construction

Construction and permanent loan fees

Loan settlement costs

Appraisal costs

Legal fees—financing

Administrative Overhead and Construction Supervision

Construction supervision

Field office expense

Bookkeeping

Home office expense

Travel and entertainment

Salaries and overhead of staff

Printing and stationery

Leasing Costs and Legal Fees

Leasing fees paid to brokers

Salaries and overhead of staff

Scale model, brochures, etc.

Legal fees—leasing

Legal fees—general

Other Overhead and Development

Market and traffic surveys

Zoning and subdivision approvals

Outside accounting and auditing

Real estate taxes

Other taxes

Insurance

Advertising and promotion of opening

Landlord's share of formation and assessments of merchants associations

Miscellaneous administrative costs

Source: Urban Land Institute.

figure 2–6
Illustrative Pro Forma Operating Statement[1]
(GLA = 900,000 Square Feet)

	Per Square Foot of GLA	Total Dollars
Income		
Minimum Rent	$18.00	$16,200,000
Percentage Rent	1.00	900,000
Real Estate Taxes	1.25	1,125,000
Common Area Maintenance	4.00	3,600,000
Utilities	2.25	2,025,000
HVAC	2.00	1,800,000
Insurance	0.15	135,000
Other Income	0.15	135,000
Gross Potential Income	28.80	25,920,000
Vacancy Allowance @ 5.00%[2]	−1.44	(1,296,000)
Total Income	$27.36	$24,624,000
Expenses		
Management /Leasing Fee @ 5.00%[3]	$1.05	$945,000
General and Administrative	0.70	630,000
Common Area Maintenance	3.50	3,150,000
HVAC	1.40	1,260,000
Utilities	1.95	1,755,000
Insurance	0.15	135,000
Advertising and Promotion	0.25	225,000
Real Estate Taxes	1.25	1,125,000
Other Expenses	0.20	180,000
Total Expenses	$10.45	$9,405,000
Net Income before Debt Service	$16.91	$15,219,000
Property Value		$174,000,000
Mortgage Amount		$130,500,000
Mortgage Constant[4]		7%
Annual Debt Service		$9,135,000

[1] For mall GLA only. Does not include department stores. Income and expenses for department stores are assumed to be on a break-even basis.

[2] Vacancy allowance at full occupancy, expected in year 3.

[3] Management and leasing fee based on 5 percent of minimum plus percentage rent.

[4] Financing is a joint venture. Lender receives interest income as well as a share of the cash flow after debt service and a portion of the resale value of the property at the end of the holding period.

ponent of the financial feasibility analysis. Such a determination should be made only by an experienced economic analyst so that the information in the survey can be related to the merchandising plan for the center. In other words, the analyst must correctly "analyze the market analysis" and interpret it to create the result desired, which is a shopping center containing stores offering the kind of merchandise at the proper prices and in sufficient quantity to satisfy demand from the trade area.

This same type of analysis with recommended store size can be applied to every potential line of merchandise to yield a picture that is close to what the tenant size and mix could be for all stores in the center. As preleasing occurs, information becomes more precise, and revenue projections can be made with a higher degree of assurance.

Feasibility studies, despite their necessity, are not infallible. Often they support conclusions that ultimately are not valid and cause a project to fail. Developers may see them only as necessary evils required to secure financing and therefore wish them to render the most optimistic forecasts. The analyst may assume the role of developer's advocate rather than independent observer. And the mortgagee may not have the staff available to evaluate the report properly and decide on its credibility. All these factors become especially critical during a downturn in the market. To avoid this situation, the developer should instruct the financial analyst on the precise nature of the study. The results should show a range of probable results and should not overstate growth projections. A downside analysis can project how the center will perform in a severe recessionary period or when unforeseen competition reduces operating revenues, and allow the developer to plan in advance for such contingencies.

Site Selection, Evaluation, and Acquisition

Selecting the right site for a shopping center is crucial, yet suitable sites for development are increasingly hard to find. And when a site is found, the location may not be zoned for commercial use, complications may develop in acquiring the property (perhaps from opposition in the community), or the land may cost too much. These factors increasingly are the realities of site selection for a shopping center.

A proposed site must exhibit the best possible combination of the following characteristics, whatever the type of center and whether or not the developer already owns the land:

- A central location relative to targeted markets;
- Easy access;
- High visibility;
- Proper size and shape relative to the proposed concept and parking requirements;
- Workable topography;
- Good drainage;
- Minimal complications in the subsoil;
- Available utilities;
- Compatible surroundings;
- Appropriate zoning; and
- Acceptable environmental impact.

The absence of any of these factors will likely have a negative effect on the project's feasibility, the length of time required to develop the project, development costs, and, ultimately, tenants' sales. Even if the shopping center developer already owns the site, the site must still be evaluated carefully to justify its use for the proposed development. Too often, shopping centers have been built simply because a developer owned a tract of land with highway frontage. A decision to build on land already owned must be based on the same market, financial, and site analyses used to purchase a parcel of land for a shopping center. If the site fails to qualify based on the analyses, the developer should acquire another site—or

forget the development. Developing an inappropriate site merely because the developer owns it can result in overdevelopment (because the best site is likely to be already developed) or the creation of a shopping center in an inappropriate location, causing sprawl, unnecessary traffic congestion, and environmental degradation. In any case, centers built on less desirable sites will most likely be less competitive than other shopping centers in the market.

Downtown and infill sites have often been overlooked as suburban markets have become saturated. They usually require the most creativity for a development, however, because such properties often come with unusual circumstances—special environmental issues, concerns involving demolition, lease encumbrances, multiple ownerships, municipal covenants, and multiple layers of approval, all of which can derail the best of intentions. Moreover, residents of surrounding neighborhoods, some of whom have lived there for decades, usually have strong

The renovation of the historic James C. Flood Building in San Francisco included preserving the existing facade and renovating three retail floors. The dense population and the excellent location on one of the busiest streets in San Francisco contributed to the project's success.

figure 2-7
Site Selection Checklist

Location

Description of location, address

Map, aerial photography

Site availability

Regional access

• Existing

• Proposed

Public transportation

Neighboring land use

• Adjacent

• Beyond (define)

Quality/stability of neighborhood

Competition

• Location (map)

• Type, size

• Quality of tenant mix

• Occupancy and turnover

Estimated trade area (map definition)

Trade area population and distribution
   (densities)

Community attitudes toward commercial
   developments

Proposed developments: residential,
   commercial

Site Data

Plat (dimensions, size)

Legal description of site(s) available

Topographical features

• Visual

• Survey

Subsoil conditions

Problems (water, rock, fill, other)

Zoning, building controls

Rezoning required?

Infrastructure elements

Ingress, egress

Visual exposure, frontage

Restrictions, easements, encumbrances

Adjacent land availability (expansion)

Current on-site improvements, if any

Daily traffic counts

Environmental constraints

Financial

Asking price and terms

Conditions of sales transfer

Options available

Property taxes

Assessment fees on sewer, gas, water,
   stormwater drains, other

Title cost

Recording taxes

Administrative

Zoning

• Current zoning and permitted use

• Zoning authority

• Planning commission

• Local zoning attorney

• Local government

Building department

• Clearances and setbacks

• Fire zone and fire department
   requirements

• Inspection requirements

Construction requirements from highway
   department

Engineering

Other, such as any local civic association

Legal

Legal description, title examination

Easements and restrictions

Filing of records

Utilities and Infrastructure

Location and map of:

• Water mains

• Sewer mains

Gas mains

Electricity supply lines

Telecommunications lines

Stormwater drains

Special requirements

• Public areas

• Special grading: streets, slow-down ramps

• Curbs and gutters

• Sidewalks

• Landscaping and screens

Miscellaneous

Any demolition required

Possible use of improvements

Source: "Shopping Centers: How to Build, Buy, and Redevelop," a workshop sponsored by ULI–the Urban Land Institute.

opinions about the nature of new development in the neighborhood. On the plus side, however, many infill and downtown sites may be more immune from variations in the economy or the oversupply of retail space because of the already built-up nature of the surrounding property that makes competitive locations unavailable.

Choosing a Location

Location is of paramount importance in the success of all types of shopping centers. The site must qualify by virtue of its trade area, the income level of the households in the area, competition, highway access, and visual exposure. Location and access are interrelated but separate aspects. The site must be easy to reach, and the roads must have extra capacity to avoid congestion during periods of high-volume traffic. The site must be easy to enter and safe to leave for customers and employees, or it must be able to be modified to make it so. Ideally, the site also should represent an impregnable economic position. Its

superior access, greater convenience, better merchant array, and improved services should make it impractical for another similar project to be developed nearby.

Recommended distances between shopping centers cannot be established precisely, either for the same or different type centers. It is not mere distance between centers, but population density, convenience, accessibility, and diverse merchandise that count. For example, multiple convenience and neighborhood centers can operate successfully within the trade area of a regional center, or even be located next to or across the road from it. Likewise, power centers and other types of community centers often are developed across from or next to regional centers to tap the already established shopping patterns of the regional center's customers. Such coexistence is possible because the two types of centers offer distinct ranges of merchandise. While shoppers at a neighborhood center want convenience in buying everyday goods and services, customers of the regional center are primarily comparison shoppers who are looking for and comparing the price, quality, size, color, and style of general merchandise.

General guidelines for location are useful as a *starting point,* but they are not definitive and will need to be modified based on the specific market and location:

- *Neighborhood centers* draw from a radius of approximately one and one-half miles, depending on the density and character of the residential area. Walking distance is not a valid criterion, particularly in suburban locations. One and one-half miles is too far to carry groceries, but in built-up areas where high-density multifamily housing and mixed uses are part of the general development pattern, walking distances as well as the site's location in relationship to other commercial areas and mass transit must be considered.
- *Community centers* draw from an area within three to five miles of the site.
- *Regional and super regional centers* draw from distances of eight miles or more. Driving time rather than distance, however, better determines these centers' area of influence. Although the maximum driving time might be 20 minutes, it may entail a distance of as few as two to as many as 20 miles, depending on traffic and highway conditions.

The drawing power for regional centers in metropolitan areas suggests that five to ten miles separate competing regional centers. In cases where regional centers have been built much closer together, the results are mixed. Inland Center Mall and Carousel Mall (formerly Center City Mall) in San Bernardino, California, for example, are only one mile apart; Center City Mall had been built in downtown San Bernardino to bring retail sales back to the downtown area after Inland Center Mall was built in the mid-1960s. Because of the short distance between the two centers, both have suffered. In suburban Washington, D.C., Tysons Galleria was built in the late 1980s across the street from Tysons Corner, a center first developed in the late 1960s and expanded in the early 1990s. Together they encompass eight department stores and more than 2 million square feet of space. Their success, however, depends on circumstances of the size and wealth of the surrounding market area and could be repeated in few other locations.

Neighborhood and convenience centers should be located on sites reached by collector streets; minor residential service streets should not serve as principal access points. If a neighborhood or convenience center is justified in a new planned unit or residential cluster development, the center should be placed where a major artery can serve the center as well as the interior residential areas of the development.

In a new, large-scale residential development, such as a satellite community or new town on several thousand acres of land, the hierarchy of shopping centers is determined by land use allocation on the master development plan during site planning. In these cases, site selection

becomes part of overall planning, and the developer and the planning team should choose the most advantageous sites for shopping centers. A major retail center should also incorporate civic and cultural facilities—offices, a library, an auditorium, and police and fire stations—as well as other uses typically found in a downtown as part of the planned center for the new community. Neighborhood and convenience centers should be located

The distance between two competing centers depends on the size of the trade area. In general, the drawing power of regional centers indicates that five to ten miles should separate competing regional centers. In selected areas with favorable growth and demographic trends, however, the market may be large enough to support two regional centers located closer together. The Lenox Square Mall, located in rapidly growing Buckhead, a suburb of Atlanta, successfully competes with the neighboring Phipps Plaza.

and designed to encourage access by pedestrians as well as automobiles.

Community centers should be located for easy access from major thoroughfares. Because their array of stores represents limited lines of shopping goods as well as convenience goods and services, these centers do not need to be accessible from an extended trade area via high-speed freeways. For off-price super community centers and power centers, however, trade areas can approach or even exceed those of some regional centers. In these cases, a location near a regional center with freeway access is preferred.

Regional centers customarily are located on sites that are the most accessible in metropolitan areas. Interchange points between expressways and freeways in suburban areas and the most visible and accessible downtown locations are preferred. Easy access to mass transit may also be important in some metropolitan areas; in Washington, D.C., for example, several regional centers—Pentagon City, Ballston Commons, Mazza Gallerie, and White Flint—are accessible from the Metro system. If a center is easily reached via freeway, travel times are reduced, congestion on local streets minimized, and access for customers, employees, and service vehicles more efficient. The distance from an interchange to a regional center ideally is less than one-half mile to a mile, depending on local circumstances; but in all cases the center should be highly visible.

Large shopping centers generate a high volume of traffic; thus, access points should not be too close to free-way interchanges because traffic can become severely congested during peak travel hours. Vehicles carrying shoppers interfere with the flow of through traffic, and the resulting congestion is intensified if stacking lanes (where cars wait to enter or exit from high-speed high-ways) are too short. Such congestion often occurs at the 1.9 million-square-foot Tysons Corner Center in McLean, Virginia.[5] By locating the access and exit points of major centers about one mile from regional freeways, cars can then be directed by signs onto various arterial streets before feeding onto the freeway, thus avoiding congestion.

In theory, a cloverleaf-type separation between two intersecting traffic routes helps draw customers by giving the center high visibility and drivers the opportunity to change travel directions easily. But in reality, a site at a cloverleaf grade separation offers poor access. The grade separation is complicated, confusing, and subject to traffic backups and accidents. Because of the higher speeds of through traffic, it is often difficult to switch to lanes leading to off-ramps that approach the center.

The only advantage for a center fronting on a restricted-access highway is that the center is highly visible. Entrance and exit points to the site require special local access lanes so that drivers can avoid left turns and other movements that might interfere with reaching the center easily. The ideal site for a regional center is one ringed by major traffic routes having access points and traffic control devices carefully designed to disperse traffic over a major street system and to handle the peak loads generated by such centers.

A good location can be convenient for a center based on distance traveled. Today, however, convenience has as much to do with saving time, stocking a range of needed items, ease of transaction, confidence and trust in stores and their merchandise, and a feeling of personal safety when shopping.

Access to the Site

Good access is an integral aspect of a suitable site, and the services of a professional traffic engineer are essential early during site analysis. If a site is not easy to enter and safe to leave, it must be made so. Traffic should flow freely toward the entrance of the site. Designing or re-designing the traffic flow at shopping center entrances requires the cooperation of traffic engineers and local highway departments. If an access road cannot carry the additional traffic and turning movements generated, the cost of necessary improvements should be considered. The bearer of those costs—the highway department, the developer, or both—must be negotiated as well as the proportion of costs each will bear.

Left turns require specially constructed lanes or an island for turning movements. Right turns on heavily trafficked routes require deceleration lanes for easy entrance and acceleration lanes for easy exit. Bottlenecks at entrances or backups on major traffic routes caused by cars moving into or out of a center can annoy customers.

Good visibility improves a center's accessibility. A shopper driving at 35 miles per hour (the speed of local traffic) can easily overshoot the entrance to the parking lot if he or she has not seen the shopping center and its entrance from the access road. Clear signage helps direct shoppers, increases visibility, and heightens awareness that a shopping center is near. Overpasses, hills, curves in the road, and heavy vegetation all impede visibility. Even though traffic flow attracts retail business, a site that fronts on a highway heavily built up with strings of competing distractions (including signs) is actually less accessible.

Configuration and Shape of the Site

The site for a shopping center should generally be somewhat regular in shape and configured in one contiguous piece. Many variations exist, however, based on the type of center planned and the character of the surrounding neighborhood. When the development concept calls for a neotraditional town center, streetfront retailing, or entertainment center, dedicated streets can bisect the site. In all cases, care must be taken so that traffic through a site does not impede the flow of pedestrians or complicate the movement of cars within the parking area.

Site depths vary widely and cannot be standardized. They depend on the type of center to be built and the total acreage available. The traditional strip commercial development of the past is an inappropriate design model for today's shopping centers, because much greater depth is now required to accommodate large-format stores, parking, and traffic circulation. A site with a regular shape—no acute angles, odd projections, or indentations—lends itself best to an efficient layout. If, however, an irregu-

Grapevine Mills, a value-oriented megamall in the Dallas/Fort Worth area, is the beneficiary of easy access from a state highway and the Dallas/Fort Worth Airport, which is just two miles away. The neon signage provides excellent visibility for the center, which draws shoppers from as far away as 100 miles.

larly shaped site is the only one available, it should still have adequate frontage for the center to be visible from access thoroughfares and for control of the center's image. Portions of an oddly shaped site may be unusable, while in other cases an odd shape could accommodate free-standing auxiliary facilities on outparcels—auto service centers, drive-in services, family restaurants, dry cleaning establishments, and financial institutions, for example.

Size of the Parcel

As a rule of thumb, each 40,000 square feet (about one acre) of site area in a typical suburban location has roughly 10,000 square feet of building area and 30,000 square feet of surface parking area (including landscaping, circulation space, delivery area, and so on)—or 25 percent coverage. For example, a 435,600-square-foot site (ten acres) can readily accommodate 100,000 square feet of building area for a conventional shopping center. A rough calculation of this sort is useful only for gauging the adequacy

of a site in an outlying suburban location, however, and would not be applicable in determining the adequacy of a downtown or infill site. In any case, requirements for lot coverage and floor/area ratio (FAR) are set forth in local zoning and subdivision regulations, and they vary from jurisdiction to jurisdiction. In dense urban areas and in some maturing suburban locations, rising land costs and competition from other land uses may make a sprawling, single-level shopping center economically unjustifiable.

In power centers and other large-scale off-price centers that contain a variety of category killers, warehouse clubs, discount department stores, multiscreen cinemas, restaurants, and side tenants, about 20 percent lot coverage is reasonable. In older centers, particularly those in dense urban areas and configured in multilevel space, coverage of at least 30 percent is normal. For downtown shopping centers where setbacks are not permitted and parking is underground, lot coverage is considerably higher.

The developer of Leesburg Corner Premium Outlets used the portions of the site not covered by buildings to create an outdoor village setting to enhance the shopping experience of customers in this outlet center in Leesburg, Virginia, about 45 minutes from Washington, D.C.

Land parcels in the future are likely to be smaller because of the limited number of sites available, the increasing use of urban infill sites, and zoning restrictions that have been enacted in response to environmental concerns. Less land may be needed for parking as well, because parking regulations are being revised to reflect parking demand more accurately. Moreover, integrating shopping centers with other forms of development to create a more convenient one-stop destination is increasingly a goal of planners and developers creating the new generation of retail centers. They recognize that a horizontal center spreading over vast acreage and separated by vast parking lots from the surrounding community can destroy the intended benefits of a shopping center—convenience and a pleasant shopping environment.

If the trade area of the proposed center is projected to grow, the developer should consider acquiring a land parcel large enough to allow for future expansion. Phasing construction as the market matures limits initial risk, construction costs, and leasing expenses. Future success, however, may depend on the ability of the center to expand and reposition itself as its market grows around it, which will depend on the size and strength of the original site.

If a shopping center reaches its projected sales volume by capturing a high proportion of the available purchasing power, others inevitably will try to tap into this success by building competing facilities nearby—if land is still available and if local zoning allows it. Given the interest of most communities in expanding their commercial tax base, open land zoned for residential use but located close to a shopping center may even be rezoned to permit additional retail space. The developer therefore may want to buy extra land to protect the location from subsequent encroachment. If the developer builds a center carefully conceived to fit its present trade area that also allows for potential growth, the center may be so successful that it actually discourages any competition. Land purchased when the center is first conceived that is not used at the outset will likely increase in value because of the construction of the shopping center itself and the general rise in land prices over time. Even if this land is never needed for expansion of the shopping center, it could prove to be a good investment because it could be developed for some other use or sold to another user. Nevertheless, high property taxes and other carrying costs may make holding undeveloped land for extended periods unprofitable.

The rising cost of land can become a dominant factor in the selection and development of a site. The high acquisition costs of a site, however, may be offset by a multiuse or multilevel configuration if permitted by zoning and justified by the market and financial analyses. Such an integrated or vertical structure would also bring parking and walking distances within comfortable ranges for those who drive to the center and make it possible for others to walk to the center. In multilevel layouts, escalators should be strategically placed to provide convenience for customers as well as to direct them past all of the stores. Each floor should have pedestrian entrances from the parking structure. Department store anchors in regional centers should have entrances on each level that heighten the visibility of and interplay among stores and between levels. In some cases, escalators should be designed to pass floors on the way up to provide express service to special attractions on upper floors. For example, a multiplex cinema can be located on the upper floors of a shopping center served directly by express escalators. On the trip down, however, escalators should be configured to pass through the lower floors so that people can shop on the way out.

As a shopping center matures and attracts a greater volume of sales and customers, additional leasable area may have to be provided, which usually requires additional parking areas that may have to be structured to accommodate the additional retail space. When the cost of land for additional parking equals or exceeds the cost of constructing parking decks, when the distance to additional land would be too great, or when alternative land uses can be developed profitably on the surrounding land, parking decks should be constructed. A parking structure not only provides parking closer to the stores but also protects vehicles from the weather, an advantage in all but the mildest climates. The design and placement of parking structures must be carefully evaluated, however, requiring the assistance of professionals who are sensitive to an appropriate relationship among the parking structure, the shopping center, and the surrounding neighborhoods.

Topography

Buildable topography is an important factor in the selection and layout of a site and in the design and construction of buildings. Fairly level or gently sloping ground is easily adaptable to shopping centers. With skill, a more steeply sloping site can be adapted to provide access for customers at different levels. It also can be used advantageously in separating retail uses from other uses, such as offices, and in reducing competition from nonretail

parkers for retail parking spaces. This approach is particularly applicable to multilevel regional centers and to mixed-use developments. For new-generation urban entertainment centers, sloping sites can be used to create intriguing pedestrian ways that draw customers through the site, provide vantage points to watch other people in the center, and permit distinctive site plans and tenant configurations.

Low areas and poor drainage complicate the subsurface construction of any center. The ideal site has minimal complications from the existing subsoil, neither solid rock nor a high water table, and a slope of less than 5 percent. If used for surface parking, a steeper slope must be cut and filled and may need detention or retention ponds to control runoff of surface water.

Public Services

The availability of utilities, including gas, water, sewerage, and electricity, on or near the site is a critical asset that

The Jerde Partnership used creative site planning to overcome the limitations of a sloped 2.5-acre infill site in Del Mar, California, to create a distinctive specialty retail center. Five terraces gently step down the natural grade of the site, and clusters of buildings knit into the hillside provide dramatic views of the Pacific Ocean.

must be considered early during site selection, because their provision can have major implications for costs—or stop the development altogether. Significant off-site improvements to connect the site to existing utility systems can require major capital expenditures and render the site financially infeasible. In some cases, local growth controls that limit utility hookups and extensions make development impossible, regardless of cost. In other areas, off-site development costs are shared with the municipality and the utility company, while in still others, the developer may have to bear the complete cost, initially or over time, if the site is located in a special utility taxing district.

For the community, the cost of providing utilities and other public services such as police and fire protection, schools, and streets is much less for commercial facilities than for residential development. In addition, commercial developments typically produce a sizable return in real estate and sales taxes to the jurisdiction where they are built—revenue that would be lost, or received by another municipality, if commercial use were not allowed. As a result, a properly located shopping center usually produces far more net income for the community than that produced from single-family residential development. A comprehensively planned shopping center development also increases the value of land adjacent to the center and as a result indirectly increases revenues to the jurisdiction from these adjacent sites.

The developer will benefit as well by encouraging development of compatible fringe uses that would generate additional business for the center while not affecting peak-hour traffic flow to the center (because most of these added customers would walk to it). Such fringe development would also concentrate traffic carrying shoppers within the vicinity of the center rather than diluting and diverting potential customers to areas beyond the center's influence. Apartments or offices developed adjacent to a shopping center site make an excellent transition zone

The Mall of Georgia at Mill Creek in Gwinnett County, Georgia, is part of a 500-acre mixed-use development that will include a 1.7 million-square-foot regional retail center resembling a town center. The retail component will be supported by the development of compatible fringe uses, such as offices and multi-family residences.

between a shopping center and a single-family residential area. A shopping center site adjacent to high-density apartment development benefits from greater walk-in trade. The ideal shopping center will become a center of community life, with such public facilities as a library, community center, and government service offices located within the complex. The era when shopping centers included only retail tenants and were separated from the community by vast parking lots is rapidly drawing to a close.

The provision of public services for a shopping center can be the flash point that leads to conflict with the community and the surrounding neighborhood, however. The added traffic that a shopping center generates, the need for new access routes or other road improvements, and the new development that the center will likely draw have led in many cases to significant opposition from neighbors, regardless of the financial benefits the community may enjoy. As a result, it is essential for shopping center developers to meet early and often with neighborhood and community representatives as plans for the center unfold to make sure that the center is *politically* possible. The tradeoffs, including the costs and benefits that the community and the developers will experience as a result of the new development, must be openly discussed, negotiations undertaken, and understandings agreed to as part of the process leading to development approvals, provision of essential public services, and mitigation of negative impacts on the community. If community opposition is strong enough, plans to build the center should be abandoned, because the costs associated with prolonged development and ill will from the neighborhood will outweigh the benefits.

Site Acquisition

The cost of land counts heavily in the development of a shopping center and therefore is a major determinant of the site chosen. In a typical suburban location, a single-level center requires approximately four square feet of land for each square foot of building area. This relationship allows one square foot of ground under the building and three square feet around it for roadways, parking spaces, landscaping, and other nonbuilding uses. But in this era of specialty, hybrid, and mixed-use centers, this ratio should not be viewed as absolute; it is simply a ballpark figure for a typical suburban configuration. Downtown shopping centers may entail lot coverage approaching 100 percent, with all parking located underground and no setbacks for storefronts from the sidewalk. In any case, the financial outlook for each project determines what land costs can or cannot be supported. As a result, even sites with abnormally high land costs may be feasible if they are developed with multilevel or vertical centers, resulting in a more economical land-to-building cost ratio.

Because land costs, building costs, and volume of sales vary greatly within metropolitan areas and from one section of the country to another, no standard figures can be set for building sites. The fact that land costs are low in a certain location does not mean that a shopping center placed there will yield the best overall income. A

Although land is more expensive in Cambridge, Massachusetts, than in more suburban locations in the Boston metropolitan area, the CambridgeSide Galleria has excellent access to two large universities and an affluent base of customers to support its blend of a regional mall and a festival marketplace.

strategic location, though more expensive, may enable a center to draw the full potential of sales from a trade area, spelling the difference between success and failure. The advantages and disadvantages of a site must be carefully weighed against a wide range of economic, financial, marketing, environmental, and social criteria. If several sites are being considered, the one selected should clearly demonstrate that it offers the strongest location for the particular project in terms of trade area, purchasing power, lifestyle characteristics, competition, potential for growth, visibility, access, configuration, traffic, shopping patterns, surrounding uses, and environmental suitability.

Several methods may be used to acquire or gain control of a site, and each offers varying financial advantages:

- Historic Ownership—If the developer has owned a site and held it for a number of years, he or she may have no further acquisition costs to pay, or such costs, if necessary, may constitute only a minimal part of the total capital outlay. For example, the site for Village Park Plaza, a 683,246-square-foot power center in Westfield, Indiana, that opened in 1991, had been purchased by the Simon Property Group in 1982 with the intention to develop it as a traditional regional shopping center. But times changed, and before developing the site as a smaller power center, the developer sold off 25 percent of the site to another developer for apartments.

- Outright Purchase—The least attractive, most costly method, outright purchase requires heavy initial investment of equity funds. It is unappealing if development is uncertain, money markets are restricted, or interest rates are high, unless the developer is contemplating a subsequent sale and leaseback or land loan.
- Purchase Contract with Options—A favored method, a purchase with options allows the developer to run the hurdles of zoning and approval without jeopardizing the bulk of the investment. The contract to purchase should provide other options subject to pertinent current conditions, such as an acceptable land title report, an accurate property survey, zoning approval of the land use, investigation of any on-site and off-site easements, site conditions, stormwater runoff, site plan clearance, and any environmental clearances. The option period should allow the developer from nine months to two years before committing to purchase the land. The developer should try not to conclude the purchase until he or she has obtained building permits. If the developer can control the property by option until potentially adverse factors have been ameliorated, the risk will be less when the property is purchased.
- Deferred Purchase with Simultaneous Sale and Leaseback—This advantageous and commonly used technique allows the developer to avoid heavy financial commitments. In effect, the developer induces the lender to buy the land and provide the money to build the center. The developer then leases the project from the lender but retains the option to buy back the development later.
- Ground Lease—A popular approach, ground leases eliminate a major initial investment in land. The principle of land leasing is that it offers the landowner an alternative to direct sale and frees the developer from an initial investment in land. The financial arrangements of a ground lease are flexible, and the tax laws have contributed to the popularity of this method of land control. A landowner who sells land that has increased in value must face a high capital gains tax, but by leasing land for a long term (up to 99 years is common), the owner can spread the return to reduce the taxes. A ground lease allows the owner to retain fee ownership while receiving, in effect, an annuity over the term of the lease. Inheritors or long-time owners of land may find ground leasing attractive, although they should first consider the many situations that could arise in the future. For example, with inflation, the fixed ground rent causes a reduction in the property's sale value until the lease term expires. There-

fore, provisions for rent escalation are important. The lessee benefits because the amount of capital required for land control is reduced, and the annual ground rent is a deductible business expense. To maximize the possibilities for financing, the developer must insist on the right to place a mortgage on the fee title to the land leased.

Under a ground lease, the developer becomes the liaison between the fee owner and the project's tenants, who produce income through rental payments. The annual ground rent is equivalent to a payment on a loan used to purchase land. The lease can provide for readjustment of the ground rental at predetermined intervals. In addition, lessors often share in the equity income from projects developed on their land, and receive annual rents of 10 to 12 percent of the land's initial value plus benefits when tenants' rents are increased as a result of inflation. Landowners may even share in percentage rent payments from tenants in lieu of other equity participation or escalation in ground rent. Two types of ground leases are common:

- *Subordinated* ground leases are the preferred arrangement for developers. The landowner submits the land to the lender as collateral should the developer default on mortgage payments. Lenders usually insist on subordination.
- *Unsubordinated* ground leases are less risky for landowners, because they do not agree to offer the land as collateral for the mortgage. Because the developer would have difficulty securing a subsequent mortgage loan, however, the landowner may not be able to lease land to the developer and both would lose. Financing with an unsubordinated ground lease, if available, usually costs more per year than for a subordinated ground lease. Giving the mortgagee the right to purchase the land in case of default can sometimes substitute for subordination, although the mortgagee may deduct the price of the land from the loan.

Ground leasing frees capital and permits the developer to raise more capital through the mortgage. For example, if the land is worth $1 million and the owner can be persuaded to lease it, the developer has an extra $1 million that could be used for capital expenditures or other purposes. When the land is leased with the right to mortgage the fee, $500,000 or more may be gained by borrowing on the land. Without the right to subordinate the fee on the land to a mortgage, the developer may not succeed in subsequent steps toward securing financing. If the developer obtains a ground lease that permits a mortgage on the fee, the financing then takes the form of a straight first mortgage on the land and buildings.

Securing Commitments from Tenants

Anchors

As a rule, a shopping center will not be built until the developer has secured commitments from key tenants.[6]

Beame Architectural Partnership

This shopping center designed by the Beame Architectural Partnership in Pôrto Alegre, Brazil, is anchored by the Renner department store.

The choice of key tenants is critical, because they heavily influence site design, building design, layout, and overall composition of tenants. In short, they determine the center's basic character and image.

It bears repeating that anchor tenants of a convenience center are usually a minimart or some other convenience service that customers are likely to visit daily. Anchor tenants for a neighborhood center are typically a supermarket and a drugstore (with a single supermarket/drugstore combination having become more prevalent in recent years in many markets); the key tenants of a community center are a discount or off-price department store, variety store, hardware/building/home improvement store, combined drug/variety/garden center, and supermarket. Key tenants of a regional or super regional center are full-line department stores (generally at least 75,000 to 100,000 square feet each), and the most successful super regional centers include at least three department stores. Few regional centers are being constructed in the late 1990s except in specialized urban locations where limited space precludes having more than one or two anchors. Power centers typically have four or more big-box category killers and often include a discount department store as well. An entertainment center is typically anchored by a new-generation cinema complex. The anchors for hybrid centers are less predictable but equally important to the center's success.

The list of tenants considered viable anchors is gradually expanding in response to changing consumer demand, evolving market niches, and the need to differentiate centers from their competitors in a generally overbuilt market. Elaborate food courts, entertainment centers, and groups of specialized tenants under the same corporate umbrella that together form a powerful draw similar to a department store increasingly are deemed anchors. In addition, as shopping centers continue to expand into previously underserved urban areas, nontraditional anchors that may not even be part of the shopping center—cultural facilities, historic districts, entertainment centers, sports facilities, convention centers, airport terminals, train stations, tourist attractions, and casinos, for example—nonetheless may perform the same function of drawing customers.

Traditionally, the commitment of an anchor tenant represents a form of partnership between it and the developer; for this reason, the anchor tenant should be carefully considered in the developer's land and building plans. Key tenants' requirements—often including firm ideas about the center's general arrangement and their locations in the center—influence the developer's decisions on leasing, financial negotiations, building treatment, architectural style, parking provisions, signage, and landscaping. Thus, before site planning or further leasing occurs, key tenants must be committed to the center.

At this stage, the project's form begins to adapt to the characteristics of the site and the potential of the trade area. In a high-income area, for example, two high-fashion stores may sign as tenants, thus creating a higher-quality

An illustrative building and site layout can be drawn before key tenants have been committed. Neonopolis at Fremont Street Experience is a 282,000-square-foot retail/entertainment center being developed in Las Vegas by World Entertainment Centers. The project is slated to open in 2000.

image for a proposed center. In this case, the quality of the market determines the type of center suitable to the area. The image of the leading tenant in turn determines the type of satellite tenants suitable to a particular center. If a discount store were the key tenant, however, all factors in planning for tenants would be different. The wrong key tenant can complicate the problem of leasing to satellite tenants. On the other hand, leasing to a mix of tenants that is too homogeneous, even in high-income areas, has proved to be a mistake. Increasingly, a mix of tenants representing a range of prices that expand the market for a particular center has proved successful. For example, Mazza Gallerie, a specialty center in Washington, D.C., includes both Neiman Marcus and Filene's Basement.

In the early stages of development, the owner/developer or the leasing agent must determine what key tenants are available—an increasingly difficult task for regional centers, given the saturation of most trade areas with department stores and the dearth of department store chains capable of entering a new market area. A competent real estate leasing agent can recognize and assess the characteristics of major key tenants, their goals for expansion, their preferred lease or occupancy provisions, the relationships they have with the developer, and commitments they have made for other projects and sites. The agent should also know under what conditions these tenants will be available or unavailable and what arrangements may make them attract other tenants.

Because of the need to deal with the subtleties of selecting tenants, the leasing agent or real estate expert must be on the development team from the start, working with the market analyst and guiding the developer and his architect, engineer, and planner. Some developers have in-house leasing experts. Successful developers who use outside agents know enough about the field so that they need not rely entirely on outside advice to resolve critical questions.

After key tenants have been committed—preferably through a "letter of intent" or other clear expression of interest (if not an actual lease or occupancy agreement)—a rough building and site layout can be prepared. Based on data from the market and economic analyses, supplementary tenant classifications can be used to produce an overall leasing plan.[7]

Leases[8] with supplementary tenants are negotiated after the major tenants have signed leases or made commitments. Commitments or expressions of interest from supplementary or satellite tenants precede firming the financing plan and any preparation of construction details. In addition, developers do not start final plans or even complete the site acquisition until they have received zoning approval, which may impose economically infeasible conditions. Final commitments from major tenants typically are subject to zoning approval.

A prospectus presented as an attractive brochure makes a useful exhibit in explaining to potential tenants findings of the market, site advantages, the tentative arrangement of building and site, commitments from key tenants, and the developer's track record and reputation. A rendering of the architectural treatment showing, for example, whether a mall will be open or enclosed and how tenant spaces will be configured is also necessary, particularly for some new forms of shopping centers, such as urban entertainment centers where anchors are positioned in complex, sometimes multilevel, configurations throughout the project to draw customers through the center. In this type of situation, negotiations with tenants can be far more complex; in fact, negotiations may have to be reopened as development evolves.

The developer should have a lease form to present to satellite or in-line tenants and should inform tenants of basic economic provisions early in the process. Matters that involve the tenant's tax participation, contributions to common area maintenance, participation in a marketing fund or a merchants' association, the rental scale, overage and percentage rents, and the promotional program should be resolved in the proposed form. Any satellite tenants should be located so that pedestrian traffic is well distributed to encourage convenience and impulse buying. For some entertainment tenants, a range of partnership options must be considered in lieu of standard lease forms.[9]

When it is not possible to have a key tenant committed to the project early in the process, developers may proceed (at their own risk) with certain efforts, such as obtaining zoning clearance, while they continue to negotiate with major department stores.

The Leasing Plan

Because the leasing plan, in the broadest sense, represents the center's potential for investment, it is the key in projecting the center's rental income. It should be prepared early in the development process and should address the following points:

- The Placement of Tenants—Tenants should be located to draw the maximum pedestrian flow past as much

store frontage as possible. Placement should consider the strength of each tenant's draw.
- Building Depths—Normally the depth for in-line tenants should not exceed 120 feet for mall shops or stores in an open center. Shops of small tenants in neighborhood centers can be 60 to 100 feet deep. Shops in malls should not exceed 40 feet wide except for courts and promotional areas. A balanced tenant mix should provide both strong, credit-rated national firms and good local merchants to meet lenders' requirements for financial credit. Building depths for anchors in malls and open-air centers are much greater. Each anchor chain has its own standardized footprint and requirements for space, although in unusual circumstances it will negotiate the dimensions.
- The Tenant Mix—The mix of tenants should be largely determined by the merchandising plan, although not all goals of the original plan will necessarily be met. Tenants' preferences and resistance to suggestions will

Location and dimensions of buildings should be specified in the leasing plan. The required depths vary based on type of shopping center and mix of tenant formats and anchor type.

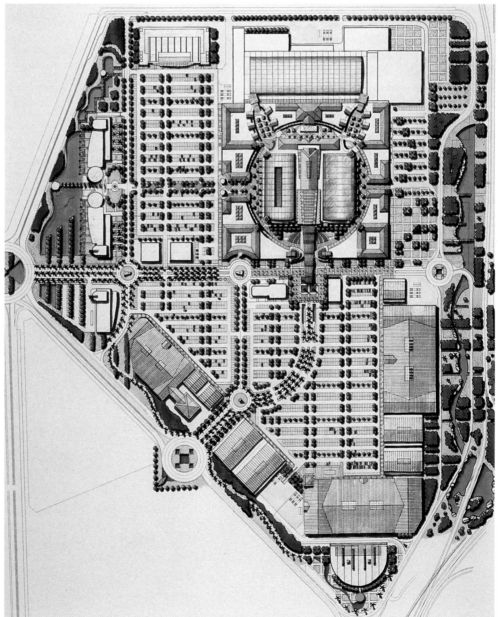

Bon Aire/Aldia, Valencia, Spain

likely result in a number of compromises, and repositioning will require constant attention if the merchandising plan is to direct leasing.

- "Pricing" for Each Store Space—Pricing depends on the tenant's size, classification, location in the project, and amount of tenant improvement allowance. This amount should be updated constantly as the project moves from speculation to a finalized program.
- Detailed Rent Schedules—Rent schedules should clearly indicate the tenant's name, classification, square footage allocated, minimum rent, and rate of percentage rent. The tenant's share of costs for HVAC should be projected. This schedule also must be continuously updated.
- Method of Handling Tenant Finishes—The preferred approach is to provide shell space plus an allowance for finishing the space to tenants' specifications. This method should be followed, even if a greater allowance is sometimes necessary to produce a "turnkey"

solution for a particular tenant. In the case of elaborate entertainment-related tenants, partnership arrangements often require the tenant to finish its own space.

- The Lease Form—The lease should require a minimum of processing, with exhibits attached showing the landlord's work, the tenant's work, HVAC rate schedules, other applicable rate schedules, and other related matters, including the site plan and criteria for signage. The lease form can be modified most easily through addenda, which provide a ready reference for changes applicable to specific tenants.[10]

The lease should provide for tenants' payments to cover the costs of operation for common areas, including maintenance, insurance, HVAC, and real estate taxes. These charges are typically prorated based on the GLA each tenant occupies; commonly exempted are key tenants, whose payment schedules are prearranged. If separate metering has not been provided, the lease should

The major income stream for shopping centers depends on the type and size of center. Regional centers, for example, receive most of their income from side-space tenants who capture shoppers fed into their smaller retail spaces by virtue of the larger anchor tenants' placement. Bluewater Park is a 1.6 million-square-foot regional center in Dartford, England, designed by RTKL.

RTKL–UK Ltd.

clearly define the responsibilities for the payment of HVAC, gas, and electricity costs. With today's unpredictable energy costs, however, separate metering is strongly recommended. "Escalator clauses" should provide for the increased costs of labor, energy, administration, and replacement parts.

Lease provisions help define the landlord's fiscal obligations. Generally, they are well known to national tenants, but local tenants, who are unaccustomed to the complexity and comprehensiveness of such provisions because of the limited scope of their operations, may resist them. The developer should nevertheless negotiate such costs with the tenants, explaining why their inclusion in the lease is essential. Owners of stronger centers can insist on reducing the fiscal uncertainty they must face, but the preceding principles are useful in structuring leases for any present-day shopping center.

Department stores in a regional shopping center are treated differently from other tenants. Key department stores may build their own stores on land bought or leased from the developer. They usually do not build their own parking areas, but they should contribute funds to the developer. The developer must have satisfactory reciprocal operating agreements that provide for handling on-site and off-site construction costs, easements, operation of common areas, operating hours, security, the marketing fund or merchants' association, the common "mall/department store" wall, and other expenses. Long-term cross-easements and agreements are extremely important to the permanent lender, the tenants, and the developer. Reciprocal easement agreements are necessary in any center with separate legal ownership or any type of site-sharing uses, such as freestanding banks, service stations, or restaurants.

To encourage department stores to enter the project on a buy/build basis, land can be sold to them at an appraised value, or at or below cost. The amount of money involved, while substantial, represents a smaller subsidy than the amount that would result from a fairly favorable gross lease. The developer typically sells to the department store not only a building pad but also necessary improvements in parking. For extremely desirable anchor department stores, the developer may even pay for construction and interior finishes, although this practice is not common. In any case, the negotiated sale price rarely reflects the prorated off-site and on-site improvement costs attributed to the land area sold.

In comparison, the income stream from a power center tends to be much flatter than the income stream from a regional shopping center. In power centers, anchor tenants' leases produce most of the cash flow, especially as anchor stores account for 85 to 90 percent of the center's GLA, a major difference between power centers and regional shopping centers. In regional centers, the anchors create the critical mass that supports the side tenants that in turn generate the majority of the income. In power centers, anchor tenants do not generate much momentum for in-line tenants. For urban entertainment centers, the income stream depends not only on rental income

but also on nontraditional sources such as partnership, sponsorship, and licensing arrangements.

Once the leasing plan has been formulated, the next step is implementation, which involves six major steps:

1. Choosing a Marketing Method—Will the developer use in-house brokers or an outside brokerage firm? What will be the method of compensation and incentives? Who will handle anchor tenants? Who will handle smaller tenants?
2. Establishing an "A" List—Only after the best tenants in each identified category have declined should a developer consider the second best.
3. Determining Techniques for "Prospecting"—This step may involve signs on the property to announce the development, direct mailings, advertising in newspapers and trade publications, involvement in trade shows, networking with other brokers, and "cold calling."
4. Pricing—In addition to considering the demand for space, the developer must consider parking access, desirable anchors, depth and width of space, special demands if the mall will be multilevel, visibility from the street, and position within the center.
5. Creating Support Material for Marketing—Marketing material should be created to support leasing: an aerial photograph, demographics of the location and trade area, a site plan that identifies the building's configuration, renderings of the project, access and visibility of the site, neighboring uses that support the identity of the center, traffic counts, news releases, and background on the development team.
6. Identifying Requirements for Tenants' Submission—The developer needs to know certain information about each tenant: legal name, address, tax identification number, financial statement, operating statement, existing locations, references, and requirements for space.

Leasing

With the leasing plan prepared and the leasing program organized, the next step is to sign leases. They may be for existing space if immediate occupancy is available or for space to be built, with occupancy projected in six to 18 months. The developer should consider the following items:

- When leasing less than an entire block of space, usually lease from the sides to the middle so that only one predetermined space will be left rather than two.
- Try to work it so that the last space could be divided in half and still meet the minimum requirements for width you have set. That is, if 15 feet is the minimum width, try to leave a 30-foot-wide space instead of a 27- or 28-foot-wide space.
- Try to lease the toughest space first or, if you are unable, keep in mind the need to beat pro forma rents on easier space so that you have flexibility on the rent required for the toughest space.
- Consider what the next tenant will be left to deal with —storefront width, column locations, signage area available, rear or secondary access, and parking required

—if the remaining space were used for a restaurant, retail space, or offices.

- On space to be built, try to build in a provision that allows the lessor to move a tenant within a certain area until a certain time. This flexibility can be very helpful in leasing.[11]

Financing

Like the shopping center industry itself, development financing continues to change considerably. Yet in the midst of these changes, a basic fact remains: a shopping center will attract debt and equity investment based on the anticipated return to all financial participants. Whatever the type of center, projected income and expenses are still the key to financing the project.

Successful shopping center developers are those who not only are aware of the marketing and economic fea-

sibility of a project but also are strongly connected to reliable sources of development capital. The source of shopping center financing depends on many variables. In the past, many regional shopping centers were financed by conventional first mortgage debt, minimizing the equity requirements and creating satisfactory returns for owners and developers. But "construction debt for new or renovated centers has become more difficult to obtain. Most lenders limit the percentage of cost they will lend. They are reluctant to assume excessive risk for this or any type of real estate projects. This has forced many developers to look for financial partners to provide the equity investment. Other developers have turned to the public financial market for sources of equity."[12]

Sources of Financing

Experienced developers have long recognized the need to maintain close contact with lenders and financial consultants. Today, this need is stronger than ever. In today's

The Teachers Insurance and Annuity Association (TIAA) of New York, a pension fund, was an equity partner with Melvin Simon & Associates in the development of Mall of America in Bloomington, Minnesota. TIAA agreed to pay off the construction loan once the project was completed in 1993 in exchange for a 55 percent share of equity.

changing capital markets, the source of financing for a particular shopping center can depend on the size of the developer, the size of the center, the tenants, and the area of the country. In any case, the financing being sought must be part of the project's overall financial plan and must fit within the economic confines of the project's potential income, cash flow, tax benefits, and appreciation of value. In some cases, more than one source of financing will be necessary.

Conventional sources of financing for shopping centers generally include insurance companies and pension funds as permanent lenders, with commercial banks and a small number of credit companies as short- and medium-term lenders. When loan delinquencies increased in the late 1980s and early 1990s because of the real estate recession, banks and insurance companies reduced their loan exposure. When they started making loans again, the only element that had changed was that standards for underwriting loans were tightened.

At least ten major sources of financing are currently used:

- Life insurance companies,
- Pension funds,
- Banks,
- S&Ls and savings banks,
- Finance and credit companies,
- Investment banks and securities firms,
- Real estate investment trusts,
- Syndications,
- Government funds, and
- Foreign investors.

Each source has its own criteria for investment. A proposed shopping center that is acceptable to one source may be of no interest to another. And as the sources change over time, deals made two or three years ago may be totally unacceptable today. Developers need to remember that lenders match types of loans with their liabilities, which could involve consumer savings accounts, money market deposit accounts, trusts and separate accounts, securities, and time deposits. As the sources of lenders' funds change, so too will the types of deals they may be willing to make.

Life Insurance Companies. Life insurance companies, for example, are experiencing a change in the sources of funds. During the 1970s, most of the funds life insurance companies loaned were raised internally from insurance premiums. Today, life insurance companies are money managers for pension funds, trusts, endowments, and foundations. Virtually all major insurance companies manage property portfolios on behalf of those investors. They also issue guaranteed investment contracts that are bought by pension funds.

Life insurance companies are not interested in all types of shopping centers. They have specified minimum loans, which will eliminate many small projects. Moreover, many life insurance companies provide financing only if they also participate in the project's cash flow and resale value. Developers must then be prepared to give up sizable equity interests. And because life insurance companies are interested in properties for their pension fund clients, developers may find that they can presell their center to the insurance company. For debt financing, loan-to-value ratios are a maximum of 75 percent, debt coverage ratios are generally 1.25 or higher, and loans mature in ten years or less.

Pension Funds. Pension funds invest in real estate directly and indirectly. Life insurance companies place large amounts of money in real estate for pension funds, which can be private funds or public funds. Private funds are those operated by corporations or unions; they must conform to the investment guidelines of the Employee Retirement Income Security Act of 1974 (ERISA) and its later amendments. Pension funds may make tax-free investments in leveraged real estate, but the income and capital gains from these projects are exempt from taxes only if the pension funds meet specific guidelines and conditions.

Public pension funds include, for example, state employee or teacher retirement funds. They need not comply with ERISA, but they may be limited in the types of investments they can make or in the size of any single investment. When investing in real estate, many public pension funds are required to focus primarily on in-state investments. Other funds may prefer residential mortgage debt, as opposed to commercial lending.

Most managers of public and private pension funds attempt to balance types of investments. Developers may find participating mortgages the dominant lending arrangement offered by many pension funds, but they will likely take longer to mature than mortgages offered by some life insurance companies. Pension funds make direct loans primarily to prime shopping center projects, and they are less likely to grant loans on smaller, riskier projects.

Banks. Commercial banks' role as a source of funds has grown in importance. Banks offer a wide range of loan types for shopping centers, and they are often more willing to offer loans for small to medium projects (although not always the case for large, money center banks). Banks are more stringent today with regard to the assumptions they will accept in a developer's pro forma. For example, at least 50 percent of the space—and sometimes 80 percent—must be preleased, and all anchors must be of high investment quality and sign a lease before construction begins. Among the types of financing banks provide for shopping centers are construction loans, interim loans, gap loans, and bullet loans.[13] Most bank real estate loans have floating interest rates.

Because many of the largest shopping center developers have gone public (in the form of REITs), many banks prefer to lend to REITs or to publicly owned corporations that own real estate rather than to privately owned development organizations. REITs typically have less debt and greater access to additional capital than the average private developer.

S&Ls and Savings Banks. The savings and loan (S&L) industry has seen many changes during the past two decades. Between 1966 and 1979, interest rates tended to fluctuate with increasing intensity, and S&Ls experienced great difficulty with rising interest rates. Moreover, ceilings on interest rates prevented S&Ls from paying competitive interest rates on deposits. Thus, every time interest rates rose, consumers withdrew substantial amounts of funds and placed them in instruments with higher rates of return. This process of withdrawing deposits (disintermediation) and the subsequent influx of deposits when rates rise (reintermediation) left S&Ls highly vulnerable. They were further restricted by not being allowed to engage in business other than accepting deposits and granting home mortgage loans.

Between 1980 and 1982, statutory and regulatory changes gave the S&L industry new hope, as they were allowed to enter new areas of business and subsequently return to profitability. In January 1982, the Federal Home Loan Bank Board reduced the net worth requirement for insured S&Ls from 4 percent to 3 percent of total deposits. Additionally, S&Ls were allowed to meet the low net worth standard of the more liberal regulatory accounting principles instead of the generally accepted accounting principles. In 1989, President Bush unveiled an S&L bailout plan, and in August, the Financial Institutions Reform, Recovery, and Enforcement Act was enacted. FIRREA abolished the Federal Home Loan Bank Board and the Federal Savings and Loan Insurance Corporation, and switched the regulation of S&Ls to a newly created Office of Thrift Supervision (OTS). In addition, a new entity, the Resolution Trust Corporation, was created to resolve insolvent S&Ls.

Today, thrift institutions continue to play an important role as residential and commercial mortgage lenders, but competition has intensified on all sides. Nonbank lenders and government-sponsored enterprises have moved strategically into the residential mortgage market, and thrifts have lost market share even though the dollar volume of their mortgages has increased. Thrifts,

Marí Cabo San Lucas is a planned open-air waterfront retail center in Cabo San Lucas, Mexico, designed by California-based architects Kaplan McLaughlin Diaz. Banks generally require at least 50 percent of a project to be pre-leased before agreeing to finance a shopping center.

like banks, have also seen their deposit base erode as the flow of money to mutual funds boomed in the last several years. Since the establishment of OTS in 1989, the thrift industry has experienced a dramatic decline in the number of institutions and level of industry assets. In December 1990, 2,539 thrift institutions held more than $1.1 trillion in consolidated assets. By December 1996, the industry had declined to 1,335 institutions holding $769 billion in consolidated assets, a 47 percent reduction in the number of institutions and a 32 percent reduction in the dollar value of assets during this six-year period. Thus, less money is available for both commercial and residential lending.

Finance and Credit Companies. Credit companies, such as the General Electric Credit Corporation, also provide funds for shopping center development. Because they usually act as intermediaries between borrowers and other financial institutions, their interest rates may be higher than those of other lenders. Yet because such firms also

often provide construction and miniperm loans on somewhat riskier shopping center projects, they serve an important function in the overall market for real estate credit.

Investment Banks and Securities Firms. Wall Street securities firms constantly communicate with investors of all types and sizes. As real estate financing involves more often the sale of securities, these firms play an increasingly important role. Other large developers have also used securities firms to raise both real estate debt and equity funds. New types of securities, such as collateralized mortgage obligations, and the strides being made to provide a rating for commercial real estate debt portend a continued role for Wall Street. Financing from Wall Street will be available only for larger developers and projects, however. Smaller developers must continue to use local institutions and mortgage bankers.

Real Estate Investment Trusts. REITs, while temporarily out of favor on Wall Street, have been important players in the 1990s, providing both debt and equity capital. REITs

The Avenue East Cobb in Atlanta is an open-air specialty retail center scheduled to open in 1999. The project is owned by Cousins, Inc., an Atlanta-based equity REIT that develops, manages, and finances shopping centers. The company has been public since 1962, and its common stock trades on the New York Stock Exchange.

are similar to mutual funds except they own real estate rather than securities. Unlike syndications, shares in REITs can be easily traded so that investors have added liquidity. Moreover, REITs can both make loans on and take equity positions in property. With such flexibility, REITs are well suited to finance shopping center development.

Syndications. Most syndicators are interested in actual ownership of proposed properties. Because developers often become general partners in shopping center syndications, they receive many of the benefits of ownership as well as project financing. Syndications can be created for small and large shopping centers. Because of the competition for investment-grade real estate projects, many syndicators are becoming more active in real estate development and construction. Syndication has also provided the means for many developers to raise their own capital. A syndication is often formed while the developer has an option on the land. Thus, its proceeds can be used just like a construction loan—to acquire the land, develop the site, and construct a shopping center. In other situations, the developer can function as a contract builder to a syndicator.

Government Funds. Rarely is government financing available for a total project. When used with funds from other sources, however, government financing programs greatly enhance a project's feasibility. To qualify for government financing, a project must serve a public purpose, stimulate economic growth, and conform to local planning and development guidelines. Shopping centers usually meet all three requirements, providing goods and services to often underserved residential areas, offering opportunities for employment, and meeting all local requirements for zoning and building.

Government financing is more often indirect than direct, and it takes different forms. Tax abatement and tax increment financing are the most commonly employed local programs that can assist in financing a project. Tax abatement reduces the property tax burden on a project, often postponing payment of the bulk of the taxes until after the first few years of a project's operation. Tax increment financing uses tax revenues from a specially created district to repay municipal bonds. The bonds can pay for land assembly and clearance, improvements in infrastructure, and parking. An otherwise infeasible project that does not have to bear these costs often becomes feasible.

Foreign Investors. Foreign investors are attracted primarily to existing centers with strong, proven operating histories. They also prefer to purchase centers outright rather than provide loans for them. Foreign lenders and investors also undertake joint ventures with U.S. developers on major commercial projects.

Financing Techniques for Shopping Centers

Shopping center financing depends on the project's economics. The developer may finance the entire construction cost through equity, debt, or a combination of both, and he or she must determine the appropriate mix of debt and equity as well as the ownership structure that will best fit the project's financial needs. Ownership can take several forms:

- A corporation,
- A limited partnership,
- A general partnership,
- A real estate investment trust, or
- A sole proprietorship.

Perhaps the key factor in deciding the ownership structure of a shopping center is the amount of equity to be placed in the project. This section identifies some debt and equity techniques used to finance shopping centers. Among the common debt techniques are construction loans, construction loans with minipermanent loans, participating mortgages, land sale/leasebacks, leasehold financing, public financing programs, and convertible mortgages. Mechanisms used for equity financing include joint ventures, limited partnerships, presale agreements, and REITs.

A real estate investment trust is a corporation or business trust that combines the capital of many investors to acquire or provide financing for all forms of real estate, according to the National Association of Real Estate Investment Trusts (NAREIT), the trade group of REITs based in Washington, D.C. The National Research Bureau has identified 62 REITs that have invested in three or more retail properties. These 62 REITs accounted for 3,193 centers and more than 1 billion square feet of total GLA of centers as of July 31, 1998.

REITs have two characteristics that distinguish them from other publicly held corporations: 1) a REIT's assets and income must be grounded principally in real estate, and 2) REITs do not pay federal corporate income taxes if they distribute their taxable income as dividends and meet other requirements for ownership and operation. Unlike a partnership, a REIT cannot pass on tax losses to investors. To maintain tax-exempt status as a REIT, a company incorporated as a REIT must earn 75 percent or more of its income from real estate, and 95 percent of its taxable income must be distributed to shareholders.

REITs can be public or private. A privately held company becomes a public REIT by issuing an initial public offering, which is how it sells "shares" or investment in the company. It is the source of raising capital. REITs typically carry less than 50 percent debt. As a result, they are less vulnerable to downturns in the industry, which should help flatten the cycles that have plagued the real estate industry in the past.

The 20 largest REITs (or approximately the top third) as measured by total GLA accounted for almost 60 percent of centers owned by REITs and almost 80 percent of the square footage held by REITs, as of July 31, 1998.

Rank		Number of Centers	GLA (Millions of Square Feet)
1	Simon Property Group	238	156.4
2	General Growth Properties	110	91.8
3	Urban Shopping Centers	111	67.5
4	The Rouse Company	58	44.0
5	The Macerich Company	59	40.4
6	Developers Diversified Realty Corp.	150	38.7
7	KIMCO Realty Corporation	271	37.0
8	Taubman Company Centers	30	32.4
9	Glimcher Realty	108	32.3
10	CBL & Associates Properties, Inc.	127	30.6
11	Westfield America	32	27.9
12	Corporate Property Investors[1]	23	27.6
13	Weingarten Realty Investors	174	21.8
14	The Mills Corporation	21	21.5
15	New Plan Realty Trust	126	19.5
16	Vornado Realty Trust	62	16.4
17	Crown America Realty Trust	29	15.0
18	Federal Realty Investment Trust	62	14.0
19	Colonial Properties Trust	50	12.9
20	Ramco-Gershenson Properties Trust	51	12.8
	Total Top 20 REITs	1,892	760.5
	Total for all Current REITs	3,193	1,001.3
	Concentration of Top 20 REITs	59%	76%

Note

1. Now combined with Simon Property Group.

Source: Excerpted from Nancy D. Veatch, "Real Estate Investment Trusts: Driving Force of the Shopping Center Industry?" *Shopping Center Directions,* Summer 1998, pp. 1–2.

■

The Florida Mall is a regional center under development in Orlando by the Simon Property Group, the largest shopping center REIT.

Options for Debt Financing. Several options are available for debt financing:

- Construction Loans—Construction loans are normally available from commercial banks, S&Ls, and, for larger projects, life insurance companies. They contain floating interest rates that change with the lender's prime rate or cost of funds index. The loan covers the entire cost of construction, and most loans have reserves that pay the interest on the loans, freeing the developer of this obligation. Many lenders require that developers obtain a takeout commitment for a permanent loan before any construction funds are advanced.

- Construction Loans with Miniperms—Recognizing the changing financial environment, banks, S&Ls, and life insurance companies are providing extended construction financing to developers. Rather than require a takeout commitment, these lenders provide fixed-rate and floating-rate term loans that extend several years beyond the construction period. Developers are then able to secure more favorable permanent financing because they have both a fully operating center and the ability to better time the move to permanent financing.

- Participating Mortgages—Participating mortgages are a major debt instrument for shopping centers. In addition to receiving interest income at a stated rate, the lender receives a portion of the income from gross sales, a portion of the net income after debt service, and a share of the property's appreciation, or some combination of income and appreciation. A developer can usually obtain a takeout commitment for a participating mortgage before construction begins or later, to refinance an extended construction loan. The lender's share of net income and appreciation varies with the interest rate charged.

- Land Sale/Leasebacks—While participating mortgages may be available for projects of all sizes, land sale/leasebacks are generally available only for larger shopping centers. As noted earlier, a land sale/leaseback involves the sale of the shopping center site to the lender or an investor. The developer then leases back the land on a long-term basis. The entire rent payment under the lease is tax deductible to the developer. Further, because a developer has all of his or her equity in the improvements, the entire value of the equity is eligible for depreciation. The lender/lessor receives rental income, a share in the project's profits, and unencumbered ownership of the land at the end of the lease term.

- Leasehold Financing—To use this method, a shopping center tenant must be a strong, nationally rated corporation or government, and the lease may not be canceled without the lender's consent. Few neighborhood or community centers are thus able to use leasehold financing.

- Public Financing Programs—Developers considering the conversion of historic properties into specialty centers should be aware of the investment tax credits available. These credits are especially attractive to investors who purchase limited partnership shares as a tax shelter.

- Convertible Mortgages—A large shopping center project may also obtain financing through a convertible mortgage, a loan that is converted into a specific equity interest in the property at a certain date. In exchange for converting equity, the lender provides a below-market interest rate to the developer. Further, the developer retains all the advantages of ownership, such as the benefits of depreciation during the loan period before conversion.

Options for Equity Financing. Options for equity financing include:

- Joint Ventures—A joint venture is the joint ownership of a project by a shopping center developer and a financial institution or large investor. Financial institutions are interested primarily in large centers, whereas

Limited partnerships are among the equity financing options available to developers of shopping centers. The First Colony Mall, a 1 million-square-foot regional center near Houston, was developed by a limited partnership between the Hines Company and Sugarland Properties, Inc.

Joe Aker/Houston

Many exclusive tenants, such as Niketown, Tiffany, and Gucci, that were not available anywhere else in the Atlanta region helped make Phipps Plaza a financial success.

other strong financial partners may invest in projects of all sizes. The amount of equity the financing partner supplies to the project varies. Institutional partners normally fund 100 percent of the development costs. Joint venture partners share in the proceeds from the development, and most joint ventures have a specified date of termination and sellout.

- Limited Partnerships—Limited partnerships may be formed in all sizes. Private offerings are more expensive to issue and are therefore feasible only for larger projects. Some "blind pool" syndications supply equity to several different projects, none of which have to be specified in the initial offering. Although the strength of the securities dealer and the issuing entity is crucial in attracting funds to blind pool syndications, it is also important in all limited partnerships. The developer may form the syndicate with his or her own project team or employ a syndicator to arrange the offering. Developers not familiar with the intricacies of syndication packaging and marketing should not attempt to do so themselves.
- Presale Agreements—A shopping center developer may find it advantageous to presell the entire project to an equity investor. The sales contract serves the same purpose as a takeout commitment in that it permits the developer to obtain construction financing. The developer receives a development profit at the sale without having to obtain it during the holding period of the investment.

- Real Estate Investment Trusts—As real estate financing techniques become more like those used in security sales, developers are organizing REITs and making other "securitized" transactions.

Preparing the Financing Package

Money is the most important ingredient in the process of developing a shopping center and the developer must exercise extreme care in creating the financing package. Whether preparing the package internally or using a consultant, the developer must disclose all project information clearly and accurately. The following items should be included in a loan package.

- A letter of transmittal that states the nature of the project and the amount of funds being requested;
- A market or feasibility study prepared by a recognized consulting firm that discusses trade area, population characteristics, competition, metropolitan growth, and all other factors that would affect the feasibility of the developer's proposal;
- A disclosure of all property characteristics, including a survey, site plan, building plans, photographs, and renderings;
- A detailed cash flow statement containing rent schedules, expenses, HVAC charges, common area maintenance costs, percentage rents, and all other items pertaining to the revenue and expenses of the proposed project;

The Simon Property Group, a self-managed equity REIT known for its ownership of high-quality, market-dominant retail properties throughout North America, purchased the Northshore Mall in the Boston metropolitan area in 1999 from the New England Development Group to increase the REIT's portfolio of northeastern retail properties.

Robert E. Mikrut

- All legal documents, including the property deed or the sales contract, the title insurance policy, any letters of intent to lease, the lease forms, and all attachments and exhibits that are part of these documents;
- A detailed cost estimate of the project along with a projected construction schedule;
- A report on the developer's experience, including a description of other projects the developer has completed.

Although this list describes the traditional requirements for a loan package, developers should also be aware of certain basic elements of equity financing for limited partnerships and REITs. All public syndications must be registered with the Securities and Exchange Commission (SEC) and with all regulating agencies in the states where the offering will be sold. Small, private offerings do not have to register with the SEC, but both public and private offerings must disclose information on the proposed syndication, including:

- Specific standards for minimum income, net worth, and tax bracket that a "suitable" investor should possess as well as the minimum amounts each partner must invest;
- The promoter's or sponsor's compensation in all its forms, such as management fees, brokerage commissions, resale profit, interest income, and interests in the partnership;
- The rights of the limited partners, including the right to inspect partnership records and to take action against the promoters or sponsors in the event of fraud or negligence;
- The agreement to make periodic reports to the investors, which, for public offerings, must be filed with the SEC and state commissions.

Developers should analyze their financing needs with the help of their lenders and consultants to derive the most appropriate financial structure for their particular projects. In all probability, side space will be leased, but the anchor space and pad space can be handled in any of three ways: sale, ground lease, or build-to-suit space. Each has its own advantages:

- Advantages of a Sale—immediate liquidity, no direct economic problems resulting from vacant space, easier documentation, faster transaction.
- Advantages of a Ground Lease—low capital requirements, limited concerns about credit, reversion of the building at the end of the lease term, more control, lower cost per square foot for financing.
- Advantages of Build-to-Suit Space—greater long-term potential for higher value, depreciability, higher base for rental escalation than for a ground lease, probable lower sale or lender cap rate with the anchor in the deal.

Other Factors Affecting a Project's Feasibility

Land Use Controls

Any site for a proposed shopping center requires favorable zoning for a developer to be able to proceed. Thus, the comprehensive plan provisions and applicable zoning in effect for a site must be carefully studied before a site is purchased. An early study explores the attitudes toward a proposed shopping center of local residents, the planning and zoning staff, and the approving body. A project's feasibility is greatly affected by current zoning regulations, as well as by time and expenses that will be required for approval or rezoning.

Areas of rapid growth generally try to streamline the approval process and to allocate adequate land for new development. In areas of rapid growth where slow growth has been advocated, permits may be difficult to obtain, restrictions profuse, and rezoning next to impossible, with little land available for new development. In areas where growth is moderate, a developer can expect any possible regulatory climate, depending on the size, staffing, and sophistication of the jurisdiction, the availability of land and its geographic characteristics, and on a host of other variables.

Each locality has to be approached as a new experience, because procedures, time frames, and dispositions vary widely from area to area. In some cases, the site proposed for a shopping center may not be planned for commercial or mixed use when the development process begins. For regional and super regional centers, the cost of accumulating large enough parcels of land on which to build a shopping center may be prohibitive if the land has not already been zoned for commercial use. In other cases, a site may be zoned for commercial use, but the ordinance may have to be modified with regard to such provisions as floor/area ratio, building height, parking requirements, lot coverage, or setbacks, to name a few.

In downtown or inner-city areas where local governments are attempting to rebuild their retail base, zoning incentives may be in place for shopping centers, although it is rare that zoning approvals are expedited, given the complexity of building *anything* in an urban environment. Condemnations, land assembly, demolition, integration with historic districts, training for residents and requirements for employment, infrastructure improvements, and construction of structured parking are some of the most important issues that must be negotiated and settled as part of the development process in most urban areas. Nevertheless, local governments are increasingly willing to work closely with shopping center developers as partners to expedite local land use controls and to create retail centers that meet public and private goals.

Avenues of Relief

If a developer is considering a project that is not consistent with the provisions of the comprehensive plan, spe-

The Third Street Promenade, a mixed-use retail/entertainment center in downtown Santa Monica, was encouraged by a public/private partnership embodied in the nonprofit Bayside District Corporation, which guided the redevelopment and management of this once foundering retail district.

A project's economics, whether for a new building or redevelopment of an existing one, has the same basic format and answers, in numbers, the same questions. Completing the project involves a certain cost, and upon completion, a revenue stream creates a return on the cost.

Cost Analysis

The cost analysis contains three sections: acquisition or land costs, hard costs, and soft costs. The first section identifies the purchase price: the cost of acquiring an existing project, a piece of land for new construction, or a combination of the two. Hard costs are expenditures attributed to the physical facility, for example, the cost of site work, utilities, buildings, finishes, signage, landscaping, reroofing, and painting. Soft costs include consultants' fees, such as fees for engineers and architects, legal costs, commissions, the cost of title policies, appraisals, points paid to lenders and fees to mortgage brokers, and the interest expense for carrying the project to the break-even point, when its income stream covers the interest on and possibly amortization of the outstanding balance of an interim loan.

The Irvine Company was required to build a shopping center at Irvine Spectrum as part of a public development agreement.

These costs can be arranged in numerous ways, as illustrated in the following example:

Cost Analysis

Land Cost	_____SF @ $_____	/SF = $_____
Less Simultaneous Sale	(_____)SF @ $_____	/SF = $_____
Net Land Cost	_____SF @ $_____	/SF = $_____

Hard Costs

Site Work	_____SF @ $_____	/SF = $_____
Shell	_____BSF @ $_____	/BSF = $_____
Finishes	_____BSF @ $_____	/BSF = $_____
Signage	_____BSF @ $_____	/BSF = $_____
Miscellaneous	_____BSF @ $_____	/BSF = $_____
Total Hard Costs	_____BSF @ $_____	/BSF = $_____

Soft Costs

Legal Expenses	_____BSF @ $_____	/BSF = $_____
Title Policy	_____BSF @ $_____	/BSF = $_____
Architectural	_____BSF @ $_____	/BSF = $_____
Engineering	_____BSF @ $_____	/BSF = $_____
Commissions	_____BSF @ $_____	/BSF = $_____
Appraisal	_____BSF @ $_____	/BSF = $_____
Financing Fees	_____BSF @ $_____	/BSF = $_____
Miscellaneous	_____BSF @ $_____	/BSF = $_____
Total Soft Costs	_____BSF @ $_____	/BSF = $_____

Interest

Land	_____% for _____ months = $_____
Hard Costs 50%	_____% for _____ months = $_____
Soft Costs 75%	_____% for _____ months = $_____

Total Project Cost	_____BSF @ $_____	/BSF = $_____

The more detailed the format, the more it can focus on specific items that make up the total cost. Site work could be broken down into off-site expenses such as utility extensions to the site and traffic signals, and on-site work such as earth moving, paving, lighting, landscaping, and striping. Engineering, a soft cost, could be separated into predevelopment testing and consultation, including soil and environmental testing and recommendations, and materials testing during construction. Almost all line items could be broken down further and could include back-up schedules identifying all costs separately.

cific avenues of relief are possible. Each avenue requires application and approval, and a developer usually hires a lawyer or employs the legal expertise on an in-house staff to work through zoning relief. The avenues available to developers fall into three main categories: rezoning, variances, and conditional use permits.

Rezoning typically involves filing an application, a review process, an appearance before an appeals board or a zoning administrator, a public hearing, and final approval by a planning board or commission. A variance involves a request, in an area already zoned for commercial use, to build something that does not comply with the specific standards of a zoning ordinance. A conditional use permit is issued through a special provision in the zoning ordinance. This provision specifies that, subject to review and approval by the local authority, special uses will be allowed that are not normally permitted in that zone. Typically, a conditional use provision states certain re-

Analysis of Income and Expenses

Gross income includes base rent, percentage rent, and contributions by the tenants for charges such as taxes, insurance, and common area maintenance. The vacancy factor, usually expressed as a percentage of the total, is subtracted from gross income to reflect the loss of income to vacancy. The vacancy factor should reflect the reliability of the income based in large part on the credit of tenants as well as market conditions. Subtracting the vacancy factor from the gross income yields total gross operating income.

The second part of the analysis of income and expenses includes charges for taxes, insurance, and common area maintenance as well as reserves for future structural and roof repairs, replacement of the parking lot if it is not covered in tenant leases, miscellaneous expenses to the ownership such as legal and tax consultants' fees, and management fees. Net operating income is derived by subtracting total expenses from gross operating income:

Income and Expense Analysis

Income		
Tenant A	_____SF @ $_____	/BSF = $_____
Tenant B	_____SF @ $_____	/BSF = $_____
Tenant C	_____SF @ $_____	/BSF = $_____
Triple Net Charges	_____SF @ $_____	/BSF = $_____
Gross Income		$_____
Less Vacancy Factor	_____%	$(____)
Gross Operating Income		$_____

Expenses		
Taxes	_____SF @ $_____	/BSF = $_____
Insurance	_____SF @ $_____	/BSF = $_____
Common Area Maintenance	_____SF @ $_____	/BSF = $_____
Management Fee	_____%	$_____
Reserves	_____SF @ $_____	/BSF = $_____
Miscellaneous	_____SF @ $_____	/BSF = $_____
Total Expenses		$_____
Net Operating Income		$_____
Free and Clear Return	_____%	

Note: SF = square feet; BSF = Building square feet.

The project's free and clear yield is the net operating income divided by the project's total cost.

The Due Diligence Process

The due diligence process involves identifying what the costs will be and what revenue stream will be created. For a new development, the cost of site work is often the most difficult to identify. Each site is different, and total cost can vary greatly from site to site. Costs for the building shell vary with quality and size. The more uncertainty in each line item under hard costs, the more the cushion that should be provided under "miscellaneous." Of soft costs, fees vary per square foot based on the size of the project. Interest costs vary based on the projected interest rate, the period of time needed to complete construction, and the period of time needed for the revenue stream to equal the cost of carrying outstanding costs. Again, the more uncertainty in each line item under soft costs, the more the cushion should be under "miscellaneous."

On the revenue side, a knowledge of market rents for the type of project proposed is crucial. Historical information is useful in identifying the expenses. Attention to detail is key to accuracy in project economics.

Acquisition

Although the format of the economics for a new development and an acquisition or redevelopment is basically the same, the processes for gathering the information (due diligence) are quite different. The following steps are involved in underwriting an acquisition.

Underwriting a project for acquisition involves evaluating the positive and negative issues associated with it that might affect operations over a given period—financial, psychological, physical, or strategic. Analyses of the market and tenant mix are also part of the underwriting process, and evaluation of all these issues is important in the final analysis.

Before considering price, a developer must perform a detailed analysis of the project's existing economics. This process involves review of:

quirements that must be met by the project (with regard to setbacks, building heights, parking, and so on) for the conditional use to be considered and granted. For both a variance and a conditional use permit, the developer goes through a similar review process, involving applications, review, and hearings before receiving or not receiving approval.

Requests for rezoning need to deal with the consistency with the community's comprehensive plan. If a site's zoning is consistent with the comprehensive plan, it is usually easier for a developer to petition for a zoning change. If the decision is unfavorable and appears unreasonable, a developer may appeal to a zoning board of appeals that operates as a quasi-judicial review arm of the local government. By this point, the developer will probably have obtained legal counsel. If an appeal of the appeals board's decision is desired, the case would be heard at a lower court of the judicial system. Further

The Court at King of Prussia was renovated with minor changes to the existing architecture.

- Operating Statement—Examine the revenues and expenses for accuracy and to determine whether operations could be more efficient, paying particular attention to third-party contracts and to expenses reimbursed by tenants. Tenants with gross leases will hurt cash flow if increases in base rent and percentage rents do not offset escalations in expenses, including replacement reserves over time. Review maintenance charges to determine where past problems have occurred and to see whether proper attention is being given to deferred maintenance.

- Rent Roll—Pay attention to tenants with long-term, fixed rental agreements. Check for caps (funding maximums) on expenses or percentage rents, and look for recapture of expenses out of percentage rents. Identify opportunities for rent increases and greater expense participation as tenants' leases expire, and check the current volume to determine whether any tenants are approaching their percentage rental break-even point.

- Debt Structure—Get details on loan structures, such as rate, term, debt service constant, amortization schedule, prepayment, and assignability.

Although the seller is bound by certain statutes to disclose substandard conditions, the buyer can assume that caveat emptor is the ruling principle in purchasing shopping centers. A buyer should look at the following items to determine the investment quality of the property and its potential for future problems:

- Sales History of Tenants—These figures are probably the best barometer of a project's health. The tenant's "health index" (total rent divided by total sales) should be compared with industry standards. If the tenants are doing acceptable volumes, most of the other problems should be solvable as long as the buyer does not pay too much for the property.

- Delinquencies among Tenants—A tenant's delinquency on rent payments is a red flag for future problems.

- Rental Rate versus Market Rate—If the center is being purchased on the "income" approach, upside potential will be adversely affected if all tenants are paying rates at or above market rates. Setting rates below market gives a developer a comfort zone if economic conditions deteriorate and market rents fall. Rolling down rental rates to market rates also gives a more accurate overall picture of stabilized income.

- Tenant Profiles—Each tenant should be interviewed at least once, but preferably by different administrative levels within the organization, to confirm the reliability of information. These interviews and other information provided by the seller should provide the follow-

appeals can be made through that system to the Supreme Court, if necessary. But this process is costly and time-consuming, and generally neither the developer nor the community wants to use it as the means to resolve a conflict.

Review of the Site Plan

In addition to zoning review and approval, most communities have instituted a process to review site plans for projects over a certain size. Such reviews involve a detailed evaluation of the project's design, including signage, parking, landscaping, design, and structural characteristics; the probable effect the project will have on the surrounding area based on environmental factors like topography, wetlands, habitats, runoff, soil characteristics, and pollution (air, water, sound, and light), needed infrastructure, and traffic; and its social impacts, especially on areas that are primarily residen-

ing information: sales history, history of delinquency, occupancy cost as percentage of sales, adequacy of the physical facility and the potential for expansion, long-term commitment to location, financial strength (credit review), competitive position in the market, possibilities of relocation or expansion, viability of the operating concept, other existing problems, the seller's history of maintaining the property, determination of the tenants most important to the project, and determination of potential new tenants.

- Legal Issues—Lease abstracts (rights of cancellation, use clauses, assignment and subletting, exclusive covenants, site plan controls, and first rights of refusal), title review, building restrictions, third-party contracts, Uniform Commercial Code as applicable, and tenant estoppels should be checked.
- Physical Inspection—If the in-house staff is inexperienced, outside consultants could be hired to complete portions of the physical inspection. This inspection involves three major components: 1) layout of the center (function versus obsolescence, store depths, dead corners, visibility from the street, parking, future expansion area of building and pads); 2) maintenance (quality of construction, structural integrity, roof, parking lot, necessity for upgraded lighting, need to conform to the local building code, cost of deferred maintenance); and 3) environmental issues, such as asbestos and contaminated soil. Many issues involved in the acquisition of an existing property are not relevant for a new building. In the same vein, acquiring properties can require a company to go beyond its capabilities and expertise.

Investors and developers who are considering an acquisition must candidly evaluate the strengths and weaknesses of their companies. Because of the different capabilities and investment objectives among potential buyers, some issues will be acceptable to one buyer but unacceptable to another. If a potential buyer's leasing staff is inexperienced and the project requires substantial retenanting, steering clear of the project may be the best alternative. Likewise, if it takes patient money to turn a project around as leases roll over and opportunities for retenanting and remixing the project present themselves, a merchant builder may need to step aside. The main point to

remember is to stay with the things your own company does well.

The following financial indexes and miscellaneous issues can be used to analyze projects objectively. These tools will help investors and developers compare projects with criteria suited to their own investment profiles.

- Cost per square foot of gross and net leasable area;
- Free and clear yield (net operating income divided by project cost, including acquisition costs and deferred maintenance);
- Return on equity (with and without amortization);
- Cash on cash (with and without amortization);
- Internal rate of return;
- Credit/noncredit ratios;
- Ratio of anchors to nonanchors;
- Aging of renewals for tenant turnover;
- Average rents versus market rents (anchor tenants and speculative space);
- Percent of expenses reimbursed by tenants.

Just as a perfect project will never be built, all the questions that need to be asked to make the right projections for an acquisition will never be asked. Moreover, all the underwriting risks may never materialize, so discounting the price for all negative possibilities may make the purchase offer too low for current market conditions. Part of the underwriting process is to determine what risks make a project infeasible or too risky and which ones can be "managed" to minimize the negative impact. A developer or investor can only hope that hard work, prudent underwriting, and luck produce an acceptable—or better—return.

Source: Excerpted from participants' manual for "Shopping Centers: How to Build, Buy, and Redevelop," a workshop sponsored by ULI.

■

tial. These considerations frequently concern citizens the most and could delay the review process during public hearings.

Municipalities have become more aware of the long-term effects of soil erosion caused by the construction of a new shopping center. They also consider more carefully the effects of development on groundwater contamination and on potential stormwater runoff and flooding. This increased concern over environmental quality is

reflected in the enactment of more specific local standards and more careful review of them during review of the site plan. Increasingly strict federal requirements apply to fragile environmental areas, particularly wetlands, plant and animal habitats, coastal and shoreline areas, and cultural and historic sites. An outside consultant specializing in environmental matters should be employed to prepare the required environmental impact statement or environmental assessment.

Sophisticated developers recognize the significance of fragile environmental areas to the neighborhood, the community, and the nation. A shopping center developer should work closely with local and federal jurisdictions during the early stages of planning to ensure that the project will not have a deleterious impact on the environment. If it becomes apparent that a favored site has serious, unforeseen environmental problems that cannot be mitigated to the satisfaction of the public, a new site should be chosen for the shopping center. In addition to the unsatisfactory environmental impact, the added time, cost, and ill will created in the community make such a site poorly suited for development.

Zoning Alternatives

Many communities have become aware of the problems inherent in designating commercial zones that try to accommodate strip commercial development, independent retail operations, and planned shopping centers within the same framework. For this reason, many communities now have planned development districts, recognizing the benefits that they can provide to the community by giving developers the flexibility to tailor development more closely to the special qualities and characteristics of the area and the population served. This special classification usually requires a mandatory site plan review by a sophisticated review staff, generally comprising engineers, architects, and planners. It also requires a high degree of cooperation among various government agencies.

Other communities have "floating zones" to accommodate shopping centers. The zoning ordinance describes a floating shopping center zone in detail, but the floating zone is not geographically located on the zoning map. The text specifies the types of development allowed and the standards that would usually be applied to a commercial district. The zone "floats" until a request is received to develop a center at a particular location. The merits of the location are then evaluated, and if it is approved, the approval process continues with a review of the site plan, after which the area under consideration is officially zoned for commercial use.

Zoning overlays are a third zoning alternative for commercial development. Such overlays specify areas where a proposal for commercial development will be considered. Any development within the overlay district is subject to certain conditions that do not exist outside the overlay zone. Zoning overlays that are not specifically geared toward shopping center development can still affect the quality of a center developed in their areas, however. For instance, a downtown revitalization overlay may give density bonuses for the inclusion of residential units in the overall design of the shopping center. A floodplain overlay district may inhibit the types of permanent building that occur in the floodplain, which decidedly affects design. An airport overlay district may have certain requirements for construction related to sound insulation and building height.

With the growing market for urban shopping centers, municipalities are faced with the problem of approving site plans for enclosed malls that incorporate existing historic structures and include necessary parking areas. In such cases, municipalities often create historic overlay districts with regulations to preserve historic structures and other urban features.

Federal, State, and Regional Regulations

Beginning in 1969, the federal government became more visibly involved in environmental regulation with the passage of the National Environmental Policy Act and numerous environmental laws and their amendments. Of these pieces of federal legislation, the Clean Air Act and amendments perhaps have had the greatest impact on shopping center development. This legislation makes localities more responsible for the regional and local impacts on air quality caused by traffic-generating development. Concern about the regional impacts of development on both the environment and on transportation systems has stimulated increasing state involvement in local land use regulation, as well as in the creation of regional authorities to oversee local activities.

Development Agreements and Exactions

A major trend that has emerged in the development approval process is the use of development agreements —negotiated agreements between developers and local jurisdictions, often arbitrated by an attorney. The developer is given permission to build in exchange for providing certain on- or off-site improvements, known as exactions, for the local governing body. Originally, development agreements were created in response to the expenditures local communities had to make on additional improvements because of new developments. Municipalities began to require that developers instead pay for the off-site improvements necessitated by their projects. These improvements might include building and widening roads, adding traffic signals, running water and sewer lines to

the project, and making other changes directly related to the development. In the case of Woodfield Village Green, a 623,000-square-foot power center in Schaumberg, Illinois, the developer provided stormwater retention for his own site and several adjacent parcels, provided right-of-way improvements to a boulevard on the east edge of its site, paid a traffic impact fee, paid another impact fee for village services, paid an exaction for off-site widening of the intersection on the southwest corner of the site, and provided funding for part of a possible Illinois tollway interchange from one of the center's access roads.[14]

When a developer has already received permission to build, a development agreement frequently involves other types of tradeoffs; for example, the developer negotiates for increased density or for other features such as a lower parking requirement in exchange for providing or paying for a public improvement. These agreements, often called bonus agreements, involve careful arbitration to reach a final proposal from which both parties feel they will benefit. Having gained popularity, bonuses are frequently used in overlay or other special districts and are often incorporated in the text of the zoning ordinance.

Many local jurisdictions have found exactions a convenient way to finance municipal improvements and thus prevent new development from being an added burden. In many areas, however, exactions are becoming less directly related to the needs caused by the development itself. Developers have successfully challenged unreasonable requests made by cities, and the courts have determined in some cases that these requests were not sufficiently related to the municipalities' development-generated needs. In general, however, the use of exactions has become a legally accepted practice, and any disputes can be resolved through negotiation between the developer and the community rather than through litigation.

Participation by Citizens

Government at all levels increasingly accommodates the desire of citizens to participate in shaping the development of their communities. Reaching a consensus among citizens with vastly diverging interests on the direction and quality of development can sometimes be a frustrating and time-consuming process. Nevertheless, citizens' participation has been largely formalized and now is handled as an orderly, routine part of the review and approval process. Indeed, the astute developer recognizes the important role that citizens play in obtaining approval for a project and works with them from the early stages of project planning. Citizens, as well as public officials and developers, are also becoming more sophisticated in their involvement, recognizing that cooperative negotiation ultimately reaps benefits for all parties.

The Approval Process

The approval process customarily involves submitting proposals to and negotiating with the jurisdiction's planning staff, which recommends ultimately whether a project be approved or denied. During this process, various agencies review the project, and public hearings are held. In the past, the developer obtained appropriate zoning for the site before applying for permits. Today, as a rule, site plans must be reviewed and the project's compliance with parking and subdivision regulations considered before the developer can obtain any zoning approval. Often a developer first can submit a basic concept plan, avoiding the expense of putting together a detailed site plan until the jurisdiction has indicated the project will likely be approved.

A developer beginning project review usually elects to hire a local attorney to represent his or her interests. A local lawyer would know the specifics of local ordinances and procedures, be familiar with the local political climate, and often receives more cooperation from officials than an "outsider." Such lawyers often have their own engineers and other expert witnesses with good local credibility to testify for presentations. The lawyer helps the developer with myriad aspects of the approval process, from rezoning to Adequate Public Facilities review. APF review involves the study of roads and sewer, water, and fire service, and it is during this review that negotiations regarding exactions are conducted. The lawyer assists during the site plan review as well, negotiating optimal bonuses to be awarded based on meeting specified conditions. The attorney also can represent the client in informal meetings with the planning staff and occasionally assists the developer obtain permit approvals. The attorney makes formal presentations at hearings and other adjudicatory proceedings. The effectiveness of a developer's legal representative can cause a project to win or lose approval. Other factors influence a project's approval as well, including the community's attitudes toward the quality of the proposed development and/or the jurisdiction's receptivity to it.

A well-planned, well-documented presentation at public hearings improves the developer's chances of obtaining community support. Photographs, statistical charts, drawings, and models make presentations more vivid and comprehensible. An experienced land use lawyer can prepare an effective presentation, producing the required expert witnesses and support documents.

A community will be concerned primarily with those elements of a shopping center that pertain to the community's general welfare. Major considerations often include the effects of competition on downtown retail operations (or other retail centers in the community), traffic, noise, required utilities and infrastructure, and environmental impact. Increasingly, communities also worry about the aesthetic qualities of a shopping center, how the center will affect the character of the surrounding community, and how well it will be integrated with surrounding neighborhoods. If a developer is sensitive to these concerns when a site is chosen and designs an attractive center that is compatible with its surroundings, the approval process will likely be much easier. At Woodfield Village Green, the developer accommodated the wishes of the citizens of Schaumberg with an open-air

shopping center that has the feel of an older midwestern village downtown. Developers should make a point of contacting local residents and civic associations early in the planning process to explain their proposal and to work closely with the community as the development concept unfolds. A developer can then avoid costly delays by entering the approval process with a plan that will not take the community by surprise and generate opposition.

The developer should also want to promote good public relations in general during the approval process. A community frequently needs reassurance when it is in the midst of transition to a more urban setting. The developer can provide this reassurance by alleviating anxieties that might have been caused by the negative consequences of past development and by demonstrating how the proposed development will enhance the community. Zoning favorable to shopping center development may be in place, but developers still must carry the burden of proof and provide sound reasons for a project's approval. A shopping center usually provides more net income from real estate and sales taxes than the increased cost of the public services required by the center. Thus, a shopping center has a more favorable fiscal impact on a community than residential development. It also generates considerable full-time and seasonal employment. And because of the nature of development agreements, communities may also receive benefits from the development of shopping centers through exactions, including road and infrastructure improvements and, in some cases, community and transportation facilities. Moreover, the community does not have the burden of underwriting the center's maintenance and security.

A developer needs to address specific community concerns very carefully. In light of an overabundance of retail space nationally and in many communities, the developer must justify the need for an increase in the area's shopping facilities as well as the center's type of goods and services. Moreover, the development team should be prepared to discuss the issues of the center's architectural design, the lighting necessary for safety and security, signage, traffic circulation, and the relationship with adjoining properties. The developer's aim should be to create a shopping environment that is popular with the community it serves, fills a niche that is currently open, and reflects an understanding of consumers' emerging shopping needs.

Types, sizes, and designs of shopping centers vary according to tenants' special leasing needs, the developer's proposed innovations, and such issues as on-site parking and off-street loading requirements. And because a shopping center's goal at the outset is to respond to its market, many concerns of the community regarding good shopping center design are also the developer's concerns. As a result, allowing latitude for a flexible design while still accommodating public planning goals generally results in an improved product for all parties.

Regardless of what the developer or the community might want in the abstract, the development costs, operational costs, and desired tenant mix must fit within a feasible investment venture. For this reason, the private business aspects of a shopping center should remain primarily in the developer's province except to the extent that the community is a financial partner in the center's creation. Approval authorities need to be careful in setting forth specifications that inhibit creativity and impose excessive costs or unusual burdens on the development. Each requirement has an impact on a center's financial feasibility, and if the regulatory burden becomes too onerous, it may render the project unfinanceable and the center unbuildable.

Comprehensive development regulations and approval processes per se are not a problem for shopping center developers if they are clearly articulated and predictable. In fact, by limiting the competition, strict regulations can improve the long-term outlook for a shopping center that is approved, and they will help the community avoid overbuilding. These procedures are sometimes

Yerba Buena Gardens is a large-scale redevelopment in San Francisco that includes Sony's Metreon retail entertainment center and an extensive park and open-space network developed by several public/private partnerships. Free public concerts are often held on the Esplanade, and the Martin Luther King memorial and waterfall provides an exciting environment for children.

The Commons at Calabasas, a 200,000-square-foot community shopping center in the suburbs of Los Angeles, was built to resemble an Italian village. The project opened in 1998 following years of neighborhood opposition to development on the site. The developer of the project, Caruso Affiliated Holdings, overcame this obstacle by meeting and consulting frequently with community groups to develop a retail center that would create a unique sense of place for this suburban community.

Erhard Pfeiffer

Erhard Pfeiffer

enveloped by an adversarial atmosphere and prolonged uncertainty, however, that in effect pit public officials, citizens, and developers against one another. Such an atmosphere benefits no one. An alternative is for developers and community officials to first establish an atmosphere of cooperation and mutual trust, far better equipping themselves to negotiate with each other to their mutual satisfaction. A community needs to understand the development business, and the developer needs to understand the community. Through such an understanding, reasonable compromises can be reached. In Virginia, for example, a system of proffers has been established through state legislation that makes it possible for developers and communities to negotiate tradeoffs that normally could not be achieved through a development agreement.

Notes

1. See Richard Kateley, "Analyzing Market Demand for Shopping Centers," in *Shopping Centers and Other Retail Properties,* ed. John R. White and Kevin D. Gray (New York: John Wiley & Sons, 1996).

2. See W. Paul O'Mara et al., *Developing Power Centers* (Washington, D.C.: ULI–the Urban Land Institute, 1996), for a detailed description of tenants in power centers.

3. Kateley, "Analyzing Market Demand for Shopping Centers."

4. Capitalization of the income stream can be used to compute the value of a new center that is leased at market rents. Cost projections for the center, however, must include leasing costs required to achieve a stabilized occupancy level. For centers that have been operating for several years and have leases below current market rents, capitalizing the current income stream can be misleading in determining the center's value. To determine the value of such a center, a multiyear discounted cash flow projection is needed to show the impact of below-market leases expiring and being replaced with leases written at estimated future market rents.

5. See Dean Schwanke, *Remaking the Shopping Center* (Washington, D.C.: ULI–the Urban Land Institute, 1994), pp. 116–22.

6. Some specialty, theme, off-price, and outlet centers have been successfully developed without anchor tenants or with just a cluster of smaller tenants, such as a food court that functions as an anchor.

7. ULI's *Dollars & Cents of Shopping Centers* series provides detailed information on composition of shopping centers by tenant category for all major types of centers.

8. The word "lease" is often used in the following discussion. If the key tenant purchases rather than leases the site, the word "lease" is used rather than "occupancy agreement" for the purpose of general discussion, even though the latter term might be more accurate in some cases.

9. For a detailed presentation of these nonlease arrangements, see Michael Beyard et al., *Developing Urban Entertainment Centers* (Washington, D.C.: ULI–the Urban Land Institute, 1998).

10. Harold R. Imus, "The Developer's View of Shopping Center Finance," paper presented to ULI's Commercial and Retail Development Council.

11. Participants' manual for "Shopping Centers: How to Build, Buy, and Redevelop," a workshop sponsored by ULI, p. 40.

12. Martin Bucksbaum and Matthew Bucksbaum, "Developing and Investing in Regional and Super Regional Malls," in *Shopping Centers and Other Retail Properties,* ed. John R. White and Kevin D. Gray (New York: John Wiley & Sons, 1996), pp. 248–49.

13. These loans are all short term (from three to seven years), with all or most of the loan amount paid at the end of the term. Developers use interim loans to pay off construction loans before securing permanent financing, while gap loans cover construction costs not included in the construction loan. Bullet loans basically serve as minipermanent loans (miniperms).

14. O'Mara et al., *Developing Power Centers,* pp. 64–65.

3. Planning and Design

Once the feasibility of creating a shopping center has been determined and the decision made to proceed with the project, site planning and architectural and structural design can move beyond the preliminary stage. The detailed planning and design of a shopping center presents many challenges: in addition to the structure's housing the business of retailing, the site must accommodate vehicular parking, the building and its environment must appeal to and be convenient for desired customers and tenants, and the development as a whole must compensate the owners for their investment as well as serve the community. Additionally, the center must be designed within ever-tighter constraints on environmental protection, traffic, growth management, building design and site configuration, and energy conservation.

Architectural quality must be compatible with the type and location of the center, the topography of the site, the configuration of the buildings, and the type of center proposed. Achieving these goals requires melding the most up-to-date principles of land planning, landscaping, architectural design, and engineering with skillful merchandising, public relations, and management. Compromises will inevitably have to be made between what can be afforded and what will have to be left out, but the finished center not only must be an appealing and convenient

marketplace in which to shop but also must match the needs of the trade area. Only then can it be profitable for the community, the tenants, and the owners.

The design of a shopping center must achieve overall harmony in style while permitting reasonable variations among tenants to give them identity. Harmony, however, no longer means sameness and repetitiveness; it has taken on a more sophisticated meaning. Customers' lives are increasingly complex, a complexity increasingly reflected in the drama, diversity, and details of the shopping center itself. A harmonious design should not lead to shopping environments that are the same in Los Angeles and Washington, D.C., which unfortunately has too often become the case. The architect and planner should coordinate their skills with those of other experts on the developer's team to create distinctive shopping environments that are rooted in the locale where they are being developed, linked more carefully to the surrounding neighborhoods and to multiple means of access, and more reflective of the community's culture and heritage.

Innovative designs are increasingly necessary to create all types of shopping centers, from strip centers that too often have suffered from a poor or mediocre appearance to regional malls that too often have been isolated from their communities by enormous parking lots and are dependent on increasingly clogged access roads. It is unfortunate that shopping centers characterized by a sameness of merchandise, a hodgepodge of predictable materials, poor taste in signage, banal architecture, and uncoordi-

Cairns Central, in Queensland, Australia, provides a direct link between the interior center court to the railway station located beneath the center.

Although Pacific Place, a five-level retail/entertainment destination completed in fall 1998, occupies one of the largest blocks in downtown Seattle, it maintains a scale consistent with the surrounding neighborhood. It was designed to look like a collection of smaller buildings that grew up over time rather than one megablock.

nated development patterns have come to represent all shopping centers in the minds of an increasing number of consumers. This situation, however, is now changing rapidly as consumers are choosing new-generation shopping environments, including town centers, entertainment centers, streetfront retailing centers, multiuse commercial centers, and specialty shopping centers conveniently integrated with airports, train stations, and transit terminals. At the same time, existing shopping centers are being redesigned more often than in the past to meet consumers' more exacting standards, to withstand the competition of new-generation centers, and to compete with nonstore shopping alternatives, such as catalog and Internet shopping.

Before the framework and the details of a shopping center can be designed, a developer must know the type of center and key tenants and the general array of spaces these tenants require. Just as the exterior design is dictated by the size, shape, and location of the property, so the placement and grouping of tenants within the structure are based on the leasing or merchandising plan. Decisions about configuration, structural framing, and mechanical equipment within the limits of cost should be made before exterior architecture is determined.

Unless the center is to have a basement or underground parking, the foundation requires only simple excavation to lay column footings and grade beams to support load-bearing walls. A flat built-up roof over a long-spanning joist roof allows load-bearing columns to be spaced widely

apart, providing maximum flexibility in designing widths and depths of individual stores. Building depths, which previously were 125 to 150 feet, now typically are 80 to 120 feet, largely because the increased cost of construction has forced tenants into smaller spaces, and, rather than give up frontage, the stores have become shallower. Smaller shops may be as shallow as 30 feet, with mall stalls against otherwise blank department store or cineplex walls as shallow as 12 feet. Many shops may be no more than 30 to 60 feet deep, with the rear space designed to serve either as storage area or as overlap area for deeper adjacent units. A variety of spaces must be designed in line with the mix of tenant types being pursued. Large shopping center developers generally have on-site leasing staff who understand the detailed space requirements of different tenant types and of specific tenants. Smaller developers typically hire an experienced leasing agent with this specialized knowledge.

In addition to the structural and interior design controls imposed on the designer by the character and composition of tenants of the particular project, external controls are imposed by the public. For example, the public's concern with environmental matters has led to buildings and site designs that are more integrated than ever before with the neighborhood and that harmonize more than ever before with the character of the community. In addition, the need to limit traffic congestion and sprawl influences shopping center design as much as site location, and the need to cut operating costs leads to more efficient construction techniques, more safety- and energy-conscious designs, and the mixing of retail and nonretail land uses to leverage the real estate.

Display windows on exterior walls of regional shopping centers are being added as centers are de-malled, insulation increased to reduce heat loss or gain through walls and roofs, lights put on automatic cycles, and the use of intensive heat-producing lighting systems decreased. Graphics are improving: illuminated identification signs with black letters silhouetted on a light background are being used instead of brilliant self-lit lettering. Energy-saving devices and innovative design techniques are limited only by the ingenuity and resourcefulness of architects, designers, and engineers.

Under provisions of the Americans with Disabilities Act (ADA), today's centers must be accessible to the handicapped. ADA covers arrival and parking areas, walkways, ramps, entrances and doorways, corridors, stairs, elevators, toilet facilities, drinking fountains, public telephones, and signs. Federal, state, and local laws mandating accessibility in privately owned public buildings (including shopping centers) are incorporated into building codes. The developer and the design team must be aware of all accessibility codes and must make certain that the requirements are incorporated in the center's design. Failure to do so will add costs later, because installed features that fail to provide access to the handicapped according to codes will have to be replaced with compo-

nents that do. Such changes also take time and could delay the occupancy permit for the center.

Building efficiency has always been important, but today's costs make it essential. Designs should maximize leasable space and minimize nonleasable spaces that are not required for customers' use. With the rising cost of land, an inefficient parking layout is intolerable. Likewise, an interior or exterior that requires a great deal of maintenance cannot be allowed.

Maximum space at minimum cost is not the only goal, however. To be successful, a shopping center must be attractive and pleasant for customers. A poorly finished appearance is projected to the customer, reducing the center's appeal and thus its earning capacity. On the other hand, an ostentatious, overdesigned center may frighten away customers of a mid- or off-price mall.

Exterior Features

Building Configuration

Determining the building configuration is an important part of site planning for both developer and tenant. The developer's main consideration should be placement of the key or anchor tenants, which must be positioned so that they draw shoppers between them and past other tenants.

Building configurations have evolved steadily over the years, and the basic configurations discussed in the following paragraphs have been adapted in countless vari-

More environmentally sound and energy-conscious designs can slash operating costs. The Lebanon Food Co-op, near Dartmouth College in New Hampshire, features natural light from the cupola that saves energy and makes the interior glow. Sensors in the market detect the level of light and adjust electric lighting automatically. The market is expected to save 36 percent a year in energy costs compared with a standard grocery store.

The introduction of multiscreen cinema complexes into shopping centers is proving to be a win-win situation. Mall owners gain an additional anchor that increases the number of customers to their centers and expands the trade area beyond the reach of other retailers. They also gain a flexible tenant: cinema complexes can activate areas unsuitable for retailing or replace anchor stores that have gone dark. What is more, cinemas change their offerings weekly, generating repeat visits. Theater operators reap bottom-line benefits too. By securing a deal with a mall, a cinema chain immediately is associated with an established destination. Shared parking reduces the theater operator's site costs, and automatic ticketing machines (both inside and outside the mall) increase the cinema's prominence and add convenience. Key design issues must be mastered, however, for the marriage of movie and mall to succeed.

Site Planning

Not long ago, developers feared that movie patrons would clog mall parking spaces, retarding the turnover of shoppers. Consequently, cinemas were placed as far as possible from mall entrances. Now that consumers have less time, what used to be viewed as two separate trips to the mall is combined into one.

Recent parking surveys show that demand for mall and theater parking is complementary. Most visits to a mall occur during daylight hours, most visits to the cinema in the evening. Conflicts, if they do occur, happen on Saturday afternoons between 5:00 and 7:00 p.m., when weekly mall and cinema peaks coincide briefly. Special peaks are widely separated: mall traffic peaks between Thanksgiving and December 31, cinema traffic in the summer. As a consequence, mall parking does not need to fulfill zoning requirements for both uses. Nevertheless, the following questions must be answered for each site:

- Can the mall accommodate the theater operator's desired parking/seat ratio?
- How much parking is required by zoning? Can a zoning variance be obtained if required parking exceeds what is needed?
- Will a parking deck be required?

Concepts for placing the cinema vary from site to site, and each concept comes with its own set of challenges. At the recently opened Brass Mill Center in Waterbury, Connecticut, a stadium-style 12-plex was positioned on top of the mall. Kathleen Shields, development director for General Growth Properties, says, "The cinema functions like an additional anchor. We wanted the cinema placed in a dramatic central location where the greatest number of customers would circulate. It is conveniently accessed from the parking deck and the mall's feature

The Entertainment Center at Irvine Spectrum is anchored by the 158,000-square-foot, 21-screen Edwards Cinemas and 3-D IMAX Theater. The grand public spaces in front of the cinema serve as a gathering spot for visitors.

entry for after-hours operation. The creation of a third level enhanced the center's visibility from nearby I-84." At Greece Ridge Center in Greece Ridge, New York, an at-grade stadium-style 12-plex with access from the mall and the exterior, replaced a failed big-box anchor at one end of the retail spine.

At Solomon Pond Mall in Marlborough, Massachusetts, the addition of a stadium-style 15-plex cinema at grade filled an underused parking field at the rear of the mall. Joe Koechel, vice president and director of properties of the Wells Park Group, says, "The cinema has benefited the mall in two ways. The overall business has seen an improvement and an increase in traffic, and because Solomon Pond Mall is not located on a busy street, the cinema has helped make the mall an entertainment destination. We now offer the three tried-and-true elements that draw customers: shopping, dining, and the movies. It's been a successful marriage so far."

Planning

Planning within the mall itself is paramount in the creation of an entertainment complex at a retail mall. Several strategic issues must be resolved while planning such a cinema complex:

- What location will generate the greatest traffic flow through the mall?
- What location provides the best opportunities for physical and visual connections between the cinema and the mall?
- What location will increase the excitement of shopping and going to the movies?
- What should be the relationship among the cinema, the food court, other eating and entertainment establishments, and synergistic co-tenants such as book and music stores?

The most significant relationship between a cinema complex and a retail mall is circulation and egress, especially when the cinema complex is not located at grade. Locating a cinema complex above or below grade helps encourage people to circulate vertically in a mall, but unusually large stairs are required to accommodate those who are leaving a movie and those who are arriving. Most codes allow a portion of the cinema population to exit into a mall. In new construction, this additional traffic must be included when determining the mall's exit capacity. When a cinema is added to an existing mall and exit systems are not sized to handle the additional exit load, additional space must be carved out for exit corridors and stairs. This factor will be a negotiating point, as the square footage of above-grade exit corridors and stairs seldom is included in a typical lease for a cinema. Most mall owners are willing to accept this condition to secure a deal for a cinema multiplex in an above- or below-grade configuration.

When a cinema complex is placed in the footprint of a defunct anchor store, the location often is far from the food court, which may weaken the synergy with dining. This problem can be countered by creating an entire entertainment/recreation area around the cinema with restaurants, cafés, games, and related retail stores. One of the most interesting examples of this concept is the Shoppingtown Mall in DeWitt, New York.

At Shoppingtown, Wilmorite, the owner of the mall, and Hoyts Cinema completed a deal whereby Hoyts constructed a sloped-floor ten-plex cinema in an underused below-grade wing. The structural challenges faced by the design team were great: structural loads were transferred, footings were lowered, and all columns were extended to accommodate the volume of a theater underneath the mall. All the while, the mall above was open for business.

With the fit-out work completed and the cinema open to the public, Wilmorite used the newly established cinema destination to anchor a new entertainment zone, which includes a restaurant/pub, pushcart marketing, a laser tag game area, and a comedy club.

Special issues involving zoning, structural design, and security occur when integrating movies into the mall:

- Is a cinema complex allowed by zoning, or is a special permit required?
- Is a height variance required? Cinemas with stadium-style seating require 30 to 40 feet in building height.
- Is a signage variance required for the cinema's pylon and marquee signs?
- Can an existing structure be adapted to accommodate spacing and volume of the cinema?
- Is additional mall security available if cinema patrons have to exit through the mall after hours? Is parking lot lighting after hours accounted for in the mall's operating budget?

These challenges notwithstanding, cinema complexes increase mall sales overall. In an article titled "New Entertainment Centers Broaden Appeal" in the October 1997 issue of *Shopping Center Business*, John Bucksbaum, executive vice president of General Growth Properties, reports that "since opening a 75,000-square-foot AMC Theater in GGP's Deerbrook Mall in Houston, the in-line stores have shown a 15 to 16 percent sales increase every month, with food court tenants increasing sales by as much as 50 percent per month."

Source: Robert S. Holt and Dennis B. Carlberg, Arrowstreet Inc.

figure 3–1

Basic Shopping Center Building Configurations

Linear

A line of stores sometimes tied together by a canopy over the side-walk, which runs along the fronts of the stores. Economical for small centers but must be kept within a reasonable length to avoid excessive walking distances and difficult merchandising.

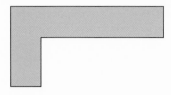

L

Basically a linear layout but with one end turned. Good for corner locations.

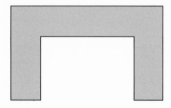

U

Basically a linear layout with both ends turned in the same direction. Good for full blocks.

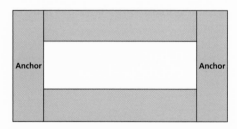

Mall

A pedestrian way, enclosed or unenclosed, between two facing linear buildings. May take many shapes.

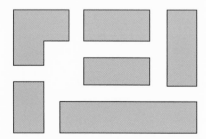

Cluster/Racetrack/Town Center

A group of retail buildings separated by pedestrian walkways or streets.

ations. The original concept of shopping centers was a linear building with parking in the rear, at the sides, or in front. The "L," "U," and "T" footprints were variations designed to fit restricted sites and special locations with respect to adjacent streets. In larger centers, stores began to turn their backs on the public street, with two strip buildings facing each other separated by parking. Later, this intervening parking space was contracted and transformed into an open and then enclosed, landscaped mall. The mall structure, with its inward-facing storefronts, became an island surrounded by parking space. Today, all types of shopping centers are more often configured toward the street once again.

The Linear Center and Variations. The linear layout is basically a straight line of stores, sometimes tied together by a canopy over a pedestrian walk that passes storefronts. The linear building is normally set back from the access street, and most of the parking is placed between the street and the building. This center design is often referred to as a "strip center." Although this term describes a particular physical arrangement that can be used for shopping centers, it is also a term that (when used in combination, as in "strip development" and "strip commercial") may not include all the factors that qualify a development as a shopping center.

The linear arrangement is most commonly applied to the neighborhood center and the power center. The most common configuration places two major units—usually a supermarket and a drugstore in a neighborhood center, a big-box retailer in a power center—at the ends of the center. Big-box retailers are also spaced regularly throughout a power center. A linear center is generally the least expensive structure to build and is easily adapted to most site conditions. With strong control over signage and good architectural treatment, the linear center can be an attractive and successful merchandising unit.

The linear center should not be too long to accommodate comfortable walking distances. About 400 feet is standard, although centers 750 feet long, and longer, have been successful. If parking is adequate in a long center, customers are tempted to drive around within a center to various sections of the center. This movement is highly undesirable and can impair vehicular circulation within the center's parking area and/or reduce parking capacity. Alternative building configurations should be carefully considered in lieu of a long linear center.

The L-shaped linear center has one end turned; the U-shaped center has both ends turned in the same direction. The major reason for using the L or U shape is to restrict the length of a center that would, if laid out in a straight line, be too long. The L can be turned in either direction according to the necessary site orientation. The L or U shape also makes the fullest use of a site that is nearly square; a linear development on such a site would waste site capacity and provide unnecessary parking. In general, the L is suitable for larger neighborhood and smaller community centers, the U for larger community centers. Because of the trend away from small shop space,

The Fountains in the Houston metropolitan region, like most suburban linear centers, is set back from the access street, with most of the parking spaces between the street and the building.

however, and toward ever-larger tenants, L-shaped centers (with too much nonvisible area and too little parking at the inside corner of the L) are proving less practical. The linear arrangement, with a straight line of stores, seems to be a more successful configuration and is less expensive to build or renovate. It is easily adapted to idiosyncrasies of the site's shape by adding slight angles or crescent shapes to the straight line.

Some shopping centers provide canopies or colonnaded roof projections along the storefronts to protect pedestrians from the weather.

The Mall. Essentially a walkway between two facing linear buildings, the mall, a pedestrian street for back-and-forth shopping movement, has become the standard pattern for the regional center and even has been applied to community-size centers. The mall may be constructed open to the sky or roofed over with skylights to allow natural lighting. The weather-protected area is heated and cooled according to the season. Although the enclosed mall has become the dominant design for regional centers, regardless of climate, this situation is changing. Customers have responded positively to the new generation of outdoor mall configurations.

Whether an indoor or outdoor configuration, however, the width of the mall must be carefully considered. If an enclosed mall is too wide, it is expensive to maintain and discourages the back-and-forth movement created by impulse buying. If it is too narrow, it becomes crowded, hard to keep clean, and difficult to use for promotional activities.

The Cluster/Racetrack/Town Center. The cluster, racetrack, and town center are variations of the same basic configuration. Tenants are arranged around pedestrian walkways or streets that may meander through the center, or be straight or offset. In traditional regional centers, the cluster may be in an "X," "Y," or dumbbell shape, with anchors at the ends of each mall and in the middle. This configuration draws customers from anchor to anchor past all the smaller tenants. In some configurations, the

cluster has evolved into a racetrack, with anchors or entrances at the four corners. Customers can circle the shopping center and finish where they started. The town center is typically an outdoor community or neighborhood variation of the cluster. Instead of a department store, the town center may be anchored in the center by a public, recreational, or entertainment feature, such as a park, ice-skating rink, cinema complex, restaurant cluster, or civic building. The retail streets typically lead to nonretail

The enclosed mall, such as the Solomon Pond Mall near Boston, has been the dominant format for regional centers, regardless of climate, for 30 years.

Perimeter Expo in Atlanta is a successful power center with second-story retail space.

anchors around the town center, such as hotels, multi-family housing, office buildings, and transit stations.

Multilevel Strip Centers. Regional malls are usually multilevel in urban areas; community and neighborhood strip centers may have one or two levels. The performance of multilevel strip center retailing depends on where the centers are, the state of the local economy, the density of the local population, and whether they still follow the rules of successful shopping centers.

Two-level strip centers have several advantages:

- They are more visible than a single-level center, and tenants' signs can be seen from a greater distance.
- Buildings become a "landmark" by providing verticality to a linear product.
- Greater floor/area ratios can be achieved.
- They can accommodate two-story tenant configurations.

They also have several disadvantages:

- The addition of stairs reduces accessibility.
- Servicing the upper stores is more difficult because of lift problems. Elevators are necessary for heavy objects and disabled customers.
- Costs are not reduced if the center needs elevators. Upper-floor costs are equal to the cost of the foundation and slab.
- A two-story community or neighborhood center may be difficult to finance.

- Customers often think it is too much trouble to walk up the stairs or find the elevator, and stores on the second floor of community and neighborhood centers may suffer.

The more successful two-story strip centers are located in highly urbanized areas with good demographics: the density of the surrounding trade area is substantial, with an extremely strong demand for retail space.

Few second-floor users in community and neighborhood centers are retail stores. They tend to be secondary uses such as insurance offices, travel agencies, military recruiting centers, dance studios, professional career centers, temporary political offices, and dentists or doctors. Few retailers have made it on the second floor; usually they are first-time operators with only the one location. Rental rates are approximately $2.00 per square foot less than on the first floor, while buildout costs for second-floor users may be higher than for the first floor.

Nevertheless, some have succeeded. One such center with second-story retail space is Perimeter Expo in Atlanta, Georgia.[1] The center's location was one of the last remaining vacant parcels in north central Atlanta. The 10.42-acre site, though small, was valuable and in demand. To achieve the critical mass of tenants, the two-story design placed anchors Linens'n Things, Marshalls, and The Sports Shoe on the second level. The floor/area ratio is 0.38, well above the 0.25 ratio typical for strip shopping centers.

Other Building Configurations. Critics of suburban shopping center development have turned in recent years to alternative models of land planning, one of which, based on its design, has acquired the name "neotraditional planning." Neotraditional planning proposes to foster neighborliness and community life through the re-creation of idealized small towns from the early 20th century.[2]

Mashpee Commons is one such example. Located in a largely rural part of Cape Cod, Mashpee Commons is a two-level, 152,058-square-foot community shopping center that involved the renovation and expansion of an 82,000-square-foot strip center.[3] The remade shopping center has traditional storefronts with offices and future residential spaces above the stores, and it is integrated physically with other downtown activities. The goal is to provide everything that a department store does in an array of individual stores.

Another variation is found in Reston Town Center in Reston, Virginia. Planned as the centerpiece of the planned community near Washington, D.C., Reston Town Center is a mixed-use suburban downtown with retail, office, hotel, residential, community, and entertainment uses. The objective was "to create a downtown that pedestrians can easily navigate, that blends interesting and inviting landscapes with active open spaces, that accommodates the automobile and puts ample parking within easy reach of shops and offices, and that creates streets with pedestrians in mind."[4]

Although the tendency is to classify building configurations according to easily identifiable shapes, a center's building configuration actually is determined by the characteristics of the particular site and by market and economic considerations. A particular site for a neighborhood center, for example, might be better suited to a bent linear configuration rather than a full L shape. Larger and therefore more complex centers have many more variations, particularly when they are used to create a special image or character. And when shopping centers are located in existing buildings through adaptive use or are integral elements of mixed-use developments, the adaptation of basic configurations can be substantial.

Stacking levels in a regional center reduces walking distances and creates a more compact shopping area. Two or three levels are called for by certain design limitations caused by the site's size and configuration. In addition, a freestanding building on an outparcel or outlot has become an accepted feature of both open and enclosed regional centers for tenants that provide convenience shopping, such as supermarkets, drive-in banks, dry cleaners and laundries, barber and beauty shops, coin-operated laundries, specialized fast-food carryouts, and shoe repair shops. Restaurants and theaters may also be placed in freestanding buildings. Such buildings provide the kind of shops that require nearby parking, quick turnover, and fast customer service.

Freestanding buildings, when skillfully positioned, create flexibility in locating tenants, provide greater convenience for customers, and make possible one-trip shopping. The customary sea of parking can be avoided, as each building has its own area of convenient parking. Tenants who prefer customer parking at their front door can thus be included in a regional center complex.

Some common design errors are found in all building patterns: unvarying widths or depths of all stores, no matter their type; smaller stores being positioned so that they are difficult to service without interfering with pedestrian or auto traffic; and dead spaces that are hard to lease because of their indirect pedestrian access. Multiple corners, setbacks, odd angles, and the like should be avoided in most small centers. In regional malls, however, these special treatments may be used to avoid a tunnel effect in the mall and to spark interest and visual excitement.

Anchor Stores. A flexible design to facilitate the future replacement of one anchor tenant with another cannot be overstated in an age when the retail industry has been so volatile and marked by bankruptcies, withdrawal from a market area, and formation of major new companies.

Reston Town Center is one of the earliest pedestrian-oriented mixed-use suburban districts. Plazas, fountains, and pedestrian walkways entice shoppers to stroll from shop to shop.

The best development projects do much more than produce the largest positive return on investment. Developers who are able to identify unmet community needs and create innovative products to satisfy those needs can reap even greater rewards. Yet identifying and meeting such needs can be difficult.

When Pacific Development Partners began to look at potential retail development sites in south Orange County, California, the firm's intent was to learn about the community and find the "missing piece" that would produce not only a financially successful retail project but also a new and exciting gathering place for the community.

The first thing the firm's executives noticed was the striking uniformity of the area's existing retail options. Most of the 10,000-acre community is master planned. Residential tracts sit side by side with occasional neighborhood strip centers, which have been planned and

Kaleidoscope as seen from I-5, with multiple levels of retail stores above the structured parking. Changing light and color illuminates the underside of the rotunda, the icon of the project, at night.

built based on the number of residents in the surrounding neighborhood. Although master-planned communities provide many benefits for both residents and businesses, in Orange County and elsewhere zoning restrictions force retail, dining, and entertainment sites into separate geographic locations.

Because master-planned communities are generally the result of preconceived and preapproved development plans, eclectic and active street scenes, like those "Main Streets" that naturally evolved in urban areas and older suburbs, cannot develop in such a community. Instead, specific spots throughout the master-planned community are dedicated to retail uses and have replaced the long commercial streets of cities and older suburbs. Unlike their urban counterparts, these communities have retail, dining, and entertainment opportunities fragmented into separate locations and thus lack the vibrant atmosphere and mixture of opportunities characteristic of the urban street scene.

Pacific Development Partners realized that if it could bring retail, dining, and entertainment options together in a single location, it could create a place where the community could come together to enjoy the southern California lifestyle without having to drive from one place to another. Based on much research and analysis, the firm planned an innovative new project: an urban entertainment/lifestyle center. The concept takes the best of the urban street scene and adapts it to a master-planned suburban setting.

The site selected for this project, known as Kaleidoscope, is a five-acre, sloping parcel in the master-planned community of Mission Viejo, California, an upper-middle-class community with more than 30,000 homes, a variety of neighborhood retail centers, a regional mall, and nearly 2.2 million square feet of office and industrial space.

Extensive market research revealed many positive factors for successful retailing at the site. Located adjacent to Mission Viejo Mall and at the intersection of the San Diego Freeway (I-5) and Crown Valley Parkway, the site has a daily traffic count of more than 300,000 cars and is completely visible from I-5, the busiest highway and the only interstate in the area. Demographic research revealed a median household income of $82,000 within a three-mile radius of the site plus a nearby—and growing—population of 450,000.

Kaleidoscope has been planned to include an exciting mix of retail stores, dining, and entertainment. The challenge to the project's developers was to physically re-create an urban street scene on a five-acre suburban parcel. The solution is a multilevel center in which the tenants, rather than being strung along a traditional commercial street, are wrapped inward and face each other. In this way, the project's design (by Altoon + Porter Architects of Los Angeles) captures the essence of the street scene while adding even more energy by increasing the number of tenants and shoppers visible from every level.

The centerpiece is a 65-foot, Teflon-coated fiberglass rotunda, which is illuminated at night. The rotunda and the center are clearly visible from Crown Valley Parkway and I-5, making the project an instantly recognizable landmark. Each level is designed to reflect the lifestyle of the community and to contribute to the total experience. Specialty food stores, convenience shops, and an upscale gourmet market are located at street level so that commuters can stop easily on their way to and from work. Larger retail tenants and specialty shops highlight the second, or plaza, level, which also features a large piazza designed to accommodate open-air dining, community events, and special performances. The upper, entertainment/cinema level combines a variety of casual restaurants with a ten-screen multiplex theater. The slope of the site allowed the developers to put some parking below street level, preserving valuable leasable space.

Wrapping Kaleidoscope's "street scene" inward not only makes efficient use of the five-acre site, but also heightens a visitor's feeling of being immersed in an invigorating urban atmosphere. While visibility and accessibility from the freeway will be the key draws for prospective tenants, the project's structure is designed to focus attention within the center, not outside it. The design removes much of the noise and visual distraction of the freeway by placing high walls on the freeway side of the project and configuring each terrace to face inward.

Kaleidoscope, completed in spring 1998, is expected to translate the dynamic urban street scene into a major amenity for south Orange County. Although the $55 million project has involved more intensive research, planning, and design than a typical suburban shopping center might, the result is an innovative product that enhances the economy and lifestyle of the surrounding area.

Source: Mark T. Burger and Don Paskewitz, "Better Retail for Master-Planned Communities," *Urban Land,* May 1997, p. 15.

Convenient and attractive parking is an essential component of a successful shopping center. Camden Park shopping center in San Jose, California, provides parking stalls immediately adjacent to store entrances to provide easy access for customers.

Clean rectangular shapes for anchors are most flexible. "Throated" entries in which shallow retail shops encroach on the frontage of a large tenant should be avoided. Natural, integral docks are preferable to truck wells and added docks. And a flatter site or an existing center in which floor slab elevation changes relatively few times is most advantageous.

Outparcels. Outparcels, outlots, or pad sites are very important to the economics of a shopping center. The placement of freestanding restaurants or retail buildings on pad sites is influenced by line of sight and parking distribution. No pad site should encroach on the field of parking influence radiated from each anchor tenant. Placing freestanding buildings as near the street as possible and in front of small shops or smaller anchors rather than large stores satisfies the criteria of parking distribution and line of sight.

New pad sites in existing centers should be used efficiently to fill gaps in parking fields. Small interrupted segments of parking around pad sites should be avoided. Instead, consider parking for the pad site an extension of the long, efficient parking aisles radiating from buildings in the main shopping center.

Parking

The act of parking marks the customer's first contact with the shopping center, and the experience should be pleasant. The parking area should support the center's prime role—providing an attractive and convenient marketplace. Although parking is not a commercial use in itself, it is essential to the commercial uses within the center. As a rule, it takes up more space than any other physical component of the center. And whether the parking is surface or in a structure, it must be carefully planned. Requirements for parking design—parking area, driveway layout, access aisles, individual stall dimensions and arrangements, pedestrian movements from the parking area to the center, grading, paving, landscaping, and lighting—are major elements of site planning.

Parking requirements vary according to size of the center and types of retail use.

©Rion Rizzo

The chief concerns in providing the parking area are the number of spaces needed and their best arrangement. The problem is complicated when requirements for off-street parking of a local zoning ordinance are not reasonably related to actual parking demand in the shopping center. When the off-street parking area required by ordinance exceeds the demand, it becomes clear to center owners and tenants that the actual demand for spaces is a more suitable basis for determining the number of spaces that should be established. Excessive zoning requirements can result in a wasteland of unused pavement, causing a poor appearance and a needless expense to the developer and tenants. And some communities have enacted regulations to limit the amount of parking provided, causing a shortfall. Although the objective of these regulations is often to control air quality or to encourage the use of mass transit, they are more likely to result in traffic congestion, frustration for customers, and a less successful center. A successful shopping center depends on adequate parking—not too much but also not too little. For this reason, parking requirements at shopping centers have received considerable attention over the years.

Parking Standards and Demand. Parking demand at a shopping center, compared with that of a freestanding store, is lessened by the fact that a customer usually visits several stores during a single shopping trip. Characteristics of multipurpose shopping, shared spaces, and the rate of turnover for parking spaces distinguish parking requirements for shopping centers from those of freestanding commercial enterprises.

Several factors affect parking demand and the provision of parking:

- Vehicle miles traveled to reach the center;
- Cost of fuel;
- Government regulations;
- Availability and cost of mass transit;
- Walk-in trade;

- Size and type of center;
- Tenant mix;
- Total GLA;
- Character and income level of the trade area;
- Cost of land.

Two terms describe the relationship of parking to the shopping center structure:

- *Parking area ratio* is the site area assigned to parking use in relation to building area.
- *Parking index* is the actual number of parking spaces per 1,000 square feet of GLA in a shopping center.

For the purposes of planning and preliminary site evaluation, the parking area ratio serves merely as a useful tool for estimating the area needed for parking; it is not a suitable measurement for establishing parking standards. Parking area ratio, when stated as 2:1 or 3:1, for example, makes only a preliminary estimate of the site's building and parking capacity; the number of spaces that will actually occupy this parking area depends on such variables as angle and size of car stalls, width of moving aisles and access drives, and the arrangement of other parking appurtenances.

The amount of retail selling space depends on type of tenant, display of goods, method of selling, the number, size, and variety of items, and other variables. For this reason, selling space is an unsuitable unit to use for statistical comparisons of building area to parking provisions. But GLA is measurable, and each tenant's GLA is stated in the lease. GLA is thus a known and realistic factor for measuring the adequacy of parking provisions in relation to retail use.

Based on a comprehensive study of parking requirements for shopping centers conducted by ULI and the International Council of Shopping Centers in 1982, the following base parking standards are recommended for a typical shopping center today:

- Four spaces per 1,000 square feet of GLA for centers with a GLA of 25,000 to 400,000 square feet;
- From four to five spaces in a linear progression, with an average of 4.5 spaces per 1,000 square feet of GLA, for centers with 400,000 to 600,000 square feet; and
- Five spaces per 1,000 square feet of GLA for centers with a GLA greater than 600,000 square feet.[5]

Recognizing differences in center size and the impact of certain uses, these standards are more complex than the single index of 5.5 spaces per 1,000 square feet of GLA previously recommended (it is necessary to read the complete ULI report to understand fully and apply correctly the recommended standards). Parking changes in renovation or expansion projects are handled in a variety of ways.

Parking based on these standards will serve patrons' and employees' needs at the 20th busiest hour of the year, allowing a surplus during all but 19 hours of the remainder of the more than 3,000 hours during which a typical center is open annually—which means that during 19 hours of each year, distributed over ten peak shopping days, some patrons will not be able to find vacant spaces when they first enter the center. Additionally, these standards will need to be adjusted depending on the quantitative presence of certain land uses.[6]

Offices, cinemas, and food services in shopping centers require additional consideration. Office space amounting to up to 10 percent of total GLA can be accommodated without providing parking in addition to that imposed by the application of the overall parking indices. Office space in excess of 10 percent of the center's GLA requires additional parking, although it requires less than a free-standing office building because of the availability of parking for dual purposes. Office entrances should be located so that office tenants do not use the best retail parking spaces. (Mixed-use developments where the primary use in building area is other than retailing were

The parking facility for the CambridgeSide Galleria was designed to blend with the urban setting of Cambridge, Massachusetts. The above-grade garage, which contains 2,600 parking spaces, features pedestrian-oriented details on the street level rather than a blank wall.

Changes to parking space in a renovation and/or expansion can range from resurfacing and restriping a lot to creating parking structures and new circulation patterns. In general, issues related to parking are important considerations in a renovation that often are not given their due. Safety and lighting in parking lots and garages are of particular concern to shoppers today, and this aspect of parking should be especially scrutinized in the renovation plan.

In addition to improving the parking environment, other changes should be considered. Because of today's smaller cars, restriping lots can be very cost effective insofar as it can reduce the amount of land devoted to parking and allow for some modest expansion. Adjusting parking angles can also yield gains in parking spaces. Some centers have implemented programs to make parking stalls diminish in size in relation to their distance from the center; the spaces closest to the buildings are the largest, because they are used most often. During peak hours, shoppers value the presence of a vacant spot more than its size; thus, smaller spaces farther away are acceptable.

At Burlington Mall in Burlington, Massachusetts, the density of parking was increased without building structured parking by reworking the parking aisles and parking spaces into a format that the police and fire chiefs actually thought was safer than what had existed. At Plaza Camino Real in Carlsbad, California, redesigning and restriping the parking lot adjusted the angle of the parking stalls from 55 degrees to 70 degrees, increasing the number of parking spaces by more than 600. This process also required reshaping 104 parking islands to accommodate the new angle.

A 1990 survey by ICSC of 14 super regional shopping centers averaging 1.2 million square feet that had been or were soon to be expanded, including new parking structures, found several interesting facts:

- The average parking structure was four levels with 1,300 spaces, but the structures ranged from two to eight levels and from 445 to 3,100 spaces per structure.
- The average cost per parking structure was $5,300, and the cost per space was 10 to 20 percent higher in structures with fewer than 1,000 spaces. The cost ranged from $3,117 to $7,680 per space.

The significant expansion program at Tysons Corner Center in McLean, Virginia, involved the addition of more than 6,000 new parking spaces in four new parking structures distributed around the center; spaces now total 10,338 with 7,843 in structures and 2,495 in surface lots. More than 17 percent of the site is now in parking structures, nearly as much as the 22 percent of the site covered by buildings. All the structures connect directly to at least one department store.

Source: Excerpted from Dean Schwanke et al., *Remaking the Shopping Center* (Washington, D.C.: ULI–the Urban Land Institute, 1994), pp. 82–83.

■

not addressed in this study, and therefore the standards set forth here may not be applied.)[7]

At centers of 100,000 to 200,000 square feet of GLA with cinemas of up to 450 seats, and at centers of more than 200,000 square feet of GLA with cinemas of up to 750 seats, patrons can be accommodated without the provision of parking spaces in addition to the overall recommended standard. Cinemas having more than this number of seats, or cinemas located at smaller centers, however, require a nominal three additional spaces per 100 seats.[8]

The amount of the center's GLA devoted to food service tenants influences the number of required parking spaces. The number of spaces to be added (or subtracted) from the amount of parking otherwise required can be calculated (using procedures presented in the study report) for centers in which up to 5 percent of the center's GLA is devoted to food service.[9]

According to the ULI study, a center generates, on a Saturday, an average of eight peak hour trips per 1,000 square feet of GLA. A trip is defined as one car driving in and one car driving out, with the peak trip period coinciding with the peak shopping period (noon to 5:00 p.m.). For a given center, the peak hour trip rate could be as much as 50 percent higher or lower than this average rate. Even during the busiest day of the year, the peak parking demands at a typical center occur for only about a two-hour period.[10]

The findings of the ULI study led to the conclusions that shopping center developers, lenders, and tenants have overestimated the demand for off-street parking, and that most zoning ordinance regulations for shopping center parking call for a substantially greater number of parking spaces than are actually necessary.[11] In *Dollars & Cents of Shopping Centers: 1997*, the median parking index for a sample of U.S. regional and super regional centers showed the parking index to be about 5.4, with the index for both neighborhood and community centers about 5.0. The parking index for Canadian centers was 5.5 for

The presence of offices, cinemas, or food services requires special consideration when figuring the necessary parking ratio for a retail center. Cinemas may or may not require additional parking spaces, depending on the size of the center and the number of seats in the cinemas.

community centers, 3.9 for neighborhood centers, and 5.5 for super regional centers.

In the past several years, however, warehouse clubs and hypermarkets have been asking for six to seven spaces per 1,000 square feet. These anchors, along with restaurants (ten to 15 cars per 1,000 square feet) and multiscreen cinemas (one car per three to four seats or 25 cars per 1,000 square feet), force land coverage down and can choke off other tenants by dominating the parking lot at peak hours.

Shared Parking. Parking demand for a shopping center that is part of a mixed-use/multiuse project or for a center that has nonretail uses is influenced by the parking accumulation of all the land uses contained in the project. Different land uses experience peak parking demands at different hours of the day, days of the week, and seasons of the year. In addition, the "captive market" effect of a mixed-use/multiuse project influences parking demand; that is, in a mixed-use/multiuse project, customers

may be attracted to two or more land uses on a single auto trip to the project. Because of these characteristics, less demand is generated for parking space in mixed-use/multiuse projects than in separate freestanding developments of similar size and character; moreover, two or more land uses may share a parking facility without conflict or encroachment. For this reason, estimated parking demand for a shopping center that is part of a mixed-use/multiuse development or for a center that has nonretail uses should be based on an estimate of shared parking demand for the entire project.

The methodology in a ULI study of shared parking includes four steps that can be used to estimate the parking demand in a mixed-use development. The methodology first requires that factors influencing peak demand for the various land uses be determined. For retail uses, the ratio in the study was 5.0 spaces per 1,000 square feet of occupied GLA on a Saturday, dropping to 3.8 spaces per 1,000 square feet of occupied GLA on a weekday. This peak parking demand then must be multiplied by the quantity of the land to produce an estimate of the peak parking demand for each use. This value is then adjusted to reflect hourly and seasonal variations as well as the presence of mass transit and the captive market effect.[12]

Changing Car Sizes. How to respond to changing car sizes has been the subject of much discussion. In almost all cases, it is extremely difficult to plan for the use of parking spaces for small cars at shopping centers. A wide range of factors would need to be considered, including the mix of large and small cars in a particular market, physical conditions and limitations of the parking lot, a profile of the center's customers, and the specific needs of the center's tenants. Most local parking ordinances relating to small cars are focused on compact or subcompact cars, usually in segregated parking areas. In general, this format does not work well for shopping centers because of the high turnover rate and lack of effective control measures.

At the time small-car-only stalls were introduced, the mix of very large and very small vehicles was very polarized. Since then, however, manufacturers have sharply downsized larger cars, and substantial confusion exists over what is and what is not a small car. And the confusion has increased with the greater number of "mid-size" vehicles and the upsizing of certain models. Moreover, small-car-only spaces are not very effective unless the parking facility can be policed to prevent the use of large-car-only spaces by small cars and vice versa.

The result is that small-car-only stalls are no longer a viable parking design. ULI believes it is time for municipalities to overhaul their parking ordinances. Where small-car-only stalls are permitted, overly generous dimensions for standard stalls virtually force owners to use small-car-only stalls to achieve an economical design. The resulting excessively large parking geometries waste resources, land, and money, and conflict with other community interests, such as increased green space and stormwater runoff.[13]

Parking Lot Design. Certain key factors must be considered when planning a new or redesigned parking lot to make the most effective use of an available area:

- Environmental and Specific Conditions—The state or locality where the center is located and all attendant parking ordinances, annual climatic conditions, terrain of the parking site, the local highway network, and access roadways;
- Shopping Center Site—The site plan, ground contours, landscaping, placement of light stanchions, plans for surface and deck parking, plans for controlled or noncontrolled parking, and free or metered/charged parking;
- Customer Profile—Areas of the parking lot where the greatest turnover will occur, and evaluation of traffic patterns and their impact on the parking areas adjacent to department stores and the general retail areas;
- Tenant Categories—Consideration of the facts that the kinds of businesses located within a center can influ-

The "captive market" effect of mixed-use projects, such as the Village at Shirlington in Arlington, Virginia, generates less demand for parking than separate freestanding centers of similar size. Parking is provided behind Shirlington's Main Street, which includes restaurants, retail stores, and cinemas.

ence parking patterns dramatically and that some tenants require parking that allows rapid turnover, while others require parking for a longer term.

The method used to design or redesign a shopping center parking lot to maximize available areas and provide adequate parking must be selected case by case. No standard formula exists. The project should be carefully evaluated with the assistance of a professional consultant on parking lot design.[14]

Layout. Ease of parking should be the guiding criterion for parking layout at any center. Parking at a shopping center must be simple, trouble-free, and safe. Shoppers should be able to move confidently through the parking area without ever having been there or knowing the layout in advance. As a rule, achieving smooth traffic circulation at a shopping center requires the advice of a qualified parking or traffic consultant.

A parking bay or parking module in a surface parking lot includes the driving aisle and the stalls on both sides. Aisles can also serve as pedestrian pathways leading to the stores. Raised walks between the bays are unnecessary and expensive. Moreover, they interfere with sweeping and snow removal. Wheel stops also complicate mechanical cleaning operations and should be used only where parking spaces are adjacent to access driveways or landscaped areas.

Access aisles should allow shoppers to walk directly toward, rather than parallel to, the building front. The maximum walking distance from a car to the stores should be 400 feet, and preferably limited to 300 to 350 feet, except for employee parking areas. Circulation for cars within the center should be continuous, preferably one way and counterclockwise. Drivers should also be able to maneuver within the site without entering a public highway. In a regional center, parking area circulation requires a roadway (a "belt") around the edge of the site and another around the building cluster. The inner belt allows for fire and emergency access and also for delivery and customer dropoff and pickup.

Main traffic aisles are of two types: entrance and exit lanes, and belt lanes. Major aisles may allow for two-way movement. Minor aisles are one way but require directional indicators, often a combination of arrows painted on the pavement and standing indicator signs.

Where the lot contains several thousand car spaces, parking stalls should not be provided along the main aisles leading to the stores, preventing congestion of the main access aisles to the center. A very large surface parking facility should be divided into sections so that customers can easily identify their parking location. Each division should contain a maximum of about 800 to 1,000 spaces.

For convenience or neighborhood centers, parking along the storefronts makes a good arrangement. This design accommodates quick visits to the stores and fast turnover of prime spaces. Wheel stops, front bumper guards, or extended curb lines are required to prevent cars from encroaching on the canopied walkway.

Several factors must be considered when planning a new or redesigned parking lot: local ordinances, shopping center site characteristics, customer profile, tenant categories, and environmental constraints. Redmond Town Center, a 120-acre mixed-use retail/office/hotel project in Redmond, Washington, includes curbside parking and four parking structures behind commercial spaces.

Access to parking should be as simple, safe, and easy as possible. The maximum walking distance from a car to the stores should be 400 feet, preferably 300 to 350 feet. The Avenue at White Marsh has parking bays adjacent to the stores to allow customers direct access.

©Whitcomb

At the Greenbrier MarketCenter in Chesapeake, Virginia, convenient parking has been made attractive by its strategic placement behind generously landscaped berms.

At one time, truck tunnels were common at regional centers to separate shoppers from freight deliveries. The costs of constructing and maintaining a truck tunnel, however, are now prohibitive. Instead, enclosed regional centers either schedule most deliveries for nonshopping hours or provide a screened or walled truck delivery court to serve a group of stores.

Patterns. Surface parking can be laid out in one of two patterns: perpendicular or angular. Perpendicular or 90-degree parking economizes on space and facilitates circulation. It also offers the advantage of two-way traffic through the aisle as well as the safety of better sight lines, greater parking capacity, and shorter cruising distances. By contrast, angular parking spaces, at either 45 degrees or 60 degrees, are easier for drivers to turn into with one motion. Diagonal parking requires one-way circulation—which is safer though perhaps less convenient than two-way traffic—and allows use of a narrower parking module.

The dilemma over perpendicular or diagonal parking is best solved by using the pattern that generally prevails in the community and is best adapted to the particular site. Each surface parking layout must be evaluated for pedestrian circulation between the parked cars and the stores, for drivers' ability to move in and out of the parking area or look for a vacant space, and for the use of space.

For perpendicular parking, the standard bay for full-size cars has been 65 feet deep, comprising two stalls, each 20 feet deep, and a center aisle of 25 feet to allow for two-way circulation. The standard stall is nine feet wide. It is likely that most new centers will reduce these measurements to 8.5 to nine feet wide and 17 to 18 feet deep. The module will be narrow, with 90-degree parking layouts having modules of 58 to 62 feet. Some tenants, such as supermarkets, prefer perpendicular parking over angle parking.

Recognizing the uncertainties of what size cars will use the center and the difficulties in managing variable stall sizes, Donald O'Hara of Barton-Aschman Associates, Inc., suggests downgrading the size of the stall in relationship to its distance from the center's buildings. That is, the spaces closest to the center's buildings would be the largest, because they are used most often (in off-peak hours, those spaces farthest from the buildings are rarely used), thereby maximizing customers' convenience. Spaces farther away would be reduced to an adequate but somewhat tighter set of dimensions and would be used during off-peak hours. During peak hours, shoppers value more highly the presence of a vacant space more than its generous size. This approach will create a greater number of spaces in a given area of land or enable less land covered by a given number of spaces. It appears to also have merit when viewed from the perspective of customer service.

Stalls. In some areas of a center, the width of stalls should not be reduced. High turnover calls for parking stalls with ample width to park easily, avoid straddling spaces, and allow car doors to be opened without bumping the adjacent car. Nine-foot widths accommodate these needs. A nine-foot stall, for example, is still best for the area close to a supermarket, as a customer laden with groceries would have difficulty loading them into a car parked with less room. This recommendation may be less applicable, however, if the practice at the center is for shoppers to pick up groceries at the curb rather than take groceries to the parked vehicle. Likewise, the design of most power centers should emphasize convenience for both retailers and consumers, and it should offer the ease of access traditionally associated with neighborhood strip centers. Shoppers want to park as close as possible to the entrances of their destination stores, because purchases at power centers tend to be bigger and bulkier than purchases at most other types of centers.

With an 8.5-foot stall, two-door cars are more likely to bump the next car unless the driver and passengers are careful when opening and closing doors. Although a nine-foot stall is preferred, an 8.75-foot stall might be an acceptable compromise, as shoppers prefer the convenience of an available parking space to the ease of loading provided by a large space. When nine-foot stalls are used, a four-inch striped hairpin or looped line painted on the pavement surface makes a good space indicator. A hairpin or looped line (16 inches between lines) is preferable to straight-line striping because it acts as a psychological aid in keeping spaces equal between cars. In any case, all space markers should be painted, because a button divider system is difficult to change if the parking pattern needs to be altered. The length of parking stalls is less important to operations than width, because the width of the aisle can compensate for a short stall and because customers who are parking a car tend not to pull all the way into the stall. Nevertheless, the length of stalls must be determined to calculate space required.

Stalls for the handicapped should be located close to center entrances and should relate to a pedestrian pathway that is level or ramped and to entrance doors that are accessible for the handicapped. The spaces should be wider than normal—the current recommendation is 12 feet wide—to accommodate special vehicles, a full door swing, and wheelchairs.

Appearance and Construction. Surface parking areas must have a substantial subbase (five and one-half to six inches) and be well drained and paved. Blacktop is the most common paving material. Parking areas need such amenities as screening, landscaping, and lighting. They must be maintained to prevent potholes from developing and to keep litter from accumulating. Stalls must be clearly marked.

Trees and shrubs can be planted in wells to avoid an otherwise barren appearance, but trees must be protected from cars and from accumulations of salt and snow in colder climates. Landscaping intermediate spots in the parking area not only requires an expenditure up front but also adds extra maintenance costs and thus increases common area charges for tenants. The aesthetic benefits, however, can be immeasurable.

Amenities such as screening, landscaping, and lighting can help prevent a barren appearance for parking areas. The rows of landscaping at the Plaza at West Covina frame the entrance to the center for approaching motorists while creating a soft edge between the main entrance and the parking areas.

Because the surface parking area is part of the open space at a shopping center, it can become one of the center's amenities when it is landscaped. Shopping center open space includes the parking area, malls, pedestrian pathways, buffer areas, and all other portions of the site not covered by buildings, except for access drives and uncovered service courts. The landscaping of parking areas and of shopping center open space in general should be designed to be both tasteful and durable. Ground cover, shrubs, and bushes massed at appropriate places on the site and occasional trees planted in wells or clusters are suitable. Components of the landscaping should be designed not to interfere with parking, maintenance of the parking area, or snow removal. Plantings should be hardy, easily maintained, and capable of thriving in the local climate.

Depressing the parking area by about two feet so that the tops of cars are below eye level when viewed from adjacent public streets increases the feeling of openness by allowing views directly from the streets to the storefronts. Berms constructed at the perimeter of the parking area can also improve the center's appearance from adjacent streets and properties. Such berms, either along public streets or between various parking sections, can also serve as landscaping features.

Proper maintenance of the parking area is essential. Management must attend to policing the area, cleanup, night lighting, orderly use, and other maintenance. Tenants pay for maintenance costs based on the proportion of space they occupy.

Employee Parking. Because employees park at the center all day, they may be allotted parking spaces eight feet wide. They should not be allowed to occupy prime spaces needed for customers, for by doing so, they could prevent customer spaces from turning over four or five times during a shopping day. Employee parking is hard to control. Regulations are usually covered in leases, which should provide that the landlord has the right to:

• Designate the number and location of employee parking places;
• Receive, on request, the car license numbers of tenants' employees;
• Cancel the lease if the tenant does not cooperate;
• Charge the tenant a specified amount per day for each employee car parked outside the designated area.

In practice, however, it may be difficult to achieve such ideal provisions.

In a linear convenience center, employee parking is best placed at the rear of the stores. A minimum width of 40 feet is required for a combined rear service and employee parking area, which allows one row of cars and a driveway along the rear property line. A better arrangement can be made if the area is 60 feet wide, which permits the rear service area to function better both as a truck delivery drive and a parking area. The rear setback should be increased when plantings are needed along the back property line as a buffer between the stores and adjacent

Parking areas near store entrances should be reserved exclusively for customers. At the Alto Avellandeda Playcenter in Buenos Aires, employee parking is placed in the rear.

residences. Or if land is at a premium, a screening wall can be placed on the property line.

In other types of centers, a special employee parking area should be assigned and the requirements for employee parking enforced. In these centers, employee parking areas should be placed at the outer edge of the site, where they will not interfere with the more desirable parking spaces closer to the stores. A center that fails to designate special employee parking areas may find its employees' cars habitually occupying the spaces closest to the stores or filling the surrounding streets, to the annoyance of neighbors. In some cities, an ordinance permits the landlord, on signed complaint, to have the police ticket and/or tow these cars. Of the total required parking, 10 percent or so can be located at the rear of stores to serve employees.

Commuter Parking. As mass transit reaches more shopping centers, thus reducing parking demand, the strong possibility arises for commuters to park in shopping center spaces. Such a situation is more likely to develop when bus routes serving the center also serve employment centers. The figures for the value of a parking space clearly spell out the economic issues. Private shopping center developers should not be expected to provide public parking lots for commuters. But like employee parking, it is difficult to police and requires the cooperation of the community.

If local laws allow police to issue parking tickets, parking lots in centers can post time limits and tickets issued to offenders. When this solution is not possible, private policing or closing the lots during the morning rush hour may be the only answer. At the same time, the shopping center developer needs to be perceived as a good neighbor in the community, and hard-line control of commuter parking may result in negative feelings in the community toward the center in general, which could result in less business for the center. If excess land is available and a conflict over parking arises, it may be possible to lease a designated portion of the site to the transit authority for parking for commuters for at least the cost of maintenance and repair. At Shoppers World in Framingham, Massachusetts, for example, the developer leases a four-acre parcel to Massport, which uses it for a park-and-ride lot for its express bus service to Logan Airport, and has constructed a ticket and hospitality facility for Logan Express commuters.[15] Requests for tax abatement may also be possible. In the final analysis, parking in shopping centers represents private parking for customers, and the developer must protect this right when other uses would be detrimental to the center's operations.

Parking and Transit. The emergence of more developed and more efficient transit systems in the past 20 years has slightly impacted parking needs of shopping centers. Thirty-six percent of the participants in a recent ULI/ICSC survey used scheduled bus service to shopping centers. Five percent of participants used some type of train service. All the centers with a scheduled bus service onto the center property provided the following amenities for transit patrons:

At the Heuvel Galerie Eindhoven, a mixed-use regional shopping, office, and residential center in Eindhoven, the Netherlands, parking spaces are reserved for bicycles near one main entrance.

- Seventy-five percent had a shelter or canopy;
- Eighty-two percent were equipped with seating;
- Seventy-two percent provided signage for bus schedules and routing;
- Twenty percent had an interior waiting area;
- Thirty-one percent had plants around the waiting area;
- Thirteen percent provided park-and-ride or commuter parking;
- One percent arranged for connections to a transit system; and
- Nine percent had some other form of transit-related amenity.[16]

Parking and Taxes. In some cities, the assessor values land used exclusively for parking at the same rate as land used for business, putting an inequitable tax load on parking at shopping centers. When commitments are made for the continued use of designated areas for parking, such as at shopping centers, the calculation of land value for tax purposes should be adjusted to the restricted use of the parking area. Although parking areas contribute substantially to a center's success, this success is also reflected in the higher taxable value of the land and structures occupied by the businesses as well as in the value of the businesses themselves. Because the shopping center's parking area is not itself a direct revenue producer, its valuation for tax purposes should be based on its use as parking, not on its business use. The valuation can also be based on acreage rather than on square feet. When

Riverside in Atlanta is a mixed-use development by Post Properties that includes residential, retail, and office space. More than 57 percent of this 85-acre riverfront site is dedicated open space.

real estate taxes on parking areas are included in common area maintenance charges paid by tenants, however, loading the taxes on the buildings to relieve the tax load on the parking area may actually impose an undue burden on the owner rather than relieving him of an economic inequity. In addition, some jurisdictions approach the value of a property on the basis of its income; land and building are not valued separately but as parts of a single package.

Structured Parking. A self-operated parking structure can alleviate excessive walking distances between parked cars and the stores in regional centers and solve space problems that may be created by a shopping center's development or its later expansion. At many centers, adjacent land for expansion of the parking area is not available or has become so costly that building a parking structure or deck may be the most economical means of providing additional parking spaces. A parking structure can be built closer to the stores, and it can be depreciated, whereas land cannot.

A parking structure has further advantages. When small cars enter the facility, they can be more effectively channeled to spaces for small cars. Less space per car can be assigned because islands and other aesthetic appurtenances are eliminated. But a parking garage also requires a ramp system (which should be as unintimidating as possible to poor drivers), overhead clearances, column spacing, and ventilation for those parts of the structure that are below grade. An entrance magazine, a temporary storage

area for cars waiting to be parked, is not needed in a self-operating parking structure. A multideck parking structure is particularly adaptable to sloping sites, where direct entrance to each level of stores can be provided. For double-level or triple-level shopping centers, entrances can also lead from each level of the parking deck to the center.

Parking structures often spring up around shopping centers because of the increased value of the land. Surface parking may no longer be the highest and best use for expanses of ground near larger retail centers. Other uses, such as hotels, office buildings, clinics, additional department stores, and commercial recreational facilities may replace surface parking, making it necessary to provide structures for existing and any additional parking.

The point at which a developer determines that a structure for additional parking would be more economical than buying more land is the point at which the value of the land that would have been acquired exceeds what it would cost to construct a parking facility. Construction costs are affected by the size and shape of the usable land area, the perimeter wall–to–floor/area ratio, the parking bay span ratio, and the elevated versus on-grade ratio (with the cost per square foot increasing with each additional parking level).[17] Should land prices and construction costs rise to a point where the provision of free parking at a shopping center is no longer economical, developers may be forced to charge customers a fee for parking or to turn parking areas over to the municipality to install parking meters and maintain the parking area.

The security of parking structures should be considered. Misfortunes to patrons range from vandalism and car theft to mugging and rape. Although these same crimes can and do occur on surface parking areas, particularly in those areas most isolated from the shopping center, customers tend to perceive structured parking as potentially riskier than surface parking. Television monitors, communications systems, adequate lighting, and the visibility of security personnel can help improve safety.

Stormwater Management

The proper handling of stormwater runoff has become a major issue in the design of shopping centers. Any strategy used to handle stormwater runoff should be developed in the preliminary stage of development planning. Peak stormwater flows and total runoff increase dramatically after a site has been partly covered by buildings and parking areas. Reducing or delaying this runoff is an important issue with significant cost implications. Communities not having excess storm system capacity—and few do—should examine such concepts as rooftop ponding, temporary detention basins (in portions of the parking area, for example), detention or retention ponds, and other mechanisms for reducing the runoff rate and total runoff after development. Likewise, potential water pollution is another problem that should be addressed.

Therefore, it is important that the developer investigate the methods of managing stormwater runoff in the community where the shopping center is to be developed.

The stormwater management system for a center should be based on the following principles:

- The design of the system must take into account the convenience and safety of the project as well as the overall safety of the drainage basin as the area becomes fully developed.
- The design of permanent and temporary ponding storage should be an integral part of the overall planning for development.
- The design of permanent storage facilities should consider safety and visual appearance in addition to the primary function of storage, and opportunities for temporary storage should be considered and planned for in the design of the system.
- Stormwater runoff systems should facilitate the recharge of aquifers when it is necessary to compensate for the removal of groundwater.
- Some communities impose a blanket per-acre storm sewer charge. The developer designing an on-site stormwater retention system should receive a credit from the community against the community's assessment charge.
- The use of overland flows and open channels and swales should blend into the natural features of the site, and they should be designed to minimize hazards.
- Stormwater management systems, parking layout, and the location of curbs and gutters should be planned simultaneously whenever possible.

The design of permanent stormwater storage should take into account safety and appearance, as exemplified by Westside in Downtown Disney in Orlando, Florida.

- The maximum flow in the deepest part of a gutter should not exceed ten cubic feet per second.
- The number and spacing of stormwater inlets should be carefully regulated, and their design should incorporate safe and efficient use.
- Any enclosed portion of a system should be designed to manage stormwater, not just to dispose of it or disperse it.
- Energy dissipaters should be designed and installed for the outfall of enclosed systems when stormwater is discharged onto highly erodible soils.
- Sizes of pipes used in the enclosed system should be based on computed hydraulic data for the system.
- The use of enclosed components in a system should be minimized, based on the ability of the existing natural systems to accommodate stormwater runoff.
- Maintenance costs and construction should be minimized.[18]

Retention ponds are generally used to treat stormwater by removing suspended materials and by providing extended contact with aquatic vegetation for removal of nutrients. By definition, retention is the impoundment of runoff (in many states usually the first inch), which is either percolated into the soil or released to the atmosphere through a combination of evaporation and plant transpiration.

This concept in its purest form is difficult to implement in areas with a high water table that do not allow rapid percolation, however. During the rainy season in such areas, retention ponds can be overburdened, causing pollutants to bypass the pond and go directly into other bodies of water. To prevent this occurrence, a well-designed retention pond usually contains a bleed-off device that releases retained water downstream over a period of five to ten days. In this way, the process of retention is actually transformed into long-term detention.

Woodbury Commons Factory Outlets in Central Valley, New York, is situated between the Schunnemunk Mountains and the Hudson highlands. This picturesque setting and the traditional architectural forms and materials provide a village-like setting.

Many local regulations stipulate that peak discharge rates for the design storm after development should not exceed peak rates from before development, and compliance typically is achieved through detention ponds that store floodwaters temporarily and release them downstream at a slower rate. Detention periods typically last several hours, compared with retention periods of five to ten days.

Topography

If a site has a slope that corresponds to grades on surrounding roads, an opportunity may exist for a two-level arrangement of buildings and parking, particularly for larger projects. Smaller neighborhood and community centers and power centers are better arranged on a single level.

Shops on both levels must be equally accessible, but concentrating the "best" stores on either level is a disadvantage for both merchants and customers. In fact, chain stores usually have very strong opinions about the level and placement of their stores in shopping centers, and some prefer the second level. With two levels of merchandising, parking must be divided to provide equal accessibility to the upper and lower levels. Neither level should dominate the center; both should be equally important.

Sensitive use of a site's topography can produce compatibility between the shopping center and the site's natural characteristics. A sloping site with specimen trees that need to be preserved can be skillfully reshaped to accommodate a stepped but single-level center. The ideal slope in a parking lot is 3 percent, which allows for sufficient drainage but helps to prevent runaway shopping carts and any difficulties with hard-to-open, heavy car doors. A slope of 7 to 8 percent is allowable in limited areas, such as at entry drives. In steeply sloped areas, a parking lot can effectively be broken into terraced pads separated by landscaped strips running perpendicular to the storefronts.

Environmental Issues

Environmental concerns have grown rapidly in our society, and sophisticated shopping center developers have become equally attuned to protecting the environment and incorporating "green" techniques into their development programs. Choosing a site with limited environmental concerns can reduce direct construction and operating costs, development time frames, and community opposition. Before acquiring or redeveloping a piece of property, a potential buyer should conduct a study to determine whether it is environmentally suited for the proposed development or tainted to a degree that could make construction costs prohibitively high or cause future liability and, if so, what the nature, extent, and costs of cleanup would be. The list of contaminating activities that may have environmentally tainted a site is a long one: recycling batteries, processing and manufacturing chemicals, commercial, industrial, or municipal landfills, storage or recycling of drums and other containers, electro-

The Brass Mill Center in Waterbury, Connecticut, was built on a former brownfield site where 15 to 20 percent of the soils were contaminated with hazardous materials. The developer, General Growth Properties, with subsidies from the state, completed a full cleanup to residential standards to satisfy the mall's anchor tenants (see case study in Chapter 7).

plating, disposal or detonation of explosives, incinerators, farmland, laundry/dry cleaning, manufacturing (other than chemical), military ordnance, open burning, ore processing and refining, sand and gravel pits, sinkholes, gasoline station with tanks above and below ground, tire storage and recycling, and wood preserving.

A professional testing company hired to perform a Phase I environmental assessment (required by EPA) can determine possible problems with the site. The assessment involves looking at the property's history, including reviewing available data such as aerial photographs, inquiries of persons familiar with the site, chain-of-title history, city directories, fire insurance maps, and so forth to identify uses that may have created environmental problems; determining from local, state, and federal regulatory agencies whether citations for noncompliance or violation have been issued in the past; visiting the site and neighboring sites, observing all operations, identifying potential polluting activities, looking for dead or stressed vegetation and

Landscaping should be used to enhance the overall appearance of parking facilities. The 7th Street and Collins public parking/retail facility in Miami Beach features seven specialty retail stores on the ground floor and a four-level, 646-space parking garage above. The entire exterior is laced with a curved and gridded fiberglass trellis and irrigated boxes planted with four different varieties of native foliage.

foliage, and taking samples to assess asbestos-containing materials; and identifying floodplains and wetlands.

The testing company should look for evidence of:

- Asbestos.
- Polychlorinated Biphenyls (PCBs)—PCBs were used in many transformers and capacitors as dielectric insulating liquid. They were banned under the federal Toxic Substance Control Act because they are carcinogenic and a threat to the environment.
- Pesticides—Highly toxic pesticides such as DDT and chlordane are now banned, but residues from these pesticides are prevalent.
- Illegal Dumping—Before the regulation of hazardous wastes, illegal dumping may have occurred on a site.
- Groundwater Contamination—Groundwater may have been contaminated by underground mines, quarry fills, underground storage tanks, and landfills.
- Other Violations of Environmental Laws—The presence of wetlands, floodplains, radon, endangered species, and historic sites can increase the problems associated with development.

A Phase II analysis, a more extensive study, includes more extensive soil and materials testing and normally involves some destruction to gain access to enclosed areas. It identifies the needed corrective actions. Depending on what further testing reveals, several approaches can be used to handle the problem or problems. Removal or abatement along with proper storage will eliminate the problem completely, but this solution may be prohibitively expensive. An operations and maintenance program—such as a formulated plan for training, cleaning, work practices, and surveillance to maintain asbestos-containing materials in good condition—can be much less expensive and still very effective. Aerating contaminated soil and removing petroleum products that have leaked into subsurfaces is effective in some cases. Professional assistance is necessary to determine the available alternatives,

but the money spent for study and advice could be minor compared with the cost of solving a problem a purchaser has unknowingly bought.[19]

Landscaping

Creative landscaping can help produce the type of memorable environment that will draw customers back again and again, while inappropriate landscaping can badly damage a shopping center's image. The most egregious example of bad landscaping is exposure of a barren expanse of parking lot to the public's view, creating a sea of asphalt that is hot in the summer and cold and windswept in winter or inclement weather. A surface parking lot must be treated as the shopping center's front yard where customers get their first all-important impression of the center. Properly designed and landscaped, it can become one of the center's amenities.

Landscaping should be used to meet design objectives and not simply to cover the site. Landscaping within a parking area should generally be confined to trees and massed plantings in wells or in clearly delineated areas. Plantings should be located where they will not interfere with parking, parking area maintenance, snow removal, or sight lines for drivers. A total landscaping budget of 3 to 5 percent of total building costs—depending on the size and character of the center—is reasonable. Performance standards allow creative design, whereas a requirement to spend a certain amount on landscaping could result in ill-conceived landscaping. Zoning requirements typically call for landscaping parking lot boundaries and property line buffer strips; those that specify a percentage of total site area for landscape treatment or that specify the placement, type, or diameter of trees can go too far in protecting the public welfare. Although the initial cost of landscaping may seem insignificant, the developer must also consider the long-term maintenance costs of any landscaped areas.

When a shopping center—generally a neighborhood center—is located close to a residential area, more substantial buffers could be necessary to insulate nearby residences. High, dense foliage planted in a strip some 20 feet wide or, when plants are not practical, masonry walls or attractive fences can provide the necessary buffer. Effective landscaping along the border provides an environmental amenity. Neither the location nor the height of landscaping features, however, should block drivers' vision.

Interior landscaping and its installation and maintenance are also part of the operating expenses for some shopping centers. Lighting plays an important role in the selection of plants for interior landscaping. Plants and seasonal floral displays appropriately placed inside the center make it much more appealing to customers, and plantings, water displays, and sculptures can transform an interior pedestrian space into a focal point for the community and a gathering place for suitable community events. Quite often the interior mall area can be included in "total landscaped area" if zoning requires it.

Building Materials

Just as the tenant mix must reflect an appropriate relationship between anchors or between anchors and local shops, building materials must be appropriate to the market. Exterior materials strongly contribute to the center's visual image and special identity. The image created should be one of harmony tempered by tasteful variation in selected details, although it need not exclude the use of more than one major material to create a distinct image. Materials should be locally available if possible, capable of being assembled and erected quickly, durable, and easily maintained. They should provide waterproofing and insulation and an attractive appearance.

Five primary factors influence the selection of materials.

- Message—Granite or marble signals upscale shops, specialty tenants, an orientation toward fashion, and expensive merchandise. Simple colorful stucco or synthetic plaster suggests an outlet or off-price center. Slate roofs and brick pavilions imply a conservative, neighborhood orientation.
- Cost—The decision about materials is influenced by how much they cost. The budget for a center can be changed by $4.00 to $8.00 per square foot by changing nothing but the materials used to clad or "skin" a structure.
- Durability—When brick is the material of choice, no one asks about ongoing maintenance costs, but the use of canvas awnings always raises the question, "How long will they last?" The answer is, "Until the next time the market demands a new look!" Durability is a desirable quality, but the ability to easily change inexpensive accessories with a five-year useful life also has advantages.
- Availability of Local Materials and Local Building Conditions—Transportation costs, the lack of skilled subcontractors, and seismic factors make brick an unlikely choice in California, so California centers

Ideally, building materials should be available locally and reflect vernacular traditions. The stucco exterior, mission bell tower, and tiled roofs at Vineyards Marketplace in Rancho Cucamonga, California, echo the Spanish Mediterranean theme common to California.

Entrances to shopping centers should be distinctive and inviting. The entrance to the Glendale Marketplace, a two-level open-air lifestyle shopping center in Glendale, California, welcomes nearby office workers with festive streetfront signs and lighting.

use a lot of stucco and ceramic tile. On the other hand, ceramic tile is never used for exterior wall cladding in cold climates, because the freeze-thaw cycle pops tile right off the facades. Most centers in the Southwest are constructed of job-cast tilt-up concrete wall panels, because they are a well-developed tradition with many contractors and because inexpensive laborers can install the system at low cost. In other regions, concrete masonry units are preferred, because they are the lowest-cost material for load-bearing walls.

- Theme—In Florida, it is not unusual to see flat-roofed centers featuring boldly colored stucco or Dryvit walls reflecting the warm sunshine and softened by rich vegetation. In the Northeast, however, this look would be foreign, and customers are more comfortable with smaller-scale forms, such as gables, hipped roofs, and towers, covered in brick with wood trim and slate roofs.

For inspiration, an architect and client should explore the center's market area to draw upon the details, materials, and history of the adjacent neighborhoods and commercial districts.[20]

Masonry is an excellent external material. In some areas, wood that has been treated for weather exposure can readily be adapted to neighborhood and convenience centers. A great many centers have resorted to metal stud enclosures with insulating plaster-type materials such as Dryvit, which can be given a variety of textures and shapes.

Consistent exterior materials are more important to department stores than similar design or detail. Because department stores are not always designed by the mall architect, they tend to call for a more distinctive look, often entailing the use of totally different materials that make the department store stand out but may, in the case of three or four stores, create a jumble of styles. To a large extent, the exterior appearance of a regional center is affected by how much control the developer is willing to exert over major tenants. Some developers seek to provide more neutral spaces between the strong architecture of the major stores; others first decide on a design theme for the mall's exterior and then work with the anchor tenants to make certain that their architecture and materials are compatible with the rest of the mall. Regardless of the method chosen, however, the mall's exterior appearance must be cohesive, welcoming, and friendly.

Architecture for power centers tends to be limited to the facade. Most power centers are single-story structures and designed like warehouses. They are often made of brick and block using tilt-up construction techniques.

Building Entrances

In an enclosed mall, entrances to the center should be prominent design features. A change of material or roof height, or a wall extension or indention may be introduced to identify the entrances and to give them a certain distinction. Attractive exterior lighting can also highlight entrances. The peak hours for shopping occur at dusk and at night. If an entrance has wonderful architectural form but is not sufficiently illuminated, customers will head for department store entrances, not the main mall entrances, reducing the possibility of visiting smaller tenants. With sufficient illumination to make it bright and attractive, a center can convey a sense of entrance to an exciting theatrical event.

Entrances to the retail component of a mixed-use development should be distinctive and inviting, as many potential customers are office workers or hotel guests who must be enticed into the retail area. Designing entrances for the retail component of a mixed-use project requires more attention to making them exciting and memorable. Shoppers should be aware that they are leaving the office environment or the hotel lobby and entering an exciting retail area. The change can be achieved through floor coverings, wall coverings, color, and ceiling treatments. At the Forum Shops, for example, a themed shopping venue attached to Caesars Palace Hotel and Casino in Las Vegas, visitors experience the sights of an ancient Roman marketplace as they walk through classically styled arches.

A different set of rules applies to shopping centers with streetfront retailing. Streetfront retail centers should blend in with the surrounding retail street, and entrances should not appear to be different from other adjacent entrances. In most cases, customers will not even realize that the stores constitute a shopping center, and, as a result, the center's success will depend on the entirety of the retail shopping district rather than the design of the shopping center itself.

Too many entrances to an enclosed mall make it difficult to concentrate traffic within the mall. An exception is downtown malls, where it is essential that the center function as an integral component of the downtown, not turn its back on the surrounding environment.

Canopies

For open malls, a colonnaded walk or arcade is the traditional means of sheltering customers and protecting storefronts from the weather. Covered walkways are essential for protection from inclement weather as well as for enjoyable shopping in any kind of weather. Twelve to 15 feet is a good width for the walkway.

Canopies may be cantilevered from the building wall or supported by freestanding columns or pillars. Their width and height are determined by proportions appropriate to the architectural style. With a canopy higher than 12 feet, the building wall below provides an ideal surface on which to place signs, which supports the architectural quality of the center and helps in an overall program to control signs. The style and materials of the canopy can be dictated or influenced by the region—for instance, roofing tiles in the Southwest, slate in New England, and cedar shake in the West.

When canopies are placed along building facades in unenclosed malls, window displays become important inducements for window shopping and impulse buying while allowing shoppers to compare prices. Customers are free to view the merchandise without having to explain that they are "just looking." Canopies increase the attractiveness of wide window displays. Windows also may be scaled to feature spot displays suited to certain kinds of shops. Mullion windows are suitable only when they are part of the center's architectural style.

Signage

Good signage should be an integral part of the building design. The shopping center's graphics are the province of the architect, whose design must prevent visual pollution. Even though a graphic designer will likely design the signs, the architect is responsible for creating a building design that provides well-planned locations for signage. These two professionals must work closely together from the early stages of preliminary design.

Signs are the retailer's lifeblood. If the architecture of the center provides the unity, then the signage for tenants provides identity. The trend today is toward vitality and freedom of expression in graphics. Each center should have well-developed criteria for tenants' signs that fairly rigidly control the type of signs allowed, the mounting system, maximum height, and allowable locations. On the other hand, good criteria are permissive when it comes to color and typeface.

In today's centers, the trend is toward more variable wall surfaces or sign fields where ever larger signs can be mounted. It is not unusual for a national tenant of a 3,000- to 4,000-square-foot space to want a sign with four-foot-high letters. For small shops, two- to three-foot-high letters are easy to read and in proper scale.

Because signage for tenants is an important source of color, vitality, and atmosphere for the center, a signage program and criteria should be the logical starting points for the skilled designer of a shopping center. The many options available today include specially shaped box signs, individual letter signs with internally illuminated Plexiglas faces, open-face letters with exposed neon, reverse channel letters with "halo effect" lighting, bare neon, with or without special backgrounds, individual letter signs mounted on a common raceway, with or without a "receiver" channel, internally illuminated sign bands, and graphics screen-printed on canvas or "Panaflex" awnings.[21]

Sign control is an important part of the shopping center management's responsibility. In fact, the shopping center industry has led the way in this area. Approval of signs is one of the conditions included in the tenant's lease, and the developer's control of the style and size of signs is often more severe than municipal regulations would be. Insisting on uniform scale, size, and placement may be a worthwhile practice for a conservative, high-end shopping center, but in other types of centers, particularly those that cater to younger, mass-market tastes and those focused on entertainment, tenants should be given more freedom to design signs that fit a total image rather than a rigid format. At the Block at Orange, an entertainment megamall in Orange, California, the developer has imposed no criteria for signs but retains final approval, working with each tenant to create dramatic, colorful, and diverse signs.

Anchors and other chain stores typically have logos, corporate colors, and other special lettering that constitutes part of their image. Such signs must be integrated with the center's overall design concept and exterior graphics. Many have added a marketing slogan or list of merchandise categories as ancillary signage, which must also be addressed in the criteria.

Signage at shopping centers typically is subject to a municipality's sign control ordinance, which also governs conventional business and commercial districts. Unfortunately, such regulations—geared primarily toward individual business properties—are rarely suitable for shopping centers. Regulations for signs are among the most controversial aspects of zoning law, and some would argue that the legal basis for such regulation is debatable, as design has to do with aesthetics. Nevertheless, regulations covering signage that include design as well as size and locational criteria have been upheld in the courts and must be taken into account when establishing a center's program of graphic design.[22]

When signage has been developed as a special element of the architectural design, the developer may find zoning authorities receptive to a carefully prepared program that deviates from the sign control ordinance—especially if the ordinance was written to control the signage for single-purpose structures rather than shopping centers. The city can assist the developer by enforcing the approved program, thus relieving the developer of the need to negotiate with tenants whose ideas about signage may be inconsistent with the developer's overall concept.

Shopkeepers want to be easily identified by customers and to be as readily identified as the competitors. And they all want that which identifies their goods and services to be distinctly their own. It has been found that when all signs in a center are required to conform to the same guidelines for size and style, tenants are more amenable to restrictions on their signage. Thus, when graphic con-

The design of Friendship Heights Mall in Washington, D.C., created varied storefronts facing the street. Each tenant was thus able to create its own distinctive identity through architectural variations and custom signage.

From exterior pylons and parking directionals to electronic message boards announcing stores and events, signs play a crucial role at shopping centers and malls. Absolutely critical, however, to ensuring a consistent message at each center is signage for tenants.

While exterior signage is influenced by design of the property and local zoning regulations, indoor signage becomes a question to resolve between tenant and landlord. Shopping center owners and managers want a look that complements the center as a whole yet also is inviting to shoppers.

Tenants, on the other hand, are concerned about creating their own image and designing signage that conveys an individual look, feel, and style. Their goal is to stand out and be remembered in the crowded, competitive field of retailing.

"Signage is vital, and you can't run a project without a lot of input," says Ken Jacobs, vice president of retail planning and design for Chicago-based General Growth Properties. Although each developer has its own bag of tricks for maintaining overall image, each retailer wants as much exposure as possible. "There is give and take from both sides, but retailers usually get what they want as long as it's in good taste," he says.

Retail property owners and managers typically set criteria for tenants' signs based on the style, theme, and location of the shopping center or mall. Tenants typically send their proposed designs while lease negotiations are in progress. Owners say creativity is appreciated and actively encourage it within limits. The boundaries imposed by center owners, Jacobs says, are a way to avoid a completely unstructured look. "There would be nothing but huge competition among retailers if there were no limits," he continues.

Most national retailers spend a great deal of money, time, and talent searching for and creating just the right image for their stores—a look revealed not only in signage but also in each store facade and throughout the entire retail space. And as retailers strive to carve a niche for themselves, the trend today is for owners and managers to be more flexible in their criteria.

"Typically, we leave it up to each tenant to do what is best for its own purposes," says Brad Smith, director of tenant coordination for Cleveland-based Forest City Management. "With the national retailers, the rules are generally not a problem, but those new to the market might need some help and guidance."

Most developers do not hesitate to ask retailers for alternate signage if necessary, but more changes are requested

The Walt Disney Company

Most national retailers spend a great deal of money, time, and talent searching for and creating just the right image for their stores.

based on physical conditions of the particular space, which can affect the size, length, and type of sign. And size is an even bigger issue as signage becomes more than just lettering atop a doorway.

"Often, tenants with themed stores or restaurants use signage in a more architectural way, making it integral to the design of the building or store," says Debra Warner, design manager for the Mills Corporation in Arlington, Virginia. "Signage is not necessarily more important than in the past, but it has become more elaborate and tenants seem to spend more money on it."

One reason signage for tenants has become more critical is that retailers now compete with other entertainment-type options as shopping center owners and managers strive to create family entertainment destinations at their centers. Ice rinks, movie theaters, food courts, children's play areas, and even children's museums all vie for consumers' dollars.

Consequently, retailers are creating more entertaining storefronts and ones that project into the mall, beckoning the shopper to come inside. "Entertainment is absolutely key to what retailers are doing with signage," Jacobs says. "With the mall being entertainment as well as a shopping destination, sometimes people see everything but the retailers."

Source: Excerpted and adopted from Esme Neely, "Shopping under a Sign," *Shopping Center World,* August 1998, pp. 69–72. © 1998 Intertec Publishing Corporation. Used with permission. ■

Tenants are being given more flexibility in designing attractive signs that fit into a total image rather than adhering to a rigid format, as shown here at Tysons Galleria in McLean, Virginia.

The ability to control the placement and design of signage is an aesthetic advantage for a shopping center over a downtown street or a commercial strip. Torrance Promenade, a community shopping center in Torrance, California, features different styles of signage that are highly visible and comprehensible for customers.

trols are uniformly applied, shopkeepers no longer feel the need to erect signs that are larger or more dazzling than those of their neighbors and competitors. In fact, proprietors in well-controlled shopping centers often find that their sales actually increase and their expenditures for signs are considerably reduced. They discover that they are able to retain their individual identities within the framework of such controls and that they become identified with the shopping center as a whole—an entity that is larger and more memorable than any individual store in it.

In this respect, the shopping center has a great advantage over a single store on a downtown street or in a detached commercial strip, because the developer of a well-managed center can insist on his own design and sign control. A shopping center normally does not need an illuminated pylon sign to be identified. Commonly found in older centers, such signs often do not conform to the concept for the shopping center; a well-designed sign is more acceptable and identifies the center equally well. At Meyerland Plaza, for example, a 900,000-square-foot power center in Houston that was redeveloped from a smaller, failed, open-air regional center, the developer elected to retain one of the center's original monument signs as a way of linking the new with the old.

Developers typically control signage by including a declaration of permitted and prohibited signage as well as an approval clause in each tenant's lease. Such declarations may forbid roof signs or larger projecting signs and favor placement at a certain level on, above, or below a canopy, depending on the architectural treatment. Both public and private sign controls commonly prohibit moving or flashing parts.

Experience has shown that both customers and merchants appreciate sign control, although battles may occur during development. Although the enforcement of the center's signage is more difficult when trademark signs are involved, a compromise can usually be reached that is compatible with the center's own specifications for size, color, and lighting.

The problems of sign control are minimized when the architectural design of the center incorporates the details of size, style, location, and lighting of signs. Effective design depends on the designer's skill in achieving uniformity in character without requiring uniformity in typography. The center's management should establish specifications, and the allowed placement of signs should be spelled out in the lease. Boring consistency, whether in size, color, or design, should be avoided in all forms of signage. Entertainment centers and food courts especially need an environment that is more entertaining, colorful, diverse, and interactive. If neon is permitted, the color of neon signs should be compatible but not the same.

Improperly handled signage can negate an otherwise carefully developed image, and many developers thus elect to control all signs, permanent or temporary, that are visible through show windows or through store entrances.

Night Lighting

Because a greater percentage of retail business is now conducted during the evening, exterior night lighting has become an important safety, as well as design, feature. It helps to protect the public at the same time it can be used to create an image and character for the center. Lighting in parking areas should provide about 1.5 footcandles at the pavement surface. Strong lighting—approximately five footcandles—should be provided in structured parking to ensure safety. In parking areas, poles should be placed in islands at the ends of parking bays. The level of intensity of outside lighting is a concern of the center's management, not of zoning specifications, although the developer could reasonably be required to ensure that the height of the standards and the direction of the lighting prevent light pollution on adjacent properties. The latest available nonglare and high-intensity lighting should be used to provide adequate illumination, to reduce spillover lighting, and to avoid excessive costs for electricity. Lighting levels can be reduced half an hour after closing time, except in areas where employees' security and safety are a problem.

An effective lighting system involves decisions about light sources, mounting height, spacing, and light control. Light sources should be evaluated based on their efficiency, durability, and color; they vary in light output (lumen), depending on the characteristics of the light. Higher-wattage lamps are more efficient than lower-wattage lights, but it may sometimes be more efficient to use a number of smaller units to light an area without wasting energy.

Modern retailing requires a heirarchy of lighting solutions to enhance shopping. The most important tasks of a comprehensive lighting system are to illuminate building facades and entrances, spotlight architectural features and landscaping, highlight shop windows and signage, define walkways, roadways, and parking, create illuminated images on walls and sidewalks, and ensure safety.

A greater percentage of retail business is now conducted during the evening, and exterior night lighting has become an important safety as well as design feature.

Sodium lighting, which has been commonly used in many locations, should be avoided, because it renders colors poorly, makes people appear sinister, and creates a menacing atmosphere. New forms of "white" lighting are now cost-effective and should be used to create an environment that customers find more appealing.

Truck Service Facilities

The delivery court has become the principal truck service facility for loading and unloading goods. It must be screened and placed out of customers' view. Small shops selling soft goods can be served by rear corridors leading from a service court. In a neighborhood or community nonmall center, occasional box deliveries from light express or parcel post vehicles can be made across the canopy walkway without distracting shoppers. Regional centers can also successfully use over-the-sidewalk delivery by regulating delivery hours. Department stores generally have separate control of their deliveries at their own service docks and, through masonry screening, at their truck service entries.

Early regional centers were designed with truck tunnels under the mall to serve all tenants. Though tunnels offered the great advantage of completely separating truck delivery traffic from pedestrian and customer traffic, tunnels were expensive to build, operate, and manage. The costs involved now have made truck service tunnels infeasible in most shopping centers, with the possible exception of mixed-use or multiuse centers or on constricted sites where land costs are high.

Interior Features

Tenant Spaces

The space a tenant has leased typically contains a certain frontage on the mall or exterior walkway, unfinished party walls separating the space from that of retail neighbors, an unfinished floor, and exposed joists for roof support. A rear door and utilities are usually indicated within the space.

Most developers use an allowance for tenants to finish such space. The developer/landlord typically lists a maximum amount per square foot of GLA for specific tenant work such as storefronts, finished floors, walls, and ceilings, primary electrical conduits, secondary wiring, and so on; interior finishes and fixtures are not installed except as part of a specially negotiated turnkey agreement. The allowance may include floors and floor coverings, but tenants pay for all light fixtures, counters, shelves, painting, and other custom fixtures and finishing. In essence, the owner furnishes the bare space. The work that the landlord is to do and the work that is the tenant's responsibility are plainly shown on working drawings and specifications and are spelled out in the lease. After the stipulated amount for an item has been reached, it is up to the tenant to pay for the rest. This system protects developers against excessive demands from tenants that can upset construction cost estimates.

Some developers, recognizing the importance of reasonably harmonious store interiors in creating a pleasing and exciting retail image for the center as a whole, assist tenants in certain phases of planning, particularly in storefront design, signs, and even color coordination of sales areas. Some developers provide an "improved shell" rather than a "bare shell" in certain situations. Conversely, other developers make tenant spaces more barren (with dirt floors and no demising walls, for example) and offer no finishing allowances. Tenant allowances depend primarily on the type of center, type of tenant, and level of local competition. Allowances can range from nothing to a full turnkey job. In small centers, developers may have to provide fully finished tenant space. Highly desirable tenants will likely demand concessions on the allowance.

Building Flexibility

Whatever the structural column spacings used in any type of center, the design should allow for a measure of

flexibility in partitioning stores. Except for intervening fire walls, the spacing of which is governed by local fire protection codes, partitions between tenant spaces should not be used as bearing walls. Partitions between tenants should be built of materials and by methods that allow for their easy removal. The design should provide for future reallocation of store space and for readjustments in fixtures needed as tenants expand or shift their locations in the center. To allow for flexible operations, structural elements such as plumbing and heating stacks, air-conditioning ducts, toilets, and stairways should be placed on end walls or on the walls least likely to be removed in enlarging a store or redividing spaces rather than on partitions between tenants.

After construction begins, changes in tenancy may require altering the arrangement of tenants to improve the groupings of related shops, to accommodate tenants' needs, or to free highly desirable locations ("hot spots") for shops that provide higher rental income or allow more intensive use. Flexible design and non-load-bearing walls allow tenant spaces to be enlarged or decreased. Good locations can be created and a plan devised that will remain workable throughout the full leasing program.

Heavy masonry piers between storefronts should be avoided in one-story neighborhood and other small centers. Such piers are expensive to install and difficult to remove, and they reduce window frontage (although such advice is impractical if the center is to have a traditional exterior architectural treatment). Small steel columns with curtain walls of gypsum wallboard or exposed concrete block should be used for interior partitions. To build the center quickly, save labor costs, and provide an incombustible structure, developers of one-story buildings can use steel beam-and-column construction with steel trusses or bar joists carrying an insulated steel roof deck and monolithic concrete floor. Often, the tenant must provide the concrete floor slab.

Continuity in the alignment of storefronts, from anchor to anchor or from anchor to small shop, promotes cross-shopping and helps to prevent one store from casting a "visibility shadow" on the next. Continuity also makes traffic circulation smoother and is highly preferred as a flexible configuration for future changes in tenanting a center.

Many of the more successful value retailers have increased the size of their prototype stores in recent years. This trend can be problematical for developers, especially when they become saddled with hard-to-lease space left vacant when the larger stores move or go out of business, or when developers seek to convert existing shopping centers to new formats but are faced with a great deal of previously built small tenant space.

Malls

The desire to separate foot traffic from motor traffic and the increased emphasis on amenities led to open pedestrian malls in shopping centers. Early malls offered the attraction of a central open space, which was improved tremendously by a garden-like treatment. Canopied walks, specimen trees, flowers, sculptures, and fountains created a park-like atmosphere where customers could rest on benches and generally relax and enjoy the surroundings. Later the appeal of this pedestrian "street" was increased by enclosing and weather-conditioning it.

A shopping center with a mall has no "best side of the street." The pattern encourages shoppers to move back and forth from one side of the mall to the other. For this reason, the mall is an asset in merchandising and a stimulus for impulse buying, as well as a pleasant and convenient place for shoppers. Pedestrian flow along the mall is encouraged by careful placement of tenants to sustain shoppers' interest. The usual arrangement of a mall center with more than one major tenant is to place one at each end of the mall. In the current generation of regional centers, open malls are rare, but they are found in places such as Hawaii where the climate is conducive to year-

No matter how spectacular the design of a shopping center's common areas, such as at Pacific Place in Seattle, the retail spaces should be built of materials that can be easily altered to allow for tenants' changing needs.

round outdoor living, and in specialty, community, and neighborhood centers.

The fully weather-conditioned enclosed mall has assets not found in open mall centers, many of which can lead to increased sales volume. The design also permits open storefronts, which save the expense of display windows. The entire mall frontage of a store can in effect become open "window" area. When benches, plants, and other mall furnishings are provided, the mall creates a setting for even greater vitality in merchandising and promotion of the center. Because of such advantages, open malls have been converted to enclosed malls—if increased sales justify the capital expense of conversion.

A straight-line mall is likely to produce an unattractive and monotonous tunnel effect if it is too long in relation to its width. To improve the visual effect and provide shorter sight distances, the pattern may assume such shapes as H, L, T, Y, or Z. A meandering traffic pattern creates more interesting movement and brings shoppers closer to storefronts. Pedestrian flow within the mall can also be directed by the strategic placement of seating areas, planters, kiosks, and other physical barriers as well as by changes in flooring, colors, and patterns. The use of mirrors and other reflective surfaces, particularly on escalator channels and along portions of the concourse walls, can provide a more dramatic feeling within the mall area. Shapes within the mall can also be varied to create a design theme.

When the direction of customer flow between anchor tenants changes, a court or widened area can be introduced. Such an area can be architecturally dramatic and premium rents charged for adjacent leasable space. It can also serve as a setting for special promotional events and displays—antique shows, for example, or holiday displays—and should be designed to accommodate large assemblies of people and large vehicles. This end can be achieved by designing the space in the style of an amphi-

A well-designed mall has no "best side of the street." The Court at King of Prussia Mall in King of Prussia, Pennsylvania, features generous landscaping and fountains to entice shoppers to roam from one side of the mall to the other.

The distinctive semicircular design of Canal City Hakata in Fukuoka, Japan, avoids the monotonous tunnel effect of a straight-line mall and provides vantage points to view programmed entertainment in the open-air courtyard.

Fukuoka Jisho

theater. Fountains, sitting areas, escalators, and sculptures can be featured attractions of the court.

Although malls generally range from 30 to 40 feet wide, the width may be increased to 60 feet or more for courts and other special areas, depending on the height and treatment of the ceiling. In multilevel malls, courts offer even greater opportunities for dramatic treatment. The ceilings can be up to 50 feet higher than in the adjacent mall area. Thirteen feet is an attractive and practical ceiling height to keep heating and air-conditioning costs within reasonable limits; the mall in a small regional center (one with approximately 300,000 square feet of GLA) may have a lower ceiling. In larger regional centers, a ceiling height of 15 feet works well. The height can be varied to avoid long straight sight lines and to provide a more interesting and pleasing appearance than that of a single-height hallway. It is also important to consider acoustics; the mall should produce no echo effect.

Because the mall customarily runs a sizable distance between major retail tenants—the department stores, or a department store and a larger variety store or food store—the architect's problem is to design this distance to seem short while still providing enough length for an array of tenants. If storefronts are appealing and varied, shoppers tend to become interested and involved with their surroundings and not mind the walk. Occasional storefronts intruding into the mall two or three feet give an undulating storefront line and make the mall more interesting. As an inexpensive solution to linearity, some developers hang banners across the mall to break up sight distances.

Developers' desire to provide enough retailing area for the stores that are part of the shopping complex while keeping the mall length to a comfortable walking distance bears directly on the depth of the stores. The GLA of enclosed malls normally equals about 84 to 89 percent of the gross building area, with the remaining space malls, courts, entrances, corridors, toilet facilities, and management facilities. In some cases, additional

leasable space may be provided by designating special areas (other than kiosks) within the mall.

Kiosks

Kiosks, or freestanding booths, are a retailing innovation in enclosed malls. They encourage impulse buying and allow the flexibility of including very small tenant spaces of about 100 square feet. Kiosks must be low enough not to interfere with the view across the mall or with the view of tenants' signs or lighting. If they are too high, they appear to be separate stores, separate traffic along the mall, and deprive nearby tenants of visibility.

The addition of carefully selected kiosks, placed in areas of heavy traffic, greatly helps to create the atmosphere of a marketplace. Counter-height kiosks are suitable for a variety of retail and service uses, such as candy, cards, keys, costume jewelry, giftware, travel agencies, ticket counters, newsstands, and insurance agencies.

Although some major tenants may seek to restrict kiosks during lease negotiations, some smaller tenants might wish to augment sales by operating kiosks in front of or near their stores. Owners or developers can receive substantial additional rental income from kiosks at little extra cost. Developers must use discretion in introducing kiosks, making certain they meet established design guidelines. Food service outlets that require on-site cooking or emit odors of any kind should probably not be permitted.

Often, particularly when older malls are being renovated or enclosed, lean-to or similar kiosks can be used to cover blank masonry walls or unwanted department store show windows. They can add excitement to previously dull and dark areas of the mall and generate substantial new income at a minimum investment for the developer. Normally, such kiosks are not roofed and require no air conditioning, heating, or sprinklers.

Multiple Levels

Vertical merchandising is used increasingly as the solution to restricted sites and the need to bring stores closer

A multilevel center, such as the Boulevard in Dallas, Texas, presents a dramatic image that draws potential customers as they drive by.

together for the convenience of shoppers. Multilevel malls reduce site coverage and walking distances between stores and between parking areas and stores. Multilevel malls also allow a regional center to include a mix of uses in compact buildings on restricted-area, high-cost sites.

Multilevel centers challenge architects, as their design requires a complex evaluation of site use, traffic movement, graphics, and amenities. This complexity is increased by the need to provide escalators, elevators, and stairways for circulation. Still, the savings in required site area can help balance the greater capital costs of multilevel design.

Multilevel centers have distinct benefits in marketing, provided tenants are distributed to the best advantage for interplay among the shopping levels. The developer must maintain careful control over tenants' locations when leasing a two-level center. Most mall tenants believe their customer drawing power depends on a well-designed connection between smaller tenants and the major stores. Therefore, the department store should have entrances from each level. Access to parking facilities from each level is also desirable and is especially easy to accomplish on a site with a natural or artificial slope or in a center with structured parking.

Visibility of the various levels is a major aspect of designing multilevel centers. The use of dramatic two-story design elements, including shops floating between levels, is a technique that has been used to prevent isolation of one level from another. The placement and prominence of

vertical transportation must also be carefully considered. End courts or central courts can feature stairways, elevators, or escalators that lead to a second gallery on the upper level and provide additional visual exposure for stores in the gallery area. Bridges may be used to connect both sides of the upper level and to offer dramatic views of activity on both levels.

Areas of vertical circulation between levels can be integrated into the overall design of a multilevel center. Necessities such as escalators and stairs can be designed to serve as attractive amenities. The space under stairways can be turned into a strong design feature, with recessed seating and carpeting installed to create an attractive rest area. The stairs, the landing, the space underneath, even the railings can be designed as an articulated amenity, creating a design element rather than just a way to get from one level to another. If they are not designed carefully, however, escalators and stairs can obscure tenants from view and create difficult areas to lease, especially in department store courts.

An old real estate adage applies to most small shopping centers—ground floor areas are rented; basements and second floors are given away—and it is seldom advisable for small centers to have two stories unless a change in grade allows direct access to both floors or the high density of development and cost of land justify it. If they are included in small centers, second floors are usually occupied by office rather than retail tenants. Office employees are all-day parkers, and office visitors are generally long-time, nonshopping parkers. Doctors and dentists make poor tenants for the second floor of a neighborhood center because of the special plumbing, wiring, and maintenance they require. Such tenants are better located in a separate medical building.

A small two-story center is likely to succeed only in an area of limited and high-cost commercial land, high population density, and a high level of disposable income. Suitable second-floor tenants are those that pull people to the center regularly and frequently, have visitors who will not park longer than an hour during shopping hours, and require no display space on the ground floor. As noted, service tenants such as beauty shops, photographers, and dance studios are appropriate for second-floor locations. Stairs to second floors should be easy to climb, with intermediate landings—another reason for designing low ceilings on the first floor. Ideally, topography of the site allows a design that provides at-grade access to the second level.

An exception to small centers with multiple levels is the current trend to convert downtown buildings, often historically certified and housing offices or warehouses, into multilevel shopping malls. Such converted buildings, usually housing a disproportionate number of restaurants and other food concessions, are often tourist attractions.

Food Courts

Over the last ten to 15 years, food courts, consisting of a cluster of quick-service food stands grouped around a common or public seating area, have become a major component of many regional malls and specialty centers. The design of a food court should provide a theme and a festive ambience; a high-quality design together with a proper tenant mix can often allow a food court to function as an anchor for the center.

To create the desired festive setting, the designer of the food court should pay close attention to features like natural lighting, the decor of public areas, design criteria for tenants, and the configuration and design of seating areas. Amenities such as terraces, water features, and landscaping are important, particularly to temper the visual impact of the seating area in a large food court. In the most successful food courts, seating encourages the pleasure of seeing and being seen. Thus, seating often borders circulation routes or overlooks a multilevel public environment. Some newer food courts feature light-menu cafés with open kitchens, creating additional opportunities for seeing and being seen.

The location of the food court is vital. If the food court is in fact an anchor, then it should be a destination sited in a location designed to draw people past other shops. If, however, it is a convenience or an "oasis," it should be located to attract the greatest number of people going from anchor to anchor—that is, in the most heavily trafficked area. Another important consideration is whether the food court's location will allow it to remain open beyond the center's normal hours of operation and be accessible to customers at various late-night entertainment

Careful attention to design details for food courts has become increasingly important, because food courts are often anchors of regional malls and specialty centers. The food court at First Colony mall near Houston features a glass skylight that creates changing shadows and light patterns on the French limestone and Indian granite interior.

RTKL, Dallas

A variety of distinctive retail tenants, rather than domination by several large anchors, can be successful in urban retail districts. Two Rodeo Drive in Beverly Hills uses street-level retail stores to create a variety of small specialty retail uses on two levels that blend seamlessly with the surrounding district.

spots within the center (such as cinemas) without creating a security problem for the center.

Whether a food court will have fixed or movable tables and seats is an important choice. Fixing them to the floor avoids the need for continually restraightening tables and chairs and reduces the risk of loss. But fixing the distance between tables and chairs means that those who are either very small (for example, children) or obese can never be completely comfortable. A frequent compromise is to fix

Shopping center developers need to have a good working knowledge of the sizes, shapes, and operational requirements of the various categories of anchor tenants. Linens'n Things, which typically requires 35,000 to 50,000 square feet, anchors the North-Point MarketCenter in Alpharetta, Georgia.

the tables and leave the chairs movable. The amount of space that should be allotted to seating is debatable, but as a rule of thumb, one square foot of seating area should be allowed for each square foot of food court GLA—or approximately 35 seats for each tenant of the food court.

The food court uses a central air-conditioning system, and, in a way, it is treated like a major tenant. Each individual tenant is in a stall, usually predesigned, with its own exhaust system and plumbing. A variable-air-volume system lends itself very well to this type of operation. Central systems for trash and garbage removal and for deliveries are essential. Sometimes, if the developer supplies trays, a common tray-washing area is necessary, and in some cases, a refrigerated garbage room may be needed. Normally, restroom and telephone facilities are centrally located for the use of employees and customers.

Storefronts

Storefronts must be architecturally integrated with the shopping center and reflect the store's merchandise and image. In malls, they may be completely or partially open, with merchandise placed before the public without the barrier of glass. With no exterior doors to open, customers can enter the sales area under the most favorable circumstances, and the full width of a store becomes the entrance. Shoplifting can become a problem, however, if the store's layout is not designed so that personnel at front sales locations can control them.

Devices for closing storefronts in enclosed malls range from sliding glass doors to roll-up grilles. The variety of attractive display possibilities for storefronts is virtually limitless. Storefronts in an enclosed mall are often less expensive to merchandise because tenants are able to do away with window backs and other expensive display materials.

Store Size

Before the advent of power centers, a saying in the shopping center industry claimed that any size store is acceptable if it is not too big. The leasing program includes plans for the sizes of stores. A merchant on a long-term lease may want the biggest store possible to accommodate possible expansion in the future. The developer/owner should have the flexibility in the lease agreements, if possible, to move tenants if they need larger (or smaller) spaces.

Small stores add character to the center. Plans for small stores must provide suitable depths, which usually entails overlapping a large, L-shaped store behind the small store. Sometimes this arrangement is not satisfactory, however. Such an arrangement slowed the leasing of a large block of space behind a small store at Village Park Plaza when the larger tenant, a drug superstore, closed.

Whatever the mix of store sizes is ultimately chosen, each tenant should be held to the minimum space needed, because it is better for the tenant to be a little tight on space than to rattle around in too much room with insufficient sales to justify the rent. This advice is especially relevant in light of today's higher building and operating costs, which are ultimately reflected in higher rents. Most tenants recognize the prudence of gauging their space to the projected volume of sales.

If possible, frontages for major tenants should be limited to permit exposure of as many different merchants as possible to pedestrian traffic. Variety in the mix of retail tenants is more important than the size of any one store. Evidence suggests that centers with a variety of retail tenants are considerably more successful than those with only a few large stores.[23] Nevertheless, shopping center development today is much more anchor-driven than ever, and the best brokers, developers, owners, managers, architects, and lenders need to have a good working knowledge of the sizes and shapes of the various categories of anchor tenants so they can choose the most appropriate mix.

Figure 3-2 lists typical store sizes for some major categories of retailers.

Understanding the most common sizes for various categories of stores can facilitate efficient planning and increase the likelihood that multiple anchors can be marketed for the same spot in a center. Stores of 8,000 to 15,000 square feet, so-called "minianchors," are an awkward size. Drugstores have grown larger, becoming "combo stores" or "superdrugs." Hardware stores and variety stores have been choked out by the Wal-Marts and Home Depots, leaving primarily video and music stores in this in-between size range. Hence, 100- to 150-foot depths should be avoided.

Width. A standard width cannot be designated for any particular type of tenant. Owners of chain stores have studied the matter for years, employing the best store planners in the field to ascertain the proper width for their stores. Merchants generally have their own ideas about store size, based on their experience and study, and usually advise the developer of their needs. Unfortunately, merchants' ideas often do not coincide with the developer's need to restrict the width of mall stores to keep the mall a reasonable length and to allow frontage on the mall for as many tenants as possible.

In most present-day centers, the architectural design calls for structures with wide spans between the structural columns. Stores are fitted into these structural steel frames without much regard for locations of the columns. With clever layout, however, columns can be disguised as part of the fixtures and often can be used as part of a store's decorative features.

Developers should keep in mind that they have only so much frontage "for sale," because usually the amount of available frontage in a center is limited. The developer should prevent a merchant from using too much of this valuable commodity for a wide but shallow store if the merchant can achieve as high a sales volume in the same square footage with a deeper store.

Depth. The ability to provide stores of varying depths is an asset to any center. A range of depths from 40 to 120 feet is often required—and feasible. When stores in the center must be of uniform depth, small stores can be carved out of deeper space, leaving rear overlap areas for the neighboring larger stores. But developers must avoid creating excessive depths for which neither they

figure 3-2
Major Non–Department Store Anchors

Selected Store Types	Size Range (Square Feet)
1. Biggs, IKEA	> 150,000
2. Warehouse Clubs (Sam's, Costco)	110,000–135,000
3. General Discounters (Kmart, Venture, Wards, Wal-Mart, Target)	100,000–130,000
4. Home Improvement (Home Depot, Lowe's, Hechinger)	100,000–130,000
5. Supercenters	125,000–180,000
6. Combo Stores (Kroger, Albertson's, Vons, Giant, Fiesta, Ukrops)	55,000–75,000
7. Sporting Goods (Sportstown, Oshmans, Sports Authority, REI)	50,000–60,000
8. Catalog Showroom (Service Merchandise)	50,000
9. Toys "R" Us	45,000
10. White Goods (Linens'n Things, Bed Bath & Beyond, Homeplace)	35,000–50,000
11. Furniture (Homelife)	35,000–40,000
12. Baby Goods (Baby Superstore)	35,000
13. Home Electronics (Circuit City, Best Buy)	32,000–58,000
14. Books (Borders, Barnes & Noble)	25,000–45,000
15. Soft Goods (TJ Maxx, Marshalls, Ross Dress for Less, Steinmart)	25,000–45,000
16. Super Pet Stores	20,000–35,000
17. Computers (CompUSA, Computer City)	25,000–45,000
18. Office Supply (Office Max, Staples, Office Depot)	20,000–45,000
19. Athletic Shoes (World Foot Locker, NikeTown)	20,000
20. Music (Virgin, Tower)	15,000
21. Drugstores (Eckerds, Walgreens)	8,600–15,000

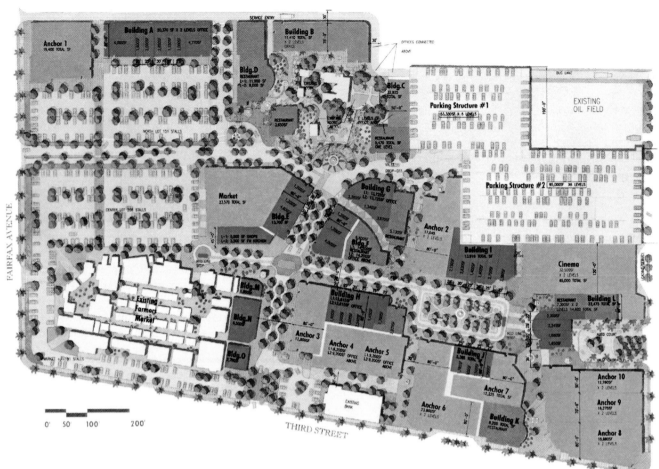

The widths and depths of stores are critical considerations when planning and designing a retail center's layout. The site plan for the proposed expansion of the Farmer's Market in Los Angeles illustrates a range of floorplate sizes and shapes to accommodate the variety of tenant types.

nor their tenants can obtain an adequate return. If shoppers travel past two rows of fronts, if delivery is at the back of the store and ground-level storage facilities have to be provided, or if the center has no basement, stores need to be deeper. Less depth is necessary if storage and service facilities are in the basement and if pedestrian traffic passes on only one side of the store. Deeper stores in regional centers are generally a product of specifically planned uses, such as large high-quality stores, multiscreen theaters, and the like. In small stores that may be enlarged later, electric panels and equipment should be placed on side walls so they will not have to be relocated if the rear wall is moved or on the rear wall if the tenant is more likely to expand by leasing an adjacent space.

Ceiling Height. The appropriate ceiling height for a store depends somewhat on the exterior architectural treatment and certainly on the total area of the store. Lower ceilings are the trend, encouraged partly because they save energy consumption in the use of heating, air conditioning, and lighting, and they are less expensive to build and maintain. On the other hand, they require architectural "breaks" to produce a pleasing appearance.

The distance from the floor stab to the underside of the bar joists holding the roof may vary from ten to 14

feet, depending on the architectural style of the building, the depth of the stores, and the type of tenants. The air space between the finished ceiling and the roof usually contains air-conditioning ducts, electrical wires, recessed lighting boxes and panels, telephone wires, plumbing lines, and other utility hardware; such equipment requires two to three feet of space between the finished ceiling and the structure.

Although many stores have 11-foot finished ceilings, some small stores may have ceilings as low as nine feet. Certain specialized tenants that use more space, such as variety stores and supermarkets, require finished ceilings as high as 13 feet. Ceilings in storage areas out of customers' view need not be finished, but many fire codes require that they have lay-in panels or other materials with a two-hour fire-resistant rating. Mezzanines used for sales or storage space require different ceiling heights.

Basements

At one time, large regional centers needed basements to accommodate their truck service tunnels. Basements were fairly easy to provide, because they could be scooped out at the same time the tunnel was dug. Today, however, with truck service courts and service delivery areas built level with the main building, basements are no longer needed and are generally considered too costly to construct when they do not provide income-producing space.

Although they are not required, basements have been used in some areas for storage and heating equipment, for office space, and for expansion of stores. Even so, a basement is an added capital cost and generally produces little income. Using concrete block foundations where subsurface conditions permit, with transverse beams providing support for the first floor, can save construction costs for a basement. This method of construction eliminates the need for basement stair headers and permits basement stairs to be relocated and widened without undue expense when store spaces and tenant arrangements are revised.

Stairways leading to a basement should be constructed of concrete or steel, and if the basement is to be used for merchandising, the stairways should be five feet wide.

Some stores, such as furniture and variety chains, specifically request basement areas for merchandising and may require elevators.

Interior Walls

Party walls between retail stores in enclosed mall centers can be constructed of any of a variety of materials, depending on local building and fire codes. Some codes require fire walls that extend to the underside of the roof. Sometimes concrete block is used; sometimes metal stud partitions with gypsum wallboard are used. The latter option provides maximum flexibility for future changes in store sizes.

Partitioning between the sales and storage areas of a store generally consists of stud and gypsum wallboard construction. The wall may be finished with anything from paint to wallpaper to painted decorations to a vinyl cover. Most fire codes require that this partitioning extend to the underside of the roof.

Most retail stores maximize their visibility by constructing storefronts almost entirely of glass. Party walls between retail stores, however, are constructed of materials dictated by local building and fire codes.

Robert E. Mikrut

Robert E. Mikrut

Robert E. Mikrut

The interior lighting by Arrowstreet designers adds a sense of playful drama at Plaza Rio Hondo in Puerto Rico.

Plumbing

Because plumbing lines often must run under the floor-slab, they are best installed while subfloors are exposed during construction. Stores that do not require special plumbing usually confine plumbing fixtures to small toilet areas and washbasins, but restaurants, beauty and barber shops, and other stores with more complex needs find plumbing a major cost for the improvements.

Plumbing requirements for shopping center tenants are essentially the same as those for freestanding stores. Tenants customarily provide any water-heating equipment needed. Restaurants and major stores provide restrooms for customers. Where permitted, a group of small tenants can be served by shared restrooms provided by the developer and maintained by the group through common area charges.

Leases should specify the developer's responsibility for providing vents and drains for tenants such as supermarkets, restaurants, and dry cleaners that require large plumbing installations. If a center has no basement, floor installations should be deferred until tenant spaces are leased, because formulation of the tenants' underfloor requirements lags behind the developer's construction schedule. Because tenants' plumbing requirements lag behind construction, the slab for the tenant space is often part of the tenant's responsibility, which can create a problem in a multilevel mall with regard to plumbing stacks and vent locations and must be taken into account.

Sprinklers must be installed in enclosed malls and in other mall buildings. The system required depends on local fire insurance rates and building codes and on available water supplies. In many instances, a sprinkler connection is brought to the tenant's lease line, and the tenant hooks up the sprinkler and does any other work within the space needed for the system to conform to the layout. Even if a mall is allowed by code to go without a sprinkler system (common in one-level malls), obtaining insurance without fire protection is virtually impossible.

Lighting

Generally, a developer provides a source of electricity at a panel, and each tenant is required to provide its own lighting and other electrical needs, all of which require the landlord's approval. Because ceilings are also usually a tenant's responsibility, the tenant, not the developer, must coordinate ceiling work with the installation of lighting.

Ceilings in enclosed mall space are frequently sky-lighted. Clerestories allow natural daylight to filter in, thus benefiting both the atmosphere in the mall and any specimen plants. Lighting enclosed mall areas is usually designed not to detract from the light intensity of the store windows while providing a pleasing, natural overall effect. Combinations of fluorescent and incandescent lighting plus indirect lighting may be used. Incandescent lighting requires more fixtures, more wiring, and greater wattage than fluorescent lighting to produce the same number of footcandles. And it generates greater heat.

Too much attention is often given to lighting store interiors rather than to lighting the merchandise. To reduce consumption of electricity, light colors could be used to eliminate the need for floodlighting. Store interiors can be designed with fewer outlets and shorter wiring runs to reduce installation and operating costs. High-lumen output lights require fewer fixtures.

Flooring

Special floor coverings are usually put over the concrete slab in tenant sales areas and often omitted in storage areas. Floor coverings range from various tile materials to carpeting. Wood flooring is not recommended for stores unless the whole decorative scheme calls for it. Stores often vary floor coverings in different parts of the sales area, depending on the character of the merchandise and the way in which the merchandise is displayed. Tenants are almost always responsible for the flooring in their spaces, which must be in accordance with criteria established by the owner and incorporated into the lease.

Floor surfaces of enclosed malls consist of a wide variety of materials—marble, polished concrete, carpets, various kinds of tile pavers, treated wood parquet (particularly on upper floors), terrazzo, and poured-in-place or precast tiles. The surface material must be durable and easy to clean and maintain. The floor must not be slippery, yet it must not be so rough that it interferes with cleaning. Quality ceramic tile floors are serviceable and economical. Flooring with repeated small designs is easier to replace if cracks appear in some heavily-used sections.

The floor of enclosed malls can appear more attractive and warmer if a carefully designed variety of materials is used rather than an unvarying, white terrazzo. The entryway of most stores can be made more dramatic and appealing if floor materials there are noticeably different from those in the mall. Designs in the flooring help break up the monotony of lengthy malls or walkways.

Heating and Air Conditioning

A shopping center can be heated and cooled by individual units for each store or by a central plant for the entire center. Tenants are responsible for their own individual units, and the shopping center's management is responsible for a central plant, which offers the greatest convenience centerwide. Hybrid systems employing large rooftop units serving several tenants are also available. One such system—the variable–air volume (VAV) system—increases or decreases the amount or volume of air to each space according to the demands of the space. A thermostat controls a VAV terminal, which controls the amount of air—usually cooling air—admitted into the space. Either a central plant or a rooftop unit senses pressure required for the system and maintains a constant temperature and pressure while varying the volume. In a conventional system, the volume is constant and the temperature varies.

With energy savings an essential criterion of HVAC systems, the mechanical engineer must evaluate all possible systems and the availability of various fuels. Good judgment, based on a thorough analysis, is necessary not only in the development of new projects but also in the improvement of operating centers. Solutions are complicated by the different requirements of various classifications of tenants.

Developers can reduce air-conditioning loads by using extra building insulation and a heat-reflective coating on the roof. In enclosed malls, engineers should be employed to check each tenant's air-conditioning system to ensure proper balance so that stores do not "bleed off" conditioned air from the mall area.

Notes

1. See W. Paul O'Mara et al., *Developing Power Centers* (Washington, D.C.: ULI–the Urban Land Institute, 1996).

2. See Owen J. Furuseth, "Neotraditional Planning: A New Strategy for Building Neighborhoods?" *Land Use Policy*, July 1997.

3. See Dean Schwanke et al., *Remaking the Shopping Center* (Washington, D.C.: ULI–the Urban Land Institute, 1994).

4. See *Mixed-Use Development Handbook* (Washington, D.C.: ULI–the Urban Land Institute, 1987), p. 327.

5. ULI–the Urban Land Institute and International Council of Shopping Centers, *Parking Requirements for Shopping Centers: Summary Recommendations and Research Study Report* (Washington, D.C.: ULI–the Urban Land Institute, 1982). Parking requirements will likely change as a result of an updated study by ULI and ICSC to be published in 1999.

6. Ibid., p. 2.

7. Ibid., p. 216.

8. Ibid., p. 17.

9. Ibid., pp. 17–18.

10. Ibid., pp. 39–40.

11. Until the ULI study in 1981, an earlier study had recommended a parking ratio of 5.5 spaces per 1,000 square feet of GLA. See *Parking Requirements for Shopping Centers* (Washington, D.C.: ULI–the Urban Land Institute, 1963).

12. *Shared Parking* (Washington, D.C.: ULI–the Urban Land Institute, 1983).

13. Robert Dunphy, ed., *Dimensions of Parking*, 4th ed. (Washington, D.C.: ULI–the Urban Land Institute, forthcoming 1999).

14. International Council of Shopping Centers, *Shopping Center Parking: The Influence of Changing Car Sizes* (New York: ICSC, 1984), pp. 4–5.

15. W. Paul O'Mara, "A Bay State Comeback," *Urban Land*, November 1995, p. 46.

16. Walker Parking Consultants, "Parking Requirements for Shopping Centers," draft (Washington, D.C.: ULI/ICSC, 1999).

17. Richard F. Roti, "Construction and Development Costs," in *The Dimensions of Parking*, 2nd ed. (Washington, D.C.: ULI–the Urban Land Institute, 1983), pp. 26–28.

18. ULI–the Urban Land Institute, National Association of Home Builders, and American Society of Civil Engineers, *Residential Storm Water Management* (Washington, D.C.: Author, 1975).

19. Participants' manual for "Shopping Centers: How to Build, Buy, and Redevelop," a workshop sponsored by ULI, pp. 83–84.

20. Ibid., p. 53.

21. Ibid., p. 56.

22. William R. Ewald, Jr., and Daniel R. Mandelker, *Street Graphics: A Concept and a System* (Washington, D.C.: American Society of Landscape Architects Foundation, 1971). *Street Graphics* is the most useful available guide to the appropriate provision and administration of sign control ordinances.

23. For median store sizes in GLA by tenant classification, see the most recent *Dollars & Cents of Shopping Centers* (Washington, D.C.: ULI–the Urban Land Institute).

4. Expansion and Rehabilitation of Existing Centers

One of the most active segments of shopping center development is expansion and rehabilitation. Several factors have made renovation of existing centers important. The inventory of shopping centers is aging and becoming physically and functionally obsolete. An estimated 65 percent are more than ten years old, and more than 63 percent are smaller than 100,000 square feet.[1] More important, numerous market forces have created a long-term market for rehabilitation, expansion, and reconfiguration of existing shopping centers:

- Overbuilt Markets—Many retail markets have become overbuilt and consequently extremely competitive. The only way to compete successfully is to keep a center looking new and attractive.
- New Concepts of Retailing—Retailing involves trends, and continuous change is the norm. The turnover of tenants is constant, with an ever-changing mix of new retailers and store styles. New kinds of stores must be accommodated.
- Financial Distress for Anchors—During the late 1980s and early 1990s, many longstanding major anchor retailers—department stores, supermarkets, discount retailers—suffered severe financial distress. Many closed their doors permanently or were consolidated with healthier chains. Many centers thus had to find new

anchors and often had to reposition themselves within the marketplace.
- Institutional Ownership—The shift away from shopping centers owned by individuals and private firms to more institutional and public ownership has led to more aggressive acquisition and management.
- Shifting Demographics—The demographics and character of the market surrounding a center can change dramatically, requiring a center to reposition itself to accommodate the new market.
- Appreciation of the Site—Many centers that were built in the 1970s and 1980s are now located on land that has appreciated significantly in value. Many owners have capitalized on their locational advantages by better using the valuable asset.
- New Preferences in Design—Rehabilitation has provided an opportunity to create higher architectural quality, inside and out.
- Greater Emphasis on Culture, Entertainment, and Service—Shopping centers now compete by combining shopping with entertainment and educational components. The trend is to make the shopping center a community and cultural center as well.
- Larger Anchors—Larger stores demanded by anchors have forced owners and developers to reconfigure their centers.
- Big-Box Retailers—Value is critical in today's retail marketplace, and value-oriented retailing is gaining market share. The rapid growth of value retailers—

The arches at the updated Fashion Island in Irvine, California, provide a view corridor to the anchor tenants.

Among the factors driving the expansion and renovation of shopping centers is the need to provide more cultural and entertainment services to stay competitive. The repositioning of the Santana Shopping Center in São Paulo, Brazil, will include the addition of a cinema as an anchor. Cinemas attract a broad demographic base of customers. They also generate multiple visits in a short period of time and are accessible day and night.

warehouse clubs, discount department stores, off-price stores, and category killers—has created opportunities not only to develop new value-oriented centers but also to reposition existing centers.

- Competition from "Nonstores"—The growth of catalog shopping has been apparent for years, but the dramatic rise of Internet shopping has taken many retailers and developers by surprise. Although the total amount of retail dollars spent through the Internet in 1999 is small relative to total retail sales, its rate of growth is expected to soar. To be successful in the coming years, retail developers and their tenants must harness the power of the Internet, or some will be consumed by it.

The long-term market forces outlined here reflect a new retail environment that requires a more dynamic approach to maintaining the competitive position of shopping centers in the early 21st century. This chapter outlines the most important issues that need to be understood and addressed for redevelopment of existing centers.[2]

Feasibility Analysis

In deciding whether to undertake the expansion or rehabilitation of an existing center, the owner must determine whether a new program is justified in terms of the potential return on investment and examine a number of factors, both internal and external. Internal factors include the history of the property, the center's tenant mix, tenants' lease terms and their sales performance, the center's market share, the relative position of the center in its market, the existing management, and the availability of land for expansion. External factors include coverage of the market area, the composition of the market and how it has evolved during operations so far, the retail potential reflected in expenditures in the market, the competition and its impact on the center, potential new competitors, the availability of new tenants to improve or expand the center's tenant mix, and an estimate of the size and timing of the proposed expansion. These factors, described in the following sections, can be evaluated in terms of the specific investment criteria established by a shopping center owner to test the feasibility of a proposed rehabilitation and/or expansion.

Analysis of Sales Performance

Unlike the developer of a new center, who has to work with estimates, the "redeveloper" of an existing center already knows the sales performance of tenants, rents and lease terms, and management capabilities of individual tenants. To diagnose the need for rehabilitation, the developer can begin with trends in sales performance over a five- to seven-year period. Total sales for the center and a comparison with those of similar retailing centers in the region are usually the first indicators of whether and to what degree to rehabilitate, reposition, and/or expand the center. For example, if the growth rate of sales for a center equals or surpasses that of its competitors, the center could probably benefit from expansion, with the prospect of updating antiquated rents. If the growth rate is lower than that of the market or if sales are declining, the center's owners should investigate the causes; rehabilitation and repositioning may be appropriate instead. Sales rates in a center thus serve as a barometer to indicate what course of action is in order.

Sales for individual tenants, classified by type, are significant not only in terms of relative growth but also as a percentage of total sales within respective categories. Tenants can be classified by performance as well. Solid performers may serve as a standard; poor ones may be given assistance in management and marketing or put on a list of tenants to be replaced. Sales trends at a particular shopping center can be compared not only with other centers in a portfolio of several centers but also with industry-wide performance averages, such as those reported in ULI's *Dollars & Cents of Shopping Centers*.[3]

Analysis of Lease Terms

The next step in determining the feasibility of remaking a shopping center is to carefully review tenant leases with regard to:

- The degree of approval rights and control vested in any one tenant;
- Duration of leases and any renewal options;
- Minimum and percentage rents compared with the current fair market value, and percentage rents assessed;
- Flexibility of lease provisions in terms of assignments, subleases, and use;
- The type and value of existing tenant improvements and who has control of such improvements at the end of the lease term;
- Taxes on real property;
- Tenants' contributions to operating expenses;
- Common areas;
- Signage.

Owners should give special attention to tenants whose terms expire in the near future, particularly those expiring within two to three years with no options to renew. Rents for these tenants could easily be raised to current market rates, provided their sales are satisfactory. Even tenants with options to renew in the near future are usually willing to renegotiate their positions when centers are rehabilitated. Poorly performing tenants whose leases expire soon should head the list of potential eliminations. The opportunity to upgrade rent and lease terms is a major signal favoring rehabilitation.

In anticipation of rehabilitation, landlords may have leases prepared to provide for stipulated rent increases should certain events occur, such as the addition of another anchor or the enclosure of an open center. Leases should require tenants to pay for common area maintenance

The renovation and expansion of Plaza West Covina included the addition of a new department store, 300,000 square feet of new retail space, and more visually exciting common areas.

Redevelopment of an existing shopping center has many possible advantages (and some disadvantages) over new development. The advantages are related to the market, public approvals, financing, construction, and operating results.

Advantages of the Market

- Availability of Prime Real Estate—Vacant prime property for new development often is located in unproved and outlying areas without fully established surrounding markets. Older shopping centers or other retail properties, such as grocery or discount store sites, can provide attractive opportunities for redevelopment in proved, mature locations. Such locations, moreover, can be accurately analyzed for development opportunities, with less guesswork about future market changes, because the market is established and not subject to significant short-term changes. In some cases, neighborhoods surrounding older retail properties actually have become wealthier, more populous, or more intensively developed since the original development.
- An Established Customer Base—A shopping center that has been in existence for many years usually has loyal customers whose shopping patterns are already set. This built-in market provides a significant advantage for a renovated center. The location also may have nostalgic or historic significance that can provide additional goodwill.
- Fewer Competitive Sites—Developed areas usually have fewer opportunities for competitors to enter the market, which limits new competition, reduces uncertainty, and increases the likelihood that the renovated center will be successful.

Advantages during the Approval Process

- Suitable Zoning Already in Place—Restrictive zoning and other development controls limit the location of new shopping centers, often because of their impact on traffic. Renovation projects often require no rezoning or subdivision approvals, which can save years and translate into significant cost savings for the developer. In some cases, the project's age may allow for variances from project codes, building setbacks, or even land use restrictions. This regulatory flexibility may permit a distinctive development plan that otherwise would be impossible to build.
- Public Support—Municipal agencies and citizens' groups often embrace projects that support neighborhood improvements, particularly in older neighborhoods that have been ignored by developers in the past. Some cities sponsor bond programs providing funding directly or through tax recovery incentives that allow the developer to recoup part of the cost. In some areas, the development agency can aid in condemnation if some leases are difficult to cancel or additional properties must be obtained. Develop-

The new Porter Square building in Cambridge, Massachusetts, was redeveloped to include specialty retail and convenience stores, such as a CVS pharmacy.

ers can obtain concessions on the parking code as part of municipal negotiations.

Advantages for Construction and Leasing

- Lower Construction Cost—The cost of buying an underperforming shopping center and renovating it is often significantly lower per square foot than building a new building.
- Faster Turnaround—The redevelopment process is likely to take less time than new construction. Public approvals are often quicker, and financing is easier because the project already has a cash flow history. The existing cash flow also reduces the lead time between beginning construction and closing the permanent loan.
- Established Operating Record—The history of the center can provide valuable information about what works and what does not work in that location in terms of market demand and tenant mix. This valuable infor-

mation generally is unavailable for a new development project. Tenants that are not doing well or that are no longer suitable for the evolving market can be bought out, sometimes at a nominal rate, and the developer can then reposition the center with a more dynamic tenant mix.

• Affordable Deals with Anchors—Because of the lower cost involved in renovating a project, anchor tenants can be offered very competitive rental rates.

Renovation also has several disadvantages:

• The center may be underperforming for good reasons that are not easily remedied.
• Even with redevelopment, certain factors of layout and design are difficult to change and may make the center less optimal than a new center.
• The costs of renovation are more difficult to estimate than those for new construction. Renovation, unlike some new construction, does not lend itself easily to a cookie-cutter approach, and some uncertainty often exists about the structure and what is required to renovate it properly.
• Existing tenants and leases may need to be bought out or removed, which can complicate development and add to costs. Special programs need to be developed to ensure tenants' involvement in the process.
• Construction usually must be managed while the center remains open, necessarily making it less efficient than new construction. Construction is often restricted to nights and early mornings, and extra safety precautions are required.
• Expansion often requires the addition of parking structures, which are more expensive than the surface lots provided with new centers.

Source: Dean Schwanke et al., *Remaking the Shopping Center* (Washington, D.C.: ULI–the Urban Land Institute, 1994), p. 15.

and HVAC costs if the mall is enclosed. The landlord whose negotiating posture is strong may also include a provision for tenants to remodel their own storefronts. Leases should clearly allow the landlord to change the center without the tenants' approval. Some landlords insist on using only short-term leases, with a view toward later incorporating such clauses when they are ready to rehabilitate the center.

Analysis of the Tenant Mix

A tenant's percentage of total floor area and share of sales in each retail category compared with total sales for the center make up the "tenant profile." Ideally, a tenant's sales profile should correspond with the trade area's current expenditure profile for identical categories, but the mathematical relationship between floor area profile and sales profile is not directly proportional. For example, department stores in a regional center might cover 60 to 65 percent of a center's total floor area but represent only 46 percent of the center's total sales, while the stores covering the remaining 35 to 40 percent of floor area are responsible for 54 percent of sales. If the expenditure profile of residents in the trade area indicates they spend equally at department stores and shops, the center is somewhat undermerchandised in terms of department stores. Similarly, overmerchandising could be strongly indicated in a category—for example, shoes—when the center's sales profile corresponds to the trade area's expenditure profile and sales per square foot of its shoe stores are static or below those of shoe stores in other parts of the trade area. Such a tenant group is not necessarily marked for elimination or redirection, however; if the center is expanded and an anchor store added, numerous shoe stores could well be in demand.

An analysis of the tenant mix therefore serves as an additional indicator for potential rehabilitation or expansion. The larger the disparity between center sales and trade area expenditures, the greater the need for rehabilitation. The tenant mix should also be analyzed with regard to how consistent it would be with the center's new image and identity after rehabilitation.

Surveys of Customers

An existing center provides the opportunity to conduct direct market interviews. Interviews of customers can reveal the public's reaction to such matters as image, design of the center, the range of tenant types, the quality of individual tenants, and the center's strengths and weaknesses in terms of customers' preferences. Such interviews also reveal how responsive customers are to marketing and who the center's competitors are. Data obtained from such interviews, if they relate to social and economic characteristics of the trade area in general, can provide information on delineation of the trade area, penetration of the market, market shares and their distribution (geographically and by economic groups), and customers' habits, preferences, and tastes. Properly structured and conducted, interviews can reaffirm or refute the need for rehabilitation.

The Streets at Mayfair, in Coconut Grove, Florida, was an inward-facing mall before its renovation in the late 1990s as an exterior pedestrian promenade. Entertainment retailers, including Planet Hollywood, News Cafe, Borders Books & Music, and Regal Cinemas, were introduced to appeal to customers seeking themed retailing in an outdoor setting.

Analysis of the Potential for Expansion

The last internal factor that should be considered is the center's physical potential for expansion, generally by one of three methods: developing outparcels, developing a portion of the existing parking area, or creating leasable space from part of the common areas. Creating additional leasable space can offset the center's remodeling costs significantly. Although many renovations involve subdividing larger stores into smaller ones, the opposite is also possible if the center needs to accommodate off-price or value retailers or specialized entertainment attractions that need a larger space.

Because of opportunities for shared parking, the development of outparcels with nonretail uses such as offices, hotels, or entertainment attractions may make it possible to create additional leasable space without the accompanying demand for additional parking. Because these nonretail uses tend to experience peak demand for parking at times other than that for retail uses, they could

share parking space with retail uses without conflict, thus eliminating the need to provide additional parking.

Restriping an existing parking lot to reduce the size of spaces or change parking angles sometimes makes it possible to provide more parking within a smaller area, thereby freeing a portion of the existing parking area for the development of additional leasable space. The inappropriate parking standards used for many older centers have resulted in a surplus of parking space even during the busiest hours of the year; such surplus space could provide additional income-producing development areas.

Blank department store walls can be lined with small, high-rent "wall shops," and tenant spaces can be reconfigured to increase the number of spaces, allowing a greater number of tenants. Large common areas in older centers also present opportunities for expansion. Early open malls were usually much wider than necessary for convenient pedestrian circulation. Many were as wide as 60 to 80 feet, twice as great as today's standard of 30 to 40 feet wide.

The updated atrium in the Santana Shopping Center in São Paulo, Brazil, exhibits the iconography and scale of a traditional city streetscape.

An important factor to consider, however, is that making a mall narrower often means deepening existing shops that are already far deeper than is suitable.

In some locations, increasing land values underneath parking lots may justify increasing the density of development and consolidating parking into structured or underground lots. This situation opens opportunities to expand the size of the shopping center, add a mix of uses that will bring new customers to the shopping center, link the center to the surrounding community, permit new retail formats and environments, enhance access for pedestrians, and create more focus for the community.

Market Analysis

The decision to rehabilitate or expand a center rests ultimately on an analysis of external factors. For instance,

American Can, an adaptive use of a former can manufacturing plant in Baltimore, includes a 200-space, two-level parking structure and some surface parking. Peak parking demand for the retail and office uses in this eight-acre facility occurs at different times, eliminating the need for additional parking space.

the locational value of the center should be reassessed based on highway improvements in the trade area, residential expansion, demographic changes such as income and lifestyle, and other commercial developments. Qualitative changes in the composition of neighborhoods should be examined for both positive and negative signs. Trade areas are in constant flux, growing or shrinking vertically and horizontally. The geographic limits of a trade area should be tested before a new anchor store is added to a center. Can the area support another store? Is the economic level of the residents compatible with the quality of the center and its proposed expansion? If an anchor store is added to a center, other companion retail tenants would likely be added in proportion to the expenditure profile of the market area. This factor would indicate the extent of expansion needed. The geographic distribution of specific income groups indicates the quality as well as the quantity of nonanchor stores needed in the center.

The effect of existing and proposed competition is measured qualitatively and quantitatively, because a market area can support only so much of any retail category. A market analysis provides information about income groups in the area and about those groups that go elsewhere to shop. The latter information should suggest the type and quality of stores lacking in the current center. If, for example, 30 percent of the households in a trade area have above-average incomes but only 5 percent of them are represented in an on-site interview sample at the center, most of them probably shop elsewhere. The market analysis helps to determine *why* they

shop elsewhere and whether and how this situation can be changed.

In short, the market analysis identifies who the potential customers are, where they currently shop, and which of their needs are not being met. It also identifies who the current and future competitors are and what needs they serve compared with the subject center. Based on a thorough market analysis, a number of hypotheses for expansion or rehabilitation can be developed. If the market analysis reveals that the addition of an anchor store would benefit the center and land for it is available, this alternative can be explored. Adding a new anchor, which in turn attracts other nonanchor tenants, reduces customers' shopping elsewhere.

When expansion of anchor stores is not possible or the market cannot support it, opportunities could still exist to expand the nonanchor portion of the center, possibly making the center more competitive. Inadequate or only moderate market support will likely rule out rehabilitation as an option. Once the developer understands the factors brought out by the market analysis, he or she can evaluate various scenarios for rehabilitation. Cost estimates developed for the proposed alternatives provide the basis for a financial pro forma.

Financial Analysis

The preparation of a financial analysis is the final step in making a decision whether to rehabilitate or expand a center, or take another course of action. The pro

figure 4-1

Illustrative Trade Area Analysis and Center Correlation to Determine Extent of Renovation/Expansion

Store Classification	Trade Area Potential Total Profile[1] (000)	(%)	Existing Center Sales Profile (000)	(%)	Center Percentage Share[2] Existing	Potential	Potential Volume and Floor Area[3, 4] Sales Profile (000)	(%)	Sales Per Square Foot	Floor Area (Square Feet)	Existing Floor (Square Feet)	Net Addition (Square Feet)
Department	$120,000	54.25	$31,130	69.52	25.94	35.00	$42,000	62.41	$120	350,000	286,000	64,000
Variety	5,000	2.26	1,300	2.90	26.00	25.00	1,250	1.86	85	14,706	20,000	−5,294[5]
Entertainment	13,000	5.88	1,092	2.44	8.40	25.00	3,250	4.83	140	23,214	9,500	13,714
Women's Apparel	22,000	9.95	2,752	6.15	12.51	25.00	5,500	8.17	165	33,333	18,500	14,833
Men's Apparel	5,000	2.26	1,274	2.85	25.48	25.00	1,250	1.86	110	11,364	13,000	−1,636
Children's Apparel	1,400	0.63	420	0.94	30.00	25.00	350	0.52	110	3,182	4,500	−1,318
Accessories	1,200	0.54	588	1.31	49.00	25.00	300	0.45	145	2,069	4,000	−1,931
Shoes	11,000	4.97	4,085	9.12	37.14	25.00	2,750	4.09	185	14,865	25,500	−10,635[5]
Furniture	17,400	N.A.[6]	881	N.A.	N.A.	N.A.	N.A.	N.A.	N.A.	8,000	8,000	0
Furnishings	7,000	3.16	588	1.31	8.40	25.00	1,750	2.60	175	10,000	4,000	6,000
Pictures/Frames	800	0.36	291	0.65	36.38	25.00	200	0.30	105	1,905	2,500	−595
Music	2,400	1.08	550	1.23	22.92	25.00	600	0.89	165	3,636	3,600	36
Electronics	7,000	3.16	0	0.00	0.00	25.00	1,750	2.60	135	12,963	0	12,963
Luggage	800	0.36	190	0.42	23.75	25.00	200	0.30	110	1,818	2,000	−182
Photo	1,600	0.72	105	0.23	6.56	25.00	400	0.59	165	2,424	1,800	624
Cards/Gifts	2,800	1.27	195	0.44	6.96	25.00	700	1.04	185	3,784	3,500	284
Jewelry	7,000	3.16	217	0.48	3.10	25.00	1,750	2.60	215	8,140	5,000	3,140
Sporting Goods	5,000	2.26	0	0.00	0.00	25.00	1,250	1.86	135	9,259	0	9,259
Books	2,400	1.08	0	0.00	0.00	25.00	600	0.89	195	3,077	0	3,077
Hobbies, Toys	4,000	1.81	0	0.00	0.00	25.00	1,000	1.49	145	6,897	0	6,897
Personal Services	1,800	0.81	0	0.00	0.00	25.00	450	0.67	145	3,103	0	3,103
Total	**$238,600**		**$45,658**		**19.14**						**527,739**	**411,400**	
Total Excluding Furniture	**$221,200**	**100.00**	**$44,777**	**100.00**	**20.24**		**$67,300**	**100.00**		**519,739**	**403,400**	**116,339**

[1]As per market analysis.

[2]Existing market share = center sales/trade area potential; potential shares based on market analysis and impact of competition (not shown).

[3]Estimated sales = trade area potential times potential center share.

[4]Floor area based on break-even sales per square foot (estimated sales/sales per square foot).

[5]Tenants to be replaced if feasible.

[6]Not included in profile calculations; tenancy optional.

forma financial analysis should include the following elements:

- Capital costs of all alternatives for rehabilitation or expansion: a full expansion to market limits, including the possibility of structured parking or the acquisition of more land if necessary; a less ambitious expansion, ruling out the addition of a major store; no expansion but rehabilitation of the existing structure; or some simple form of modification.
- Projected sales for all tenants in the center, existing and new, including estimates indicating how rehabilitation would affect marginal existing tenants, which

would help screen tenants for possible elimination and replacement. Screening could be highly subjective, but usually an existing poorly performing tenant is not eliminated unless a proven merchandiser is found to replace it. The main purpose of sales projections is to estimate potential overage rents.

- Rent schedules, reflecting current terms, anticipated gross income from new tenants, and pass-throughs.
- Estimated operating expenses.
- Capitalization (for purposes of evaluating financing alternatives).
- Mortgage and equity requirements to help determine whether to refinance the center, wholly or in part.

figure 4-2
Comparative Pro Forma Financial Analysis: Before and After Renovation
Dollars in Thousands

	Existing	Renovation	Refinance
Net Operating Income	$1,563	$2,637	$2,637
Capitalization			
Rate (%)	9.00	10.50	10.50
Value	$17,367	$25,114	$25,114
Financing			
Mortgage (Outstanding)	4,500	7,060	17,580
Equity—Buildup	10,670	11,310	7,534
Equity—Initial Cash	3,000	3,640	7,534
Total Funding	15,170	18,370	25,114
Debt Service			
Amortization	1,154	1,474	2,198
Principal Outstanding	4,500	7,060	0
Cash Equity Buildup, Cumulative	10,670	11,310	7,534
Cash Flow	409	1,163	440
Cash Flow as Percent of Equity Buildup	3.83	10.28	5.83
Cash Flow as Percent of Initial Cash Equity	13.62	31.94	5.83

- Cash flow analysis to determine present property value estimates or other investment criteria (cash or cash return, return on market equity, or internal rate of return if property is eventually sold).

A financial pro forma developed along these lines provides the ultimate framework on which to base a decision about whether, how, and to what extent to rehabilitate the existing center.

The Approval Process

The approval process for renovation is often fairly straightforward, but expansion can involve more zoning and building approvals than mere rehabilitation. Occasionally, protests by citizens can become an obstacle. It is important to ensure that the existing center is not a legal nonconforming use, because new construction could invalidate the center's legal status. To secure the necessary government approvals for rehabilitation and/or expansion, some or all of the following steps may be necessary:

- Rezoning to a higher density;
- Rezoning for new uses;
- Upgrading the structure to meet current building codes;
- Complying with environmental requirements, such as removing hazardous materials (PCBs or asbestos, for example);

- Complying with provisions of ADA;
- Complying with new sign controls and ordinances; and
- Securing approvals for new road improvements, entrances, turning lanes, and parking configurations.

Changes in Physical Design

Shopping centers generally need to be physically updated every five to ten years because of the intense competition and the fickleness of American consumers, who demand the most up-to-date retail formats, tenant mix, and physical environment. Updating can range from cosmetic improvements to complete rebuilding. If the developer decides to proceed with physical rehabilitation and expansion, detailed plans will be required that consider every aspect of the property—all interior and exterior components of the structures, and all site elements, such as access roads, parking, and landscaping. Although not all elements and components will require physical changes, each must be examined as part of the comprehensive redevelopment to determine which upgrades are required to achieve the envisioned design concept and draw the targeted customers.

Buildings and Common Areas
The condition of existing buildings must first be studied to determine the amount of rehabilitation needed. Signs of deficient maintenance must be corrected, and build-

ings must be made to comply with building codes. A developer considering the acquisition of an older center for rehabilitation and expansion might do well to meet with the local building inspector to get some idea of the extent of rehabilitation necessary to correct existing problems with the overall structure, roofs and skylights, elevators and escalators, entrances and exits, storefronts and signage, flooring, plumbing and the sprinkler system, the HVAC system, lighting and sound systems, security systems, restrooms, merchandise delivery and trash removal systems, and access for handicapped patrons.

In addition to determining necessary functional rehabilitation, the development team must determine the extent and nature of aesthetic rehabilitation needed to improve the center's overall appearance and general shopping environment. Today more than ever the environment of a shopping center is critical to its success, as customers have so many options for buying comparable merchandise. Both the exterior and interior design should be examined for how up-to-date the center is, how well it reflects the desired image, and how attractive and convenient it is for shoppers. An enclosed center built in the 1970s or 1980s, for example, with dark interior finishes, low ceilings, and minimal amenities might require a redesign that includes more architectural diversity; new, lighter finishes; higher-quality materials; skylights; more up-to-date signage and lighting; and the addition of more appealing interior or exterior landscaped areas and pedestrian walkways with fountains, art and sculpture, and seating areas.

For an older open center, it might be advisable to cover parts of existing walkways with arcades or canopies to convey a more intimate character and to protect shoppers from the weather. Creating varied facades, setbacks, materials, and signage along pedestrian walkways could add visual interest as well as the elements of surprise and diversity to the shopping experience.

In the 1970s and even into the 1980s, some older open-air malls were successfully transformed into enclosed malls. In the 1990s, however, the trend has been reversed and some enclosed centers are being demalled to draw customers in from the sidewalk, to create livelier retail districts with streetfront retailing, and to provide a type of shopping experience that is at once "new" and nostalgic. In some locations, town centers are gaining favor. Old Orchard Center, in Skokie, Illinois, for example, is an upscale regional center that kept its open-air form when renovation in 1995 added more than 500,000 square feet of GLA (see the case study in Chapter 7). This approach responds to changing demand from customers and differentiates the shopping center from its many enclosed competitors. The decision whether or not to enclose a center must be based on a thorough analysis of the concept being considered, the competition, consumers' preferences, the site, the climate, and the cost.

Walkways must be carefully examined, as pedestrian surfaces in newer shopping centers are at once more varied and use higher-quality materials. The developer also needs to determine whether they are adequate for

Redevelopment of a central city site in Eindhoven, the Netherlands, created a multistory mixed-use center that includes shopping, offices, and residential uses. Relatively limited retail offerings in the surrounding retail trade area convinced city officials that the concentration of many uses would bring shoppers back downtown.

High demand has fueled rents in Santa Monica's publicly sponsored Third Street retail/entertainment center, even during the recession of the early 1990s. The center has become one of the major nightime gathering places in the Los Angeles area.

The expansion of Phipps Plaza in Atlanta during the 1990s included the rezoning of adjacent property from single-family residential to commercial use. Rezoning required the approval of the city of Atlanta as well as careful consultation with several neighborhood groups.

the efficient and comfortable circulation of pedestrians. In older strip centers, walkways may need to be widened, narrowed, resurfaced, or reconfigured. In any case, interesting and decorative materials should be investigated for use. Ordinary concrete can be made more interesting with brick or wooden spacers, or the concrete itself can be enhanced with color or stamped patterns or textures so that it resembles more costly materials. A high-end renovation might merit walkways made of brick, stone, or clay tiles. In all cases, a key factor in designing walkways and deciding which materials to use is safety. Slippery or otherwise dangerous surfaces must be avoided. Varied surfaces should be considered to differentiate sections of the shopping center with different characters.

Rehabilitation of Facades

The building's facade offers the greatest opportunity for creating a new image that can help to reposition a center, and altering building facades is one of the easiest ways to change dramatically a center's character and appearance. Options to consider range from a minimal program of repainting, adding awnings, and updating signage to a comprehensive rehabilitation that provides an entirely new profile for a center. Either approach is valid, depending on the goals to be achieved and the market potential for recouping the investment.

If the buildings are structurally sound, it may be possible to construct new facades around them, thus avoiding demolition and rebuilding and significantly reducing rehabilitation costs. Constructing new facades around the existing structures also makes it easier for tenants to remain in operation during rehabilitation. Opportunities to reduce the visual impact of an older strip center's length should be examined when rehabilitating the center's facade. Vertical design details (such as clock towers) can provide visual diversity and minimize the effect of the center's horizontal form.

One way to update the physical appearance of a shopping center is to create a memorable architectural theme by creating a visual focus or landmark through towers, a dramatic entry, or an identification sign. A center can be given a skyline through the use of architectural detailing. Better-located, larger, and more visible signage for tenants often improves the appearance of a center at minimal cost. Another way is "rehabilitation by subtraction," that is, removal of dated design features such as canopies.

Differentiating among anchors or developing a hierarchy between anchor tenants and local shops through design elements can update the center's appearance. Special, oversized entry canopies for anchors, a profile involving raised parapets, or striking colors could be used for identification. Removing bulkheads can increase storefront exposure for smaller, nonanchor shops, and it might be desirable to reduce anchor tenants' storefronts to allow greater visibility for smaller stores.

Establishing a budget for rehabilitating a facade requires considerable experience and comparative data. Budgets can vary significantly, depending on the extent of the work to be done. They can range from about $400

Center City Retail Trust is renovating a two-story enclosed mall in Schaumburg, Illinois, transforming it to the Streets of Woodfield. The center will be changed to a pedestrian-oriented neo-traditional town center by rehabilitating the facade to include street-level storefronts oriented toward the sidewalks.

per linear foot of storefront for a minimal facade rehabilitation to as much as $2,000 per linear foot for a more extensive redesign. Spending a great deal on renovating the facade of a relatively shallow store is less cost-effective than renovating a narrow storefront for a deeper store for which the costs of renovation can be recouped by greater square footage within the store.

Lighting

Because lighting is such an important factor in the center's overall appearance, security, and energy consumption, both exterior and interior lighting systems should be carefully inspected and evaluated. Recent innovations in lighting technology have brought better aesthetics along with greater energy and cost-efficiency. Inexpensive sodium vapor lighting is commonly used in parking lots and other exterior common areas of older retail centers, even though it has certain well-known negative attributes. This type of lighting can now be readily avoided, however, with the advent of cost-effective "white" lighting that renders colors well and avoids sodium lighting's eerie and menacing effect. If a center is more than ten years old, chances are that the lighting is outdated and should be upgraded to current standards. And the design of light standards must be compatible with the center's overall design.

Lighting interior common areas is an art, not a science, and it should be carefully coordinated with the center's overall hierarchy of lighting. It must be sufficient to give the shopping environment an engaging and safe appearance without any glare, but it must also create an intimate atmosphere that highlights individual shop windows and their merchandise. Special consideration must be given to the lighting of mall entrances, signs, architectural features and landmarks, and areas of pedestrian circulation. Interior plants, particularly tropical plants, may require special lighting. Lighting can also be used for purely aesthetic reasons and to attract shoppers to the center at night. In a specialty or entertainment center where

Inside and outside, the level of lighting at a shopping center is linked to retailing, entertainment, and potential sales. The right lighting creates a mood, encourages safety, and can boost sales. A poorly lit store renders the merchandise dull and does not encourage lingering. Lighting outside stores enhances the mood for shopping, playing a big part in whether shoppers visit at all.

Car parking facilities are now perceived, often rightly so, as dark, dingy places that are a veritable haven for muggers, keeping shoppers away and sending them elsewhere. Sarah Palliser, retail lighting expert at the Design Solution, offers some observations: "Perceived brightness plays a major role in car park lighting, as brightness is linked to the feeling of safety, which is particularly relevant to female consumers. The problem is not really sodium lighting. This light source is cost-effective and that is why it is used, but it has considerable failings. Sodium renders green, blue, and yellow very badly, so it is often difficult to locate your car in a full car parking facility, because you cannot tell one car from another. More important, flesh tones are rendered badly. With the low level of lighting and the shadows, anyone walking toward you can look menacing."

The right lighting scheme, such as the one designed by the Jerde Partnership for the Beursplein in Rotterdam, creates mood, encourages safety, and can boost sales.

Palliser goes on to offer a solution for car parks: "It is now possible to light car parks with white light using compact fluorescent and even mercury discharge lamps. These light sources are rapidly becoming very cost-effective and have all the advantages of good color rendition and a feeling of safety for customers. If an environment is lit with a white light, everyone can be seen, and that is bad news for criminals."

Floodlighting a building exterior attracts attention and creates a favorable impression with passersby. For storefronts, floodlighting is often a subtle and dignified yet highly effective form of advertising that has the power to attract tourists, especially in major cities, and new retail businesses. Floodlighting old or distinctive buildings also has great potential—not only because the buildings have great architectural features, but also because lighting helps reinforce the image of an area as one of exciting retail streets and parks, even when the shops are closed. In Paris, for example, buildings in the city center are illuminated using only white light, and floodlighting has worked well.

Lighting can be used to link areas, guiding shoppers with a kind of subliminal signage, and to create a mood. Lower floors can be gently dappled with light and have higher ambient light levels than floors above, creating visual interest.

Palliser explains the lighting principles in some of Europe's shopping malls: "In Europe, particularly in Spain, Italy, and France, you have greater use of white light, partly because people there are more nocturnal and it is a way of providing 'daylight.'"

Perhaps the era of interactive video imaging on the fronts and sides of stores will not be far behind. In the meantime, let us just have fewer sodium-lit retail car parks and a better view of our retail entertainment centers.

Source: Excerpted from Steve Thomas Emberson, "Light Entertainment," *Retail Week,* November 14, 1997, p. 15.

themed lighting may be used, however, care must be taken to balance aesthetics with the need for adequate illumination. And because interior lighting should provide a pleasant, natural effect, opportunities to increase natural lighting through skylights and clerestories should be considered.

Signage

Because coordinated signage is an essential component of a center's design, most rehabilitation requires all signs to be replaced. New signage must be compatible with the overall image projected. Although signage needs to be large enough to convey information from appropriate distances, it must not be so large that it overpowers the design of the buildings. Signs vary, depending on whether they are meant to be read from streets or highways adjacent to the center, the parking area, or storefronts. And although graphics should be coordinated, they must strike a balance among the envisioned aesthetic concept, the need for interesting and diverse styles, colors, and designs,

and adequate identification for tenants. Retailers are concerned with maintaining their own identities, which must be taken into consideration.

Parking

The design of the parking lot can be a critical factor in the success of a rehabilitation/expansion project. Parking must be convenient, plentiful, and safe. In considering the possibilities for modifying the existing parking area, a developer should analyze ease of ingress and egress, conflicts between pedestrians and vehicles, and the overall configuration and appearance of the parking area.

Poorly designed entrances and exits not only present a traffic hazard but also cause congestion that can negatively affect a center's image. Vehicular access to the center often can be improved and congestion minimized on adjacent roadways by redesigning entrances so that they penetrate farther into the site and provide stacking space within the parking area. Deeper entrances also facilitate the use of traffic counters. Exiting can be improved by establishing double left-turn lanes out of the center or by providing more sophisticated traffic signals. Possibilities to reduce the number of existing exits and entrances should also be considered. Many older centers have too many curb cuts, making it difficult to control traffic flow. Eliminating some of the superfluous access points makes it easier to control traffic flow. Reducing the number of exits and entrances can also create space for more parking.

Redesigning a shopping center parking lot may also present an opportunity to create more efficient links with neighboring developments. In too many older commercial areas, movement from one shopping center to another requires exiting onto an arterial road rather than traversing a linked parking area. This design creates unnecessary traffic congestion, inconvenience for shoppers, and lost sales because shoppers may be unwilling to try to figure out the traffic maze between centers.

Retail's New Hook

It is happening in London, New York, Cleveland, Santiago, and Singapore: the rediscovery of Main Street is an international phenomenon. Shoppers, retailers, and developers recognize that the alternatively elegant and gritty urban shopping street possesses timeless intangibles. Those intangibles are at the source of the new flow of shopping environments. Traffic noise, the hustle and bustle of crowds, street vendors and musicians, shoppers of every stripe, and eye-catching display windows are all part of the pageantry. Without Main Streets, one cannot fully experience Paris or Chicago or Santa Monica.

Concepts for new retail destinations resemble movie storyboards as much as architectural designs. The intangibles —how people feel while they are there—are now programmed. What do shoppers see first? What sounds do

they hear? What is the story of the destination? How can that story be told in material, color, sound, and signs? The language of retailing has come to include scripting and choreography as developers struggle to capture an increasingly diverse shopping public. Indeed, these same intangible factors are reshaping retailing in many venues —in de-malled malls, in newly urbanized suburban town centers, and in resurgent inner cities.

According to the President's Council on Recreation and Natural Beauty, "By the year 2000, nearly eight out of ten Americans will consider home as an urban setting—not only the place of residence, but the site of most experience." Make no mistake, people want a brand new version of the old downtown. They are willing to demand it, vote for it, and find a way to fund it. The renewed focus on

©Whitecomb 4/98: RTKL Associates Inc.

The Avenue at White Marsh, near Baltimore, re-creates an ideal Main Street through the use of stores fronting the limited-width throughfare, head-in parking, and street trees.

Conflicts between vehicles and pedestrians must be minimized. Ideally, the parking area should be redesigned so that pedestrians walk parallel to moving cars, making visibility better for both drivers and pedestrians. Whenever feasible, raised and landscaped walkways should be provided within parking lots. Because the greatest conflict between pedestrians and vehicles occurs in the "cruising" or fire lane located immediately adjacent to storefront walkways, this lane must be carefully designed to discourage rapidly moving vehicles as well as vehicular movement through the center using this lane. Methods to slow traffic such as speed bumps or narrow lanes may serve this purpose. Vehicular circulation through the site must be directed away from the fire lane to the outer edge of the parking lot where there are fewer pedestrians.

Changing the configuration and appearance of the existing parking lot may also be necessary. The parking revitalization has resulted in incentive programs, including business improvement districts, empowerment zones, and tax-free districts that encourage investment. Early results are in, and urban entertainment districts and Main Street retailing are leading the way.

Even smaller cities are enjoying a renaissance of inner-city retailing. The National Trust for Historic Preservation's National Main Street Center reports that downtown associations in many small towns are successfully recruiting retail tenants from suburban strip centers—many of whom had deserted their Main Streets in the 1970s and 1980s. Small and medium-sized cities are experimenting with new retail strategies, stealing what they can from the big-city models but tailoring the components to their unique locations. "Living over the store" is once again possible in urban neighborhoods in downtown San Diego, San Francisco's Mission District, Dallas's Uptown District, Denver's LoDo and Uptown District, and West Palm Beach, to name a few.

Across the country, developers and their design teams are finding ways to turn malls inside out and create areas that have the vitality of urban shopping streets. The trick to changing a mall is not to contrive a street but to allow the freestyle development of a real street. For example, at the new Citrus Park Town Center in Tampa, Florida, which was completed in 1999, tenants built their own building facades, without a neutral bulkhead above or demising piers between tenants. As tenants change, new lessees will simply take over the previous tenant's "building." Storefronts will not be replaced; rather, building facades will remain, just as they do on a street. Signs, awnings, paint colors, doors, and display windows may be updated, but the sense of the "street" will stay the same.

With competition from both the newly fashionable Main Streets and the recently repositioned regional malls, many secondary shopping centers are losing their drawing power. Astute local governments are searching for new uses for these failing shopping centers. Situated at the confluence of residential areas yet safely distant from major highways, these 70- to 90-acre sites provide excellent opportunities for redevelopment. Through cooperative ventures with local municipalities, these sites can be sculpted into urban blocks and woven into the surrounding street systems. For many classic suburban bedroom communities, these parcels can be transformed into a lively urban core with a combination of office, retail, and medium-density residential space, along with a village green.

What elements are needed in this transformation? Thirty-degree head-in parking, street trees, well-placed traffic lights, limited-width thoroughfares, and carefully integrated parking structures—all of which can be combined to create authentic Main Streets for suburbia. The key lies in allowing greater densities and in resisting the temptation to replace the mall with yet another power center. Success depends on cooperative financing, ownership, and maintenance of the entire development. Suburban communities that long for a small-town center of commerce and a sense of identity are finding the means to achieve them through thoughtful urban planning, careful partnering, and appropriate financing.

The future of retailing is more and more the future of community. Located in revitalized inner cities or on a suburban site enhanced by increased density and a full mix of uses, the new urban villages provide the next development model. People are citizens, workers, and consumers simultaneously. Consequently, they demand more complex and satisfying environments to engage them.

Source: Jeff Gunning et al., "Retail's New Hook," *Urban Land,* July 1998, p. 52.

Bayou Place is a multiuse entertainment destination developed by the Cordish Company in the late 1990s. Renovation and transformation of a closed and deteriorated 1960s convention center created a distinctive pedestrian-oriented destination in the heart of Houston.

lot typically is placed at the front of the center and thus must be made an integral part of the center's overall design. An unattractive parking lot detracts considerably from the center's curb appeal. One of the most logical ways to improve the appearance as well as the functioning of the parking area is to break up the sea of asphalt by installing strategically placed plants and berms, which might include along the perimeter of the site as well as landscaped islands in the parking area. In addition to improving aesthetics, landscaping can aid drainage and lessen the environmental impact of large parking lots. The introduction of attractively designed outparcels adjacent to access roads can also improve the aesthetics of the parking lot.

In most older centers, parking lots need to be restriped and/or repaved, offering the chance to change the size of stalls, angles, and the widths of bays to make more

efficient use of the parking area. Rearranging an existing parking area to accommodate compact cars can also improve capacity, adding spaces in the same area or maintaining the same number of spaces in less area (although, as noted earlier, it is difficult to estimate how many small parking spaces would be used at shopping centers).

Another consideration is whether to expand parking by means of structured or underground garages. When a large expansion is considered and additional land is too expensive or unavailable, structured parking may be the only option. It is also expensive, however, typically costing about $10,000 per stall. Thus, the feasibility of adding structured parking must be carefully considered as part of the process to determine whether the proposed expansion makes economic sense.

Like all other elements of the shopping center, a parking garage should be designed to enhance the center's overall look. Safety is a major issue, and large, multistory parking garages should be equipped with roving security guards and/or electronic monitors. Good lighting in parking lots is crucial for customers' and employees' safety and security.

Landscaping and Street Furniture

In the rehabilitation of an existing center, improving the landscaping may range from a simple refurbishment of existing landscaping to its total replacement. Plants must be carefully selected and placed to soften the center's appearance while not blocking views of signage and storefronts. Landscaping must also allow adequate sight distances within parking areas and at vehicular entrances and exits. Plantings, both exterior and interior, should provide as much permanent, year-round greenery as possible and should be highlighted with color from seasonal flowering plants. Indigenous plants are preferred for exterior landscaping, because they are most likely to withstand local climatic extremes and cost less to maintain. They also add to the local character and authenticity of the shopping environment. Interior plants should be

figure 4-3

Most Frequently Found Outparcels in U.S. Super Regional and Regional Shopping Centers

In Descending Order

Super Regional Centers	Regional Centers
Bank	Bank
Restaurant (with liquor)	Restaurant (with liquor)
Restaurant (without liquor)	Hamburgers
Supermarket	Automotive
Liquor/Wine	Cinema
Cinema	Restaurant (without liquor)
Automotive (TB&A)	
Toys	
Service Station	

Source: *Dollars & Cents of Shopping Centers: 1997* (Washington, D.C: ULI–the Urban Land Institute, 1997).

chosen for the drama they impart to the center's overall appearance, the cost of installation and maintenance, and the need for special lighting or temperatures.

Furniture (benches, planters, and trash receptacles) should be selected for its design and durability. Furniture in an older center usually needs to be replaced, as it most likely is worn and its design out of date. Although the cost of new mall furniture is generally small compared with the project's total cost (1 percent or less is typical), the effect of mall furniture on the center's overall appearance is significant.

Marketing

Coordination of Tenants

Renovation and expansion of any older center generally involves more than physical changes to the center. The rehabilitation must be coordinated carefully with tenants. And because it must be consistent with the new image and identity being created for the center, the tenant mix must likely be changed or upgraded.

Successful rehabilitation requires the enthusiastic support and cooperation of tenants, which will depend on the developer's frequent communication and consultation with them. The developer should not announce the rehabilitation to tenants without first thoroughly reviewing and analyzing the existing mix and the status of all leases to locate possible obstacles to the rehabilitation.

Following this tenant-by-tenant analysis, the developer will be in a position to inform the tenants of impending rehabilitation by meeting with them to review the rationale for the renovation, the planned architectural design, changes to signage, the construction schedule, the period of time that tenants will be without identifying signage, and the steps that will be taken to minimize the inconvenience to tenants and shoppers. If some tenants are expected to move to a new position within the mall permanently or temporarily while their spaces are being redeveloped, the terms must be negotiated privately with the affected tenants. Adjustments to rent during the disruption will likely be required, and some desirable tenants may choose to leave the center during reconstruction. These realities need to be factored into the economic equation before renovation is undertaken.

The developer also needs to let tenants know what is expected of them during and after renovation with regard to increased common area maintenance and operation costs, additional merchants' association assessments to pay for the grand reopening, the removal of old signs and acquisition of new ones, and similar items. Most important, the developer must convince tenants at this meeting that the renovation is in their best interests by reviewing with them the concept for the renovated center and the advantages they can expect as a result of the reconstruction. Tenants must be reassured and convinced that sales lost during reconstruction (if any) and their increased operating costs following rehabilitation will be

The entrance to the rehabilitated historic One Colorado in Pasadena includes extensive landscaping and street furniture to attract pedestrians into a once abandoned alley.

more than offset by a greater number of shoppers and higher sales volumes.

After this initial meeting, the developer is in a position to renegotiate leases with individual tenants, keeping in mind that existing tenants can be an excellent source of referrals for other potential tenants. Although lease renegotiation varies from tenant to tenant, tenants generally seek several changes during renegotiation: additional renewal options, an extended term in which to

City Halls in the Malls

Where do you go to renew your driver's license, pay your water bill, return your library books, process your passport application, or receive free math tutoring? Increasingly, your local shopping center.

As a way to increase efficiency in providing services to citizens, many local jurisdictions are opening "storefronts" in their neighborhood malls. A distinctive addition to the tenant mix of shopping centers, these city storefronts—satellite city halls, citizen service centers, and city halls in the mall as they are typically called—are being met with much enthusiasm by local residents.

Information on programs and services offered by city departments, city job listings, reference materials related to city codes and ordinances and the comprehensive city plan, and board and commission agendas and summaries are typically available at these city storefronts. In addition, local jurisdictions usually make available the ability to pay bills, drop off job applications, return library books, register for city recreation programs, and renew or obtain licenses for your dog, your moped, or your bicycle at these locations.

- The city and county of Honolulu processes building permits at various satellite facilities on a daily rotating schedule.
- The county of Palm Beach, Florida, in partnership with the city of Boynton Beach and Bethesda Memorial Hospital, offers blood pressure checks, classes in CPR, and other programs through the hospital physicians.
- The city of Tallahassee provides materials for hurricane and other disaster preparedness.
- The city of Stockton, California, offers adoptions of rescued dogs and cats and provides weekday afternoon math tutoring for high school students.

Source: Jeffrey L. Hinkle.

amortize interior store improvements, a contribution from the developer for the cost of new signage, opportunities to expand or relocate the store, and a construction allowance for leasehold improvements and/or a new storefront. Developers usually seek a capital contribution from the tenant for the cost of rehabilitation, an increase in rent, the conversion of gross leases to net leases, extensions of lease terms for key tenants (an important factor in obtaining new financing for the rehabilitation), an increased contribution for common area maintenance, modification of restrictive covenants, tenants' rehabilitation of storefronts and store interiors, and the possible expansion of key tenants when space is available.

Scheduling and Logistics

Rehabilitation or expansion should be carefully planned and scheduled to allow the center to remain fully operational during the construction period. Interference with traffic carrying shoppers must be minimized to avoid the loss of sales revenue and to protect against potential liability. Entrances and exits to the center (both vehicular and pedestrian) should not be blocked during construction, and it is essential that the site be kept as clean as possible (with daily cleanups by the general contractor). Arrangements should also be made for temporary services needed to provide a convenient, safe atmosphere (temporary lighting, warning signs, barricades, security guards, and so forth). Building materials should not be delivered during peak shopping hours. And construction generally should not occur during the peak retail season; ideally, construction should start after Easter and be completed before Thanksgiving.

Finally, it is imperative that the developer explain the objectives for rehabilitation and expansion to all members of the development team. Rapport must be established among members of the team, and they must agree on the project's proposed schedule and meet the required deadlines. A tenant coordinator is a key member of the team and should be on board before and during construction to assist tenants.

Marketing the New Center

A complete promotional campaign should be developed for the project consisting of preconstruction announcements, promotion during the renovation, promotion for the grand reopening, and the grand reopening itself. A well-executed promotional campaign, capitalizing on the excitement of the renovation, can actually increase sales activity during construction. When renegotiating leases, the developer/owner should make certain that an assessment for the grand reopening is included in all new leases.[4]

Problems in Rehabilitation and Expansion

Renovation of a shopping center is a complex undertaking. Although the rewards can be significant, numerous problems can arise. Being aware of them can help the developer avoid, or at least plan for, them. The following list describes major problems that can arise during the course of rehabilitation or expansion:

- Unexpected Building Obsolescence—An aging physical plant, particularly roofs, parking lots, and mechanical systems, can be costly to replace or repair. Structural failure can result from lengthy exposure to the elements during reconstruction, and the penetration of

water into the subsurface over a period of years may have caused heaving of slabs and paving, and possibly structural movement.

- Inadequate Structural Design—Roof loads for new mechanical equipment often exceed the building's original capacity. Additionally, any new facade contemplated could require new structural support. Adding such structures can be expensive and disruptive

The expansion of Oak Park Mall in Overland Park, Kansas, included this new wing designed by RTKL. The new wing created additional space for Nordstrom, an existing anchor tenant.

David Whitcomb/RTKL

A pilot project to offer one-stop employment services to retailers has been enacted by National Retail Federation (NRF) of Washington, D.C., American Express Travel Related Services Co. of New York, Kravco Co. of King of Prussia, Pennsylvania, and the commonwealth of Pennsylvania. Located at the Plaza and Court at King of Prussia (owned by Kravco), the Retail Skills Center assists retailers in recruiting, training, and placing employees.

The retail industry has undergone profound changes in recent years, notes Tracy McMullen, NRF's president. "The need for highly skilled workers in our industry has never been greater," he explains. "This partnership helps bring together the resources and technology needed to create a strong, competitive workforce."

The impetus for the skills center was the expansion of the Court at King of Prussia (the mall has more than 400 stores), which has increased the demand for skilled retail sales associates. In addition to unemployed workers or adults in transition, the skills center is open to high school and community college students who are entering the job market. It is also open to the Court's current sales associates who want to improve their skills and options for a retail career.

The Retail Skills Center at the Plaza and Court at King of Prussia combines computerized instruction and workshops.

The Retail Skills Center combines self-paced, computerized instruction with workshops to provide skills in customer service, selling and promoting products, monitoring inventory, maintaining a store's appearance, protecting company assets, and teamwork. Job placement, mentoring, and career guidance also are part of the program.

The center's standards for skills were set by NRF using guidelines provided by the National Skills Standards Board. Leading retailers such as Sears, Federated Department Stores, JCPenney, Crate & Barrel, Circuit City, and Nordstrom also contributed to the process. Nonprofit training vendors TRAC/USA of Alexandria, Virginia, and Public/Private Ventures of Philadelphia developed materials for training and assessment, as did NCS/London House of Minneapolis.

Staffing and operating expenses for the center are paid with a three-year grant from American Express. By 2000, King of Prussia's Retail Skills Center will be self-sufficient, NRF predicts. The federation anticipates ongoing support from labor and employment organizations, and local educational institutions. It also expects to institute a fee for employed program participants.

Expectations are high for the center. "Time and time again, we've heard from employers that they can't find workers with the skills to succeed," says Pennsylvania Governor Tom Ridge. "This unique partnership helps ensure that this is not the case in King of Prussia. And for those desiring the skills to go to work, this program lends that helping hand."

NRF reports that it will roll out the concept of the Retail Skills Center in additional shopping center and retail locations.

for existing tenants, and can inconvenience and discourage shoppers.

- Inadequate Utility Service—Utility service to a building may be adequate for its current or previous use but may be woefully inadequate for additional demand. Some uses require significantly more electrical, water, and/or sanitary sewer service. Subdividing a large space into two or more uses and thus providing individual service to each user usually requires at least more electrical service but can also require extending sewer lines and cutting out the floorslab. Sometimes the sewer line is not deep enough to extend it. Each utility should be checked for adequacy based on the new design.

- Inappropriate Depths in Stores—Older centers may have many 100- to 140-foot-deep nonanchor stores, and newer centers may have too many shallow stores. It is easy to handle the deeper stores by lowering the rent or sizing down the space with interior partitions and leasing the remaining areas as warehouse space as long as the economics of the center make it possible. Expanding the depth of shallow space, however, is much more costly, especially if utilities exist on the rear walls.

- Asbestos—With renovation of a building more than ten to 15 years old, demolition will probably involve asbestos abatement, a costly and time-consuming process. Before beginning acquisition or renovation, the developer must have appropriate environmental testing performed. Failure to do so could be very costly.

- Trauma to Tenants during Construction—Unless visibility and access during construction are handled appropriately, some small tenants may go out of business. This risk is a major problem to overcome during renovation.

- Loss of "Grandfather" Protection—Depending on municipal codes, some redevelopment may mandate bringing the center up to current zoning and building codes for parking requirements, accessibility for the handicapped, sprinklers, use of noncombustible building materials, and landscaping requirements. Moreover, many municipalities now impose impact fees, often requiring the developer to provide significant improvements to off-site infrastructure before approvals will be granted.

- Higher Real Estate Taxes—Renovation will probably trigger a higher appraisal for real estate taxes. If the property has been significantly undervalued, the developer must consider the impact on operating expenses passed on to tenants. The developer must also consider the potential for reduced cash flow in leases where expense pass-throughs are not the full responsibility of the tenant.

- Renegotiation of Long-Term, Low-Rent Leases—Long-term leases with low market rents may need to be renegotiated. Such negotiations can be very difficult if the tenant recognizes the value of the leasehold interest.

- Onerous Lease Provisions—The developer needs to determine what degree of approval rights existing

Aging structures or physical plants can make rehabilitation costly. A prime location in downtown Sydney, Australia, near mass transit and heavy pedestrian traffic, however, makes the restoration and expansion of the historic Grace Bros department store feasible.

tenants have in the shopping center. Site plan controls may require tenants' approval before any additions are made, and existing tenants may have very liberal subletting provisions that inhibit the developer's ability to control the space. Old leases may contain onerous provisions for the contribution of extra charges. Some leases require that architectural approvals be obtained before any modifications to the shopping center begin.

- Stigma of Failure—If the building housing anchor tenants has been the home of several failed retail operations, customers and tenants may resist the location. The developer should determine such intangible factors early, neutralizing them by meeting them head on.

- Financing—Lenders are generally skeptical of redevelopment projects until substantial preleasing has occurred. It is often difficult to obtain satisfactory appraisals, and permanent lenders may be skeptical about making forward commitments on the project.[5]

Notes

1. *Shopping Center Directory* (Chicago: National Research Bureau, 1998), p. 1.

2. For more detail, see Dean Schwanke et al., *Remaking the Shopping Center* (Washington, D.C.: ULI–the Urban Land Institute, 1994).

3. *Dollars & Cents of Shopping Centers* provides comprehensive and authoritative data for shopping center sales as well as for sales for more than 175 different categories of tenants in each of the various types of centers.

4. See Schwanke et al., *Remaking the Shopping Center,* for examples of successful marketing and promotion campaigns.

5. Participants' manual for "Shopping Centers: How to Build, Buy, and Redevelop," a workshop sponsored by ULI, pp. 65–67. See also Schwanke et al., *Remaking the Shopping Center,* for a more detailed discussion of the renovation and expansion of shopping centers, as well as case study examples.

5. Tenants

The retail tenants of a shopping center are its lifeblood, and ultimately it is the tenants that make a center viable. But it is the developer who melds all the components of a center—its tenants, its building structure, and its site attributes—into an environment that gives a shopping center its competitive edge, particularly as many tenants appear in more than one shopping center in the same trade area. Despite the importance of the preliminaries in planning for the type and size of a center, site work and building construction cannot begin until anchor tenants are identified, selected, and committed. The need to secure anchor tenants cannot be overemphasized. At the beginning, reliable commitments rather than agreements to precise lease provisions are sufficient. Specific terms can be negotiated later. Whether or not anchor tenants are to lease space in a shell or in a finished building, or are to lease space independently or to buy land, binding overall commitments should be obtained before building begins and final site layouts are prepared.

The anchor tenants—whether supermarkets, discount stores, category killers, or full-line department stores—should be tied in closely with the development team at the planning stage. They will influence the developer's decisions on building layout and architectural style and even on parking, lighting, signage, and landscaping. Moreover, at the early stages of planning, major tenants should

Tenant spaces in Universal CityWalk are individually crafted to create a livelier and more entertaining shopping environment.

agree to items such as common area maintenance, taxes, and participation in the center's promotional programs.

Anchor Tenants

A center's tenant mix cannot be decided by a formula; each community and each shopping center are different. Any list of tenant classifications most frequently found in a given type of center can serve only as a guide in selecting tenants. Based on market and feasibility studies, a shopping center's composition is determined ultimately by the developer's search for and negotiation with tenants. It also depends on the type of center to be built. Once a developer knows the characteristics of the market the center will serve, he or she can decide first on anchor tenants and then on smaller stores.

The following outline describes anchor tenants for various types of centers (see also Chapter 1):

- The anchor tenant in a *convenience center* is typically a minimarket, although some convenience centers are organized around a specialized service such as food, personal services, or office services.
- A supermarket or a megasupermarket/drugstore combination is the key tenant in a *neighborhood center*. Other principal tenants may be a drugstore and/or a variety store. Neighborhood centers also usually include personal services, food services, and convenience goods

Phillips Place, a suburban mixed-use center near Charlotte, North Carolina, includes a 130,000-square-foot retail component that is designed to be like an old Main Street. The Harris Group actively sought national tenants that were not already present in the Charlotte market. Strong population growth and high median family incomes in the area convinced the development team that national tenants would be successful.

tenants. In lieu of a supermarket as the anchor tenant, some neighborhood centers have a combination of food tenants that are equivalent to a supermarket.

- The anchor tenant for a *community center* is most often a discount or off-price department store, a specialty store (such as a hardware/building/home improvement store), or a combined drug/variety/garden store. A junior department store or a large variety store may also serve as the anchor tenant in the community center, although this practice is no longer as common as it was in the past. Supplementary tenants include those that might be found in a neighborhood center, with added representation in shopping goods, particularly in apparel and home furnishings. A community center may also include banking and professional services, recreational facilities, and tenants that are unlikely to be found in a regional center, such as hardware, garden, and building supply stores. A community center does not have a full-line department store as anchor.

- *Regional centers,* by definition, include at least one full-line department store with at least 75,000 square feet of GLA. A majority of regional centers include two or more such department stores. The roster of supplemental tenants draws upon all classifications of tenants. Several stores from the same category are customarily included, allowing the final composition of tenants to represent as closely as possible the ranges in price and merchandise once found only in downtowns.

- *Super regional centers* include three or more full-line department stores of generally no less than 100,000 square feet each and a total center GLA of at least 500,000 square feet. Some super regional centers may have up to five or six department stores and a gross leasable area of more than 1.5 million square feet.

- By definition, *power centers* have four or more big-box anchors containing at least 20,000 or more square feet and a large off-price discount department store or warehouse store of at least 100,000 square feet. These anchors contain at least 25 percent of the center's gross leasable area.

- *Specialty centers* do not need an anchor tenant from the traditional categories. The grouping of tenants is determined by the special nature of the trade area or according to the tenants' suitability to a specific structure, such as a rehabilitated historic structure. In some specialty centers, a group of tenants such as a food-service cluster, high-fashion shops, home design stores, or a cinema complex may effectively serve as an anchor.[1]

The gross leasable area of specialty centers may range widely, depending on the special circumstances of type and location. Although the center's size and market area are not directly related, a specialty center's market—neighborhood, community, or region (including tourists)—is a guide to the center's size. A variety of tenants—boutiques, import shops, high-fashion or specialty apparel shops, arts and crafts stores, hobby shops or other specialty stores, food stores, entertainment, and food-service outlets—may be suitable, depending on the character, quality, and drawing power of the location.

Any specialty center must have at least one prime or anchor tenant (or a group of tenants that serve as a "cluster" anchor, such as the food-service and food tenants in a food court). The key tenant varies with the type of specialty center and its market. A tourist-oriented retail or retail entertainment center, such as South Street Seaport in New York or CocoWalk in Miami, typically has a high percentage of GLA devoted to specialty restaurants and food vendors. Retail goods at these centers tend to emphasize impulse and specialty items. Such centers are typically linked to surrounding pedestrian-oriented commercial districts and form anchors for the retail, entertainment, historic, and cultural activities found there.

In all types of centers, the developer needs to be flexible and creative in selecting tenants and negotiating with them. Numerous adjustments will likely be made in interior arrangements and leases during development to accommodate the evolving tenant mix, especially in urban entertainment centers, where anchor tenants typically are spaced throughout the center. Under normal conditions, key tenants commit themselves to a substantial percentage of the center's planned GLA before final construction drawings are made; otherwise, the development takes on aspects of a speculative enterprise.

Classification

Tenants are classified in several ways, including categories of merchandise, overall credit rating, and ownership. Some definitions are useful in describing prospective tenants by classification of ownership:

- A *national chain store* operates in four or more metropolitan areas in three or more states.
- An *independent store* has no more than two outlets in only one metropolitan area.
- A *local chain store* falls into neither of the preceding two categories.

The classifications by type of merchandise (see Figure 5-1) are those established for ULI's *Dollars & Cents of Shopping Centers: 1997*. The principal groups are generally related to major standard industrial classification codes.[2]

Placement of Anchors

Placement of anchor tenants usually follows two simple guidelines: locate them so that shoppers must walk past the storefronts of supplementary tenants to reach them, and separate them so that all supplementary tenants are passed on the way to and from the anchors. They should be placed at opposite ends of a strip center or mall, for example, rather than side by side near the center. Multiple anchors should be spaced in a way that draws customers through the center and leaves no walkways without

Entertainment features have been added to the list of upscale tenants at South Coast Plaza, a super regional center in Orange County, California, to broaden the center's appeal.

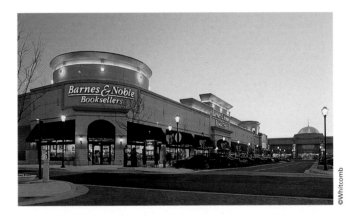

The Avenue at White Marsh in Maryland strategically spaces major tenants to ensure that enough spillover traffic reaches the smaller tenants in the center.

an anchor. Major building entrances and exits, whether to the street or to parking, should be arranged so that customers can move to and from the key tenants conveniently while also being exposed to as many other tenants as possible.

Tenants may have strong and seemingly arbitrary views about where they will or will not be located in a center. A location, or level, that is advantageous for one type of business may be entirely inappropriate for another, and placement in relation to the overall composition of tenants is often critical. Grouping tenants in the center may follow either "mix" or "match" principles so long as it sustains the interest of customers and draws shoppers through the entire center. Stores may be arranged in affinity groupings, such as an entertainment-oriented wing, but even in this case mixing specific tenant types is essential and complex.

Logical clusters include service and repair shops, food and food services, high-fashion stores, entertainment, and home improvement, appliance, and home furnishings stores. The merchandising principles involved in determining the array of tenants in a shopping center are similar to those used by successful full-line department stores to determine locations for the various departments within the store.

Stores offering convenience goods or personal services should be easily and quickly accessible from the parking area. A long walk into a mall to reach a convenience store is neither welcomed by customers nor appropriate for tenants. Certain stores, such as supermarkets, dry cleaners, and carryouts, are not usually tenants in malls because their purposes, market areas, and rent structures are not those of typical mall tenants. Because customers visit them frequently, they are usually located closer and more conveniently to peoples' homes or places of employment.

A developer should consider several factors in locating tenants in any type of center:

figure 5-1
Tenant Classifications

General Merchandise	Pretzel Shop	Maternity	**Home Appliances/Music**
Full-Line Department Store	Cookie Shop	Hosiery	Appliances
(owned)	Sandwich Shop	Hat Shop	Audio/Video
Full-Line Department Store	Hot Dogs/Corn Dogs	Children's Wear	Sewing Machines
(unowned)	Hamburgers	Men's Wear	Record/Tape
Junior Department Store	Barbecue	Family Wear	Musical Instruments
Variety Store	Seafood/Fish and Chips	Fur Store	Gourmet Cookware
Discount Department Store	Potatoes/French Fries	Jeans Shop	Computer/Software
Showroom/Catalog Store	Pizza	Leather Shop	Electronics, General
Warehouse Club	Chicken/Turkey	Uniform Shop	
Dollar Store/Novelties	Salads/Fruit	Special Apparel–Unisex	**Building Materials/Garden**
	Coffee/Tea	Costume Jewelry	Paint and Wallpaper
Food	Drinks/Juice/Lemonade		Hardware
Meat, Poultry, and Fish	Bagels	**Shoes**	Home Improvements
Specialty Food	Chinese Fast Food	Family Shoes	Specialty Hardware
Delicatessen	Japanese Fast Food	Women's Shoes	
Bakery	Other Asian Fast Food	Men's Shoes	**Automotive**
Candy and Nuts	Mexican Fast Food	Children's Shoes	Automotive (TB&A)
Dairy Products	Other Latin American	Athletic Footwear	Service Station
Health Food/Supplements	Fast Food		Automobile Showroom
Supermarket	Greek Fast Food	**Home Furnishings**	
Warehouse	Italian Fast Food	Furniture	**Hobby/Special Interest**
Convenience Market	Other European Fast Food	Lamps	Sporting Goods, General
Gourmet Grocery	Middle Eastern Fast Food	Floor Coverings	Hobby
	Popcorn	Curtains and Drapes	Art Gallery
Food Service	Steak/Roast Beef	China and Glassware	Cameras
Restaurant without Liquor	Caribbean Fast Food	Bath Shop/Linens	Toys
Restaurant with Liquor	Other Fast Food/Carryout	Home Accessories	Bike Shop
Cafeteria		Cutlery Store	Arts and Crafts
Cocktail Lounge	**Clothing and Accessories**	Kitchen Store	Coin Shop
Doughnut/Muffin Shop	Women's Specialty	Container Store	Outfitters
Ice Cream Parlor	Women's Ready-to-Wear	Closet Store	Game Store
Yogurt Shop	Bridal Shop		Science/Nature Store

- The tenant's suitability for the location, as well as the amount of rent the tenant is able to pay;
- Local preferences for certain tenants;
- Compatibility and complementary status among adjoining stores;
- Compatibility of the tenant's merchandising practices with those of adjoining stores;
- Parking needs generated by the tenant;
- Convenience for customers.

Tenant Mix

The tenant classifications by type of center shown in the *Dollars & Cents of Shopping Centers* series might suggest common tenant mixes. However, the exact tenant mix for a specific center is naturally affected by the specific circumstances of leasing, financing, and availability of tenants for a particular trade area (see *Dollars & Cents of Shopping Centers: 1997* for a suggested mix of tenants by type of center). In fact, a tenant appropriate for one center could be a mistake in another. The selection of types of stores must be left to individual developers, who will base their choices on varying income ranges and other characteristics of the market area, local buying habits, store sizes, and merchandising practices in different site conditions and various geographic areas. Nevertheless, certain types of stores tend to be prevalent in particular types of centers. Nearly every neighborhood center, for example, except for the new specialty or high-fashion centers, contains a drugstore and a food-service store and supermarket.

Leasing brokers, appraisers, landlords, and shopping center operators have learned some lessons about grouping certain kinds of businesses:

- Men's stores—shoes, clothing, and sporting goods—tend to increase each other's volume.

Religious Store
Collectibles
Medical/Health and
  Wellness Equipment

Gifts/Specialty
Imports
Luggage and Leather
Cards and Gifts
Candle Shop
Books
Decorative Accessories
Stationery
Newspapers/Magazines
Movie Studio Store
Christmas Store
Party Store
Baby Store
Aromatherapy Store
Calendar Store

Jewelry
Jewelry

Liquor
Liquor/Wine

Drugs
Drugstore/Pharmacy

Other Retail
Fabric Shop
Tobacco

Pet Shop
Flowers/Plant Store
Telephone Store/Telecom
Eyeglasses/Optician
Cosmetics/Beauty Supplies
Office Supplies
Clocks/Watches
Sunglasses
Other Retail

Personal Services
Women's Hair Salon
Men's Barber
Shoe Repair
Dry Cleaner
Laundry
Photographer
Formal Wear/Rental
Interior Decorator
Travel Agent
Key Shop
Unisex Hair
Film Processing
Photocopy/Fast Print
Rental Shop
Video Tape Rentals
Tailor
Weight Loss Center
Mailing/Packaging
Nail Salon
Tanning Salon
Picture Framing
Tattoo Parlor

Day Spa
Massage
Other Services

Entertainment/Community
Post Office
Music Studio and Dance
Bowling Alley
Daycare and Nursery
Lottery
Health Club
Martial Arts
Armed Forces Recruiting
Learning Center/College
House of Worship
Cinema, General (tickets & concessions)
Cinema, Special Format (tickets & concessions)
Video Arcade
Childrens's Play Gym
Gaming/Wagering Parlor
Performance Club
Other Specialty Entertainment Attraction

Financial
Bank
Savings and Loan
Finance Company
Brokerage
Insurance
Real Estate

Automatic Teller Machine

Offices (Other than Financial)
Optometrist
Medical and Dental
Legal
Accounting
Employment Agency
Government
Veterinary
Other Offices

Parking at community centers, such as Perimeter in Atlanta, should provide easy access to each of the center's stores.

Kieran Reynolds

Outlet centers have no specific anchor tenant, although one or more of its most famous brand names may perform this role.

- Similarly, women's apparel, shoes, and children's clothes and toys perform better if located close to each other.
- Food product businesses—groceries, meat and fish markets, delicatessens, bakeries, doughnut shops, and confectioners—do well when grouped together.
- Stores selling personal services and conveniences are naturally compatible.

It is difficult to quantify the effect of store types and groupings because so many variables come into play. One immeasurable factor is the ability of a particular merchant to work as a member of the merchandising team—the team that ultimately becomes the shopping center.

Theoretically, in a well-laid-out shopping center, all locations are good, and each carries equal advantage for some tenant's high-volume retailing. As a result, the long-established retail theory of the "100 percent location" that was once applied to downtowns should not be reflected

in well-designed shopping centers. Certain types of tenants do not require prime locations in a mall or center, and, in fact, what is prime for one tenant may not be prime for another.[3] Banks, travel agencies and other services, and restaurants are suited to side corridors, pad sites, or other locations that would be undesirable for stores selling, say, impulse goods.

When choosing stores for a center in a new growth area, the developer must secure shops that can render a service to the trade area and that have the financial stamina to weather a pioneering period until the trade area matures. Other special points to consider are tenants' credit rating, profit and loss statements, advertising policy, type of merchandise, class of customers, housekeeping practices, long-term operational record, merchandising policy, and integrity.

Certain axioms about grouping stores have grown out of experience with shopping centers. Tenants should be arranged to provide the greatest amount of interplay

Universal CityWalk, a regional entertainment center, benefits from visitors to Universal Studios, who are attracted to CityWalk's theaters, restaurants, and entertainment stores. UCLA leases space on the second level for continuing education courses.

Stephen Simpson

among stores. In neighborhood and community centers, the location of a supermarket should be carefully chosen because of the heavy demand for parking spaces. If the supermarket (or a cinema, for that matter) has no convenient parking, there will be no customers.

A supermarket is typically the major tenant in a neighborhood center, with a drugstore often occupying the second highest percentage of total GLA. Community centers provide a greater array of tenants than neighborhood centers. Classifications of tenants for regional and super regional centers depend first on lease negotiations with anchor tenants (typically department stores). In super regional centers, the merchandising plan requires even greater care than in smaller centers to place small tenants in the path of pedestrian circulation among the larger department stores, specialty stores, and quality restaurants.[4]

A regional center must be all-inclusive and self-sufficient, suggesting the importance of grouping stores. To be self-

sufficient, the center must have not only stores with big drawing power but also a full range of merchandise available to shoppers, including nearly every retail offering once found in downtown shopping districts. The amount of sales space for each category should be based on the estimated sales volume that can be captured in each retail segment, based on the market analysis. Increasingly, tenants in regional and super regional centers are chosen for their lifestyle orientation, brand identity, and merchandise setting, which closely reflect customers' aspirations and interests. The environment that these tenants and their merchandise create provides a powerful draw for customers who might otherwise be tempted to shop at off-price centers or to shop online.

When discussing anchor tenants and other tenants most frequently associated with a certain shopping center type, one tends to assume the absence of all other tenant types. But each type can occur at different frequencies in different centers. The success of a shopping center's

In summer 2000, Phoenix-based Westcor Partners will introduce Denver area shoppers to the retail concept it hopes will increase dwindling mall traffic while meeting the competition posed by power centers and reemerging urban downtowns. FlatIron Crossing, a new 1.5 million-square-foot regional mall slated to open northwest of Denver in Broomfield, Colorado, will merge an upscale fashion mall with an outdoor park and a contemporary main street.

With its combination of indoor fashion offerings and outdoor Main Street shopping, dining, and entertainment, FlatIron Crossing aims to offer many vistas that will encourage visitors to stay until the late movie ends.

"We've concluded that future regional malls need to be upscale in design and fashion merchandise, and they need to offer a lifestyle experience. We focus on the word 'experience' rather than entertainment, a direction other developers have taken," says Dave Scholl, Westcor's senior vice president.

The idea of combining an enclosed shopping center with an outdoor village gives rise to an exciting leasing strategy for FlatIron, according to Fred Collings, senior vice president of leasing for Westcor. "We have an opportunity, probably one of the first ever, to commingle these two concepts on the same property," he says.

"In FlatIron Village [the Main Street of shops, restaurants, and entertainment venues], we hope to create a host of restaurant opportunities," Collings continues. "We also hope to have a gourmet grocery, a pharmacy, a hardware store, a garden shop, financial services offerings, and basic services such as shoe repair and dry cleaning. The idea of the village is to provide a whole range of services

so that the village and the mall together become a true one-stop shopping destination."

Westcor intends to focus leasing in the village on local tenants. Executives note that because the area has been underserved by national retailers, shoppers have come to rely on a number of popular local merchants. Toward the end of Main Street, for example, leasing plans call for a major bookstore, an amphitheater, and a 16- to 20-screen theater complex that may include feature independent films.

The enclosed mall will house four additional anchors, including Nordstrom, Foley's, and Lord & Taylor. Specialty retail space in the mall will total 650,000 square feet. Collings hopes to assemble a roster of upscale retailers consistent with those in other Nordstrom-anchored centers to fill that space. "We have had extremely positive responses from a host of retailers already," he says.

Collings sees an added bonus in his leasing prospects for FlatIron Crossing. Area customers tend to be very interested in outdoor recreation: hiking, camping, fishing, biking, running, and golfing. "This opens up opportunities for us to talk to major sporting goods players that you wouldn't traditionally find in suburban and metropolitan market malls," he says. "We are very excited about the opportunity to develop a property that encompasses the whole Colorado lifestyle and experience."

The Colorado way of life is reflected in the mall's design. Cottonwood Canyon, the common area and outdoor park, will lie on the north side of the mall, where a series of community hiking trails meander around creeks and lakes. The trails eventually will intersect at the mall and lead into FlatIron Village.

FlatIron Crossing will combine an enclosed shopping center with an outdoor village. Dining, entertainment, and services (such as dry cleaning and shoe repair) will characterize the outdoor Main Street shopping experience. The indoor shopping will focus on fashion-oriented retail such as Nordstrom.

The common spaces of the mall will include community hiking trails, meandering creeks, and spaces for shoppers to stroll and sit.

Among the trails on the north side of the mall, Westcor plans to establish an outdoor try-before-you-buy pavilion, to be operated by a sporting goods retailer or by mall management as a service for several retailers. From the pavilion, paths will lead to a climbing wall or tower that visitors can scale themselves or watch others test their skills. An entrance will lead to an escalator and up into the food court, where visitors can turn left or right and shop at the mall or pass through large sliding glass window-walls to enter FlatIron Village.

With its combination of upscale retailers and lifestyle-based design, Westcor hopes FlatIron Crossing will replace the original mall model developed in the 1950s. Not simply "just another mall," FlatIron Crossing will challenge conventional retailing to merge two shopping experiences under one roof. This new shopping destination is expected to rise high above the competition.

Source: Excerpted from Michael Fickes, "Expanding the Limits of the Regional Mall," *Shopping Center World*, February 1998.

tenant mix lies not in including or excluding a specific tenant type, but rather in selecting and combining a group of mutually reinforcing tenants that will serve the needs of the particular market.

Evaluation of Tenants

Shopping center operators must regularly evaluate tenants' performance. If tenants' sales volumes are low, they can be replaced, provided they are on short-term leases; otherwise, problems can be corrected through negotiations. Operators of new centers must monitor and encourage tenants' performance, particularly the performance of any tenants who are first-time entrants into a shopping center.

Developer/owners who decide to reduce the proportion of triple-A credit-rated national chains and to increase the number of local chains and independent merchants (who have built-in customer appeal, merchandising expertise for the area, and operational knowledge of the area) must continuously evaluate their performance and assist the independent businesses in their merchandising. In enclosed malls, the ability of tenants to pull customer traffic into and along the mall may be a greater test of productivity than the clauses of a lease. An anchor tenant in particular is expected to deliver a sizable number of customers to the rest of the tenants.

Developers seeking tenants must consider not only the services that a center is to offer a community but also current trends in classifying tenants and in merchandising. They must avoid fads, yet they must take into account the effects of economic conditions. Conducting surveys and studies of societal trends and consumers' changing behavior and preferences, learning about the experiences of other shopping centers, perusing the latest industry journals and periodicals, and attending technical conferences can help the developer determine these effects.

To select a tenant mix that is on target for the center's trade area, a developer must also remember that the leasing strategy will need to be continuously fine-tuned; for example, it is not enough to know that the tenant mix should include two sit-down restaurants of so many seats. The situation must be further studied to determine the specific types of restaurants that would be most appropriate, and to identify and analyze specific restaurant chains or restaurateurs that should be wooed. Such determinations should be based on the center's proposed type and focus, detailed demographic studies of the center's trade area, and customer surveys and focus groups.

To calculate the potential rental income stream from a certain mix of tenants, the developer can choose to trade higher rents for some spaces to attract particularly attractive tenants that are in great demand and will be powerful draws. Rents per square foot vary widely not only by retail category and location within a shopping center, but also within categories according to the bargaining strength, price points, and anticipated sales and profit of a particular store. As a result, all types of stores cannot and should not pay the same rent per square foot, and each tenant is, or should be, aware of this situation.

Certain types of establishments may pay comparatively low rents and may even be loss leaders for their centers. Such tenants, however, are valuable to high-rent tenants for their drawing power, for rounding out a center's tenant mix, and for providing essential services to the community, which are all important for maintaining continued patronage and good will. In regional centers, for example, department stores typically pay rent of only $1.00 to $2.00 per square foot if they are in space owned by the shopping center; they often pay nothing but a small charge for common area maintenance if they occupy their own space. They pay low rents because they have high advertising budgets that supplement the center's own advertising, strong name recognition, and well-known reputations that draw customers to the center. Some convenience services pay low rents because their customers

Plaza Frontenac's New Attitude

For nearly 20 years, Plaza Frontenac, a 440,000-square-foot fashion center in suburban St. Louis County, Missouri, boasted the largest assemblage of high-end stores in the region, featuring Gucci and Mark Cross plus anchors Saks Fifth Avenue and Neiman Marcus. That situation changed in 1991, when an aging shopping center nearby was transformed into the successful Saint Louis Galleria. The new super regional center siphoned tenants and customers away from Plaza Frontenac.

When Robert Perlmutter, chief executive officer of Heitman Retail Properties, purchased Frontenac in 1993, he realized that breathing new life into the tired center called for a major makeover. Rather than fashioning the old center to compete with the Galleria, Perlmutter believed it would be possible for the two centers to work together as one regional destination offering different, but complementary, shopping experiences. To distinguish it from the supercharged mall, Frontenac would offer a more leisurely, intimate shopping experience in a country club–like setting that blended hospitality with casual elegance.

The metamorphosis of Plaza Frontenac into a lifestyle center with upscale restaurants and a mix of understated, entertainment-based tenants evolved slowly but steadily and was completed in spring 1998 with the opening of several art galleries, the Green Door Spa, and Landmark's six-screen Plaza Frontenac Cinema.

St. Louis–based architects David Dale Suttle and Michael Mindlin, who headed Frontenac's redesign with Hellmuth, Obata + Kassabaum, offered a "clear retail strategy before designing the handrails and skylights," says Perlmutter. Their strategy called for repositioning Frontenac as a lifestyle center that was more than just a place to shop, offering a more diverse merchandising mix, and designing a physical environment that expressed the values of both merchants and customers.

The architects envisioned Frontenac as a place of hospitality that also would invite shoppers to dine, take in a movie, refresh themselves at a spa, or enjoy a classical concert. To increase evening activity, they recommended adding a major restaurant anchor on the ground floor. Besides drawing an affluent business market at lunch, the 6,500-square-foot Cardwell's restaurant, which opened in 1994, pulls many of the same customers back at night for dinner with their families.

To expand the customer base, the remerchandising concept, which revolved around food and home furnishings, was targeted to tenants representing a broad price range, from Williams-Sonoma to Pottery Barn. Remerchandising also drew some top fashion tenants, including Ann Taylor, Banana Republic, Liz Claiborne, Talbots, and J. Crew. These tenants as well as the center's anchors "speak less about actual price than about attitude and sophistication," says Suttle.

Challenged by a modest budget, the architects retained existing features where they could and focused on the interior public spaces that mattered most to customers—main circulation halls, telephone areas, and women's lounges. The design aimed to project Plaza Frontenac's new image without alienating longtime customers. Suttle and Mindlin chose a classic modern look and cleaned up many of the cluttered, colonial-style design elements of the old center. They used existing columns to create a series of intimate living room spaces. In the center court, they installed new escalators off to the side to form a grand lobby space that is punctuated by a custom-made wool Oriental rug. Reinforcing the notion of casual luxury, elegant leather chairs and couches—much like the furniture one finds in a boutique hotel—can be found throughout the center.

One year following the renovation in 1994, sales at in-line shops had increased some 35 percent. Today, more than 70 percent of Plaza Frontenac's stores have remerchandised, and sales at in-line stores exceed $400 per square foot. The foreign film cinema sells out on Friday and Saturday nights. The strategy for turning around this once beleaguered center was based on the premise that its customers would consider the shopping experience as important as the transaction itself. "Our retail concept and design address this particular market segment, which looks to shopping as an essential expression of lifestyle and identity," says Mindlin.

Source: Excerpted from Terry J. Lassar, "Plaza Frontenac's New Attitude," *Urban Land*, July 1998, p. 90.

■

come to the center often to use their service. Some famous and highly regarded tenants may pay lower rent than stores selling similar merchandise because they raise the center's image and profile and give it a cachet that it otherwise would not have.

Retail spaces in any center need to be reconfigured from time to time, and certain tenants need to be relocated. Some tenants outgrow their original spaces, while others will require smaller spaces. Still others may need

The transformation of Plaza Frontenac included the creation of intimate living room spaces on the interior. The grand lobby is furnished with a custom-made wool Oriental rug and elegant leather chairs and couches.

to be shifted to strengthen the overall operations of a center or to concentrate certain types of tenants in a particular part of the center. Many merchants fail or perform poorly because they start with too much space and must carry its additional overhead. As a result, some tenants continue to move toward smaller spaces to encourage higher productivity and more intensive use of the space. In other cases, however, spaces, especially those designed for big-box category killers and lifestyle and entertainment-oriented retailers, have been growing to provide space for deeply merchandised presentations and elaborate shopping environments. In all types of centers, however, a mix of different sizes of retail space is essential to have the flexibility to adapt space to tenants' changing needs.

The rest of this chapter discusses the major categories of tenants found in shopping centers. Each type includes examples and a description of the type of center or centers where such a tenant would typically be found.[5]

Food and Food Service

Supermarkets and Other Food Stores

A supermarket is the anchor tenant in a traditional neighborhood center and a key tenant in community centers. It is rarely included in a regional center except in Canada and in old, small-town American malls. (Century City in Los Angeles is an anomaly.) Today, the term "supermarket" is applied to a number of distinct store types, ranging from a conventional supermarket to a food warehouse to a superstore. *Chain Store Guide: Supermarket, Grocery Stores, and Convenience Store Chains,* published annually by Business Guides, defines a conventional supermarket as a complete full-line, self-service market with an annual sales volume of at least $2 million. It defines a "superstore" as one with more than 30,000 square feet of sales area and an annual sales volume of at least $5 million. In reality, these definitions are losing their meaning, because most new supermarkets are larger than 40,000 square feet. In fact, the median size of all supermarkets is more than 40,000 square feet, according to *Dollars & Cents of Shopping Centers: 1997,* and more than 10 percent (usually superstores that contain a supermarket/drugstore combination) are larger than 60,000 square feet. A food warehouse is a variant of a supermarket. It offers products in bulk, cut-rate prices, and minimal ambience.

The developer may also have to decide whether to build one or more supermarkets in a strong location, taking into account the fact that rates for percentage rents on food items are between 1 and 1.75 percent of sales, whereas rates on nonfood items could be as high as 8 percent if sold by stores other than the supermarket. Because of the differences in percentage rates for various classes of merchandise, it is important to clearly understand the specific internal characteristics of a supermarket. The fact that food items are sold at low markups is well known. The proportion of nonfood sales to total GLA varies widely and changes somewhat each year. In general, however, supermarkets today increasingly sell a larger pro-

The Lebanon Food Co-Op, a 55,000-square-foot grocery store near Dartmouth College, is the anchor for this center, which draws customers because of its proximity to the school.

Arrowstreet Inc.

portion of nonfood items. In addition, most supermarket chains target each store to the demographics of its specific trade area in terms of both the store's design and the merchandise mix.

Supermarkets have special land use requirements that need to be addressed. Parking spaces must be adequate for heavy customer turnover, and entrances to the supermarket should open directly onto the parking areas. The number of required parking spaces, which is typically controlled by local zoning, varies from location to location. Supermarkets also require loading docks for trucks, truck turning areas, and special trash storage and pickup spaces. The best architectural treatment for these areas is a court, behind the store and screened from customers' view.

In general, supermarkets are not appropriate for regional or super regional centers, because people cannot carry their groceries from store to store as they shop, but they can be sited within a power center or other value retailing format. Often supermarkets in these centers are larger and can sell many more items in bulk than regular supermarkets. The smaller the center, the more important supermarkets become. In those centers where the supermarket is a preferred tenant, its drawing power is its greatest contribution to the center as a whole.

Small specialty food shops—delicatessens and stores that offer meats, fish, and poultry, candy and nuts, baked goods, or dairy products—when effectively merchandised, can be valued tenants in neighborhood and community shopping centers, but only specific merchandisers, such as coffee merchants or chocolatiers, work well in regional and super regional centers.

Restaurants

Virtually all shopping centers provide some form of eating facilities. Even a small neighborhood center should have at least a sandwich shop or ice cream parlor. Community centers often include fast-food operations and/or one or more restaurants providing table service. In a regional or super regional center, a broad range of eating places, from counters to fancier restaurants, is desirable.

Restaurants vary greatly as to classification and type of operation. They may be independently owned or part of a national chain. They may range from the small, quick-order, limited-menu counter service to the distinctively decorated, destination-quality establishment providing table service. They may be family-oriented and moderately priced or serve alcohol and cater to a more sophisticated market. They may offer traditional American food or ethnic cuisine. They may have an entertainment or themed environment or be located near a food court. All types have succeeded and failed in all types of centers; there is no set formula for success. Because the rate of failure is notoriously high, a carefully selected format and an experienced operator are crucial to a restaurant's success. The format and price point of the restaurant must be compatible with those of the overall center and its market.

If the developer can lease restaurant space only by providing fixtures and furniture, he or she should select the best locally known successful proprietor and advance the necessary funds, based on the assumption that the investment will eventually be recovered.

The location of a restaurant is a crucial factor in its success. A large restaurant that depends on wide market support typically requires highway visibility, while a coffee bar is more likely to serve only the shoppers on site and therefore requires visibility only within the shopping center. A pad for a freestanding restaurant on the shopping center site permits drive-through service and specially assigned parking spaces. It can also bring the shopping center out to the street and fill in gaps in the parking field. It should be easily accessible and readily identified, and it should provide adequate and convenient parking. It may also be located so that it is accessible from a mall or plaza, thus drawing traffic to an area that might otherwise receive light pedestrian traffic. Ideally, a restaurant that is part of a mall structure should also have convenient outside access.

Main Street–style centers and entertainment-oriented centers are exceptions to some rules about location. These kinds of centers are destinations, and for them to succeed, pedestrian traffic and repeat visits are key. As a result, visibility from major roadways is often unlikely and unnecessary. Even in these centers, however, a restaurant's location and visibility are crucial components of its success, and it must be carefully sited as part of a center with several anchors to help draw customers through the center.

Besides providing an amenity for shoppers, restaurants draw clientele to the center during weekday evenings, a time that may not otherwise draw customers for shopping. Indeed, a carefully conceived and well-patronized restaurant can become the signature of a smaller shopping center and an important part of the tenant mix in a larger one. A high-quality restaurant with an excellent reputation can draw patrons from throughout a trade area. By expanding the market area and extending the period of use, restaurants can broaden the shopping center's appeal and increase its market potential.

Food Courts

Food courts have become major components of many regional malls and specialty centers. They consist of a cluster of food service (and occasionally food-related) tenants grouped around a common or public eating area. The goal in the design and leasing of a food court is to create a festive atmosphere as well as a synergy that will result in a high volume of sales and customer traffic for the center. Sometimes food courts are leased by a single master tenant with a licensing arrangement for individual tenant spaces, while in other cases the shopping center has leasing arrangements separately with each food service tenant. Special assessments are sometimes made in addition to a shopping center's normal charges for common area maintenance to maintain the food court's common areas.

The Commons at Calabasas has half a dozen restaurants that benefit from the overflow pedestrian traffic from the Edwards Cinemas in the center.

The food court has been a significant staple of the regional mall for several years now, and it continues to be important in its success. But what about power centers and those newly created entertainment venues with a multiscreen theater and a few retailers? Where's the food court? Bud Lauria wants to create one for them—not just any ordinary food court, but one that acts like a themed restaurant and a food court in one.

The Lost City Food Resort, Lauria's creation that involves a series of food and entertainment venues, will feature the theme of an ancient tropical temple—complete with waterfalls, an active volcano, and a 25,000-gallon salt water reef aquarium—and plenty of eating options.

With the creation of Lost City, quick-service vendors will find the answer to their expansion needs, and big-box power centers and multiscreen theater operators will find a food and entertainment value they have been looking for.

The idea was a revelation to Lauria, principle of Voorhees, New Jersey–based VJL Development Corporation, who wants to pull the theme out of restaurants and put it into food courts. The concept of Lost City is unlike a typical food court in that it will rely heavily on a theme. It is also different because it will be developed by an outside operator. But most important, it will add an element of entertainment to the center. "We've created a total family fun, dining, and entertainment experience at a price everyone can afford," says Lauria.

VJL plans to develop a number of Lost City Food Resorts next to multiscreen theaters, and it is working with a number of theater operators around the country to figure out which venues would support the concept. VJL

The Lost City Food Resort puts a twist on the food court to create a new model for family fun and entertainment.

is developing a system so that customers eating at Lost City can see previews of movies showing at the theater next door on a large screen. All Lost City venues will be equipped with automatic ticket machines so customers can easily purchase tickets to see movies.

Lost City will initially be developed in two sizes. The larger one will have two levels and more than 32,000 square feet. More than 9,000 square feet on the first floor will be dedicated to quick-service vendors, while 12,000 square feet on the mezzanine level will have two full-service restaurants with bars. The smaller one will have 21,000 square feet, with 9,000 square feet for express restaurant vendors, each averaging 600 square feet.

The concept of Lost City is inspired in part by the surge of phenomenally successful themed restaurants such as the Rainforest Cafe, Planet Hollywood, and Hard Rock Cafe. Unlike most other themed restaurants, however, Lost City Food Resorts will be located in regional centers, not necessarily in destination locations. "We want to bring the same concept as a themed restaurant to regional power centers," says Lauria, "and to do that, we have to be conscious of price."

A lot of discussion has transpired in the industry on how to achieve power centers' full potential. Lauria also hopes to remedy their need for entertainment with Lost City, helping quick-service restaurants with their expansion plans. With fewer enclosed malls being built, adding a variety of quick-service vendors to power centers will help satisfy the needs of the $106 billion a year fast-food industry, says Lauria.

"The food court has become an anchor for the mall. You can't have a successful regional mall today without a successful food court," he says. "The fast-food industry needs to reposition itself to be competitive in the future. And power center developers have come to the same conclusions."

"I'm ready to bring the concept of Lost City to the world," says Lauria.

Source: Excerpted from Beverly Cox Clark, "A Theme for the Food Court," *Shopping Center Business,* September 1998.

Food court tenants in regional centers often occupy harder-to-lease space on the top floor.

L&B Realty Advisors, Inc.

The need for strong thematic organization of as many elements as possible has led to a mix of tenant categories, from an exclusive food service mix to a food-related retail program, such as cleverly packaged and merchandised gourmet items, coffees, and spices, or cookware and kitchen gadgets. Mixing categories of tenants can expand the drawing power of a food court as well as reinforce a chosen theme. A successfully implemented theme may have numerous benefits:

- The center's marketing potential will be strengthened.
- Participants can share marketing, overhead, and direct expenses.
- By having a unified theme, the project can be more easily identified and memorable for customers.
- Tenants will be more easily encouraged to strive for individual quality in the preparation and presentation of their foods.

The objective of a food court should be to obtain a variety of tenants while at the same time protecting the concept of a food cluster. Complementary, not competitive, menus should be the goal, with a variety of comfort foods, ethnic foods, desserts, and specialty items. Menus should reflect local tastes. If space is leased to operators who offer distinctive local specialties, a highly desirable goal in the abstract, several potential problems must be avoided or dealt with:

- The developer will probably face higher tenant allowances among potentially undercapitalized local entrepreneurs than for fast-food chains or franchise operations.
- Spin-offs that are not yet highly organized chains can easily become "stepchildren." The successful skills of the parent operation must be re-created by a dedicated operator, and absentee management should be avoided.
- Because of the individuality and quirkiness of local operators, management's control of the operation may be more difficult.

A successful food court makes the most of competition among its various operations, keeping quality, performance, and aspirations high. Sometimes food courts may have a single operator behind a facade of differing menus, giving only the illusion of diversity. Having only one operator simplifies lease negotiations, for a single lease ensures fewer duplications of equipment (with one master kitchen and central supplies) and even simplifies solutions to the space-consuming problems of access. But quality typically suffers. A well-managed, themed food court usually requires more than one kitchen.

In addition to kitchens, a food court requires washing and cold-storage facilities. All food court tenants are typically on separate percentage leases and therefore pay a higher overall rent than a single restaurant tenant. Management must carefully and continually monitor, evaluate, and solve problems of maintenance, cleanliness, and placement within the center. Other details must be worked out, including ownership of fixtures and furnishings, the practical and financial arrangements for procuring and maintaining these items, and arrangements for day-to-day supplies and services.

Fast-Food Outlets

In a regional or super regional center, the chain fast-food outlet is most likely treated like any other mall tenant, although in more upscale malls, fast-food tenants, if they exist at all, are collocated with the food court and away from the high-end shops. The situation is different in community and neighborhood centers, however. Most fast-food chains have distinctive building designs and specific on-site circulation and parking patterns related to their method of operation. In most cases, a shopping center developer planning to include such tenants should apply the same standards of design that would be applied to any other tenant.

Beursplein, a large mixed-use development in downtown Rotterdam, includes four department stores, which funnel heavy volumes of pedestrian traffic into smaller retail shops located between the main anchors.

General Merchandise and Apparel

Department Stores

Regional centers, by definition, are anchored by one or two full-line department stores containing at least 75,000 square feet of GLA (50,000 square feet in small towns). Super regional centers include three or more department stores, each containing at least 100,000 square feet of GLA, usually more. In addition to full-line department stores, they may contain other anchors, such as discount department stores. They also contain a full range of comparison or shoppers goods that customers need periodically but not every day.

Department stores are often the main generators of customer traffic. If a center has more than one department store, the center's configuration must be designed to separate them so that the movement of pedestrians is directed through the mall. Supplementary tenants are positioned between them to benefit from the flow of customers between the department stores. Parking must be balanced and directly accessible to each department store as well as to the other mall tenants. Providing for a safe and convenient customer flow between the parking areas and the building entrances while drawing pedestrians through the mall is the crux of good site planning and building design for regional centers.

Department stores are sometimes referred to as "full-line department stores," but this phrase is really a misnomer because in many cases they do not offer full lines of merchandise. Over the years, many have dropped unprofitable lines such as furniture, toys, appliances, and books. As a result, some, such as Saks Fifth Avenue, Neiman Marcus, Nordstrom, and Lord & Taylor, are really multidepartment apparel and housewares stores, although they are still categorized and thought of as department stores. On the other hand, some stores, such as Macy's, Marshall Field, and Sears, continue to carry a more traditional, wide range of department store goods.

When negotiating for department stores, developers should understand customers' loyalties, the segment of the market the department store serves, and the store's policies, price lines, merchandising image, management skills, and financial viability. The volatility in the department store industry in the 1980s and early 1990s is well known. Consolidations and bankruptcies of many well-known and highly regarded department store chains created turmoil for many regional and super regional malls, which suddenly found themselves without anchors and few prospects for replacement. While this segment of the retailing industry has regained its balance and re-established its prominence in malls, it is more essential than ever for developers to examine the financial health of the individual department store chains it is considering as potential anchors.

In metropolitan areas, one or more department store chains usually serve each market segment in a trade area. These stores may already be operating in the market, and the success of a new regional center may depend on whether the developer can pull a particular department store or stores into the center. Other department store chains that wish to establish new market outlets generally prefer to be associated with stores that are already established in the region. In smaller markets, there may be only one or two department store chains (local, regional, or national), and they will each serve all local market segments. High-end shoppers in smaller markets typically shop for comparison goods in nearby major cities or even travel to large cities like New York and Chicago for goods that are unavailable in their hometown markets.

To determine the number of department stores appropriate for a super regional center, a developer must be sure that additional anchors actually will increase the center's drawing power, that the deal to be struck with an additional anchor is economically feasible, and that the trade area can support another department store. The developer certainly does not want one department store in a center to cannibalize another. In any case, the options for department stores for many centers are few, because the market for malls—and department stores—is saturated in many trade areas.

The long-term trend continues away from traditional leasing arrangements in which a department store leases GLA from the shopping center owner in much the same way as other stores in the center. Today, each department store typically buys its own land (including a portion of the parking areas) from the shopping center developer/owner. In some cases, the developer gives the land and the building to a highly desirable department store and, in extreme cases, finishes the interior store space. Customers, however, never see any physical evidence of a difference in ownership between the department store and the rest of the center, because the department store remains an integral part of the center's design. In smaller markets, a gross lease may be preferred for department stores.

When anchor department stores build and own their units, a complex set of legal operating arrangements and cross-easements becomes necessary. Various agreements between the department stores and the shopping center owner must cover such items as the type of department store to be operated, the hours of operation, the continuation of store operations, participation in the operation and maintenance of common areas (including the parking area), and participation in the merchants' association (if one exists) and advertising and promotional programs. The content and thoroughness of these agreements are particularly significant to lending institutions.

Because full-line stores are such major attractions, the quality of the architectural design must be dictated by the character of the trade area and the marketing concept. Each department store, with its own standards in merchandising and quality, should complement the other stores and should help set the tone for the entire center.

Off-Price and Discount Retailers

Once anathema to malls, off-price stores and discount department stores have found a home in many regional

Outlet Centers in Europe

If Europe's famous shopping boulevards are starting to look the same, if the prices make you wince and the products make you sigh, do what the locals are beginning to do: go for the factory stores.

Bicester Village is one of a growing band of factory outlet centers taking Europe by storm. And while the whereabouts of these bargain lairs are still well-guarded secrets, determined shoppers are ferreting out the marked-down merchandise in droves.

In the United Kingdom alone, 17 centers have opened since 1992, when the first British outlet threw open its doors to shoppers, according to retail researcher Corporate Intelligence. The company says plans are pending to develop 16 more outlet malls throughout Britain, and a host of projects are targeted for continental Europe.

"We haven't begun to do what we know we can do," says Scott Malkin, head of Value Retail, with a sweep of his hand. Already, Malkin's consortium has won permission to open a factory outlet center at the doorstep of Disneyland, Paris. That site is scheduled to open in summer 2000, Malkin says. Meanwhile, Value Retail is launching a 60-store complex near Barcelona. Malls in Madrid and Munich will follow. Other commercial operators have also jumped on the bandwagon. BAA McArthur Glen, a leader in the development of outlet centers, says it has projects planned for France, Austria, Germany, and Belgium.

Outlets offer the genuine article—Lacroix, Prada, Armani, and more—at prices from 25 to 60 percent off the regular retail value. And while slaves to this season's latest craze might grumble, most shoppers can find stylish bargains only a step behind the hottest fashion trend.

Most outlets in Europe keep a low profile, banding together in out-of-the-way spots where they won't pose a threat to local retailers. In fact, unless you're a well-informed local, you're likely to need detailed directions to sniff out the bargains.

Source: Excerpted from Caitlan Randall, "Outlet Centers in Europe," *Business Life*, June 1998, pp. 67–68.

■

centers. Both power centers and traditional regional centers mix value retailers and traditional retailers, and the distinctions between the two types of centers is beginning to blur. As noted, off-price stores and discount stores are common anchor tenants in a community center, filling the role that junior department stores and variety stores once filled. Discount department stores include Wal-Mart, Kmart, and Target, off-price stores Ross, Marshalls, and TJ Maxx. Both off-price and discount department stores are self-service operations, which keeps down overhead and allows customers to make purchases at lower prices. These stores also keep down prices by buying in volume, working with lower profit margins, receiving merchandise directly from manufacturers, and using sales areas as storage areas (thus reducing storage space to as little as 10 percent of GLA). In contrast, traditional department stores generally use from 20 to 40 percent of their floor area for storage and other nonselling purposes.

Off-price stores and discount stores offer merchandise at lower prices than traditional department stores, and they typically differ in the type of merchandise offered. Off-price stores cater to middle- and upper-middle-income buyers who are price sensitive and seek quality, brand-name merchandise at a discount. Discount stores usually cater to middle- to lower-income buyers who are more cost conscious and buy lesser-quality merchandise at a discount because they may not be able to afford better merchandise on a regular basis.

If an off-price or discount store is to be a key tenant in a community center, its practices of merchandising, advertising, and signage must be compatible with those of side tenants, the shopping center management, and the target market. The developer should also bear in mind that percentage rents for off-price and discount tenants typically are lower than those paid by traditional retailers —usually about 1 percent lower for comparable locations. Sales per square foot for off-price and discount tenants,

Plaza del Atlantico, a regional center in Arecibo, Puerto Rico, was renovated to provide a more colorful environment for its mid-priced tenants.

Some outlet and value-oriented centers and malls increase sales and profits by catering to the motorcoach business, which brings in organized groups for a day of shopping.

Now comes the RV trade, which—thanks to Overnighters Association (OA)—could increase shopping by people traveling in motor homes and other recreational vehicles. Overnighters, based in Punta Gorda, Florida, launched a program in 1998 in which outlet, value-oriented, and other shopping centers will allow people traveling in RVs to park overnight in their parking lots for a fee of $5.00 a night. The RVs will have to be self-contained because there will be no sewer, electrical, water, or other service hook-ups. The centers get $2.00 of the fee, but the main advantage to them and their tenants is the likelihood that RVers will shop during their stays.

"Shopping centers will benefit by having a new market of RV owners with discretionary buying power," says Orren Hall, vice president of OA. "We can deliver a new, profitable, and mobile consumer base to centers on a repeat basis in exchange for simple benefits to these consumers."

According to the Recreation Vehicle Industry Association, 25 million RVs travel the highways. "Overnight arrangements for self-contained units average from $15.00 to $55.00 or more per night" at parks, campgrounds, and other facilities, Hall says. But "reservations are not always accepted, sites frequently charge for hook-ups not needed by self-contained units, campgrounds are often poorly maintained, and locations are hard to reach. Motor home owners can spend as much as $1,500 a month on services when they travel," he adds. "If that expense were reduced by lowering the cost of overnight stays and pro-

viding them with new shopping venues, the result would be increased buying at participating centers."

Here's how the system works: RVers can enroll in OA for $29.95 per year, and OA's database lists each member, giving name, address, type and size of RV, and other pertinent data. OA publishes a directory of participating shopping centers for its RV members at no cost to the centers.

For their part, participating centers each designate five to ten reserved and marked drive-through spaces in their parking lots for the RVs. OA contracts with Habitat for Humanity and other nonprofit groups to monitor the RV parking in each center.

RVers can call an 800 number for OA to make reservations and pay the $5.00 fee using a credit card. OA then faxes or E-mails information about reservations to each shopping center. Monitoring organizations check to make sure each overnighting RVer has a reservation. Shopping centers are also free to make their own checks and to market the centers by handing out fliers or having signs visible at the RV sites.

Once a month, OA sends checks to centers for their $2.00 cut of each overnight fee. Habitat for Humanity and other monitoring organizations get the remaining $3.00, Hall says.

According to Hall, about 300 shopping centers participate in the system, and more are added all the time.

Source: Excerpted from Donald Finley, "Outlet Centers May Host RVs Overnight," *Value Retail News,* June 1998, p. 26. ∎

however, are often much higher than those generated by traditional retailers because of their higher sales volume.

Warehouse Clubs

Warehouse clubs are big-box retailers that sell a wide range of goods in bulk quantities—often including groceries, beer and wine, electronics, tires, office supplies, clothing, hardware, and jewelry—at wholesale or near-wholesale prices. They offer little depth of selection or brand for any given product. Whereas discount department stores may carry upward of 60,000 items, warehouse clubs usually stock 3,000 to 5,000 items. Although the number of warehouse club stores has proliferated, the number of operators has declined, and the warehouse club market is dominated by only three major players: Sam's Club (a division of Wal-Mart), Costco, and BJ's. Warehouse clubs have felt competition from new and existing supermarkets using club-like promotions for bulk goods and from large category killers.

Category Killers

Category killers are large specialty retailers that serve a single market segment with a single class of merchandise. Rather than selling everything from tires to tomatoes, like warehouse clubs, category killers concentrate on providing depth of merchandise. If a customer goes to Home Depot, for example, looking for a hammer, she will find a wide selection of brands, sizes, and types from which to choose. Consumers interested in a wide selection might also shop at Circuit City for electronics, Bed Bath & Beyond for linens and housewares, the Sports Authority for sporting goods, and Borders or Barnes & Noble for books. Category killers are increasingly common anchor tenants in community and regional shopping centers. They range in size from 25,000 to more than 100,000 square feet. Their large size can be an advantage for suburban sites and for customers who like this kind of format, but some operators are developing scaled-down versions of their stores to fit into the confines of

Cousins Market Centers, Inc.

Category killers provide a wide selection of goods for one single class of merchandise. Cousins Market Center in Orlando, Florida, features a Circuit City offering shoppers a wide variety of electronic goods.

the urban landscape and to cater to customers who are intimidated by big-box stores and prefer a quick shopping trip over a large selection. Office Max, for example, developed a prototype 7,500-square-foot store stocked with about one-third the number of items carried in its larger stores.

Clothing and Accessories

Tenants in the apparel category cover a wide range of store types, quality, style, and price points. Independent merchants, local chains, national chains, custom clothing shops, ready-to-wear outlets, and accessories are all part of the mix. In a neighborhood center, an apparel store usually offers a limited range of goods that are a convenience for the local market, but the situation is changing as some high-quality specialty apparel stores for men and women find an advantage to being closer to their customers in local neighborhood centers.

Except for anchor tenants, apparel stores typically represent the largest proportion of space in community, regional, and super regional centers. Men's, women's, children's, and family clothing lines demand an environment conducive to comparison shopping, and developers look for apparel chains and specialty apparel stores with the highest productivity in terms of store area, sales, and rents.

Community, regional, and super regional centers may contain groups of high-price, high-fashion, and other specialty apparel stores for both men and women. In the right trade area, such stores can dramatically strengthen a cen-

ter's drawing power. For example, a group of women's apparel stores offering distinctive merchandise can provide the stimulus for special-purpose shopping trips from within and beyond the trade area. During the 1980s and early 1990s, however, an overreliance on women's apparel stores in many shopping centers led to increased vacancies and a shift to more lifestyle-oriented shops.

Jewelry Stores

Jewelry stores typically are located in super regional and regional shopping centers, and few are found in neighborhood and community centers. Although they occupy a small amount of space, jewelry stores' sales per square foot are among the highest of all tenants, typically ranging from $500 to $700 per square foot, and up to $2,500 per square foot is not uncommon. With sales figures and productivity per square foot so high, it is not surprising that the best performers in the jewelry category are among the most highly sought-after tenants. Costume jewelers are a subset of the jewelry category, but their sales figures are much lower, typically in the same range as apparel stores. Costume jewelers, however, are also important tenants, because they attract a much greater volume of traffic and a different demographic group from fine jewelers, and they complement adjacent apparel stores. As with the apparel category, shopping centers typically provide a variety of jewelry stores at different price points to broaden their market and provide a full range of jewelry products and services.

Shoe Stores

Neighborhood and community shopping centers do not always have a shoe store, but regional and super regional centers almost always include several of them, usually regional or national chains. Because competition within the lines bolsters sales volumes, it is usually feasible to include multiple men's, women's, and family shoe stores in the same center. Stores must be carefully selected to provide a range of prices; a smaller proportion of shoe stores for men than for women and children is desirable, because men buy fewer pairs of shoes per season.

Shoe stores are a key component of super regional and regional shopping centers. After general merchandise and apparel stores, shoe stores occupy the third largest amount of space, nearly 10 percent of the center's GLA, and bring in the third largest amount of sales per square foot, also nearly 10 percent, in super regional centers. Shoe stores typically are scattered throughout a shopping center so that customers pass other stores as they comparison shop. They are coveted tenants because they bring customers back to the center again and again.

Furniture and Home Furnishings

A furniture store produces little traffic and a low sales volume per square foot of GLA, as the average household purchases furniture infrequently and makes a special shopping trip for it. Furniture stores usually require large display and storage areas, necessitating low rents per square foot. A full-line furniture store can occupy 50,000 square feet or more. Furniture stores fit into suburban locations, and they are better suited to freestanding locations or centers designed specifically for them than to regional shopping centers. If a furniture store is to be placed in a regional center, it may be suitably located in a lower-rent portion, such as a basement or other space away from the principal shopping area.

At Natick Mall and Shoppers World in Framingham, Massachusetts, a redeveloped 1.1 million-square-foot super regional center and a 1950s regional center that became an 828,000-square-foot power center, the Jordan Marsh department store spun off its furniture department into a freestanding store called Furniture Gallery.[6] Similarly, Sears has spun off its home furnishings department into separate Home Life stores in many locations.

Although full-line furniture stores seldom are appropriate for regional malls, specialty home furnishing merchants may be suitable. Such trend setters as Crate & Barrel, Pottery Barn, and the more establishment-style Bombay Company are often successful mall tenants. Unlike full-line furniture stores, these merchants focus on accessories and offer a few furniture items. Sales per square foot are higher, and the store can be much smaller.

Home Appliances/Music

Home appliance and music-related stores are found in all types of shopping centers, although they are more likely to be found in super regional, regional, and power centers. This category includes kitchen appliances and cookware as well as all types of home and office electronic equipment from audio/video equipment to computers and computer software. As consumer spending has shifted slowly from apparel to items for the home, home appliance/music stores have become more important to shopping centers. Although not in the top tier of tenants in super regional and regional centers, the new generation of specialty home electronics and computer stores has become an essential part of the tenant mix, providing an increasingly strong presence.

Natick Mall and Shoppers World is an example of a failing regional center that was redeveloped into a power center. Its longtime tenant, the Jordan Marsh department store, spun off its furniture department into a freestanding store.

The major impact of home appliance/music stores, however, has been felt in power centers, and large category-killer appliance stores have proliferated, as most items sold in this category are commodities that lend themselves to a big-box selling environment. Big-box stores that specialize in one type of appliance (such as CompUSA for computers) or all types (such as Best Buy) have become important anchors in power centers around the country.

Hobby/Special Interest

Hobby and special-interest stores are found in all types of shopping centers. Even though they have a reputation for being found primarily in neighborhood centers close to hobbyists and enthusiasts, in fact they occupy more space in super regional, regional, and power centers. They are among the major tenants in power centers in terms of occupied space and sales per square foot. Like home appliance/music stores, however, hobby/special-interest stores are not in the top tier of tenants in regional and super regional centers. Nevertheless, they are essential for creating the character of the center, expanding the center's draw, and helping such centers provide a comprehensive range of products to sell.

A wide variety of store types are included in this category—sporting goods stores, hobby shops, art galleries, cameras, toys, bicycles, arts and crafts shops, coin shops, outfitters, game stores, science and nature stores, religious stores, collectibles, antiques, and medical health and wellness stores. Sporting goods, outfitters, and toys are increasingly found in big-box stores in power centers, although smaller specialty stores in these categories are still found in more traditional shopping centers.

Gift and Specialty Stores

Gift and specialty stores have long been staples of all types of shopping centers, particularly super regional and regional centers; however, many of these tenant types in this broad category have emerged only recently as stand-alone specialty stores. As a result, this category is one of the most dynamic and rapidly changing of the major tenant categories. As a group, they typically represent 5 to 7 percent of both tenant space and sales in super regional and regional centers. Although not among the most frequently found tenants, they nevertheless are visited more often by shopping center customers than most other tenant types and are therefore important tenants to round out the tenant mix.

This category of tenants is a broad one, encompassing imports, luggage, cards and gifts, candles, books, decorative accessories, stationery, newspapers and magazines, items related to movie studios and Christmas, party goods, baby goods, aromatherapy, calendars, fabrics, tobacco, pets, flowers, telephones, eyeglasses and sunglasses, cosmetics, office supplies, clocks, and watches. Every year, additional types are added to this list based on the findings of *Dollars & Cents of Shopping Centers*. Of this list, only books are found in big-box stores.

Home Improvement, Hardware, and Garden Centers

Hardware stores have largely become a subgroup of big-box category killers. The expanding do-it-yourself and home improvement market has transformed the small traditional hardware store into a large building equipment and materials, home repair, and garden center. With the ambience of a factory or warehouse, stores display merchandise in concrete-floored aisles on shelves to the ceiling. In season, the sales area spills out into the parking lot with plants and garden supplies. Such centers are usually freestanding or located in big-box centers or on an outparcel of a shopping mall. Convenient and ample parking and loading areas must be available. Much consolidation has taken place in the home improvement industry, with Lowe's and Home Depot remaining major players.

Small specialty hardware and home improvement stores such as Restoration Hardware represent an emerging subset of this traditional category, and they are being sited in high-end regional malls, specialty centers, and standalone street-front locations. A boutique for specialty

Drugstores are key tenants in many neighborhood centers, such as Shepherd Square in Houston.

Ontario Mills, about 40 miles east of Los Angeles, combines the concept of a value megamall with large doses of entertainment. The megamall, as large as 38 football fields, includes off-price retailers, 54 movie screens, a video arcade, and an "environmental" center that combines 70 species of live animals with a simulator ride and interactive displays.

hardware, paint, and home improvement items, these stores offer an updated, lifestyle-oriented adaptation of an old-fashioned Main Street hardware store.

Garden shops require space for outdoor sales and displays. The display area must be adjacent to the store itself with direct access, necessitating special attention to arrangement of the site and to security after hours. During prime seasons, home improvement outlets and other merchants may add a garden shop that is converted to other uses during the rest of the year. Today, plants and garden merchandise are sometimes included with a drug/variety/garden center that may serve as the principal anchor tenant for a community center. They also may be offered by discount department stores such as Wal-Mart. A plant store or florist is frequently found in all types of shopping centers.

Drugstores

Drugstores are key anchor tenants in neighborhood centers. They are also desirable tenants in nearly any other type of center, although they are not often found in high-end fashion or specialty centers. Community and regional centers may have two drugstores, which may be prescription pharmacies, traditional drugstores, or drug superstores. Increasingly, most drug outlets are part of national chains. The term "drugstore" is gradually losing its appeal and is being replaced by "pharmacy."

A prescription pharmacy usually contains 650 to 1,200 square feet of GLA, a traditional drugstore about 5,000 square feet, and a drug superstore more than 10,000 square feet (some have 25,000 to 30,000 square feet). Developers must generally choose between a chain drugstore and a strong independent merchant. Because of its size, a drug superstore may fill the center's need for a variety store. It also frequently competes directly with the nonfood areas of supermarkets. Therefore, it is important to maintain a careful balance among the drug superstore, the supermarket, and variety store tenants in neighborhood and community centers.

Personal Services

Tenants providing personal services are common to all types and sizes of shopping centers, although they occupy a much higher percentage of total GLA in neighborhood than they do in regional centers. The range of personal services provided in shopping centers continues to expand dramatically, with new types of tenants constantly emerging. Hair stylists, tanning salons, weight loss centers, photocopiers, print shops, video tape rentals, picture framing, dry cleaners, mailing and packaging centers, nail salons, shoe repair shops, key makers, health spas, interior decorators, travel agents, and other service shops are all important for the convenience of shoppers. Service tenants are usually independent merchants who pay high rents per square foot of store area.

Service shops are traffic builders in a neighborhood center and traffic users in a larger center. They need locations that provide direct access to parking, because much of their trade is the "run-in, run-out" kind. In an enclosed center, service shops are usually placed in secondary locations or apart from the center in a freestanding building.

Entertainment and Recreational Tenants

Entertainment and recreational facilities have become a greater part of many types of centers. The amusement industry has come of age, with sophisticated venues appealing to every market niche. The amusement/video center has matured into vast entertainment complexes that cater to both children and adults. Young children have their birthday parties at themed indoor playgrounds and parks. Preteens frequent high-tech game centers or indoor rock-climbing spaces. Adults have Internet cafés, brewpubs, dance clubs, and more. All age groups frequent health clubs, martial arts training centers, bowling alleys, themed restaurants, entertainment-oriented retail stores, specialized entertainment attractions, and cinemas, the most important entertainment tenant of all. And all of these facilities are successfully linked with shopping.

figure 5-2
Multianchor Urban Entertainment Centers

Type of Anchor	Function	Examples
Activity Generator (mainly entertainment-based venues)	• Draw broad segment of consumer market • Extend geographic range • Enhance penetration	• Cineplex/megaplex • Large-format theaters • Game-based attractions, such as GameWorks • Sports-based attractions, such as ESPN Club • Location-based entertainment attractions, such as American Wilderness Experience • Live performance venues
Activity Extender (mainly dining venues)	• Enhance length of stay • Elevate repeat visitation (penetration) • Extend multisegment appeal • Support daytime and evening activities	• Signature restaurants, such as Il Fornaio, Cheesecake Factory • Themed restaurants, such as Planet Hollywood, Rainforest Cafe • Entertainment restaurants and clubs, such as Wildhorse Saloon, House of Blues
Activity Inducer (mainly icon retailers)	• Extend geographic range for unique shopping experience • Create shopping itinerary	• Icon retailers, such as Barnes & Noble, Williams-Sonoma, Crate & Barrel • Brand retailers, such as Sony Style Store, Nike-Town, Virgin Records, Viacom Brands Store

Source: MRA International.

Entertainment-oriented tenants such as game arcades were once given secondary locations in malls, away from prime shopping areas, and some concern was always raised about the boisterous teenagers who were their prime market segment. Cinemas were hidden away in leftover space that was not suitable for prime tenants. Today, however, more sophisticated entertainment venues are becoming key tenants, sometimes helping to set the theme for the center and rejuvenating faded retail properties.

The issue of whether to include recreation and amusement components in a regional center should be carefully considered, because the markets for traditional retailers and entertainment tenants are somewhat different. If an amusement/entertainment component is to be part of the center, the mix of tenants must be carefully planned by experts who understand the operational requirements of this new form of development, which are much greater than for traditional forms of retail development (see Figure 5-2).[7]

Cinemas

Cinemas are the major entertainment component in shopping centers. New-generation, multiscreen cinemas have grown significantly in size, with up to 30 or more screens and more than 100,000 square feet. At this size, they are becoming key anchor tenants in all types of shopping centers. When combined with other entertainment-related tenants such as themed restaurants, attractions, lifestyle stores, and entertainment retail stores, they also can function as anchors in regional centers. Cinema complexes are being designed to anchor a wing of a regional center or to draw customers to the top floor of a center rather than placing them on freestanding pad sites where their energy is dissipated.

New-generation cinemas have changed more than any other type of shopping center tenant in the past decade. In addition to the vast increase in the number of screens, the movie-going environment has improved markedly. Stadium-style seating, ergonomically designed seats, dramatic design and more attractive finishes, more sophisticated food, state-of-the-art projection and sound systems, and larger screens are the most important improvements.

Operating hours for cinemas are longer than for traditional retail stores, and so they extend the hours of the shopping center and keep people in the center for longer periods of time. Peak parking hours are different from those for the rest of the shopping center, and shared parking thus becomes feasible. They also help to expand the center's customer base, generating customer traffic through the shopping center before and sometimes after the shows. Good bookings and active promotion are major factors in successful cinema operation, and successful operation helps the rest of the shopping center. Like any anchor, cinemas do not pay high rents per square foot. Revenue percentages from the theater's vending machines help to determine the rents cinemas pay to the center.

Specialized Office Tenants

Specialized office tenants are largely found in neighborhood shopping centers, where they may occupy about

4 to 5 percent of the space. Most such offices have no goods to sell, but they offer important services—legal, accounting, employment, government, veterinary, medical, and dental—that draw customers to the center.

Such offices are often located on the second level of a shopping center or in other secondary spaces that may not be suitable for retail tenants because they have low visibility and indirect access. In some cases, these offices may be placed on outparcels. For example, a freestanding clinic building could be designed on the site or on an adjacent property, eliminating the need for and cost of running elevators and extensive plumbing to a second level.

Banks and Other Financial Services

Banks are common tenants in community and neighborhood shopping centers, although in regional and super regional centers, it is increasingly unusual to find banking services other than automatic teller machines (ATMs). Banks are frequently located in a freestanding building on a pad or outparcel so they can offer the convenience of drive-through service. They must have good visibility, easy traffic access in and out of the parking lot, and adequate stacking areas for bank customers waiting in their cars to use the drive-through windows. Circulation must be arranged so that it does not block the shopping center's walk-in entrances or traffic. The appropriate number of windows and stacking spaces depends on the volume of customers expected. Banks sometimes have ground leases and pay their own construction and outfitting costs. Net leases are quite common in freestanding buildings. If a ground lease is executed with a bank that will construct its own facility, the bank must become party to cross-easements and operating agreements.

The advent of the ATM, which pays very high rent per square foot, has dramatically changed the way banking services are provided. Placed in kiosks in a mall or even within stores, ATMs can eliminate the need for branch banks. Likewise, cyberbanking eliminates the need to

Carillon Point, a 31-acre mixed-use center in Kirkland, Washington, includes retail, office, and residential uses. The waterfront public esplanade creates dynamic views as well as a convenient pedestrian link among the various uses.

The Newhall Land and Farming Company developed a Main Street retail center in Valencia, California, adjacent to offices, hotels, and multifamily residential sites. Proximity to such diverse uses will help generate demand for shops along Valencia Town Center Drive, which opened in 1999.

The Service Side of Strips

Medical and other service tenants are hardly as sexy as entertainment retailing, which gets most of the credit for breathing new life into today's shopping centers. But services should not be overlooked. Many strip developers say nontraditional tenants are quickly and quietly becoming a greater part of a strip's landscape. "There are a tremendous number of alternative uses that everyone is looking at," observes David Rosen, principal of Rosen Associates Management Corp., Jericho, New York.

In Doylestown, Pennsylvania, for example, a local dress shop in Vesterra Corp.'s Mercer Square Shopping Center was replaced not by another apparel store but by the 7,000-square-foot Doylestown Rehab and Sports Medicine physical therapy facility.

The increase in these types of tenants, particularly health care and financial services, can be traced to changes in their respective industries as well as to retail trends affecting unenclosed shopping centers. In strip centers across the nation, big boxes are getting bigger. Category killers like Staples are expanding to larger prototypes, and supermarkets are opening boutique shops within their stores. Thus, less room is available, and there is less need for smaller specialty shops, leaving holes for nontraditional retailers, such as check-cashing stores, says Peter Framson, partner at KLNB Inc., a commercial real estate service company in Baltimore.

Consolidation and technology are changing how people bank. Yet the new banking system, characterized by electronic transactions, higher fees, and fewer branch locations, leaves in its wake a population of underserved customers. "There are still a lot of people who require a walk-in financial services institution," says Gerald Divaris, president of Divaris Real Estate Inc., Virginia Beach, Virginia. Divaris and others believe check-cashing stores are poised to keep filling this void by diversifying their services, extending hours of operation, and adding locations where banks have closed, many in suburban strip centers.

Check-cashing stores are hardly new to strips, but as they continue to grow and reinvent themselves, the industry's biggest obstacle is perhaps its own seedy reputation. Many

actually go to a bank. Nonetheless, many banks now offer in-store bank branches—in effect bringing the bank to the customer. Several banks have struck deals to put small banking centers in supermarkets. Such centers are built-in facilities or modular facilities that can be installed and/or removed quickly. For the latter type of installation, the entire facility is treated as furniture, with a much quicker depreciation schedule than a built-in facility, which is treated as real estate.

Other types of financial services provided in shopping centers include savings and loan offices, finance companies, brokers, and insurance and real estate offices.

Auto Supply Stores and Gas Stations

Auto accessory stores are minor tenants in shopping centers today. They are usually located in neighborhood, community, or power centers and are not often found in regional shopping centers. This type of store, often known as a tire, battery, and accessory (TB & A) store, is usually placed in a secondary or freestanding location if it includes auto repair services so that parking and car service will not interfere with the center's general customer parking or detract from the center's appearance. Some department stores, such as Sears and Wards, have their own TB & A stores to supplement customer services.

Adding a new gas station to a shopping center, done less frequently than in the past, is likely to be only marginally profitable. If a gas station site is sold before a center is developed, however, the station will most likely be-

come part of a neighborhood center or be located on a corner site that has been developed independently of the shopping center. Until the 1970s, most community and regional shopping centers encouraged gas stations to join the complex as a freestanding facility, either through an independent franchise operation or through a direct oil company landownership or ground lease, to provide an added convenience for shoppers and store employees. Today, many petroleum companies build convenience

retailers, developers, and the public harbor a not-in-my-neighborhood mentality. The industry, however, is working hard to overhaul its image, and Ace Cash Express of Dallas, one of the nation's largest check-cashing chains, is leading this effort to revamp the industry's image.

During the late 1980s and 1990s, the check-cashing industry nearly doubled its store count. Today, about $60 billion in checks is cashed at check-cashing facilities each year, says Henry F. Shyne, executive director of the National Check Cashers Association in Hackensack, New Jersey. More than cashing checks, the stores transfer money, write consumer loans, issue money orders, and accept payments for utility bills.

Like check-cashing facilities, medical services such as opticians, chiropractors, and dentists are long-time staples of strip malls. But a new and increasing variety of walk-in health care–related tenants are finding homes in unenclosed shopping centers.

The competitive and cost-conscious nature of health care is one reason many medical professionals seek the same visibility and curb appeal that retailers require, notes Richard Baker, president of Purchase, New York–based National Realty & Development Corp. At the same time, these tenants are not as picky about where in the strip they reside. "Medical tenants don't always have to be in a prominent location. They can be on the side or around the back," says Alan E. Smith, executive vice president of Konover & Associates.

In addition to opticians, chiropractors, and dentists, hospitals are opening more outpatient satellite facilities in locations like community shopping centers, where mandatory space and parking already exist. By locating away from the medical campus, hospitals can cut overhead costs, increase visibility, and improve access. "Hospitals want to be located in places that are convenient and accessible," says Paula Crowley, CEO of Anchor Health Properties. "To be competitive, they need to go to where the customer base is." That's why shopping centers located in the heart of communities make attractive sites.

Not everyone, however, agrees that patients with time to kill also make good retail customers. The idea that a complementary relationship exists between traditional and nontraditional retail tenants goes against what many people have believed for years: service providers hurt rather than stimulate surrounding stores' sales.

"Nobody shops while waiting for the doctor," says Don Dauphin, director of real estate for 72 Superfresh stores. Like other supermarkets, Superfresh dislikes any tenant that demands a large amount of parking. To that end, many food anchors' and drugstores' leases stipulate how much office space can exist in a center.

To retailers who shun having a doctor's office next door, some retail consultants say, "Stop whining!" Instead, they recommend that retailers take advantage of this captive audience. They note service providers like medical practices enjoy a built-in frequency and a higher level of customer loyalty than many retailers do. Anyone in a health plan visits a medical provider at least twice a year, which generates a lot of traffic, according to Dan Zelson, principal at Charter Realty in Greenwich, Connecticut, which recently made a deal with managed-care provider Sierra Health Services at Groton Square in Connecticut.

In the years to come, that loyalty to service chains may prove a boon rather than a bust for retailers who can turn patients—and even check cashers—into impulse shoppers.

Source: Excerpted from Joanne Gordon, "The Service Side of Strips," *Chain Store Age,* February 1998, pp. 136–38.

stores with gas islands or strike deals with fast-food outlets to offer two lines of products on a single site.

Two types of lease agreements—fixed payment and variable payment—are commonly used for gas stations. The fixed-payment arrangement involves a flat monthly rent, while the variable payment is based on the monthly volume of sales. Like other leases, a variable-payment lease provides that the tenant pay a minimum rate even if sales should drop. Because most gas station operators

lease their stations from the oil company, most developers' leases are made directly with the oil company.

The location and design of gas stations in relationship to a shopping center have become important issues, especially in neighborhood and community centers, where oil companies have customarily sought corner locations so that the shopping center site is often wrapped around the station. It is particularly important that the shopping center developer maintain control over design to keep

The redevelopment of the retail center in Beaver Creek, Colorado, in the late 1990s by East-West Partners included the construction of a community ice-skating rink.

the station's design compatible with that of the main building. Cross-easements for joint access are also important. The design and location of gas stations have received a great deal of criticism, and the developer may find that public approval for a shopping center hinges on proper design and location. When a service station site has been sold before a shopping center has been developed, control over design and joint access may be difficult to obtain. This situation is to be avoided, because it may require compromises in design to overcome adverse effects. Environmental issues are also a major concern related to gas stations.

Special Services

In a nonstop effort to remain competitive and in response to consumers' demands for time-saving services, many centers provide new and innovative conveniences to their customers, among them valet parking, a concierge, personal shoppers, fashion and wardrobe consultants, busi-

ness gift shoppers, gift wrapping, translation services for foreign customers, group tour arrangements, and Internet and other forms of interactive shopping services.

Other Tenants in Mixed-Use Retail Developments

As shopping centers and their suburban neighborhoods mature, demand for mixed-use development is increasing. Offices, hotels, and residential and institutional developments are being linked with shopping centers. These ancillary developments may be managed as part of the larger development, although their tenants are not considered shopping center tenants even though ownership may be the same.

Office buildings designed for a single corporation or for multiple tenants that are collocated with shopping centers create additional markets for the center. In the past, offices in a shopping center were located in freestanding buildings; today, however, they are often successfully integrated into the shopping center complex, such as Pentagon City in suburban Washington, D.C., and the Galleria in Houston. Because offices generate business for shops and restaurants, their construction on regional shopping center properties has followed naturally. If an office building is part of the development, the site must be adequate to handle the separate parking and traffic that offices generate, and it must be able to accommodate all-day parkers without negatively affecting the shopping center. An important consideration is that the combined parking demand for office space and retail uses will be less than the demand generated by each use individually. Opportunities for shared parking must be carefully evaluated.[8]

The demand for office parking (which peaks on weekdays between 9 a.m. and 5 p.m.) normally does not conflict with peak shopping hours. For this reason, the parking standard for shopping centers will accommodate office tenants until the net rentable area of the offices reaches 10 percent of the center's GLA. When this point is reached, additional parking space should be constructed.

To determine whether an office component will enhance the center's bottom line, the developer should evaluate the market potential for office space and the feasibility of locating office development on the site. In some cases, the office property may be located in a section of the shopping center where high-density retail facilities or other facilities of greater benefit to the project would not be feasible. In other cases, a more integrated approach is preferable.

Today, many developers are creating urban-style complexes with retail stores on the first level and office space above. Such projects can be complicated and difficult to design and manage as a result of the need for separate entrances, lobbies, and elevators to the upper floors and to underground parking. In the right setting, these developments are quite successful, with synergies created that enhance both the office and retail components. In a town center setting, office space on a second level may not lease as rapidly as the retail space, although as this configuration becomes more common again, this situation will likely change. If the shopping center management places enough emphasis on office leasing, most second-story office spaces are eventually filled, but rental rates could be lower than expected.

The presence of a retail center in the same complex enhances the marketability of residential and hotel developments, but as is the case with office buildings, access, parking, and separate building systems must be coordinated.

Concluding Thoughts

The creation of the perfect tenant mix in a particular type of shopping center is a laudable goal, but it is doubtful such a thing exists. The mix of tenants must be viewed as the best possible compromise that meets the greatest number of criteria established by the developer for the project: maximizing rents, signing targeted anchors and high-impact brand-name tenants, successfully concluding favorable lease negotiations and achieving a broad range of tenant types and services, and accommodating tenants' physical requirements and customers' parking needs, all within the constraints imposed by the public sector and the financial backers. Some of these goals may be contradictory; for example, a shopping center made up entirely of jewelry stores would theoretically generate incredibly high rents based on average rent per square foot. In reality, of course, such a center would likely fail.

Moreover, a shopping center's tenant mix is, by its very nature, transitory. Economic and social conditions change constantly, and they are reflected in the changing nature of shopping centers and in the particular mix of tenants most suitable at any given moment. In fact, the constant turnover in tenants (perhaps 10 percent a year) is driven as much by the need to keep the shopping center fresh as it is to accommodate better tenants and new retail concepts. The creation of the optimal mix of tenants in every type of shopping center is as much an art as it is a science.

Notes

1. For detailed information about anchors in urban entertainment centers, see Michael Beyard et al., *Developing Urban Entertainment Centers* (Washington, D.C.: ULI–the Urban Land Institute, 1998).

2. These codes are described in ULI's *Dollars & Cents of Shopping Centers* and in *The Standard Industrial Classification Manual*, prepared by the Statistical Policy Division of the Executive Office of the President, Office of Management and Budget. Definitions and classifications found in the SIC manual are used by government, industry, and trade associations for statistical purposes.

3. See *Dollars & Cents of Shopping Centers: 1997* for sales and rent figures for different types of tenants by location and level in regional shopping centers.

4. The lists of tenants for neighborhood, community, regional, and super regional centers come from *Dollars & Cents of Shopping Centers: 1997,* which will be updated in the 1999 edition.

5. For detailed definitions of the types of stores in these categories and the goods sold in them, see *North American Industry Classification System* (Washington, D.C.: Executive Office of the President, Office of Management and Budget, 1997).

6. See W. Paul O'Mara, "A Bay State Comeback," *Urban Land*, November 1995, p. 45.

7. See Beyard et al., *Developing Urban Entertainment Centers.*

8. See Barton-Aschman Associates, Inc., and ULI–the Urban Land Institute, *Shared Parking* (Washington, D.C.: ULI–the Urban Land Institute, 1983).

6. Operation and Management

The Lease as an Operational Tool

The lease document provides the foundation for the successful operation of a shopping center. Its detailed provisions not only establish the level of income that the developer/landlord anticipates from his enterprise, but also itemize the contractual rights and obligations that have been successfully negotiated between the tenant and the landlord. Shopping center leases differ significantly from other commercial leases.

A shopping center lease is a contract through which a landlord gives a tenant the use and possession of designated premises for a specified period of time in exchange for payments of specified amounts. Leasing refers to such conveyance. The conveying party is the lessor, and the party to whom the right of terminable use is conveyed is the lessee. In real estate, the right of terminable use conveyed to the lessee is a leasehold. Rents are based on estimates of the value of the leased premise.

Issues regarding leasing should be part of the earliest stages of the development venture, regardless of the type or location of the shopping center, because the leasing strategy dramatically affects the center's feasibility and shapes its ongoing planning. The lease document's treatment of details and its handling of the many facets of the

shopping center's operation in large measure determine the center's character, customer appeal, and financial success. Because the lease is a legal instrument, a lawyer specializing in the field should draft it. No universal leasing document can be made that applies to all shopping centers, all tenant types, and all jurisdictions.[1] The following sections present the practices currently employed in shopping center leasing that balance the landlord's risk with tenants' performance.

Percentage Leases

A shopping center developer/owner is confronted with two basic economic needs: an adequate income stream to meet the shopping center's fixed expenses and a return on the developer's equity that reflects the value of the property. If properly structured, the combination of minimum guaranteed rent plus percentage rent, or rent as a percentage of sales, can answer both needs.

Besides providing a basic return on investment, minimum rents should cover the fixed expenses of operating the shopping center—principal and interest on the mortgage, real estate taxes, insurance, maintenance, housekeeping, and other operating expenses. The percentage rent, when added to the minimum guaranteed rent, should provide for the potential of an increasing return on investment for the developer if the center is successful and allow the developer to share in that success. The adequacy of the minimum rent structure is ensured by special lease provisions, such as escalator clauses and

Programmed events, such as the fashion shows at Beachwood Place in Dallas, Texas, are an important part of retail centers' operations.

the establishment of a formula for shared common area charges and real estate taxes, which protect the landlord against inflation.

In the retail field, the percentage lease has become the most widely used kind of rental contract for both tenant and landlord. In its simplest form, the percentage lease is an instrument in which the tenant agrees to pay a rent equal to a stipulated percentage of the gross dollar volume of the tenant's sales. In shopping centers, the most common type of percentage lease is one in which the tenant agrees to pay a specified minimum rent, even if the negotiated percentage of gross sales is less than the agreed-upon minimum. This combination of minimum rent and percentage rent takes the needs of both landlord and tenant into account; the guaranteed minimum protects the shopping center owner if the tenant's sales are not high enough to produce the necessary rental income. The owner thus receives enough income to cover amortization and operating costs, plus a basic return on investment. But the owner receives less when times are rough and during the early years of a development, and more as the tenant's business prospers, as total rent charges fluctuate with the volume of business.

Percentage lease rates and the amount of the minimum rent should be based on the kind of business, the volume of business per square foot of leased space, the markup on merchandise, the business value of the tenant's space and of the shopping center location, the amount of competition, and other factors.[2] Percentage rents for regional and super regional centers range from about 2 to 10 percent, with most non-fast-food tenants ranging from 5 to 8 percent. Fast-food tenants typically pay 8 to 10 percent, while anchor department stores typically pay only 2 percent. At community shopping centers, percentage rents are slightly lower, ranging from about 1 to 8 percent, with most tenants ranging from 4 to 6 percent. At neighborhood centers, percentage rents are slightly lower still, although in recent years, they have moved upward so that they now approach rents for community centers in many cases.[3]

The breakpoint in gross sales volume, that is, the point above which the percentage rent applies, can be determined mathematically once the minimum rent and the rate of percentage rent are established. For example, if the minimum rent is set at $6,000 and if the agreed-upon percentage rate is 6 percent, gross sales of $100,000 would be the breakpoint. But if gross sales fall below this figure, say to $50,000, the tenant would still pay $6,000. On the other hand, with a straight percentage lease (with no minimum), the owner would receive only $3,000 in this example. When sales exceed $100,000, the percentage rate applies only to the overage. Thus, if sales reach $150,000, the tenant pays the landlord the base rent of $6,000 plus 6 percent of $50,000, for a total of $9,000. The overage offers the shopping center owner a financial cushion; this cushion becomes the balance after operating expenses, known as net operating balance.

Because it balances tenants' and the landlord's interests, the percentage lease with a minimum guarantee is commonly used for most types of shopping center tenants. Some exceptions are nonretail tenants such as banks, service shops, and offices for such tenants as insurance agencies, doctors, and dentists. When only fixed guarantees are involved, the developer would be wise to consider short-term leases or leases that escalate based on a series of specified steps or on the consumer price index. With fixed rents, the owner is at a disadvantage because he or she does not share in the center's profits, which are the result in large measure of his or her expertise in creating the center in the first place. If a percentage lease is not possible, owners typically opt for a short-term lease so that they are better able to adjust rental incomes in line with the rising value of the center's location, higher operating costs, and other changing circumstances. Of course, tenants prefer longer leases in the same circumstances.

When negotiating percentage rent, the owner should consider several options:

- Offsetting any higher finish allowances by subtracting the amortization of the expense from the calculation of the breakpoint.
- Accelerating the percentage rate as sales increase.
- Recognizing the difference in the ability of different types of users to pay a higher percentage of sales relative to occupancy costs.
- Letting establishment of the breakpoint be based on the lesser of the negotiated amount or sales for a specified lease year, ensuring percentage rent on incremental sales over the base year, regardless of the negotiated breakpoint. The base year should not be a year in which sales are likely to peak.
- Changing the percentage rate or converting percentage rent to base rent in the event of assignment or subletting.
- Setting the percentage breakpoint as the economic breakpoint for the tenant's profitability.
- Changing the percentage rate and/or breakpoint in the event of a change in use.[4]

The income stream from power centers tends to be much flatter than from traditional community or regional shopping centers, and as a result little upside potential exists for power center owners. In power centers, the anchor tenants' leases produce most of the cash flow. Creditworthy power center tenants are able to keep their long-term rent costs at 1 to 3 percent of sales.

Although percentage lease clauses are included in many leases for anchor tenants in power centers, the breakpoints are set so high that very little percentage rent, if any, is collected. According to ULI's *Dollars & Cents of Power Centers: 1997,* the median overage rent paid to power center developers was only $0.16 per square foot.

The Lease Document

An attorney can draft a lease, but the developer should establish the business terms upon which the document is based. A well-constructed and well-drawn lease is also

The percentage lease is the most common kind of rental contract in the retail field. Regional centers such as Fashion Island, located on an 87-acre site overlooking the Pacific Ocean in Newport Beach, California, command larger percentage lease rates than community or neighborhood centers.

Mizner Park's high volume of retail sales has allowed this mixed-use center to command competitive retail lease rates. The retail component was 90 percent leased before the grand opening in the early 1990s.

a management tool, as it sets down the rules and regulations of conduct for both tenant and landlord. Any sample lease form for a shopping center should be used only with caution. The developer must avoid any legal form based on another jurisdiction, because many factors prevent a leasing formula from being applicable everywhere. Lease provisions must also conform to the circumstances and requirements of the particular type of shopping center. Above all, it is unwise to enter into any important transaction, such as a long-term lease for a commercial property, without the counsel of an attorney who resides in the city where the center is located and who is familiar with statutes, ordinances, and court decisions applicable to the development and operation of a shopping center in that jurisdiction.

Besides establishing obligations, responsibilities, and leasehold arrangements, the lease incorporates the means of preserving the shopping center's character and appearance over time. When drafted properly, lease provisions

establish beneficial relationships between the developer and tenant. For a well-planned operation, the lease should cover these items, which are discussed in the following sections:

• Description of the premises;
• Term of the lease;
• Rental terms: the minimum guaranteed rent and the rate of percentage rent based on gross sales (including a definition of gross sales);
• Tenant's share of operating expenses, property taxes, and other expenses;
• Permitted use of the premises, including hours of operation and merchandise to be sold;
• Alteration and improvement of the premises;
• Assignment and subletting;
• Landlord's lien;
• Indemnification and insurance;
• Landlord's right to enter the premises;

- Damage or destruction to the premises, building, or common area;
- Condemnation;
- Default;
- Surrender of the premises;
- Other issues affecting leasing;
- The merchants' association or marketing fund;
- Miscellaneous provisions;
- A site plan and building layout indicating the demised premises, as an exhibit appended to the document.

Lease Forms. Although anchor tenants or national chains sometimes have the economic power to insist upon the use of their own lease forms, if possible all tenant leases in a shopping center should be written on the landlord's form. The form should take into account the particular operational and physical characteristics of the center, market trends, competition, and the relative financial strength of the center owner. A major regional shopping center developer can probably impose a more extensive lease form than can the owner of a small neighborhood center. The longer form may contain provisions for a merchants' association or promotional fund, restrictions on hours and methods of operation, use of common areas, tenant improvements and alterations, and a clause prohibiting the tenant from owning or operating another store within a specified distance of the premises. The lease form must also reflect the requirements of any relevant state laws, municipal ordinances, deed restrictions and covenants, and conditions and restrictions. The landlord usually needs a different lease form for the first tenants in a center to address such issues as the tenant's initial improvements and participation in a grand opening, as well as the initial basis on which the tenant's share of taxes and operating expenses is calculated.

Once the lease form has been developed by the developer/owner and an attorney and reviewed by knowledgeable leasing brokers, it should be printed in a format that permits all variable data—such as the name of the tenant, the term, the rent, the use, hours of operation and address for notices—to be inserted on a separate sheet (called "basic lease information" or "fundamental lease provisions") that can be reviewed at a glance. The designation of the tenant on the signature page of the lease form should also be added. A printed form psychologically impedes the use of amendments, but if any are made, they should be set forth in a separately prepared addendum to the lease. This approach facilitates the review of individual leases, and the economic terms of each lease and any departures from the basic form or additional terms can quickly be noted by reviewing the basic lease information and any addenda.

Description of the Premises. The area and general location of the premises should be described in the lease. A lease for a new center may need to describe the area of the premises as built. A floor plan attached to the lease should describe the exact area, location, and configuration of the space the tenant will occupy. If the landlord gives the tenant exclusive responsibility for maintenance of a certain area or allows the tenant to use additional space—for example, part of the common area in front of a shop—such responsibility or use should be granted as a license. If the premises are described to include common areas or portions of the structure and the landlord or other tenants interfere with the use of those areas, the tenant could have cause to demand an abatement of rent based on constructive eviction.

Tenants want confirmation that their premises include the use of parking areas and malls. Such confirmation should be granted as a nonexclusive license, and areas used for these purposes should not be described as part of the premises. The landlord should reserve the right to grant similar nonexclusive use to other tenants, to promulgate rules and regulations regarding the use of such facilities, to designate specific parking areas for employees or for the use of any tenant, to change the parking layout and perhaps to withdraw property from use for parking, and to close temporarily and/or redesign all or any portion of the common areas. The right to close and/or redesign common areas can be quite important in leases for older centers where remodeling or refurbishment is being considered.

Term of the Lease. The appropriate term of the lease depends on the market, the tenant's size, strength, and credit, and the landlord's desire to maintain stability at the center while at the same time protecting future options. As a rule, economically weaker tenants and smaller spaces warrant shorter lease terms. Shop tenants, even national chains, typically are given leases with five- to ten-year terms, with rental increases during that term built into the lease. Shorter leases allow the landlord to renegotiate with the majority of smaller tenants more frequently, and to weed out poorly performing tenants. Certain tenants, such as restaurants, require longer lease terms to finance their furnishings, fixtures, and equipment; the landlord's primary incentive in accepting longer terms derives from having lease provisions that require rents to be periodically readjusted to market value. If an option to renew is granted a small tenant, not only should the rent be readjusted to the market, but it also may be advisable to condition the right of renewal upon the tenant's achievement of a certain level of gross sales.

The lease term may begin at a different date from the date rental payments begin. Tenants may be granted a rent-free period in which to install fixtures on their premises, and major tenants may be able to insist that their rental obligations not begin until certain other designated major tenants and perhaps a specified number of shop tenants are also open for business. In those leases where certain events are tied to anniversaries of the commencement of rental payment rather than to the commencement of the term, the landlord and tenant may need to execute, and sometimes to record, a memorandum documenting the relevant date.

Rental Terms. Most shopping center leases require monthly payments of both minimum rents and percent-

Monarch Court is one of the focal points of Phipps Plaza in Atlanta.

age rents based on gross sales. Gross sales should be defined as broadly as possible and should always include receipts for merchandise and services sold in or from the premises by the tenant and the tenant's subtenants, licensees, and concessionaires. They should also include gross receipts from merchandise and services sold as a result of orders received at the premises by mail, telephone, video, or other electronic, mechanical, or automated means, whether such orders are filled on the premises or elsewhere.

Excluded from gross sales are sales or excise taxes collected from customers and the amounts of any refunds or credits made for returned merchandise—but only if the receipts for such merchandise were included in an earlier calculation of gross sales. Gross sales should be reported monthly within a fairly short period—perhaps ten days—after the end of each month. Ideally, the tenant's report should show daily sales as well as sales broken down among the tenant and each of its subten-

ants, licensees, and concessionaires, as well as an itemization of all deductions from gross sales. An independent accountant should audit tenants' sales once a year.

Although it once was unrealistic to expect smaller tenants to produce monthly reports (even though the landlord received monthly payments of percentage rents), it is no longer the case because computers have simplified the task. If it remains a problem, the tenant should be required to make monthly payments equal to the monthly average of the percentage rents paid the previous year, with an adjustment at the end of the year. The requirements for auditing and reporting are particularly important for a tenant that operates other stores whose gross sales are not yet sufficient to require payment of percentage rents or whose percentage rents are lower.

The lease should designate the location where the tenant will maintain its computerized accounts and account records relating to gross sales. It should require that these records be retained for at least three years, and should permit the landlord and his representatives to audit such books at any time after giving reasonable notice. Leases may call for the tenant to adopt and maintain a procedure to keep adequate daily records of sales and to provide the landlord access to any records or reports relating to sales or excise taxes as well as to the results of an audit of the tenant's business by a certified public accountant. The tenant should pay for the audit if the audit indicates that statements of gross sales previously made by the tenant fall short of the amount of actual gross sales by more than 2 percent.

Tenant's Share of Operating Expenses, Property Taxes, and Other Expenses. From the landlord's point of view, the preferred lease arrangement requires the tenant to pay its share of all property taxes and assessments as well as all operating expenses incurred in connection with the shopping center. In new projects, because taxes and expenses for the first year will be artificially low, tenants may be reluctant to pay increases in operating expenses and property taxes thereafter. To ward off this problem, the landlord can calculate taxes and operating expenses for the base year as though the building were 90 to 95 percent occupied. In mixed-use projects, another issue concerns the allocation of property taxes and operating expenses among parking, office, and retail areas. To preserve flexibility with respect to operating expenses, the lease should simply state that such allocations will be based on generally acceptable accounting practices. Property taxes may be handled most directly by allocating to each component of the project explicit percentages for payment of the taxes.

Taxes, tax assessments, and operating expenses should be defined to include standard and special assessments as well as any governmental impositions—for example, special transit service, street improvements, contributions in lieu of the developer's providing housing or parkland, or business improvement districts. In states such as California, where assessed values may be readjusted to reflect the sale price when property changes hands, tenants may ask for a provision that protects them from tax increases resulting from the reassessments. The landlord obviously wishes to avoid this provision and might argue that until reassessment following sale of the center, tenants enjoy artificially small increases in property taxes because assessments are not regularly increased to reflect increases in the market value of the shopping center.

Common area expenses or operating expenses should be broadly defined to include costs incurred in connection with the operation of the particular building where the tenants are located as well as all related areas, including parking lots, service roads, HVAC for an enclosed mall, snow and trash removal, utilities, security, landscaping, elevator/escalator maintenance, and any expenses that might be incurred under a reciprocal easement agreement.

Operating expenses should also include the obvious expenses of general repair and maintenance of buildings and roofs, operation of any central utility system, insurance (liability, property, and any special insurance,

A key issue in determining a tenant's share of operating expenses, property taxes, and other expenses in mixed-use centers such as Reston Town Center involves the proper allocation of property taxes and operating expenses among parking, office, hotel, and retail areas.

such as earthquake or flood insurance), advertising and promotion, and general and administrative costs, as well as the depreciation of machinery and equipment used to maintain the premises and reasonable replacement reserves.

Capital expenses should be included to the extent that they cover the cost of improvements made to the building after the lease goes into effect if these improvements are reasonably anticipated to reduce operating expenses or are required under a law not applicable to the building at the time the lease was executed, amortized over the reasonable useful life of such improvements. In addition, capital expenses should include the landlord's interest cost on funds borrowed to pay for such capital improvements. Management fees, or a specific percentage ranging from 5 to 15 percent, for administrative and overhead expenses, calculated on the basis

The Shops at Sunset Place

A New Wave of Shopping Center Operations

Sunset Place is a 550,000-square-foot entertainment-anchored retail destination developed in South Miami by the Simon Property Group in association with the Comras Company. The project is representative of a new type of development being pursued by Simon across the United States that is designed to perform as a regional destination through the application of multianchoring and branding, and the creation of distinctive, people-oriented environments. Simon recently created a $1 billion venture fund with investment bankers Donaldson, Lufkin, Jenrette to develop such entertainment-enhanced destination projects.

Multianchoring at Sunset Place comprises a variety of entertainment venues, including a 24-screen AMC theater, a 450-seat IMAX theater, and a 40,000-square-foot, two-level GameWorks entertainment center; a number of brand and icon retailers, including a Virgin megastore, NikeTown, FAO Schwarz, Barnes & Noble, and Z-Gallerie; and signature restaurants new to Miami, such as New York's Coco Pazzo and China Grill, the Santa Fe Beer Factory from Mexico City, and new dining concepts such as the Country Store Restaurant and Swampy's Wilderness Grill.

Simon has also emphasized the importance of creating a distinctive sense of place to distinguish Sunset Place as a destination in the context of competitive projects such as the Bayside Festival Market Place, CocoWalk, and a recently announced retail complex in Coral Gables.

Stan Eckstut of Ehrenkrantz Eckstut & Kuhn Architects was charged with developing a plan that complied with South Miami's Hometown Plan (which requires integration of the project within the existing urban fabric) while creating a one-of-a-kind experience. Miami's Wolfberg, Alvarez and Partners executed the architectural design and oversaw the integration of scenographics and landscape. McBride & Company created the environmental treatments and special effects used throughout the project's public spaces.

Context

The street plan developed for Sunset Place connects with the surrounding grid of streets while subtly introducing a more romantic, curvilinear system of internal streets. The internal streets open onto a Grand Plaza and a Grand Stair, suggestive of the colonial cities of the Caribbean in which the grid plan is juxtaposed with streets that curve to address the challenges of a hill, the tropical sun, or the entrepreneurial verve of local merchants.

The internal streets have been planned to allow for penetration by cars into the block of the project for both valet parking and garage access. The automobile, which is very much part of Miami's urban culture, is meant to be part of this environment. Pedestrian streets are an extension of these vehicular entryways into the project, with lush plantings and colorful sidewalk mosaics signaling the transition.

The plan also addresses the significant challenges of vertical circulation by treating stairways, escalators, and elevators within the context of a city center. There is a bit of the feeling of great colonial fortresses that over time became integrated within an expanding city fabric. The most dramatic example of this feeling is the Grand Stair, which is carved into the block of the project as the central feature. It provides seating for people watching and street performances and access to the second and third levels of shops and entertainment.

Choreography

Considerable effort has been directed at creating a "guest experience" at Sunset Place by paying attention to visitors' itineraries. The curvilinear streets invite exploration, rewarding patrons with surprises as they round a corner to discover a piazza, a lush tropical water garden, a special effects show, or the drama of the Grand Stair.

The designers have in effect choreographed the experience for visitors from the multiple entries into the block to the sequence of experiences that lead through the project. For example, at the Sunset Entry, visitors enter the project through the organic lattice of a banyan tree. This transition from the heat of the city streets is reinforced by natural tropical sounds and Caribbean music, along with flowering ground cover and water features. After emerging from the banyan tree, visitors find themselves in a large rotunda with two levels of shops shaded by a second higher canopy modeled on a grove of banyan

of all other specific operating expenses, are typically included in general and administrative costs.

Pass-throughs of operating expenses outlined in this section are always based on the tenant's percentage share of the total area to which the particular operating expenses or property taxes are applied. This pass-through should be drafted to reflect an agreed-upon number of initial total square feet of such improvements, with a provision that permits an adjustment in the percentage share if the rent-able area of the improvements to which such expenses relate changes. In mixed-use projects, the lease should recognize that certain expenses may be allocated to an office or residential portion and certain expenses allocated to all portions of the project, and that the landlord's accountant will allocate expenses among such portions. Similar apportionment is required when particular tenants pay directly all of certain expenses that would otherwise

The back story at Sunset Place is based on the notion of a festive Latin city within a city to be discovered behind an ancient banyan grove and the stone walls of a triangular stone fortress.

trees and designed to provide a mix of shade and filtered light by day and a chiaroscuro of colored light and dappled shadows by night.

Special effects are used several times a day to create a storm in the rotunda, complete with thunder and lighting but without the downpour that accompanies Mother Nature's version.

Back Story
No literal story serves as the theme for Sunset Place, but a back story informed design decisions. Based on the notion of a festive Latin city within the city, it is meant to be discovered behind an ancient banyan grove and the stone walls of a triangular colonial fortress. The back story allows for a mix of images, a kind of temporal collage in which Sunset Place has evolved from colonial fortress to Caribbean village to a vibrant Latin city center. Images of colonial arches are juxtaposed with the graceful angles of Caribbean village architecture with its pastel hues and steel roofs. A fanciful red steel bridge is symbolic of the Flagler Overseas Railroad, which once connected Miami to Key West.

Brand Identity
Sunset Place is designed to evoke a powerful brand identity by creating a distinctive sense of place and a unique experience. The word "sunset" is meant to be more than a place name, connoting the moment of transition in which the memories of the day fade in anticipation of the evening. The architecture, graphics, and lighting effects are meant to reinforce this image subtly and directly. The entry along heavily traveled U.S. Highway 1 features the abstract image of a sailboat gliding past a setting sun. The 120-foot elevator tower looks like a grand ruin overrun by tropical plants by day, which transforms into a beacon of lighting and laser effects by night.

The positioning of Sunset Place as a destination has as much to do with its distinctiveness as a place and an experience as with its critical mix of tenants and multiple anchors. Sunset Place's brand identity is intended to convey the project's appeal as a destination for both daytime and evening excursions.

Source: Michael S. Rubin, MRA International.

■

Canal City Hakata in Japan is operated as a series of special districts with a canal as its main street. The center, which opened in 1996, was designed by RTKL to encourage social interaction among visitors so they can experience it as "urban theater."

be included in operating expenses, for example, heat and air conditioning within the store spaces themselves.

The lease should always permit the landlord to estimate property taxes and operating expenses to be incurred during the calendar year and should require the tenant to pay these estimated amounts monthly. The landlord should have the right to revise his share of the estimate and adjust the lessee's payments if he determines the estimate will be significantly off.

The lease should provide that the tenant pay on time for all utilities used in the premises, as well as for all taxes and assessments on the lessee's inventory, furnishings, fixtures, and equipment, and any gross receipts taxes or other taxes chargeable to rentals paid under the lease. This provision gives the landlord grounds for eviction or other action should a tenant attempt to continue business on a marginal basis.

Permitted Use of the Premises. Use clauses are of critical importance in maintaining a proper tenant mix and for enforcing restrictions on assignment and subletting. The permitted use should be described as specifically as possible. If a tenant is to sell women's clothing, the permitted use can be described in terms of articles of clothing, price range, and sometimes even primary lines to be carried. Restaurant leases can describe the types of food to be served as well as items to be included, or sometimes excluded, from the menu.

For the landlord's protection, some leases include a "radius clause" that restricts the tenant from owning or operating another establishment within a specified distance from the subject center. The distance depends on the type of business involved. This provision can be coupled with one that gives the landlord the option of permitting the operation of the nearby store but requiring that all or a portion of gross sales from that store be included in the calculation of gross sales from the leased premises to determine the tenant's percentage rent.

Powerful tenants cannot insist that lease provisions grant them exclusive rights to sell certain price and merchandise lines. They cannot control advertising by other tenants, prohibit discount selling in the center, prevent the inclusion of certain other tenants in the center, or limit the amount of space leased to other tenants. Major tenants do, however, retain the right to negotiate lease clauses that will protect the location of their stores and establish a reasonable range of categories of uses from which the landlord may select tenants to be located near the major tenants. Restrictions on tenants' activities should be aimed toward preserving the quality of the center rather than stifling competition in pricing. Any exclusive rights provided should be reviewed with an attorney, as the landlord's activities may be subject to scrutiny under federal or state antitrust law. In addition, the fact that a major tenant is a joint venture partner with the landlord may lead to greater scrutiny under antitrust laws.

Use clauses should also contain general language that prohibits a tenant from using the premises in a manner that is illegal, that affects the rate of insurance on the building or premises, and that interferes with or annoys other tenants. Specific limitations may be necessary for uses such as restaurants, which might introduce undesirable noises or odors.

A clause specifying certain minimum hours of operation is essential, particularly when tenants are located in malls. Requirements may also be needed concerning the lighting of window displays and interiors during operations and after closing hours to maintain or enhance the attractiveness of the center.

Alteration and Improvement of the Premises. The lease should tightly control the tenant's ability to alter the interior or exterior of the tenant's premises without the landlord's consent. The landlord should also fully control initial improvement of the premises. The lease should prevent the tenant from placing any sign, awning, canopy, advertising matter, or any other material on the glass at the exterior of the premises or on any other portion of the exterior of the premises without the landlord's consent, and should also regulate placement of any merchandise, equipment, or furniture outside the premises. These restrictions are necessary to control the appearance of the center and should be strictly enforced. The restrictions on alterations should also address the installation of radio or television antennas, satellites, loudspeakers, or any other devices on the exterior of the premises.

Additional language in the lease should describe the means and methods by which the tenant may carry out alterations, including a requirement that the premises and the building be kept free from liens arising out of work performed on the premises. In some states, the law provides that mechanics' liens will not attach to the landlord's interest in property if the landlord posts or files a notice of nonresponsibility before the tenant's construction begins. In such cases, the lease should stipulate that even after the landlord has consented to the tenant's improvements, the tenant should notify the landlord of the work before it begins.

In some states, even the posting of a notice of nonresponsibility may not protect the landlord from liens arising out of tenant improvements if the landlord contributed to the cost of the improvements or, as provided in many leases, the landlord is given ownership of the improvements after they are completed. If the landlord lacks protection from liens, the lease should require the tenant to provide labor and materials and completion bonds before starting work.

Assignment and Subletting. For the tenant to sublet the premises or assign the lease should always require the landlord's consent. This restriction, together with the use clause, gives the landlord control over the use and occupancy of the premises. The landlord's consent to such subletting or assignment is, as a general rule, not unreasonably withheld; in fact, in some states, this condition is legally implied. It is a matter to be determined with local counsel. In some states, a lease provision imposing a requirement for "reasonableness" on the landlord's refusal to consent to assignment or subletting may leave the landlord wide latitude, while in other states, the basis for withholding consent is limited to the proposed subtenant's or assignee's credit or business experience. These provisions should be carefully considered in light of local law.

Even if a reasonableness limitation is imposed on the landlord or implied by law, it is not always clear whether the limitation extends to subletting part of the premises as well as the entire premises. Situations may arise, particularly with regard to large stores, in which the landlord does not want to permit balkanization of the premises with multiple subtenancies.

The definition of "assignment" should be drafted to recognize the transfer of various interests in the entity that is the tenant, as for example, a sale of partnership interests or the controlling stock of a corporate tenant. A restricted assignment should also be defined to include those that occur "by operation of law" as well as assignments for the benefit of creditors or in connec-

Kings Waterfront is a proposed urban retail center in Liverpool, England, being designed by RTKL–United Kingdom. Preleasing is underway.

tion with voluntary or involuntary bankruptcy or reorganization, although the latter provision may, in fact, be unenforceable.

If any tenant has been given a lease without a percentage rent provision, the landlord should be compensated with a provision calling for the tenant to pay some portion or all of the consideration he receives in connection with the transfer of his leasehold interest. The landlord may then share in the tenant's profit from a bargain lease.

Landlord's Lien. The furnishings and fixtures that a tenant installs may be an asset to the landlord in re-leasing the premises should the tenant default and the landlord terminate the lease. For that reason, the lease should contain language creating a lien on furnishings and fixtures to secure payment of the tenant's obligations under the lease. As a practical matter, however, many tenants either lease furniture and equipment or finance its acquisition. For this reason, the landlord should be prepared, either in the lease form or in an addendum, to subordinate the lien to that of any bona fide lessor, supplier, or lender, and to execute and deliver any documents that may reasonably be required as evidence of this subordination.

Indemnification and Insurance. All leases should contain a provision by which the tenant waives any claims against the landlord for damage to property or injury to persons in, on, or about the premises arising from any cause other than from the negligence or willful act of the landlord. The exact wording of this provision should reflect state negligence law. The lease should also protect the landlord from liability for any damage to the property of the tenant or others located on the premises caused by theft or resulting from fire, explosion, water leakage, or the failure of utilities. In other words, the tenant maintains coverage for any damage to his property or interruption of his business. In addition, the tenant's coverage should include a provision that holds the landlord harmless from any claims or expenses incurred by the landlord in connection with the tenant's use of the premises, unless the landlord caused such expenses or claims. The landlord maintains insurance to protect himself against tenants' claims; however, the indemnification language of the lease establishes the primary responsibilities for such indemnification and insurance coverage.

The tenant should be required to obtain and maintain at his expense insurance coverage for general public liability, naming the landlord as additionally insured, as well as coverage for the cost of full replacement of the tenant's improvements to its premises. The exact language of the insurance requirements should be drafted with the help of an experienced insurance adviser with an eye toward special situations, such as liability for the storage or use of hazardous materials. Occasionally, a tenant that is a major national corporation prefers to insure itself rather than purchase insurance. This option may be acceptable if the tenant is likely to retain adequate financial resources.

Insurance provisions should always contain a waiver of subrogation as well as a requirement for both the landlord and tenant to seek these waivers from their respective property and liability insurers. Such waivers tend to speed settlement of claims.

Landlord's Right to Enter the Premises. The landlord should have explicit rights to enter the tenant's premises during normal business hours to inspect, repair, or reconstruct any part of the building, to install or repair improvements to or within parts of the building adjacent to the tenant, to perform any work required because the tenant has defaulted under the lease, to post notices of nonresponsibility, and to show the premises to prospective lenders, purchasers, and replacement tenants. Without the right of entry to repair or improve the building and adjacent premises, the landlord may be stymied in preparing adjacent spaces for other tenants. The landlord should also have the right to enter the premises at any time and without notice during an emergency. The tenant should be required at all times to provide the landlord with keys to all areas of the premises except to the tenant's safe or other similar designated areas.

Damage or Destruction. The exact drafting of this provision depends, to some extent, on the relative bargaining power of the landlord and tenant. Several combinations of damage may be considered involving partial or complete damage to the premises and partial or complete damage to the building or the common areas. Each party will want the option to treat damage or destruction as an opportunity unilaterally to decide whether or not to continue the particular lease. While the language of this provision in leases with major tenants may be subject to considerable negotiation, the lease form for smaller tenants should contain certain standard provisions. Typically, if only the tenant's area is damaged, the tenant receives no abatement of rent and must reconstruct the damaged section as soon as possible. This arrangement presumes that the tenant maintains adequate insurance. If the damage is to a portion of the building beyond the exterior boundary of the tenant's premises but necessary for the tenant's occupancy, the landlord usually agrees to repair it if the repairs can be made within a reasonable period, perhaps 90 days. If the landlord is committed to make the repair, the lease remains in effect. Even if the repair requires more than the stated length of time, the landlord should have the right to keep the lease in effect if he has notified the tenant within a shorter period after the damage occurred, say 30 days, of his commitment to make the repair. Any abatement in minimum rent related to damage extending beyond the tenant's area should be in the proportion that the damaged area of the premises bears to the total premises. No abatement should be allowed if the damage resulted from the acts or negligence of the tenant or his employees. Some tenants may justifiably insist upon a rent abatement if damage to the building or common area affects the volume of their sales. Before agreeing to this provision, the landlord should be satisfied that his insurance or rental losses will cover revenues lost for this reason.

Sacramento's Downtown Plaza provides an open-air shopping experience for residents of California's capital city.

©Tom Myers 1995

Condemnation. Even though the exercise of eminent domain is uncommon, it provides another area in which substantial negotiation can occur between the landlord and a major tenant. (It does not affect other tenants, however, with whom the landlord should still use the unmodified lease form.) The provision for condemnation should address at least two situations—a total or "material" taking, and a partial taking. When any portion of the tenant's premises is taken in a manner that interferes with the tenant's use, either the landlord or tenant should have the right—after giving notice to the other within a reasonably short period after the taking (perhaps 30 days)—to terminate the lease as of the date of the notice. In addition, the landlord may want the right to terminate the lease if any major tenant—for example, one occupying more than 10,000 square feet—terminates its lease or abandons its premises as a result of the taking, or if more than half of the area of the shopping center

The Camden Park shopping center was built in San Jose, California, during the recession of the early 1990s, when some tenants were struggling. Landlords of shopping centers can protect themselves with a default provision in the lease that provides remedies in the event a tenant fails to fulfill obligations or goes bankrupt.

or more than 20 percent of the area of the premises is taken.

In the case of a partial taking of the premises that does not result in terminating the whole lease, that part of the lease applying to the taking should terminate and the rent adjusted equitably. If the building or premises must be repaired because of the partial taking, the landlord's responsibility for the repair should be limited to the condemnation monies awarded for this purpose.

The lease should provide that, in any event, all awards for condemnation be payable to the landlord. The tenant is entitled to awards—up to the point that they do not diminish the awards otherwise due to the landlord —only for the taking of his fixtures and personal property and for relocation expenses.

Default. A provision for default has two major aspects: a definition of the default and a description of the landlord's remedies. Typically, a tenant is in default when any of the following events occur:

- The tenant fails to pay rent for more than a designated period after the time due, typically five to ten days. This provision may be modified to provide that the grace period will not apply if a tenant has failed more than two or three times in any 12-month period to pay rent when due. Tenants often request that an event of default not occur until a specified period after receipt from the landlord of a notice that rent is unpaid. This provision puts an additional administrative bur-

den on the landlord and extends the notice periods that generally are already provided by law before eviction proceedings can begin. For this reason, lenders regard the provision with disfavor.

- The tenant fails to perform any other obligations under the lease, including paying other amounts that may be due, for as long as ten days or some other reasonable period after notice.

- The tenant goes bankrupt or becomes insolvent, or engages in any fraudulent transfer of assets to protect itself from creditors.

- A receiver is appointed for a substantial portion of the tenant's assets or the levy on the lease or any estate of the tenant by attachment or execution, and the tenant fails to have the attachment or execution "vacated" within a specified period, typically 30 days. A receiver is likely to be appointed at the request of creditors, again typically in the context of a bankruptcy. A levy by attachment is ordered by a court upon the request of a party that has initiated a suit against the tenant and has convinced the court that the tenant is likely to dissipate his assets before they can be used to pay a judgment. The levy of execution then occurs when someone has won a judgment against the tenant. Either of such events may indicate a tenant's weak financial state, and both are included as events of default because the landlord will likely not want a receiver or judgment creditor as tenant.

- The tenant abandons the premises.

Leases are contracts, and the remedies available to a landlord when a tenant defaults are normal contractual remedies, subject in some states to statutory constraints. As a basic concept, if the tenant defaults, the landlord is entitled to the benefit of his bargain, which includes, first of all, the right to treat the lease as terminated. Until the landlord has declared the lease terminated, however, the landlord is entitled to the rent accruing under the lease, together with interest at the rate provided in the lease, or otherwise at the legal rate.

If the landlord finds a new tenant before terminating the lease, the landlord should be entitled to brokerage commissions and some or all of the remodeling expenses incurred in connection with the new tenant. After the lease is terminated, the landlord should be entitled to the benefit of his bargain, measured by the present value of the lease payments he would otherwise have received, less any loss he could have avoided by re-leasing the premises. Typically, the tenant bears the burden of

providing the amount of loss the landlord should have avoided. If the lease rate when the tenant defaulted was significantly below market, the landlord will want to find a new tenant and terminate the lease as soon as possible. If the market is soft and the defaulting tenant or his guarantor has substantial assets, the landlord may refrain from terminating the lease and permit unpaid rent to accrue, pending trial.

There may be many other reasons for not permitting a space to remain vacant during this period. If, on the other hand, it is clear that the tenant is insolvent and may file for bankruptcy, the landlord may be wise to terminate the lease as soon as possible to regain possession of the premises before the tenant is protected by a "stay" in bankruptcy. Once the tenant has come under the protection of the Bankruptcy Act, the landlord becomes a general unsecured creditor with respect to amounts owed and, if the trustee in bankruptcy rejects the lease, a limit is placed on the landlord's recovery for "benefit of the

Skylights permit sunshine to bathe the interior of the Rouse Company's Beachwood Place in Cleveland, Ohio.

Dave Whitcomb/RTKL

bargain" damages related to future rents. Strategies for dealing with defaulting tenants who may go bankrupt, or have already sought protection under the statute, should be reviewed with counsel expert in this area of the law.

When a tenant files for protection under the Bankruptcy Act, it can seek to liquidate its assets or make an arrangement with its creditors, perhaps in connection with a reorganization. Once the tenant files for protection under the act, its trustee in bankruptcy or the tenant itself as debtor in possession must decide within 60 days to "assume" or reject the lease, and during that period it must perform the tenant's obligations under the lease. Of course, trustees in bankruptcy and debtors in possession may not have the funds with which to perform such obligations. In addition, delays may occur in surrendering possession of the premises upon rejection of a lease while fixtures, equipment, and inventory on the premises are moved to storage or are sold.

Shopping center owners are provided with certain particularly explicit protections when the bankrupt tenant or its trustee wants to assume the lease. To assume the lease, the bankrupt tenant or its trustee must provide "adequate assurance" with regard to curing existing defaults and performing under the lease provisions. Adequate assurance must be given regarding the source of rent. The tenant or its trustee must also ensure that the percentage rent due under the lease will not decline substantially, that assumption or assignment of the lease will

not breach any provision relating to radius, location, use, or exclusivity, and that assumption or assignment will not disrupt the center's tenant mix or balance. If such assurance can be given, the tenant or its trustee can assign the lease to a third party unless a provision prohibits or conditions the assignment.

The lease should also contain language explicitly permitting the landlord to pay any amount, other than rental, on behalf of the tenant, or to perform any other act that the tenant has failed to perform on its own behalf. The landlord could then consider these expenditures as additional rent due under the lease.

Surrender of the Premises. Typically, a tenant is obligated to surrender the premises in good condition and repair and to remove its property upon the expiration or earlier termination of the lease. The lease also contains a provision that permits the landlord to remove any personal property that he finds on the premises upon termination or expiration of the lease and eventually to sell such property on behalf of the tenant's account. If the landlord comes into possession of the tenant's personal property, the landlord cannot dispose of the property freely but must follow legal requirements and be prepared to provide an accounting for the proceeds of any sale.

Other Issues Affecting Leasing. A lease may address a number of issues that might arise in connection with the financing or refinancing of a shopping center. Occasionally, the lease is made contingent upon the landlord's obtaining financing for the property; if the landlord is

Owners of large shopping centers, such as Centro Augusta in Zaragoza, Spain, often prefer to use a marketing or promotional fund rather than a merchants' association.

RTKL–UK Ltd.

figure 6-1
Percentage of U.S. Shopping Centers with Merchants' Associations and Promotional Funds

Type of Center	Super Regional (n = 125)	Regional (n = 104)	Community (n = 365)	Neighborhood (n = 324)
Centers with Neither Merchants' Association nor Promotional Fund	4%	7%	61%	80%
Centers with Merchants' Association Only	15	27	15	10
Centers with Promotional Fund Only	63	58	21	9
Centers with Merchants' Association and Promotional Fund	18	9	3	1
Total	100%	100%	100%	100%

Source: *Dollars & Cents of Shopping Centers:1997* (Washington, D.C.: ULI–the Urban Land Institute, 1997), p. 396.

unable to obtain acceptable financing within a specified time, the tenants are released from their commitments and the landlord from further obligations. In this situation, additional language should be inserted, if possible, calling for the tenant to consent to nonmaterial modifications in the language of the lease if required by the lender. If the tenant refuses to consent to such a modification, as well as to other possible remedies, the landlord should have the right to cancel the lease. The landlord should no longer be able to request lender-oriented lease modifications after delivering possession of the premises to the tenant.

The lease must always require the tenant to execute and deliver an estoppel certificate (a statement setting forth facts of lease, such as rent and concessions) to the landlord within a certain period after the landlord's request for such a certificate. In connection with such a certificate, the tenant should provide any reasonable information requested concerning the status of the lease and the premises. Ideally, this provision should also oblige the tenant to deliver its most recent financial statement if requested by a lender.

The lease should also contain a provision stating that, unless a mortgagee, trustee, or ground lessor elects otherwise, the lease is subject and subordinate to any ground lease, deed of trust, or mortgage placed upon the building and to any and all advances made in security thereof. This provision is subject to negotiation with major tenants, who usually insist that their subordination be conditioned upon the execution and delivery of an explicit nondisturbance agreement from a ground lessor or lender providing generally that, even if a lessor's ground lease is terminated or the building is foreclosed and sold under a trust deed or mortgage, as long as the tenant is performing its obligations under the lease, it will not be disturbed.

Merchants' Association or Marketing Fund. The merchants' association can be an essential factor in the successful operation of a shopping center. The lease should contain a paragraph giving the landlord the option to establish a merchants' association and requiring the tenant to join and make contributions. The tenant usually contributes to the merchants' association a specific amount per square foot of gross leasable area, with a

guaranteed minimum (for example, $500 a year), subject to escalation related to inflation. An alternative arrangement requires the tenant to contribute on the basis of gross sales, but this arrangement may not benefit the association because shops with the lowest gross sales typically require the greatest assistance from the merchants' association. The shopping center management often contributes to the merchants' association.

Many owners, particularly owners of large shopping centers, prefer to use a marketing or promotional fund rather than the merchants' association (see Figure 6-1). In some cases, they have both. The developer, subject to advice from a tenants' advisory board, controls expenditures from a promotional fund. This arrangement is a natural outgrowth of the promotional assessment for the grand opening that is often included in leases for new shopping centers. The money collected by either a merchants' association or promotional fund typically amounts to $0.02 (in neighborhood centers) to $0.23 (for super regional and regional centers) per square foot of GLA, with anchor tenants contributing a smaller amount per square foot than small tenants. Management usually contributes a larger share, ranging from about $0.03 (in neighborhood centers) to $0.14 (in super regional and regional centers) per square foot.

In addition to these requirements, or sometimes as an alternative, some leases require each tenant to contribute a stated percentage of gross sales for advertising.

Miscellaneous Provisions. Some of what are often referred to as "miscellaneous" provisions may in fact be of great significance in determining the outcome of disputes with tenants.

- Additional Rent—Some jurisdictions may require leases to state that any sums that may be payable to the landlord are additional rent, because the statute providing a summary proceeding for eviction does so only for nonpayment of "rent."
- Attorneys' Fees—This provision is necessary to enable the landlord to recover attorneys' fees spent in bringing actions against a tenant. It should be worded carefully so that reimbursement is not conditioned upon bringing such actions to final judgment.

RTKL Associates Inc.

RTKL Associates Inc.

The lease establishes many of the details of center management such as common area maintenance, signage, hours of operation, and employee parking. At Brandon Town Center in Florida, management sets the standard with the center's entrance sign and sculptural fountain.

- Sale of the Premises—This provision provides that, upon sale of the premises, the landlord is released from any further lease obligations accruing or attributable to any period after the landlord's ownership is terminated.
- Notices—This provision states that a notice is effective upon the earlier of 1) its delivery to a responsible employee of the tenant at the premises, or 2) a specified period after the notice has been mailed, addressed as set forth in the basic lease information and with postage prepaid.
- Waivers—A waiver is needed to make clear the fact that the landlord's failure to enforce a provision of the lease on one occasion does not necessarily jeopardize the landlord's right to enforce that provision later.
- Complete Agreement—The lease must state that no oral agreements exist between the landlord and the tenant affecting the premises and that the lease incorporates and supersedes any and all previous writings, such as letters of intent, between the parties.

Many of the details of shopping center operation and management are established in the lease. Through the lease provisions, the shopping center management establishes control of the tenant mix and the assessments for common area operation and maintenance, and provides for the enforcement of controls on signage, hours of operation, employee parking, tenant housekeeping, and maintenance of interior premises. Additionally, through the organization and operation of the merchants' association or marketing fund, as detailed in the lease, the center's management fosters and strengthens an image for the center that is attractive to shoppers in the trade area.

The lease provides for smooth operation and management by clearly dividing responsibilities between the landlord and the tenant; it describes what the tenant is obliged to maintain and what the landlord is required to perform. Structural maintenance and capital improvement of the buildings, for example, are the owner's responsibility, as is the repair of outside walls, roofs, sidewalks, and canopies, subject to reimbursement by tenants. The owner, with contributions from tenants, also maintains and repairs parking lots and landscaped areas, while tenants are responsible for the repair and maintenance of their own spaces.

In addition to allocating work responsibilities to the tenant and the landlord, the lease establishes who will pay for the upkeep and operation of the various areas of the center. In most centers, this distribution of financial support is simplified by separating each tenant's rental payment from the tenant's contribution to common area operation. The lease then describes which expenses the owner will cover and which will be considered common area expenses. Lighting the parking area, for example, is considered a maintenance cost and is therefore charged to the tenants through a provision in the lease. The distribution of charges for air conditioning depends on whether the system involves a central plant or individual units. In either case, capital costs and operating charges are divided between landlord and tenant and, as in all other areas of operation and maintenance, the chosen arrangement must be made legally enforceable through inclusion in the lease.

The lease can also be seen as the second of three steps that help ensure the center's proper operation and management and its ultimate success as a business venture. The first step involves the consideration of such development criteria as a strong location with respect to access from the trade area, proper site planning, good tenant mix, and appropriateness of store sizes and building layout for individual tenants' merchandising abilities and for the needs of the trade area.

The second step includes the leasing program and the many operational arrangements set forth in the lease. The third step is the ongoing operation and management of the center. Only so much groundwork can be laid; after that point, it is up to the management, in its day-to-day decisions and policies, to guide the center toward success for both the owner and the merchants. For a center to succeed, it must have strong and enthusiastic merchants, a general manager who is given a free hand and who possesses promotional skills and a knowledge of merchandising, and a developer/owner who is keenly interested in promoting the center. For a promotional campaign to succeed, the market and the various techniques of marketing—buying, inventorying, display-

ing, pricing, selling to please customers, promoting, and advertising—must be understood by the developer and employed by the merchants. The shopping center is no longer simply a real estate operation; it is a complex merchandising business.

Although no one has yet found a way to measure the energy, know-how, or capability of management, the intangible qualities of managerial efficiency and effectiveness are important in making a center profitable. The shopping center manager and the staff can contribute only so much to the success of the center, however. The mechanics of management and the decisions made by the manager cannot ensure a thriving marketplace. Likewise, the developer can provide only the setting for success, because it is largely the merchants who determine the customer draw and who cause the center to succeed or fail. For this reason, the most important responsibility of the shopping center's management is to stimulate the merchants to create a marketplace that is outside the ordinary. The merchants must be encouraged to tailor their range of merchandise, services, and overall environment to the ever-changing demands of the buying public.

Management of a Successful Center

Because a shopping center must be treated as an ongoing merchandising operation rather than as a straightforward real estate venture, management must be as

Depending on the arrangements in the lease, the shopping center owner/developer manages the center or turns over the center's operations to a management firm. Del Mar Plaza is a specialty retail center managed by a contracted management firm.

The Big Hulk. The Winning Guest. Fried Chicken of Kentucky. These literal Chinese translations of McDonald's, Pizza Hut, and Kentucky Fried Chicken exemplify the first wave of western food service and retail operators entering the Asian market. In a market dominated by large well-capitalized and well-connected Asian retailers, western counterparts until now have remained largely on the sidelines. To capitalize on opportunities in the fastest-growing retail market in the world, western firms need to know how to overcome the various barriers to entering the Asian market.

Overview of the Asian Market

Asian markets can be categorized by their various stages of political and economic evolution. Markets range from "undeveloped" (Vietnam, Myanmar [Burma]) to "emerging" (China, Indonesia, Malaysia, the Philippines, India, Thailand) to "mature" (Taiwan, Japan, South Korea, Singapore, Hong Kong). In general, the economic situation has grown more liberal throughout the region, with retail markets opening that historically have been protected by government policies such as licensing requirements, tariffs, and limited foreign ownership. Although barriers to entry still exist in some countries, they increasingly are being relaxed. Taiwan and South Korea, for example, opened their markets in the late 1980s. China liberalized its major markets (Shanghai, Beijing, and Guangzhou) and special economic zones in the early 1990s. Japan, with its 1998 New Large-Scale Store Law, has dramatically changed its local retail distribution systems and opened up its retail industry to foreign stores and brands.

A common denominator among Asian markets is the growth of the middle class, with its sophisticated tastes (frequently enhanced by foreign travel and education) and pent-up demand for retail, entertainment, and recreational activities—especially for western labels. The young middle class clearly prefers value-oriented merchandising and is decidedly influenced by foreign brand names and media. China, for example, has 250 million TV sets, many of them receiving satellite feeds from Hong Kong and Japan. These consumers are the MTV generation, eastern style.

Retail markets across Asia are changing rapidly. The traditional Asian department stores, streetfront retail shops, and "night markets" are gradually yielding to western retail formats, specialty boutiques, entertainment concepts, and even discount retailing.

While Asian markets offer substantial opportunities for retailing, they are growing at different rates and have vastly different political economies. Asia is not a homogeneous market, and the "one-size-fits-all" approach frequently used in the United States will not work. The cultural characteristics and opportunities of each Asian country are distinctive; hence, development strategies must be tailor-made for each market.

Retail Trends in Asia

Asia, now part of the global economy, is subject to influences and trends similar to those that affect western retail markets. Its cultural, political, and economic influences, however, superimpose a distinct set of market trends on these nations. Prevailing Asian retail currents emphasize three major categories.

Selection and Price/Value. As in the United States, Asian consumers are becoming more discerning. Although brand conscious, they are bargain hunters by nature, just like U.S. consumers. They believe locally made products are just as good as foreign products and prefer low-price/high-value merchandise. This penchant is validated by the success of discount retailers like Costco (United States), Carrefour (France), Makro (the Netherlands), and Lotus Superstores (Thailand), which capitalize not only on consumers' price sensitivity but also on their desire for selection, competitive pricing, and product differentiation.

Entertainment/Recreation. Many Asian consumers have newfound leisure and have the expanded income to support it. China, for example, recently adopted a five-day work week, releasing enormous pent-up demand. A 38 percent savings rate means consumers have disposable income to spend. In addition to the ubiquitous and traditional KTV (karaoke television), Asians are seeking movies, bowling, nightclubs, theme parks, interactive shopping experiences, water theme parks, and virtually anything that spells "fun."

The Family, the Child, and the Home. Perhaps the single largest market segment consists of the 20- to 35-year-old professionals who are starting or already have families. Strong family-based cultures in Asia tend to have large extended families that live, eat, play, and shop together. As a result, children become focal points of consumption and gifts. Retail sales are especially strong in children's items and household furnishings, reflecting a strong market among those forming households.

Retail Development in Asia

Over the past few years, traditional eastern retail and local department stores and general merchandise stores have begun to face intense competition from large Asian retailers such as Sogo, Isetan, Watsons, Jusco, Wellcome, and Seibu, as well as from western firms like Printemps (France), Benetton (Italy), and Toys "R" Us (United States). Even specialty stores and outlet shopping are slowly working their way into the Asian retail vernacular.

A variety of shopping centers, megamalls, and urban retail entertainment centers are now sprouting up on the Asian

Canal City Hakata in Fukuoka, Japan, typifies retail development in Asia. The center is a vertical mixed-use center that combines food, entertainment, and family activities. Most of Canal City's customers rely on public transportation or bicycles to get to the center.

landscape. They typically are mixed-use projects with multiple destination anchors and an emphasis on food, entertainment, and family activities. Compared with their U.S. counterparts, some are vertical in design—generally in excess of three stories and many over five.

These projects are often as large as 1 million square feet, while some, like Canal Place Hakata in Fukuoka, Japan, are large mixed-use projects well over 1 million square

feet. Parking is limited, and consumers rely heavily on public transportation or bicycles.

Because good locations and centers are limited, demand for retail space had been high and rents rising until the Asian economic crisis hit. This situation, however, will not last indefinitely: currencies have begun slowly recovering, and the problem of nonperforming loans was gradually being resolved during 1999. Structural changes in most Asian markets portend well for the future of Asian retail development.

Asian markets are no longer a luxury or an experiment; they are a strategic necessity. The opportunity costs of not pursuing a consistent Asian strategy may result in less growth, profitability, and value per share. In short, not competing in Asia carries a high price.

Case Study: Japan

The Japanese market provides an instructive example of both the opportunities and obstacles generally facing Asian retail development. As the world's second largest economy, Japan was the last Asian nation to fall victim to the financial crisis that devastated other regional markets. Its $5.1 trillion economy remained relatively stable because of its strong underlying fundamentals: high per capita incomes (25 percent higher than in the United States), a solid homogeneous middle class, retail expenditures approximately 30 percent higher than in the United States, and retail sales productivity almost four times greater than in the United States.

The strengths and weaknesses of the Japanese market have contributed to the prolonged economic stagnation and recession. Those sectors are strong that the government has opened up to international competition, particularly manufacturing industries, such as automobiles and consumer electronics, can withstand the competition. But major weaknesses exist in sectors protected from competition, including financial services, retailing, and construction (a sector that is particularly important in Japan as it accounts for more than 10 percent of employment).

Japan's regulation of the market differs from the U.S. government's more open approach. The government's regulation of the banking system has heavily influenced the allocation of capital in Japan since World War II. The result of the allocation practices was the country's banking crisis that emerged in the late 1990s and the related crunch in liquidity. Japan's banks became undercapitalized and, burdened by nonperforming loans, were not in a position to provide new loans as late as 1999. Many major Japanese corporations became overleveraged and unprofitable. Bankruptcies reached a record level in the late 1990s. According to many economists, the situation in 1999 is likely to get worse in the near term, at least into 2000 and perhaps for a prolonged period of approximately three years.

The modern history of Japan suggests, however, that the country will solve its problems. The solution will probably be somewhat unique to Japan, accommodating some of the fundamental cultural differences between Japan and the West, especially the United States. The Japanese cultural need to build consensus before fundamental change is adopted means that solutions will probably take longer to achieve than would be the case in the United States.

The existence of massive personal savings and a continued high personal savings rate must be recognized in assessing Japan. The large majority of these savings are invested in low-yield accounts with the government-controlled postal savings system and with Japanese domestic banks. Although it is expected that these savings will move to higher-yield opportunities as a result of Japan's financial reforms in the late 1990s, demographic and cultural considerations suggest that a large portion will remain concentrated in yen-denominated assts. If so, Japan will not require foreign capital over the medium and longer term, and a strong demand should exist for investment-grade income-producing Japanese real estate by Japanese investors.

Many Japanese laws and business practices related to real estate, including the provision of financing, are quite different from those in the United States. Although regulations are changing, Japanese cultural considerations will likely preclude a complete transformation to U.S. practices. Hence, it is difficult to predict the pace and precise outcome of this evolutionary process. Japan is a very complex market to be entering near the dawn of the new millennium; it is not a place for short-term investors.

Changing retail distribution systems, a relaxation in government regulations, and decreased land and building rents have reduced barriers for foreign retailers trying to enter Japan's retail market. In addition, such changes have provided local retailers with greater freedom to expand into underserved suburban markets and create new alliances with foreign and local developers.

Japanese consumers' shopping habits are also changing significantly. The driving forces in the market are single working women in their twenties and newly married couples in their thirties. Consumers are now conscious of value, price, and selection, and tend to be more individualistic and less oriented toward mass consumption than their parents. Moreover, greater leisure time has increased expenditures on entertainment and recreation, and has opened the door to western brands, retail trends, and shopping formats.

New shopping formats have emerged as a result of the recent shifts in retailing and demographics. Multianchor suburban shopping centers are starting to be developed by retailers such as Seibu and Jusco as well as by local real estate companies like Diamond City, Aeon Kosan, Nomura, and Mitsubishi Estates. Outlet centers are beginning to be developed by both local developers (Mitsui) and a U.S. REIT (Chelsea). Also popular are urban entertainment centers, like ones developed by HUMAX, a local developer, that combine cinemas, themed restaurants, and spas with specialty retail stores.

And this is just the beginning. Japan in general is an underserved retail market with only four square feet of retail space per capita. In comparison, the United States, with less income per capita, has about 19 square feet per capita, and Singapore, at the other (overbuilt) extreme, has 36 square feet per capita.

During the first decade of the new millennium, Japan's retail markets and shopping center industry will continue to shift dynamically. The following trends will be the driving forces of the future:

1. From Shopping Centers with a Single Anchor to Centers with Multiple Anchors—Changes in laws and distribution systems, and continued suburban growth will force department stores and general merchandise stores out of urban locations into multianchor shopping centers.
2. Greater Balance between Local and Global Retailers—Again, changed laws have reduced barriers to entry for foreign tenants, such as Tiffany, The Gap, Ralph Lauren/Polo, and Toys "R" Us, whose brand names are in demand by the young consumer-driven market. New strategic alliances and joint ventures between Japanese and international retailers will facilitate this trend.
3. From Urban to Suburban Shopping Centers—In the 1970s and 1980s, Japan's population experienced rapid suburbanization, yet retail and office development did not follow. As a result, many suburban markets are understored. Great mass-transit and highway transportation systems have created tremendous opportunities for shopping center development.
4. From Older to Younger Shoppers—The baby boomers are now entering their prime spending years. Led by western influences, Japanese 16- to 30-year-olds will continue to drive changes in the retail market and formatting well into the next century. The success of foreign retailers like Body Shop, Tower Records, AMC Theatres, Oshman's Sporting Goods, and Starbucks is testimony to the power of the youth market.
5. From Marginal Retailers to Competitive, Progressive Retailers—A shakeout of the retail industry is occurring, and it affects every segment—from small mom-and-pop stores to larger (and now bankrupt) general merchandise stores like Yaohan. Even old-line department stores like Mitsuoshi, which will close 11 stores, are not immune. Exciting new local retailers like Sazaby, Muji, and Loft, and foreign retailers like Armani Exchange and HMV Mega Stores will continue to challenge and dominate the first-generation retailers

because of their ability to effectively address the under-30 market.
6. From Loyalty to Store Brands to Value and Price Orientation—Japanese consumers are becoming increasingly fickle. Price matters, as does trendiness. Young consumers are no longer lifelong devotees of a single department store, as their parents once were.
7. From Return on Retail Sales to Return on Assets—Retailers have built stores and shopping centers as a means of generating sales and capturing market share, rather than maximizing return on assets. Hence, many retailers' balance sheets are burdened with nonperforming investments that reduce liquidity for their core retail business. Retailers will increasingly sell nonproductive assets and focus on returns from their core business.

The Japanese shopping center and retail industry will face significant obstacles as it enters the 21st century. The country's ongoing banking crises and stagnant economy will exacerbate the liquidity crisis; land and building prices, however, continue to drop precipitously, thereby reducing the cost barriers to entering the Japanese market. Underneath it all is a silver lining, however: a fundamentally strong and underserved retail market that needs modern shopping centers and retail entertainment facilities. Therein lies the opportunity for western developers.

Source: Kenneth Munkacy, managing director, TrizecHahn Asia-Pacific.

Decorative night lighting will make Neonopolis, scheduled to open in fall 2000 in downtown Las Vegas, a dynamic and safe environment for shoppers and tourists.

responsive as possible to the center's needs, knowledgeable about the evolving changes in the shopping center industry, and attuned to changes in society and among consumers. The owner, whether or not he is also the manager, must provide leadership and drive.

Depending on the size of the center and the arrangements for operation worked out earlier in the lease negotiations, the shopping center owner/developer provides for maintenance and management in one of the following ways:

- The owner/developer acts as or employs a manager to supervise the maintenance and management force, including the supervision of promotion and advertising, whether this work is handled by outside contract or by the center's management staff. The owner also retains the promotion director as a key member of the management staff. In some arrangements, the owner pays the promotion director's salary as part of his contribution to the merchants' association or marketing fund.
- The owner/developer turns over the center's operations to a management firm if this capacity does not exist in the developer's own organization. This practice is common in neighborhood centers.

When a management firm handles a center's operations, the fee paid to the firm is usually determined by negotiation. The fee depends on the extent of services rendered; the firm would charge a higher fee if the contract called for it to be responsible for advertising, promotion, and coordination of the merchants' association.

A leasing and management contract should be considered as two separate agreements. If a management firm is only to secure leases and perform no other management functions, the prevailing rates for real estate management in the local area may be used as a guide. In shopping center leasing, commissions paid to the broker who secures a lease from a tenant are usually similar to those paid for securing commercial leases. For management alone, fees are generally based on a percentage of the gross rentals collected.

In addition to maintenance and other facets of shopping center operation, a number of management concerns may be troublesome and require the landlord's special attention—including sign control, enforcement of parking regulations, evening and Sunday operations, real estate taxes, and accounting.

Sign Control

As discussed in Chapter 3, the owner and manager should maintain control over the size, location, quality, and design of all signs and other graphics in line with the center's design concept. If management directives are to succeed in preventing poor or incompatible signage, controls must be incorporated into the lease in a form that is strongly enforceable. Lease clauses should regulate the amount of space that tenants' signs may occupy, require that no signs be placed on the roof (unless that is part of the concept), and provide that any lettering to be placed on glass be approved by the landlord.[5]

Shopping center management should be wary of offering concessions in matters of sign control. Some tenants, such as chain drugstores, favor the placement of paper signs on display windows to promote certain merchandise or to advertise sales. But the effectiveness of the practice is dubious and can give the center as a whole a cheap, shabby appearance.

When the renovation of an existing center involves a new signage program, the owner would do well to "give a little and take a little" by offering to pay a portion of the cost of new signs. Whatever policy is adopted, all tenants should be offered the same arrangement.

Enforcement of Parking Regulations

A considerable number of employees' cars must be accommodated at any center. In fact, parking standards typically include an allotment of 10 to 20 percent of the total parking area to accommodate parking for employees in those cases where separate off-site employee parking has not been provided. Regulations designating certain portions of the parking area for employee parking are included in the lease; the lease further provides that flagrant violations can lead to cancellation of the lease. These provisions are necessary as the center's parking areas are private property and thus the parking regulations cannot be enforced by local police. At any rate, the center's management must continually check to see whether regulations are observed and must work with individual tenants and through the merchants' association to enforce the regulations. Otherwise, employees will occupy prime parking spaces best used for customers' vehicles.

Parking violations by the public are another matter. Because persons who misuse parking spaces may also be customers of the center, diplomacy and finesse must be used in dealing with violations. The greatest problem arises when commuters find the shopping center a convenient place to leave their cars all day. These parkers either work nearby or park their cars at the center and take another form of transportation to their place of employment. Peripheral parking might be turned into an opportunity, however. If parking is abundant, an area on the outer edges might be formally designated as commuter parking, thus providing a community service and drawing after-work shoppers at the same time.

Evening and Sunday Operations

Evening shopping is a major force in retailing, especially when entertainment attractions are added to the shopping center. The practice has shifted the peak hours of trade and the traditional shopping schedules to such a point that most centers now stay open at least six nights a week. Evening sales typically account for 30 to 40 percent of a center's trade. The challenge faced by management is to achieve greater trade volumes in off-peak hours through effective advertising and promotion.

Operation after dark requires better lighting for walks and parking areas and greater attention to both interior and exterior lighting for stores. Lighting can add glamour to a center at night, but it should not consume excessive energy. Sodium vapor lighting should be avoided, because its yellowish light casts an eerie glow that renders colors badly and makes people look menacing. Holding down the costs of lighting and heating or air conditioning while expanding the hours of evening operation calls for skillful planning and design by the center's management and tenants.

Most shopping centers are also open on Sundays. Shopping center operators report that weekend shopping accounts for an ever-greater proportion of sales volume, as more women have entered the workforce and have only weekends to shop. Weekend shopping is even more apparent at new-generation shopping centers where shopping is increasingly entertainment and environment oriented. Business activity starts building on Thursday and reaches its peak on Saturday afternoon, the heaviest shopping day. In some locales, however, Sunday openings produce the highest sales volumes per hour of the week.

Store hours can be regulated by agreement or by specification in the lease. The lease should explicitly prohibit independent action by a tenant who chooses not to remain open during regular daytime, evening, or Sunday hours. Most centers are open six nights per week and a limited number of hours on Sunday. Hours for small tenants should be tied to the hours established by the major tenants. In most centers, tenants are permitted to be open for longer hours than required, if they choose. For example, a tenant that relies on breakfast traffic may choose to open earlier. Restaurants, clubs, and cinemas and stores that cater to the same market often choose to be open later.

Real Estate Taxes

Real estate taxes and assessments create another special problem for the shopping center owner, because real estate taxes represent one of the landlord's greatest operational expenses. As reported in *Dollars & Cents of Shopping Centers: 1997,* real estate taxes in 1996 accounted for about 17 percent of total operating expenses in super regional and regional centers, about 30 percent in community centers, and about 34 percent in neighborhood centers. To protect the owner from increases in real estate taxes, a clause in the lease should provide that tenants pay for tax hikes through increases in rent. Tenants therefore will be concerned about local assessment practices and may be more inclined to get involved in tax-relief efforts. Future taxes are often underestimated. To be on the safe side, taxes should be figured at the local rate and at the full assessed value based on whatever assessment method the local assessor uses. Although centers are reassessed frequently, the trend is ever upward.

The difference in value between land used for buildings and land used for parking should be reflected in the tax assessment of the shopping center property. The land used for parking should be valued as parking area, not as commercial property similar to that occupied by the commercial structure. Shopping center parking areas used for the public's benefit support the thesis that more reasonable valuations are needed for shopping centers.

Accounting

ULI's *Dollars & Cents of Shopping Centers* analyzes the balance left in shopping center operations after operating expenses are subtracted from gross receipts. From this balance must be subtracted depreciation, debt service, and income taxes to arrive at the actual return on investment. *Dollars & Cents* presents current data on the various components of shopping center income and expense (as well as other data on centers in the United States and Canada), providing a reference source for finding and evaluating levels of performance in shopping center operations.

The categories of measurement used in *Dollars & Cents* and the accounting methods that the presentation of data reflects are based on ULI's *Standard Manual of Accounting for Shopping Center Operations.*[6] Whereas *Dollars & Cents* is intended as a reference work on current shopping center performance, the *Standard Manual* was developed because of the need for uniform shopping center accounting methods to provide consistent information and meaningful comparisons of operating results. Special accounting methods were not required for asset and liability accounting, because methods are much the same for shopping centers as for other businesses, but income and expense accounting needed special and standardized methods. Income accounting in shopping centers is largely a reflection of the revenue received through provisions in tenant leases, including rental income from tenants, income from common area services, income from the sale of utilities to tenants, and income from miscellaneous sources. Expense accounting in shopping centers, on the other hand, must be tailored to provide center owners, developers, and managers with useful data for budget projections and for comparison within the industry. The *Standard Manual* was designed to meet these accounting needs and to facilitate the sharing of information to improve the practices of shopping center management and performance and operation of shopping centers. Much of the following information is based on the *Standard Manual.*

Income Accounting. Total income or total operating receipts are derived from all money received from rent, common area charges, and other income. Total rent is the income from tenants for the leased space, including the minimum guaranteed yearly rent (or the straight percentage rent when no minimum guarantee is set) and the overage rent received as a percentage of sales above the established breakpoint. Because of the many different rental arrangements commonly used, only the figures contributing to the total rent are useful for rental comparisons (including those found in *Dollars & Cents*) across the industry. But in income accounting for individual shopping centers, the records should readily show

the data in each of the following categories as established in each tenant's lease:

- GLA in square feet;
- Sales (annual volume and per square foot of GLA);
- Rate of percentage rent;
- Percentage rent when no minimum guarantee is established;
- Minimum guaranteed yearly rent;
- Overage rent earned for the year;
- Charges to tenants for common area services, including charges for heating and air conditioning an enclosed mall;
- Charges under the escalator clauses, accounted separately for each type of charge;
- Utility charges for the year, where applicable;
- Miscellaneous income, including revenue from such facilities as public telephones and vending machines;
- Total rent and total charges.

Expense Accounting. The standard system of expense accounting is based on two objectives, the first and more important of which is the need to classify and present accounting data according to the accounting and information needs of the shopping center's management. The second objective is to provide accounting methods that facilitate the industrywide gathering and analysis of operating expense data. To accommodate these two objectives, shopping center expenses are categorized in two ways: by functional category and by natural category. The functional categories can be applied to all centers they provide the framework for comparison across the industry. The natural division of expenses, on the other hand, ties functional expenses with the primary objectives of expenditure. Functional expense categories include building maintenance, parking lots, the mall, and other public areas, central utility systems, office area services, advertising and promotion, expenses of financing, depreciation and amortization of deferred costs, real estate taxes, insurance, and general and administrative costs. Natural expense categories include payroll and supplementary benefits, management fees, contractual services, professional services, leasing fees and commissions, materials and supplies, equipment, utilities, travel and entertainment, communications, taxes and licenses, contributions to the merchants' association, insurance, losses from bad debts, interest, depreciation, amortization of deferred costs, and ground rent.

Taken together, the two groups of categories provide a logical basis for analytical comparisons of results for individual shopping centers with industry data as well as day-to-day information. The standard system is designed to serve as the expense classification for a complete system of accounting, with two exceptions—financing costs and depreciation of the structures (real and appurtenances). Consequently, it is essential that the shopping center developer and his accountant be totally familiar with current tax laws.

Expense accounting for shopping centers should be based on two objectives: providing data for the shopping center's management and gathering data useful for industry-wide surveys.

RTKL Associates Inc./Los Angeles

Because regional, community, and neighborhood centers differ substantially in size and complexity, management's needs for accounting information also vary. If the manager of a large shopping center wants to use the standard system of expense accounting as a tool for financial planning and budgetary control, he or she should also establish for internal use a subdivision of functional categories or an expansion of natural divisions with assignments of responsibility and supervisory personnel.

Marketing and Promotion

A successful center is a well-promoted center. By building shopper traffic and increasing sales for all tenants in the center, effective promotion affects the level of percentage rents and thus plays a major role in determining the rate of return to the developer/owner. For this reason, promotion is essential for all sizes and types of shopping centers and should be a well-conceived program.

Strategies for promotion and marketing should focus on the center as a cohesive whole rather than on a collection of individual stores.

David H. Ramsey

The successful marketing of a shopping center is a complex task that must follow a careful plan, the goal of which is to produce profit for the center's tenants and owner. All elements of the plan must be thought out well in advance and should be the result of a coordinated effort among all the center's merchants; the plan should be targeted specifically to the customers in the center's trade area. A good plan goes beyond advertising, sales promotion, and presenting a series of special events, however. Rather than a program derived through trial and error, a marketing plan should be a deliberate series of actions taken to bring a center to its potential volume and beyond.

Positioning the shopping center is the basis of a successful marketing plan. To position the center, management must carefully analyze how the center compares with its competitors in terms of location, tenant mix, architecture, and accessibility. The marketing program must then capitalize on the center's strengths and the competitors' weaknesses.

The promotional program must be formulated to meet the individual needs of the specific shopping center. Some basic guidelines are necessary, however, to plan and implement a successful promotional program.

- Financial participation in the center's promotional activities should be mandatory for all tenants, and a clause to this effect should be included in the lease.
- An aggressive publicity program should be instituted at least six months before the center's opening (or reopening).
- Preferably six months to a year before opening (but no later than three months), the center should have an operational merchants' association or a steering committee of merchants structured as a marketing fund.
- All promotion for the center should be developed and implemented by the center's marketing director or advertising agency.
- The center and its stores should be promoted as a single, cohesive unit. In this regard, all print advertising for the center should appear as a unit with a cohesive theme. Similarly, radio and/or television advertising must promote all stores as a unit and use an identical theme.
- The promotion of merchandise should be supported by and coordinated with an event that is designed to further attract the public to the center. And major promotional events should be coordinated with some type of merchandise promotion.
- The center should be involved in community affairs to build good will and to increase traffic to the center. For example, the center might financially support major community endeavors, share the use of shopping center facilities, plan and participate in civic events, and so forth.
- The center's promotional unit and the merchants should always be in communication with each other.

Merchants' Association

A merchants' association typically is responsible for the promotion of a shopping center. It acts as a clearinghouse for suggestions, ideas, and programming of promotional events. A lease clause is the recommended vehicle by which to establish a merchants' association. Most lease agreements stipulate that an association will be formed, that the tenants will pay a specified rate per square foot to the association, and that the developer will pay a certain percentage of the annual costs. Generally, the lease further stipulates that the developer and tenants pay a specified amount of the center's preopening and opening costs and that bylaws, personnel, and detailed programs and budgets will be developed later, but before the first organizational meeting of the association. Preferably, the association should be operational at least six months before the center opens.

Bylaws establish the specific purposes, organization, and requirements of the association and should be programmed by an individual or an agency with experience in the operation and promotion of shopping centers.

Since the Hohokam Indians first farmed the Valley of the Sun in 400 B.C., the waters flowing through their extensive network of irrigation canals have been the lifeblood of the Phoenix region. Today, following a "modern" update of the canal system in the 19th century, the canals can be seen traversing the urban area as they bring irrigation and drinking water to the desert city.

Although these canals have been used as informal linear parks for more than a century, their potential as an amenity for commercial and residential activities has been completely overlooked. But the Scottsdale Waterfront, a development by Mashburn-Hope Limited with its partner Starwood Capital Group, plans to change that oversight.

The Scottsdale Waterfront is the culmination of many years of discussions between the private developers and the city of Scottsdale's redevelopment interests to turn a section of the long-ignored banks of the Arizona Canal in downtown Scottsdale into a major shopping and tourist attraction.

Situated between the 1.9 million-square-foot Scottsdale Fashion Square (the fifth highest grossing mall per square foot in the country) and Scottsdale's downtown shopping and arts district aimed at tourists, the Scottsdale Waterfront is the first of two projects designed to tie these two separate shopping districts together, using the canal as the centerpiece of the development. (The second project, the Canals of Scottsdale, is in preliminary planning.

It includes additional canals weaving through an entertainment district and a proposed Smithsonian affiliate museum at the former Scottsdale Galleria, an upscale mall that closed in the early 1990s.)

The developers of the Scottsdale Waterfront, Lee Mashburn and Phil Hope, have put together a 12-acre project that includes 300,000 square feet of specialty retail space, 50,000 square feet of restaurant space, a 35,000-square-foot multiscreen theater, 100 luxury condominiums, and approximately 2,000 underground parking spaces.

Modeled after the concept of a Main Street, the Scottsdale Waterfront's character will include storefronts lining the edges of interior streets, shaded gathering places, fountains, and public art. The focus of the project, however, will be the canal, with stores and restaurants lining its bank; dining barges, interactive water features, lush landscaping, and bridges will also be featured.

Scheduled to open in the fourth quarter of 2000 with flagship stores Borders Books & Music and FAO Schwarz and a number of retailers and restaurants distinctive to the Phoenix market, the Scottsdale Waterfront will finally use the canal system for more than a conduit of water. The project will celebrate those waters for their role as the lifeblood of the desert community.

Source: Jeffrey L. Hinkle.

The Scottsdale Waterfront will include lively, pedestrian-friendly streetscapes.

They should be reviewed and approved by attorneys before they are printed and should be available before the association's first meeting. Bylaws set forth all pertinent information, including rules governing election of officers, duties of officers, a quorum, order of business for monthly meetings, date of annual meeting, appointment of committees, and, usually, establishment of a board of directors consisting of a president, vice president, secretary, and treasurer. The usual standing committees cover the areas of finance, advertising, special events, and publicity. The authority to assess dues and fees for advertising, promotion, seasonal decoration, and other activities is spelled out in the formal lease document. In joining the association as required in the lease, the tenant also agrees to abide by the association's charter and bylaws.

The owner can rely on either of two operational policies with respect to the merchants' association. He can act merely as the agent for the association, relying on the members' interests to guide the operation of the center, in which case an executive secretary or professional promotions director will be hired and paid by the association, or he can actively run the association, relying on the officers, members, and committees to cooperate in advertising and promotional programs.

The owner must take on certain responsibilities in promoting the center. The association's members should approve a comprehensive promotions program and a promotions director hired to execute the program. When the owner pays the salary of the director, the owner maintains control of promotions, even in small centers. Associations have trouble when the landlord leaves the center's merchants to their own devices; in general, tenants are slow to appreciate what an association can do for them.

An association may be organized as a for-profit corporation with a charter and bylaws. Although a nonprofit corporation has tax advantages, its activities are limited. The for-profit organization operates more broadly and can escape taxes at the end of the year by investing all its assessments from tenants in promotional events and other activities.

A part-time or full-time paid secretary is essential for successful operation. No member alone can assume the multiple responsibilities of correspondence, preparation of a newsletter, notices, billings, and other duties; members must always concentrate their primary efforts on making their own stores profitable. In small centers, the association may not have the resources to maintain a staff. In such cases, staff work must become part of the owner's responsibilities.

If the association does not employ a staff promotions manager, it can contract the services of a public relations firm. Even though a large agency that is not locally based can be used, the representative who handles the center's work should be local. In general, the more local the management, the better the operation.

The merchants' association can be charged with a wide range of activities—joint advertising of the center, including the use of the center's name on advertising mastheads, letterheads, bill heads, and statements; spe-

The merchants' association can provide an effective strategy for promoting a center. The retail component, as well as the entire mixed-use center, at Carillon Point, in Kirkland, Washington, benefits from promotional activities organized by the local retail merchants' association.

cial centerwide promotions; seasonal events and decorations; enforcement of parking lot regulations, particularly those regarding parking for employees; business referrals and credit systems; store hours and night and holiday openings; a directory of merchants; and centerwide news bulletins or special newspapers for distribution in the trade area. The importance of involving the merchants cannot be overstated. Unless they are actively involved, merchants will merely accept what is offered.

The basis of assessment for contributions to the cost of the association's activities varies widely. The most equitable and usual method is that all tenants contribute to the advertising fund according to each tenant's GLA. In less common arrangements, contributions might be based on a straight percentage of gross sales, a formula combining the percentage of sales volume and the number of square feet occupied, front footage occupied, a percentage of the tenant's annual rent in relation to the total annual rent of the center, individually negotiated assessments unrelated to the merchant's size or volume, and combinations of these methods, although formulas that combine several of these methods may be difficult to administer.

Tenants such as banks, whose leases do not include percentage clauses, should contribute to the promotion fund on the basis of square footage occupied. A lease can also specify the amount to be contributed for preopening and grand opening promotions and for the first year of operation. The developer generally pays one-quarter to one-third of the association's annual budget. As a rule of thumb, most budgets for the grand opening range from 50 to 100 percent of the annual assessment and budget.

The landlord must take action against any tenant that fails to pay its dues, thus violating terms of the lease. Terminating the lease is preferable to a lawsuit, which neither the tenant nor the landlord wants. The owner/developer must not only organize the merchants' association but must also participate in and guide its activities. He must contribute to the operating fund. An effective association needs an active and energetic owner who will stimulate interest, originate and launch promotions, prepare budgets, and coordinate all activities of the association.

To stimulate the merchants, a monthly association bulletin can be distributed that includes increases and decreases in sales volume from the previous month and year. This information can be presented by tenant classification —shoes, women's apparel, and so forth. Tenants report their sales monthly, and management can then incorporate these figures to formulate and report overall sales volumes and trends without revealing the sales volumes of individual tenants. The monthly bulletin, as part of the educational program for merchants, should also contain other news and information about future programs of interest to merchants.

Marketing or Promotional Fund

An alternative to the establishment of a merchants' association is the newer approach of a marketing or promotional fund to promote the center. Tenants are still assessed to provide funds to promote the center, but unlike a merchants' association, the marketing fund is totally controlled and administered by the center's developer/owner. The fund is administered by a marketing director, who reports to the developer/owner rather than to a merchants' association. Tenants pay fees directly to the developer/owner and do not play an active role in the development of the

promotional program (although a steering committee of tenants is sometimes appointed to operate as advisers).

The advantage of a marketing fund over a merchants' association is that the owner/developer maintains full control rather than relying on the elected directors of a merchants' association, who may lack the necessary expertise in marketing, promotion, and publicity or may not promote the interests of the center as a whole over the interests of their individual stores. Another advantage of the marketing fund is that it frees the marketing director from the many organizational details and internal politics of the merchants' association, allowing him or her to concentrate on marketing and promotion rather than on details. In addition, the marketing fund enables long-term promotional goals and programs to be established, which may be difficult to do under a merchants' association, with its frequent change of leaders. With a marketing fund, it is particularly important for the developer and the marketing director to maintain clear lines of communication with tenants to sustain their cooperation.

If a center has an existing merchants' association, a number of factors should be carefully examined before deciding to convert from an association to a marketing fund. The following advice is not new, but it still applies. The existing merchants' association should be retained if:

- Merchants work well together and participate in group promotional activities.

San Antonio's Riverwalk has grown into an international tourist destination. The Rivercenter benefits from its physical connection as well as the name recognition associated with Riverwalk.

- The association's leadership is consistent and strong, tending to the business of marketing the center, without interfering in operational matters.
- The association board acts as a creative advisory body, allowing the professional marketing director to do an effective long-term marketing job with well-defined programs.
- The association maintains tight financial controls, not subjecting its members to the liabilities of a deficit or to taxes on a profit.
- The association is an effective two-way mechanism for communications, and the leadership uses peer pressure to encourage good merchandising and participation for the benefit of the entire center.
- The shopping center owner receives a satisfactory return on his investment in the activities of the merchants' association.
- The shopping center owner does not wish to be responsible for marketing the center.
- The shopping center owner is not sufficiently knowledgeable about retailing and marketing and is not able to guide a strong marketing program.
- The center's finances, leasing record, and/or operations are too weak to take the steps necessary to convert an association to a marketing fund.[7]

On the other hand, conversion to a marketing fund is appropriate if:

- Merchants are apathetic and not participating in group promotional and advertising activities.
- Leadership allows merchants' meetings to turn into grievance sessions with little discussion of marketing.
- The turnover of store managers is high, resulting in frequent changes in association leadership and in the marketing program.
- The association's board continually acts in the interest of a few merchants rather than for the good of the entire center.
- The association's funds are spent on nonproductive activities or are continually overspent.
- Decision making is ineffective, resulting in only mediocre or short-term marketing programs.
- The center is unable to attract or to keep professional marketing talent because of the frustration of working with the association.
- Meetings and administration take up too much time.
- The center's owner is better able than an association to guide and administer the marketing effort and is willing to accept this responsibility.[8]

If a decision is made to convert an association to a marketing fund, the following steps should be taken:

- An attorney should prepare an amendment to the lease to provide for the marketing fund.
- Agreements should be obtained from anchor tenants stating that they will resign from the merchants' association, will continue funding the promotion of the center through a marketing fund, and will participate on an advisory committee.
- Tenants agreeing to the change should sign lease amendments redirecting payments from the association to the marketing fund.
- For those tenants who do not agree to convert, the merchants' association should continue to operate on a token basis. Meetings should be held, officers elected, contributions collected, and all lease obligations and legal requirements of the merchants' association satisfied. Those tenants wishing to remain members of the association should assume administrative responsibilities.
- The marketing fund should be operated independently of the merchants' association, should one still exist. Only contributors to the marketing fund should be included in promotional activities paid for by the fund.
- Conversion to a marketing fund should be included as a condition in lease renewals, lease modifications, and operational requests by hold-out tenants.
- When the last tenant has converted to the fund, the merchants' association should be legally dissolved.[9]

Finally, it should be remembered that the process of conversion may take several years and may result in acrimony between the owner and tenants.

Types of Promotion

Whether a center's promotion is handled by a merchants' association or a marketing fund, important decisions must be made about the types of promotion to be undertaken. Promotional and special events can be used to make a community more aware of a center and to attract shoppers. Promotional events may take any number of forms, but the style of the events should reflect the character of the shopping center. An upscale center would not benefit from a carnival-type promotional event. Nor would a discount center benefit from a black-tie event. Whatever form they take, promotions must be aimed at attracting customers, not just curious crowds.

Developers emphasize that promotions for a center should be planned around a major tenant's individual promotion. Timing and merchandise offerings should not be duplicated. Most developers have found it helpful to focus on five or six major promotions during the year, supplemented by appropriate minor events. Promotional events and activities should be set up and budgeted a year in advance, and association members should be given a full description of the program and budget. A record should be kept of each promotional event so that the owner or promotions director can review completed promotions to identify why they succeeded or failed.

Christmas, Easter, Halloween, and other holidays provide occasions for special promotions and seasonal decoration of the center. Other worthwhile promotional schemes include "giveaways," children's attractions, and special sales on holidays or other occasions. For example, a "mothers' day out" or a fitness fair can replace the traditional midsummer clearance sale.

The Bayside Development Corporation, a nonprofit corporation established by the city of Santa Monica, runs the promotional efforts for the Third Street Promenade.

In addition to promotional events, the center can be promoted through advertising, which should help the public to associate individual shops within the center with the image of the center itself. The market area of the media selected as most effective to promote the center should match that of the center as closely as possible. For example, it does not seem logical for a neighborhood center to use costly television promotions to advertise to an area that is 40 or 50 times larger than its market. Television ads *are* often appropriate for a super regional center with a large market area, however.

Newspaper and radio advertising is most frequently used for other kinds of centers. Newspaper ads are relatively inexpensive and can be widely distributed. Radio is considered one of the most effective forms of advertising in today's market, and because of the size of the market that it reaches, it can also be inexpensive. It reaches only certain market segments, however, depending on the target markets of the particular radio station. Other advertising possibilities include direct mail, billboards, and advertising on mass-transit vehicles. The Internet is another medium that should be explored. Establishing a Web site for the shopping center can be an inexpensive and effective way to get the message out. No hard-and-fast rules exist as to the advertising mix that should be implemented. Advertising varies widely from center to center, depending on the center's needs, its target market, and the funds available.

Notes

1. See the sample lease in Appendix 1. This lease is presented only as an example and is not intended to be a definitive or universally applicable document.
2. Median and ranges of percentage rents by tenant classification and by type of shopping center are detailed in the most recent edition of *Dollars & Cents of Shopping Centers* (Washington, D.C.: ULI–the Urban Land Institute).
3. Ibid.
4. Participants' manual for "Shopping Centers: How to Build, Buy, and Redevelop," a workshop sponsored by ULI, p. 51.
5. See the sample agreement in Appendix 2.
6. *Standard Manual of Accounting for Shopping Center Operations* (Washington, D.C.: ULI–the Urban Land Institute, 1971).
7. "Jones Report for Shopping Center Marketing," April 1980.
8. Ibid.
9. Ibid.

7. Case Studies

Circle Centre, Indianapolis, Indiana
An 800,000-square-foot mall in downtown Indianapolis. Skillful blend of new construction and historic structures includes two department store anchors and entertainment uses.

Crossroads Shopping Center, Bellevue, Washington
A 475,000-square-foot partial demolition/renovation of an existing center. Public art and music performances contribute to the center's reputation as a community gathering spot.

Dadeland Station, Miami, Florida
A 350,000-square-foot, three-level shopping center adjacent to the Dadeland North Metrorail Station. The center includes value-oriented retail and a six-level parking facility for 1,470 cars.

The Forum Shops at Caesars Palace, Las Vegas, Nevada
A 250,000-square-foot retail center designed to resemble an ancient Roman streetscape, anchored by Caesars Palace Hotel and Casino. Combines upscale retail stores with entertainment attractions.

Great Mall of the Bay Area, Milpitas, California
A 1.2 million-square-foot, value-oriented shopping center located in a former Ford Motor Company assembly plant.

Grove City Factory Shops, Grove City, Pennsylvania
A 533,000-square-foot outlet center located 45 miles north of Pittsburgh in an open-air, village-like setting.

Irvine Spectrum Center, Irvine, California
A 260,400-square-foot freestanding entertainment center about 40 miles south of Los Angeles that is anchored by a 21-screen theater complex including the first IMAX 3D theater on the West Coast.

The Marketplace at Cascades Town Center, Loudoun County, Virginia
A 417,000-square-foot retail center located in an outer suburb of Washington, D.C., featuring a neotraditional, pedestrian-friendly design. Offers regional, community, and neighborhood shopping.

New Community Neighborhood Shopping Center, Newark, New Jersey
A 55,000-square-foot shopping center anchored by the first supermarket to be built in the central ward, an inner-city neighborhood, since the civil disturbances in the summer of 1967.

Old Orchard Center, Skokie, Illinois
A 1.8 million-square-foot shopping center that was renovated and remerchandized in two phases, adding more than one-half million square feet of new space.

Portland International Airport Concessions Expansion/Renovation, Portland, Oregon
Renovation, reconfiguration, and expansion of airport retail and food concessions in the main terminal and concourse, featuring high-quality specialty retail shops.

The Promenade at Westlake, Westlake, California
A 210,000-square-foot community shopping center that aspires to be the town center of a suburban community about 45 minutes from Los Angeles. Features neighborhood and entertainment-oriented retailers.

Sycamore Plaza at Kenwood, Cincinnati, Ohio
A 345,000-square-foot upscale power center that resulted from the demalling, redevelopment, and repositioning of a devalued mall.

The Waterside Shops, Pelican Bay, Florida
A 250,000-square-foot, open-air mall featuring a central courtyard with an elaborate 350,000-gallon waterscape that creates an exotic environment.

The Westchester, White Plains, New York
A 2.5 million-square-foot regional mall in downtown White Plains anchored by two department store chains. Includes nearly 150 upscale tenants.

Circle Centre

Indianapolis, Indiana

Circle Centre is something of an anomaly among shopping centers—a mall that does not look like a mall. Opened in 1995, the 800,000-square-foot downtown Indianapolis center incorporates nine historic facades and parts of two historic structures in a skillful blend of new construction with old. The existing street pattern is maintained, and the two and one-half blocks of the center are connected by bridges and by underground parking. Bridges also connect the center to adjacent hotels, office buildings, the convention center, the RCA dome, and additional parking.

Though urban in appearance, Circle Centre was designed to succeed as a retail mall. The center includes two department store anchors—a 206,000-square-foot Nordstrom and a 144,000-square-foot Parisian—as well as 70,000 square feet of the Limited stores (in 11 shops throughout the mall). In addition to the retail uses, an entire floor is devoted to entertainment—cinema, games, nightclubs, and restaurants—to extend the mall's hours into evenings and weekends. With retail sales approaching $400 per square foot and daily traffic as high as 70,000 persons (particularly during the NCAA basketball tournament), it appears that Circle Centre has found the right formula for downtown retailing.

The future was not always this bright, however. Conceived in the 1980s as an answer to declining retail business in downtown Indianapolis, the center was more than ten years in the making. The site sat vacant for much of that time, a two-block hole in the ground, while various financing schemes were developed and tenants pursued. Ultimately, the city provided over half the project's financing through tax increment financing, and the Indianapolis business community stepped into the breach and provided almost another one-quarter.

Site and Development Process

Circle Centre is located one block south of Monument Circle, the heart of downtown. In the early 1980s, when the first plans were drawn, retail uses were being replaced by high-rise office buildings, several major hotels, a convention center, and a sports stadium. In this precarious context, the city approached Melvin Simon & Associates —which had the distinction of being both a premier builder of shopping centers and an Indianapolis-based organization—to develop plans for a downtown mall.

In 1987, a memorandum of agreement was signed that set guidelines for preserving historic elements of the site and surrounding area. The agreement committed the city and developer to preserve the L.S. Ayres department store building and to retain or reconstruct the fa-

cades of several other historic structures. The agreement also defined allowable heights and mandatory setbacks for any new construction on the site.

Financing was a long-term problem, even following the city's commitment to bond financing. Traditional lenders were reluctant to finance a shopping center during the recession of 1990 and 1991, particularly a downtown center. To close the gap, the mayor turned to the Corporate Community Council, a civic organization that includes some of the largest businesses in Indianapolis, including Lilly Industries, BankOne Indiana, and others.

Some of the businesses that responded to the mayor's call viewed their participation as essentially a charitable venture. Others, like the Lilly Pension Fund, were constrained by their fiduciary obligations and looked at the project in terms of its economic soundness as a portfolio investment. After extended negotiations, 12 organizations joined to form the Circle Centre Development Company (CCDC). Eventually 20 organizations, including the Simon DeBartolo Group, Inc. (now the Simon Property Group), participated in CCDC as the project's capital requirements grew.

Planning and Design

Circle Centre is laid out in a traditional "dumbbell" plan, with retail anchors at each end and mall shops between. At the north end is the Parisian department store, which occupies three floors of the historic L.S. Ayres building. At the south end is Nordstrom, which occupies a half block at the street level and a smaller footprint on two floors above. Five historic facades have been incorporated into the Nordstrom building.

Where possible, the designers of Circle Centre, Ehrenkrantz & Eckstut Architects, integrated the preserved historic elements functionally as well as visually. For example, a historic interior has been converted into the Nordstrom espresso bar. Several other historic structures remained in private ownership, including the venerable Canterbury Hotel and the St. Elmo building, and the Circle Centre project was built around them or they were only partially incorporated.

Parking for the project is provided under the mall, below street level, and in a multilevel parking structure across the street that is connected to the center by a bridge. Pedestrian entries to the center are located at the major street corners, and service docks are located inconspicuously off the minor cross street between the blocks.

The primary circulation spine of the mall is a skylighted space that doubles as a bridge spanning the street

The ArtsGarden, bridging a primary intersection adjacent to the site, has become an icon of the city.

between the Parisian block and the Nordstrom block. Above the retail shops on the fourth floor is the center's entertainment component: cinemas, games, food court, restaurants, and nightclubs.

To further knit Circle Centre into its urban context, the designers of the center proposed a bridge crossing the primary intersection at the northwest corner of the site. Ultimately, the bridge was built as the Indianapolis Artsgarden. The 12,500-square-foot barrel-vaulted structure, which has become an icon of the city, serves also as a performance space and exhibition area for the Indianapolis arts community.

Financing and Ownership
The development of Circle Centre was, in many respects, a public/private partnership. The city owns the land and buildings, with the exception of the Nordstrom building. Circle Centre Development Company was officially the developer of the project. CCDC, in turn, is a partner-

The project integrates several restored historic facades with well-scaled new elevations.

The expansive skylighted space of the ArtsGarden serves as a performance and exhibition area for the Indianapolis arts community.

ship between the Simon Property Group, Inc., acting as managing general partner, and a limited partnership of 19 business and corporate investors, acting as a second general partner.

The city provided approximately 60 percent ($187 million) of the $307.5 million cost of the project through the sale of tax increment bonds. Initially offered in 1987, the Circle Centre bonds were refinanced in 1992 to take advantage of lower interest rates. Almost a quarter of the financing ($75 million) was equity raised by CCDC, and the remainder (approximately $45 million) was provided in the form of a construction loan from the United Bank of Switzerland and the Hypo Bank.

The city assembled the project site, including acquiring and preserving the existing historic structures. The city's responsibilities also included site preparation and construction of the mall core and shell and parking garages. CCDC was responsible for construction of tenant improvements and the fourth-floor entertainment component.

In return for its investment, the city receives parking revenues, rent from CCDC, and a share of the project's net operating income.

Leasing and Marketing
The Simon organization recognized that to bring customers downtown and to compete with suburban malls, Circle Centre would have to offer something different. Thus, the leasing team cast a wide net, looking for tenants not yet represented in the market area as well as for new and different retailers.

Nordstrom, for one, was new to Indianapolis, and Parisian had just one relatively new store in the metropolitan area. In total, nearly half the center's tenants were new to the metropolitan area. Supplementing this effort was an "entrepreneur" program, in which the developer has worked to cultivate promising startup businesses. Eight tenants are businesses that were harvested from this program.

The Simon organization looked to entertainment attractions that would draw workers and visitors to the mall in the evenings and bring workers back downtown on the weekends. The attractions include a nine-screen United Artists cinema; the "Starport," a collection of high-tech and virtual-reality games owned and operated by United Artists; the Showscan ride simulator; several restaurants (in addition to a food court); and five theme nightclubs.

Circle Centre's marketing program promotes the mall as a unique, sophisticated urban attraction. Most of the center's advertising is on network TV, reaching over a 200-mile radius to include cities such as Cincinnati, Louisville, and Dayton, in addition to Indianapolis.

Experience Gained
- Success for the developer has meant success for the city. By its presence and potential, Circle Centre has bolstered existing downtown development and stimulated new development. Hotel occupancy downtown

A narrow retail arcade modeled on traditional urban shopping streets connects the two courts in Circle Centre; at the north end, activities in Parisian Court are enhanced by the food court terrace and upper-level entertainment attractions.

has improved, and convention center bookings are up since Circle Centre opened.

- One key to Circle Centre's success is its urban design strategy. Although a mall by definition looks inward, the effort to connect with the city has paid dividends by making the center a more inviting and memorable destination.
- A second key to Circle Centre's success is its market strategy, which differentiates the center from its suburban competition and provides a more urban, round-the-clock environment based on a strong entertainment component.
- The final—and perhaps the fundamental—key to Circle Centre's success is the sustained commitment of the city of Indianapolis and the hands-on participation of the Indianapolis business community, without which Circle Centre could not have happened.

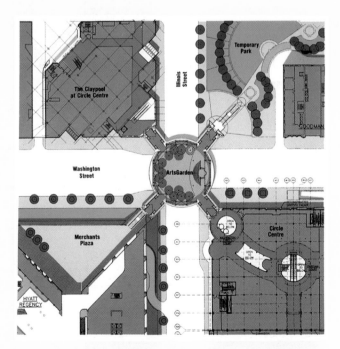

Placement of the ArtsGarden over the intersection of Washington and Illinois Streets has created convenient pedestrian access between Circle Centre and the adjacent hotels and offices and the nearby convention center.

Street-level plan.

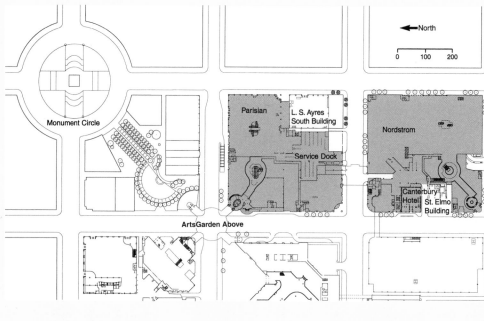

Second-floor plan.

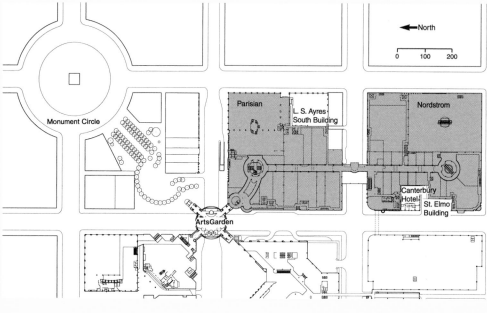

Fourth-floor plan.

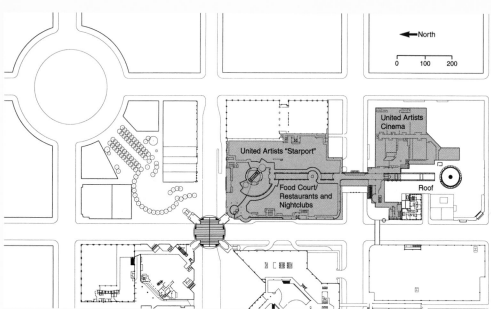

Project Data: Circle Centre

Land Use and Building Information

Site Area	9.2 acres
Gross Building Area	960,000 square feet
Gross Leasable Area (GLA)	793,755 square feet
Floor/Area Ratio	3.1
Levels	4
Parking	2,780
Surface spaces	0
Structured spaces	2,780

Land Use Plan

	Acres	Percent of Site
Buildings	7.2	78
Parking structures	2.0	22
Total	9.2	100

Retail Tenant Information

Classification	Number of Stores	Total GLA (square feet)
Food	5	4,112
Food service and food court	17	49,634
Clothing and accessories	25	132,194
Shoes	5	23,112
Home furnishings	3	8,660
Home appliances/music	1	23,035
Hobby/special interest	3	14,092
Gifts/specialty	11	34,001
Jewelry	1	1,226
Other retail	6	7,548
Personal services	2	2,334
Recreation/community	7	117,277
Financial	1	597
Offices (other than financial)	1	150
Vacant	4	25,783
Parisian		144,000
Nordstrom		206,000
Total		793,755

Lease Terms

Average length of lease	7–15 years
Typical lease provisions	Operating requirements, minimum hours of operation, common area maintenance, taxes
Annual rents	$20–40 per square foot

Average Annual Sales

Including all mall tenants	$330 per square foot
Excluding entertainment tenants	$400 per square foot

Development Cost Information[1]

Site acquisition cost	$55,000,000
Site improvement	10,300,000
Mall construction	62,200,000
Parking structure	27,400,000
Tenant improvements	124,000,000
Soft costs	28,600,000
Total Development Costs	$307,500,000

Annual Operating Expenses (1996)

Taxes	$378,000
Insurance	36,000
Services (security, landscaping, advertising)	1,881,000
Maintenance	794,000
Janitorial	393,000
Utilities	236,000
Management	847,000
Miscellaneous	269,000
Total	$4,834,000

Financing Information

City of Indianapolis	$187,000,000
Equity partners	75,000,000
Construction loan	45,000,000
Total	$307,000,000

Development Schedule

1992	Site purchased	11/1992	Construction started
1984	Planning started	1989	Leasing started
1992	Approvals obtained	9/1995	Project opened

Developer

Circle Centre Development Company
Simon Property Group, Inc.
Managing General Partner
115 West Washington Street
Indianapolis, Indiana 46204
317-636-1600

Design Architect

Ehrenkrantz & Eckstut Architects
23 E. 4th Street, 5th Floor
New York, New York 10003
212-353-0400

Coordinating Architect

Centre Venture, Indianapolis
a joint venture of
Browning, Day, Mullins, Dierdorf, Inc., *and* CSO, Inc.
Indianapolis, Indiana

Notes

[1]Not including ArtsGarden, whose $12 million cost was funded separately.

Crossroads Shopping Center

Bellevue, Washington

The 475,000-square-foot Crossroads Shopping Center—once a shabby hodgepodge of shops and vacant storefronts—has become the social hub and unofficial town center of east Bellevue, offering live music four nights a week and the most extensive selection of ethnic restaurants in suburban Seattle. The redevelopment of the former public market with international eateries and a comprehensive program of free concerts and multicultural activities draws customers from around the region and has repositioned Crossroads as an entertainment center.

At the intersection of 156th Avenue N.E. and N.E. 8th Street, the 41-acre site is located on the east edge of Bellevue, Washington, in the Crossroads neighborhood, a suburban community some 15 miles east of downtown Seattle. In addition to its entertainment component and its status as a community gathering place, the center provides a mix of regional big-box retailers, community services, and shops serving the immediate neighborhood.

Site History

Originally built as an open-air community shopping center, Crossroads was enclosed as a mall in the late 1970s. Poor access—it is located one and one-half miles from any freeway—and the redevelopment in the early 1980s of nearby Bellevue Square into Seattle's premier super regional center hastened Crossroads's decline.

Once known mainly as an affluent bedroom community of Seattle, Bellevue had emerged by the mid-1980s into a commercial center with active real estate development and a growing number of financial and technology firms. (Microsoft's headquarters in Redmond is about a mile north of Crossroads Shopping Center.) By the mid-1980s, national retailers recognized the Seattle area, including Bellevue, as a desirable metropolitan region in which to locate. Crossroads's demographics also were favorable: the center serves a population of more than 250,000 people, and average annual family income is approximately $84,000. But no large parcels were available for new retail development in the Crossroads primary trade area. These factors motivated San Francisco–based real estate syndicate Terranomics Equity Investments (TEI) to acquire the center in 1985. The company formed a limited partnership, Terranomics Crossroads Associates (TCA), which purchased the leasehold interest in the center and assumed the long-term ground lease from Crossroads's developers for $17 million.

Development Process

When Terranomics took over the foundering center in 1987, it was on the brink of bankruptcy. TCA's strategy was to develop a 40,000-square-foot public market—modeled after Pike Place Market in downtown Seattle and Granville Island Market in Vancouver, British Columbia—complete with fish, produce, and restaurants, at the central mall entrance. Leasing was a formidable challenge. Crossroads, which lacks the spectacular water views and urban synergy of the Seattle and Vancouver markets, failed to draw the tourists that help them maintain their vitality. Moreover, TCA underestimated the high startup costs and the time required to build momentum and had to subsidize tenant operating costs and marketing much longer than anticipated. By 1987, the public market appeared unable to survive, let alone attract additional retailers and turn the center around.

Acknowledging that Crossroads was on a downward slide, the investors divided into two factions: one group wanted to salvage the situation, the other to cut its losses. At this point, minority partner Merritt Sher, chair of Terranomics, and his brother Ron, who represented one of the limited partners and was living in the Bellevue area, decided to assume management and control of the center. The partnership was restructured in late 1987 with more than $6.5 million in new capital, most of which came from Eurodevelopment, a French investment partnership that had invested in other projects with the Shers. Eurodevelopment and the Shers bought out the syndicate's dissenting limited partners at a discount, with TEI subordinating its equity interest to the Shers, Eurodevelopment, and the remaining partners. The restructuring placed Ron Sher and Terranomics Development in control of the development, management, leasing, and marketing of Crossroads.

For Crossroads to succeed, Terranomics Development knew it needed to offer something different from the traditional shopping experience. The company envisioned a retail center that would celebrate the Crossroads community, the most ethnically diverse neighborhood in the Seattle area, and that would serve as the downtown of east Bellevue. Whereas many shopping center developers seek out locations next to affluent residential neighborhoods, Ron Sher viewed the ring of modest apartments encircling the center as an asset rather than a negative attribute.

Many of the residents were first-generation immigrant families who moved to the neighborhood in search of affordable housing. Terranomics Development recog-

The design of Crossroads makes the center look less like a typical suburban mall and more like a village main street. The standard elements of traditional main street design—awnings, individual storefronts, and signage—were used as unifying elements throughout the center.

nized that these residents, who live in small spaces with no backyards, would probably welcome a place nearby where they could read a newspaper or book, play a game of cards, or just interact with other people. Sher wanted Crossroads Shopping Center to be a lively "third place," a concept he later read about in Ray Oldenburg's *The Great Good Place.* The idea is that while home and work are important places, most people benefit from spending time in a third place. Although the English have their pubs and the French their cafés and city parks, most Americans living in suburbia have few third places where they can linger and mingle with others in the community.

The *Seattle Post-Intelligencer* (January 11, 1997) called Crossroads Shopping Center the "people-packed heart of the Crossroads community." Here turbaned East Indians share tables with Microsoft workers on their lunch break. Russian men play chess. Recent immigrants take English language courses at the mini–city hall, and music fans flock to the center on Friday and Saturday evenings to enjoy free jazz, folk, or world music concerts.

The first hurdle was to overcome the many negative perceptions of the center. The shopping center had been sorely neglected over the years. Roofs leaked. Vacant storefronts were boarded up. Teenagers and purported drug dealers cruising the parking lot scared away many shoppers, and the center's image was tarnished further by rumors of neighborhood gangs and criminal activity. To show that Crossroads was changing, Terranomics moved first to demolish the three dilapidated, empty commer-

cial buildings at the center's main southwest corner and replace them with a new retail structure (Building A) that included a 7,000-square-foot Blockbuster Video store. An art deco design with jazzy neon elements, reminiscent of early theater marquees, was selected for Building A to emphasize Crossroads's new image as a place for entertainment. A ceremonial archway with a minipark and benches was created for this new front door to the center.

At the same time, Crossroads Cinemas built an expanded movie complex diagonally across from Blockbuster at the northeast corner of the site. It immediately became one of the top-performing cinemas in the region, helping to boost Crossroads's new image as a high-energy, urban destination.

Terranomics Development focused next on the center's interior, renovating the public market area into a food court and bringing new tenants into the mall building. It then renovated the exterior of the main building facing 156th Avenue N.E. This movement between the inside and outside characterized the developer's overall incremental approach to redeveloping the center.

Rather than developing a new master plan for the entire center, Terranomics chose instead to proceed with small, discrete pieces, allowing the center to evolve over time. By not locking into a formal plan in advance, the company could respond more directly to individual opportunities that surfaced during redevelopment.

The city of Bellevue facilitated redevelopment of the shopping center—and the neighborhood—by establishing a single-user local improvement district to fund a capital improvement program for the area. The main arterial streets were widened to five lanes, signals were installed, sidewalks were constructed, and landscaping was added at the front of the center. Half the $1 million cost was assessed against the center, to be repaid over ten years.

One of the greatest obstacles to redevelopment was the land lease on the center. Terranomics in 1985 had assumed the long-term lease on the land underlying the shopping center, which was controlled by an adjacent landowner. Although the lease would not expire for another 37 years, the rental rate was scheduled to jump from $138,536 annually to market rates in 17 years. Sher felt that if he did not purchase the land, his ability to manage the center for the long term would be compromised and securing financing would be difficult. Terranomics paid $5.2 million for the land in 1989.

Once the land was purchased, Terranomics demolished an old movie theater, some small stores, and a small medical building on the north end to make way for the new mall anchor—QFC, a strong supermarket chain in the Northwest. At the same time, 7,000 square feet of stores was added. The public market was extended to the supermarket entrance so that QFC shoppers could participate in the market experience.

Planning and Design

Terranomics's incremental development strategy resulted in a design that includes far more variety than usually is found in shopping centers. The developer disliked the bland concrete box architecture that characterizes many suburban centers. Tenants at Crossroads were encouraged to create individualistic storefronts and to break up flat rooflines with distinctive features. Although it departed from corporate design, Barnes & Noble went along with a book motif created by the architect for the roof of its main corner tower, and Coyote Creek Pizza finished its rooftop with a coyote. Creating different identities along the center's facade and giving the smaller buildings their own character was part of Terranomics's strategy to make Crossroads look less like a mall and more like a village or main street. Nevertheless, the new exterior had to be harmonious and cohesive. The standard elements of traditional shopping streets—awnings, individual storefronts, and signage—were used as unifying elements. Bright primary colors and a black-and-white checkerboard pattern also were applied throughout redevelopment.

Public art is a prominent feature of the development. One of the works—a family of pipe people constructed of air vents—was created and loaned by a frequent Crossroads visitor. Other art pieces include a 19th-century replica of a 17th-century French fountain and a rock-like sculpture of a Volkswagen in front of the Crossroads vehicle licensing station.

Tenants

When Terranomics Development first took over Crossroads, one goal was to attract community-minded tenants to serve neighborhood residents. The company also wanted tenants that shoppers would patronize frequently. For that reason, the center includes few tenants, such as furniture stores, that usually draw shoppers no more than every couple of years. Unlike many retail centers, where local tenants are rare, Crossroads supports a healthy mix of national and local retailers. Terranomics specifically sought out mom-and-pop stores as a way to distinguish Crossroads from typical suburban centers and to avoid the cookie-cutter syndrome.

Most of the public market tenants that were brought in as part of the 1985 makeover failed miserably. These

Crossroads has been repositioned from a declining enclosed mall to a vibrant shopping center that serves as a community gathering place.

Tenants were encouraged to break up flat rooflines with distinctive features, such as this departure from the Barnes & Noble corporate design.

one-unit operations suffered because they were not visible from the street and were hard pressed to absorb the high common area maintenance (CAM) charges. Nonetheless, Terranomics liked the concept and sought to retain the ambience of a marketplace. In place of the greengrocers, it brought in 17 eateries, most of which were local ethnic restaurants. These restaurants, which serve Indian, Italian, Vietnamese, Mediterranean, Russian, Thai, Mexican, Japanese, Korean, and French cuisine, constitute the largest collection of ethnic restaurants outside downtown Seattle. Ethnic food was not part of the initial strategy; it just happened that many of the small restaurants looking for a location in the Seattle area were ethnic, so Terranomics seized the opportunity. The decision affords the adjacent Crossroads residential neighborhood, which contains the largest ethnic population in the region, a variety of dining options. Besides the restaurants, the 40,000-square-foot public market area also contains a fresh-fish market, a world-class newsstand, a large used-book store, and a coffeehouse.

To help these small businesses survive the hefty startup and management expenses, Terranomics paid most of the CAM charges at first. Rent was sometimes deferred until tenants were strong enough to afford the full payment. Although Crossroads is about 97 percent leased today, its dismal reputation 11 years ago made attracting tenants difficult. And to attract the types of tenants it wanted, Terranomics in some instances created its own tenants.

If Crossroads was to become a gathering place for the entire family, it needed stores for children as well as a daycare center. A children's store operator wanted to locate at Crossroads but had no capital, so Terranomics created a partnership through which it financed, designed, and built a store that was leased to Kids' Club. Terranomics was the major partner. The operator was not successful, but because the store significantly bolstered development momentum, Terranomics took over ownership and hired a manager to operate the store. After

the takeover, the store generated annual sales of more than $1 million in its second year.

Terranomics also used creative leasing structures in the early years to attract tenants. One of the toughest locations was a secondary concourse called Death Valley because it had been plagued by chronic vacancies since the mall was first enclosed. Terranomics's solution was to reconfigure the shops and include the concourse in a 22,400-square-foot superstore for Pacific Linen, a regional chain. Persuading Pacific Linen to locate there, however —with no external entrance in an area that was more than twice as large as that of other Pacific Linen stores— would be a hard sell. Terranomics convinced Pacific Linen's president to travel to California and visit such stores as Bed Bath & Beyond and other retailers in its category.

A creative leasing structure with significant financial inducements finally convinced Pacific Linen to sign on, but the company lacked capital. Terranomics offered to pay $500,000 to construct the store and lent the chain $200,000 to pay for inventory. The rent agreement was structured so that if Pacific Linen performed well, Terranomics would benefit, but if Pacific Linen failed, Terranomics would absorb much of the loss. The Crossroads Pacific Linen store became the prototype for the chain's western expansion and one of its top performers.

From the start, the selection of tenants was based on the retailer's ability to reinforce the heart of the center —the public market. When Starbucks first negotiated for a Crossroads location in the early 1990s, it wanted to be on the western edge of the center with an external presence facing the main arterial street. But Terranomics rejected the proposal because it felt that Starbucks's presence there would detract from the energy of the public market. Instead, Terranomics convinced Starbucks to move in next to the used-book store, reinforcing the public market area. Starbucks also opened one of its early drive-through stores on the south end of the site.

By 1993, Crossroads had reached critical mass as a destination center. Despite its location off the beaten path

Live music concerts are featured in the public market area. The developers installed a high-quality sound system for the performances, which draw audiences from around the region.

and far from any freeway, large national retailers began to seek it out. In 1994, Barnes & Noble opened a 14,452-square-foot store north of the QFC supermarket that immediately became one of the chain's best-performing stores. Next, Sports Authority opened a 43,257-square-foot store in a new building on the northwest edge of the site, where several small, freestanding restaurants once stood. Circuit City followed in 1995 in a new building south of the cinema. These well-known national stores created greater traffic volume, which helped the smaller specialty shops.

Marketing and Management

A primary marketing strategy for repositioning Crossroads as the unofficial downtown of east Bellevue was to provide first-rate, free entertainment. A stage with a high-quality sound system was built in the market area. Live music concerts are featured four evenings a week with late-night concerts on Fridays and Saturdays, when the

market restaurants remain open until 10:30 p.m. When the "Late Night at the Market" concerts first started in 1991, it was difficult to attract professional musicians, who disdained performing in a shopping mall. But the excellent sound system, no-smoking rule, and enthusiastic audiences—sometimes standing room only—changed their minds. Performances now draw audiences from around the region, and many serious jazz lovers regard Crossroads as one of the best jazz venues in the region.

Crossroads employs a booking agent who lines up performers for the programs, which feature a broad range of music, from jazz to folk. Thursday open-mike night routinely features more than 20 performers. The "Late Night at the Market" program, which sometimes draws audiences of 1,500 people on Friday and Saturday nights, gets most of the credit for boosting overall public market sales, which climbed 25 percent in 1993.

Audiences at Crossroads are an international mix, mirroring the multicultural makeup of the adjacent residential neighborhoods. Ethnic folk groups and bands perform regularly. For several years, audiences have flocked to "Cultural Crossroads," three days of nonstop entertainment from around the world. Programs have featured music and dance from Israel, Bosnia, Ireland, and Alaska, along with Egyptian belly dancers and tango dancers from Argentina.

In addition to the music and dance events, Crossroads features other entertainment, such as a Brobdingnagian-scale chessboard across which players, many of whom are Russian, move two-foot-high chess pieces. In fact, one ongoing problem was monopolization of the chessboard. Crossroads's management organized a "summit meeting" with the players to address the issue. A timer was installed, and designated game tables were set up for playing chess, cards, and checkers.

Patrons are encouraged to sit for a while in the market area, which offers tables and seating for more than 900 people. Visitors feel comfortable sitting there and browsing through books they bought at one of the two

Phase I of the renovation included the addition of a 7,000-square-foot Blockbuster Video store.

In addition to international restaurants, the 40,000-square-foot public market area contains a fresh-fish market, a world-class newsstand, a large used-book store, and a coffeehouse.

bookstores or magazines from the Daily Planet, a newsstand that features newspapers and magazines from around the world. Visitors are invited to linger in Crossroads's giant "living room," conversing with friends or just taking in the scene.

Although much of the entertainment at Crossroads is multicultural, Terranomics Development never targeted specific ethnic groups as part of a formal marketing strategy; its approach was more inclusive, aimed at celebrating the Crossroads community at large. For example, the Crossroads neighborhood supports a large population of physically disabled and handicapped people. When business lagged in the early years, some retailers feared that customers might be put off by seeing large numbers of these individuals. But Crossroads's management, determined to make them feel welcome, provided various features to accommodate them, before state and federal law required businesses to do so.

Crossroads is the most culturally diverse community in the region. The last census showed that about 75 percent of the area's housing comprises multifamily units. Almost one in five people living in Crossroads is foreign born, compared with one in seven in Bellevue overall. In about 5 percent of those households, no one older than 14 speaks English. Two of the largest ethnic groups are Asian and Russian, while the fastest-growing ethnic group is Hispanic.

Several years ago Bellevue opened a Crossroads mini–city hall where residents can pay utility and tax bills and obtain information about employment; bus schedules published in Spanish, Russian, Vietnamese, and Chinese; and job applications. The city hall sponsors classes in English as a second language, and the management of Crossroads offers the classes to Crossroads employees, many of whom are foreign born.

Experience Gained

- Terranomics's initial plans called for a more intensive mixed-use development. The outbuildings were first designed with second-floor office space. With Microsoft's campus less than a mile away, the developer reasoned that high-tech users would be demanding additional office space with large floor plates. Despite numerous efforts, however, the developer could not make the second floor office space economically feasible.

- Instead of adhering strictly to a formal strategy, Terranomics used a more flexible approach that allowed it to take advantage of opportunities as they arose. For example, most shopping centers do not feature used-book stores in prime locations. When the owner of Half Price Books approached Terranomics about becoming a tenant, the store was placed in a prominent location so that it could contribute to the overall character of the center.

- Late-night concerts at the Marketstage now draw as many as 1,500 people. Terranomics learned that smaller performances, such as poetry readings, work better in a more intimate space. A program of poetry readings was canceled after running for almost a year.

- Crossroads's success as a "third place" where people linger in what is now regarded as east Bellevue's new town center inspired Terranomics to embark on a new business venture. Third Place Books, a new retail format, will blend some of the same elements offered at Crossroads, featuring books, restaurants, and entertainment for every age group. It also will include plenty of opportunities for people watching, which Ron Sher regards as the highest form of entertainment.

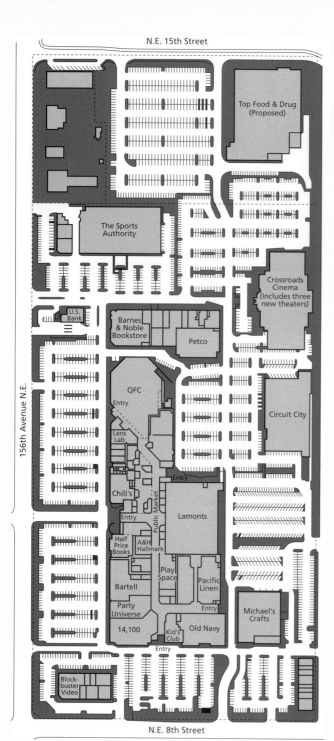

N.E. 15th Street

Top Food & Drug
(Proposed)

The Sports
Authority

156th Avenue N.E.

U.S.
Bank

Barnes
& Noble
Bookstore

Petco

Crossroads
Cinema
(Includes three
new theaters)

QFC
Entry

Circuit City

Lens
Lab

Entry

Chili's

Public Market

Lamonts

Entry

Half
Price
Books

A&H
Hallmark

Play
Space

Pacific
Linen

Bartell

Party
Universe

Entry

Michael's
Crafts

14,100

Kid's
Club

Old Navy

Entry

Block-
buster
Video

N.E. 8th Street

Site plan.

Project Data: Crossroads Shopping Center

Land Use and Building Information

Site Area	41 acres

Gross Building Area

Before renovation	419,000 square feet
After renovation	533,000 square feet

Gross Leasable Area (GLA)

Before renovation	365,000 square feet
After renovation	475,000 square feet

Floor/Area Ratio	0.27

Total Surface Parking Spaces

Before renovation	1,817
After renovation	2,292

Land Use Plan

Use	Before Renovation (acres)	After Renovation (acres)	Percent of Site
Buildings	9.6	12.2	30
Paved Areas	22.9	24.9	61
Landscaped Areas	1.0	3.9	9
Vacant Areas	6.5	0	0
Total	40.0	41.0	100

Development Cost Information

Leasehold costs	$17,000,000
Land costs	5,000,000
Site improvement costs	2,000,000
Construction and soft costs	25,000,000
Total	$49,000,000

Financing Information

Leasehold Acquisition

Principal financial group	$7,500,000
Seller financing	4,000,000
Equity and loans from developer's affiliates	5,500,000

Land Acquisition

Principal financial group	$5,000,000

Construction Financing

Northwestern Mutual Life (with takeout financing)	$18,000,000
Equity and loans from developer's affiliates	9,000,000
Total	$49,000,000

Retail Tenant Information

Classification	Number of Stores	Percent of Total	Total GLA (square feet)	Percent of GLA
General merchandise	3	4	44,307	10
Food	25	31	25,794	6
Clothing and accessories	6	8	113,603	25
Shoes	1	1	487	–
Home furnishings	3	4	29,053	6
Home appliances/music	2	2	41,741	9
Hobby/special interest	13	16	67,206	15
Gifts/specialty	5	6	8,060	2
Jewelry	1	1	2,522	1
Drugs	1	1	14,016	3
Cinema and other retail	3	4	41,122	9
Personal services	6	8	9,304	2
Recreation/community	2	2	8,174	2
Financial offices	3	4	5,968	1
Offices (other than financial)	6	8	5,725	1
Vacant space under construction	–	–	35,270	8
Total	80	100	452,352	100

Leasing Information

Major Tenants

Average length of lease	19 years
Annual rent	$9 per square foot
Annual sales	$273 per square foot

Mid-Sized Tenants

Average length of lease	12 years
Annual rent	$14 per square foot
Annual sales	$247 per square foot

Small Shops

Average length of lease	7 years
Annual rent	$17 per square foot
Annual sales	$191 per square foot

Restaurants

Average length of lease	7 years
Annual rent	$21 per square foot
Annual sales	$378 per square foot

Development Schedule (Terranomics Development)

1987	Control assumed
1987	Planning started
1988	Approvals obtained
1988	Construction started
1987	Re-leasing started
1990	Land lease acquired
1998	Project completed

Owner

Terranomics Crossroads Associates
320 108th Avenue, N.E./Suite 406
Bellevue, Washington 98004
425-453-0324

Developer/Manager

Terranomics Development
320 108th Avenue, N.E., Suite 406
Bellevue, Washington 98004
425-453-0324

Architect

The Callison Partnership
1420 5th Avenue/Suite 2400
Seattle, Washington 98101
206-623-4646

Dadeland Station

Miami, Florida

Miami's Dadeland Station is an effective marriage of two components previously thought to be inconsistent: value-oriented retailing and an urban infill setting. Five big-box retailers have been stacked vertically in a three-story structure that is connected to a six-level parking facility for 1,470 cars; a six-story canopied galleria provides direct access to the garage. Dadeland Station is located next to the Dadeland North Metrorail station on a 7.25-acre triangular parcel, formerly the site of a surplus county-owned parking lot.

The design of the shopping center incorporates a pedestrian link to Metrorail, a 21-mile, electrically powered, elevated rapid-transit rail system built from the Dadeland area to Hialeah at a cost of $1.03 billion. Ridership totaled slightly over 13.4 million in 1998; average weekday ridership at the Dadeland North station totaled 5,341.

Site

Designated a "metropolitan diversified activity center" in the Dade County comprehensive master development plan, the property is located within a rapid-transit zone, which permits a wide variety of mixed uses, including retail, residential, hotel, and office. The site is bordered on the south by the Dadeland North Metrorail station, a three-acre parcel used for surface parking, the Snapper Creek Canal, and a 2,000-car county parking garage; on the north by the Snapper Creek Expressway (SR 878); on the east by U.S. Route 1; and on the west by SW 70th Avenue and Dadeland Mall. Dadeland Mall, one of the area's premier super regional shopping centers, with 1.5 million square feet of retail space, is anchored by Burdines, Saks, Lord & Taylor, and JCPenney. Its owner, the Equitable Life Assurance Society of the United States, plans to expand the mall's footprint eastward, with an additional 800,000 square feet of retail space and 4,000 new parking spaces.

U.S. Route 1, a six-lane divided highway with average daily traffic of 91,500 vehicles, offers convenient access to south Dade County as well as to I-95 to the north. The Snapper Creek Expressway handles approximately 30,000 daily trips. The Palmetto Expressway (SR 826) runs on the west side of Dadeland Mall. It also links I-95 and north Dade County, ending at U.S. Route 1 just south of the Dadeland Station site. Substantial changes are planned to the Palmetto Expressway as a result of the Dadeland Mall expansion. A new roadway design will allow for a direct route from the Palmetto Expressway not only to Dadeland Mall but also to the Dadeland

North Metrorail station and the Dadeland Station shopping center.

Development Process

The Green Companies was the successful bidder on a request for proposals issued in the 1980s by Dade County seeking developers for the 12-acre property. Green negotiated unsuccessfully for many years to acquire a ground lease with the county. In 1995, after the county had initiated efforts to terminate its negotiations with the Green Companies, Berkowitz Development Group acquired the development rights to the retail portion of the development and successfully negotiated a 90-year unsubordinated ground lease with the county. A special county requirement mandated that 25 percent of the design work, 20 percent of construction, and 50 percent of the smaller shops be reserved for minority or woman-owned business enterprises.

The shopping center, a joint development of Berkowitz Development Group and the Miami-Dade Transit Authority, is only one component to be built on the 12-acre site. The entire site had been used as the primary surface parking lot serving the Metrorail station; the surface lot subsequently was replaced by a 2,000-car parking structure, developed by Dade County with state and federal funding, adjacent to the station itself. With the shopping center occupying a little over seven acres, the Green Companies retained the development rights for the office and hotel portions of the project on the remaining three acres, which must be completed within ten to 15 years.

The ground lease with Berkowitz Development was approved in June 1994, development approvals were obtained by April 1995, and construction started in September 1995. The shopping center officially opened in October 1996, having been 100 percent leased before construction.

Dade County provided significant support throughout the lease negotiation, planning, and permitting phases of the project. During construction, the county was instrumental in assisting the developer in securing a major new signalized intersection, opening access to the site from U.S. Route 1 (South Dixie Highway) under the existing elevated Metrorail tracks. In addition, the county paid 20 percent of the development costs for such items as signage and the intersection at U.S. Route 1.

The project generated over $1 million in impact and permit fees during construction and is estimated to produce more than $100 million for taxpayers over the 90-year lease term. For the owners, the project has generated

Visible on the Miami skyline, Dadeland Station adapts the concept of a suburban power center to an urban infill location with a challenging density requirement.

Dadeland Station successfully compresses five big-box retailers and nearly 306,000 gross leasable square feet and 1,500 parking spaces onto a mere 7.25 acres. The development's density is four and one-half times higher than that of traditional power centers, resulting in the use of 80 percent less land.

better than $5 million in net operating income. Approximately 600 permanent jobs were created.

A construction loan of $35 million with SunTrust Bank of Alabama, N.A., has been replaced by a 20-year permanent loan with New York Life Insurance Company. The construction lender wanted a permanent takeout lender in place before any construction began.

Planning and Design

While the development of Dadeland Station gave big-box retailers the opportunity to enter the Dadeland market, the developer still had to convince them that the vertical concept would satisfy their respective operational requirements, many of which revolved around adequate parking close to a store's front door. The project was conceived as consumer friendly to both those arriving by car and those using the transit system.

Best Buy and Michaels are located on the first retail level, Target on the second, and Sports Authority and

The project incorporated the use of air rights over an existing four-lane road to accommodate retailer's floorplates; Target, with over 120,000 square feet, was able to locate on the second retail level.

Bed Bath & Beyond on the third. Best Buy had to be located on the first level because of its car radio installation facility; Target physically could not fit on the first level with its typical store footprint (100,000 square feet plus), as that would have necessitated closing SW 70th Avenue permanently. In the end, the project incorporated the use of air rights, with 60,000 square feet of retail space constructed over the existing four-lane SW 70th Avenue. The five major anchor tenants occupy 97 percent of the center's gross leasable area (GLA). The floor/area ratio is 1.1, significantly above the 0.25 ratio typical for strip shopping centers.

With 23-foot ceilings for each retail level, the developer could provide two parking levels with ten-foot ceilings for each retail level. The project includes an additional 9,500 square feet of small shops and restaurants adjacent to the pedestrian link between the station and the shopping center to serve the needs of Metrorail commuters.

To accommodate shoppers arriving by car, the parking garage design allows customers to drive directly to the retail level of their choice by incorporating two 80-foot-diameter ingress and egress helixes to transport cars vertically to an open, rampless parking level. A computerized tracking system directs incoming automobiles to their specific retail destination. Parking for Dadeland Station is provided at a ratio of 4.6 parking spaces per 1,000 square feet of GLA.

Shopping carts were accommodated by building two banks of oversized, glass-enclosed traction elevators, allowing up to nine shoppers at one time to enter with carts from the retail side and to exit at any one of the six parking levels.

Concerns about security in the garage were addressed by painting the interior of the garage white, providing lighting far in excess of the minimum requirements (six footcandles versus one-half footcandle), installing an elaborate panic intercom system and 24-hour color camera surveillance of the entire parking garage, and making security personnel and equipment visible to shopping center patrons.

A secure loading facility is provided on the north side of the site for each anchor tenant, with the exception of Michaels, whose loading dock is to the west. Individual elevators or conveyors transport goods securely to the upper-level tenants.

Each tenant is separately metered for heating and cooling. Vertical and horizontal easements allow the ductwork to be located within the building. Target built out its own space.

Dadeland Station soon will feature a six-story sculpture entitled *Welcome* by international artist Romero Britto. It will be located between the shopping center and the train station.

Leasing and Marketing

Leasing began in May 1994 and essentially was completed before construction started in September 1995. Unlike the other big-box tenants, which opened when the project opened in October 1996, Michaels did not open until 1997.

Two extra-wide helixes vertically transport cars to open, level parking fields.

Through a network of escalators and pedestrian and cart elevators, customers have convenient access to all five anchor stores, permitting more cross shopping than in traditional power centers.

Dadeland Station, with its vertical orientation, presented anchor retailers with an opportunity to enter the Dadeland market, where land for a typical power center simply is not available.

In 1993, there were 217,000 households within a seven-mile radius of Dadeland Station, which is considered the trade area. That number was projected to increase to 246,000 households in 1998. Average annual household income in 1993 was estimated at $51,000. (Within a three-mile radius, average annual household income is over $70,000.) The population is well educated: 50 percent have had some college education or have graduated from college, and 67 percent of the working population have white-collar jobs. The average age is 37.

All the major tenants have reported strong sales exceeding their projections. The Dadeland Sports Authority store is presently the number-two store in the south Florida area and is ninth of all Sports Authority stores in terms of sales per square foot. Likewise, Target ranks second in sales within its district, following the number-one store at Sawgrass Mills.

Experience Gained

- Locating all the retailers close to one another permits more cross shopping than in a traditional power center. Consequently, the parking lot is hardly ever full. Levels one, three, and five, which offer the most direct access to the individual stores, typically fill up first. The project allows consumers direct access through a vertical transportation network consisting of escalators and pedestrian and cart elevators to all five anchor stores without having to get back in a car and drive across a large parking lot to another retailer. The garage/galleria retail configuration allows shoppers to shop in a protected environment.

- At first glance, the structure of Dadeland Station can be a little imposing. To make this nontraditional center customer friendly, the developer spent a significant amount of money up front on security, extra signage, and two extra-wide open helixes for ingress and egress. Target contributed money upfront for the security system; all the tenants contributed to the upgraded signage.

- In the absence of many comparable projects, in Miami or elsewhere, the anchor retailers had to be convinced that the vertical space configuration facing a parking garage would meet their needs. Despite these concerns, the project provided the big-box retailers with the opportunity to enter the much-sought-after Dadeland market, because few, if any, large land parcels were available for development as traditional strip centers.

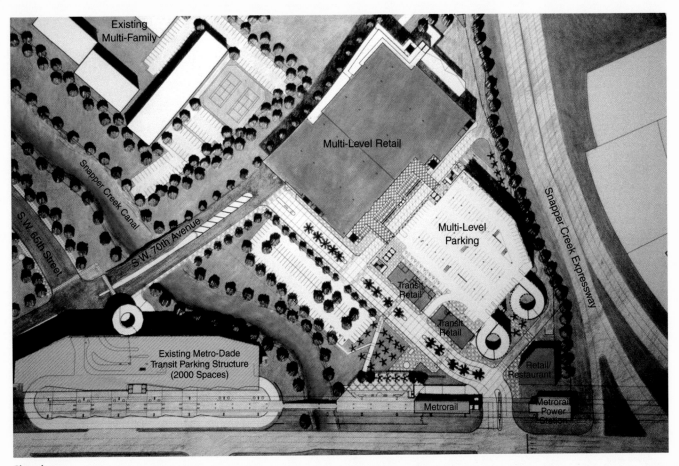

Site plan.

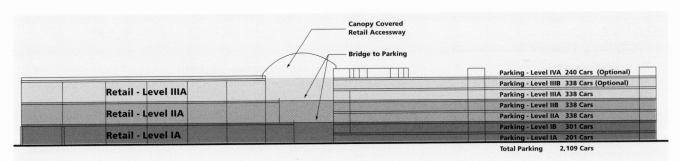

**Canopy Covered
Retail Accessway**

Bridge to Parking

Parking - Level IVA	240 Cars	(Optional)
Parking - Level IIIB	338 Cars	(Optional)
Parking - Level IIIA	338 Cars	
Parking - Level IIB	338 Cars	
Parking - Level IIA	338 Cars	
Parking - Level IB	301 Cars	
Parking - Level IA	201 Cars	
Total Parking	**2,109 Cars**	

Retail - Level IIIA

Retail - Level IIA

Retail - Level IA

Section.

Project Data: Dadeland Station

Land Use and Building Information

Site Area   7.25 acres

Gross Building Area (GBA)   350,000 square feet
(excluding parking structure)

Gross Leasable Area (GLA)   315,298 square feet

Target	123,112 square feet
Bed Bath & Beyond	60,000 square feet
Best Buy	58,000 square feet
Sports Authority	45,249 square feet
Michaels	19,478 square feet

Floor/Area Ratio   1.1

Levels

Shopping	3
Parking	6

Parking Spaces   1,470

Parking Ratio   4.6 spaces per 1,000 square feet of GLA

Land Use Plan

	Acres	Percent of Site
Buildings	2.06	28
Parking structures	2.18	30
Paved area[1]	1.21	17
Landscaped areas	1.80	25
Total	7.25	100

Development Cost Information

Site Acquisition Cost[2] $750,000

Site Improvement Cost

Excavation/grading	$187,360
Sewer/water/drainage	817,330
Paving/curbs/sidewalks	746,029
Landscaping/irrigation	100,000
Other	1,226,830
Total	$3,077,549

Construction Cost

Superstructure	$7,465,495
HVAC	500,000
Electrical	1,211,000
Plumbing/sprinklers	658,000
Elevators	1,450,000
Fees/general conditions	1,650,000
Finishes	1,751,000
Graphics/specialties	600,000
Parking structure	7,374,185
Tenant improvements	3,247,000
Total	$25,906,680

Soft Costs

Architecture/engineering	$927,500
Project management	400,000
Marketing	625,000
Legal/accounting	250,000
Taxes/insurance	100,000
Title fees/testing	98,000
Construction interest/fees	3,500,000
Art in public spaces	225,000
Permits/impact fees	1,000,000
Other (document stamps, inspection, etc.)	250,000
Miscellaneous	600,000
Total	$7,975,500

Total Development Cost $37,709,729

Total Development Cost per Gross Square Foot of GBA $107.75

Annual Operating Expenses (1997)

Taxes	$669,094
Insurance	465,028
Services	337,609
Maintenance	105,306
Janitorial	156,473
Utilities	173,624
Legal	197,801
Management	205,776
Miscellaneous	218,439
Total	$2,529,150

Notes

[1] Surface parking and roads.

[2] For acquisition of rights to ground lease.

Retail Tenant Information

Classification	Number of Stores	Total GLA	Percent of GLA (square feet)
General merchandise	1	123,112	39.0
Food service	3	5,180	1.6
Home furnishings	1	60,000	19.0
Home appliances/music	1	58,000	18.4
Hobby/special interest	1	45,249	14.4
Gifts/specialty	1	19,478	6.2
Jewelry	1	831	0.3
Other retail	1	1,340	0.4
Personal services	1	970	0.3
Vacant	1	1,138	0.4
Total	12	315,298	100.0

Lease Terms

Average annual rent	$14–28 per square foot
Average length of lease	15–20 years
Typical lease provisions	Net net. Landlord pays for roof and structural maintenance.

Development Schedule

5/1994	Leasing started
6/1994	Ground lease between developer and county approved
4/1995	Development approvals obtained
9/1995	Construction started
10/1996	Shopping center opened

Developer

Berkowitz Development Group
2665 South Bayshore Drive/Suite 1200
Miami, Florida 33133
305-854-2800

Architect

Robin Bosco Architect & Planners, Inc.
2937 SW 27th Avenue/Suite 207
Miami, Florida 33133
305-442-2345

Leasing

Florida Shopping Center Group
1110 Brickell Avenue/Suite 509
Miami, Florida 33131
305-374-4370

The Forum Shops at Caesars Palace

Las Vegas, Nevada

The "Shopping Wonder of the World" reads the advertising copy for the Forum Shops, and with sales exceeding $1,200 per square foot, the words are no idle boast. Lured by its ancient Rome–themed "streets," its vaulted cloud-painted ceilings lit to reflect the changing colors of the sky, and its "animatronic" sculptures that simulate human movement, some 50,000 visitors flow through the center each day—almost 20 million visitors a year.

And when not looking at the "sky," listening to Bacchus, or watching the sinking of Atlantis, a good number of the 20 million shop. For the well-heeled and the lucky roulette players, shops offer fashions by Gucci, Bernini, and Louis Vuitton. For the rest, the Forum Shops includes less patrician retailers, such as Guess, Brookstone, and Victoria's Secret, and, in a bow to the emerging family atmosphere in Las Vegas, a Warner Bros. Store and a Disney Store.

Phase II has a similar tenant mix, with strong name-brand retailers such as Abercrombie & Fitch, DKNY, Hugo Boss, Diesel, Lacoste, NikeTown, Polo/Ralph Lauren, Virgin Megastore, and Bernini Collections. Completing the mix are high-profile restaurants, such as Spago, Planet Hollywood, and the Stage Deli. The center is anchored by Caesars Palace Hotel and Casino.

Site

The Forum Shops is situated on a 12-acre site just north of Caesars Palace on land that formerly was used for employee parking and as a Grand Prix racetrack. Phase I of the center is L-shaped, with the long leg facing Las Vegas Boulevard and the short leg abutting and tied into the Olympic Casino of Caesars Palace. Phase II extends the long leg of the center westward from the Fountain of the Gods. The center's shops are primarily on one level, raised above the lower-level vehicle circulation area, which leads to the valet parking entrance as well as a self-parking area in the rear. A Cyberstation (games arcade) and Cinema Ride (motion simulator 3-D ride) also are located on the lower level.

From the street outside, one approaches the Forum Shops on a one-way moving walkway that passes through a series of five triumphal arches. Inside, the visitor proceeds along the Roman "street" as it bends and turns, passing through a series of gathering points—piazzas—and eventually exiting directly into the casino. Going the other way, hotel and casino patrons pass through a monumental portal into the Forum Shops. As a result of a grade change as well as the one-way moving walkway at the end of the "street," a journey through the Forum Shops that starts at the casino also ends back at the casino.

Development Process

In the late 1980s, as lavish new hotels were booming all around Caesars, it became clear that employee parking was not the highest and best use for eight acres facing Las Vegas Boulevard. The "Street of Dreams," as the Forum Shops was initially conceived, represented to Caesars the opportunity to reestablish its preeminent place in the pantheon of hotel/casinos by offering the most unusual, most upscale shopping environment in Las Vegas. Not incidentally, the plan also was intended to drive more people through the casino. The Simon Property Group and Gordon Group Holdings Ltd., developers of premier shopping centers across the country, were brought in to realize the vision.

The Forum Shops was constructed on land leased to the project by Caesars World. Construction for Phase I was financed by Yasuda Trust and Banking Co. Ltd., along with equity contributions from the Simon Property Group. In 1996 the United Bank of Switzerland provided permanent financing for the project.

Development of the specialized architectural and entertainment elements of the Forum Shops involved the efforts of a wide range of designers, artists, and artisans working under the direction of Dougall Design Associates and Marnell/Corrao, the center's design/build architect and contractor. Achieving the complex special effects and authentic-looking faux finishes envisioned for the project required an extended series of models, mock-ups, and material samples.

Because of the project's complexity, the Simon Property Group retained Marnell/Corrao under a design/build arrangement. As executive architect, Marnell/Corrao developed the construction documents from Dougall Design Associates's models; thereafter, as contractor, Marnell/Corrao was responsible for building the project for a guaranteed maximum price. As a further control, the Simon Property Group placed two of its in-house construction personnel on site for the duration of construction.

The primary difficulty encountered in the otherwise smooth construction process involved unanticipated delays in the completion of storefronts because of the extensive number of castings and faux finishes required and the limited number of firms retained to do this specialized work.

Design and Architecture

In both materials and layout, the Forum Shops is intended to evoke the feel of a Roman city. Floors in the common

In the Roman Great Hall, the sinking of Atlantis is a dazzling display of cutting-edge technologies in projection, animation, and hydraulics.

area, for example, are of stamped concrete, patterned to look like the rough stone of a Roman street. The storefronts are two stories high, with display windows below and Roman streetfront facades above, replete with shuttered windows, balconies, lanterns, and tile roofs.

Arching over the "street" is a vaulted ceiling painted to look like a cloud-filled sky. Computer-controlled devices light up the "sky," changing its appearance from that of an orangy dawn to a clear blue midday to a purple dusk, all in a one-hour rotation. The layout of the Forum Shops also contributes to its varying ambience. The narrow street alternates with wider piazzas, and the street itself bends, producing a series of vistas as one proceeds along the route.

The first highlight of the procession—judging by the crowds—is the Festival Fountain, a large rotunda and fountain with figures of Bacchus, Apollo, Venus, and Pluto, who come to life once an hour through the magic of audio animatronics. For seven minutes, the characters are heard chatting, moving their lips and other parts of their bodies in sync.

Offering more sedate charms is the larger Fountain of the Gods piazza. In addition to some of the upscale shops, the Fountain of the Gods offers an "outdoor" café (Bertolinis) at which customers can sip coffee and watch the passing parade. Roman statuary crowns the facades along the piazza.

Phase II is a seamless integration of more entertainment and shopping options into the existing fabric. The centerpiece of the new addition, which extends westward

from the Fountain of the Gods, is the Roman Great Hall; of heroic proportions, it measures 160 feet in diameter and 85 feet in height. Located within the great hall is a spectacular new attraction featuring both humans and talking statues in regularly scheduled performances of the sinking of Atlantis, Las Vegas style. The mind-boggling display combines cutting-edge technologies in projection, animation, and hydraulics. The expansion also includes a 50,000-gallon marine aquarium designed to represent the legendary sunken city of Atlantis. Overseen by three staff biologists, the aquarium contains a wide variety of fish from a geographic range of 10 to 15 degrees north latitude, just above the equator in the Caribbean. Many new statues made of fiberglass and weighing between 1,500 and 2,000 pounds each adorn Phase II's Piazza IV, including four large horses, a winged siren, two warriors, and a lion.

Marketing and Management

Marketing the Forum Shops to financiers as well as potential tenants before development was not the easy sell that in retrospect it might seem. In their favor, the developers had a strong location, a strong concept, and quotable sales figures from retailers in Las Vegas. On the other hand, at that time Las Vegas was known to most retailers as a casino market, not as a shopping market or family market. By opening day for Phase I, however, the center was 90 percent leased. Phase II, which opened four years later, also was nearly leased at opening.

The fantasy design of the Forum Shops reflects a classic Roman theme with columns, pilasters, balconies, and statuary. Storefronts are two stories tall, with display windows below and Roman streetfront facades above. The vaulted ceiling is painted to look like a cloud-filled sky.

The entrance corridor to the Forum Shops from the casino features a statue of the goddess Fortuna and integrates gaming facilities with the retail environment.

Eric Figge Photography © 92

Construction activities were the source of much of the initial publicity for the center, and hard-hat tours were organized for the news media to cover events such as the painting of the sky ceiling. In addition, the development team marketed the center through airport displays, billboards, in-flight magazines, tourist publications, and, to a lesser extent, radio and television. The team also staged a series of preopening events, including separate hosted evenings for the local chamber of commerce, taxi and limousine drivers, and Caesars Palace employees.

More than 15 million people visited the center in its first year—50 percent more than initially projected. Almost all the center's tenants have exceeded projected sales, and several are the leading sales locations in their chains. Only one tenant (a restaurant) has failed, and two have been bought out and replaced with new tenants.

The shops typically are open from 10:00 a.m. to 11:00 p.m. and until midnight on weekends. The common areas remain open 24 hours a day, 365 days a year.

Because of the extended hours and the large crowds, maintenance and security are critical, and management and security personnel are on duty around the clock. Nearly 50 employees are on staff, including management office personnel, security officers, building engineers, and housekeeping staff. To support these operations, common area maintenance charges are high, but, as a percentage of sales volume, they are not unlike those in more typical centers, according to Deborah Simon of the Simon Property Group.

As a result of Phase I's record sales and number of visitors, Phase II broke ground just four years after the opening of Phase I. The 276,000-square-foot expansion, which opened in August 1997, effectively doubles the size of the center. The entertainment and shopping experience has been enhanced by the re-creation of the sinking of Atlantis as well as by the addition of 35 strong name-brand tenants. Unlike for Phase I, little marketing was required for Phase II. The unmitigated success of Phase I

The Fountain of the Gods piazza contains the Temple of Neptune.

FAO Schwarz is one of many brand-name retailers—including Abercrombie & Fitch, DKNY, Hugo Boss, Diesel, Lacoste, NikeTown, Polo/ Ralph Lauren, Virgin Megastore, and Bernini Collections—to take space in Phase II.

and the promise that Phase II would offer even more shopping and entertainment options were the keys to marketing Phase II. Ninety percent of the new retail space was preleased, and it is now completely leased. Referring to the record sales at the Forum Shops, David Salz, CEO of Alfred Dunhill USA, an upscale men's wear store, said, "I would have to be catatonic not to do business in this center" (*Daily News Record*, September 5, 1997).

Experience Gained
- Both entertainment and environment attract visitors to the Forum Shops. The center's architectural theme and its supporting amenities, including the animatronic displays, combine to create a "must see" attraction in Las Vegas.
- Design and development required extensive production of custom finishes and complex installation procedures, increasing both hard and soft costs and prolonging construction. These finishes, however, significantly con-

tribute to the innovative design theme that has played an invaluable role in the complex's success. Through creative design and tenanting, the integration of retailing and entertainment can serve as a valuable complement to a casino and hotel complex, creating a strong identity in a crowded market.

THE FORUM SHOPS AT CAESARS

WOMEN'S APPAREL
116 Ann Taylor
188 bebe
179 Cache
130 DKNY
121 Escada
200 Express
158 Max Mara
190 St. John
148 Shauna Stein

SPECIALTY APPAREL
139 Abercrombie & Fitch Co.
131 A/X Armani Exchange
194 Banana Republic
103 Beyond the Beach
147 Diesel
152 Emporio Armani
174 French Room
150 Gap
124 Gianni Versace
120 Guess
203 Images by Crazy Shirts
138 Lacoste
133 The Polo Store/Ralph Lauren
173 Rose of Sharon–Size 14 & Up
162 Sloanes
169 Versus
114 Victoria's Secret

SPECIALTY SHOPS
155 Alfred Dunhill
145 Bath & Body at Home
207 Christian Dior
186 Davante
115 The Disney Store
165 Estée Lauder
195 Field of Dreams
149 Guess Home Collection
105 Magic Masters
142 NIKETOWN
185 Porsche Design
202 Sports Logo
110 Sunglass Hut International
128 Swatch
136 Victoria's Secret Bath
      & Fragrance
144 Virgin Megastore
178 Warner Bros. Studio Store

LEATHER
164 El Portal Luggage
156 Fendi
122 Gucci
125 Louis Vuitton

ENTERTAINMENT
204 Cinema Ride
205 CyberStation
140 Race For Atlantis –
      The IMAX 3-D Ride

JEWELRY
184 Bvlgari
160 Fred Joaillier
153 Hyde Park
111 M.J. Christensen Jewelers
182 N. Landau Hyman
161 Opals & Gems of Australia
113 Roman Times
196 Zero Gravity

SHOES
172 Avventura
134 Footworks
197 Just For Feet
137 Salvatore
127 Salvatore Ferragamo
170 Shooze at The Forum
181 Stuart Weitzman
119 Via Veneto

ART GALLERIES
108 Antiquities
118 Galerie Lassen
163 Galleria di Sorrento

GIFTS
112 Brookstone
175 Caesars Exclusively
193 Crystal Galleria
101 The Endangered Species Store
159 Ice Accessories Las Vegas
100 Lalique
167 The Museum Company
192 Planet Hollywood Superstore
189 West of Santa Fe

RESTAURANTS
183 Bertolini's
146 Caviarteria
143 The Cheesecake Factory
154 Chinois
107 La Salsa
171 Palm Restaurant
191 Planet Hollywood
180 Spago
104 Stage Deli

SPECIALTY FOOD
104 Cafe Express
106 Chocolate Chariot
109 David's Cookies
109 Heidi's Yogurt
198 Sweet Factory
109 Swensen's Ice Cream

MEN'S APPAREL
126 Bernini
151 Bernini Collections
168 Cuzzens
157 Hugo Boss
176 Kerkarian
117 The Knot Shop
201 Structure
166 Vasari

CHILDREN'S APPAREL & TOYS
102 Animal Crackers
149 Baby Guess
132 FAO Schwarz
150 Gap Kids
177 Kids Kastle

SERVICES
206 Allstate Ticketing & Tours
    ATM Bank of America ATM/Cash
206 Business/Postal Service
206 Customer Service Center
199 Foto Forum
    PC Phone Card Machine

GENERAL INFORMATION
123 Management Office/Security

TELEPHONES
VALET PARKING
ELEVATORS
RESTROOMS
ATM
PHONE CARD MACHINE
OPENING SOON

Site plan.

Many famous retailers line the narrow street bustling with activity between Piazza IV and the Roman Great Hall.

Project Data: The Forum Shops at Caesars Palace

Land Use and Building Information

Site Area

Phase I	8.4 acres
Phase II	3.6 acres

Gross Leasable Area (GLA)

Phase I	229,499 square feet
Phase II	258,440 square feet

Levels

One retail level with valet parking entrance and video arcade on a sublevel. Several tenant spaces include mezzanine levels.

Parking Spaces

Parking Spaces	2,100

Retail Tenant Information

	Phase I		Phase II	
	Number of Retailers	GLA (square feet)	Number of Retailers	GLA (square feet)
Food	3	2,967	0	0
Food service	6	52,062	3	29,729
Clothing and accessories	24	81,606	13	77,428
Shoes	6	21,739	2	3,261
Hobby/special interest	3	0	0	10,515
Gifts/specialty	8	22,014	2	1,707
Jewelry	5	3,766	3	3,146
Other retail	13	31,058	9	109,354
Personal services	2	851	1	100
Recreation/community	2	13,436	1	23,200
Total	72	229,499	34	258,440

Average Length of Lease

Average Length of Lease	10–12 years

Annual Rents

Annual Rents	$70–200 per square foot

Average Annual Sales

Average Annual Sales	$1,200 per square foot

Annual Operating Expenses (1995—pre-Phase II)

Taxes	$471,996
Insurance	218,000
Services	65,100
Maintenance	1,074,000
Janitorial	496,900
Utilities	301,000
Management	225,352
Miscellaneous	2,694,419
Total	$5,546,767

Development Cost Information (Phase I)

Site Acquisition Cost

Site Acquisition Cost	$5,000,000[1]

Site Improvement Costs (on and off site)

Excavation/grading	$500,000
Sewer/water/drainage	250,000
Paving/curbs/sidewalks	200,000
Landscaping/irrigation	100,000
Fees/general conditions	200,000
Other	750,000
Total	$2,000,000

Construction Costs

Superstructure	$11,000,000
HVAC	3,000,000
Electrical	4,000,000
Plumbing/sprinklers	2,000,000
Elevators	200,000
Fees/general conditions	6,200,000
Finishes	15,800,000
Graphics/specialties	500,000
Parking structure	5,000,000
Tenant improvements	17,000,000
Total	$64,700,000

Soft Costs

Architecture/engineering	$2,500,000
Project management	100,000
Marketing	1,500,000
Legal/accounting	1,000,000
Taxes/insurance	500,000
Construction interest and fees	7,600,000
Other	600,000
Total	$13,800,000

Leasing and Development Fees

Leasing and Development Fees	$4,500,000

Total Development Cost

Total Development Cost	$90,000,000

Development Schedule

	Phase I	Phase II
Site purchased	Ground lease	Ground lease
Planning started	1988	1992
Sales/leasing started	1988	1992
Construction started	2/1990	5/1995
Project completed	5/1992	8/1997

Developers

Simon Property Group, Inc.
115 W. Washington Street
Indianapolis, Indiana 46204
317-636-1600

Gordon Group Holdings Ltd.
3500 Las Vegas Bouldevard South
Las Vegas, Nevada 89109
702-650-9111

Architect

Marnell/Corrao Associates
4495 South Polaris Avenue
Las Vegas, Nevada 89103

Interior Designer

Dougall Design Associates, Inc.
35 North Arroyo Parkway
Pasadena, California 91103

Note

[1]Reimbursement to Caesars Palace for existing site improvements.

Great Mall of the Bay Area

Milpitas, California

For 25 years, the anonymous-looking industrial building in Milpitas, California, served up a menu of Ford automobiles: Mustangs, Falcons, Fairlanes, Cougars, Pintos, and Escorts. Its 2 million-square-foot plant employed 5,000 workers, catering to the demand of the post–World War II era for cars. By 1983, however, the plant had closed, a victim of changes in consumers' tastes and auto industry economics.

A decade later, in 1994, the stripped-down and retooled former Ford Motor Company San Jose assembly plant was rechristened Great Mall of the Bay Area, reopening for business as a value-oriented megamall. To accomplish that metamorphosis, all of the original outbuildings and pieces of the main plant were removed, interiors were gutted, new mechanical and electrical systems were installed, and the building was seismically strengthened. A new, looping "racetrack" circulation system replaced the former assembly line, and the concrete tilt-up exterior walls were reskinned.

The conversion, which cost approximately $120 million and took 15 months to complete, provides for 14 anchor tenants (12 currently are in place) and 201 mall shops, including a 715-seat food court. For the most part, the mall contains outlet shops of manufacturers and major retailers and value-oriented, off-price retail stores. Some stores, however, are more traditional, crossing over from the standard regional mall format. In addition, following in the footsteps of other regional malls, Great Mall has embraced the entertainment/retail concept, introducing virtual-reality and arcade game tenants and theme design revolving around the site's past association with transportation.

Site and Development Process

Great Mall is located in a low-density suburban commercial/industrial area, approximately one-quarter mile east of I-880. The site is bordered on two sides by rail lines, one of few reminders of its industrial past. Nearby are business parks and research and development facilities. Access to the site is via the Great Mall Parkway exit of I-880, which was planned before the mall was developed but completed and named a year after its opening. Approximately 6 million people live within a 50-mile radius.

While the site generally was suitable for a major shopping center, the placement of the main building within the 147-acre site was less so. Parking areas were available on all four sides of the building, but the potential parking field on the main entrance side was too narrow. Dealing with this problem required "surgery," and the

southwest corner of the assembly plant was sheared off. Conversely, in some locations, the plant building had to be enlarged to provide sufficient depth for anchor tenants.

As Timothy J. Ridner, Ford Motor Land Development's western region development and operations manager, summarized the process, the adaptive use of the plant entailed "a little addition and a lot of subtraction." In all, about 500,000 square feet of space was demolished to make way for the mall. Much of this material was recycled within the project: 150,000 tons of concrete and asphalt were crushed and reused for walkways and parking lots; hundreds of miles of piping were melted down; and more than 12,000 tons of iron, tin, copper, and aluminum were recycled off site.

Soon after the assembly plant closed in 1983, the site was sold to a developer who intended to convert the building to high-tech, R&D office use. The venture did not succeed, and in 1987, Ford Motor Land Development Corporation bought back the facility. Several uses were considered for the site and rejected: office use because of market conditions, and a regional mall because of existing competition.

The idea of value-oriented shopping, whose viability had been established in several locations around the country, made the most sense; the South Bay market was huge, and there was little real competition in that category. Studies confirmed the feasibility of the idea, and the required environmental impact statement, which used the former 5,000-person assembly plant as a comparison, cleared the way for construction.

The city of Milpitas supported the retail concept for the site and assisted financially by providing needed off-site improvements. Street widening and other traffic-related improvements were required, which cost approximately $8.5 million total. The project otherwise was privately developed and financed.

Planning and Design

While the high ceilings and open structure of the assembly plant were conducive to the development of a shopping mall, significant upgrading was required, given the plant's age and current building code requirements. Several structural improvements were necessary, some of which were planned, some not. An initial round of seismic improvements was undertaken as part of planned construction, and the walls and ceilings were "buttoned up" as scheduled. After the Northridge earthquake of January 1994, the city of Milpitas called for further testing and analysis of the assembly plant's structure. Substantial

The center's five major entrances are tied to the theme of the court within. The five themes—"Great Autos," "Great Railroads," "Great Ships," "Great Planes," and "Great Eats"—are advertised with tall space-frame structures with large graphic panels.

While the site provided ample space for parking areas, the potential parking field on the main entrance side was too narrow. To widen the area, the southwest corner of the assembly plant was sheared off.

Great Mall of the Bay's circulation system is designed as a continuous 0.7-mile-long loop to maximize use of space within the existing footprint of the assembly plant.

The original exterior concrete tilt-up panels with punched windows were considered too unattractive for a shopping mall. Outer panels were removed and replaced with a metal stud structure that was then finished with a combination of synthetic stucco and painted, corrugated metal panels.

additional seismic reinforcing of the steel structure was required, necessitating removal of a major portion of the finish work, lead paint abatement (the paint previously had been encapsulated by the finish work), and round-the-clock construction to meet the project's September 1994 opening.

A second area of work was environmental remediation. More than 140 pits left over from the assembly plant operation had to be cleaned and filled under the purview of environmental agencies. In addition, because the site was located above an aquifer, the regional water authority required remedial drainage work to ensure that the project would not contribute to the degradation of the water supply. A third area of remediation was roof repair. Detailed inspection revealed that substantial portions of the metal roof deck were corroded, requiring considerably more roof replacement than initially was budgeted for.

The exterior skin of the plant building, while sound, was considered too unattractive for a shopping mall. The original walls were concrete tilt-up panels with punched windows. The original base course of concrete panels (approximately eight feet high) was retained; the remaining panels were removed and replaced with a metal stud structure. The resulting concrete and metal stud wall was then finished with a combination of synthetic stucco and painted, corrugated metal panels.

Five major entrances were created, each tied to the theme of the court within. The five themes—"Great Autos," "Great Railroads," "Great Ships," "Great Planes," and "Great Eats"—are advertised with tall space-frame structures with large graphic panels. Additional portals and graphics identify each anchor tenant.

The interior courts were designed to create landmarks for visitors to use to orient themselves and to provide areas where they can rest at intervals along the circulation course. The theme of each court is carried out in exhibits, seating, lighting, and graphics. The focal point of the Great Autos court, for example, is a restored 1957

Ford Skyliner on a rotating platform. Every 15 minutes, the car's soft-top roof rises up and folds into the trunk and then returns to its original position. Supporting elements include seating groups composed of bucket and bench-style car seats, original Coke machines, 1950s-style gasoline pumps, and other period details. Storefronts along the Great Autos court tie into the theme through the use of forms, patterns, and colors typical of the 1950s. Similar coordinated theme environments are provided for the Great Railroads, Ships, and Planes courts, as well as for the Great Eats food court, which includes elements from all modes of transportation.

In a departure from the usual mall design, Great Mall's circulation system is designed as a continuous 0.7-mile-long loop, or "racetrack," to maximize use of space within the existing footprint of the assembly plant. The loop allows for easy and equal access to a large number of anchor and in-line stores and helps to eliminate low-traffic "cold spots." The great length of the loop, however, has proven frustrating for some shoppers, who on customer response forms have indicated the desire for a cut-through path to facilitate access through the mall to particular shops.

Ownership and Financing

Ford Motor Land Development Corporation (Ford Land), owner and joint developer of Great Mall of the Bay Area, is the real estate branch of Ford Motor Company. It is involved in development, management, acquisition, and sale of land and facilities for Ford worldwide. Since its inception in 1970, Ford Land has been the developer of the 2,360-acre Fairlane mixed-use project in Dearborn, Michigan; Detroit's Renaissance Center; and other major projects.

Petrie Dierman Kughn, codeveloper of Great Mall, specializes in the development, leasing, and management of shopping centers. Over the past eight years, the McLean, Virginia, company has developed or codeveloped more than 5 million square feet of retail projects,

The high ceilings and open structure of the assembly plant were conductive to the development of the shopping mall, including the themed courts. The focal point of the Great Autos court is a restored 1957 Ford Skyliner on a rotating platform; the Great Ships court features a fountain and a nautical theme.

including City Place (Silver Spring, Maryland) and the Center at Salisbury (Salisbury, Maryland).

Development of Great Mall was financed primarily by Ford. Ford Land contributed the site and building and financed the construction through Ford Holdings, a Ford Motor Company subsidiary. The Ford Holdings loan is a seven-year miniperm loan covering construction and approximately five years of operations. The only outside source of funds was a pledge of $8.5 million in sales tax revenues by the city of Milpitas to pay for off-site improvements. Through a sales tax revenue–sharing agreement, 50 percent of the incremental sales tax revenues generated by the project are devoted to repaying the $8.5 million (plus interest) fronted by the developer.

Leasing, Marketing, and Management

Great Mall was 68 percent leased at its opening in fall 1994; occupancy in 1997 was approximately 85 percent. Leasing has been challenging because of what Ford Land's Ridner calls "sensitivity issues." Some retailers, according to Ridner, have been ambivalent about outlet retailing and value centers. Some have questioned whether having an outlet in Great Mall could interfere with sales at their traditional stores in nearby conventional malls, and others have requested that their company name not be used in mall advertising out of concern for their relationships with the traditional department stores that also carry their goods.

The mall reaches out to the entire Bay Area, including the San Jose, San Francisco, and Oakland markets, through TV, radio, and direct mail advertising. Says John Petersen, general manager of Great Mall, the message is an appeal to value: "Now, anybody can afford to look like a million bucks."

Beyond the usual advertising media, Great Mall also appeals directly to tourists. The Great Mall marketing department works directly with tour operators and advertises in hotel and tourist publications. In addition, the mall has an annual reception for concierges and tour operators. Notes Petersen, "You have to sell the salespeople." The effort has proved quite successful: in 1996, approximately 800 busloads of shoppers were enticed to visit Great Mall. Approximately 60 percent of these tour groups were Japanese visitors.

In another innovation, the marketing department is reaching out to cybershoppers. During the holiday season, the mall operates ASAP! (A Shopping Assistance Program), through which shoppers can visit Great Mall's Web site via the Internet. Shoppers can electronically submit information about whom they are shopping for, and Great Mall's personal shoppers will e-mail back gift suggestions from Great Mall stores within 24 hours.

Great Mall's information-age savvy is displayed on site as well. Sixty-eight TV monitors are located throughout the mall, showing video loops produced in house by the mall media department. Some of the segments are produced in an on-site studio, although most are filmed directly in the tenant spaces.

Security provisions at the mall are extensive. Sixty-five closed-circuit television (CCTV) cameras scan the mall, inside and out, and a monitoring panel and dispatch unit is staffed 24 hours a day. In addition, the Milpitas police department has a substation in the mall that is staffed on weekends and holidays. The police department also provides foot and squad-car patrols on mall grounds. According to general manager Petersen, the investment in preventive security measures is worth the cost. The police presence deters vandalism and crime, and the CCTV system, while costly, pays for itself over time by requiring fewer security personnel.

Experience Gained

- Working with an existing building, while offering economic and environmental benefits, presents a whole new set of challenges. Because it is sometimes difficult to predict accurately the extent or difficulty of renovation required, additional leeway, both in terms of budget and time, should be built into planning for this kind of project.

- Also worthy of further consideration is the difficulty of phasing development in a renovation project like Great Mall. Unlike at many new outlet centers, which add space as demand warrants, at Great Mall the entire perimeter skin of the assembly plant had to be renovated and a high level of interior improvements completed before opening day to create the desired environment and image.

- Overall, the experience at Great Mall hints at the promise in reusing the increasing stock of surplus industrial property in the United States. Like Great Mall of the Bay Area, many of these properties—outdated but well located—have intrinsic economic value and can be reconditioned, providing environmentally efficient and economically profitable service.

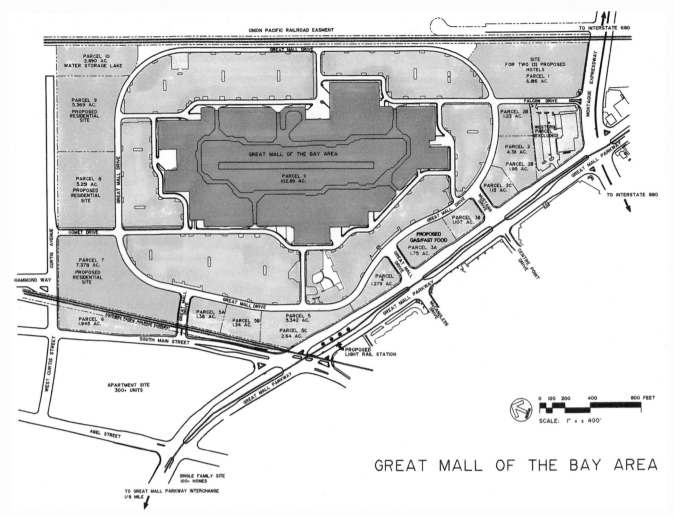

Site plan.

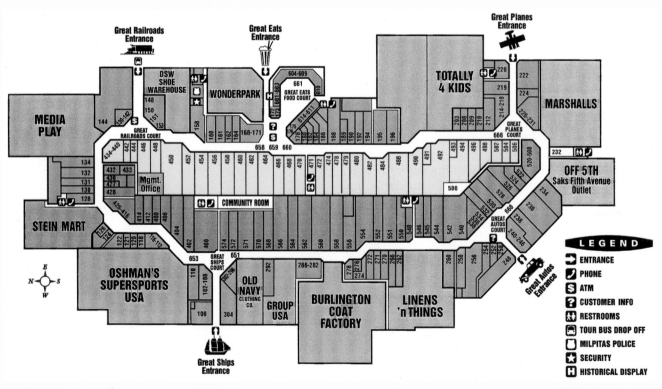

Mall layout.

Project Data: Great Mall of the Bay Area

Land Use and Building Information

Site Area	146.88 acres total
	(106.34 acres + 40.54 acres of outparcels)
Gross Building Area	1,548,171 square feet
Gross Leasable Area	1,247,662 square feet
Parking Spaces (surface)	6,352

Land Use Plan[1]

	Acres	Percent of Site
Buildings	35.54	33.4
Paved areas	51.96	48.9
Landscaped areas	15.95	15.0
Other	2.89	2.7
Total	106.34	100.0

Retail Tenant Information

Major Tenants	Square Feet
Off 5th (Saks 5th Avenue)	25,250
Burlington Coat Factory	81,656
Old Navy	20,134
Group USA	20,847
Oshman's Supersports	84,982
Media Play	49,409
Wonder for Kids	52,554
Marshalls Superstore	52,504
Linens'N Things	42,327

Lease Terms

Average length of lease	6–7 years
Typical lease provisions	Standard
Annual rents (in-line stores)	$18–30 per square foot
Average Annual Sales	$228 per square foot

Development Cost Information

Site Acquisition Cost	$33,900,000
Site Improvement Costs[2]	$9,770,000

Hard Costs

Mall/box fit-up/site work/demolition	$47,951,000
Anchor store fit-up/allowances	25,332,000
Seismic and roof repairs	8,041,000
Theme courts	3,354,000
Security system	436,000
Test borings	263,000
Other	706,000
Total	$86,083,000

Soft Costs

Architectural/mechanical and electrical engineering	$3,896,000
Marketing	2,602,000
Developers' fee	4,000,000
Legal/accounting	6,208,000
Taxes/insurance	1,127,000
Title fees	37,000
Construction interest	4,730,000
Other	1,978,000
Total	$24,578,000

Total Development Cost	$154,331,000

Operating Expenses

Taxes	$2,000,000
Insurance	425,000
Maintenance/janitorial	1,260,000
Utilities	300,000
Management	1,225,000
Marketing/advertising/promotions/tourism	1,800,000
Total	$7,010,000

Development Schedule

2/1989	Site purchased
Fall 1992	Planning started
Spring 1993	Approvals obtained
Summer 1993	Construction started
Spring 1993	Leasing started
9/1994	Project opened

Developer

A joint development of
Ford Motor Land Development Corporation
1900 McCarthy Boulevard/Suite 106
Milpitas, California 95035
408-232-9832
and
Petrie Dierman Kughn
1430 Springhill Road/Suite 520
McLean, Virginia 22102
703-749-4500

Architect

Wah Yee Associates
34405 West 12-Mile Road/Suite 225
Farmington Hills, Michigan 48331

Theme Design

Space Design International
311 Elm Street
Cincinnati, Ohio 45202

Notes
[1] Excluding outparcels.
[2] $8.5 million of total financed by city.

Grove City Factory Shops

Grove City, Pennsylvania

Manufacturers' outlet centers ranked in the 1990s as one of the fastest-growing segments of the shopping center industry: 294 outlet centers with a gross leasable area (GLA) of 57.2 million square feet were open as of May 1999.

An example of the current genre of outlet center is Grove City Factory Shops, 45 miles north of Pittsburgh. With 533,000 square feet of GLA and 139 shops, Grove City is one of the largest outlet centers in the country.

Grove City Factory Shops is a development of Prime Retail, L.P., of Baltimore, the largest developer of outlet centers in the United States. Prime Retail is a self-administered and self-managed real estate investment trust engaged in the ownership, development, acquisition, leasing, marketing, and management of outlet centers throughout the United States and Puerto Rico. Prime Retail's portfolio includes 28 centers in 20 states with approximately 7.5 million square feet of retail space. Grove City Factory Shops, which opened in August 1994, was the eighth outlet center developed by Prime Retail.

Site

The 70-acre, mostly rectangular site is located at the intersection of north/south I-79 and Pennsylvania Route 208, one exit south of east/west I-80. Youngstown, Ohio, is 30 miles west; Erie, Pennsylvania, is 70 miles north; and Cleveland, Ohio, is 90 miles northwest.

I-79 forms the project's eastern boundary, Pennsylvania Route 208 its northern boundary. To the west and south is farmland. Prime Retail owns approximately 40 acres adjacent to the southern boundary of the center, but it has no immediate plans for additions to the center.

Development

Prime Retail differentiates itself from its competitors in the outlet center industry by developing larger outlet centers in highly accessible locations, providing a larger and more diverse merchandising mix, extensive food vendors and recreational amenities, and high-quality architecture and landscaping designed to create an upscale environment in which to showcase merchandise. The company generally will not start construction of a new center unless at least 50 percent of the GLA is preleased. Typically, a center is 80 to 100 percent leased at the grand opening.

The average outlet center in the company's portfolio contains 270,500 square feet, 73 percent larger than the average outlet center (156,506 square feet) nationwide, according to *Value Retail News* (May 1997). Prime Retail

believes that the larger size of its centers and its established base of national and international manufacturers of designer and brand-name merchandise enhance its competitive position within the industry. Prime Retail has established the Manufacturers Forum, an organization of over 100 manufacturers that conducts four to six industry meetings per year to discuss ideas, trends, data, and other issues pertinent to the outlet center industry.

The company's outlet centers compete for customers primarily with traditional regional shopping centers, off-price retailers, and other outlet centers. To avoid direct competition with major retailers and their full-price stores, Prime Retail locates its outlet centers at least 20 miles from the nearest regional mall.

Grove City Factory Shops was built in four phases. A total of 235,000 square feet opened in August 1994, followed by 95,000 square feet in November 1994, 85,000 square feet in November 1995, and 118,000 square feet in November 1996, for a total GLA of 533,000 square feet. The developer's philosophy is to establish a center with a sustainable critical mass and add to it as the market matures. In this way, the developer can maximize returns from the outlet centers through higher effective net rents from the new merchants based on the proven success and drawing power of the previous phases.

The site was purchased and construction started in October 1993. Planning and leasing started in February and June 1992, respectively. The project officially opened in August 1994 with 45 shops.

Grove City Factory Shops was developed by Prime Retail and Fru-Con Development Corporation as joint partners. On November 1, 1996, Prime Retail purchased Fru-Con's 50 percent interest in the shopping center.

Planning and Design

Grove City Factory Shops is a one-story, open-air facility in a village-like setting. Its architecture exhibits regional architectural influences; several roof treatments, for example, were influenced by Amish buildings. The brickwork is reminiscent not only of the buildings on the nearby Grove City College campus but also of the Allegheny County Courthouse in Pittsburgh, designed by Henry Hobson Richardson in 1884. Dormer windows, old-fashioned lamps, wrought iron and wooden benches, and gardens of flowers and shrubs add to the ambience.

There are six sets of two buildings that face each other across pedestrian-oriented village streets. Parking is located on the east, west, and south sides of the site.

Grove City Factory Shops responded to pent-up retail demand in the Pittsburgh market with a more than 500,000-square-foot project that serves as both an outlet center and a regional shopping center.

A decorative gristmill mimics the mill in the town of Volant nearby.

Amenities include a food court, a children's playground, a post office, stroller rental, wheelchair loans, and an ATM. Because of the center's large size, the developer now provides free shuttle bus service that runs in a loop around the perimeter of the center.

The developer paid to have Grove City's sewer system extended to the site. The developer received a property tax abatement and is paying off the sewer debt in lieu of taxes. The Buhl Community Water Company underwent a $1.5 million expansion (with a state grant and two loans) to improve its service and run a water line to the shopping center. The shopping center uses 10 million gallons of water annually.

At peak times, shoppers have found it difficult to get to the center. The developer spent $900,000 to add turning lanes on Route 208 and has committed $3.3 million for highway improvements at the I-79 interchange.

Leasing and Merchandising

Grove City Factory Shops is 100 percent leased with a broad mix of nationally recognized manufacturers of designer and brand-name merchandise such as Ann Taylor, Brooks Brothers, Corning-Revere, Danskin, Eddie Bauer, Guess?, Donna Karan, Levi Strauss, Nautica, Nike, Off 5th, Reebok, Philips/Van Heusen, Polo/Ralph Lauren, Sara Lee, Tommy Hilfiger, and VF Corporation.

A total of 4.6 million shoppers visited the center in 1997—453,000 in the one month between November 28 and December 28. Three-fourths of the customers are repeat visitors, a high percentage that usually foretells sustained high performance. Thirty percent of all customers come from southwest Pennsylvania, 30 percent from northwest Pennsylvania, and 24 percent from Ohio. Visitors and tourists to the area account for the remaining 16 percent.

In 1996, more than 1,400 buses brought more than 40,000 people to the center. To bring more tour buses to the outlet center, Prime Retail actively pursues the companies that book the tours—a standard practice throughout the outlet center industry.

Prime Retail advertises its centers using a wide variety of media that can include television, radio, and print advertising; promotions; and special events. Advertising for the Grove City Factory Shops tends to be concentrated in the Youngstown, Erie, and Pittsburgh markets, as well as in the local market. The busiest times of the year for the Grove City center are during the summer and early fall (back to school) and late November and December (Christmas).

The average shopper at Grove City Factory Shops travels 68 minutes to reach the center and stays an average of three hours and 12 minutes.

Dormer windows, old-fashioned lamps, wrought iron and wood benches, and gardens of flowers and shrubs enhance the village-like setting.

Amenities at Grove City Factory Shops include a food court, a children's playground, a post office, stroller rental, wheelchair loans, and an ATM.

Experience Gained

- Part of the success of Grove City Factory Shops stems from the familiarity of shoppers in Pennsylvania with outlet shopping, having had long experience with established outlets in places like Reading. (Vanity Fair, now VF Corporation, opened the first multitenant manufacturers' outlet center in 1974, leading the way for other such projects.) As an additional bonus, Pennsylvania charges no sales tax on most shoe and apparel purchases.

- In retrospect, Prime Retail wishes it had purchased more land around the center to take advantage of the land values it now has created for others by developing the shopping center.

- The developer underestimated the success of the Grove City project. Consequently, the developer has been working with the community to correct an ingress/egress problem at the center during peak shopping days.

- Development of large regional shopping centers and big-box retailing did not occur in the greater Pittsburgh area in the 1980s. Consequently, pent-up demand for any type of retailing meant that Grove City was the right project at the right time for both the local and the regional markets. At more than 500,000 square feet, Grove City Factory Shops serves as both an outlet center and a regional shopping center.

Regional architecture was the influence for the red brick, cream-colored walls, and dark-green trim of the center's exterior.

The project creates the effect of six pedestrian-oriented village streets. Covered walkways line the storefronts along the streets.

Parking is located on three sides of the site.

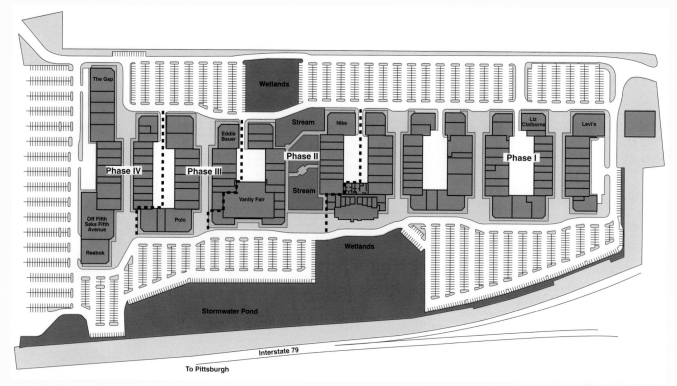

The Gap

Wetlands

Stream

Nike

Liz
Claiborne

Levi's

Eddie
Bauer

Phase II

Phase I

Phase IV

Phase III

Vanity Fair

Stream

Off Fifth
Saks Fifth
Avenue

Polo

Reebok

Wetlands

Stormwater Pond

Interstate 79

To Pittsburgh

Site plan.

Project Data: Grove City Factory Shops

Land Use and Building Information

Site area	70 acres
Gross building area	555,000 square feet
Gross leasable area (GLA)	533,000 square feet
Floor/area ratio	0.18
Levels	1
Buildings	12
Parking (surface spaces)	3,000
Parking Ratio	5.6 spaces per 1,000 square feet of GLA

Land Use Plan

	Acres	Percent of Site
Buildings	15	21.4
Paved area[1]	37	52.9
Landscaped areas/detention	18	25.7
Total	70	100.0

Development Cost Information

Site Acquisition Cost	$1,120,000
Site Improvement Cost	$9,450,000
Construction Cost	$37,010,000

Soft Costs

Architecture/engineering	$2,030,000
Project management	1,790,000
Marketing	570,000
Legal/accounting	270,000
Construction interest/fees	1,100,000
Other	6,690,000
Total	$12,450,000
Total Development Cost	$60,030,000
Total Development Cost per Gross Square Foot	$108.16

Retail Tenant Information

	Number of Stores	Percent of Total	Total GLA	Percent of GLA (suqare feet)
Food	2	1.4	3,997	0.7
Food service	9	6.5	5,951	1.1
Clothing and accessories	77	55.4	337,257	63.3
Shoes	13	9.4	61,808	11.6
Home furnishings	18	13.0	63,780	12.0
Home appliances/music	6	4.3	23,668	4.4
Jewelry	2	1.4	2,477	0.5
Other retail	12	8.6	34,062	6.4
Total	139	100.0	533,000	100.0

Annual Rents	$20–40 per square foot
Average Length of Lease	7 years

Sales

$325–350 per square foot

Major Tenants	Square Feet
Off 5th	20,188
Calvin Klein Outlet	6,200
Sony Electronics	6,026
Eddie Bauer Outlet	8,395
VF	26,842
Brooks Brothers	5,682
J. Crew	7,028
Gap Outlet	9,097

Annual Operating Expenses (1997)

Taxes	$1,221,085
Insurance	68,204
Services	154,320
Maintenance/janitorial	443,679
Utilities	285,030
Management	320,867
Miscellaneous (trash removal)	111,191
Total	$2,604,376

Development Schedule

2/1992	Planning started
6/1995	Leasing started
10/1993	Construction started
8/1994	Phase I opened
11/1994	Phase II opened
11/1995	Phase III opened
11/1996	Phase IV opened

Developer

Prime Retail, L.P.
100 East Pratt Street
Nineteenth Floor
Baltimore, MD 21202
410-234-0782

Architects

Design Collective, Inc.	KA Incorporated
100 East Pratt Street	1468 West Ninth Street
Baltimore, MD 21202	Cleveland, OH 44113
410-685-6655	216-781-9144

Civil Engineering

Civil and Environmental Consultants, Inc.
601 Holiday Drive
Foster Plaza 3
Pittsburgh, PA 15220
412-921-3402

Note

[1]Surface parking and roads.

Irvine Spectrum Center

Irvine, California

Irvine Spectrum Center (Phase I) is a $25 million, 260,000-square-foot, freestanding destination entertainment center approximately 40 miles south of Los Angeles. The project is one of the first freestanding entertainment-only centers in the nation. Instead of emphasizing shopping, the center has responded to increasing consumer demand for exciting experiences; it features a variety of high-tech entertainment tenants and signature restaurants where a high level of energy, good service, the menu, and the atmosphere are all of equal importance. It is designed to offer consumers a complete, synergistic experience involving entertainment, food, people watching, and shopping.

Irvine Spectrum Center is anchored by the world's largest theater complex, the 158,000-square-foot, 6,400-seat Edwards Theater (known as "the Big One"), which features 21 state-of-the art motion picture screens, including the West Coast's first 3-D IMAX theater. The festive outdoor center also features a variety of entertainment-oriented tenants, including four world-class restaurants, a food court, a virtual-reality center, book and music shops, a coffee shop, and colorful carts and kiosks; 4,100 surface parking spaces; and valet parking. Blending a Moroccan design theme with futuristic innovations such as computer-generated laser lighting, the center provides a memorable experience.

The project, which is 100 percent leased, averages sales of over $400 per square foot, excluding the theater. Moreover, restaurants' average gross revenues are 30 percent higher than their own projections, and 10,000 cars a day visit the center. The center's combination of location, demographics, tenant mix, and architectural theme has resulted in a project that is dramatically exceeding revenue projections.

Phase II, which broke ground in July 1997 and was completed in July 1998, doubles the size of the center and greatly expands the entertainment and retail offerings. Dave & Buster's (a thirty something–oriented place for dining, billiards, and a variety of games) anchors Phase II, along with restaurants that are more affordable than those in Phase I. Parking spaces were added in preparation for Phase II. Altogether, 3,350 spaces are available on site, with another 2,500 spaces in commercial areas next to the center; shuttles and valet service are available for customers' convenience.

A third phase of the center, currently in planning, will add another 450,000 square feet. This phase will be primarily retail and feature large national retailers and specialty shops. Construction of Phase III is scheduled to start in January 1999.

Site and Trade Area

The project serves as an urban center for Orange County, California, and for Irvine Spectrum, a 3,600-acre master-planned business community developed by the Irvine Company. Irvine Spectrum currently has more than 100 industrial and commercial buildings totaling 7 million square feet and is home to more than 2,200 firms and 36,000 employees. The site for Irvine Spectrum Center was zoned for a regional mall, with all entitlements in place for up to 1.75 million square feet of regional retail development.

The flat, 56-acre site is ideally located at the convergence of Orange County's two busiest freeways—I-5, the Santa Ana Freeway, and I-405, the San Diego Freeway. Known as the "El Toro Y," it is the world's largest interchange, with 26 lanes at its widest point. An estimated 500,000 vehicles drive by the center each day. Four exit ramps and 30 lanes of arterial roads feed directly into Irvine Spectrum.

In addition to outstanding visibility and accessibility, the center enjoys excellent demographics. Ninety percent of Orange County households (2.4 million people) are located within a 20-minute drive of the center. Residents of the center's trade area are affluent and well educated. Average annual household income in the primary trade area is $86,000, and 30 percent of the households have an annual income of more than $100,000. Further, 70 percent of all Orange County households with an income of more than $100,000 and 85 percent of households with an income of more than $150,000 reside in the primary trade area. The center draws not only from Orange County, with its population of more than 2.8 million, but also from as far north as Los Angeles County and as far south as San Diego County.

Project History

The project originated in response to the need for retail facilities (particularly places for people to meet and eat) to serve the 36,000 employees at Irvine Spectrum. Although the original plan was to locate several restaurants on the site, planners soon recognized that while the restaurants would have built-in lunchtime business, it would be difficult to attract business in the evening and therefore to attract signature restaurants. An anchor tenant was needed to draw people to the area after business hours and on weekends.

The Irvine Company decided to pursue a multiscreen cinema as the anchor tenant and approached Edwards Theaters to discuss the concept of developing a ten-screen

Nighttime at the Irvine Spectrum Center. As people wend their way through the center, the circulation network changes into a series of more intimate paseos.

The heart of the project, the central plaza, links restaurants, tented food courts, and entertainment-oriented stores with the Edwards Theater. The plaza features the center's open bazaar, an area of carts and kiosks.

The center is anchored by the 158,000-square-foot, 21-screen Edwards Theater, which has a 3-D IMAX theater. Grand public spaces near the cinema serve as a place for people to gather and orient themselves on arrival.

cinema adjacent to the proposed restaurants. Edwards Theaters had a record of great success in southern California (currently operating 470 screens at 86 locations) as well as a strong working relationship with the Irvine Company. After reviewing the project's demographics, Edwards decided that it wanted to do more than a ten-screen theater, and the original concept gradually evolved into a 21-screen complex with a 3-D IMAX theater. The cinema site was leased to Edwards; eventually the project concept was expanded to include an entertainment center requiring about 30 acres to provide for the buildings, public space, and parking. RTKL Associates was hired to prepare a master plan and to implement the design theme set by Irvine's chair, Donald Bren. Bren envisioned the center as an escape, "a destination resort for those in search of a smile—a place that demands that you leave your cares in the parking lot." Burton Associates of San Diego was retained as landscape architect for the project.

Phase I, which started as a place to meet the lunchtime needs of the rapidly growing number of employees in Irvine Spectrum, evolved into a successful entertainment destination for a much wider audience. The more than 5 million visitors per year from surrounding counties and around the world, coupled with their eagerness to spend, resulted in sales of $400 per square foot in the first year of operation. In response to the unmitigated success of Phase I, the Irvine Company broke ground for Phase II less than two years after the opening of Phase I.

Planning and Design
The primary planning and design objective for Phase I was to create an entertainment/retail destination with a distinct sense of place and a variety of vibrant, exciting spaces. It was achieved by using a Moroccan village theme featuring a distinctive blend of indoor and outdoor spaces and the bold forms and rich colors of Moroccan and other North African cities. The Moroccan design was selected for its compatibility with southern California's predominantly Spanish Mediterranean architecture as well as its ability to balance the more intimate, human-scale environment of the center's retail buildings with the massive cinema complex. The five one-story restaurant/retail buildings (containing 100,000 square feet) were designed to be one and one-half stories high to provide the proper balance. The buildings in the center are outlined by five miles of neon lighting, enhancing the project's visibility and visual excitement after dark.

The heart of the project is the central plaza—a major public space in front of the cinema complex for people to gather and orient themselves upon arrival. The plaza is paved with splashes of color—copper, turquoise, and purple—and links the Edwards cinema building with the restaurant buildings, the tented food court, and the entertainment-oriented stores. The plaza also features the center's open bazaar, an area of carts and 15 kiosks. Near the cinema, the public spaces are wide and open, but the circulation network gently changes into a series of more intimate paseos. Subdued patterns and clustered elements outline gathering areas and draw people into the heart of the project. The center was planned to be a series of spaces framed by buildings and landscape, and as much attention was given to designing spaces where people can interact as to designing the buildings.

The layering of Moroccan-inspired elements enhances the sense of adventure for customers as they stroll through the center. Recurring domes in reds, greens, and golds; neon lighting around the buildings; intricately patterned paving; landscaping; fountains; bright graphics (including 150 banners in a variety of shapes and colors); a variety of portable kiosks and carts; narrow canvas-shaded passageways; 150 palm and 100 olive trees; and a tented food court provide visual excitement and a fantasyland for visitors. Working closely with the city of Irvine, which has strict sign controls, the architects created an 80-foot-high Plexiglas pyramid to serve as the center's landmark. A computerized lighting system changes the colors of the pyramid by day and night. The pyramid is the only one of its type in the United States and provides a dynamic landmark for the center.

Overlooking the central plaza, the $27 million Edwards Theater building was envisioned as a Moroccan palace. Grand stairs connect the building to the central plaza and the rest of the center. The building's facade features twin 80-foot towers with vertical, cantilevered blade signs. A cornice frieze with decorative three-dimensional patterns wraps around the entire building. Inside, the 42-foot-tall, 15,000-square-foot lobby evokes images of the grand movie palaces of the 1920s and 1930s, with 40-foot-tall mosaics and murals, bright neon piping, seven concession stands, and brass and marble finishes. Each of the four giant-screen (40- by 80-foot) theaters in the complex features a design theme: Hollywood, ancient Egypt, imperial China, and 1920s movie palace. The theater complex also houses the 3-D IMAX theater (with a 90-foot-tall screen) and two large theaters with tiered stadium seating.

The design of Phase II was inspired by the Alhambra, a 13th-century castle in Granada, Spain, that features an exotic blend of classic architecture with the colorful overlay of Moorish detailing. The buildings of the Alhambra are connected by magnificent courtyards, including the Court of Lions and the Court of the Myrtles. Similar courtyards have become a main feature of Phase II of the center. Irvine Spectrum Center's Cuarto Dorado, for example, includes a 92-foot shadow-lit bell tower, the highest point of the center. The Court of Lions features a fountain inspired by the lion fountain at the Alhambra, along with colored arcades and giant palms. In the Court of the Myrtles, architectural elements include a reflecting pool with arching jets of water, arcades, and seating areas shaded by palms. The *souks*—or shopping streets between the courts—feature special overhead trellises and hanging awnings that cast decorative shadows on the pathways both day and night. The *souks* connect the three courts.

Tenant Mix

The developer pursued three general categories of tenants: high-tech, interactive multimedia tenants; trend-setting eateries; and specialty retail stores focused on entertainment and recreation. One key objective was to locate viable, high-quality merchants with extensive experience and the demonstrated ability to innovate and adapt to consumers' changing preferences. The developer also sought tenants that would do whatever they do in an entertaining way and offer a participatory experience to consumers of all ages. To minimize financial risk, 33 restaurants and stores were leased before construction started on Phase I. Five of the tenants have established their first California operations in the center. Phase II also was significantly preleased before ground was broken.

Major tenants in Phase I include four signature restaurants, each with a different theme, which were selected for their presentation, the quality of their food, and a one-of-a-kind dining experience: Bertolini's Authentic Trat-

A Moroccan village theme helps the center to achieve a distinct and vibrant sense of place.

toria, Champp's Americana, P.F. Chang's China Bistro, and the Wolfgang Puck Cafe. The 11 tenants in the upscale Oasis food court offer a variety of gourmet items. The center has 50,000 square feet of restaurant space with 1,700 seats, including outdoor seating for 400. Entertainment retail tenants include a 20,000-square-foot, two-story Barnes & Noble Superstore. Barnes & Noble is connected to Diedrich's, an upscale coffee shop, and features cozy couch settings and book and poetry readings. A Blockbuster Music store includes a state-of-the art CD listening bar. Other key tenants include Sega City (a 15,000-square-foot virtual-reality center) and California's first Sloppy Joe's Bar, a dance bar modeled on the bar frequented by Ernest Hemingway in Key West, Florida. The center also features 1,600 square feet of specialty retail space in carts, kiosks, and wall shops.

Similar tenants were sought for Phase II. Dave & Buster's, a 55,000-square-foot complex, anchors Phase II. The Dallas-based entertainment/restaurant chain markets itself as the ultimate place for "big kids" to play, combining upscale quality dining with classic and state-of-the-art amusements. Dave & Buster's includes two full-service bars, world-class pocket billiards, "Play-for-Fun Blackjack," full-swing golf simulators, table shuffleboard, and the Million Dollar Midway with more than 200 interactive amusements, including virtual-reality games, classic carnival games, and simulator rides.

Restaurants that are more affordable than those in Phase I were chosen to round out dining opportunities. Among the full-service restaurants are the Cheesecake Factory, Rock Bottom Brewery (a microbrewery), Speedway Cafe (which has an auto-racing theme), and Johnny Rockets (hamburgers). Other retailers include Coffee Bean & Tea Leaf, Wetzel's Pretzels, Jamba Juice, Skechers (family shoe store), Dapy (gift shop), Glow (gift shop), NASCAR Silicon Motor Speedway (ride simulator), Big Entertainment (entertainment memorabilia), Brookstone, Electronics Boutique, O'My Sole (casual footware), Limbo Lounge (apparel and accessories), and Quicksilver Boardrider (surfwear).

Experience Gained

- It was important to stay focused on an entertainment theme in creating the tenant mix. The customer is not confused about the center's purpose; it is clearly a place to dine and enjoy movies and other attractions. Opportunities to buy are all entertainment related.
- An entertainment center requires a trade area with a population that has the disposable income to spend on entertainment and that is large enough to supply good repeat business. A key factor in the success of the project was the critical mass of jobs and affluent households in Irvine Spectrum and Orange County.
- The center must feature only viable merchants with high-quality operations, preferably with national stature and experience at keeping up to date and staying ahead of trends.
- Safety and security and the perception of safety are important considerations in an entertainment center.

The design for Phase II was inspired by the Alhambra, a 13th-century castle in Granada, Spain, that features an exotic blend of classic architecture with a colorful overlay of Moorish detailing.

Including a police substation within the center and working with the local police department to provide uniformed officers at appropriate times ensures that customers feel comfortable returning to the center regularly.

- A strong anchor with the ability to draw from a large trade area was essential to the center's success. The Edwards Theater complex, the largest movie theater in the world and the most advanced 3-D IMAX theater in the country, fulfills this role.

- Conventional shopping center parking ratios are not adequate for an entertainment center that includes a megatheater. Counting the center's original 1,350 surface on-site parking spaces and the 2,000 spaces in adjacent shared lots, the center had more than three times the code-required parking (five spaces per 1,000 square feet). To meet demand, however, 1,000 new spaces were added on site three months after the center's opening. The project now has a parking ratio of 17 spaces per 1,000 square feet.

- An entertainment center draws people who want to be entertained, not conventional shoppers. Originally, some of the carts and kiosks in the plaza were stocked with too many conventional clothing items and accessories instead of merchandise that appeals to the customer's sense of fun and to the impulse to buy.

- Larger service areas and a larger on-site management office should have been provided. The higher-than-anticipated customer traffic has placed increased demands on center operations, specialty retailing (carts and kiosks), maintenance, and security. Allowing additional space for service areas would have allowed all deliveries and service to be confined to designated service areas.

- More and larger trash compactors should have been provided. High-volume stores and restaurants generate a lot of trash, leading to higher operating costs as a result of more frequent trash service.

- The frequent use of valet parking was not anticipated in planning the center. Many customers (more than 13,000 cars per month) take advantage of the convenience of valet parking, even in a center where surface parking is available within a reasonable walking distance.

- If the physical layout of the site and the surrounding road system permit, main vehicular entrances should be kept away from pedestrian areas, particularly in a project like the Irvine Spectrum Center, where the vehicular traffic volume is very high.

- Entertainment options must be well rounded. The center needed to offer enjoyment to consumers of all ages—from business people looking for relaxation on a lunch break, to the thirty-something professional stopping by after work, to the family on weekends, to the southern California tourist.

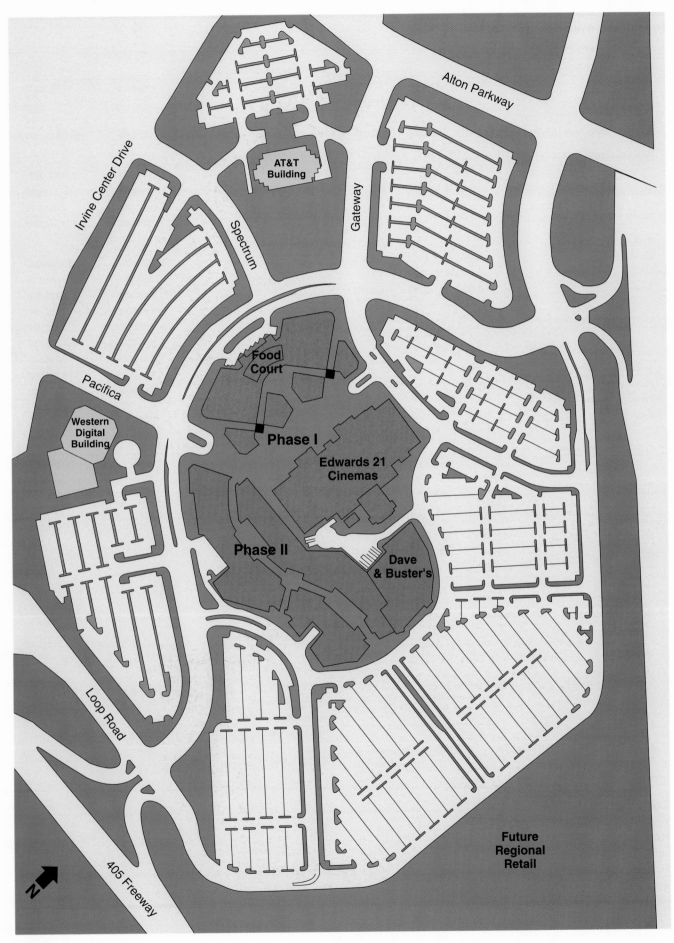

Alton Parkway

Irvine Center Drive

Spectrum

Gateway

AT&T Building

Pacifica

Western Digital Building

Food Court

Phase I

Edwards 21 Cinemas

Phase II

Dave & Buster's

Loop Road

405 Freeway

N

Future Regional Retail

Site plan.

Project Data: Irvine Spectrum Center

Land Use and Building Information

	Phase I	Phase II	Total
Site Area (acres)	29	27	56
Gross Building Area (square feet)	277,050	228,500	505,550
Gross Leasable Area (GLA) (square feet)	258,728	221,600	400,328
Floor/Area Ratio	0.205	0.205	0.205
Levels	1[1]	1	

Parking

	Phase I	Phase II	Total
On-site surface spaces	2,247	1,108	3,355
Off-site shared spaces	1,857	650	2,507
Total	4,104	1,758	5,862

Land Use Plan (Phases I and II)

	Acres	Percent of Site
Buildings	11.4	20.5
Service and amenity areas[2]	8.6	15.5
Paved areas[3]	29.4	53.0
Landscaped areas	6.1	11.0
Total	55.5	100.0

Retail Tenant Information

	Phase I Total GLA (square feet)	Phase II Total GLA (square feet)	Total GLA (square feet)
Cineplex	158,000	55,000	213,000
Entertainment/retail	48,228	129,100	177,328
Restaurants	40,900	35,000	75,900
Food court	10,000	0	10,000
Specialty retail (carts, kiosks, wall shops)	1,600	2,500	4,100
Total	258,728	221,600	480,328

Lease Terms

Length of lease	5–10 years
Typical lease provisions	Minimum rent plus percentage of sales, common area expenses, real estate taxes, and promotional fund
Annual rents	$28–60 per square foot
Average Annual Sales	Over $400 per square foot (excluding theater)

Development Cost Information

	Phase I	Phase II
Site Acquisition Cost	–	–
Site Improvement Costs	$6,132,000	$10,648,000
Construction Costs		
Building costs	$8,681,000	$18,936,000
Graphics/specialties	890,000	710,000
Tenant improvements	3,487,000	9,018,000
Total	$13,058,000	$28,664,000
Soft Costs		
Architecture/engineering	$2,042,000	$3,806,000
Project management	667,000	301,000
Marketing	150,000	400,000
Legal/accounting	75,000	160,000
Taxes/insurance	100,000	342,000
Fees/permits	709,000	1,675,000
Construction interest and fees	1,045,000	1,828,000
Leasing	954,000	1,714,000
Total	$5,742,000	$10,226,000
Total Development Cost	$24,932,000[4]	$49,538,000

Annual Operating Expense (Phases I and II)

Taxes	$884,000
Insurance	82,000
Services	720,000
Maintenance	488,000
Janitorial	619,000
Utilities	159,000
Legal	50,000
Management	1,036,000
Miscellaneous	117,000
Total	$4,155,000

Development Schedule

	Phase I	Phase II
Planning started	12/1993	4/1996
Leasing started	2/1994	9/1996
Approvals obtained	7/1994	2/1997
Construction started	1/1995	7/1997
Project opened	11/1995	7/1998

Notes

[1]With some mezzanine space.

[2]Plazas, paseos.

[3]Surface parking and roads.

[4]Excludes theater development costs of approximately $25 million. Theater transaction is a ground lease, and all theater development costs were paid by the lessee.

Developer

The Irvine Company
550 Newport Center Drive
Newport Beach, California 92660
714-720-2000

Architect

RTKL Associates
333 South Hope Street
Los Angeles, California 90071
213-627-7373

Landscape Architect

Burton Associates
12760 High Bluff Drive #120
San Diego, California 92130
619-794-7204

General Contractor

Snyder Langston
17962 Cowan
Irvine, California 92614
949-863-9200

The Marketplace at Cascades Town Center

Loudoun County, Virginia

The Marketplace at Cascades Town Center is an unusual marriage of a regional open-air shopping center with a neotraditional grid design. The 419,000-square-foot shopping district is the central focus of the 105-acre town center of Cascades, a new, 3,000-acre planned unit development in exurban Loudoun County, an outer suburb of Washington, D.C. The center embodies the feel of both an urban shopping district and a small-town main street, while serving as a neighborhood, community, and regional shopping district.

The Marketplace represents an evolution of new urbanism, designed in neotraditional style but incorporating the pragmatic adjustments necessary to keep from compromising retail viability. The retail complex is user driven, blending a pedestrian character with the access and parking required for big-box retailing.

Planning and Design

In the late 1980s, the original land developer planned a neotraditional town center combining residential, business, and retail uses in multistory structures for Cascades. This mixed-use center formed a key component of the 6,500-unit Cascades community, the largest new community to be approved in the county.

Like many other new large-scale residential communities, the development found itself unable to sustain the tremendous initial investment in infrastructure required in the face of a major slump in homebuying during the recession of the early 1990s. After obtaining ownership, the lender began seeking buyers for the town center, including its retail component. The lender approached GFS Realty, Inc., which after much deliberation purchased the retail portion of the town center site at the end of 1992.

The town center was laid out on a neotraditional street grid with the infrastructure already in place; the approved master plan provided for multi- and single-story buildings opening on sidewalks to promote pedestrian access. GFS needed to determine whether the changes to the original plan that they felt were required for successful retailing would be politically acceptable. Moreover, GFS had no open-air shopping centers of recent vintage built on a grid pattern it could point to as proof that the concept would work.

GFS and its design team, Development Design Group, Inc., of Baltimore, began developing design criteria based on their understanding of the users of the shopping center —first the tenants and then the customers. If retailers could not be persuaded to lease the stores, the approved concept would not get off the ground.

Design criteria were based on both the approved planning goals for the project and the retail objectives of potential anchor tenants. A key criterion was that regional tenants, whose customers were destination shoppers, could not interfere with community and neighborhood tenants, whose customers were convenience shoppers. The first piece of the design puzzle fell into place during early negotiations with Home Depot, a regional tenant that purchased and developed its site outright. To be successful, Home Depot required a traditional big-box location and parking lot so that its customers could drive in and park conveniently, and its site, at Route 7 and Cascades Parkway, easily met that requirement.

The second major design criterion was that multiple grids had to be accommodated within the overall grid pattern, and a subsequent decision had to be made as to whether the grids should be independent of each other. Ultimately, independent grids were created to meet the needs of regional, community, and neighborhood retailers and shoppers. The needs of each retailer and how it could best serve its trade area were of paramount importance; they determined the character of each grid. The 105,000-square-foot Home Depot took one grid, oriented toward the major highways and the Cascades planned unit development. The 77,000-square-foot Village Shops, anchored by a Giant supermarket and pharmacy, created a neighborhood shopping grid with a more interior location oriented toward the immediate Cascades residential neighborhood.

The 87,000-square-foot 7th Avenue Shops, anchored by Marshall's, Linens'N Things, Cosmetic Center, and Zany Brainy, a children's educational toy store, created a community/regional shopping grid. The 7th Avenue Shops, like Home Depot, is oriented toward the cloverleaf interchange of Route 7 and Cascades Parkway, the entry to the new Cascades community. A major street passes by the rear of these stores, allowing additional easy access.

Southbank Commons, a fourth grid anchored by an Old Navy clothing store, was created as an intimate shopping block to provide the critical connection among the grids. The merchandising plan for the town center provided for destination tenants for this interior, shop-lined street. Southbank Commons, lined with restaurants and sidewalk cafés, contains a highly visible and distinctive clock tower that provides visual identity for the center. It forms the link between the Village Shops and the 7th Avenue Shops; each maintains a distinct retail identity. The design adheres to the original require-

Featuring neighborhood, community, and regional retail tenants, the Marketplace at Cascades Town Center offers the feel of an urban shopping district while accommodating the realities of modern retailing.

ment that convenience and destination retailing not interfere with each other.

A future phase of the center was designed as a regional grid oriented toward the Home Depot grid and the others. The ability to expand the Marketplace as the project progressed, depending on the initial absorption of retail space, was critical to the developer. The town center plan therefore was amended to incorporate a retail site of up to 125,000 square feet, which required moving a residential area included in the original town center plan to another location. The 100,000-square-foot Shops at Park Place was completed in 1998; it is anchored by Sports Authority, Pier 1 Imports, and Staples, and includes a dental practice and a brew pub.

A city park was completed at the juncture of the Shops at Park Place, Southbank Commons, and the Village Shops, further connecting the grids and reinforcing the center's identity. The park contains a fountain reminiscent of those found in Italian towns and a wall mural of a city park scene in which children are playing basketball.

In choosing designs, the developer turned to psychological marketing and merchandising techniques that have been successfully applied in interior retail design in many regional malls—music, product choice, and color, lighting, and variety in visual displays—to create a sense of fun and excitement that engages the senses and moves customers through the stores without their being conscious of the distance they walk. The same techniques

were applied to draw customers through the streets and parking lots of the center. The park and the sidewalk cafés at Southbank Commons create a sense of intimacy. The streets, while narrow, still allow for parallel parking, and they slow traffic and heighten the connection between the retail shops on opposite sides of the street. Although most buildings contain only ground-floor retail space, a variety of small windows below the rooflines make them look like two-story buildings, enhancing the small-town feel.

Southbank Commons creates an image that is maintained throughout the Marketplace by facades of varying materials, colors, elevations, and roof pitches, reminiscent of European villages; old-fashioned gas lights and signage; colorful canopies and identifying banners; wrought iron fencing and pedestrian furniture; and tree-lined sidewalks. Cars may park along the street, and they are forced to proceed at a measured pace past strolling pedestrians. The interior parking lots are enclosed by the retail anchors on one side and small retail buildings, some with a back entrance to the parking lots.

Approvals

The site's original street grid and the boundaries of the land parcels were included in approvals for the Cascades planned unit development. The developer thus was faced with a potentially lengthy effort to obtain approvals for any changes in planning and design. Fortunately, Loudoun County, the local jurisdiction, concerned about commercial development at the site, the success of the Cascades community, and the resulting improvement to its tax base, was cooperative.

While strict neotraditional planning calls for small town centers with multistory streetfront retail stores and a mix of residential and commercial uses in each building, the developer felt that large retailers and parking lots were essential for a financially viable retail center. The developer's first step in negotiating with the county was to establish that large retail anchor stores with large parking

Southbank Commons, based on a traditional shopping street, features broad sidewalks, street trees and flowers, and colorful canopies and banners to create a sense of intimacy. The design of Southbank Commons separates the regional tenants from the community and neighborhood tenants.

areas would have to be accommodated before negotiations could proceed.

Negotiations with the county began while GFS determined whether the project's retail goals could be met within the framework of the platted parcels. During preleasing negotiations, the developer obtained sufficient information from critical anchor tenants to determine what design parameters the project would need to meet and what tradeoffs might be made to satisfy the county. The anchor tenants would not commit to the site until they were assured that the county would approve the necessary design changes.

GFS approached the county with the retailers' perspective. Subsequent discussions were based on the understanding that maintaining the major goals of the approved plan—the street grid, the concept of shopping streets, ease of pedestrian access, and the small-town feeling—would be paramount. Tenants, however, would have to agree to any proposed changes to their requirements or the developer could not agree to them.

Because so many individual tradeoffs had to be made with each major tenant, the county was willing to negotiate and provide more than one solution in certain situations. This approach assured the county that neither solution would compromise the major goals of the plan and gave the developer the room needed to negotiate agreements with tenants.

Negotiations with McDonald's, for example, show the kinds of compromises that were necessary to work within the approved grid. McDonald's felt that it required the typical two-sided drive-through and did not believe that a sidewalk orientation would increase sales. The company finally agreed, however, to a one-sided drive-through and a building that backed up to the sidewalk. McDonald's was uncertain how the layout would affect sales and put in a smaller unit than it would have otherwise. Now, after a few years of proven sales, the company has enlarged the unit.

Development of the project also was expedited by the county's agreement to the use of private roads within the parcel. The codes for public streets do not allow for aesthetic liberties such as narrow roads, which slow drivers and make it easy for pedestrians to cross the street to explore shopping opportunities on the other side.

The county also was willing to make some concessions in the materials called for in the approved plan. Most rear facades had to be treated aesthetically because many buildings backed up to the front facades of other stores, but the project could not afford all-brick facades or all-brick pavers throughout. Sidewalks are cement, and more affordable colored concrete panels are used in the rear of some buildings for an aesthetic treatment.

Loudoun County's flexibility was essential to the success of the venture. Without compromising key goals, the county allowed the developer some latitude in designing the shopping center without having to obtain separate approvals for amendments during each lease negotiation. The county accepted the difficulty of convincing retailers to adopt a new design and trusted the

The complex features a neotraditional grid street layout. Grids were designed independently to ensure that regional destination shoppers did not interfere with community and neighborhood retail users.

developer to adhere to the broad design goals of the original plan.

Since the start of construction of the shopping district, a mixture of uses built on adjacent properties has begun to enhance the "Our Town" feeling of the town center. These facilities include a Marriott hotel, a senior citizens center, a farmers' market, a regional library, and in-town townhouses. Future plans include a nearby office complex, additional restaurants, a post office, and possibly a second hotel. The town center is expected to be built out in three or four years.

Experience Gained

- A patient and understanding lender willing to accept the risk of financing a development with an unproven retail layout is critical. The additional time required to negotiate solutions with tenants and the county increases carrying costs. An unproven layout that emphasizes pedestrian access and requires compromises in design on the part of the tenants will not command high initial rents.
- Buildings built on a grid pattern have to be built in squares surrounding parking lots. They cannot be built in phases as they are leased, as often can be done in a linear format. GFS, as a major corporation, was fortunate in having sufficient equity capital to sustain the inherent risks and carrying costs.
- Local officials' cooperation was crucial to the project's success. Had the county not been willing to compromise, the cost of the design elements initially required would have escalated project costs to the point that the pro forma would have been unworkable.
- Loudoun County allowed GFS some flexibility and preapproved more than one solution to several design issues that could be deal breakers for major tenants. Unlike in jurisdictions where developers have to return for repeated approvals of plan details, elevations, or other matters, the county approved concepts and ma-

Old-fashioned gas lights and signage and wrought iron fencing help to define the image of Southbank Commons.

terials and trusted GFS to remain true to the approved goals of the master plan.

- A regional draw was necessary to lease the small shops built to complete the grid design and to promote the intimate shopping experience desired. The destination tenants in Southbank Commons, which contains only street retail shops oriented toward the sidewalks, would not have leased space without the regional draw.

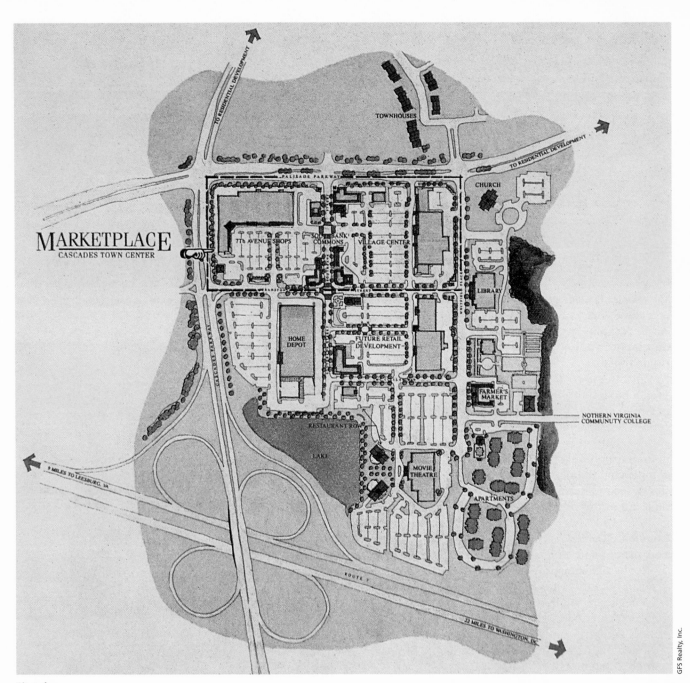

Site plan.

Project Data: The Marketplace at Cascades Town Center

Land Use and Building Information

Site Area
21.6 acres

Gross Leasable Area (GLA)
Phase I	215,000 square feet
Phase II	99,000 square feet
Home Depot[1]	105,000 square feet
Total GLA	419,000 square feet

Floor/Area Ratio
0.45

Parking Spaces
989

Development Cost Information

	Phase I	Phase II
Site Acquisition Cost	$7,980,000[2]	$3,220,000[2]
Construction Costs	11,500,000+	5,508,000
Soft Costs	2,000,000+	972,000
Total	$21,500,000+	$9,700,000+[3]

Total Development Cost
$31,200,000+

Retail Tenant Information

	Number of Stores
Food	1
Food service	7
Clothing and accessories	4
Shoes	1
Home furnishings	1
Home appliances/music	2
Hobby/special interest	1
Gifts/specialty	2
Drugs	1
Other retail	1
Financial offices	1
Offices (other than financial)	2
Vacant (new construction)	5
Total	29

Major Tenants

	Square Feet
Home Depot[4]	105,000
Giant Food	60,811
Old Navy	12,665
Marshalls	30,000
Linens'N Things	30,000
Zany Brainy	12,421
Pier 1 Imports[5]	8,000
Staples	24,000
Sports Authority	40,000

Average Length of Lease
10–15 years

Average Annual Sales
$300 per square foot

Development Schedule

10/1992	Site purchased
10/1992	Planning started
4/1993	Approvals obtained
5/1993	Construction started
12/1992	Leasing started
8/1994	Phase I opened
1997/1998	Phase II opened

Developer

GFS Realty, Inc.
P.O. Box 1804
Washington, D.C. 20013
301-341-8440

Architect/Planner

DDGI Development Design Group, Inc.
7 St. Paul Street
Baltimore, Maryland 21202
410-962-0505

Notes

[1] Separate ownership.

[2] Includes site improvement costs. Off-site costs, such as those for road improvements, including a share of the Route 7/Cascades Parkway interchange, infrastructure, and utilities, are included in the acquisition price.

[3] To date.

[4] Freestanding.

[5] Possible expansion being studied.

New Community Neighborhood Shopping Center

Newark, New Jersey

Like the phoenix rising from the ashes, the New Community Neighborhood Shopping Center has risen out of the devastation that resulted from civil disturbances in Newark, New Jersey's central ward in the summer of 1967. The 47,000-square-foot Pathmark supermarket that anchors the shopping center is the first major supermarket in the central ward in more than 20 years—nothing short of a miracle in the inner city. For residents of the predominantly low-income, African-American central ward, the miracle occurred on July 26, 1990, at the grand opening of the supermarket. Jack Kemp, then Secretary of Housing and Urban Development, was one of many politicians on hand for the ribbon-cutting ceremony.

Other mainstream businesses found in abundance in suburban America occupy the remaining 8,000 square feet in the center. Dunkin' Donuts, strategically located on the southeast corner of the shopping center, is open 24 hours a day. Mail Boxes Etc. provides postal, business, and communications services to customers and small businesses, with 24-hour key access to mailboxes. With its state-of-the-art equipment, NC Print & Copy Shop helps individuals and small business owners produce stationery, invitations, flyers, brochures, booklets, and business cards. The need for transportation in a neighborhood where only one in three residents owns a car is filled by Grocery Delivery, a van service that transports customers, their packages, and often their children. The World of Foods has fostered New Community Corporation businesses with its Southern Kitchen and New Community Neighborhood Bakery. In 1996, Pizza Hut, Taco Bell, Magic Fountain, and Nathan's were added to the World of Foods court. Despite the growing list of national franchises, the crown jewel of the center is undeniably the Pathmark supermarket.

New Community Corporation

The civil unrest of July 1967 strengthened the resolve of a handful of residents who already had begun meeting in Queen of Angels Catholic Church to discuss methods of breaking the cycle of abandonment and decay plaguing their neighborhood. In January 1968, the residents, led by Father William J. Linder, a priest at the church, officially incorporated as New Community Corporation (NCC), a nonprofit community development corporation. Today, NCC is the largest community development organization in the nation, with programs and services touching the lives of 35,000 people daily. NCC has assets in excess of $300 million, with a 1997 cash flow of $200 million. Since its inception, NCC has formed many public/private part-

nerships, with partners such as Hartz Mountain Industries, Bellemead Development Corporation, Pathmark Stores, Inc., Colgate-Palmolive Company, Ford Motor Company, Bloomfield College, Essex County College, Seton Hall University, Fairleigh Dickinson University, Rutgers University, and all levels of government. These partnerships, together with the tenacity of NCC's grass-roots board of directors, have made many of the accomplishments possible.

Improving the neighborhood's quality of life has been the driving force behind all the projects undertaken by NCC. Responding to the desperate need for good-quality, affordable housing that broke the typical public housing mold, NCC developed its first housing units in October 1975. Against all odds, NCC convinced local politicians and influential business and community leaders that families should not be housed in towering high rises, which can become breeding grounds for crime. Consequently, the 120 units were contained in five-story buildings. Each unit has an entrance fronting on an elevated walkway. Since 1975, NCC has built or managed over 3,000 units housing more than 7,000 residents in 18 developments in Newark, Englewood, Eatontown, and Jersey City.

Jobs also were desperately needed. In 1968, NCC's goal was to create 1,100 jobs in 20 years, based on the number of households in the central ward on welfare. NCC has far surpassed that goal in creating permanent jobs for former welfare recipients of the central ward and other areas. Currently, the NCC network employs over 1,500 people. In 1997, it provided job training for 500, placed another 1,000 clients in jobs through its employment services, and counseled 3,000. NCC has increased its job training and placement activity as a result of welfare-to-work activities in 1998 and will double its current capacity for training and placement with the opening of its new Workforce Development Center in late 1998. In addition, NCC manages its own properties, employing many more individuals. NCC is now one of Newark's largest employers, one of only ten organizations and companies in the city that employ more than 1,500 people. NCC also has its own security force, which grew out of the need to provide security for its many housing complexes; the security force now provides protection for the patrons of New Community Neighborhood Shopping Center and other NCC facilities.

The creation of jobs and training for central ward residents reinforced the need for daycare for children of the large number of single mothers who now looked

The Pathmark supermarket is the first to come into the central ward since the 1967 civil disturbances, which sent major chains packing. Although smaller because of its site limitations, the store follows the prototype used in Pathmark's suburban stores.

(photo credit: Laura Comppen)

to jobs, not welfare, for their future. Today, Babyland Family Services, Inc., provides daycare to some 800 infants and toddlers at affordable rates. Its full range of programs serves 1,500 families. The aging of central ward residents gave rise to the need for geriatric care and assisted living services. The New Community Extended-Care Facility provides first-rate care for elderly residents who might otherwise be forced to live in nursing homes far from their friends and neighborhood, as well as adult medical daycare at four sites. NCC also offers in-home health services and short-term transitional housing for the county's homeless population. Its credit union has over 2,400 members and assets of $3 million. St. Rose of Lima School, another NCC network partner, offers an alternative to the troubled public school system for educating children in kindergarten through the eighth grade.

It was the desperate need for high-quality, affordable food that gave rise to the New Community Neighborhood Shopping Center. The Pathmark supermarket has meant

not only affordable food, but also jobs with a career path for nearly 300 employees, most of them Newark residents. Another 100 are employed in the satellite businesses.

Land Assembly and Acquisition

Land assembly is a difficult process in the inner city, where ownership of land typically is fragmented and absentee landlords are common. Assembling the parcels for the New Community Neighborhood Shopping Center was no exception. Between 1980 and 1984, NCC assembled land for the shopping center. The site comprised 62 parcels, 15 of which were owned by the city; 25 others had buildings on the property. Relocating owners who were willing to move required extensive research and negotiation.

Land acquisition was another hurdle. In 1985, NCC began to buy individual lots for the site, acquiring 56 lots without resorting to condemnation. Condemnation of the remaining six parcels was sought because their nonresident owners were asking extremely high prices. In May 1985, the board of the New Jersey Housing Mortgage Finance Agency authorized the New Jersey Attorney General and Department of Transportation to proceed with condemnation of the lots, but the New Jersey Superior Court issued a decision favorable to the six property owners and several months later dismissed the agency's complaint that it needed the property for a public purpose. That decision was overturned by the appellate division of the superior court, which determined that the condemnation powers of the agency are valid when public benefit prevails, as it did in the case of the shopping center. In March 1987, the property owners filed notice of appeal to the Supreme Court of New Jersey to stay the condemnation process, but in a final ruling in May 1987, the supreme court denied the property owners' request that the court review the case further.

The zoning also had to be changed before breaking ground for the new shopping center. In October 1987, the board of adjustment voted unanimously for NCC's right to build the supermarket. One final holdout of the original six property owners filed a complaint against the board of adjustment and NCC to have approval of the variance and site plan overturned; the court quickly dismissed the challenge.

The site is located at the intersection of South Orange Avenue, a main east/west artery, and Bergen Street, a main north/south artery, with the shopping center facing South Orange Avenue. Across Bergen Street to the east

of the shopping center is the University of Medicine and Dentistry of New Jersey and University Hospital. Small-scale commercial development largely characterizes land uses to the east and south of the site. To the north and west, use is primarily residential.

Ownership, Leasing, and Financing

Finding a supermarket anchor proved less problematic than land assembly and acquisition. In the early 1980s, Father Linder approached Supermarkets General, Pathmark's parent company, about the possibility of locating a store in the central ward. Pathmark, which remained a strong partner throughout the ten-year development campaign, agreed; it looked like a good business proposition, given the population density and lack of competition in the area. A 1980 study commissioned by NCC showed that, with 93,000 residents within a one-half mile radius, the site was a virtual magnet for shoppers, given appropriate commercial development. At the time, more than 90 percent of these residents shopped at lower-priced supermarkets outside Newark.

Pathmark also benefited from the site's location in an urban enterprise zone, which allows Pathmark to charge half the state sales tax and eliminates the sales tax on the store's equipment purchases. The company was also entitled to a $1,500 tax credit for each hiree from Newark who had been unemployed for three months. Pathmark's commitment to revitalizing the central ward was sustained during its leveraged buyout by Equitable Life, Inc., and

Shoppers can grab a bite to eat at one of several fast-food establishments—including Taco Bell, Pizza Hut, the Magic Fountain, and Nathan's—at the World of Foods, which also includes a bakery owned by the New Community Corporation. Employees of the establishments are primarily graduates of a comprehensive job training program offered by NCC.

The Pathmark supermarket looks like its suburban counterparts. It is renowned for its fresh produce and fish, which were unavailable in the few convenience stores that characterized the central ward.

Laura Comppen

Merrill Lynch. In fact, one term of the transaction was that Supermarkets General would continue to work with NCC to bring affordable food to the residents of the central ward.

In August 1987, NCC and Supermarkets General ironed out the ownership and lease arrangements. Under the terms of the agreement, NCC owns two-thirds of the joint venture market, which is managed by Pathmark, ensuring that it will be run like any other store in the chain. Supermarkets General owns one-third of the market. Community Supermarkets Corporation was formed to be the decision-making entity. It meets monthly to discuss issues affecting the community and to decide how to respond to the community's changing needs. The corporation consists of four NCC members and three Pathmark members. NCC is the sole developer and full owner of the shopping center. The satellite stores are mostly national chain franchises that are owned and operated by NCC.

The search for financing began in earnest in 1983. The first financial boost came as a seed loan for $275,000 from the New Jersey Department of Community Affairs. In May 1984, the New Jersey Housing Mortgage Finance Agency approved the withdrawal of $130,000 from a community development escrow account to partially fund development costs, land acquisition, and technical fees. In January 1989, NCC began intensive negotiations with lending institutions. Nearly 10 percent of the total development cost of $12.9 million was funded by NCC itself, 56 percent was funded by a loan from the Prudential Insurance Company, 14 percent was funded by the federal government through the urban development action grant and community development block grant programs, and nearly 20 percent was funded by the state of New Jersey through various programs.

Design

The focal point of the New Community Neighborhood Shopping Center is the Pathmark supermarket, which accounts for 47,000 of the center's 55,000 square feet.

NCC did not design the store but had it built to Pathmark's specifications. The prototype is Pathmark 2000, the model for all Pathmark stores; the design had to be adapted slightly because the New Community store is somewhat smaller than Pathmark's suburban stores. Pathmark originally thought it could perhaps do without the fresh seafood and deli departments, but community surveys indicated that they were precisely the departments the residents were most interested in. Today, the fresh seafood department is thriving, just as surveys predicted. Unlike its suburban counterparts, Pathmark does not have an on-site bakery, but pastries, cakes, and the like can be purchased at the center's New Community Neighborhood Bakery, which is owned and operated by NCC. Pathmark constantly evaluates product sales and adjusts its stock accordingly. For example, the fresh flower and plant department was eliminated after several months of lackluster sales.

The design of the remainder of the shopping center was dictated largely by the design requirements of the Dunkin' Donuts and Mail Boxes Etc. franchises, but the natural limitations of the site also played a role. At only 3.3 acres, the site is smaller than the five to eight acres typical of many such centers in a suburban setting. Because the site slopes, a retaining wall was necessary on the west side, also limiting the design of the center. The southwest corner of the site reflects the final holdout in land sales. Because the owner wanted more than $1 million for the small parcel, NCC determined that it was not essential and decided to build around it. The only impact on design was a reduction of about ten parking spaces and a rather oddly shaped site.

Security is an important issue for shopping centers, in the inner city or the suburbs. At the Pathmark store, security costs constituted about 1.4 percent of operating expenses in 1996. A sophisticated in-store surveillance system ensures customers' safety, and the entire center is protected around the clock by at least three NCC security guards, one of whom is stationed in a security booth

New Community Corporation runs a delivery service to transport senior citizens and other central ward residents to and from the shopping center for a nominal fee. This service is critical in the central ward, where many residents do not own an automobile.

at the east entrance of the parking lot. In addition, at least one Newark city policeman is always on duty. The parking lot is illuminated by extra outdoor lighting and is completely fenced, making for very limited access to the center. Access is further limited by geography and traffic patterns. But the most important feature of the shopping center's security system is the watchful eyes of its patrons. It had taken nearly a decade to make the shopping center a reality, and patrons are determined to protect their Pathmark from petty theft.

Experience Gained
- Federal, state, and local governments' agreement with NCC that high-quality, affordable food was desperately needed in the central ward led NCC to believe fewer obstacles would be encountered to the shopping center's development than for commercial development projects in general. This wide-eyed optimism led to disappointment as NCC encountered one obstacle after another. Land assembly, plagued by multiple absentee landowners, took from 1980 through 1984. Once that hurdle was cleared, the protracted condemnation process lasted another two years.
- Commitment and the ability to roll with the punches are key to realizing commercial development in inner-city neighborhoods. Construction on the New Community Neighborhood Shopping Center was expected to begin in fall 1984. In fact, ground was not broken until May 1, 1989—nearly five years later.
- The joint venture with Pathmark was a critical element in the center's success. In addition to contributing one-third of the working capital, Pathmark brought expertise in management, which provided a well-merchandised, customer-driven store, and expertise in store design and layout. It also brought previous experience in a successful joint venture with a nonprofit community organization, the Bedford Stuyvesant Restoration Corporation in New York City. That experience taught Pathmark about retailing in the inner city.

For example, sales skyrocket twice a month, coinciding with the receipt of welfare and social security checks. By recognizing the different sales patterns and buying habits of inner-city residents, Pathmark could plan for the increase.
- A project's economics must be favorable for a retailer to come to the inner city, no matter how strong the retailer's commitment. This joint venture has been an unmitigated success for Pathmark. Its initial sales projections have been far surpassed, and sales per square foot have catapulted the store to the ranks of the top 10 percent of supermarkets in neighborhood shopping centers throughout the United States. For the past several years, its sales per selling square foot have been twice the supermarket industry average.
- The success of the shopping center and the Pathmark supermarket has come from listening and responding to the community's needs. Pathmark undertook several surveys of central ward residents to determine what products they wanted. The ethnicity of the neighborhood is reflected in many products that are not sold at suburban locations. Moreover, even before the electronic benefit transfer system was put in the store so that welfare transactions could be handled discreetly, Pathmark accepted food stamps and cashed customers' welfare checks at no charge.

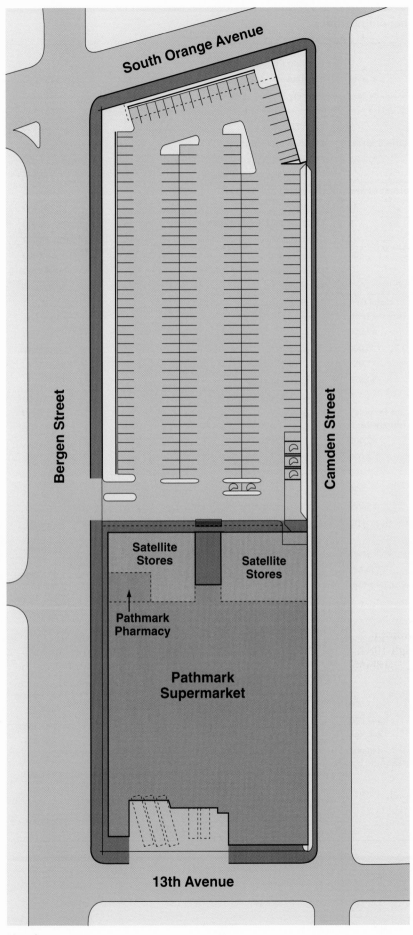

South Orange Avenue

Bergen Street

Camden Street

Satellite Stores

Satellite Stores

Pathmark Pharmacy

Pathmark Supermarket

13th Avenue

Site plan.

Project Data: New Community Neighborhood Shopping Center

Land Use Information

Site area	3.3 acres
Gross building area	55,000 square feet
Gross leasable area (GLA)	55,000 square feet
Levels	1
Parking	227 surface spaces

Land Use Plan

	Acres	Percent of Site
Buildings	1.5	45
Parking structures	0.0	0
Paved areas	1.8	55
Total	3.3	100

Retail Tenant Information

	Number of Stores	Total GLA (square feet)
Food	1	47,000
Food service	2	6,000
Personal services	2	1,950
Total	5	54,950

Major Tenants

	Space Occupied (square feet)
Pathmark	47,000
Dunkin' Donuts	2,000
Mail Boxes Etc.	1,400
NC Print & Copy	550
World of Foods	4,000

Lease Terms

Length of lease	1–20 years
Typical lease provisions	Triple net
Annual rents	$18 per square foot

Development Cost Information

Land Acquisition	$1,574,780
Demolition	$672,462

Site Improvement Costs

General conditions	$433,500
Earthwork	342,000
Site utilities	496,595
Site improvements	440,000
Total	$1,712,095

Building Construction Costs

Concrete	$757,000
Masonry	440,221
Structural steel and miscellaneous iron	461,100
Carpentry	61,500
Moisture protection	20,000
Roofing and skylights	293,850
Doors, frames, and hardware	162,600
Drywall	235,500
Finishes	154,330
Metal ceilings, loading dock	7,000
Canopy	47,000
Metal screens	28,800
Miscellaneous specialties	47,700
Plumbing	204,000
Sprinkler	99,000
HVAC	203,000
Electrical	476,000
Total	$3,698,601

Professional Fees

Architectural/engineering	$350,000
Surveying	12,500
Legal	125,000
Accounting	20,000
Other professional fees	30,000
Planning and development	110,000
Total	$647,500

Financing Costs	$199,600
Construction Interest	$600,000
Real Estate Taxes	$12,000
Contingencies	$642,962
Equipment	$1,900,000
Working Capital	$1,200,000
Total Project Cost	$12,860,000

Annual Operating Expenses (Pathmark)

Total labor and store direct expenses	$4,895,916
Total advertising and promotion	487,476
Total maintenance	242,165
Rent	591,996
Real estate taxes	148,000
Utilities	251,600
Insurance (nonlabor related)	204,425
Other expenses net of other income	613,693
Total	$7,435,271

Financing Information

Source	Amount
Prudential Insurance (permanent)	$7,200,000
New Jersey Local Development Finance Fund	1,380,000
Urban Development Action Grant	1,530,000
New Jersey Office of Community Service	500,000
Community Development Block Grant	300,000
New Jersey Economic Development Authority	717,000
New Community Corporation	1,233,000
Total	$12,860,000

Development Schedule

3/1979	Planning started
1980 through 1984	Land assembly
1985 through 1987	Condemnation process
1987	Approvals obtained
5/1989	Construction started
7/1990	Project opened

Developer/Owner

New Community Corporation
233 West Market Street
Newark, New Jersey 07103
201-623-2800

Architect/Planner

Bomad
47 Newark Street
Hoboken, New Jersey 07030

Builder

Turner Construction Company
265 Davidson Avenue
Somerset, New Jersey 08873
908-627-8300

Old Orchard Center

Skokie, Illinois

The 86-acre, 865,075-square-foot Old Orchard shopping center opened in 1956 as one of the country's first regional shopping centers. Located in Skokie, just one block east of I-94, the link between the North Shore and downtown Chicago, the center boasts a trade area population of 1.2 million and average annual household income of more than $71,000. Marshall Field's, Saks Fifth Avenue, and Montgomery Ward originally anchored the open-air center, which served Chicago's affluent North Shore communities. In 1977, Old Orchard was expanded by the addition of Lord & Taylor.

For many years, the center was regarded as the premier shopping destination in the Chicago area. But by the mid-1980s, the 30-year-old-center had lost its dominant position in the marketplace. With Montgomery Ward's departure, a significant portion of the center stood vacant, and plans for its reuse failed to come to fruition. Competition from Northbrook Court, a 1 million-square-foot regional center, was also beginning to undermine the success of the aging mall. Located about seven miles from Old Orchard, Northbrook Court was anchored by Nieman Marcus and targeted many of the same high-income communities as Old Orchard. In addition, with fewer than 75 small tenants, Old Orchard's small-tenant roster was undersized compared with that of the competition. Old Orchard also lacked the entertainment and restaurants expected in today's regional shopping centers.

A recent renovation added more than 500,000 square feet of gross leasable area (GLA) to Old Orchard, nearly doubling the number of small tenants. This renovation enhanced the center's original open-air, parklike design and reestablished it as a dominant shopping center in its market.

Development

Redevelopment occurred in two phases. The first phase began in January 1993 and was completed in October 1994. It featured the construction of a two-level, 200,000-square-foot Nordstrom store, which replaced Montgomery Ward. Nordstrom's commitment to its second store in the Chicago area was one of the catalysts for the expansion and renovation of Old Orchard. The undersized Lord & Taylor store (60,000 square feet) was replaced by a new 115,000-square-foot store. New shops for small tenants; a seven-screen movie theater complex; a 600-seat food court; and a five-level, 1,175-space parking structure also were added during this phase. Renovations involved the interior of an adjacent professional building and an existing 860-space parking structure. All mall common areas were renovated, including walking surfaces, landscapes, fountains, directories and graphics, lighting, seating, and customer amenities. These improvements highlighted Old Orchard's open-air design and complemented the center's trademark seasonal flower displays.

Phase II of the renovation began in August 1994 and was completed in September 1995. The centerpiece of Phase II was the construction of a three-level, 200,000-square-foot Bloomingdale's department store. The addition of Bloomingdale's, the company's second store in the Chicago area, helped secure Old Orchard's competitive position. Also added during the second phase were 150,000 square feet of small retail shops on two levels; a six-level, 2,100-space parking structure; and a 90-space underground parking garage that serves the professional office building.

The GLA of the new Old Orchard is 1.8 million square feet, a net addition of over half a million square feet. The number of stores increased from 75 to 140, and 1,121 parking spaces were added.

Planning and Design

Old Orchard's original site plan featured a 446,000-square-foot Marshall Field's at the mall's center, a 200,000-square-foot Montgomery Ward at the mall's south end, and a 60,000-square-foot Saks Fifth Avenue at the north end. The center lacked a common pedestrian connection between the north and south anchors. Over the years—and even with the addition of Lord & Taylor at the north end and the enlargement of Saks—Old Orchard had become polarized. Middle-market comparison-shopping, convenience, and service tenants concentrated in the south mall around Montgomery Ward, while higher-end fashion stores clustered around Saks and Lord & Taylor in the north mall. The bulk of Marshall Field's in the middle of Old Orchard interrupted any visual or physical connection.

The redevelopment set out to remedy the problem. The catalyst was Nordstrom's interest in replacing the vacant Ward store and the construction of Bloomingdale's at the center's northwest corner, west of Saks. The objective was to create a complete outdoor pedestrian path linking Nordstrom on the south to Marshall Field's in the center, Saks and Lord & Taylor to the north, and Bloomingdale's to the west. For the first time, a pedestrian arcade connected the north and south malls with the shops added east of Marshall Field's.

The goals for the expansion and updating of Old Orchard Center were architectural as well as market

The landscaping and sculpture at the center's entrance emphasize its garden theme.

driven. The owner and the design team sought to maintain the distinctive open-air landscaped courtyards and to enhance the pedestrian scale, paying particular attention to preserving open sight lines and views throughout the center. They also sought to emphasize and reinforce existing design elements, such as water features, landscaping, and sculptural elements that would enhance public use and enjoyment of the mall common areas.

At the same time, the owner and the design team needed to increase the number and variety of tenants and their offerings and to update the facility to attract several upscale retail tenants currently in or considering entry to Chicago's suburban North Shore market. The team also needed to increase the food and entertainment offerings throughout Old Orchard.

The owner and the design team chose a design theme that would enable Old Orchard to remain a vital retail center well into the future. The theme, which deliberately respected and enhanced some of Old Orchard's original design elements while providing for the needs of contemporary retail shoppers, comprised three components: the master plan, the building plan, and the garden plan.

The master plan oriented the new construction toward a village street by offering straightforward vehicular and pedestrian circulation. The building plan connected the existing and proposed north and south retail buildings in a manner that provides varied public spaces and amenities, enhancing the retail experience for shoppers. The

architectural and landscape design theme is reminiscent of a European town center, with interior tree-lined walkways and courtyards carved out to create various public spaces and environments throughout the center.

The garden plan built on the open-air, parklike character of the center, allowing Old Orchard's all-season garden to become the center's dominant theme. The plan called for new plant species to offer variety as well as for fountains, park seating, and other amenities. The hardscape was held to a minimum; the balance was landscaped in a manner suggestive of an English garden. Each courtyard has an individual theme, with plantings selected to enhance its character. The new plantings and landscaping are extremely "people friendly," allowing visitors to sit on the grass and use the fountains.

Construction

Construction and renovation had to overcome several challenges. The first was maintaining utility services to existing tenants while new service was installed or relocated. The second was coordinating construction activity so that existing retailers remained accessible and visible and experienced as little disruption in their business as possible. The third was saving the shopping center's mature trees. Ninety-four mature trees were transplanted around the perimeter of Old Orchard; only four were lost. The transplanting not only saved the lives of the trees but also provided the center with a new, mature look—even before construction began.

Water features and landscaping in the north court create a parklike setting.

Extensive efforts were made to preserve the existing mature trees during renovation.

A rear view of the grand entrance in its formal garden setting.

The construction agenda included two projects that would benefit the community of Skokie. Old Orchard, like Skokie, had a combined sanitary and storm sewer system. Part of the construction process called for the installation of separate sanitary and storm sewer systems at Old Orchard to accommodate Skokie's future water disposal needs. In addition, the Montgomery Ward Auto Center was demolished to build a new on-site stormwater retention facility as a component of Skokie's stormwater control program. The retention pond will help alleviate the flooding problems that formerly plagued Old Orchard and surrounding neighborhoods.

Tenants

The renovation, retenanting, and repositioning of Old Orchard have transformed the center into a distinctive shopping destination and the premier retail center in the Chicago/North Shore marketplace. Today, the center features five anchor tenants, 135 specialty stores, restaurants, and a seven-screen theater complex. The realization of the goals of increasing the number and variety of tenants and their offerings and expanding the center's food and entertainment components has exceeded expectations.

Experience Gained

- An effective project team, including the owner, development manager, architect/design team, contractors, on-site management, those responsible for leasing, merchants, and local public officials and staff, works together and communicates from the earliest planning stages through the execution of the plan and completion of the center's renovation.
- Extensive preplanning is important to ensure that existing merchants remain in business during construction and that shoppers continue to patronize the center. Plans must be developed for construction phasing, utility connections, accessibility and visibility of merchants, customer parking, signage, advertising, and safety of shoppers and employees.
- Surveying the existing condition of a center and its infrastructure during the planning stage is critical in that it is extremely difficult to document existing conditions once construction begins. Surveying allows construction plans to reflect existing conditions, minimizing cost overruns and delays.
- Identifying major existing and prospective tenants early is essential to ensure that tenants' needs are accommodated during initial planning. Doing so eliminates costly delays and change orders during construction.
- It is important to review all existing leases for clauses that will be difficult to maintain during construction or after renovation and to renegotiate them. It may not be possible to adhere to specific clauses in a lease if a center is undergoing extensive redevelopment.
- It is critical to intervene as soon as possible once a center begins to lose its competitive edge. Assume a proactive posture, upgrade facilities, and secure new tenants to prevent the center from losing its image or dominance.

The garden court serves as the connection to the two-level Nordstrom store. Construction of the store was one of the catalysts for Old Orchard's renovation and expansion.

An interactive children's play area in the south court is part of the people-friendly landscape.

- The developer must establish open communications with the municipality during initial planning. The redevelopment process will progress more smoothly and with fewer problems if the developer establishes a good relationship with the community.
- Open-air malls are feasible, even in a cold climate. It is imperative to build on the center's strengths, such as its image, location, tenant mix, restaurants, entertainment offerings, design, appearance, and customer and pedestrian friendliness.

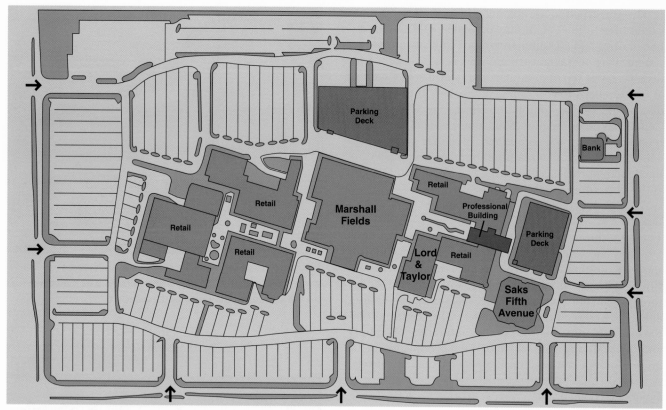

Site plan before renovation.

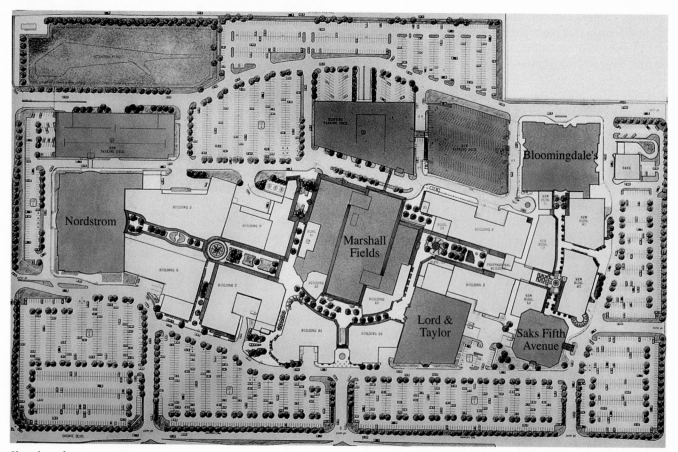

Site plan after renovation.

Project Data: Old Orchard Center

Land Use and Building Information

Site Area

86 acres

Gross Leasable Area

Before renovation	1,288,000 square feet
After renovation	1,786,000 square feet

Total Parking Spaces

	Surface	Deck	Total
Before renovation	5,224	1,296	6,520
After renovation	3,480	4,161	7,641

Redevelopment Cost Information

	Phase I	Phase II	Total
Hard Costs			
Shell and core construction	$33,233,000	$15,593,000	$48,826,000
Site improvements	4,858,000	950,000	5,808,000
Parking decks	7,335,000	13,199,000	20,534,000
Landscaping/graphics/ furniture/amenities	2,269,000	1,157,000	3,426,000
Asbestos abatement	719,000	0	719,000
Office building renovation	2,752,000	0	2,752,000
Food court	3,136,000	0	3,136,000
Total	$54,302,000	$30,899,000	$85,201,000
Soft Costs			
Professional fees	$6,073,000	$2,601,000	$8,674,000
Legal fees	2,506,000	607,000	3,113,000
Marketing	96,000	321,000	417,000
Development/leasing coordination	5,942,000	3,018,000	8,960,000
Financing costs	2,210,000	819,000	3,029,000
Preopening/start-up costs	452,000	381,000	833,000
Total	$17,279,000	$7,747,000	$25,026,000
Tenant Allowances	$16,613,000	$7,439,000	$24,052,000
Total Project Costs	$88,194,000	$46,085	$134,279,000

Retail Tenant Information

	Number of Stores	Total GLA (square feet)	Percent of GLA
Department stores	5	1,063,717	59.5
Cards	2	3,917	0.2
Restaurants	8	73,104	4.1
Clothing and accessories	43	217,207	12.2
Shoes	11	26,004	1.5
Home furnishings	10	95,624	5.4
Music/books	3	54,216	3.0
Health/beauty	9	21,212	1.2
Eyewear	4	8,771	0.5
Jewelry	4	4,951	0.3
Food court/other food	17	25,851	1.4
Toys/educational	4	22,996	1.3
Other retail	4	8,910	0.5
Services	5	29,396	1.6
Theater	1	40,642	2.3
Retail vacancy/storage	10	29,362	1.6
Offices	–	60,521	3.4
Total	140	1,786,401	100.0

Development Schedule

1956	Original project opened
1993	Renovation started
1994	Phase I completed
1995	Phase II completed

Owner's Representative

Urban Shopping Centers, Inc.
900 North Michigan Avenue
Chicago, Illinois 60611
312-915-2000

Development Manager

Urban Retail Properties
900 North Michigan Avenue
Chicago, Illinois 60611
312-915-1725

Portland International Airport Concessions Expansion and Renovation

Portland, Oregon

Located 12 miles northeast of downtown Portland, Portland International Airport (PDX) was one of the first airports in the country to offer travelers upscale shopping. Development of the concessions area was an outgrowth of a major airport renovation in the late 1980s and expansion in the early 1990s that extended the terminal north by 200 feet, added two new concourses, and provided 22,000 square feet of new space for additional concessions. The first development phase, the Oregon Market, began in 1988. It consists of six specialty retail shops aligned along what resembles a typical city retail street; the shops feature a diverse selection of high-quality retail goods sold by local businesses. The main focus of the 1994–1995 development phase—a new food and beverage program —added a full-service restaurant, a nine-unit food court, and three additional specialty retail shops, creating a secondary retail street around a "town square."

Development

At the start of the airport expansion during the 1990s, passenger growth had been hovering at just above 5 percent annually and was expected to continue at a rate of over 4 percent annually. Since that time, however, growth has skyrocketed. PDX has been sustaining increases in growth rate of about 16 percent for the past five years, making it one of the fastest-growing airports in the country. Nearly 6.4 million passengers flew in or out of PDX in 1991. In 1994, the year Southwest Airlines started service out of Portland, the passenger level hit nearly 10 million. PDX expected 12.4 million passengers in 1998.

Many observers consider Southwest Airlines and other no-frills carriers as the driving force behind PDX's growth and expansion. They also look to the region's population, which continues to burgeon, a product of the state's strong economy. Oregon industries continue to prosper, spurring more business travel and cargo flights.

The Oregon Market, part of the Phase I expansion, increased retail revenues at PDX by 125 percent in its first year of operation. The project paid for itself within five and one-half years. Customers' satisfaction with PDX's food and beverage operations was a different story, however. Like many other airports, PDX had a traditional food and beverage concession program operated by a master concessionaire. The program's approach ignored current trends in the food industry. Food and beverage revenues at PDX had not increased in proportion to the Oregon Market's retail sales. Revenues had been flat or declining each year since 1986 and had not kept pace with increases in passenger traffic.

Market research studies showed that passengers wanted quicker service, higher-quality food, wider selection, and competitive pricing. Given that PDX was nearing the end of a long-term contract with its existing concessionaire, the timing was right to consider a comprehensive overhaul of the concession program.

Because Portland International Airport is a public facility operated by the Port of Portland, the selection of retail tenants and concession vendors depended on a public request for proposals (RFP). The port promoted available spaces by using standard mall marketing techniques. It developed a marketing brochure, made numerous public presentations, and met with over 120 local and national concessionaires. Nonetheless, many local operators were unfamiliar with the RFP process. Accordingly, the port reformatted the standard RFP application and streamlined the process. As a result, the port received 56 responses for the ten food and beverage contracts let in the 1994–1995 expansion (Phase II).

Tenant improvement allowances were offered to food and beverage units with interior seating, while tenant participation packages were developed for local tenants, many of whom had not previously operated in an airport location and thus might have found it difficult to secure a loan. As a public entity, the port technically does not make loans, but it did purchase the tenant improvements and lease them back to the individual operators. Three local tenants participated in this program, enabling them to submit competitive bids and further the general goal of establishing a level playing field.

The port's strategy in the Phase II expansion was to build on the success of the Oregon Market retail shops and continue to feature local businesses whenever possible. Analysis showed, however, that profits would be maximized by mixing local and national tenants. The port achieved its target goal—60 percent local, 40 percent national, with 29 percent disadvantaged business enterprise participation. "Portland is fortunate," noted PDX concession program manager Jeanne Raikoglo, "to support such a rich selection of well-run, home-grown companies such as Nike and Norm Thompson that are also nationally known and bring great name recognition. Not all cities can draw from such strong resources."

The port deliberately sought retailers with easily transportable merchandise that would make appealing gifts. Made in Oregon, for example, features food sundries such as small jars of Oregon jams, packages of smoked salmon, and chocolate-covered hazelnuts—items that fit easily into a suitcase or shopping bag. Port staff were sur-

Portland International Airport was one of the first airports in the country to offer travelers upscale shopping. Oregon Market consists of specialty shops aligned along a main street with a clock tower in the middle.

©Ed Hershberger

Skylights were added to provide natural light, and flat storefronts were replaced with expansive bay windows, showcasing merchandise and making small shop spaces look larger. The use of extra-wide open portals adds to the sense of spaciousness.

©Ed Hershberger

©Ed Hershberger

prised to learn that one of the best-selling items is luggage. At the Norm Thompson airport store, luggage remains the strongest single merchandise category.

Gross sales in specialty shops before the 1988 renovation totaled $2.15 million per year. In its first full year of operation, the Oregon Market produced sales of slightly more than $5 million, more than doubling retail revenues. Now, following the 1994–1995 renovation/expansion, gross sales per square foot for the retail shops range from $400 per square foot to over $1,500 per square foot—about three times the national average for regional malls. Factoring in food and beverage as well as news and gift shops, the average sale per enplaning passenger—more than $7.00—is one of the highest in the country. Some 15 percent of purchases are made by individuals who come to the airport just to shop. The airport's proximity to Washington State, which unlike Oregon has a sales tax, undoubtedly attracts some shoppers from the Vancouver, Washington, area. As an additional attraction,

retailers offer reduced parking rates to customers who make purchases.

The concession program at PDX is also a profit enhancer for the airlines. Under PDX's modified residual plan, revenue generated from concessions is used to offset operating expenses. It was estimated that increased revenues from expansion of the concessions could reduce the average terminal rental rate by as much as $3.00 per square foot in the first year of operation.

Market Research

For both the 1988 and the 1994–1995 renovation/expansions, the port undertook extensive market analysis and surveys relating to dwell time (time spent in the airport), travelers' needs, traffic counts and projections, traffic flow, and demographics of travelers. It made extensive use of direct-intercept surveys, especially useful for collecting information about dwell time and demographics as well as for assessing passengers' needs and satisfaction, to keep abreast of the ever-changing market.

As hands-on manager of its concessions, the port continuously collects data and undertakes market analyses and surveys to keep informed of current trends in the concession business and their effect on airport concessions. The port uses the information to improve concession management and to plan future concession development. Information on traffic flow helps in projecting revenues, much the way that traffic counts are used for shopping center development. One of the most useful analyses was a market-share study of concessionaires undertaken in combination with a traffic flow survey. It counted people as they entered the terminal and tracked them as they passed several key airport locations. Individual merchants tracked the number and amount of sales per hour over a week, enabling the port to determine the percentage of the passing traffic each shop captured in any given time period and the dollars converted into sales from that traffic. The information was validated by comparing market-share percentages for each concession for the test period with the same percentages of annual gross sales. The findings helped the port identify specific management problems with individual locations as well as overall traffic problems.

For example, traffic flow surveys showed a significant difference in traffic patterns and habits at each end of the terminal. Further examination indicated that the difference was largely attributable to the type of food service available at each end during the peak early-morning hours. The port concluded from the studies that the south end of the concession lobby would benefit from a pastry or coffee shop located in the highly visible area across from the specialty retail shops. Such an establishment would capture the popular breakfast market as well as increase the Oregon Market's traffic, thus benefiting all the shops.

The port regularly conducts direct-intercept surveys of airport users, passengers, and meeter/greeters. One survey analyzed the composition of the concession lobby population. Of the people in the Oregon Market area, 56 percent had entered from the ticket lobby, 44 percent from security. Other survey data showed that deplaning passengers and friends and relatives who greet arriving passengers generally do not stop to shop on their way to the baggage claim area. Yet the data showed that high percentages of persons return from the secure concourses to the Oregon Market. Follow-up questions indicated that 27 percent of enplaning passengers are likely to return through security checkpoints to shop or eat in the central concession lobby. This pattern differs from that at most airports and is likely a consequence of PDX's manageable size and centralized concessions. Further, projected traffic patterns showed that the central concession lobby was the preferred location for new concessions. The centralized location minimizes any potentially negative impacts on existing concessions and maximizes the benefits of spinoff associated with established retail operations. This information influenced the decision to locate additional specialty shops within the Oregon Market as part of the 1994–1995 renovation/expansion.

Demographic surveys showed that PDX passengers have higher incomes and more education than the average tricounty resident. The information supported the initial decision to feature upscale specialty retail shopping in the Oregon Market instead of the more typical nationally franchised news and gift shops that dominate most airports. The port is currently conducting studies that break down the demographics for each airline and each concourse to develop a better understanding of the specific spending patterns for each and to provide the appropriate concessions in those particular locations. PDX is now home to several low-fare carriers, such as Southwest Airlines, whose passengers are, for example, more apt than first-class passengers to stock up on fast food at the airport before boarding their flight.

Planning and Design

Architect John Schleuning, whose firm, SRG Partnership, spearheaded the design for both the original Oregon Market and the 1994–1995 expansion, notes that from the start PDX never "felt like your generic airport." It had always featured natural materials from the Northwest—plenty of wood instead of laminates, carpeting to soften sound, and comfortable upholstered chairs to make passengers feel at home. A main design goal for the 1988 development of the retail shops was to expand on these local features to create a distinct sense of place so that passengers flying into PDX would know from looking at the materials, colors, and merchandise in the shops that they were in Portland, not Chicago or Denver.

Phase I. Although some retail experts warned that the project would fail without the usual complement of national retailers that occupy space in most major U.S. airports, the 1988 renovation/reconfiguration introduced six specialty retail shops that were Portland-based businesses. These shops were organized along a "main street" with a clock tower in the middle. The tower—instead of the more usual suspended clock—created a focal point and meeting place, much like the clock in New York's Penn Station.

To create a critical mass of high-quality specialty shops, the news and gift concessions that carried more generic convenience goods—souvenir mugs, T-shirts, and drugstore items—were moved from the central Oregon Market area to locations on the sides closer to the gates. The higher traffic counts at those peripheral locations provided retailers with an incentive to relocate.

The port's strategy for elevating the caliber of the retail shops was similar to that taken by many shopping malls to draw upscale tenants—upgrade the design and finishes and offer high-quality merchandise. The addition of skylights brought in natural light. For many of the local stores that had never operated in a shopping center—much less in an airport—the need to coordinate with other retailers required reeducation. The port played a more active role in unit design than is typical at other retail centers. From the start, port staff and designers collaborated directly with tenants and their architects to complete the six retail shops.

Flat storefronts were replaced with oversized bay windows that better showcase merchandise and make small shop spaces look larger. The use of extra-wide, open portals adds to the sense of spaciousness. The open frontage also makes it easier for shoppers, many of whom carry luggage, to maneuver through the shops. The storefronts are finished with light-colored native woods—maple, cherry, and Douglas fir.

At many shopping malls, stores are designed to "pop out" and call attention to themselves. At PDX, in contrast, a primary goal was to minimize confusion by creating a harmonious street edge. Instead of diversity, the storefronts were designed to be compatible with one another and to achieve a certain uniformity. A series of freestanding street lights, interspersed with colorful banners, creates the effect of a continuous stream of activity and reinforces the main street theme.

Because one of an airport's primary functions is to move passengers from the entrances to the gates, directional signs must be highly visible and easy to read. Signage at PDX follows a deliberate hierarchy. The functional blue and white directional signs with straightforward block letters are clearly distinguished from the more elaborate retail signs with script lettering. Flashing neon signs, used in many traditional retail settings, are not permitted at PDX because they could confuse and distract passengers from finding their way to the gates. Double-sided signs with store logos grace the main shopping street. They hang perpendicular to the storefronts and are easily seen from both ends of the street.

Phase II. The second half of the renovation/expansion focused mainly on upgrading the food concessions. The original plan called for consolidating the fast-food units into a food court at the terminal's far north end, away from the retail shops. The architects, however, took a different approach and looked instead to the model of the European street whose shops, open-air food markets, and restaurants are typically integrated into mixed-use corridors. Instead of isolating the food establishments from the main shopping core, the architects dispersed them to create separate zones of activity.

The food court is centrally located on the main street across from the specialty retail stores. A mix of local eateries and national fast-food outlets sits across from the shops, aligned in an arc to create a secondary street and a town square. This configuration opened the common seating area to sweeping exterior views of the runways and planes that diners can enjoy while eating.

Coffee People, one of Portland's best-known espresso drink purveyors, was selected for the central food court. Although known for its friendly service and no-nonsense slogan, "Good coffee, no backtalk," Coffee People's sophisticated design and high-quality finishings and materials make it perfectly compatible with the upscale shops across the street. The "aero mocha" logo (a flying coffee cup reminiscent of a DC-3) was specially designed for Coffee People's airport store.

The Red Lion restaurant is strategically positioned at one of the airport's points with the highest circulation. Passengers using the north concourses pass by the restaurant on departure before entering the gate area and on arrival on their way to the baggage claim area. The full-service restaurant, operated by a local hotel chain, resembles a resort lodge, such as Timberline Lodge at nearby Mt. Hood. The front lounge features a large stone fireplace with a roaring fire and oversized leather chairs, inviting passengers and shoppers to linger and relax—a respite from the harried pace of the airport. Serving as an anchor for the food and retail shops, the Red Lion is flanked by three new retail shops added in the 1994–1995 expansion.

Like many other airports, PDX had always operated an employee cafeteria. With development of the food court and a street pricing policy that ensures reasonably priced food, the airport no longer has to provide separate eating facilities for employees. The cafeteria was recently converted into a lounge for airport staff.

At many shopping malls, stores are designed to "pop out" to call attention to themselves. At PDX, the goal was to minimize confusion by creating a harmonious street edge.

©Ed Hershberger

The 1994–1995 renovation of the food concession area ensured that it would reflect the high quality of the overall airport environment. Comprehensive design standards required some tenants to deviate from their usual design programs.

©Sally Painter

To ensure that the food concession area would reflect the high-quality design of the overall airport environment, the port staff and SRG Partnership developed a set of comprehensive design standards. General design standards address issues such as signage, lighting, and overall image and character. They encourage the use of natural materials, such as wood slat ceilings and granite for the wall bases and door thresholds. The use of stone, metal, wood, glass, or tile is encouraged for counterfronts, whereas materials that simulate wood and brick are discouraged. Likewise, standards relating to signage prohibit exposed neon as well as signs that "flash, move, or make noise."

In some situations, the standards required tenants, especially the national chains that tend to follow formulas, to deviate from their usual design programs. For example, Wendy's typically uses a standard black and white checkerboard pattern on its counter fronts. The PDX design standards, however, called for a larger pattern that was better suited to the scale of the public space. The standards also promoted the use of three-dimensional logos that look more like sculptures. Wendy's initially submitted a large styrofoam hamburger as its logo. SRG worked with the chain to create a logo that was more compatible with the food court design and complied with the guidelines. Instead of the typical food poster or portrait of Wendy's owner, Dave Thomas, an oversized sculpture of a metal and glass hamburger hovers above Wendy's front counter. Although the three-dimensional logo was far more expensive than the usual framed poster, Wendy's management was so taken with the bold image that it is considering using it for several new stores in other cities.

Management

Although PDX had successfully managed its first six specialty retail shops, the airport used expansion of the concessions as an opportunity to consider alternative management options—a master concessionaire, a developer, or continued reliance on the airport as developer/manager. Whereas most airports do not develop and manage their concessions, the port decided to continue its management for several reasons: greatest profit potential; enhanced opportunities for local participation; direct involvement in tenant selection and direct contact with individual operators and owners, giving PDX more control over pricing, operating standards, and facility design; and greater flexibility, enabling PDX to select the concepts that best reflect the specific preferences and needs of passengers and the local community.

The port ultimately decided to drop the master concessionaire, whose 30-year lease was expiring, and to enter into separate contracts with ten different food and beverage concessionaires. Leases for retail shops and food concessions average seven to ten years. The 12,924-square-foot, full-service Red Lion restaurant secured a longer lease—15 years—to account for its greater capital investment. Although rents tend to be higher than at other local locations, Red Lion pays no common area maintenance charges. Food court tenants, however, pay a proportionate share of food court common area maintenance charges.

Concession program manager Jeanne Raikoglo notes that the mercurial nature of the airport environment requires a seasoned, entrepreneurial manager to run an airport retail shop. For example, when the airport is fogged in and flights are delayed for several hours, the opportunities to maximize revenues are tremendous. In fact, a shop can generate two to three times its normal daily sales volume. The store manager must, however, have the authority to bring in additional staff (perhaps from other locations) and, if necessary, secure additional inventory. A new shop or restaurant might take as long as a year to learn all the intricacies of operating in this complicated environment.

The peaks and valleys at airport shops also tend to be more extreme than at traditional shopping centers. The busiest peak at PDX is 5:00 a.m. to 9:00 a.m., with a second peak at 4:00 p.m to 7:30 p.m. and a peak for international travelers at 10:30 a.m. to 1:30 p.m. Market

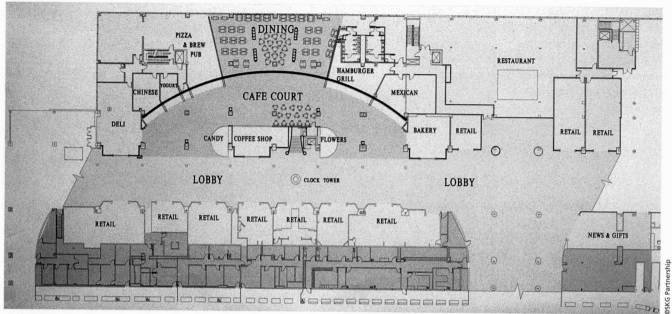

Site plan.

research showed that sales volume was significantly higher before 7:00 a.m. than originally anticipated, prompting some shops and food vendors to open earlier. As the airport grows and airlines run more flights throughout the day, the nonpeak shopping hours will become less frequent, while the peaks remain constant. Typical shop hours are 6:00 a.m to 9:00 p.m daily; food and beverage hours are longer, beginning as early as 5:00 a.m. and running as late as 11:00 p.m.

Airport shoppers have significantly less time to make purchasing decisions than shoppers at traditional retail centers. At PDX, shoppers spend about an hour in the airport and average one-half hour to make a purchase. To help customers make speedy decisions, shops find it useful to limit choices by stocking fewer selections within a specific merchandise category. Research also showed that some PDX shops had a much higher conversion ratio (actual sales as opposed to browsing), because staff gave customers more personalized attention. For these reasons, some PDX shops have created two separate tiers of manager positions. Managers staffing airport shops tend to have more experience than those at other locations.

Experience Gained

- Hindsight points to the advisability of having made the project much larger. When the second development phase started in 1991, PDX had not yet experienced the three years of dramatic growth that would increase passenger numbers by almost 50 percent. Seating at the food court, which seemed ample at the time, is filled every day. Almost every retail tenant has requested additional shop space.
- If basic airport layout does not change significantly in the future, current traffic patterns can provide the basis for projected traffic patterns and increases in enplanements. This type of analysis provides an estimated traffic flow for any point in the airport and

is critical in determining the optimal location for new concessions.

- Focusing on local products and retailers has worked well at PDX. Airport retailing provides an opportunity to promote local companies and products and to offer high-quality shopping and culinary choices not generally available at most airports.
- Assiduous market research and comprehensive analysis have produced the right mix of merchandise and food services at PDX, pushing overall sales per enplaning passenger to one of the highest rates in the country.
- Operating successfully in an airport is challenging even for experienced operators. Notes Raikoglo, "It can take as long as a year to become accustomed to the constantly changing environment and to maximize revenue potential. Those who are able to adapt can reach sales thresholds that are significantly higher than in more traditional retail environments."

Project Data: Portland International Airport Concessions Expansion and Renovation

Land Use and Building Information

Gross Building Area   993,000 square feet[1]

Gross Leasable Area (GLA)

Before expansion	54,000 square feet
After expansion	76,000 square feet

Floor/Area Ratio

Before expansion	.054
After expansion	.076

Levels

First floor: operations and storage

Second floor: concessions and passenger level

Third floor: offices and airline VIP lounges

Retail Tenant Information

	Number of Stores		Total GLA (square feet)	
	Before Expansion	After Expansion	Before Expansion	After Expansion
General merchandise	6	8	7,628	12,632
Food	18	25	34,363	37,301[2]
Clothing and accessories	2	3	2,983	3,456
Gifts/specialty	4	8	7,510	11,159
Total	30	44	52,484	64,548

Major Tenants   Square Feet

Made In Oregon	2,192
Powell's Bookstore	1,507
Norm Thompson	1,840
Nike	1,143
Red Lion	12,924
Wendy's	4,583
Concessions International	8,916
Coffee People	3,245

Lease Terms

Length of lease	7–10 years
Typical lease provisions	Zero base rent, plus percentage over base[3]
Annual rents	$50–150 per square foot[4]

Average Annual Sales $550 per square foot

Retail	$1,100 per square foot
Food and beverage	$400 per square foot

Development Cost Information

Construction Costs

Superstructure	$4,564,000
Tenant improvements	2,065,000
Total	$6,629,000

Soft Costs

Architecture/engineering	$1,690,000
Project management	466,500
Other (lease buyouts)	1,590,000
Total	$3,746,500

Total Development Cost $10,375,500

Annual Operating Expenses (1995–1996)

Taxes	Paid by tenant
Services	$94,750
Maintenance	63,700
Janitorial	138,000
Utilities	Paid by tenant
Miscellaneous	22,000
Total	$318,450

Development Schedule

1/992	Planning started
6/1993	Approvals obtained
11/1993	Construction started
1/1994	Leasing started
10/1994	Project opened
10/1995	Phase I
10/1995	Phase II

Owner/Manager

Port of Portland

Portland International Airport

7000 N.E. Airport Way/Third Floor

Portland, Oregon 97218

503-231-5000

Architect/Planner

SRG Partnership, Inc.

621 S.W. Morrison Street/Suite 200

Portland, Oregon 97205

503-222-1917

Notes

[1] Airport terminal and concourses.

[2] Plus 11,346-square-foot common area for food court.

[3] A fixed minimum annual guarantee applies in each year of the lease term. In the first year, the monthly lease is either one-twelfth of the minimum annual guarantee or a certain percentage of the previous month's gross sales, whichever is higher. In the second and subsequent years of the lease, the minimum annual guarantee adjusts to 90 percent of the previous year's rent. Monthly rents are calculated in the same manner as during the first year of the lease.

[4] $400 per square foot in the duty-free shop.

The Promenade at Westlake

Thousand Oaks, California

The Promenade at Westlake is a 210,000-square-foot community shopping center that aspires to be a traditional downtown. Every detail, from the selection of tenants to the design of building facades, is intended to foster a sense of place and collectively to establish a new social destination for the affluent residents of Thousand Oaks. In the words of developer Rick Caruso, of Caruso Affiliated Holdings (CAH), the goal for the Promenade was nothing less than "to create the center of town."

Like a downtown, the Promenade has a variety of tenants that generate activity throughout the day and evening, from shops serving local needs, like a dry cleaner, to entertainment-oriented retailers, including restaurants, cafés, a bookstore, a cinema, and a Club Disney for children. And as in a traditional town center, spaces and structures are highly articulated. Each tenant, large or small, has its own design identity, and the bulk of the mall has been broken up into a series of smaller "buildings," as if built over time. The site includes a variety of outdoor spaces for sitting, dining, and strolling.

The intention, according to Caruso, was to reverse the process of development. Instead of building a place to shop, Caruso wanted to "create a place that people want to go to," the assumption being that visitors would stay to shop.

The entertainment theory of retailing has been proven correct at the Promenade by several indicators, among them that retail sales have been averaging $450 per square foot, and that provisions for percentage rents came into play after just one year of operation. Behind these statistics is another barometer of success: people spend four to five hours at the Promenade on average, traveling from beyond the expected trade area for a project of this size. The city of Thousand Oaks was so pleased with the design of the project that it is using the Promenade as the design standard for adjacent and future projects.

Development

The 22.5-acre Promenade parcel was known locally as a difficult site. Two other developers tried and failed before CAH acquired the property. Though the site had good access to the freeway, excellent demographics, and no serious development limitations, it was not considered to be a retail area, and the neighborhood residents had objected to earlier attempts to develop the site.

Knowing this—and because of it—Caruso considered it to be an ideal site. Caruso believes having prior unsuccessful developers "creates a road map for you," not to mention lowers seller's expectations for the sale price. Moreover, notes Caruso, a slow-growth or antigrowth environment "by nature creates a barrier to the entry of competition" and usually means the area is underserved.

Before the project could get off the ground, however, two constituencies had to be convinced of its merits: the neighbors and potential retail tenants. For the neighbors, the strategy was simple and effective: "Give the residents what they want, and they will support you," says Caruso. The developer met with the presidents of some ten different homeowners associations and "sat with a blank piece of paper," taking notes on what the residents wanted and what they did not want. For the most part, the developer was able to deliver what the residents asked for: a bookstore, cafés, a gourmet food store, and a low-scale design with traditional materials. On the other hand, Caruso explained the limits of accommodation; the parking, for example, could not be hidden from view.

A second strategy for winning over the local residents (and city officials and potential tenants as well) was the development of an animated computer model of the project. The La Jolla Group Interactive, in cooperation with the Ayres Group of San Diego, developed a virtual-reality walk-through of the project. The presentation showed the project rendered in full detail, as if one were actually strolling past the storefronts, courtyards, and fountains, allowing for an informed discussion of signage, heights, views, traffic, and access.

At the city council hearing for the project, each council member viewed the presentation on an individual monitor, while the audience viewed it on a ten-foot projection screen. The presentation aired on local cable television as well. As a result of the developer's careful and serious wooing of the neighbors, the project won strong support from area residents and passed both the planning commission's and the city council's reviews with unanimous votes, a first for Thousand Oaks.

The developer also deployed community enthusiasm to help convince retailers that the Promenade site would be a strong retail location. To that end, Caruso "turned the residents loose on the retailers," having them write letters to several target tenants. And if the residents' letters and computer model did not make the point finely enough, Caruso flew prospective tenants over the site in a helicopter. By the time the developer closed escrow on the site, the project was 90 percent leased (and by opening day, 100 percent).

Design

With some noteworthy exceptions, the site design for the Promenade follows the standard model for a community

Each tenant at the Promenade at Westlake, large or small, has its own design identity; as in a traditional town center, spaces and structures are highly articulated.

shopping center: The main block of shops is set back from the street, with anchor tenants at each end, a parking lot in front, and several freestanding retail buildings along the street. The exceptions come in the finer site planning, principally for pedestrians. The main block of shops is actually two blocks, with a landscaped watercourse in between. This breezeway-like space, which has a fountain at the sidewalk, is used for outdoor dining for the adjacent restaurants and doubles as a pleasant passageway to a section of rear parking. Fountains, each with a bronze sculpture or other feature and special-effects lighting, are also located at focal points throughout the site.

The 15- to 20-foot-wide sidewalk—the promenade—in front of the main retail areas is paved with a variety of colored and stamped concrete and natural stone pavers, echoing and reinforcing the individuality of the various storefronts. Bollards, trees, stone pots, and custom-designed pole lighting add to the mix of textures, and carts and kiosks help provide retail energy and interest along the route.

While the streetscape design is clearly successful, David W. Williams, vice president of architecture at CAH, notes that next time he would prefer to include an even wider sidewalk, perhaps with street trees and a parkway, so that pedestrians would not be aware of being on the edge of a parking lot.

In a departure from usual industry practice, the Mann cineplex allowed the Promenade's developer to locate several small retail tenants along the theater's frontage, thus reducing the theater's apparent bulk and providing livelier street frontage. This simple design strategy not only makes for a better streetscape, but also, according to Williams, makes the cineplex site a more desirable theater destination as well.

Building facades are highly articulated and finished in a variety of materials to evoke a traditional village center. Each tenant's facade is distinctive: elevations are

The main block of shops is split by a landscaped watercourse; marked by a fountain at the sidewalk, the breezeway-like space is used for outdoor dining by the adjacent restaurants and doubles as a pleasant passageway to rear parking areas.

canted or projected in or out from the primary building line, and rooflines are raised, lowered, and topped with a variety of hip roofs, cornices, and domed towers. For a "living-above-the-store" effect, many of the facades have faux second stories, complete with windows, shutters, and lighting. As a matter of corporate philosophy, CAH strives to give each tenant its own identity, treating smaller tenants with the same dignity afforded anchor tenants.

Exterior finish materials include a variety of stone veneers, smoothly troweled plaster, cast cornices and trim, and multicolor, barrel-shaped roof tiles. Twenty-two different paint colors were used on the plaster and trim. Carmen Perri, executive vice president for development at CAH, likens the process of building the Promenade to custom homebuilding; like that for a custom home, design and construction of the Promenade was highly detailed, with a variety of custom-designed elements and special finishes such as lime-wash paint from Australia, which was used to create a weathered look.

Lighting design for the Promenade is also detailed, varied, and customized. The developer and architect searched out special sources for the decorative pole lighting and the internally illuminated stained glass tower dome. Supplementing these light sources are wall-mounted coach lights and lighting for the pitched roof surfaces, as well as general facade and signage lighting.

Financing and Construction

CAH financed site acquisition for the Promenade. Construction was funded through a conventional, fixed-rate commercial bank construction loan, though construction was about 30 percent complete before this funding was in place, according to Caruso. Permanent financing was provided by Massachusetts Mutual Life. No outside investors participated in the project.

Construction is wood frame and fully sprinklered. The primary phase was compressed into a scant 29 weeks to meet the November 1996 opening date. A second phase, approximately 15,000 square feet, opened in July 1997. Most recently, CAH purchased and renovated a two-story office building adjacent to the Promenade and incorporated its site into the project.

Leasing and Marketing

The Promenade's tenant roster spans from Fazio Cleaners, a local business, all the way to Club Disney. The common denominator is the creation of a town center. The intent, according to Caruso, was to create a place for multiple types of activity to generate morning, afternoon, and evening trips. The emphasis is on social activities: dining, cinema, bookstore, Disney. The Barnes & Noble bookstore, for example, is complete with lounge areas and café and is open until 11 p.m.

Club Disney was a late addition to the Promenade's entertainment lineup, but it fits comfortably with the concept. Club Disney is billed as "an interactive environment

The promenade in front of the main retail areas is paved with a variety of colored and stamped concrete and natural stone pavers. Bollards, trees, and custom-designed pole lighting add to the mix of textures, and carts and kiosks help provide retail energy and interest along the route.

The lighting design of the Promenade at Westlake is detailed and varied. Custom-built pole lighting and the illuminated tower dome incorporate imported glass and ironwork. Supplementing these light sources are wall-mounted coach lights, lighting for the pitched roof surfaces, and general facade and signage lighting.

for parents and children." Aimed at children up to 12 years old, Club Disney offers computer games, make-your-own animations, games of skill, dress-up costumes, a three-story climber, and other activities. A restaurant is included and party rooms are available. Unlike at some similar facilities, parents are required to attend with their children.

Club Disney provides regional visibility for the Promenade, notes Dan Burgner, senior vice president for operations at CAH, and brings visitors from outside the traditional trade area. It attracts school field trips from as far as 30 to 40 miles away.

Overall, the Promenade is marketed through center and tenant events. The on-site management team schedules an array of activities, including regular Friday and Saturday evening musical performances. In addition, the center publishes "The Promenade Post," a calendar of events with a circulation of 3,000 to 5,000.

Experience Gained
- Strong community participation during planning and design is essential in obtaining support for a project in a slow-growth or antigrowth environment.
- With its quality design and detailing, pedestrian-friendly environment, and entertainment-focused leasing strategy, the Promenade has shown that the standard community shopping center can become an attraction for many types of activities throughout the day.

- Though it may not be a town center in the historical mold, the social and environmental clues the Promenade has drawn from the traditional town center model represent a promising direction for community shopping center development.

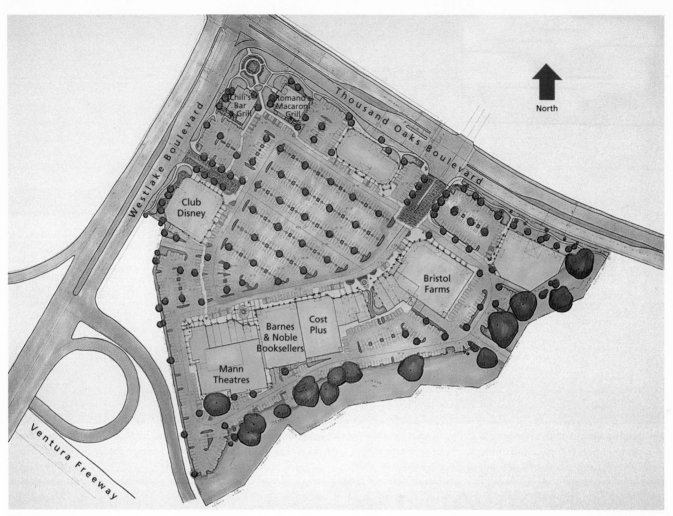

Site plan.

Project Data: The Promenade at Westlake

Land Use and Building Information

Site area	22.5 acres
Gross building area	210,000 square feet
Gross leasable area (GLA)	201,572 square feet
Floor/area ratio	0.214
Levels	1
Total surface parking spaces	1,296

Land Use Plan

	Acres	Percent of Site
Buildings	5	22
Paved areas[1]	10	44
Landscaped areas	3	14
Dedicated space[2]	4.5	20
Total	22.5	100

Retail Tenant Information

	Number of Stores	Total GLA (square feet)
Food	1	31,067
Food service	10	30,458
Clothing and accessories	5	9,326
Shoes	1	1,195
Home furnishings	1	18,930
Hobby/special interest	2	27,818
Gifts/specialty	6	21,745
Personal services	2	2,667
Entertainment	2	58,336
Total	30	201,542

Major Tenants

	Square Feet
Club Disney	25,804
Bristol Farms	31,067
Cost Plus	18,930
Mann Theaters	32,562
Barnes & Noble	20,600

Length of Lease 5–25 years

Annual Rents $24–72 per square foot

Average Annual Sales $450 per square foot

Development Cost Information

Site acquisition cost	$12,465,786
Site improvement costs	$ 8,427,615
Construction costs	$10,553,178
Soft costs	$10,192,641
Total	$41,639,220

Financing Information

Permanent Loan

Massachusetts Mutual (debt)	$39,000,000
Equity investment	2,639,220

Construction Loan

Tokai Bank of California	$33,000,000

Development Schedule

8/1995	Planning started
8/1995	Leasing started
12/1995	Site purchased
1/1996	Approvals obtained
2/1996	Construction started
11/1996	Project opened

Developer

Caruso Affiliated Holdings
100 Wilshire Boulevard/14th Floor
Santa Monica, California 90401
310-458-0202

Architect/Planner

Altevers & Associates
8910 University Center Lane/Suite 250
San Diego, California 92122
619-534-9777

Landscape Architect

James Dean Group
573 Raquet Club Lane
Thousand Oaks, California 91360
805-454-0623

Lighting Specialist

Francis Krahe & Associates, Inc.
580 Broadway/Suite 100
Laguna Beach, California 92651
949-376-0744

Notes

[1] Surface parking and roads.

[2] Arroyo.

Sycamore Plaza at Kenwood

Cincinnati, Ohio

Sycamore Plaza at Kenwood is a 345,000-square-foot power center in Cincinnati. The $18.7 million project involved the "de-malling," redevelopment, and repositioning of devalued Kenwood Mall into an upscale power center. The result is a hybrid shopping center that successfully combines the design, amenities, and entertainment focus of a regional mall with the convenience and value offered by category-killer merchants.

Originally opened in 1966, Kenwood Mall was anchored by a Lazarus department store and furniture gallery. The mall performed well as the immediate neighborhood's population and average income grew. In 1988, however, Kenwood Mall lost its only anchor tenant to Kenwood Towne Center, an upscale super regional center directly across the street. Shortly thereafter, Kenwood Mall lost seven additional in-line tenants to the adjacent competition. With that, the mall experienced a seemingly irreversible decline in traffic, sales volume, and occupancy.

When Compass Retail assumed management of the original center in 1991, it undertook a thorough analysis to determine the site's highest and best use. Among the several alternative uses under consideration was the redevelopment of the center as an upscale super regional mall that would compete directly with Kenwood Towne Center. Compass Retail decided, however, that instead of trying to compete with the adjacent mall it would convert Kenwood into an upscale power center that would capitalize on the site's excellent location and demographics, a strong interest in the site from national and regional category-killer merchants, and the shift in consumer preferences value retailing.

Redevelopment of Kenwood Mall began in March 1994 and was completed in November of that year. The new Sycamore Plaza at Kenwood has been highly successful. The center was 80 percent preleased before ground breaking and is exceeding sales projections.

Site and Trade Area

The 31.1-acre, football-shaped site enjoys an excellent location in Cincinnati's northern suburbs in one of the fastest-growing and most desirable retail markets in the city. It is bordered by I-71 to the south and east and by two major arterials, Montgomery Road and Kenwood Road, to the north and west. More than 96,000 vehicles per day pass the site on I-71, and two I-71 interchanges are located just to the north and south of the center. The site slopes from north to south with a change in grade of approximately 19 feet.

Surrounding uses include a strip center to the west, an office building and a strip center to the north, and the 1.15 million-square-foot Kenwood Towne Center directly across Montgomery Road to the north. Surrounding this commercial hub is a mix of single- and multifamily residential neighborhoods. The center's trade area includes Cincinnati's most affluent suburbs. The trade area population of 617,748 accounts for 239,580 households with an average income of $43,700 and a median age of 39.

During development, Compass Retail worked closely with Sycamore township officials, who were then beginning a program to rename the Kenwood area Sycamore Center. The center's name, Sycamore Plaza at Kenwood, was selected to merge the 28-year-old center's original name with the new identity for the area. The center has had a favorable impact on the community, providing the additional critical mass needed to make the Sycamore Center district the premier shopping destination for the entire Cincinnati metropolitan area. In anticipation of increased traffic volume in the community, ERE Yarmouth, the successor to Compass Retail, is now working closely with township officials to improve transportation.

Renovation

The chief objectives of renovation were to provide an environment that would work for both big-box and some smaller tenants; to increase the center's critical mass and visibility (from both I-71 and the local community); to provide a strong, distinctive identity for the project; and to use as much of the existing building as possible, a primary factor in the project's economic feasibility. The renovation turned the structure inside out by eliminating the existing mall's interior common areas and reorienting the storefronts to the center's exterior. To give the center a more contemporary look, the exterior was reclad with brick and tan Dryvit plaster. An inviting, landscaped pedestrian plaza constructed at the center's main entrance to the west accommodates smaller tenants and restaurants and increases the center's visibility from Montgomery and Kenwood Roads. The center's opposite side, to the east, accommodates large space users and attracts shoppers from I-71.

To enhance the project's physical presence and create the image of an upscale power center, two atriums were added (a two-story atrium to the west and a three-story atrium to the east). The atriums feature lush interior landscaping, marble floors, and vaulted ceilings. They create a larger-scale presence for the individual stores and echo the design of a Cincinnati icon, Union Terminal (a 1930s train station that is now the Cincinnati Museum Center). The soaring east atrium provides a common entrance to

LAZARUS

Bookse

To create the image of an upscale power center, two atriums with marble floors and vaulted ceilings were added. A central elevator and escalators in the east atrium provide convenient access to the second and third floors.

Dick Loesch, CAM-TECH

The renovation increased the center's mass and visibility and created a strong image while using as much of the existing building as possible.

Dick Loesch, CAM-TECH

The east atrium provides a common entrance to four big-box stores. The facade of the atrium has a layered appearance, with the juxtaposition of solid and opaque planes providing an animated, billboard-scale exterior overlooking the interstate highway.

Dick Loesch, CAM-TECH

four big-box stores and offers excellent visibility for the center from I-71. The center's east facade has a layered appearance, with the juxtaposition of solid and opaque planes providing an animated, billboard-scale exterior overlooking the interstate highway. A central elevator in the east atrium and escalators in both atriums provide convenient access for shoppers to the second and third floors and increase the ease of shopping in the center's three-level core. Generous signage and dramatic night lighting increase the center's visibility from I-71.

Tenant Mix and Leasing

Strong interest in the site from national and regional category-killer tenants expedited leasing. The center is currently 100 percent leased and occupied. The center's tenant mix reflects the trade area's upscale demographics, with category-killer tenants ranging from 15,000 to 71,000 square feet; they include Dick's Sporting Goods, Barnes & Noble, Loehmann's, Old Navy, Staples, Linens'N

Things, and Toys "R" Us. These large tenants are complemented by a variety of smaller tenants, including several restaurants new to the Cincinnati market selected to offer a distinctive dining and entertainment experience. Five of the current tenants were previously located in Kenwood Mall when work began (Wilson's Paint, Staples, Firestone, Lenscrafters, and Lazarus Furniture). Since redevelopment, these tenants, some in relocated spaces, have all seen a significant increase in traffic and sales.

Leases are a mix of space leases and ground leases. Leases for more than half the large users and one of the outparcels were negotiated by using the tenants' lease forms, while those for the others were negotiated by using the landlord's form. Leases typically contain some restrictions on each party's use of its respective area, which required a careful balancing of interests. The center's hybrid nature (with both traditional mall and strip center tenants) resulted in extensive negotiations over the allocation of maintenance expenses. Because the project

With the lush interior land-scaping, marble floors, and vaulted ceilings, shoppers and many tenants expected all the typical mall amenities, such as public telephones, special events, and entertainment.

Escalators to the second floor highlight the center's vertical component and facilitate cross-shopping, an unexpected result of the hybrid design.

was a renovation, the landlord's and tenants' construction obligations also were a point of significant negotiation.

Experience Gained

- For today's time-poor, destination-oriented shopper, traditional enclosed malls do not always provide the desired retail choices. By providing discounted merchandise in highly specialized categories and a variety of restaurants in an upscale, attractive, contemporary environment, the center complements rather than competes with the adjacent super regional mall.
- In today's intensely competitive retail market, the conversion of a declining enclosed mall into a hybrid power center may offer a feasible alternative to regional mall owners who are unable or unwilling to commit the capital necessary to ensure the market dominance and long-term value of their centers as regional malls. While the project offers a blueprint for resurrecting a devalued retail property into a viable asset, de-malling

is not the solution for every ailing mall. Successful de-malling requires demand from power center tenants, an appropriate location, good trade area demographics, and the ability to undertake the project in an economical manner.
- Based on the project's mix of category-killer tenants, the center was expected to attract destination-oriented shoppers with minimal interest in cross-shopping. In reality, many shoppers at the center are cross-shopping, resulting in the need for additional signage and directories in each atrium.
- Given that retailers drive the success of a power center, it is critical to secure the right tenant mix and then to design the center in response to tenants' needs and requirements.
- When a power center includes an enclosed public space, shoppers and many tenants expect all the typical mall amenities, such as public telephones, special events, and entertainment. The project's hybrid nature

The existing mall's interior common areas were eliminated, and the storefronts were reoriented toward the center's exterior.

also has presented some unusual challenges in dealing with tenants. Traditional mall tenants located in the center expect the same level of service provided at their mall locations. For tenants who historically have occupied strip centers, allocation of maintenance expenses was an area of significant negotiation. The relatively expansive enclosed common areas in the center, as well as its focus on entertainment, created challenges. In addition, some of the center's tenants accustomed to locations in strip centers have failed to secure the proper approvals from management to conduct special events.

• The center requires more management than expected. In the original concept, a satellite manager was to be responsible for the center's management. The first few months of operation proved, however, that tenants expect an on-site manager who communicates with them regularly.

• The center's upscale design (with a number of mall amenities) and hybrid tenant mix facilitated the review and approval process with Sycamore township officials. The township was seeking an eye-catching, upscale center that would be consistent with the quality of the adjacent regional mall. The center's hybrid tenant mix with upscale design elements responds to the demographics of the trade area.

• It was decided to lease unfinished space to most tenants and to provide larger-than-normal tenant finish allowances. The strategy did not work as well as antic-

ipated; most tenants expected additional concessions at the time leases were negotiated because of the condition of the space. In retrospect, the developer should have provided a higher level of tenant finishes and a reduced tenant allowance.

Site plan before renovation.

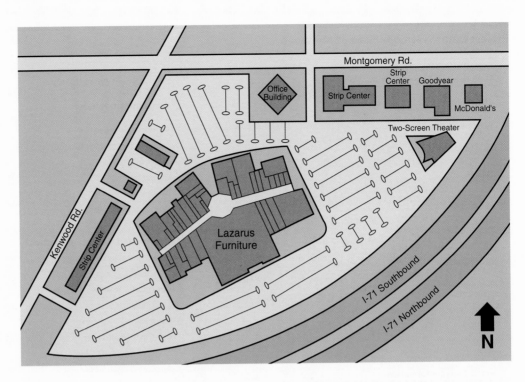

Site plan after renovation.

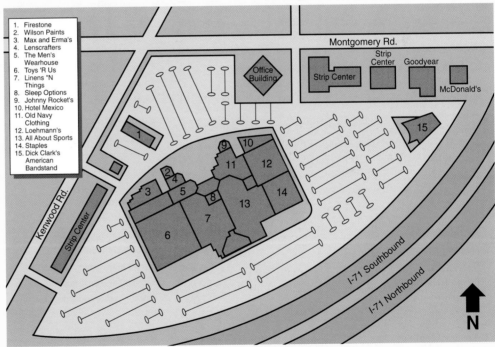

1. Firestone
2. Wilson Paints
3. Max and Erma's
4. Lenscrafters
5. The Men's Wearhouse
6. Toys 'R Us
7. Linens 'N Things
8. Sleep Options
9. Johnny Rocket's
10. Hotel Mexico
11. Old Navy Clothing
12. Loehmann's
13. All About Sports
14. Staples
15. Dick Clark's American Bandstand

Project Data: Sycamore Plaza at Kenwood

Land Use and Building Information

Site Area — 31.1 acres

Gross Building Area — 404,156 square feet

Gross Leasable Area (GLA) — 345,000 square feet

Levels

East side	3
West side	2

Parking (surface spaces) — 2,156

Land Use Plan

	Acres	Percent of Site
Buildings	6.4	21
Paved areas	22.7	73
Landscaped areas	2.0	6
Total	31.1	100

Retail Tenant Information

	Number of Stores	Percent of Total	Total GLA (square feet)	Percent of GLA
Food service	4	23.5	20,582	6
Clothing and accessories	3	17.6	43,529	13
Home furnishings	3	17.6	107,177	33
Building materials/hardware	1	5.9	2,200	1
Automotive	1	5.9	6,600	2
Hobby/special interest	1	5.9	41,684	13
Toys	1	5.9	46,000	14
Office supply	1	5.9	19,054	6
Books	1	5.9	35,000	11
Personal services	1	5.9	4,000	1
Total	17	100.0	325,826	100

Anchor Tenants

	Square Feet
Lazarus Furniture	69,491
Dick's Sporting Goods	41,684
Barnes & Noble	35,000
Linens'N Things	35,385
Toys "R" Us	46,000

Average Length of Lease — 10 years

Annual Rents — $7–30 per square foot

Average Annual Sales (1997) — $250 per square foot

Development Cost Information

Site Acquisition Cost — $12,656,035

Construction Costs

General requirements/conditions	$592,500
Site work	790,777
Concrete	828,745
Masonry	92,018
Woods and plastics	779,759
Metals	1,372,618
Thermal and moisture protection	294,675
Doors and windows	763,622
Finishes	1,323,438
Conveying systems	587,500
Mechanical	768,148
Electrical	454,450
Contractor contingency	174,186
General contractor fee	281,068
Approved change orders	1,062,814
Pending costs/value engineering	240,616
Interior landscaping/furniture	55,000
Testing and inspection	55,000
Site graphics	140,000
Project contingency	124,162
Property allocation	(200,000)
Total	$10,581,096

Soft Costs

Architecture/engineering	$720,000
Other consultants	7,200
Legal fees	50,000
Marketing/promotion	85,000
Reimbursables	130,000
Developer's fee	661,320
Project management fee	127,532
Broker's commission	135,250
Tenant allowances	5,537,902
Rebuild Lazarus finishes	324,079
Miscellaneous/predevelopment	367,431
Total	$8,145,714

Total Development Cost — $31,382,845

Annual Operating Expenses (1998)

Reimbursed Expenses

Common area maintenance costs	
Repairs and maintenance	$233,805
Cleaning	115,100
Utilities	92,400
Landscaping	33,500
Security	126,050
Miscellaneous	43,800
Administration	139,335
Total common area maintenance costs	$783,990

Real estate taxes	$456,000
Utility expenses	$462,020
Other reimbursed expenses	$20,940
Total reimbursed expenses	$1,722,950

Owner's Expenses

Management fees	$183,472
Bad debts	16,500
Professional fees	22,550
Marketing expenses	7,933
Owner's operating expenses	20,550
Miscellaneous expenses	3,750
Total owner's expenses	$254,755

Total Operating Expenses	$1,977,705

Development Schedule

1991	Acquisition of management contract
1991	Planning started
1992–1993	Approvals obtained
1992	Leasing started
3/1994	Construction started
11/1994	Project completed

Developer

ERE Yarmouth Retail, Inc.
5775 Peachtree Dunwoody Road/Suite 200-D
Atlanta, Georgia 30342
404-303-6100

Architect

Baxter Hodell Donnelly Preston, Inc.
3500 Red Bank Road
Cincinnati, Ohio 45227-4188
513-271-1634

Contractor

Danis Building and Construction Company
9918 Carver Road
Cincinnati, Ohio 45242
513-984-9696

Planning Consultant

R.B. Shirk Design Collaborative
Cincinnati, Ohio

The Waterside Shops

Pelican Bay, Florida

A specialty retail center designed and developed to accommodate a rapidly growing resort, retirement, and second-home community, Waterside Shops is the upscale retail component of the Pelican Bay master-planned community. Developed by a limited partnership of the Courtelis Company and the Westinghouse Communities of Naples (WCN), Waterside Shops comprises 47 retail boutiques and two anchor department stores. Located near Naples, Florida, the 250,000-square-foot, open-air mall features a central courtyard with an elaborate 350,000-gallon waterscape that creates an exotic atmosphere. Cascading waterfalls form a series of focal points amid an extensive array of interconnected ponds and lagoons. Covered walkways and expansive common areas make for an unusual, park-like shopping environment.

The Waterside development team faced several formidable challenges commonly encountered by today's retail developers, including regulatory limitations on gross leasable area, which significantly reduce the pool of potential department store anchors; stringent underwriting criteria requiring extensive preleasing with credit-worthy tenants; and the need to differentiate the product using innovative design.

Site and Development

Waterside Shops is located in Pelican Bay, a 2,104-acre master-planned community on Florida's Gulf Coast immediately north of Naples. Pelican Bay, which is approximately 85 percent complete, contains a mix of residential, recreational, commercial, and institutional uses. At completion (projected for 1999), the community will include approximately 8,600 residential units, 1.1 million square feet of office/commercial space, and 1,336 hotel rooms.

Waterside Shops is situated on a 28-acre lot on the southernmost corner of Pelican Bay, along U.S. Route 41 (the Tamiami Trail), a major transportation arterial. The small regional center was designed and developed to accommodate the Pelican Bay community while simultaneously capturing regional traffic flow.

As the master developer of Pelican Bay, WCN approached the Courtelis Company in 1986 about working together to emulate and enhance the upscale, open-air, waterscape mall design that Courtelis had implemented in the development of the Falls, a 450,000-square-foot center in Miami. After several months of negotiation, WCN and the Courtelis Company created a limited partnership for the development of Waterside Shops. The partnership secured an option on the parcel and acquired it from WCN in October 1987 for $5.6 million. (WCN

sold the parcel to the limited partnership in which it was a partner.)

Before the formation of the Waterside joint venture, WCN had secured regulatory approvals for the site and had established primary infrastructure improvements, reducing the partnership's upfront risk exposure. Regulatory entitlements were largely dictated by Florida's DRI (development of regional impact) process, which limited the site's retail/commercial buildout to 265,000 square feet of gross leasable area (GLA). Such limitations on GLA created a significant challenge to the Waterside partnership's development of a retail center with two department store anchors and a diverse tenant mix.

Tenants

Understanding the importance of securing anchor tenants, the Waterside development team approached Saks Fifth Avenue and Jacobson's department stores early during predevelopment. The developers targeted the department stores because of their willingness to occupy anchor spaces of under 50,000 square feet as well as their ability to cater to the targeted upscale market. Jacobson's (currently Waterside's larger anchor) originally was not interested in the site. Saks Fifth Avenue, on the other hand, was interested in both the Naples marketplace and the site's physical attributes, and asked the developers to retain a market analyst chosen by Saks. Based on the results of the marketing study, Saks decided to occupy one of Waterside's anchor stores. Two weeks after that decision, however, the project encountered a major setback when the retailer's parent company became the target of a hostile takeover attempt. Saks put the Waterside project on hold for approximately two years until ownership of the retail chain was transferred. Throughout this two-year transition period, the Waterside development team kept in touch with the retailer's top decision makers, who continued to remain interested in the site.

Ultimately, in August 1990, the developers successfully secured a prelease agreement with Saks. Soon after signing a letter of intent with Saks, the developers again contacted Jacobson's, which agreed to open a store in the project. The two-year delay in Waterside's development perhaps worked to the developers' advantage, allowing the Naples market to further mature.

As a small upscale regional center, Waterside has a mix of tenants, including an assortment of national chains—for example, Polo/Ralph Lauren, Ann Taylor, the Banana Republic, the Gap, Williams Sonoma, and the California Pizza Kitchen—and a variety of local boutiques, giving

An elegant retail environment surrounding an elaborate waterscape has enabled the Waterside Shops to achieve significant differentiation in the market.

the property a familiar retail setting as well as a Gulf Coast flavor. The average tenant improvement allowance for Waterside retailers was approximately $60.00 per square foot.

Financing

The Waterside development partnership was structured as a limited partnership, with the Courtelis Company acting as general partner and initially securing a 65 percent interest in the project, and WCN retaining a 35 percent interest.

With ground breaking in November 1991, fast-track construction was necessary to open the center in one year and enable Waterside to capture the market's upswing during the peak shopping season. As a direct result of those time constraints, construction initiatives began before construction financing was secured. The Waterside partnership, however, was able to use equity resources and a $5 million bridge loan provided by WCN to finance Waterside's initial construction. As compensation for originating the bridge loan, WCN received a greater interest in the Waterside partnership, bringing its limited partnership interest to 40 percent. WCN also received interest on the loan.

In July 1992, five months before the project's opening, the partnership closed on a $30 million, five-year construction and miniperm loan originated by the Canadian Imperial Bank of Commerce. To close and draw upon the loan, however, Waterside's developers were required

to satisfy the lender's stringent prelease stipulations, including 105 percent debt service coverage with qualified leases. The lender's underwriting criteria also established strict guidelines for the percentage of national tenants as well as for lease terms and contingencies. Waterside appears to have met the lender's criteria: with occupancy rates exceeding 90 percent, Waterside's gross sales were approximately $66.2 million in 1994.

Design and Construction

Waterside's site planning, tenant mix, and common area walkways were designed largely around the center's distinctive waterscape. Situated in the mall's central courtyard, the series of interconnected waterfalls and extensively landscaped lagoons create a sense of discovery. The development team was able to improve upon previous mall designs with waterscapes by reducing the size of the water feature and intensifying landscaping and enhancing the level of construction finishes. By decreasing the size of the waterscape, the design team was able to reduce the distance between storefronts, enhancing circulation patterns as well as the project's sense of place.

The development team adopted a Mediterranean style of architecture that integrates Waterside with the Pelican Bay community. The project's retail structures are typical concrete block buildings with stucco walls and steel-frame roofs. A high level of construction finishes, including barrel-tile roofs, stone walkways and columns, and cov-

The Mediterranean architectural design helps to integrate Waterside Shops into the context of the Pelican Bay planned community.

Ed Chappell

ered breezeways with brass-accented mahogany railings, accentuate the casual but elegant design.

Given the rectangular shape of the site, designers devised a circular parking configuration similar to that of a conventional regional mall. The configuration allowed the design team to create seven mall entrances, significantly increasing access for pedestrians as well as air circulation throughout the mall. Ceiling fans above the walkways also enhance airflow.

AERIALVENTURES Incorporated

The open-air mall design of Waterside Shops, located at the southernmost corner of the Pelican Bay planned community, is well suited for the rapidly expanding resort, second-home, and retirement community.

Waterside is home to Saks Fifth Avenue's prototype resort-format store. Significantly smaller than conventional Saks stores, the single-story, 31,671-square-foot store has selected merchandise that targets the upscale resort community market. The project also includes a 10,000-square-foot U.S. Trust Bank and a 23,328-square-foot freestanding Barnes & Noble bookstore on two separate one-acre outparcels.

Experienced Gained
- An open-air waterscape can provide a resort community with a distinctive retail product, but if the project does not incorporate the proper tenant mix, the waterscape will serve only as a tourist attraction and will not successfully capture the increasing number of primary residents in the resort community.
- Although disproportionate numbers of common area walkways and extensive landscaping significantly increased the project's construction costs, Waterside's exotic, parklike setting has allowed the project to achieve considerable differentiation in the market.
- A limited number of anchor department stores would consider occupying a store of under 47,000 square feet. Within a resort/second-home community, however, opportunities exist for securing upscale anchor tenants interested in occupying smaller, boutique-like stores.

Site planning, common area walkways, and the tenant mix at Waterside Shops were largely designed around the specialty center's waterscape, in which cascading waterfalls form a series of focal points amid an extensive array of interconnected ponds and lagoons.

Ed Chappell

The project's casual but elegant design is accentuated by a high level of construction finishes, including stone walkways and columns and brass-accented mahogany railings.

Ed Chappell

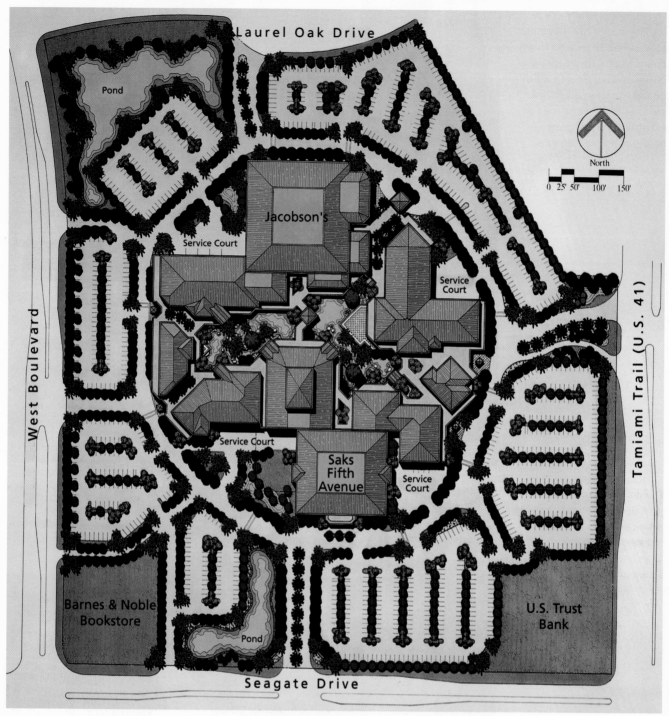

Laurel Oak Drive

Pond

North

0 25' 50'   100'   150'

Jacobson's

Service Court

Service Court

West Boulevard

Service Court

Saks Fifth Avenue

Service Court

Tamiami Trail (U.S. 41)

Barnes & Noble Bookstore

Pond

U.S. Trust Bank

Seagate Drive

Site plan.

Project Data: The Waterside Shops

Land Use and Building Information

Site area	26.3 acres
Gross leasable area (GLA)	234,670 square feet
Levels	1
Total parking spaces	1,167

Land Use Plan

	Acres	Percent of Site
Buildings	202,600	17.7
Paved areas[1]	513,990	44.8
Landscaped areas	430,870	37.5
Total	1,147,460	100.0

Retail Tenant Information

	Number of Stores	Total GLA (square feet)
General merchandise	2	77,670
Food service	5	14,702
Clothing and accessories	21	75,051
Shoes	2	2,310
Home furnishings	2	6,678
Music	1	2,370
Gifts/specialty	7	9,797
Jewelry	1	1,242
Bookstore	1	23,973
Personal services	3	2,488
Financial	1	10,000
Offices (other than financial)	1	1,652
Vacant	1	2,175
Other	2	4,562
Total	50	234,670

Major Tenants

	Square Feet
Saks Fifth Avenue	31,671
Jacobson's	45,670
U.S. Trust	10,000
Barnes & Noble	23,973
The Gap	11,670
The Limited	7,396
Banana Republic	6,627

Development Cost Information

Site Acquisition Cost	**$5,630,625**

Site Improvement Costs (on and off site)

Excavation/grading	$250,000
Sewer/water/drainage	450,000
Paving/curbs/sidewalks	871,000
Landscaping/irrigation	667,000
Site lighting	500,000
Waterscape	530,000
Total	$3,268,000

Construction Costs

Specialty tenants, shell	$6,010,000
Saks Fifth Avenue	3,000,000
Jacobson's	3,721,000
Impact fees	990,000
Tenant improvements	7,777,000
Other	300,000
Total	$21,798,000

Soft Costs

Architecture/engineering	$600,000
Project leasing	641,000
Marketing	175,000
Taxes/insurance	150,000
Construction interest and fees	1,180,000
Other	250,000
Total	$2,996,000

Total Development Cost	**$33,692,625**

Development Schedule

10/1987	Site purchased
1/1991	Planning started
11/1991	Approvals obtained
11/1991	Construction started
8/1990	Leasing started
11/1992	Project opened

Developers

Courtelis Company
701 Brickell Avenue/Suite 1400
Miami, Florida 33131
305-379-8467

WCI Communities Limited Partnership
(formerly Westinghouse Communities of Naples)
801 Laurel Oak Drive/Suite 500
Naples, Florida 33961
941-597-6061

Architect/Planner

Dorsky Hodges & Partners, Inc.
2700 Cypress Creek Road
Fort Lauderdale, Florida 33309
305-975-8138

Note
[1] Surface parking and roads.

The Westchester

White Plains, New York

The Westchester is a 2.5 million-square-foot regional mall on a tight infill site in downtown White Plains, New York. Anchored by a 200,000-square-foot Nordstrom and a renovated 143,000-square-foot Neiman Marcus, the $250 million multilevel center targets an affluent, well-educated market. The project includes nearly 150 upscale tenants (among them Abercrombie & Fitch, Tiffany, Ann Taylor, FAO Schwarz, Crate & Barrel, and Williams Sonoma); a 500-seat food court; and 3,200 parking spaces in a ten-level parking deck and three levels of underground parking.

Extensive market research during planning helped ensure that the center would satisfy the needs of the affluent, sophisticated shoppers in its trade area. The Westchester's design, finishes, tenant mix, and services were carefully orchestrated to provide customers with a comfortable, memorable shopping experience. The mall features upscale amenities including two valet parking stations, a concierge, carpeted walkways in the upper levels, an extensive sculpture collection, historic exhibits, 14-foot-high Doric columns, marble flooring and wall facings, brass railings, and an abundance of skylights. Since its opening in March 1995, the center has averaged sales of $400 per square foot.

The Westchester also is playing a key role in the revitalization of downtown White Plains as a retail center for Westchester County. The city boasted the first suburban department store in the United States after B. Altman & Company opened there in 1930, and over the years Macy's, a new Altman's, Saks Fifth Avenue, Bloomingdale's, and several other department stores followed. But by the 1990s competition from other suburban centers and changes in the retail industry were contributing to an overall decline in White Plains's status as a retail center. With the opening of the Westchester, the city, county, and state are benefiting from increased tax revenues and White Plains has once again become a shopping destination for the area.

Site and Trade Area

Located at the intersection of Bloomingdale Road and Westchester Avenue at the edge of downtown White Plains, the site benefits from excellent access. It is adjacent to an interchange at I-287 (the Cross Westchester Expressway) and is within three miles of many other highways, including I-684, I-95, and the New York thruway. I-287 is the major east/west highway crossing Westchester County, and virtually all major roads feed into it.

The site's proximity to this extensive network of highways and its character and tenant mix have allowed it to draw from an unusually large trade area. It attracts shoppers not only from southern Westchester County and southwestern Fairfield County in Connecticut, but also from northern Westchester and Putnam counties to the north, Rockland and Bergen counties to the west, and New York City to the south. Within its primary trade area resides a population of approximately 600,000 with an average annual household income of nearly $100,000. In addition to its high household income, the trade area contains an unusually high percentage of single-income households (nearly 30 percent) and an unusually low amount of GLA per person (roughly 2.7 square feet). With its excellent demographics and accessibility, the site is considered one of the premier retail locations in the Northeast.

The site is located across the street from a freestanding Saks Fifth Avenue and several blocks from a freestanding Bloomingdale's. Other nearby retail uses include the Westchester Pavilion (a 173,000-square-foot power center), the Galleria (an 880,000-square-foot regional mall anchored by JCPenney and Sterns), a freestanding Macy's, and a freestanding Sears. Other nearby land uses include a Holiday Inn Crowne Plaza, office buildings housing more than 250,000 office workers in downtown White Plains, multifamily residential buildings to the north, and the New York Hospital/Cornell Medical Center to the east.

The site's natural features and configuration presented several challenges during design and construction. The northwest corner of the site is solid bedrock and drops 55 feet in grade, while the eastern portion of the site is only four feet above the water table. In addition, the 12.1-acre L-shaped site was unusually small for the development of a mall the size of the Westchester.

Development and Financing

The project was initiated in 1989 during the real estate recession, making it unusually challenging to get the project started and to maintain momentum. As a result of the unprecedented credit crisis, it took 14 months to move from marketing the project to finally closing the construction loan in 1992. Financing from U.S. banks was unavailable. Four foreign banks (Bank of Montreal, Hypo Bank, Crédit Lyonnaise, and Sumitomo Bank) provided the $160 million construction loan, and $100 million in equity from the owners was required. In addition, the lenders required that all 40 trade unions to be involved in the project accept a job agreement stipulating that no strikes or work stoppages would occur. Finally,

Targeting an affluent, sophisticated market through its amenities and mix of stores, the Westchester is playing a key role in the revitalization of White Plains, New York.

the lenders required that at least 125,000 square feet be preleased. CIGNA provided permanent financing.

Land assembly was complex. Six parcels and air rights were acquired; two of the parcels had existing freestanding department stores (Neiman Marcus and B. Altman), each with structured parking. A plan was prepared that was predicated on bringing in Nordstrom as an anchor for the mall while also using the two freestanding department stores as anchors. In 1989, Nordstrom signed a letter of intent for a 200,000-square-foot store, and site planning and predevelopment began. During the project's predevelopment phase, however, the B. Altman chain went bankrupt, leaving the project with only two anchors.

A second plan was drawn up extending the mall to include an additional parcel of land that would connect it to downtown White Plains. This elongated L-shaped plan involved purchasing a city parking lot and a small piece of land that was included in an estate, as well as vacating a portion of a city street. The absence of a third anchor tenant required a creative solution—the addition of a specialty retail pod at the top end of the L (consisting of specialty retail tenants requiring unusually large stores and a food court that would in effect serve as a third anchor), with Nordstrom at the heel of the L and Neiman Marcus at the toe.

The site, which had been zoned for freestanding retail, required rezoning; the process was complicated by an election that changed the composition of the city's common council. The new council required approval of an environmental impact statement in addition to rezoning and site plan approval. The O'Connor Group, the developer, decided to pursue all approvals at the same time instead of sequentially.

With approvals from the city in hand, the developer decided to begin preliminary site work, spending approximately $2 million even though project financing had not yet been secured. An elaborate phasing scheme was required to allow the existing Neiman Marcus to remain open for business and to make certain that site work could be reversed if the financing were not approved. Structural modifications were made to the B. Altman garage to allow part of it to be used by Neiman Marcus customers. Once this work was done, the Neiman Marcus garage was demolished so that excavation could begin.

Early in 1993, as soon as construction financing had been secured, the first element of the mall was constructed—the ten-level precast concrete parking garage. Excavation for the garage required a number of well points and a pumping station to keep the site dry, as the water table was only four feet below the surface. Upon completion of the new parking structure, the B. Altman garage was demolished, and construction of the rest of the mall began during the Christmas season of 1993 as soon as the certificate of occupancy for the new garage was issued.

Located on an infill site at the edge of downtown, the project benefits from excellent access and a larger-than-normal trade area.

Planning and Design

Planning and design were also challenging: the mall required placing a large amount of retail space on a compact, steep, L-shaped site; integrating the mall with the adjacent downtown; providing excellent vehicular and pedestrian access to the mall; providing 3,200 parking spaces on site in a visually unobtrusive manner; and creating an upscale ambience for shoppers.

The mall's L-shaped design features three retail levels on one leg of the L and two levels on the other. The food court/specialty retail pod was placed on the top level at the end of the two-level leg, abutting White Plains's central business district and convenient for downtown office workers.

The project involved major improvements to existing roads, which were undertaken by the city and the county. Bloomingdale Road (to the east of the site) was realigned to improve access to and from I-287, to soften the mall's exterior design by allowing an attractive landscaped area to be created, and to allow for greater capacity at one of the key entrances to the parking garage. Other road improvements included the widening and realignment of the I-287 entrance/exit ramps so that they would feed directly into the main parking garage, the widening of Westchester Avenue (to the north of the site), the relocation and widening of Paulding Street (which runs through the center of the site), and improvements to the intersection at the southeast corner of the site (near the existing Neiman Marcus). The mall had to be built over

the widened Paulding Street. Because the city would not allow columns in the median, a bridge configuration was designed with trusses hanging from the roof.

Parking was provided in a ten-level tower and a three-level underground garage. The tower has a precast concrete exterior and provides two levels of parking at each retail level; a double helix was used to move vehicles in and out. Conveniently located elevators, escalators, and stairs provide access for shoppers to and from the mall. Mall finishes were carried through to elevators, escalators, stairs, and lobbies of the parking garage. The garage is painted white, is well lighted, and has excellent signage to direct shoppers. The mall's two valet parking areas, which shoppers use often, convey the ambience of a first-class hotel.

The mall's exterior is red brick with extensive precast concrete neoclassical detailing, including arched pedestrian and vehicular entrances. A key goal in the exterior design was to minimize the project's massiveness by using a stepped configuration. The building's eastern wall along Bloomingdale Road has been set back and curved; its appearance is also softened by extensive exterior landscaping. At the westernmost end of the mall (near the food court), a pedestrian entrance facilitates access by downtown office workers and nearby residents. Display windows and awnings also help to integrate the project with the surrounding streetscape.

The mall's interior emphasizes the neoclassical motif with 14-foot-high Doric columns. Marble floors are used in the first level, carpeted floors on the upper. The carpet, in earth tones, burgundy, and green, helps to convey the ambience of a hotel. A terrazzo floor was installed in the food court. Other features of the interior design include brass railings, marble fountains, attractive landscaping, and an extensive sculpture collection. The mall features an abundance of skylights, including three domes that flood the interior with natural light. The liberal use of vaulted ceilings further enhances the mall's open, airy feeling. Providing outstanding vertical access was a top priority. The Westchester has ten sets of escalators, three staircases, and eight elevators. Several elements of local historical interest also were incorporated in the mall, including a permanent exhibit about the old New York, Westchester & Boston Railroad terminal (which occupied the B. Altman site until 1937) and a marble fountain, hand carved in 1905, that once graced the B. Altman store in Manhattan.

Tenant Mix

The project includes an unusually broad, distinctive tenant mix that reflects the affluent demographics of the trade area. In addition to such popular names as the Gap and Gap Kids, Warner Bros., Abercrombie & Fitch, Brooks Brothers, and the Sharper Image, the Westchester contains many tenants not typically found in malls—Tiffany's, Armani Exchange, Hanna Andersson, Oilily, the Franklin Mint, Timberland, and Eileen Fisher. Many stores are larger than normal, particularly in the specialty retail/

food court pod; for example, the FAO Schwarz store (which contains a complete "Barbie" shop) is 15,000 square feet, and the two-story Crate & Barrel is 33,000 square feet. The mall also contains an unusually high percentage of tenants offering women's, men's, and children's apparel and shoes.

Marketing and Management

The Westchester benefited considerably from an aggressive public relations program during development. The project received extensive media coverage before and during its grand opening, including coverage by the major television networks, local newspapers, and the *New York Times*. The O'Connor Group and the Historic Hudson Valley Foundation cohosted an elaborate grand opening party. All proceeds from the charge of $75.00 per person went to the foundation. The project's newspaper advertisements feature simple, elegant design, and some direct-mail promotion has been used. Special events have included evening jazz concerts and a back-to-school week with daily learning demonstrations. The mall's marketing fund has a budget of just under $1 million, with mall tenants contributing approximately $2.00 per square foot.

A mission statement prepared for the Westchester before it opened serves as the cornerstone of the center's management. Outside firms, whose staffs must understand and work toward the center's mission, are used for security, garage operations, and housekeeping. The O'Connor Group runs a one-week training seminar for

Interior design elements create an attractive, upscale ambience. A part of the Westchester's extensive sculpture collection—"Horses at Play"—enhances an interior court.

The mall's interior features clerestories, skylights, vaulted ceilings, and carpeted floors on the upper levels.

Pedestrian-only entrances, display windows, and awnings help to integrate the project with the surrounding streetscape.

contractors' employees to make certain that the quality of their work will be consistent with and reinforce the mission statement. The O'Connor Group has a nine-person in-house management staff to manage the outside contractors and to work with tenants. Quarterly meetings are held with all store managers, as well as with tenants in smaller groups by tenant category.

Experience Gained
- Although the New York City area is notorious for its difficult trade unions, the developer encountered no problems with union members, which can be attributed to a great extent to the upscale character of the project and to a concerted effort by the developer to get union members excited about the project's quality and distinctiveness. By taking pride of ownership in the project, union members were motivated to do quality work and to complete the job on schedule.

- A specialty retail/food court pod can be used successfully as a third anchor in a regional mall. When the Westchester's third anchor tenant was lost, planners were concerned that the specialty retail/food court concept with several large users might not be viable. In reality, the concept has been very successful, proving to be the easiest section of the mall to lease.
- It can be difficult to attract sit-down, white-tablecloth restaurants to a mall, even if the mall has a reputation as a one-of-a-kind, upscale center.
- The decision to use carpet on the mall's upper levels has worked well. Designed by the architect, the carpeting has helped to convey the desired ambience for the project and offers the advantages of being quieter than marble floors, safer for children, and easy to replace so that the mall can be given a fresh look in a few years. The one disadvantage is that additional light-

The Westchester's exterior is red brick with extensive precast concrete neoclassical detailing. A stepped configuration relieves the project's mass.

Placing the food court and specialty retail tenants requiring large stores, such as Crate & Barrel and FAO Schwarz, at one end of the mall served as a creative solution to the loss of a third anchor.

ing may be needed, as carpet absorbs light instead of reflecting it.

- A project of this complexity requires problem solving and hands-on management, particularly in the few months before opening.
- In a jurisdiction that has very detailed, rigidly enforced codes, it is advisable to bring in a tenant coordinator to work with the local jurisdiction and with tenants' architects and contractors to minimize problems with code compliance.
- To expedite the review and approval of tenants' plans by the city, the developer offered to pay for any overtime that the city's plan review staff had to work. The city accepted the offer, which helped to complete the project on schedule.
- By continuing to emphasize the project's financial benefits to the city, the developer eventually was able to convince the city to accept responsibility for needed road improvements.

- The successful use of outside contractors for mall management requires enlightened leadership daily from the in-house mall management team. Whenever possible, it is best to hire contractors who have a presence in the local market.

First-level plan.

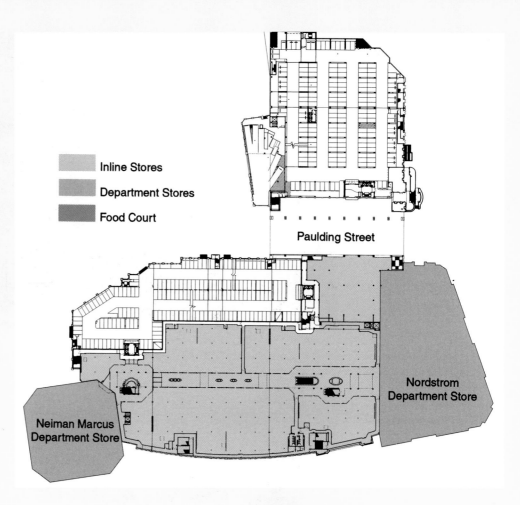

Inline Stores

Department Stores

Food Court

Paulding Street

Nordstrom
Department Store

Neiman Marcus
Department Store

Third-level plan.

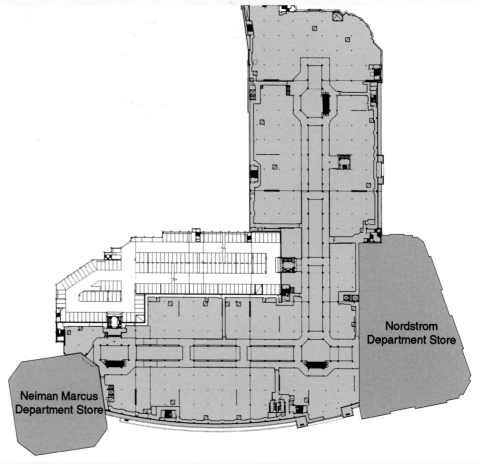

Nordstrom
Department Store

Neiman Marcus
Department Store

Second-level plan.

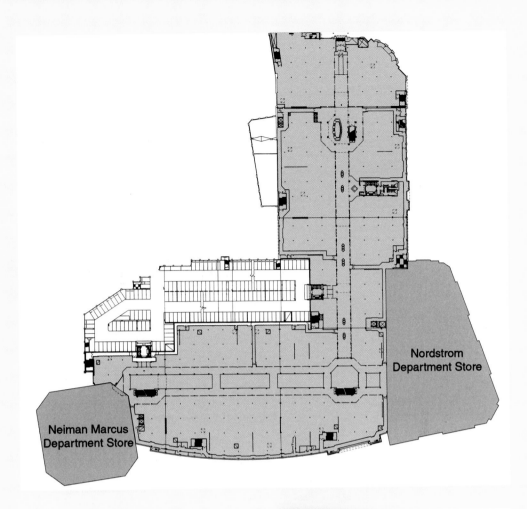

Fourth-level plan.

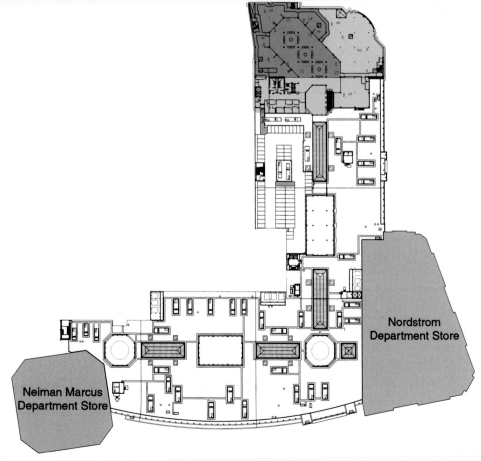

Project Data: The Westchester

Land Use and Building Information

Site area	12.1 acres
Gross building area[1]	2,460,000 square feet
Gross leasable area (GLA)	829,000 square feet
Floor/area ratio	1.9
Parking (structured spaces)	3,200

Land Use Plan

	Acres	Percent of Site
Buildings	10.0	83
Parking structures	1.4	11
Landscaped areas	0.7	6
Total	12.1	100

Retail Tenant Information

	Number of Stores	Percent of Total	Total GLA (square feet)	Percent of GLA
Women's apparel	28	20.0	101,630	23.1
Men's apparel	8	5.7	35,716	8.1
Family/children's apparel	18	12.8	69,337	15.8
Shoes	13	9.2	22,336	5.1
Home furnishings	8	5.7	60,845	13.9
Home entertainment/ electronic	3	2.1	15,454	3.5
Jewelry	4	2.8	9,148	2.1
Miscellaneous/specialty	32	22.7	97,465	22.2
Fast-food restaurants	17	12.0	18,581	4.2
Services	10	7.0	8,805	2.0
Total	141	100.0	439,317	100.0

Anchor Tenants

	Square Feet
Neiman Marcus	143,000
Nordstrom	200,000

Average Length of Lease 5–15 years

Typical Lease Terms Base rent plus percentage rent and charges for common area maintenance, real estate taxes, marketing, HVAC

Annual Rents $35–100 per square foot

Average Annual Sales $400 per square foot

Development Cost Information

Site Acquisition Cost	$49,100,000

Site Improvement Costs

Demolition and site preparation	$4,150,000
Excavation and grading	6,400,000
Sewer, water, and drainage	5,900,000
Sidewalks, curbs, and paving	1,450,000
Landscaping and irrigation	400,000
General conditions and fees	4,300,000
Total	$22,600,000

Construction Costs

Superstructure	$32,125,000
Parking structure	32,100,000
HVAC	5,900,000
Electrical	10,350,000
Plumbing and sprinklers	4,675,000
Vertical transportation	2,975,000
Finishes	18,300,000
Graphics and specialties	2,025,000
Tenant improvements	27,750,000
General conditions and fees	11,650,000
Total	$147,850,000

Soft Costs

Architecture/engineering	$8,900,000
Project management	2,550,000
Marketing	400,000
Legal/accounting	6,650,000
Taxes and insurance	4,000,000
Title insurance and fees	750,000
Construction interest and fees	6,650,000
Total	$29,900,000

Total Development Cost	$249,450,000

Note

[1] Including 1.4 million square feet of structured parking.

Annual Operating Expenses

Taxes	$4,300,000
Insurance	300,000
Services (garage expenses)	840,000
Maintenance	155,000
Janitorial	620,000
Utilities	2,400,000
Legal	75,000
Management (fees/salaries)	2,100,000
Miscellaneous	600,000
Marketing	1,000,000
Total	$12,390,000

Development Schedule

12/1992	Site purchased
4/1989	Planning started
8/1991	Approvals obtained
1/1993	Construction started
6/1991	Leasing started
3/1995	Project opened

Developer

The O'Connor Group
40 West 57th Street
New York, New York 10019
212-307-0404

Architect

RTKL Associates, Inc.
2828 Routh Street/Suite 200
Dallas, Texas 75201
214-871-8877

Construction Manager

The Whiting-Turner Contracting Company
4 Armstrong Road
Shelton, Connecticut 06484
203-926-9200

8. Future Directions

Innovation in the shopping center industry has been continuous and pervasive since this form of development was introduced to this country in the early 20th century. As a society, we often seem to measure our progress by the amount and quality of change we experience, and the retailing world reflects this approach in spades. In fact, changes in retailing are accelerating—not only as new ideas arise but also, and perhaps more important, as old ideas are revived and adapted to modern social, economic, and demographic trends.

Today, shopping center owners and developers must be more creative, more nimble, and more customer savvy than ever before to provide and maintain the type of shopping environment that consumers want. The necessities reflect not only a heightened competitive environment but also an environment that constantly demands new forms of shopping centers, new types of tenants, new retail formats, new shopping environments, new experiences for customers, new locations, and new ways of linking shopping centers with the broader communities around them. It is no longer enough simply to identify the best location with the highest visibility and access; the build-it-and-they-will-come approach no longer works.

Taichung, a proposed mixed-use retail development in Taichung, Taiwan, includes a shopping center that is designed along a serpentine outdoor pedestrian way. It will be lined with retail stores, entertainment venues, and restaurants in the midst of a dense high-rise commercial and residential environment.

Although this simple strategy worked well in underserved suburban markets as the shopping center industry matured from the 1950s until the 1990s, it will work no longer. In the new millennium, remaking existing centers to create a stimulating and entertaining environment that people want to be part of and exploiting niche markets by building highly focused new centers targeted to emerging market segments will be the keys to success.

Although retail development during the next ten years will continue to evolve in unexpected ways, major trends are increasingly apparent that will shape its future face. These trends reflect changes in demographics, consumers' preferences, real estate development practices, and technology. Regardless of where these trends take us, however, it must be clearly recognized that retail development is and always will be a business venture, and so its future direction will ultimately be defined by its profitability.

Both earlier editions of *Shopping Center Development Handbook* (1977 and 1985) focused on two trends: the importance of renovation and expansion and the movement toward new downtown shopping centers. The 1977 edition also predicted the difficulty of getting financing, the reduced opportunities to develop shopping centers in general, and the increasing share of shopping center business that smaller regional centers would attain. The 1985 handbook, on the other hand, predicted an increase in mixed-use development, increasing segmentation of shopping center types, and more financing options.

To some extent, the perceived trends have materialized; in other ways, however, the crystal ball was foggy. Both editions were correct that renovation and expansion of existing centers would be an important trend, but it was a safe prediction because as a general rule, shopping centers need to be updated every five to ten years to remain competitive. This trend continues today, and it is an even more important phenomenon than ever before.

The prediction that development of downtown shopping centers would be a major growth industry proved to be more wishful thinking than based on reality. While downtown retail success stories continue to appear—the latest being MacArthur Center, a new regional mall opened in April 1999 by the Taubman Company in downtown Norfolk, Virginia—only a limited number of downtown shopping centers have opened compared with the vast number of suburban centers opened since 1977. Nevertheless, new shopping centers in some cities have

undeniably played key roles in their ongoing downtown redevelopment strategies, including Circle Centre in Indianapolis, Arizona Center in Phoenix, the Pavilions in Denver, Union Station and Georgetown Park in Washington, D.C., the Galleria and Harbor Place in Baltimore, and the granddaddy of them all, Faneuil Hall Marketplace in Boston.

In some cases, however, downtown centers that opened to great fanfare in the 1980s have since been buffeted by cyclical economic trends that have forced a downscaling of their original concepts and a scramble to find new concepts that will work in today's marketplace—for example, St. Louis Center in Missouri, the Gallery at Market East in Philadelphia, and the Shops at the Old Post Office Pavilion and National Place in Washington, D.C. As described later in this chapter, the development of entertainment venues is one of the concepts proving to be remarkably successful in reinvigorating the downtown retail environment.

Jockey Plaza, a retail "village" being developed in São Paulo, Brazil, will include an outdoor Main Street environment. The development of this center will revitalize what was once one of Brazil's most prominent equestrian racetracks and will include a megaplex, a 1,000-seat food court, themed restaurants, and a bowling alley.

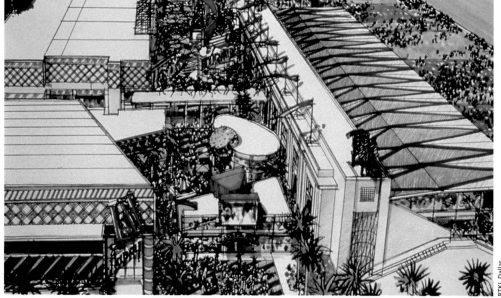

One of the hottest topics in the real estate industry today is the concept of merging entertainment with retail development. Whether we call this phenomenon urban entertainment centers, destination retail projects, entertainment/retail projects, or location-based entertainment, it's a business that everyone—from retail real estate owners and developers to entertainment providers—wants to be in.

Not everyone, however, understands the full range of opportunities embodied in this new development trend. Many in the industry want to characterize these new development products in terms of something familiar. Real estate developers look for the next anchor department store, while entertainment providers seek the next-generation theme park. But this narrow definition will not suffice. The new development trend of entertainment/retail projects encompasses a wide variety of components and product types.

Entertainment development and retail operations have been on a converging course for a number of years for several important reasons. On the retail development side, the industry is more competitive than ever. Traditional shopping centers are being affected by new development trends such as power centers, big boxes, and factory outlets, as well as changes in the product distribution system, including catalog sales, home shopping, and, in the future, interactive television.

From the perspective of the entertainment provider, the dominance of the major media companies has led to the search for new products to fully exploit the value of their intellectual properties and brand identities. In addition, technology is forcing change by creating ever smaller attractions in the form of motion-based simulator rides, virtual-reality attractions, and the like. These new technologies make it possible to create theme park–caliber experiences in a compact, relatively inexpensive form based on software.

In the entertainment/retail mix, retailing looks to entertainment components to enhance and extend the shopping experience and the drawing power of a center, while entertainment needs the retail environment to provide new product outlets and to justify urban land values. In some cases, these new combinations create new urban destinations, while in others, the objective will be to enhance or differentiate an existing retail center.

This discussion outlines a range of entertainment/retail components and project types. Some of them are familiar, others new. Because this new development trend is dynamic, we can expect to see these components and projects evolve dramatically over the next several years.

Cinema Complexes

Cinema complexes typically are a key component of entertainment/retail projects. They attract a large audience with a desirable demographic profile that is also interested in other activities at the center, including shopping and eating. The newest version of the cinema, which is creating the most interest in the development community today, is the category killer cinema complex. These complexes can total up to 24 screens and 100,000 square feet of space.

Themed Restaurants

Themed restaurants, a business that has grown dramatically in recent years, also can be a major component of entertainment/retail centers. Most observers trace the origin of the business to the founding of the Hard Rock Cafe in London in 1971. Themed restaurants provide high business volumes, brand name appeal, and destination drawing power. Major brand name identities include Hard Rock Cafe and Planet Hollywood; newer concepts include Hotel Discovery and NASCAR Cafe.

Entertainment-Oriented Retailers

The retail component in new urban entertainment centers usually incorporates a mix of major retailers and smaller specialty shops. Major retailers considered top candidates for new centers include brand name merchandisers and entertainment-oriented stores. Brand name retailing encompasses manufacturers and owners of powerful brand name licenses that have developed their own stores to sell directly and to showcase their entire product line. Key examples include Nike Town, Disney Stores, and Warner Bros. Studio Stores. Major entertainment-oriented retailers that fit well the customer profile for these types of centers include major music stores such as Virgin Records megastores and HMV, and large bookstores such as Barnes & Noble and Borders.

Family Entertainment Centers

Adapting traditional family entertainment centers to shopping centers is a growing development trend throughout the United States and overseas. Indoor centers in shopping environments can range from 20,000 to 100,000 square feet. They include typical components such as carousels (for example, Carousel Mall in San Bernardino, California), amusement rides, miniature golf, and games. Because many of the activities are participatory, they are highly repeatable, and they appeal directly to families with young children, a target market prized by regional mall operators.

While family entertainment centers as part of regional shopping centers have been accepted in the marketplace, they generally have achieved only modest economic success. They are often viewed as a form of anchor tenant for a shopping center, however, and as such add value to the center by providing the ambience of entertainment, enhancing overall drawing power, increasing the potential of repeat visits, and extending the visitor's length of stay at the center.

High-Tech Entertainment Centers

Urban centers featuring arcades and high-tech attractions have become important development opportunities in recent years, and they are expected to increase in importance in the near future. While electronic arcades have been on the scene for some time, the next generation of arcades will feature much more than video games, offering a variety of entertainment experiences, simulation experiences, virtual reality, immersion environments, and other high-tech entertainment features. New arcades will range in size up to 100,000 square feet. At the high end, these projects will become small, high-tech, indoor theme parks, such as Disney Quest.

Specialty Film Venues

IMAX pioneered the large-screen, high-definition film format primarily for use in museums and theme parks. More recently, specialty film formats have been incorporated into urban retail locations. An example of a commercial giant-screen theater is the Sony/Loews Theaters complex at Lincoln Square in New York. Simulator experiences have been incorporated into freestanding commercial locations such as the Showscan simulator Cinemania at CityWalk in Los Angeles. Cinetropolis by IWERKS incorporates several high-definition film technologies into one location—a large-screen theater, a 360-degree theater, and a simulator ride. The prototype Cinetropolis is located at the Foxwoods Casino in Connecticut.

Nighttime Entertainment Centers

Nighttime entertainment complexes feature a variety of nightclubs and other entertainment components grouped together in one facility and operated by one entity. Two projects found in Orlando—Church Street Station and Pleasure Island—were the forerunners of this type of complex. Such projects have served as models for several similar entertainment projects: America Live complexes include up to seven nightclubs and restaurants in one location, and Dave 'N Busters incorporates bars, restaurants, billiards, and interactive arcades.

Live Entertainment Attractions

Various projects use live entertainment venues as key attractions. Locations around the country are hoping to capture some of the magic of Branson, Missouri, with indoor music theaters featuring name entertainers, typically country music performers. In the home of country music, Nashville, Gaylord Entertainment recently unveiled its Wild Horse Saloon, a 50,000-square-foot live music/dance/television venue, which could be developed at locations around the United States.

Entertainment-Driven Retailing

A new category of retail project—entertainment-driven retailing—is the logical outgrowth of trends in specialty shopping center development over the past 30 years. In the 1960s, specialty shopping centers appeared featuring historic locations and interesting shops, for example, Ghirardelli Square and Pier 39 in San Francisco. In the 1970s and 1980s, the Rouse Company developed the festival marketplace, with Faneuil Hall/Quincy Market in Boston and Harborplace in Baltimore.

These centers increased the number of programmatic activities offered and the importance of food as a drawing card. Recently, a third generation of retail shopping has emerged—retail centers driven by key entertainment activities.

CityWalk in Los Angeles was designed to take advantage of the more than 8 million visitors to the Universal Studios complex each year. It provides retail stores and food service along with its own entertainment components. The design of the facility borrows a great deal from theme parks in its over-the-top use of architectural icons, sets, and props. The Forum Shops in Las Vegas offers an extremely entertaining shopping and eating experience that takes advantage of the vast numbers of visitors to Caesar's Palace. One of the most successful shopping centers in this country as measured by sales per square foot, this complex incorporates about 500,000 square feet of retail space, restaurants, and entertainment features.

Extending the entertainment-driven retail concept to the maximum are several proposed entertainment village developments, which will be on the scale of regional shopping centers, with major entertainment venues to draw crowds. Entertainment villages or districts of this type may include music theaters, nightclubs, dinner theaters, specialty film venues, programmatic entertainment, a range of major retailers and specialty stores, and a variety of restaurants and other food opportunities. A future phase of development of the Forum Shops will match this description.

Public-Sponsored Entertainment Development

The importance of entertainment attractions and nighttime activities has not been lost on city planners in the United States. Two examples of public-sponsored development of entertainment-driven retail projects include the Santa Monica Promenade and Yerba Buena Gardens. The Santa Monica Promenade was a derelict downtown area in upscale Santa Monica. The addition of three movie complexes to the three-block area served as a catalyst to bring nighttime crowds, which led directly to the development of an assortment of restaurants, followed by retail shops. The area is now a thriving nighttime entertainment center for the region. Yerba Buena Gardens, in downtown San Francisco, is a large-scale, mixed-use urban center designed from the outset to incorporate entertainment, recreation, and cultural attractions as a catalyst for the development. The entertainment retail component, Metreon, includes cinemas, interactive entertainment, an IMAX theater, restaurants, and retail space.

Themed Attractions in Malls

A number of indoor theme parks attempted in the United States have been major disappointments. The most recent indoor theme park, however, Camp Snoopy at the Mall of America in Minneapolis, has been very successful. Several key factors differentiate Camp Snoopy from other unsuccessful indoor theme parks:

- It was designed as an integral part of the shopping center.
- It functions as the center court with free access so that all shopping visitors can walk through and be entertained.
- It was designed and is operated by a successful theme park operator.
- It was designed to incorporate natural light and greenery so that it is appealing in good weather as well as bad.

This type of complex, featuring an enclosed indoor amusement park along with shopping opportunities, is expected to have strong potential in locales with extreme climates. Southeast Asia in particular, because of its high-density population base of key cities and the attractiveness of its climate-controlled environment, is expected to be a good location for this type of development.

Retail Entertainment Attractions in Casinos

The development of gaming locations is growing rapidly throughout the United Stares. In many cases, gaming establishments are incorporating entertainment attractions and activities. In major markets such as Las Vegas, large-scale casinos like MGM Grand, Aladdin, and Luxor are adding entertainment to expand the overall market by attracting families and to differentiate themselves in a highly competitive environment. In other locations throughout the United States, proposals to develop new gaming opportunities often incorporate entertainment activities to provide a diverse drawing power and to differentiate themselves in the selection of a developer.

Retail Entertainment Attractions at Sports Venues

Developing new professional sports venues is a strong trend in the United States, stemming from the fact that, even though many major sports venues throughout the country are structurally sound, they are economically obsolete because they lack luxury suites, preferential club

RTKL Associates Inc., LA

The Desert Passage at Aladdin–The Lost City is a 450,000-square-foot retail entertainment center being developed in Las Vegas by TrizecHahn Corporation. Anchored by a major casino and hotel, the elaborately themed retail environment will include specialty retail stores and restaurants designed to enhance visitors' sense of romantic adventure.

seating, and high-revenue concourse activities. Often, new arenas like Staples Center in downtown Los Angeles and stadia like Pacific Bell Park in downtown San Francisco are being built in urban areas in association with retail and entertainment activities. Major sports teams, in conjunction with real estate developers, are looking for ways to combine entertainment activities on site to take advantage of the draw of the teams during the season, as well as to provide year-round activities on site.

Source: Adapted from "Urban Entertainment Destinations," *Urban Land* Supplement, August 1995.

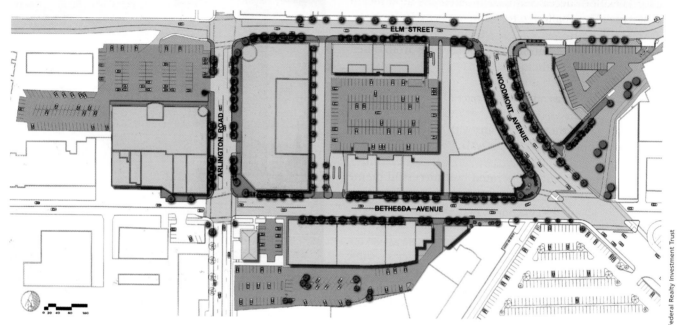

Bethesda Row does not look like a community shopping center to the casual observer. Designed as infill development along the streets of Bethesda, Maryland, it is being built block by block in line with demand. Consumers in this urbanizing suburban downtown near Washington, D.C., strongly support streetfront retailing. The complex includes a below-ground, eight-screen cinema, more than 50,000 square feet of ground-level restaurants and specialty stores, and 71,000 square feet of offices on the upper levels.

The prediction in 1977 that financing would be hard to come by and that there would be fewer opportunities to develop shopping centers in the future would have been timely if it had come ten years later. During the 1980s, shopping center construction reached its zenith and led to the severe overbuilding that is only now being worked off. And the expectation that smaller regional centers would be where development action would be proved to be flat-out wrong. In 1981, about 19,000 shopping centers, about 1,100 of them regional centers, were located in this country. By 1997, about 23,000 new centers had been added to the inventory, only about 500 of them new regional centers. The vast majority of new centers built since 1977 have been neighborhood and community centers (including off-price centers), and among enclosed malls, the development trend has inexorably been toward large super regional centers rather than smaller regional centers.

The greatest failing of previous predictions, however, is that both editions failed to foresee the dramatic over-

building that has plagued the shopping center industry for the last ten years and the changing shopping patterns of today's consumers, which are buffeting the industry as never before and leading to unprecedented development and redevelopment challenges in the future.

The following points summarize the major trends that ULI believes will affect shopping center development in the next ten years.

Emerging demographic trends mean new retail opportunities.

As the 21st century dawns, the U.S. Census Bureau projects population growth in the United States to slow to its lowest rate in over 60 years—just 0.8 percent annually from 2000 to 2010. But this trend masks a dramatic change in the characteristics of the population that will render obsolete many existing shopping centers and open new retail opportunities around the country.

Retail management and operation in Asia have not yet matured to that found in the United States. Throughout most of the Pacific Rim, retail space is bought like condominiums rather than leased. Independent merchants own their businesses as well as their shops. No business incentive exists for the kind of collegiality found in U.S. centers. And one of the major challenges facing retailing in Asia is whether or not the business culture can adjust to a new relationship between landlord and tenant.

Merchants, retailers, and developers in Asia are only beginning to exploit successfully the North American business prototype. The challenge for developers and designers alike is to provide the physical amenities to support this evolution within the broader cultural context.

Sociological factors that affect density generate pressure on the development/design team to re-create the retail mall on a different—Asian—scale. Wider walkways are required to provide room for three generations—six or seven family members—shopping together. Food courts must accommodate as many as 1,200 customers at one sitting. And when daily visitors number 90,000 to 100,000 (compared with 20,000 to 30,000 in U.S. malls), traffic circulation is critical.

In Asia's sultry climates, environmental issues also play a role in design. The reliability of the infrastructure will be tested by heat, wind, and monsoon rains. Although the equatorial sun rules out skylights, vast expanses of windows are used instead to bring daylight inside and create an inviting setting.

The lack of a full range of major department stores to serve as anchors means Asian centers will rely on other "anchor" attractions tied to local cultural and economic demands, such as supersize food courts and entertainment centers with everything from real snow to virtual reality. With very few international brand-name merchants available as tenants because of laws limiting trade and other import issues, mom-and-pop stores dominate retail trade, with all the idiosyncrasies those establishments entail.

Source: *Urban Land,* Asia Supplement, May 1997, p. 29. ■

Retail malls in Asia must be re-created on an Asian scale; for example, walkways must be wider to provide room for three generations of family members shopping together. The Tao-Yuan Shopping Center in Taipai, Taiwan, a suburban regional center in southern Taiwan near Shin-Yin, is located on a 25-acre site and contains a total gross floor area of 780,000 square feet and structured parking totaling 395,000 square feet. A 737,000-square-foot department store and a 108,000-square-foot cinema are located in the center.

Altoon + Porter Architects

The reduced rate of population growth is the result of lower birthrates among native-born European Americans that is not entirely compensated for by the relatively fast growth in minority populations resulting from immigration and natural increase. By 2010, the minority share of the overall U.S. population is expected to reach 32 percent, up from 24 percent as recently as 1990.

Net immigration over the next decade is officially projected to average 820,000 annually; however, it is increasingly likely that this estimate will prove to be conservative, given the high rate of illegal immigration and the pressures to expand immigration quotas to feed the need for more entry-level workers. In the past, 75 percent of annual immigrants were from Latin America (50 percent) and Asia (25 percent). Although the balance may shift somewhat in the future, immigration will continue to be predominantly from developing countries of Latin America, Asia, and Africa. This trend will have a profound effect on the need for shopping centers to retarget their marketing to serve emerging ethnic communities whose buying habits are different.

Despite the slower but still increasing overall population growth projected over the next 15 years, the growth of households will likely remain steady because of smaller household sizes. What will change, however, is the age and profiles of those households. The strongest household growth will continue to be among 45- to 64-year-olds, i.e., those in their peak earning years. This cohort will also include many of the married-couple households without minor children (empty nesters) that will also grow at an increasingly rapid rate to become the fastest-growing family type by 2000.

By 2010, 36 million households—slightly less than a third of the total number of households—will be empty nesters. These consumers largely have what they need. Their high discretionary income, their sophisticated tastes that demand high-quality, specialty merchandise, and

their desire to be stimulated, educated, and entertained will have a profound effect on the nature of future shopping environments.

Single-parent households, on the other hand, are expected to experience slower growth over the next 15 years. Although single-person households will increase numerically, more than a third of these households will be in the over 65 category; the number of single-person households under 45 will drop by 6 percent by 2010.[1]

The U.S. population balance continues its tilt to the South and West, but growth continues in all regions. The share of the U.S. population in these two regions is 57 percent, up from 48 percent in 1970, and it is likely that this shift will continue. It is estimated that 60 percent of the U.S. population will live in these regions by 2010, with more than 25 percent of the total residing in California, Texas, and Florida alone. As the newer Sunbelt communities grow larger and become more urban, the demand for more and different types of shopping environments

The demand for new shopping environments in downtowns, suburban town centers, neighborhood streetfronts, mixed-use developments, transit stations, and waterfronts will grow in all parts of the country. The Avenue of the Peninsulas, being developed by Cousins Properties in Rolling Hills, California, will introduce open-air Main Street shopping to this suburb of Los Angeles.

Hollywood & Highland
Hollywood, California

Baby boomers and Gen-Xers both will be drawn to exciting retail destinations that give them an opportunity to eat out, go to the movies, educate themselves, and spend money on lifestyle goods relating to self-improvement, health, hobbies, entertainment, and recreation. Hollywood & Highland will provide all these things in a destination that will be a key anchor in the revitalization of Hollywood Boulevard in Los Angeles.

will grow, including downtowns and town centers, street-front retailing, mixed-use developments, and transit-linked developments—the types of retail development that have existed for years in more mature parts of the country.

The North and East, on the other hand, contain the oldest stock of shopping centers as well as the nation's highest income levels. This combination will continue to generate a strong market for rehabilitation of aging shopping centers to reflect the latest retailing concepts that high-income consumers demand.

Shifting consumer behavior will change the way people shop.
Despite the fact that, in a typical month, 185 million adults (94 percent of the population over 18 years of age) shop at shopping centers, Americans still are making fewer trips to the mall and are spending less time there—68 minutes per average shopping trip, down from 90 minutes —than they did in 1982.[2] Two-income families and everyone else are simply too busy to spend lengthy periods of time at the mall, particularly with all the alternatives available. Convenience is the new watchword, and neighborhood and community centers are happy to provide many of the goods and services that used to be found exclusively in malls. This trend will increase.

The flashy spenders of the 1980s were replaced by the cost-conscious, value-oriented consumers of the 1990s, and they are being replaced by the entertainment shoppers of the 2000s. Shoppers from two-wage-earner families will always be concerned with how much time shopping takes, and they will continue to look for quality merchandise that is fairly priced, well designed, and durable. But do they have to go to a shopping mall to get it? Today they can go to outlet, off-price, power, and other types of value-oriented centers and pay less. Tomorrow they may choose not to go to a shopping center at all if they can buy much of the same merchandise over the Internet or through catalogs. While the type of merchan-

dise that can be purchased in a nonstore environment (mostly commodities like books, toys, electronics, office supplies, and computers) will be limited, this trend will have a profound effect on power centers and other value-oriented shopping centers that sell primarily commodities. Shopping centers of all types will respond by creating environments that provide an experience that people enjoy being part of. Shopping will be only one part of this equation.

Clearly, the two age cohorts that will have the greatest impact on shopping center retailing for the foreseeable future will be the baby boomers (those born between 1946 and 1964) and the so-called Generation X (teens and 20-somethings). Baby boomers' current focus is on technological, service- and home-oriented pursuits, those things that offer convenience and pampering. They have most of the things they need, and so their purchases will become more and more discretionary. Although boomers are aging, they are not getting old, and their interests and their purchases will more and more tend toward the types of goods that used to be associated with younger people exclusively. Their current focus will likely be augmented in the future by increased spending on recreation, travel, entertainment, self-improvement, health, hobbies, and other self-indulgent pursuits.

In contrast to the boomers, the Gen-Xers:

- Grew up with television advertising and became shoppers at an earlier age;
- Don't earn much yet (still living with their parents and not paying rent enable this generation to devote a higher percentage of income to possessions or travel);
- Spend money eating out, going to movies, concerts, and sporting events, at electronics and record stores, and buying clothing and cosmetics;
- Have less loyalty to particular brands;
- Think multiculturally; and
- Like self-service because they already consider themselves knowledgeable consumers.[3]

The revitalized area in and around Yerba Buena Gardens, south of Market Street in San Francisco, contains numerous cultural institutions (the Yerba Buena Center for the Arts and the San Francisco Museum of Modern Art), the Moscone Convention Center, retail establishments (the San Francisco Center anchored by Nordstrom), and restaurants (Chevy's, Max's Diner) that attract visitors and residents alike to the neighborhood. In the past, however, "south of Market Street" was considered an isolated location where commercial development was infeasible.

Against this backdrop, Sony Retail Entertainment (SRE) has completed work on Metreon, a Sony Entertainment Center overlooking Yerba Buena Gardens Esplanade. In so doing, the company hopes to create a model for future successful urban entertainment development.

What distinguishes Metreon is that Sony Retail Entertainment chose to approach it as a retail business venture rather than as a more traditional real estate project. It partnered with Millennium Partners of New York and WDG Ventures of San Francisco, which developed the physical site. SRE assumed the role of master tenant and leased the entire building from the San Francisco Redevelopment Agency. This approach allowed Sony to focus on its primary concern—ensuring that each component of the center operates as a profitable business. An SRE division, Sony Development, worked with designers and marketing specialists to refine the center's look, feel, and mix of offerings.

The four-story, 350,000-square-foot project includes a 15-screen Sony Theaters complex, a Sony IMAX theater, themed attractions, new restaurants, and retail shopping, all of which are reached through a central area called Metreon Gateway. Technology-based entertainment features an interactive 3-D show and presentation of the book *The Way Things Work* by David Macaulay, as well as a PC-based electronic game and virtual-reality experience called "Airtight Garage" created by the French graphic-novelist Möebius. The SRE team also worked with author and illustrator Maurice Sendak on a large family attraction featuring the characters and story lines from Sendak's well-loved books, including *Where the Wild Things Are*.

Source: Daniel C. Scheffey.

Metreon, created by Sony Development, WDG Ventures, and Millennium Partners in downtown San Francisco, opened in spring 1999 to rave reviews. A destination retail entertainment project that has been collocated with the city's Museum of Modern Art and the Moscone Convention Center, it is responding to the new demographics of American cities.

Dolphin Mall is a 1.65-million-square foot themed value retail mall being developed in Miami. Plans call for a public entertainment plaza flanked by cafés and boutiques. The entertaining environment will draw customers who might otherwise shop on the Internet to find value.

Baby boomers are quite flexible in their outlook, and it is likely they too will adopt many of the buying habits of the Gen-Xers and accelerate the changing nature of consumer behavior.

The distinctions among shopping center types will continue to blur as developers strive to broaden their customer base, reduce risks, and fill market niches.

The term "specialty center" once meant a type of center that did not fit the standard categories in terms of market served or tenants represented. Today, however, there are more varieties of specialty centers than there are standard shopping center categories: megamalls, off-price megamalls, off-price entertainment megamalls, urban entertainment centers, power centers, entertainment/power centers, outlet centers, airport centers, town centers, streetfront retail centers, transit centers, resort centers, tourist retail centers, and minimalls, to name the most common. To complicate matters further, full-price and off-price stores are being mixed in some centers, others that have a regional draw may not have department store anchors, and still others may be sized like neighborhood centers but serve far more than a single neighborhood.

The mix-and-match qualities of new shopping centers reflect the dynamic retail environment and consumers' changing behavior and preferences. And this trend will intensify as the amount of retail space per capita continues to increase—it is now more than 19 square feet per person. As a result, many new types of centers will continue to fill specialized niches and replace obsolete, traditional retail centers that are still operating but clearly on their way out.

Now that the shopping center industry is mature, both making and remaking centers will require greater levels of sophistication in shaping the character of tenants and the nature of the shopping environment to meet more precisely the specific needs of prospective consumers—and tenants. This process will be a continuation of one that has been around for a long time. The earliest specialty centers had no anchor tenants; in fact, for some time this trait defined a specialty center, and the high-end fashion center represented the first clear strategy on the part of larger centers to target market segments. The festival center, geared toward specialty foods, food services, and tourists, was also strategically developed to meet a need.

Off-price, power, and outlet malls were originally seen by some as a whole new type of shopping center and by others as a temporary accommodation for tenants that were threatening to conventional retailers but would likely be welcome later in more traditional centers. And the variety of entertainment-oriented shopping centers currently available reflect the latest in a long line of specialty niches. Segmentation and hybridization will continue to occur simultaneously as the shopping center industry intensifies its revitalization and renovation activity; in fact, identifying new market segments and niches and creating retail environments that exploit them will likely be the

David Whitcomb

Washingtonian Center, under development in Gaithersburg, Maryland, is a pedestrian-oriented power center that includes an open-air Main Street. The massing of the big-box stores is masked by small shops placed along their otherwise blank walls.

keys to the successful renovation, expansion, or development of new shopping centers in the coming decade.

Older and smaller regional shopping centers are finding it hard to compete, and the situation will only get worse.

In the face of competition from dominant super regional centers and off-price centers, most older one- and two-anchor malls will find it increasingly hard to compete. A large percentage of these centers cannot be expanded because they are landlocked. Their trade areas, once adequate to support their retail offerings have been eroded by changing demographics or by newer, more powerful centers within easy driving distance. To compound the problem, many older centers have not been continuously renovated to reflect consumers' changing tastes.

Between 1995 and 1998, according to ULI's *Dollars & Cents of Shopping Centers,* total operating receipts of regional centers (those anchored by only one or two department stores) declined dramatically, from $18.98 to $13.93 per square foot, while net operating balances declined from $10.85 to $8.95 per square foot. The Darwinian situation among regional centers will increasingly lead to several solutions. Centers in the direst straits, perhaps as many as 10 percent, will simply close, as did Cinderella City in suburban Denver and Sherman Oaks Galleria in Sherman Oaks, California (which is being torn down and redeveloped as a mixed-use office/retail/entertainment center). The next group, which has more options, will remake themselves into new shopping center types, particularly off-price centers, as did Worcester Mall in downtown Worcester, Massachusetts, and Seven Corners Center in Falls Church, Virginia. The third group includes centers with great potential to be renovated and expanded because of their locations and the demographics of the surrounding areas, such as Mazza Gallerie in Washington, D.C.

Rehabilitation and expansion of shopping centers, a trend throughout the 1990s, will accelerate.

The United States is overstored and overmalled, and many existing shopping centers are ripe for rehabilitation and expansion. Thousands of the shopping centers constructed between the 1950s and the 1990s are now aging and obsolete because they have not kept pace with the changing consumer environment. Although this trend has been apparent for years, the urgency of renewing shopping centers continues to grow because of the tremendous competition.

Since 1961, more than 2,000 neighborhood and community shopping centers were built every five years, and almost three-quarters of all neighborhood and community centers opened before 1986. Likewise, from 300 to 600 enclosed malls were constructed during each five-year period, with more than four-fifths opening before 1985.[4] By 1998, more than 42,000 shopping centers containing more than 5.1 billion square feet were open. And according to F.W. Dodge, construction continues: 583 new shopping centers totaling 51.9 million square feet were started in 1996. Of this number, 445, or 76 percent, were neighborhood centers containing less than 100,000 square feet.

Old Orchard Center, located outside Chicago and one of the nation's first regional shopping centers (see the case study in Chapter 7), was rebuilt between 1993 and 1995 to include entertainment, restaurants, and new and enlarged anchors, all in an open-air setting. Mazza Gallerie, an enclosed mall in uptown Washington, D.C., is being de-malled. Window displays are being punched into its austere stone-paneled facade, and some of its tenants are being repositioned to face the sidewalk instead of the enclosed central court. A cineplex is being added on the top floor, space that had always been difficult to lease.

Downtown and inner-city locations continue to represent major overlooked shopping center markets.

The suburban growth rate is likely to slow somewhat in the next ten years as a result of increasing congestion, distance from employment centers, and limitations on

The de-malling of Mazza Gallerie in Washington, D.C., will create a more dynamic, pedestrian-oriented facade. It is part of a major trend toward streetfront retailing and toward the rehabilitation and repositioning of smaller regional centers.

Pacific Place, a spectacular new regional center in downtown Seattle, has tapped into the significant buying power of revitalized downtown markets.

Mimi Rodriguez of New York City loves to shop. Every year, she shells out about $2,000 on clothes, filling her wardrobe with the trendiest styles and hottest brand names.

While she spends her weekends shopping, she never buys anything from stores near her Harlem home.

"There just aren't good stores around here," says the 25-year-old New Yorker. "If I want good clothes, I have to go downtown or to the malls in New Jersey or Long Island."

Two studies released in June 1998 by the Boston-based Initiative for a Competitive Inner City found that cities are largely underserved by retailers, who favor rural and overseas expansion to urban development. One study focused primarily on Atlanta, Boston, Chicago, Miami, Oakland, and New York's Harlem. A second study surveyed 1,205 inner-city households nationwide.

According to the studies, consumers in this country's inner cities possess more than $85 billion in annual retail spending power, accounting for nearly 7 percent of the total retail spending in the United States. But that demand is largely unmet. Only a handful of national retailers like Sears and Pathmark Stores operate stores in urban America; virtually no discount chains, like Wal-Mart, are located in inner cities.

"Prejudice in this country exists beyond social circles; it extends into business," says John Konarski, vice president of research at the Council of Shopping Centers, a New York trade group. "For many years, there have been stereotypes that cause retailers to shy away from opening stores in inner cities.

"But there is good money to be made in the inner cities," he says. "People there need to eat, they need clothing, they need things for their homes, and they have money to spend."

In fact, inner-city consumers spend about 21 percent more each year on men's clothing and 24 percent more on children's clothing than the average American shopper, the studies found. Grocery store sales can be as much as 40 percent higher per square foot in inner cities, while sales at drugstores in those areas can be as much as twice the regional average.

"Incomes in inner cities have grown dramatically, and people want to shop," says Drew Greenwald, president of Grid Properties, which is building Harlem USA, a large shopping complex in upper Manhattan that will include a Disney Store, The Gap, HMV Records, and Old Navy. "Give them good stores, and they will come," he says. "But when they can't find them, they take their shopping elsewhere."

Source: Associated Press, New York.

The Power Plant, an adaptive use of a former power plant in downtown Baltimore, has been transformed into a retail entertainment center.

Entertainment will be added to all types of shopping centers as they reposition themselves to remain competitive in the 21st century. This multiplex theater was added in the mid-1990s to the Woodland Hills Promenade, a regional center in suburban Los Angeles.

growth as suburbanites try to protect what they have and to hold down taxes. As a result, much suburban shopping center development will likely cannibalize existing but obsolete centers because these areas are already saturated with shopping centers of all types. On the other hand, many older cities, particularly those that have the most to offer, will begin to grow more rapidly. Cities like New York, Boston, Portland, Oregon, Seattle, and San Francisco are already growing and increasingly perceived as among the most dynamic places to live.

It has been widely predicted that continued advances in telecommunications, particularly the ubiquity of the Internet, may encourage some companies in older metropolitan areas to move some or all of their business to lower cost, less dense areas. It has been further predicted that because skilled workers will be able to work anywhere, these older metropolitan areas will gradually wither. Certainly some businesses that are highly dependent on low labor costs will continue to move to cheaper areas in the Sunbelt or off-shore. But it already seems clear that the engines of wealth creation and job growth in the future will be primarily the industries that are capital, information, and technology based. And these industries and the wealth they generate in the future will be in places that offer the highest quality of life and have the best educational, cultural, and recreational environment—the mature metropolitan areas.

As older central cities continue their long-term efforts to rebuild, they will increasingly cater to a population desiring culture, entertainment, and other sophisticated pleasures and intellectual stimulations associated with the best of city living. Other cities will follow these trend setters and try to emulate their success. Coupled with the acute shortage of retailing in urban neighborhoods, local governments' nascent efforts to form partnerships to revitalize neighborhood commercial strips, and the dramatic reduction in crime, opportunities in urban neighborhoods should prove to be an irresistible lure for retail developers over the next ten years.

The New Community Neighborhood Shopping Center in Newark, New Jersey, is a shopping phoenix, having risen from the ashes of Newark's central ward and proved that buying power in central city neighborhoods is currently being neglected. Harlem USA, a retail and entertainment center under construction on 125th Street in New York City to be anchored by a Cineplex Odeon and a Disney Store, will lure residents as well as visitors from outside the neighborhood to Harlem (see the case studies in Chapter 7).

Entertainment will be added to all forms of shopping centers as they are repositioned to reflect 21st century lifestyles.

Retailers are reintroducing fun into shopping. "Entertainment in the form of information (infotainment), ideas, or fashion," says J'Amy Owens of the Seattle-based Retail Group, "has emerged as a critical element in retailing. An estimated 70 percent of shoppers who have ex-

Hawkstown, in Fukuoka, Japan, will include elaborate landscaping and water features to welcome visitors and create a destination that customers will be drawn to even when they have no intention of shopping. This environment augments and reinforces existing department store anchors.

perienced entertainment in a retail setting return for another visit—a figure three to four times the industry standard. Forty percent of Americans consider shopping a source of entertainment and would like more entertainment in the future."[5] Among the concepts that seem to be proliferating are practice areas to try out goods like sporting equipment, relaxation retailing (tearooms, coffeehouses), megaplex cinemas, film studio stores, virtual reality attractions (including indoor golf and skiing simulations), motion simulators, museums in the mall, indoor playgrounds, themed restaurants, and lifestyle-oriented shops.

The Mall of Georgia at Mill Creek in Gwinnett County, for example, will include a 1.5 million-square-foot regional mall with six anchor stores, a 130,000-square-foot Main Street village, a 20-screen theater, a seven-story IMAX 3-D theater, a 500-seat amphitheater, an 80-acre nature park with a creek, and 9,000 parking spaces. At Circle Centre, a new downtown mall in Indianapolis, the Simon Property Group used entertainment—a cineplex, nightclubs, and restaurants—as one important element to create a regional draw and has succeeded in bringing suburban shoppers downtown to shop and enjoy themselves. And in April 1999, the Mills Corporation added 300,000 square feet of retail entertainment attractions to Sawgrass Mills, its 1.8 million-square-foot off-price megamall in Sunrise, Florida. Named the Oasis, this outdoor entertainment expansion connects the mall to the National Car Rental Center Arena, home of the NHL Florida Panthers, and features waterfalls, palm-lined pedestrian ways, and numerous opportunities for dining outdoors.

Strong anchors are still essential for long-term success, but they are not always the same anchors as in the past. In the old days, anchor department stores competed with one another to take coveted anchor locations in regional shopping centers. Then came the 1990s, with bankruptcies and consolidations of department stores decimating the industry and dramatically reducing the number of viable and desirable chains available to lease space. Many of the chains that disappeared were regional and local stores that had been anchors of shopping centers since they first appeared. Replacing them with other department stores proved impossible for some older centers, and they were forced to rent anchor space to discount department stores or big-box stores. In some cases, it has been a blessing in disguise, because the discounters are stronger draws than the old-line department stores they replaced. In other cases, strong national department store chains like Nordstrom, Macy's, and JCPenney have moved aggressively to help fill the void left by department stores in some centers.

Increasingly, however, developers of regional centers have recognized that department stores are not the only potential anchors. Elaborate food courts, entertainment centers, and even nonretail uses such as convention centers and sports stadia are seen as potential anchors that would complement the department stores and add a strong unconventional draw to the mall. Shopping cen-

Located near Tijuca, considered one of Rio de Janeiro's most prestigious residential districts, Shopping Center Iguatemi Rio, completed in 1996, occupies a corner site that was formerly a soccer field in a dense urban area. The developer, La Fonte Participações, recognized the potential of the abandoned site and the needs of the surrounding community, and the mall has helped to revitalize the neighborhood. Now a local gathering place and a center for entertainment and shopping that serves a trade area of more than half a million people, it encompasses 280,000 square feet of GLA, including a collection of small shops, a supermarket, two department stores, a seven-screen cinema complex, a large food court, and a themed family entertainment area.

To design the mall, La Fonte Participações called on Coral Gables, Florida–based Beame Architectural Partnership, a firm it had worked with on several other malls in Brazil that was experienced in the design of retail/entertainment facilities. With two main facades broken down into pedestrian-scale elements, Iguatemi Rio's contemporary exterior blends well with the scale and texture of the surrounding neighborhood. The center is topped by a soaring cross-vaulted steel truss structure covered with skylights. Stone-clad columns in tropical colors rest on patterned terrazzo and granite paving.

A racetrack configuration was used because of the site's deep rectangular shape and the need to develop an efficient multilevel layout for a myriad of small shops. Because it was feasible to place only one level of parking below grade because of a large rock formation that protruded into the site, the mall's three retail levels are sandwiched between a single level of structured parking below grade and four levels of parking adjacent to the third retail level and above. Placing easy-to-use, economical parking on the roof while still admitting ample tropical sunlight into the center was a challenge that was met by placing skylights in strategic areas.

Iguatemi Rio has brought vitality back to the neighborhood by providing a festive experience for visitors and accommodating a diverse clientele elegantly yet casually. In May 1998, Beame Architectural Partnership accepted a top design award for the center from the International Council of Shopping Centers. With more than 240 tenants and average sales of $470 per square foot, the center has exceeded early pro formas and provides an example of how good planning and a strong tenant mix in the right location can make up for a difficult site.

Source: Lawrence Beame, "Rio de Janeiro Shopping Center Revitalizes Neighborhood," *Urban Land,* July 1998, p. 20.

©Thomas Delbeck Photography

©Thomas Delbeck Photography

The center's atmosphere is elegant yet festive and spirited, created by the use of colors; design details such as steel trusses, high-end stone paving, and skylights; and an open floor plan.

E Walk is a retail entertainment destination being developed on 42nd Street in Times Square by the Tishman Urban Development Corporation in the expectation that people would rather play here than sit at home and play on the Internet.

ter developers and retailers also recognize that being part of a larger commercial district is to be an anchor in and of itself. The presence of adjacent streetfront specialty shopping, spaces for the performing arts, galleries and clubs, museums, and other cultural and historic facilities also provides powerful anchors for retail centers.

In community centers, the traditional anchors are discount department stores, supermarkets, junior department stores, drugstores, and variety stores, and they are still the most common anchors. Developers increasingly see cinemas, family clothing stores, furniture stores, and sporting goods stores as anchors in community shopping centers, however. Even owners of small neighborhood centers are looking for new types of anchor tenants that may not have been interested in small neighborhood locations in the past. National credit tenants, including specialty and apparel stores, more than ever are looking at well-located neighborhood centers to remain competitive, while at the same time, neighborhood centers are shying

away from leasing space to local or regional tenants if they can. As in the past, all types of centers with second- and third-tier anchor tenants will continue to be a risk.

Value retailers and traditional retailers increasingly will be found together in many different types of shopping centers.
Until the 1990s, it was almost unheard of for full-price and off-price tenants to be found in the same shopping center. In fact, many of the strongest tenants had such clout that they would never have allowed it to happen, and most developers would have been aghast at how combining them would have affected the image of their centers. Times have certainly changed, and the overbuilding and lack of enough highly desirable tenants to fill the available space have made developers recognize that a broader range of prices may actually attract more customers. Old formulas are being ignored, and the result is a blurring of distinctions among shopping center types and the

A dramatic glass-and-steel entrance was created for Centro Oberhausen, an indoor/outdoor megamall in Oberhausen, Germany. It is evocative of the industrial plants that previously occupied the site.

ongoing breakdown of the old rules about what is and what is not a suitable tenant in a particular center.

Discount stores and category killers have been moving into spaces vacated by department stores. For example, IKEA replaced a Broadway store at Carson Mall in Los Angeles and Filene's Basement became one of the anchor stores in the upscale Mazza Galerie in Washington, D.C. Some full-price tenants are being added to off-price centers, and the Simon Property Group, among others, has successfully added selected off-price tenants to its regional malls. At the Mills Corporation's off-price megamalls, full-price entertainment attractions, cineplexes, restaurants, and specialty retailers coexist happily with outlet and off-price stores.

Shopping center developers will harness the power of the Internet to counteract its threat.

Nonstore alternatives for shopping have led to much uncertainty and concern within the shopping center industry.

Part of the concern is that the issues surrounding nonstore shopping are not well understood, and many in the shopping center industry still have their heads in the sand. Nonstore shopping usually refers to three ways to shop: television shopping networks, catalog shopping, and the Internet. Catalog shopping has been around a long time and is predictable. As a result, the shopping center industry is not concerned. And despite the presence of the Home Shopping Network and QVC, home shopping on television also does not pose a serious threat to retail stores, because choices are limited.

The third choice, retail commerce on the Internet, or "cybershopping," is expected to become a $7.3 billion business by 2000, with households that are online making 120 transactions per year, up from the current nine.[6] Contrast that figure with overall retail sales in shopping centers of $973.6 billion (representing 52 percent of total retail sales in the United States, excluding sales by automobile dealers), and it does not look alarming. More-

The retail development field is on the threshold of the most challenging and exhilarating era it has faced in many years. The old formulas are for the most part out —yet no one seems to have completely defined the new ones. The definition of anchor, for example, is changing even as this is written—from "department store" to "entertainment destination." Multiplex cinemas are now commonly considered viable—even essential—shopping center anchors.

Debates about design and merchandising are raging over such issues as clustering techniques for food and entertainment uses or enclosed versus open courtyard spaces and storefront access. Developers lament that traditional funding sources, including pension banks and overseas investors, are not as readily available without preleases

for, in many cases, up to 70 percent or more of the tenants. The sure-fire development planning cost formulas of x dollars per square foot for a given commodity no longer apply. The ever-present issue of variable costs associated with integrating amusement and leisure facilities in and around retail developments—the unanswered questions regarding useful life, true costs, security, and maintenance—is but another of the major concerns the industry must wrestle with as the next century quickly approaches.

But what are the factors behind—or perhaps beyond— the current entertainment phenomenon that will drive the retail development industry into the new millennium? The future of development, and particularly the development of the worldwide shopping center industry, must be

The success of Universal Studio's CityWalk indicates the preference of contemporary consumers for state-of-the art entertainment design and technology, a wide range of foods, and a pedestrian orientation.

viewed in the context of current and projected global economic and social realities.

Youth Culture

First and foremost, retailers' interaction with the international youth culture must be recognized as a manifestation of globalization. The trend toward an increasingly international and pervasive youth culture will no doubt continue into the next century, at least partly because of increased use of the Internet. Leading technology firms estimate that revenue from goods and services purchased via the Net will reach $600 billion in the next five years. It is particularly noteworthy that virtually every survey points out that the vast majority of "surfers" and "surf-shoppers" are under 35. Merchandising and tenant mixes must evolve to accommodate this changing consumer demographic.

International Growth

Across the Pacific, the rampant growth and economic development of Asia is undeniable. As national populations grow and the availability of suitable land shrinks, demand undoubtedly will continue for increased density in projects throughout the region, both in new developments and in horizontal and vertical expansion of existing successful projects.

Ecodevelopments

Many countries, such as those in southeast Asia that are now considered the worst culprits in environmental degradation, will be (at the rate of their phenomenal economic growth) at the forefront of the "ecodevelopment" wave into the 21st century. Dedicated to building new towns, all with new shopping centers, for their rapidly expanding middle-class populations, these nations already are far ahead of the western world in the creation of low-pollutant systems for everything from mass transportation to recycling.

Urban Cores

Sweeping the United States is a strong emphasis on revitalizing urban cores. Cities are feeling the need to create —or re-create—downtown retail, amusement, and leisure developments to increase jobs and improve life for all segments of the urban community. The social and economic trend to look to the past for clues to the future—to go back downtown to shop, to eat, to attend the theater— is challenging the very definition of shopping center. Shoppers once again are seeking the small shops and intimate boutiques of the 1930s and 1940s Main Street. While demanding state-of-the-art technology and a wider range of buying options than ever, consumers now show a marked preference for a small-town feeling and presentation: witness the overwhelming success of developments like CityWalk and the Forum Shops at Caesars. Although vastly different in themes (one is high funk California,

the other Romanesque Italy), both employ high technology and claim as tenants the hottest retailers around. Yet both present themselves as somewhat chaotic gatherings of "organically grown" shops along a meandering "city" street.

Diversity

Shopping centers must begin to change more dynamically than merely by incorporating leisure/entertainment uses and must begin to include (as some do already) even more nontraditional uses, such as libraries, hospitals, places of worship, cultural attractions, supermarkets, specialized schools, hotels, farmers' markets, community facilities, live theaters, museums, and more. Why not create assisted housing for the elderly on the upper levels of a project, with upscale shopping, convenience retail shops, dining, and entertainment below, for the easy accessibility of older residents?

In an ever more competitive commercial atmosphere— and to contest the growing array of video and home-based shopping options, malls must soon become total destinations. And ironically, as shopping centers and urban centers begin to merchandise themselves more as fairgrounds—diverse uses and attractions for all ages—they will face the paradoxical need to control the spontaneity they encourage and promote.

Source: Excerpted from Roy H. Higgs, "From Country Store to Cybercade," *Urban Land*, July 1997, p. 46.

over, many of the products that can be sold successfully on the Internet tend to be commodities that men purchase, because the majority of computer users still are male and the biggest source of sales on the Internet is computers and computer-related items. "As long as computer use continues to be dominated by males," say Patricia Johnson and Richard Outcalt, "cyberspace will not soon be a hotbed of retail activity. Few men choose to shop, or enjoy shopping. Why would men use the Internet to browse a shopping mall?"[7]

But what is true today may not be true in the future. It is not unrealistic to expect that over the next ten years, women will become just as adept on the computer as men. In addition, the ease of purchase on the Internet and the availability of reliable comparative data that allow product comparisons for a much wider range of goods will become routine. Although projections of sales on the Internet are speculative at best, it is likely they will skyrocket. Within the next few years, the Net could pose a major threat to commodity-based shopping centers—especially power centers—but it should not be a major threat to the overall health of regional shopping centers or traditional neighborhood and convenience centers because of their inherent advantages for shopping. After the next few years, the impact will depend on how successful shopping centers themselves are at changing their shopping environments to create stimulating and entertaining social gathering places that people want to be part of. Shopping centers' success also will depend on how well they are able to harness the power of the Internet to drive customers toward rather than away from shopping centers. It is too early to predict, but it is possible that the Internet will actually help to increase shopping in many shopping centers by educating people about shopping opportunities, products, choices, and bargains. Already, the major shopping center developers are looking into ways to make it happen.

The historic Farmers Market in Los Angeles is currently surrounded by nondescript surface parking lots. Renovation plans for the center include retaining and building around the historic core and adding a new Main Street of shopping and entertainment on existing parking space.

Citrus Park Town Center is a new regional mall being built in northwest Tampa, Florida. The mall will attempt to create the feel of a traditional Main Street.

Power centers and outlet centers, a powerful trend in the 1990s, may themselves be at risk from nonstore shopping alternatives in the 2000s.

Although traditional shopping centers are typically known for quality, variety, service, and environment, value retailing centers—power centers and outlet centers—are known for value. If a better alternative arises, such as E-commerce, that offers better value, value retailing centers will be at risk. At the moment, shopping on the Internet is an immature industry. Potential customers have trouble finding the items they want, getting enough information to comparison shop, trusting that their credit card information will be safe, and learning the real cost of the item they want to purchase upfront, including service, mailing, and handling charges. And the Internet can be frustratingly time consuming, with no guarantee that the search will lead to a successful purchase. The situation is changing rapidly, however, as retailers' Web sites, merchandise search mechanisms, and cost comparisons become more

sophisticated and easier to use, and customers become more comfortable with shopping online. As the Internet becomes more customer friendly, which it inevitably will, value retailers will have to provide more reasons to shop out of the home or they will risk failure.

To the extent they can, value retailing centers will have to provide a better shopping experience, adding fun to the bargain hunting. This ability is hindered somewhat by the need to provide value, but it can be done cost-effectively. The Mills Corporation opened the Block at Orange in December 1998, a 600,000+-square-foot mega-mall in Orange, California, that is 75 percent off-price retailing. It has a strong entertainment orientation, including cinemas, along with an energized, high-intensity pedestrian environment that has made it a destination for fun as well as shopping. Prime Retail has opened numerous outlet centers, including the Prime Outlets in Hagerstown, Maryland, in 1998, that are designed as street-

The vision for Minami Senri in Osaka, Japan, designed by KMD, is of a vibrant and dynamic shopping experience that will induce shoppers to stay late into the evening, thereby spending more time and money at the center.

Much has changed since malls were introduced more than 40 years ago. Today, regional malls cater to different customers and face far greater competition. Certain issues will continue to affect regional malls:

- Demographic Changes—A large percentage of the population is either diverting income to savings or shopping at discount stores. The result is fewer visits to the mall.
- Social Changes—Many retailers are missing the big shift to casual dress in America and the net result that less money is spent on apparel.
- The Reengineered Economy—Despite efforts by department stores to restructure, regional malls symbolize the old economy of high costs.
- New Retail Competitors—The biggest change in retailing has been the rise of stores oriented toward value, which means lower prices. To keep costs low, value-oriented retailers have avoided the high occupancy costs of regional malls.
- The Retail Building Boom—Unlike other real estate investments, retail development has had almost no slowdown in the wake of overbuilding in the 1980s. And value retailers are leading the charge, because existing centers do not meet their requirements for space.

Several factors are critical to the success of malls over the next decade:

- The increasing size of centers (to over 800,000 square feet);
- Higher-income trade areas;
- Strong department stores with long-term leases and operating covenants;
- Dominance in their trade areas;
- Updated physical plants; and
- Limited competition from power centers, discounters, and other formats, which may enable some malls to restructure themselves as value-oriented centers.

In the long run, the survival of a successful regional mall will require a combination of strong department stores and innovative strategies to attract customers. As new low-density housing is built on the fringes of metropolitan areas, residents of almost all these areas are becoming more widely dispersed. Older regional malls are facing the combined impact of aging consumers, declining densities, and new competition by discounters. At the same time, new regional malls in growth areas chip away at the older mall's trade area.

The cost of information technology continues to fall by 50 percent every 18 months, creating tremendous opportunities for retailers with capital to reduce costs, serve customers better, or both. Many retailers' extensive investment in technology has led to greater productivity per employee, reduced inventory, and shortened replenishment time. Computers have enabled retailers to reduce shipping, storage, and distribution costs. Companies like Wal-Mart that have been in the forefront have reduced prices and margins accordingly. Leading-edge retailers now deal directly with manufacturers.

The bankruptcies of the 1980s and the subsequent consolidations have left fewer strong department store operators. The largest mall anchors, such as Sears, JCPenney, Federated/Broadway, May Company, Wards, and Dillard's, have absorbed competitors and streamlined operations. Or they have created special niches, as Nordstrom has with its superior service. Many department stores have increased their focus on apparel, to the detriment of specialty apparel stores in malls. Small regional department stores continue to struggle and will have difficulty competing with larger, better-capitalized chains. For regional malls, this situation has meant fewer options for anchor stores and much less favorable leases with department stores. Some retail areas—furniture, appliances, and computers, for example—have seen strong increases in sales that should continue for the rest of the decade.

As entertainment and social gathering places for suburban residents, malls can compete with downtown areas and freestanding facilities. Access, safety, and free parking are the obvious advantages.

Overall, the supply of retail space is growing much faster than retail expenditures. A record 260 million square feet was delivered in 1995. New development is occurring in growth areas and in established areas with new formats. Few regional malls have been built since the early 1990s, but the list of announced projects is becoming longer, especially in the Sunbelt and Mountain states, with a few planned for the outlying suburbs of slow-growing cities in the Northeast and Midwest. New malls that follow population growth continue to attract tenants and developers.

Despite the problems facing regional malls, operating results have not been catastrophic. But although significant renovations and additions have occurred at many malls, sales per square foot have been declining slowly for more than ten years, after adjusting for inflation. There clearly have been winners and losers, with winners adding strong anchors and achieving dominance in their markets. The losers have either adopted other retail formats or are barely surviving with no strategy for redevelopment on the horizon.

As an investment, malls have not provided returns that compensate investors for the risk. Between 1983 and 1995, regional malls owned by institutional investors provided an average income yield of 6.8 percent of appraised value. Much of that return, however, was reinvested in the form of capital improvements, resulting in lower cash yields.

To survive, malls will have to compete more directly in the areas of price, convenience, and service, or they will have to provide distinctive tenants and products. The continued shakeout of specialty retailers will cause problems all around, with stores closing at low-volume centers. On the other hand, the remaining specialty stores should be stronger financially and will have a chance to catch up with discounters and department stores in the areas of technology, relationships with suppliers, and more targeted merchandising.

Malls in upper-income areas (less than 20 percent of all regional malls) are somewhat insulated from the shift in buying patterns. Other malls likely to survive include those with strong anchors and stable or improving demographics. These malls must implement innovative strategies to remain appealing to consumers, however. Whether the right strategy includes entertainment, value shopping, or something else depends on the specifics of the trade area and the competition; what is certain is that significant investment will be required for older malls.

Malls with weak or lost anchors or in areas with declining demographics may not survive the next five years. Indeed, several malls around the country have been de-malled. Anaheim Plaza in Orange County, California, for instance, is now a power center. Others, such as Meyerland Plaza in Houston, have turned into value-oriented malls with minimal interior space. Redevelopment is not always feasible; many department stores own or control their sites yet do not have operating covenants and can effectively block redevelopment or reuse of their space.

Entertainment is unlikely to be a strategy for fading malls with little else to draw shoppers. It takes a sizable investment to create an entertainment venue that draws customers. Entertainment uses can also be located at nonmall locations, and many of the new entertainment concepts are likely to become outdated quickly.

The restructuring of the retail industry has placed regional malls in a new position in the pecking order. In some communities, they are still the dominant retail venues. In others, they are one of many options available to shoppers. The survivors will be those who meet consumers' requirements for value or provide goods, services, and entertainment not available at other retail locations.

Source: William J. Maher, "The Future of Regional Malls," in Laurence C. Siegel, "The Changing Face of Value Retail," *Urban Land*, May 1996, pp. 30–31.

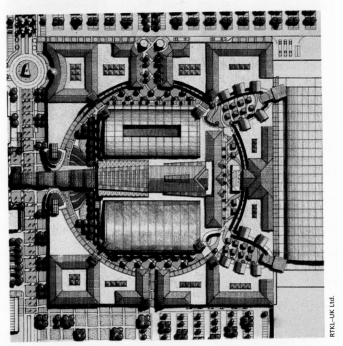

Bon Aire/Aldia, a retail center designed by RTKL in Valencia, Spain, will feature many of the characteristics of future malls: culturally based architecture, an outdoor pedestrian environment, and a site plan carefully linked to the surrounding community.

approaching the same level of saturation, because they cannot be built in the densest, most populated areas (within 25 miles of the center of a metropolitan area) without undermining the manufacturers' business relationships with full-price stores in other types of shopping centers. Consequently, outlet stores are usually not convenient enough to pose a serious threat to other forms of value retailing. And the sheer size of megamalls, which can approach 2 million square feet, usually limits them to one or two per metropolitan area.

The prototypical, stand-alone shopping center surrounded by a sea of parking is transitional; it too shall pass.
In the past few years, we have heard a considerable amount about new forms of shopping centers: transit-linked centers, town-center retailing mixed with civic and cultural uses and designed around pedestrian-oriented public spaces, streetfront retailing with offices and residences above the stores, retail entertainment centers, lifestyle centers, mixed-use centers, in-city shopping centers, and shopping centers physically and functionally linked with their communities wherever they are located. All of these concepts are represented in the case studies chosen for this handbook because they are in the vanguard of where the retailing industry is heading. And all of them foretell a different world of shopping that is just being born. They represent the beginning of a shift in how, why, and when people shop.

When we look back from the vantage point of the 21st century, we will recognize that the first generation of shopping centers represented the nuclei of emerging communities. They were not finished, and they never will be. And they are still evolving as the cities around them evolve. As communities mature and become more dense, more diverse, and more urban, the next generation of shopping centers will have to adapt themselves to these new social and economic conditions, becoming reintegrated with their communities physically, functionally, and socially.

Parking, of course, will continue to be provided, but increasingly it will be designed in new configurations—behind, beside, above, and below the commercial activity—and other modes of access will become more important. As a result, the old parking lots that separate thousands of shopping centers from their suburban surroundings will slowly disappear as centers are remade to form communities and neighborhoods. New configurations, new mixes of uses, new connections, new tenants, and new functions will make going to a shopping center an experience to be enjoyed and not simply an exercise in consumption. In fact, the term "shopping center" may disappear as developers reintegrate shopping into the fabric of daily life—which of course will not occur overnight. It will likely take decades.

A major retail entertainment development being built by TrizecHahn in Hollywood, California, will be integrated with other streetfront retailing along Hollywood Boulevard. Its name will be the name of the intersection where it is located—Hollywood & Highland. DDR OliverMcMillan is extending the streets of Long Beach, California, to form

Belo Horizonte is being designed by RTKL as an open-air Main Street for retail and entertainment uses that will extend and enhance the vibrant streetlife of the Savassi district in Belo Horizonte, Brazil.

front shops or town centers providing an enjoyable outdoor shopping experience.

As nonstore shopping alternatives expand, competition among outlet centers, power centers, and off-price megamalls undoubtedly will grow. As a result, limitations on the construction of all types of off-price centers, which already are apparent, will likely become even tighter. Power centers have already saturated most markets, and construction has slowed to a crawl. Outlet centers are rapidly

the shape of a planned neotraditional retail center and link the downtown with the convention center, aquarium, harborfront promenade, and marina. Federal Realty and CCR McCaffery Development are creating infill retail centers that do not look like shopping centers along traditional streetfronts. The goal of all these centers is to blend into the surrounding commercial development so that customers are unaware that they are separate. In all these cases, the goal is to achieve success by joining

the city—not being walled off from it. This is the future of shopping centers.

The recent turmoil in the shopping center industry, the acknowledged obsolescence of some of its earlier prototypes, and the growing preference of many shoppers for streetfront retailing and E-commerce have led some commentators to predict the slow demise of the shopping center as a land use type. It won't happen. No matter how much they may be criticized, shopping cen-

The American Wilderness Zoo & Aquarium

Ogden Entertainment's American Wilderness Zoo & Aquarium (AWZA), a division of Ogden Corporation based in New York, opened in Ontario Mills, California, in 1998. The first of almost a dozen to be built, the $10 million AWZA center is located in Ontario Mills shopping mall rather than in a science center or nature museum, where one would more likely expect to find such an attraction.

Although the location is different, it speaks volumes to the changes in shopping malls and their interest in providing diverse entertainment for customers. Shopping malls are becoming the new social centers for urban communities, and AWZA, as an "edutainment" center, offers mall visitors a chance to learn about American ecology and its animal inhabitants. It is essentially an attraction designed to bring nature indoors and make it accessible to urban dwellers.

Traveling to the local wilderness is not always easy, particularly for residents who are caught up in urban living. Thus, the idea of installing AWZA facilities in shopping malls was not so much to make it a destination site as it was a matter of convenience—because that's where people are. "To go into the wilderness for a camping trip is something that has to be planned; it takes thought and time," notes Billy Warr, vice president of operations for American Wilderness Zoo & Aquarium. "Taking AWZA to a shopping mall was a matter of bringing it to a place where a great many people gather. If it's there, people will visit it."

The flagship American Wilderness Zoo & Aquarium, designed by the McBride Company, is packaged in a 30,000-square-foot anchor site in Ontario Mills shopping center; it incorporates several components, including the Wilderness Grill, a themed restaurant where patrons dine under redwoods and food is served on split-rail tables. The menu includes wilderness delights such as wild west roasted soup, achiate chicken salad, and dirt apple bacon burgers. Naturally Untamed is a retail shop with merchandise and memorabilia geared to the great outdoors.

The first stop for visitors to AWZA is the Wild Ride Theater. Designed by SimEx in Toronto, the motion simulator theater presentation of the American wilderness tells

of the importance of animals' coexisting with humans, including a preshow video celebrating animals in their own habitats.

At the completion of the show at the Wild Ride Theater, visitors approach a set of giant doors that open into the Redwood Forest, where they are invited to "hike inside the great outdoors." At this point, visitors move on to the five biomes that are the centerpiece of AWZA, each complete with its appropriate flora, fauna, and geological environment. The selected California regions include the redwood forest, the high Sierras, the Mojave Desert, and the Pacific shore; the Amazon Valley is the fifth choice.

AWZA's contact with the community is bidirectional: people come to AWZA and AWZA in turn works very hard to build a strong educational relationship with nearby school districts. "We built a school curriculum for San Bernardino County schools (from kindergarten through 12th grade)," says Warr. "After completing the curriculum for the schools, we invited teachers to visit AWZA. It's been an overwhelming success, and we're now booking thousands of kids into the facility. It's a multipart experience for students; they begin by studying wilderness curriculum guides at school, then come here and see firsthand the animals and their habitats, and then go back to school and review what they have learned."

"We're also sponsoring overnight adventures in which students come and spend a night camping out at a biome where they see animals up close and get a feeling of a wilderness experience," says Warr. "We've had local Girl Scout and Boy Scout troops, church groups, and even families who want to come and enjoy the overnight program."

The next sites for AWZA are under construction in Grapevine, Texas, and Tempe, Arizona. The new facilities' biomes will have a regional flavor to them but will also showcase the best of North America, which could be the Rocky Mountains, a typical desert, a valley, or even a rain forest.

Source: Excerpted from Louis M. Brill, "The American Wilderness Zoo & Aquarium Brings the Great Outdoors to an Urban Area," *Funworld*, August 1998, p. 35.

Big Boxes

Changes in the prevailing retail model are rarely the result of consumers' wishes alone. The big-box phenomenon is driven by economics—a single product line, high margins, large quantities, efficient distribution, and low overhead in low-cost, often out-of-town sites. And the trend is not going away just yet, given the enduring success of numerous examples. In densely urban areas that depend on public transportation—including New York, Chicago, and much of Europe—however, category-killer, off-price retailing has yet to take hold. Still, big boxes like Bed Bath & Beyond, Old Navy, and others are a success on lower Sixth Avenue in Manhattan, and BAA McArthur Glen is having a fine run with outlet malls in the United Kingdom.

Showcase Stores

"Brand Lands." "Retail churches," the superstores of Nike, Disney, and their brethren, are another example of economics' leading retail evolution. What were once distinct lines between the hospitality, entertainment, and retail sectors have disappeared in the new "brand" environment. Entertainers such as Warner Bros. and Disney have become retailers; retailers like Jigsaw, Levi's, and Nike have become entertainers. What is more, the concept of retail showcase is still evolving. As the battle for sustainable identity continues, more corporations are exploring the strength of industrial tourism, which features appealing displays, education and entertainment, and the ability to buy both at the factory and other locations. In Vermont, Ben & Jerry's Ice Cream Factory has become a major tourist destination by selling a story along with its ice cream.

Try It! The next stage in the evolutionary process may be the new educational/experiential stores that look not quite like retail outlets. The Discovery Channel store resembles a museum, Seattle's REI store offers more sports play sites than most gyms, and Color-Me-Mine in Santa Monica could be an arts and crafts school instead of a pottery store.

There is more to do in these environments than shop or be entertained with multiscreen visions of action heroes. Here the customer is center stage in a venue that pushes the boundaries of retailing with extensive interactive displays, activities, and educational opportunities. Learn to climb at REI or fly fish at Bass Pro and then buy the equipment you need for your sporting vacation. These retailers bring entertainment to the shopping experience, and for many, it is working. REI executives report that they met their five-year sales goal after only two years. Look for further variations on this trend.

www.shopping.com

Upward of 10 percent of new cars purchased in the United States are sold through the Internet. Does this newfound avenue mean the end of the dealer? It is more likely that the rise of Internet purchases will transform the dealer into a different kind of merchant. The impact of Net shopping on the marketplace will be much like the influence of the video store on the cinema. In spite of dire predictions, cinemas, video stores, and pay-per-view alternatives are all booming. The Internet increases alternatives, and retail providers will become players in the broader process. People use the Internet to find everything in print, but they still use the bookstore/café for books and company. Both are part of an expanding distribution channel.

Source: Jeff Gunning et al., "Trends to Watch," *Urban Land,* July 1998, p. 35.

The Karasuma Center in Kusatsu, Japan, is being designed by RTKL. The center will make customers the center stage with interactive displays amidst a stunning waterfront setting that will create a special shopping experience.

Rael Slutsky/RTKL

Rael Slutsky/RTKL

The Bangkok Bus Terminal is a 13-level transit-oriented mixed-use center being developed in Bangkok, Thailand. The center will include a shopping center, office, and hotels at the terminus of major rail and bus lines.

ters have proved to be among the most flexible and successful of all land use types, shown time and again as they have reinvented themselves to meet consumers' changing demands.

As old retail concepts fade, shopping centers are reborn to reflect shoppers' latest preferences. If enclosed centers fall out of fashion, centers are de-malled; if auto-oriented centers wane, they are made pedestrian friendly; if the traditional mix of tenants is considered too boring and predictable, some entertainment is brought in; if standalone retailing is considered too one-dimensional, mix in other uses to create a town center; if the old tenants and tenant types no longer reflect what people want, get rid of them and bring in new tenants; if the design is too standardized, boxy, and characterless, create a new experience that people will want to return to again and again; and if people want to shop in new locations, build new centers and convert the old ones to something else.

Shopping centers of all types are in the midst of a historic transition as communities and consumers mature around them. The nature of this transformation will vary widely. And that is the point! The era of the standardized, predictable, formula-driven, standalone shopping center that looks the same in Los Angeles or Washington, D.C., is drawing to a close. The future belongs to those who create shopping *environments* that people want to be part of, that provide social gathering places where people can interact in a comfortable and secure environment, that reflect the emerging lifestyles, interests, and aspirations of the new consumers, that provide experiences that people find entertaining and educational, that give people the opportunity to do more than just shop, and that are integrated physically and culturally with their communities. Will these emerging places still be called shopping centers in the future? Perhaps not, but that is what they still will be.

Notes

1. "Demographic and Income Trends," National Association of Home Builders, *http://www.nahb.com/demographic.html*.

2. Marcia Berss, "Oversupply Opens Opportunities," *Forbes*, April 8, 1996, pp. 57–58.

3. M. Leanne Lachman and Deborah L. Brett, "Retail Trends: Consumers, Goods, and Real Estate," *Commentary*, Summer 1994, p. 7.

4. See Dean Schwanke et al., *Remaking the Shopping Center* (Washington, D.C.: ULI–the Urban Land Institute, 1994).

5. J'Amy Owens, "Retail in the 90s: Big Winners, Big Losers," *Seattle Journal of Commerce*, at *http://www.djc.com/special/cmarket/c10006506.html*.

6. Jennifer Kingson Bloom, "Net Commerce, Chip Cards to Gain Fast, Study Predicts," *American Banker*, January 29, 1997, p. 12.

7. Patricia M. Johnson and Richard F. Outcalt, "'Myths' of Retail May Be Hurting Your Business," *Seattle Daily Journal of Commerce*, *http://www.djc.com/special/cmarket/c10006615.html*.

Appendices, Bibliography, and Index

Appendix 1
Sample Shopping Center Lease

ARTICLE I. Basic Lease Provisions; Enumeration of Exhibits

SECTION 1 .01. Basic Lease Provisions.

DATE: _____

LANDLORD: _____

ADDRESS OF LANDLORD: _____
_____

TENANT: _____

ADDRESS OF TENANT: _____
_____

PERMITTED USE (Section 3.02): _____

TENANT'S TRADE NAME (Section 3.02): _____

SHOPPING CENTER (Section 2.01): _____
("Shopping Center"), situated in the City of _____,
County of _____, State of _____ .

PREMISES (Section 2.01): That portion of the Shopping Center outlined in red on the site plan attached hereto as Exhibit A (the "Site Plan") with the following approximate dimensions and area:
Width: ____ ft. Depth: ____ ft. Area: ____ sq. ft. Space Number: ____ .

LEASE YEAR: If the Commencement Date is other than the first day of a calendar month, the first Lease Year shall be the period of time from said Commencement Date to the end of the month in which said Commencement Date shall occur plus the following twelve (12) calendar months. Each Lease Year thereafter shall be a successive period of twelve (12) calendar months.

LEASE TERM AND COMMENCEMENT DATE (Section 2.05):
_____ (_____)
Lease Years to commence _____ (_____) days after notice by Landlord that the Premises are available to Tenant ready for Tenant's work, or the date Tenant opens for business, whichever is sooner ("Commencement Date").

FIXED MINIMUM RENT (Section 3.01):
   (a) _____ Dollars ($_____) each calendar month of any Partial Lease Year and (each Lease Year) (the first through the ___ Lease Year inclusive); and
   (b) _____ Dollars ($_____) each calendar month of the Lease Year through the ___ Lease Year inclusive.

PERCENTAGE RENT RATE (Section 3.02): _____ percent (_____%)

OPERATING COSTS (Section 4.01): Proportionate Share

REAL ESTATE TAX EXPENSE (Section 4.01): Proportionate Share

ADVERTISING AND PROMOTION (Section 5.01): Tenant Costs

PREPAID RENT: $_____ paid upon execution of this Lease to be applied to the first installment(s) of Fixed Minimum Rent due hereunder.

SECURITY DEPOSIT (Section 3.07): _____ Dollars ($_____)

GUARANTOR: _____

GUARANTOR'S ADDRESS: _____
_____

SECTION 1.02. Significance of a Basic Lease Provision.
Each reference in this "Lease" to any of the Basic Lease Provisions contained in Section 1.01 of this Article shall be deemed and construed to incorporate all of the terms thereof. The Basic Lease Provisions shall be construed in connection with and limited by any such reference.

SECTION 1.03. Enumeration of Exhibits.
The exhibits enumerated in this Section and attached to this Lease are incorporated in this Lease by this reference and are to be construed as a part of this Lease.
* Exhibit A. Site Plan of Shopping Center*
* Exhibit B. Specifications (Landlord's Work, Tenant's Work, and Sign Criteria)*

*(Not included in this book)

ARTICLE II. Demise of Premises and Quiet Enjoyment

SECTION 2.01. Description and General Obligations.
Landlord warrants to Tenant that it owns or controls the land shown on Exhibit A, together with the certain proposed buildings and improvements thereon depicted, all of which constitute the Shopping Center. In consideration of the rents, covenants, and agreements reserved and contained in this Lease, Landlord hereby leases and demises the Premises to Tenant and Tenant rents same, in order that Tenant shall continuously operate its retail business operations thereon in accordance with its Permitted Use, subject only to the terms and conditions herein contained and all liens, encumbrances, easements, restrictions, zoning laws, and governmental or other regulations affecting the Shopping Center. The approximate location of the Premises is outlined in red on the site plan attached hereto as Exhibit A (the "Site Plan").

The Premises shall include only the appurtenances specifically granted in this Lease with Landlord specifically excepting and reserving for itself, the roof, the air space above the roof, the space below the floor, the exterior portions of the Premises (other than the storefront), and the right to install, maintain, use, repair and replace pipes, ductwork, conduits, utility lines, and wires in the Premises. Landlord agrees that where possible all work in the Premises shall be performed in a manner which shall not unreasonably interfere with the normal business operations of Tenant.

SECTION 2.02. Use of Additional Area.
The use and occupation by the Tenant of the Premises shall include a revocable license to use in common with the others entitled thereto, the Common Areas, as may be designated from time to time by the Landlord, subject however to the terms and conditions of this Lease

and to rules and regulations for the use thereof as prescribed from time to time by the Landlord. The purpose of the Site Plan is to show the approximate location of the Premises. Landlord reserves the right at any time to relocate the building, automobile parking areas, and other Common Areas; to change the number of buildings, buildings' dimensions, the number of floors in any of the buildings, store dimensions, Common Areas, the identity and type of other stores and tenancies, and the right to construct other buildings or improvements in the Shopping Center from time to time and to construct double-deck or elevated parking facilities, provided only that the general location and size of the Premises, reasonable access to the Premises and the parking facilities shall not be materially impaired. The term "Common Areas" as used in this Lease shall mean all facilities furnished in the Shopping Center and designated by Landlord for the general use, in common, of occupants of the Shopping Center, including Tenant, its officers, agents, employees, and customers, which facilities may include, but are not limited to, the parking areas, streets, passenger vehicle roadways, sidewalks, walkways, service areas, roadways, loading platforms, drainage and plumbing systems, roof, canopies, ramps, landscaped areas, and other similar facilities available for common use which may from time to time exist. Landlord shall have no obligation to permit any of the Common Areas to be operated beyond the hour designated by Landlord in Section 3.02 hereof. All Common Areas not within the Premises, which Tenant may be permitted to use and occupy, are to be used and occupied under a revocable license, and if the amount of the Common Areas be diminished, Landlord shall not be subject to any liability nor shall Tenant be entitled to any compensation or diminution or abatement of rent, except as otherwise provided elsewhere herein, nor shall such diminution of the Common Areas be deemed constructive or actual eviction.

SECTION 2.03. Construction/Possession.

Landlord and Tenant hereby agree that Tenant's taking possession of the Premises shall be deemed conclusive evidence of Tenant's acceptance of the Premises in satisfactory condition and in full compliance with all covenants and obligations of Landlord in connection therewith. Tenant agrees that it will accept possession of the Premises in an "as is" condition and that no representations or inducements respecting the condition of the Premises have been made to Tenant by Landlord or its authorized representatives. Similarly, Tenant hereby acknowledges that no promises to decorate, alter, repair, or improve the Premises, either before or after the execution hereof, have been made by Landlord or its authorized representatives. Tenant further agrees that no representations have been made to Tenant that any other tenants have leased or will continue to lease space within the Shopping Center or that Tenant has any exclusive right to sell merchandise of any type and character (it being agreed and understood that Landlord shall have the right to lease other space in the Shopping Center to tenants selling merchandise similar to the merchandise to be sold by Tenant). Tenant shall perform all Tenant work in the Premises in accordance with Exhibit B attached hereto and shall thereafter install such stock, fixtures, and equipment and perform such other work as shall be necessary or appropriate in order to prepare the Premises for the opening and continuous operation of its business thereon. Tenant shall observe and perform all of its obligations under this Lease and shall pay charges for temporary water, heating, cooling, and lighting from the date upon which the Premises are made available to Tenant for its work (or from the date when Tenant commences to perform its said work, if earlier) until the Rental Commencement Date.

SECTION 2.04. Quiet Enjoyment.

Landlord covenants that Tenant, upon paying all sums due from Tenant to Landlord, hereunder "Rent," and performing and observing all of Tenant's obligations under this Lease, shall peacefully and quietly have, hold, and enjoy the Premises and the appurtenances throughout the Lease Term without interference by the Landlord, subject, nevertheless, to the other terms and provisions of this Lease.

SECTION 2.05. Statement of Lease Term.

When the Commencement Date and termination date of the Lease Term have been determined, Landlord and Tenant shall execute and deliver a written statement in recordable form specifying therein the Commencement Date and termination date of the Lease Term.

SECTION 2.06. Failure of Tenant to Open.

In the event that Tenant fails to open the Premises for business fully fixtured, stocked, and staffed on the Commencement Date of the Lease Term, then the Landlord shall have in addition to any and all remedies herein provided the right at its option to collect not only the Fixed Minimum but additional rent at the rate of 1/360th per day of the annual Fixed Minimum Rent.

SECTION 2.07. Joint Opening.

Tenant shall cooperate in an endeavor to effect a joint opening of the Shopping Center and accordingly, if so requested by Landlord in writing, will delay the opening of its store until the joint opening date stated in such written request by Landlord; in such event, notwithstanding any provisions to the contrary herein contained, the Lease Term and Tenant's obligation to pay rent shall commence upon said joint opening date.

ARTICLE III. Rent

SECTION 3.01. Fixed Minimum Rent.

During the entire Lease Term, Tenant covenants and agrees to pay to Landlord, in lawful money of the United States, without any prior demand and without any deduction or setoff whatsoever, the Fixed Minimum Rent as provided in Section 1.01. The payment of Fixed Minimum Rent by Tenant to Landlord shall be made in advance on the first day of each calendar month during the Lease Term hereof, except that the first monthly installment shall be paid prior to the Commencement Date. Fixed Minimum Rent for any partial calendar month during the Lease Term shall be prorated on a per diem basis.

SECTION 3.02. Percentage Rent.

As a further inducement for Landlord's entering into this Lease with Tenant, Tenant agrees, in addition to its covenant to pay Fixed Minimum Rent, to pay to Landlord in the manner and upon the conditions and at the times hereinafter set forth for each Lease Year an amount equal to the product of Tenant's Gross Receipts (as hereinafter defined) in excess of _____ Dollars ($_____) (the "Percentage Break Point") multiplied by the Percentage Rent Rate (hereinafter sometimes referred to as the "Percentage Rent"). Percentage Rent shall be due and payable on or before the tenth (10th) day of each calendar month during the term hereof and on or before the tenth (10th) day of the first (1st) calendar month following the termination hereof. On or before the tenth (10th) day of each calendar month during the term hereof, Tenant shall furnish Landlord with a written statement certified to be correct by Tenant showing the amount of Gross Receipts for the Premises from the beginning of the Lease Year to the end of the previous calendar month or portion thereof. If, by the end of any such preceding calendar month, _____ percent (_____%) of the Gross Receipts in the Premises shall have exceeded the Fixed Minimum Rent payable for such Lease Year, Tenant shall pay Landlord the Percentage Rent due hereunder on the basis of such Gross Receipts less the aggregate of Percentage Rent previously paid by Tenant during the Lease Year. Tenant hereby acknowledges that Tenant's business reputation, intended use of the Premises, potential for payment of Percentage Rent, and ability to generate patronage to the Premises and the Shopping Center were all relied upon by Landlord and served as significant and material inducements contributing to Landlord's decision to execute this Lease with Tenant. Tenant hereby covenants and agrees: (i) to operate in the Premises only under the Trade Name set forth in Section 1.01 and under no other name or Trade Name whatsoever without Landlord's prior written consent, (ii) to continuously use, occupy, and operate the whole of the Premises for the retail sale of its goods or services in accordance with its Permitted Use (Tenant hereby agreeing to minimize the space utilized for nonsales activities to ten percent (10%) or less of the area of the Premises), during minimum business hours of _____ to _____ , _____ days per week, or such other hours not to exceed _____ as are from time to time designated by Landlord, and for no other purpose whatsoever, and (iii) not to own, operate, or be financially interested in, either directly or indirectly (by itself or with others), a business like or similar to the business permitted to be conducted hereunder, or which employs the same or similar Trade Name, within a radius of three (3) miles of the perimeter of the Shopping Center, except for those which Tenant has in operation as of the date hereof. Without limiting Landlord's other available remedies, in the event Tenant should violate covenant (iii) above, Landlord may, at its option, (a) terminate this Lease upon thirty (30) days' written notice to Tenant, (b) enjoin the operation of the violative store, or (c) include all Gross Receipts generated by any violative store as Gross Receipts in calculating the Percentage Rent due under this Lease.

SECTION 3.03. Gross Receipts Defined.

The term "Gross Receipts" is hereby defined to mean receipts from all sales of Tenant and of all licensees, concessionaires, and tenants of Tenant, from all business conducted upon or from the Premises by Tenant and all others, and whether such sales be evidenced by check, credit charge account, exchange, or otherwise, and shall include, but not be limited to, the amount received from the sale of goods, wares, and merchandise and for services performed on or at the Premises, together with the amount of all orders taken or received at the Premises or sales completed by delivery at the Premises, whether such orders be filled from the Premises or elsewhere, and whether such sales be made by means of mechanical or other vending devices in the Premises. If any one or more departments or other divisions of Tenant's business shall be sublet by Tenant or conducted by any person, firm, or corporation other than Tenant, then there shall be included in Gross Receipts for the purpose of fixing the Percentage Rent payable hereunder, all sales of such departments or divisions, whether such sales be made at the Premises or elsewhere, in the same manner and with the same effect as if the business or sales of such departments and divisions of Tenant's business have been conducted by Tenant itself. Gross Receipts shall not include sales of merchandise for which cash has been refunded, or allowances made on merchandise claimed to be defective or unsatisfactory, provided such sales have been included in Gross Receipts. Gross Receipts shall not include the amount of any sales, use, or gross receipts tax imposed by any federal, state, municipal, or governmental authority directly on sales and collected from customers, provided that the amount thereof is added to the selling price or absorbed therein, and paid by the Tenant to such governmental authority. No franchise or capital stock tax and no income or similar tax based upon income or profits as such shall be deducted from Gross Receipts in any event whatever. Each charge or sale upon installment or credit shall be treated as a sale for the full price in the month during which such charge or sale shall be made, irrespective of the time when Tenant shall receive payment (whether full or partial) therefor. No deduction shall be allowed for uncollected or uncollectible installment or credit accounts.

SECTION 3.04. Tenant's Records.

For the purpose of ascertaining the amount payable as Percentage Rent, Tenant agrees to prepare and keep on the Premises, for a period of not less than three (3) years following each of the dates upon which Tenant delivers to Landlord each of the written statements required in Section 3.05, adequate records for the period reported upon by such statement which shall show inventories and receipt of merchandise at the Premises, and daily receipts from all sales and other transactions on or from the Premises by Tenant and any other persons conducting any business upon or from the Premises. Tenant shall record at the time of sale, in the presence of the customer, all receipts from sales or other transactions whether for cash or credit in a cash register or in cash registers having a cumulative total which shall be sealed in a manner approved by Landlord, and having such other features as shall be approved by Landlord. Tenant further agrees to keep on the Premises for at least three (3) years following the end of any partial Lease Year and each Lease Year the gross income, sales, and occupation tax returns with respect to said partial Lease Year and Lease Years and all pertinent original sales records. Pertinent original sales records shall include: (a) cash register tapes, including tapes from temporary registers; (b) serially numbered sales slips; (c) the originals of all mail orders

at and to the Premises; (d) the original records of all telephone orders at and to the Premises; (e) settlement report sheets of transactions with subtenants, concessionaires, and licensees; (f) the original records showing that merchandise returned by customers was purchased at the Premises by such customers; (g) memorandum receipts or other records of merchandise taken out on approval; (h) such other sales records, if any, which would normally be examined by an independent accountant pursuant to accepted auditing standards in performing an audit of Tenant's sales; and (i) the records specified in (a) to (h) above of subtenants, assignees, concessionaires, or licensees. Landlord and Landlord's authorized representative shall have the right to audit and otherwise examine Tenant's records aforesaid during regular business hours. If such audit shall disclose a deficiency in Percentage Rent, Tenant shall promptly pay such deficiency. If such audit shows Gross Receipts to be understated by _____ percent or more, Tenant shall pay the cost of such audit in addition to any deficiency, and if such audit shows Gross Receipts to be understated by _____ percent or more, Landlord shall have the right to terminate this Lease upon five (5) days' written notice to Tenant, in addition to any other remedies provided for Tenant's default hereunder.

SECTION 3.05. Reports by Tenant.

In addition to the written statement of Gross Receipts required pursuant to Section 3.02, Tenant shall submit to Landlord on or before the sixtieth (60th) day following the end of each Lease Year at the place then fixed for the payment of rent a written statement signed by Tenant and certified by it to be true and correct, by either a certified public accountant or a financial officer of Tenant reasonably acceptable to Landlord, showing in accurate detail the amount of Gross Receipts during the preceding Lease Year. The statements referred to herein shall be in such form and style and contain such details and breakdown as Landlord may reasonably determine.

SECTION 3.06. Termination by Landlord for Insufficient Percentage Rent.

In the event Tenant's Gross Receipts for the third Lease Year or any subsequent Lease Year during the Term (or any extension or renewal thereof) are insufficient to produce Percentage Rent equal to at least _____ percent of the Fixed Minimum Rent for that year, Landlord may at its election, terminate this Lease and the tenancy thereby created by giving to Tenant, within one hundred eighty (180) days after the expiration of said period, written notice of Landlord's election to do so. The termination shall be effective not less than ninety (90) days after Landlord's election; provided, however, Landlord's termination as aforesaid shall be ineffective if Tenant within thirty (30) days after receipt of Landlord's notice, shall pay to Landlord the amount of such rent deficiency and shall submit a written agreement increasing Tenant's obligation to pay Fixed Minimum Rent by an amount equal to _____ percent of Fixed Minimum Rent thereafter payable.

SECTION 3.07. Security Deposit.

Tenant has concurrently with the execution of this Lease deposited with Landlord the sum set forth in Section 1.01 (hereinafter sometimes referred to as the "Security Deposit") as security for the full performance of every provision of this Lease by Tenant. Landlord may apply all or any part of the Security Deposit to cure any default by Tenant hereunder, and Tenant shall promptly restore to the Security Deposit all amounts so applied upon invoice. If Tenant shall fully perform each provision of this Lease, any portion of the Security Deposit which has not been appropriated by Landlord in accordance with the provisions hereof shall be returned to Tenant without interest within thirty (30) days after the expiration of the Lease Term. Landlord may deliver the funds deposited hereunder by Tenant to the purchaser or transferee of Landlord's interest in the Premises in the event that such interest be sold or transferred, and, in the event the purchaser or transferee assumes the obligations of Landlord, thereupon Landlord shall be discharged from any further liability with respect to such deposit.

SECTION 3.08. Additional Charges.

In addition to Fixed Minimum Rent and Percentage Rent, all other payments, including but not limited to Operating Charges and Charges for Taxes, to be made by Tenant, either to Landlord or the Promotion and Advertising Fund, shall be deemed to be and shall become "Additional Rent" hereunder whether or not the same be designated as such, and shall be due and payable on demand together with any interest thereon; and Landlord shall have the same remedies for failure to pay same as for a nonpayment of Minimum or Percentage Rent. (Minimum Rent, Percentage Rent, and Additional Rent are hereinafter sometimes collectively referred to as "Rent.") If Tenant shall fail to make any payment of Rent when due as required under the applicable provisions of this Lease, Tenant shall pay a late charge in accordance with Section 3.09 hereof.

SECTION 3.09. Past Due Rent and Additional Rent.

If Tenant shall fail to pay, when the same is due and payable, any Rent or any Additional Rent, or amounts or charges of the character described in Section 3.08 hereof, such unpaid amounts shall bear interest from the due date thereof to the date of payment at the rate which is the lesser of eighteen percent (18%) per annum or the maximum interest rate permitted by law. Tenant shall in addition pay as Additional Rent a fee of Fifty Dollars ($50.00) for processing of late payments.

ARTICLE IV. Common Areas and Operating Costs

SECTION 4.01. Operating Costs.

During each month of the Lease Term, Tenant shall pay, along with its monthly installments of Fixed Minimum Rent and without demand, deduction, or setoff, as Additional Rent to Landlord, Tenant's proportionate share of all costs incurred by Landlord in maintaining, repairing, replacing, improving, operating, managing, administering, and insuring the portions of the Shopping Center which are the responsibility of Landlord hereunder (herein sometimes referred to as the "Operating Costs"), including, without limitation, the total costs of operating, repairing, replacing, lighting, cleaning, landscaping, maintaining, painting, securing (if Landlord shall so elect), managing, and insuring (including, without limitation, premiums for insurance policies whether under master or blanket policies or separate policies, and shall include, without limitation, commercial general liability insurance for personal injury, wrongful arrest or detainer, death and property damage, rent insurance, workers' compensation insurance, fidelity bonds for personnel, and plate glass insurance) the Shopping Center; costs incurred in complying with governmental laws, ordinances, rules, and regulations; and paying all taxes, public charges, and assessments of whatsoever nature directly or indirectly assessed or imposed upon the land, buildings, equipment, and improvements constituting the Shopping Center and the rents therefrom, including, but not limited to, all real property taxes, rates, duties and assessments, local improvement taxes, import charges or levies, whether general or special, that are levied, charged, or assessed against the Shopping Center by any lawful taxing authority whether federal, state, county, municipal, school, or otherwise (other than income, inheritance, and franchise taxes thereon), plus an administrative cost equal to fifteen percent (15%) of the foregoing costs.

* *

[ALTERNATE PROVISION TO BE USED FOR ENCLOSED MALL]

During each month of the term of this Lease, Tenant shall pay, along with its monthly installments of Fixed Minimum Rent and without demand, deduction, or setoff, as Additional Rent to Landlord, Tenant's proportionate share of Landlord's total costs (including appropriate reserves) for operating, managing, administering, maintaining, repairing, replacing, or improving the portions of the Shopping Center which are the responsibility of Landlord hereunder and Landlord's total costs for all insurance covering the Shopping Center, the cost of all deductibles paid by Landlord, ground lease payments, and Landlord's cost for furnishing heating, ventilating, and air conditioning in connection with all or any part of the Shopping Center ("Operating Costs"). Without limitation of the generality of the foregoing, Operating Costs shall include the cost to Landlord of the following: premiums for insurance policies whether under master or blanket policies or separate policies,

and shall include, without limitation, commercial general liability insurance for personal injury, wrongful arrest or detainer, death, and property damage; all risk (special form) insurance; rent insurance; workers' compensation insurance; fidelity bonds for personnel; and plate glass insurance; lighting, cleaning, snow and ice removal, landscaping, painting, policing, providing security (if Landlord shall so elect), fire protection, drainage, heating, ventilating, and air conditioning; depreciation of machinery and equipment used in connection with the Shopping Center and the maintenance thereof, the maintenance and replacement of the roof of the enclosed mall and the enclosed mall building, the maintenance and operation of the sprinkler system installed in the Shopping Center; costs incurred in complying with governmental laws, ordinances, rules, and regulations together with Landlord's expenses in determining the amount of any charges or assessments levied on the Shopping Center; all on-site costs and personnel expenses incurred by Landlord in managing the Shopping Center (including all contributions and payments required to be paid by the employer and all fringe benefits); and paying all taxes, public charges, and assessments of whatsoever nature directly or indirectly assessed or imposed upon the land, buildings, equipment, and improvements constituting the Shopping Center and the rents therefrom, including, but not limited to, all real property taxes, rates, duties, and assessments, local improvement taxes, import charges, or levies, whether general or special, that are levied, charged or assessed against the Shopping Center by any lawful taxing authority whether federal, state, county, municipal, school, or otherwise (other than income, inheritance, and franchise taxes thereon), plus an amount for administration equal to fifteen percent (15%) of the total of all Operating Costs.

* *

The net amount of Operating Costs paid to Landlord by any "Department Stores" (defined for purposes of this Lease as stores occupying _____ square feet or more of the gross leasable area) or tenants of freestanding buildings in the Shopping Center shall be deducted from Operating Costs prior to computing Tenant's proportionate share of Operating Costs, and accordingly, the gross leasable area of such Department Stores and tenants of freestanding buildings in the Shopping Center shall be deducted from the gross leasable area of the Shopping Center for purposes of computing Tenant's proportionate share of Operating Costs. Tenant's proportionate share of Operating Costs as adjusted pursuant to the foregoing sentence shall be computed by multiplying Operating Costs by a fraction, the numerator of which shall be the number of square feet of floor area of the Premises and the denominator of which shall be the number of square feet of gross leasable area of the Shopping Center. Tenant shall pay its proportionate share of Operating Costs in advance based on estimates made by Landlord from time to time. Estimates shall be revised annually on the basis of actual Operating Costs for the preceding year of operations. Should Operating Costs be underestimated, Tenant shall pay any deficiency along with the payment of Fixed Minimum Rent next due and thereafter pay its adjusted proportionate share of Operating Costs in equal monthly installments as herein provided. Any excess payments shall be credited against the payment of Operating Costs next due.

ARTICLE V. Advertising and Promotion

SECTION 5.01. Tenant Costs.

It is understood and agreed that it is in the best interest of Landlord and Tenant to advertise and promote the Shopping Center. Accordingly, Tenant shall pay to Landlord for such purposes in equal monthly installments, as Additional Rent, a promotion charge equal to the greater of (i) _____ ($ _____) per square foot of gross leasable area in the Premises, or (ii) _____ ($ _____), payable in advance along with Tenant's payment of Minimum Rent hereunder.

ARTICLE VI. Utilities

SECTION 6.01. Tenant Responsibilities.
Tenant shall make application for, obtain, pay for, and be solely responsible for all utilities required, used, or consumed in the Premises, including, but not limited to, gas, water (including water for domestic uses and for fire protection), telephone, electricity, sewer service, garbage collection services, HVAC maintenance services, or any similar service (herein sometimes collectively referred to as the "Utility Services"). In the event that any charge for any utility supplied to the Premises is not paid by Tenant to the utility supplier when due, then Landlord may, but shall not be required to, pay such charge for and on behalf of Tenant, with any such amount paid by Landlord being repaid by Tenant to Landlord, as Additional Rent, promptly upon demand. Additionally, if Landlord shall elect to supply any of the Utility Services, then Tenant shall pay to Landlord the cost of its utility consumption, along with the cost of installing separate metering devices, if necessary. Landlord agrees that the cost to Tenant of any Landlord-provided utility service shall not exceed the amount Tenant would have had to pay had it independently obtained said utility service from the local utility supplier. Landlord and Tenant hereby agree that Landlord shall not be liable for any interruptions or curtailment in utility services due to causes beyond its control or due to Landlord's alteration, repair, or improvement of the Premises or the Shopping Center.

ARTICLE VII. Installation, Maintenance, Operation, and Repair

SECTION 7.01. Tenant Installation.
Tenant shall, at Tenant's sole expense, install all trade fixtures and equipment required to operate its business (all of which shall be of first-class quality and workmanship). All trade fixtures, signs, or other personal property installed in the Premises by Tenant shall remain the property of Tenant and may be removed at any time provided that Tenant is not in default hereunder and provided the removal thereof does not cause, contribute to, or result in Tenant's default hereunder; and further provided that Tenant shall at Tenant's sole expense promptly repair any damage to the Premises resulting from the removal of personal property and shall replace same with personal property of like or better quality. The term "trade fixtures" as used herein shall not include carpeting, floor coverings, attached shelving, lighting fixtures other than freestanding lamps, wall coverings, or similar Tenant improvements which shall become the property of Landlord upon surrender of the Premises by Tenant for whatever reason. Tenant shall not attach any fixtures or articles to any portion of the Premises, nor make any alterations, additions, improvements, or changes or perform any other work whatsoever in and to the Premises, other than minor interior, cosmetic, and decorative changes which do not exceed One Thousand and No/100 Dollars ($1,000.00) in the aggregate per Lease Year, without in each instance obtaining the prior written approval of Landlord. Any alterations, additions, improvements, changes to the Premises, or other work permitted herein shall be made by Tenant at Tenant's sole cost and expense in the manner set forth in Exhibit B.

SECTION 7.02. Maintenance by Tenant.
Except as provided in Section 7.01 hereof, Tenant shall, at Tenant's expense, at all times keep the Premises (interior and exterior) and appurtenances thereto in good order, condition, and repair, clean, sanitary, and safe, including the replacement of equipment, fixtures, and all broken glass (with glass of the same size and quality), and shall, in a manner satisfactory to Landlord, decorate and paint the Premises when necessary to maintain at all times a clean and sightly appearance. In the event Tenant fails to perform any of its obligations as required hereunder, Landlord may, but shall not be required to, perform and satisfy same with Tenant hereby agreeing to reimburse Landlord, as Additional Rent, for the cost thereof promptly upon demand. Tenant shall make any and all additions, improvements, alterations, and repairs to or on the Premises (including, without limitation, all modifications to any fire sprinkler system located within the Premises), other than

those required for the structural repair and maintenance of the roof, foundation, or exterior walls, which may at any time during the Lease Term be required or recommended by any lawful authorities, insurance underwriters, Inspection Rating Bureaus, or insurance inspectors designated by Landlord. Landlord may, but shall not be obligated to, deal directly with any authorities respecting their requirements for additions, improvements, alterations, or repairs. All such work shall be performed in a good and workmanlike manner in accordance with the requirements set forth in Exhibit B. All Tenant work (as set forth in Exhibit B) and all such additions, improvements, and alterations thereto shall become the property of the Landlord upon the expiration or earlier termination of this Lease.

SECTION 7.03. Signs, Awnings, and Canopies.
Tenant will not place or suffer to be placed or maintained on any exterior door, wall, or window of the Premises any sign, awning, or canopy, or advertising matter or other thing of any kind, and will not place or maintain any exterior lighting, plumbing fixture, or protruding object or any decoration, lettering, or advertising matter on the glass of any window or door of the Premises without first obtaining Landlord's written approval and consent. Tenant further agrees to maintain such sign, awning, canopy, decoration, lettering, advertising matter, or other thing as may be approved in good condition and repair at all times.

SECTION 7.04. Tenant Shall Discharge All Liens.
Tenant will not create or permit to be created or to remain, and will discharge, any lien (including, but not limited to, the liens of mechanics, laborers, or materialmen for work or materials alleged to be done or furnished in connection with the Premises), encumbrance, or other charge upon the Premises or any part thereof, upon Tenant's leasehold interest therein, provided that Tenant shall not be required to discharge any such liens, encumbrances, or charges as may be placed upon the Premises by the act of Landlord. Tenant shall have the right to contest, in good faith and by appropriate legal proceedings, the validity or amount of any mechanics', laborers', or materialmen's lien or claimed lien. In the event of such contest, Tenant shall give to Landlord reasonable security as may be amended by Landlord to insure payment thereof and to prevent any sale, foreclosure, or forfeiture of the Premises or any part thereof by reason of such nonpayment. On final determination of such lien or such claim for lien, Tenant will immediately pay any judgment rendered, with all proper costs and charges, and shall have such lien released or judgment satisfied at Tenant's expense, and upon such payment and release of satisfaction, Landlord will promptly return to Tenant such security as Landlord shall have received in connection with such contest. Landlord reserves the right to enter the Premises to post and keep posted notices of nonresponsibility for any such lien. Tenant will pay, protect, and indemnify Landlord within ten (10) days after demand therefor, from and against all liabilities, losses, claims, damages, costs, and expenses, including reasonable attorney's fees, incurred by Landlord by reason of the filing of any lien and/or the removal of the same.

SECTION 7.05. Maintenance by Landlord.
Landlord shall keep the exterior supporting walls, the foundations, roof, and spouting of the Premises in reasonable repair, provided that Tenant shall promptly give Landlord written notice of the necessity for such repairs, and provided that the damage thereto shall not have been caused by negligence of Tenant, its concessionaires, officers, agents, employees, licensees, or invitees; in which event Tenant shall be responsible therefor. Landlord shall have no obligation to repair, maintain, alter, or perform any other acts with reference to the Premises or any part thereof, or any plumbing, heating, ventilating, electrical, air conditioning, or other mechanical installations therein.

SECTION 7.06. Hazardous Substances.
Landlord hereby warrants that to the best of its knowledge and belief as of the date of this Lease there are no Hazardous Substances (as defined hereinbelow) currently existing on, in, or under the Premises or the Shopping Center and that there are no underground storage tanks under the Premises or the Shopping Center. Tenant hereby covenants and agrees that it shall not discharge any Hazardous Substances on, in,

or under the Premises or the Shopping Center. Each party shall fully indemnify and hold the other party harmless from any liability, damage, loss, cost, or expense that either party might otherwise suffer from the other party's breach or default of its warranties or covenants, as the case may be, in this Section 7.06. The indemnity of this Section 7.06 shall survive the expiration or other termination of this Lease. "Hazardous Substances" means and includes any of the substances, materials, elements, or compounds that are contained in the list of hazardous substances adopted by the United States Environmental Protection Agency (the "EPA") and the list of toxic pollutants designated by the United States Congress or the EPA or any substances, materials, elements, or compounds affected by any other federal, state, or local statute, law, ordinance, code, rule, regulation, order, or decree now or at any time hereafter in effect regulating, relating to, or imposing liability or standards of conduct concerning any hazardous, toxic, dangerous, restricted, or otherwise regulated waste, substance, or material, as now or at any time hereafter in effect.

ARTICLE VIII. Operating Rules, Regulations, Surrender

SECTION 8.01. Rules and Regulations.
Tenant agrees to comply with and observe the following rules and regulations:

(1) All loading and unloading of goods shall be done only at such times, in the areas, and through the entrances designated for such purposes by Landlord.

(2) The delivery or shipping of merchandise, supplies, and fixtures to and from the Premises shall be subject to such rules and regulations as in the judgment of Landlord are necessary for the proper operation of the Premises or Shopping Center.

(3) All garbage and refuse shall be kept in the kind of container specified by Landlord, and shall be placed outside of the Premises, prepared for collection in the manner and at the time and places specified by Landlord. If Landlord shall provide or designate a service for picking up refuse and garbage, Tenant shall use same at Tenant's cost. Tenant shall pay the cost of removal of any of Tenant's refuse or rubbish.

(4) No radio or television or other similar device shall be installed without first obtaining in each instance Landlord's consent in writing. No aerial shall be erected on the roof or exterior walls of the Premises or on the grounds without, in each instance, the written consent of Landlord. Any aerial so installed without such written consent shall be subject to removal without notice at any time.

(5) No loudspeakers, televisions, phonographs, radios, or other devices shall be used in a manner so as to be heard or seen outside of the Premises without the prior written consent of Landlord.

(6) If the Premises are equipped with heating facilities separate from those in the remainder of the Shopping Center, Tenant shall keep the Premises at a temperature sufficiently high to prevent freezing of water in pipes and fixtures.

(7) The exterior areas immediately adjoining the Premises shall be kept clean and free from snow, ice, dirt, and rubbish by Tenant to the satisfaction of Landlord, and Tenant shall not place or permit any obstructions or merchandise in such areas.

(8) Tenant and Tenant's employees shall park their cars only in those parking areas designated for that purpose by Landlord. Tenant shall furnish Landlord with State automobile license numbers assigned to Tenant's car or cars, and cars of Tenant's employees, within five (5) days after taking possession of the Premises and shall thereafter notify Landlord of any changes within five (5) days after such changes occur. In the event that Tenant or its employees fail to park their cars in designated parking areas as aforesaid, then Landlord at its option shall charge Tenant Ten Dollars ($10.00) per day per car parked in any area other than those designated, as and for liquidated damage.

(9) The plumbing facilities shall not be used for any other purpose than that for which they are constructed, and no foreign substance of any kind shall be thrown therein, and the expense of any breakage, stoppage, or damage resulting from a violation of this provision shall be borne by Tenant who shall, or whose employees, agents, or invitees shall, have caused it.

(10) Tenant shall use at Tenant's cost such pest extermination contractor as Landlord may direct and at such intervals as Landlord may require.

(11) Tenant shall not burn any trash or garbage of any kind in or about the Premises, the Shopping Center, or within one mile of the outside property lines of the Shopping Center.

(12) Tenant shall not make noises, cause disturbances, or create odors which may be offensive to other tenants of the Shopping Center or their officers, employees, agents, servants, customers, or invitees.

(13) Tenant shall not commit or suffer to be committed any waste upon the Premises or any nuisance or other act or thing which may disturb the quiet enjoyment of any other tenant in the building in which the Premises may be located, or in the Shopping Center, or which may disturb the quiet enjoyment of any person within five hundred feet of the boundaries of the Shopping Center.

(14) Tenant shall, at Tenant's sole cost and expense, comply with all of the requirements of all county, municipal, state, federal, and other applicable governmental authorities, now in force, or which may hereafter be in force, pertaining to the Premises, and shall faithfully observe in the use of the Premises all municipal and county ordinances and state and federal statutes now in force or which may hereafter be in force, and all regulations, orders, and other requirements issued or made pursuant to any such ordinances and statutes, including, without limitation, Title III of the Americans with Disabilities Act of 1990 ("ADA") and the U.S. Occupational Safety and Health Administration ("OSHA"). Notwithstanding the foregoing, Landlord shall cause the structural portions of the Shopping Center, including the Premises, to comply with all applicable statutes, ordinances, rules, regulations, orders, and requirements now or hereafter applicable thereto; including, but not limited to, any requirements imposed under ADA or OSHA; provided, however, if with respect to the Premises, such compliance is necessitated by reason of Tenant's particular manner of using the Premises, then such compliance will be accomplished by Tenant at its expense. Tenant agrees to comply with and observe the rules and regulations set forth above. Tenant's failure to keep and observe said rules and regulations shall constitute a breach of the terms of this Lease in the manner as if the same were contained herein as covenants. Landlord reserves the right from time to time to amend or supplement said rules and regulations, and to adopt and promulgate additional rules and regulations applicable to the Premises and the Shopping Center.

ARTICLE IX. Insurance

SECTION 9.01. Tenant's Coverage.
Tenant shall maintain at its sole expense during the term hereof commercial general liability insurance with insurance companies satisfactory to Landlord covering Tenant, and naming Landlord and Landlord's mortgagee as an additional insured, providing single limit coverage of not less than $3,000,000.00 bodily injury, including death and personal injury, and property damage for any one occurrence in the Premises, and $3,000,000.00 per location general aggregate. Tenant shall also keep in force rent insurance as well as fire and extended coverage, vandalism, and malicious mischief insurance, including, but not limited to, a standard "all risk" policy insuring and protecting against all risk of physical loss or damage to Tenant's improvements and property, including, but not limited to, inventory, trade fixtures, furnishings, and other personal property for the full replacement cost thereof. Tenant will cause such insurance policies to name Landlord as an additional insured. In addition, Tenant shall keep in force workers' compensation or similar insurance to the extent required by law. Tenant shall deliver said policies or certificates thereof to Landlord at least five (5) days prior to the commencement of Tenant's Work. Should Tenant fail to effect the insurance called for herein, Landlord may, at its sole option, procure said insurance and pay the requisite premiums, in which event, Tenant shall pay all sums so expended to Landlord, as Additional Rent following invoice. Each insurer under the policies required hereunder shall agree by endorsement on the policy issued by it or by independent instrument furnished to Landlord that it will give Landlord thirty (30) days' prior written notice before the policy or policies in question shall be altered or canceled.

SECTION 9.02. Increase in Fire Insurance Premium.

Tenant shall not keep, use, sell, or offer for sale in or upon the Premises any article which may be prohibited by the standard form of fire insurance policy. Tenant agrees to pay any increase in premiums for fire and extended coverage insurance that may be charged during the Lease Term on the amount of such insurance which may be carried by Landlord on the Premises or the Shopping Center, resulting from the type of merchandise sold by Tenant in the Premises, whether or not Landlord has consented to the same. In determining whether increased premiums are the result of Tenant's use of the Premises, a schedule, issued by the organization making the insurance rate on the Premises, showing the various components of such rate, shall be conclusive evidence of the several items and charges which make up the fire insurance rate on the Premises.

In the event Tenant's occupancy causes any increase of premium for the fire and/or casualty rates on the Premises, Tenant shall pay the additional premium on the fire and/or casualty insurance policies by reason thereof. The Tenant also shall pay, in such event, any additional premium on the rent insurance policy that may be carried by the Landlord for its protection against rent loss through fire. Bills for such additional premiums shall be rendered by Landlord to Tenant at such times as Landlord may elect, and shall be due from, and payable by, Tenant when rendered, and the amount thereof shall be deemed to be, and be paid as, Additional Rent.

SECTION 9.03. Indemnification.

Tenant hereby agrees to indemnify and hold Landlord harmless from any and all claims, damages, liabilities, or expenses arising out of (a) Tenant's use of the Premises or the Shopping Center, (b) any and all claims arising from any breach or default in the performance of any obligation of Tenant, (c) any act, omission, or negligence of Tenant, its agents, or employees. Tenant further releases Landlord from liability for any damages sustained by Tenant or any other person claiming by, through, or under Tenant due to the Premises, the Shopping Center, or any part thereof or any appurtenances thereto becoming out of repair, or due to the happening of any accident, including, but not limited to, any damage caused by water, snow, windstorm, tornado, gas, steam, electrical wiring, sprinkler system, plumbing, heating, and air conditioning apparatus and from any acts or omissions of cotenants or other occupants of the Shopping Center. Landlord shall not be liable for any damage to or loss of Tenant's personal property, inventory, fixtures, or improvements, from any cause whatsoever, except the affirmative acts of proven negligence of Landlord, and then only to the extent not covered by insurance to be obtained by Tenant in accordance with Section 9.01 hereof.

SECTION 9.04. Mutual Release, Waiver of Subrogation.

Landlord and Tenant hereby release each other and anyone claiming through or under the other by way of subrogation from any and all liability for any loss of or damage to property, whether or not caused by the negligence or fault of the other party. In addition, Landlord and Tenant shall cause each insurance policy carried by them insuring the Premises or the Shopping Center, or the contents thereof, to be written to provide that the insurer waives all rights of recovery by way of subrogation against the other party hereto in connection with any loss or damage covered by the policy.

ARTICLE X. Casualty and Condemnation

SECTION 10.01. Fire, Explosion, or Other Casualty.

In the event the Premises are damaged by fire, explosion or any other casualty to an extent which is less than fifty percent (50%) of the cost of replacement of the Premises, the damage, except as provided in Section 10.02, shall promptly be repaired by Landlord at Landlord's expense, provided that Landlord shall not be obligated to expend for such repair an amount in excess of the insurance proceeds recovered or recoverable as a result of such damage, and that in no event shall Landlord be required to repair or replace Tenant's stock in trade fixtures, furniture, furnishings, floor coverings, and equipment. If: (a) Landlord

is not required to repair as hereinabove provided, or (b) the Premises shall be damaged to the extent of fifty percent (50%) or more of the cost of replacement, or (c) the building of which the Premises are a part is damaged to the extent of twenty-five percent (25%) or more of the cost of replacement, or (d) the buildings (taken in the aggregate) in the Shopping Center shall be damaged to the extent of more than twenty-five percent (25%) or more of the cost of replacement, then Landlord may elect either to repair or rebuild the Premises or the building or buildings, or to terminate this Lease upon giving notice of such election in writing to Tenant within ninety (90) days after the occurrence of the event causing the damage. If the casualty, repairing, or rebuilding shall render the Premises untenantable, in whole or in part, and the damage shall not have been due to the default or neglect of Tenant, a proportionate abatement of the Fixed Minimum Rent shall be allowed from the date when the damage occurred until the date Landlord completes its work, said proportion to be computed on the basis of the relation which the gross square foot area of the space rendered untenantable bears to the floor area of the Premises. Nothing in this Section shall be construed to permit the abatement in whole or in part of the Percentage Rent, but, for the purpose of Section 3.02 hereof, the computation of Percentage Rent shall be based upon the revised Fixed Minimum Rent as the same may be abated pursuant to this Section 10.01.

SECTION 10.02. Landlord's and Tenant's Work.

The provisions of this Article X with respect to repair by Landlord shall be limited to such repair as is necessary to place the Premises in the same condition as when possession was delivered by Landlord. Promptly following such condemnation, Tenant shall, at Tenant's expense, perform any work required to place the premises in the condition pursuant to Exhibit B and Tenant shall restore, repair, or replace its stock in trade fixtures, furniture, furnishings, floor coverings, and equipment, and if Tenant has closed, Tenant shall promptly reopen for business.

SECTION 10.03. Condemnation.

If the whole of the Premises, or so much thereof as to render the balance unusable by Tenant, shall be taken under power of eminent domain, or otherwise transferred in lieu thereof, or if any part of the Shopping Center is taken and its continued operation is not, in Landlord's sole opinion, economical, this Lease shall automatically terminate as of the date possession is taken by the condemning authority. No award for any total or partial taking shall be apportioned, and Tenant hereby unconditionally assigns to Landlord any award which may be made in such taking or condemnation. In the event of a partial taking which does not result in the termination of this Lease, Fixed Minimum Rent shall be apportioned according to the part of the Premises remaining usable by Tenant.

SECTION 10.04. Condemnation Award.

All compensation awarded or paid for any taking or acquiring under the power or threat of eminent domain, whether for the whole or a part of the Premises or Shopping Center, shall be the property of Landlord, whether such damages shall be awarded as compensation for diminution in the value of the leasehold or to the fee of the Premises or otherwise, and Tenant hereby assigns to Landlord all of the Tenant's right, title, and interest in and to any and all such compensation; provided, however, that Landlord shall not be entitled to any award specifically made to Tenant for the taking of Tenant's trade fixtures, furniture, or leasehold improvements to the extent of the cost to Tenant of said improvements (exclusive of Landlord's contribution), less depreciation computed from the date of said improvements to the expiration of the original term of this Lease.

SECTION 10.05. Restoration.

In the event of a taking in respect of which this Lease is not terminated, this Lease and the term hereof shall continue in full force and effect and Landlord forthwith shall attempt to restore the remaining portions of the Premises and the Shopping Center to an architectural whole; provided, however, that in no event shall Landlord be required to expend in connection with such restoration more than the amount of any condemnation award actually received by Landlord.

ARTICLE XI. Default and Remedies

SECTION 11.01. Definitions.

In the event that Tenant (a) fails to pay all or any portion of any sum due from Tenant hereunder or pursuant to any exhibit hereto within five (5) days following notice; (b) fails to cease all conduct prohibited hereby immediately upon receipt of written notice from Landlord; (c) fails to take actions in accordance with the provisions of written notice from Landlord to remedy Tenant's failure to perform any of the terms, covenants, and conditions hereof; (d) fails to conduct business in the Premises as herein required; (e) commits an act in violation of this Lease which Landlord has previously notified Tenant to cease more than once in any year; (f) becomes bankrupt, insolvent, or files any debtor proceeding; takes or has taken against Tenant any petition of bankruptcy; takes action or has action taken against Tenant for the appointment of a receiver for all or a portion of Tenant's assets; files a petition for a corporate reorganization; makes an assignment for the benefit of creditors, or if in any other manner Tenant's interest hereunder shall pass to another by operation of law (any or all of the occurrences in this said Section 11.01(f) shall be deemed a default on account of bankruptcy for the purposes hereof and such default on account of bankruptcy shall apply to and include any Guarantor of this Lease); (g) commits waste to the Premises; or (h) is otherwise in breach of Tenant's obligations hereunder and shall not have cured same within ten (10) days following written notice from Landlord; then Tenant shall be in default hereunder and Landlord may, at its option and without further notice to Tenant, terminate Tenant's right to possession of the Premises and without terminating this Lease reenter and resume possession of the Premises and/or declare this Lease terminated, and may thereupon in either event remove all persons and property from the Premises, with or without resort to process of any court, either by force or otherwise. Notwithstanding such reentry by Landlord, Tenant hereby indemnifies and holds Landlord harmless from any and all loss or damage which Tenant may incur by reason of the termination of this Lease and/or Tenant's right to possession hereunder. In no event shall Landlord's termination of this Lease and/or Tenant's right to possession of the Premises abrogate Tenant's agreement to pay rent and additional charges due hereunder for the full term hereof. Following reentry of the Premises by Landlord, Tenant shall continue to pay all such rent and additional charges as same become due under the terms of this Lease, together with all other expenses incurred by Landlord in regaining possession, until such time, if any, as Landlord relets same and the Premises are occupied by such successor, it being understood that Landlord shall have no obligations to mitigate Tenant's damages by reletting the Premises. Upon reletting, sums received from such new lessee by Landlord shall be applied first to payment of costs incident to reletting; any excess shall then be applied to any indebtedness to Landlord from Tenant other than for Fixed Minimum and Percentage Rent; and any excess shall then be applied to the payment of Minimum and Percentage Rent due and unpaid. The balance, if any, shall be applied against the deficiency between all amounts received hereunder and sums to be received by Landlord on reletting, which deficiency Tenant shall pay to Landlord in full, within five (5) days of notice of same from Landlord. Tenant shall have no right to any proceeds of reletting that remain following application of same in the manner set forth herein. The Percentage Rent for which Tenant remains prospectively liable under the provisions hereof shall be a sum equal to the greatest amount of Percentage Rent paid by Tenant for any Lease Year since the Commencement Date multiplied by the number of years remaining in the term at the time of such termination.

SECTION 11.02. Rights and Remedies.

The various rights and remedies herein granted to Landlord shall be cumulative and in addition to any others Landlord may be entitled to by law or in equity, and the exercise of one or more rights or remedies shall not impair Landlord's right to exercise any other right or remedy. In all events, Landlord shall have the right upon notice to Tenant to cure any breach by Tenant at Tenant's sole cost and expense, and Tenant shall reimburse Landlord for such expense upon demand.

SECTION 11.03. Bankruptcy.

If Landlord shall not be permitted to terminate this Lease as hereinabove provided because of the provisions of Title 11 of the United States Code relating to Bankruptcy, as amended ("Bankruptcy Code"), then Tenant as a debtor-in-possession or any trustee for Tenant agrees promptly, within no more than fifteen (15) days upon request by Landlord to the Bankruptcy Court, to assume or reject this Lease and Tenant on behalf of itself, and any trustee agrees not to seek or request any extension or adjournment of any application to assume or reject this Lease by Landlord with such Court. In such event, Tenant or any trustee for Tenant may only assume this Lease if it (a) cures or provides adequate assurance that the trustees will promptly cure any default hereunder, (b) compensates or provides adequate assurance that Tenant will promptly compensate Landlord for any actual pecuniary loss to Landlord resulting from Tenant's defaults, and (c) provides adequate assurance of performance during the fully stated term hereof of all of the terms, covenants, and provisions of this Lease to be performed by Tenant. In no event after the assumption of this Lease shall any then existing default remain uncured for a period in excess of the earlier of ten (10) days or the time period set forth herein. Adequate assurance of performance of this Lease, as set forth hereinabove, shall include, without limitation, adequate assurance (1) of the source of rent reserved hereunder, (2) that any Percentage Rent due hereunder will not decline from the levels anticipated, and (3) that the assumption of this Lease will not breach any provision hereunder. In the event of a filing of a petition under the Bankruptcy Code, Landlord shall have no obligation to provide Tenant with any services or utilities as herein required, unless Tenant shall have paid and be current in all payments of Operating Costs, utilities, or other charges therefor.

SECTION 11.04. Self Help.

If either party defaults in the performance of any obligation imposed on it by this Lease and does not cure such default within thirty (30) days after written notice from the other party specifying the default (or does not within said period commence and diligently proceed to cure such default), the other party, without waiver of or prejudice to any other right or remedy it may have, shall have the right, at any time thereafter, to cure such default for the account of the defaulting party, and the defaulting party shall reimburse the other party upon invoice for any amount paid and any expense or contractual liability so incurred. If Landlord is the defaulting party and fails to reimburse Tenant within ten (10) days after invoice, then Tenant shall have the right to offset the amount due thereunder, together with interest at the rate of two percent (2%) above the then current prime lending rate published in the *Wall Street Journal*, against Fixed Minimum Rent due from Tenant to Landlord under this Lease until Tenant has been completely reimbursed for its expenses. The foregoing to the contrary notwithstanding, except in cases of emergency as provided hereinbelow Tenant shall have no right to cure any default hereunder unless and until Tenant has given not less than thirty (30) days' prior written notice of such default to the holder of any mortgage, deed to secure debt, or deed of trust on the Premises or the Shopping Center of which Tenant has received notice from Landlord and such holder fails to cure or cause Landlord to cure said default.

In the event of emergencies, or where necessary to prevent injury to persons or damage to property, either party may cure a default by the other before the expiration of the waiting period, but after giving such written or oral notice to the other party as is practical under all of the circumstances.

ARTICLE XII. Assignment and Subletting

SECTION 12.01. Assignment and Subletting.

Tenant acknowledges that Tenant's agreement to operate in the Premises for the Permitted Use set forth in Section 1.01 hereof for the fully stated term hereof was a primary inducement and precondition to Landlord's agreement to lease the Premises to Tenant. Accordingly, Tenant's interest in the Premises shall be limited to the use and occupancy thereof in accordance with the provisions hereof and shall be nontransferable. Any attempts by Tenant to sublet the Premises in whole or in part or to sell, assign, lien, encumber, or in any manner transfer this Lease or any interest therein shall constitute a default hereunder, as shall any attempt by Tenant to assign or delegate the management or to permit the use or occupancy of the Premises or any part hereof by anyone other than Tenant. Landlord and Tenant acknowledge and agree that the foregoing provisions have been freely negotiated by the parties hereto and that Landlord would not have entered into this Lease without Tenant's consent to the terms of this Section 12.01. Any attempt by Tenant to sublet all or any portion of the Premises, to encumber same, or to in any manner transfer, convey, assign Tenant's interest therein, allow the use or management thereof, shall be void ab initio.

SECTION 12.02. Change of Control.

In furtherance of the provisions of Section 12.01 hereof, if Tenant is a corporation and if the person or persons who own a majority of its voting shares at the time of the execution hereof cease to own a majority of such shares at any time hereafter, except as a result of transfers by gift, bequest, or inheritance by or among immediate family members, Tenant shall so notify Landlord. In the event of such change of ownership, whether or not Tenant has notified Landlord thereof, Landlord may terminate this Lease by notice to Tenant effective sixty (60) days from the date of such notice from Tenant, or the date on which Landlord first has knowledge of such transfer, whichever shall first occur. This Section 12.02 shall not apply as long as Tenant is a corporation, the outstanding voting stock of which is listed on a recognized security exchange. If Tenant is a partnership and if any partner or partners withdraw from the partnership, or if the partnership is otherwise dissolved, Tenant shall so notify Landlord. In the event of such withdrawal or dissolution, Landlord may terminate this Lease by notice to Tenant effective sixty (60) days from the date of notification from Tenant or the date on which Landlord first has knowledge of such withdrawal or dissolution, whichever shall first occur. If Tenant is a sole proprietorship, in the event of his incapacity or death, Landlord shall have the option to terminate this Lease upon sixty (60) days' prior written notice to Tenant or his legal representative.

SECTION 12.03. Dissolution of Partnership.

If Tenant is a partnership and if any partner or partners withdraw from the partnership, or if the partnership is otherwise dissolved, or control of the partnership changes, Tenant shall so notify Landlord. In the event of such withdrawal or dissolution, Landlord may terminate this Lease by notice to Tenant effective ninety (90) days from the date of such notice from Tenant or the date on which Landlord first has knowledge of such withdrawal or dissolution, whichever shall first occur.

ARTICLE XIII. Right of Entry

SECTION 13.01. Right of Entry.

Landlord or Landlord's agents shall have the right to enter the Premises at all times to examine the same, and to show them to prospective purchasers or tenants of the building or Shopping Center, and to make such repairs, alterations, improvements, or additions as Landlord may elect to make, and Landlord shall be allowed to take all material into and upon the Premises that may be required therefor without the same constituting an eviction of Tenant in whole or in part, and the rent reserved shall in no wise abate while said repairs, alterations, improvements, or additions are being made, by reason of loss or interruption of business of Tenant, or otherwise. During the six months prior to the expiration of the Lease Term or any renewal term, Landlord may exhibit the Premises to prospective tenants or purchasers, and place upon the Premises the usual notices "To Let" or "For Sale," which notices Tenant shall permit to remain thereon without molestation.

ARTICLE XIV. Tenant's Property

SECTION 14.01. Taxes.

Tenant shall be responsible for and shall pay before delinquency all municipal, county, or state taxes, levies, and fees of every kind and nature, including, but not limited to, general or special assessments assessed during the term of this Lease against any personal property of any kind, owned by, or placed in, upon, or about the Premises by the Tenant and taxes assessed on the basis of Tenant's occupancy thereof, including, but not limited to, taxes measured by Rents due from Tenant hereunder.

SECTION 14.02. Notices by Tenant.

Tenant shall give immediate telephone or telegraphic notice to Landlord in case of fire, casualty, or accidents in the Premises or in the building of which the Premises are a part or of defects therein or in any fixtures or equipment and shall promptly thereafter confirm such notice in writing.

ARTICLE XV. Succession to Landlord's Interest

SECTION 15.01. Attornment.

Tenant shall attorn and be bound to any of Landlord's successors under all the terms, covenants, and conditions of this Lease for the balance of the remaining term.

SECTION 15.02. Subordination.

This Lease shall be subordinate to the lien of any mortgage or security deed or the lien resulting from any other method of financing or refinancing now or hereafter in force against the Shopping Center, any portion thereof, or upon any buildings hereafter placed upon the land of which the Premises are a part, and to any and all advances to be made under such mortgages, and all renewals, modifications, extensions, consolidations, and replacements thereof. The aforesaid provisions shall be self-operative, and no further instrument of subordination shall be required to evidence such subordination. Tenant covenants and agrees to execute and deliver, upon demand, such further instrument or instruments subordinating this Lease on the foregoing basis to the lien of any such mortgage or mortgages as shall be desired by Landlord and any mortgagees or proposed mortgagees, and hereby irrevocably appoints Landlord the attorney-in-fact of Tenant to execute and deliver such instrument or instruments within ten (10) days after written notice to do so.

SECTION 15.03. Mortgagee's Approval.

If any mortgagee of the Shopping Center requires any modification of the terms and provisions of this Lease as a condition to such financing as Landlord may desire, then Landlord shall have the right to cancel this Lease if Tenant fails or refuses to approve and execute such modification(s) within thirty (30) days after Landlord's request therefor, provided said request is made prior to the Commencement Date. Upon such cancellation by Landlord, this Lease shall be null and void and neither party shall have any liability either for damages or otherwise to the other by reason of such cancellation. In no event, however, shall Tenant be required to agree, and Landlord shall not have any right of cancellation for Tenant's refusal to agree, to any modification of the provisions of this Lease relating to: the amount of rent or other charges reserved herein; the size and/or location of the Premises; the duration and/or Commencement Date of the term; or the reduction of the improvements to be made by Landlord to the Premises prior to delivery of possession.

SECTION 15.04. Estoppel Certificate.

Within ten (10) days after request therefor by Landlord, or in the event that upon any sale, assignment, or hypothecation of the Premises and/or the land thereunder by Landlord, an estoppel certificate shall be required from Tenant. Tenant agrees to deliver, in recordable form, a certificate to any proposed mortgagee or purchaser, or to Landlord, certifying that this Lease is unmodified and in full force and effect (or, if there have been modifications, that the same is in full force and effect as modified, and stating the modifications), that there are no defenses or offsets thereto (or stating those claimed by Tenant), and the dates to which Fixed Minimum Rent, Percentage Rent, and other charges have been paid.

ARTICLE XVI. Surrender of Premises

SECTION 16.01. Condition on Surrender.
At the expiration or earlier termination of this Lease, Tenant shall surrender the Premises to Landlord broom clean and in the same condition as when tendered by Landlord, reasonable wear and tear and insured casualty excepted. Tenant shall promptly repair any damage to the Premises caused by the removal of any furniture, trade fixtures, or other personal property placed in the Premises.

SECTION 16.02. Holding Over.
Should Tenant, with Landlord's written consent, hold over at the end of the term, Tenant shall become a Tenant at will, and any such holding over shall not constitute an extension of this Lease. During such holding over, Tenant shall pay rent and other charges at the highest monthly rate provided for herein. If Tenant holds over at the end of the term without Landlord's written consent, Tenant shall pay Landlord as liquidated damages a sum equal to twice the rent to be paid by Tenant to Landlord for all the time Tenant shall so retain possession of the Premises; provided that the exercise of Landlord's rights under this clause shall not be interpreted as a grant of permission to Tenant to continue in possession.

ARTICLE XVII. Miscellaneous

SECTION 17.01. Waiver.
The waiver by Landlord of any breach of any term, covenant, or condition herein contained shall not be deemed to be a waiver of such term, covenant, or condition or any subsequent breach of the same or any other term, covenant, or condition herein contained. The subsequent acceptance of rent hereunder by Landlord shall not be deemed to be a waiver of any preceding breach by Tenant of any term, covenant, or condition of this Lease, other than the failure of Tenant to pay the particular rental so accepted, regardless of Landlord's knowledge of such preceding breach at the time of acceptance of such rent. No covenant, term, or condition of this Lease shall be deemed to have been waived by Landlord, unless such waiver be in writing by Landlord.

SECTION 17.02. Accord and Satisfaction.
No payment by Tenant or receipt by Landlord of a lesser amount than the monthly rent herein stipulated shall be deemed to be other than on account of the earliest stipulated rent, nor shall any endorsement or statement on any check or any letter accompanying any check or payment as rent be deemed an accord and satisfaction, and Landlord may accept such check or payment without prejudice to Landlord's right to recover the balance of such rent or pursue any other remedy in this Lease provided.

SECTION 17.03. Entire Agreement.
This Lease and the Exhibits and Rider, if any, attached hereto and forming a part hereof, set forth all the covenants, promises, agreements, conditions, and understandings between Landlord and Tenant concerning the Premises, and there are no covenants, promises, agreements, conditions, or understandings, either oral or written, between them other than as are herein set forth. Except as herein otherwise provided, no subsequent alteration, amendment, change, or addition to this Lease shall be binding upon Landlord or Tenant unless reduced to writing and signed by them.

SECTION 17.04. No Partnership.
Landlord does not, in any way or for any purpose, become a partner of Tenant in the conduct of its business, or otherwise, or joint venturer

or a member of a joint enterprise with Tenant. The provisions of this Lease relating to the Percentage Rent payable hereunder are included solely for the purpose of providing a method whereby the rent is to be measured and ascertained.

SECTION 17.05. Force Majeure.
If either party shall be delayed or hindered in or prevented from the performance of any act required hereunder by reason of strikes, lockouts, labor troubles, inability to procure material, failure of power, restrictive governmental laws or regulations, riots, insurrection, war, or other reason of a like nature beyond the reasonable control of a party (but not for the inability to meet its monetary obligations hereunder), the period for the performance of any such act shall be extended for a period equivalent to the period of such delay.

SECTION 17.06. Notices.
Any notice, demand, request, or other instrument which may be or are required to be given under this Lease shall be delivered personally or sent by either United States certified mail postage prepaid or expedited mail service and shall be addressed (a) if to Landlord at the address provided in Section 1.01 for Landlord or at such other address as Landlord may designate by written notice and (b) if to Tenant at the address provided in Section 1.01 for Tenant or at such other address as Tenant shall designate by written notice. Notices shall be effective upon delivery unless delivery is refused or cannot be made, in which event notice shall be effective on mailing.

SECTION 17.07. Captions and Section Numbers.
The captions, section numbers, article numbers, and index appearing in this Lease are inserted only as a matter of convenience and in no way define, limit, construe, or describe the scope or intent of such section or articles of this Lease nor in any way affect this Lease.

SECTION 17.08. Tenant Defined, Use of Pronoun.
The word "Tenant" shall be deemed and taken to mean each and every person or party mentioned as a Tenant herein, be the same one or more; and if there shall be more than one Tenant, any notice required or permitted by the terms of this Lease may be given by or to any one thereof, and shall have the same force and effect as if given by or to all thereof. The use of the neuter singular pronoun to refer to Landlord or Tenant shall be deemed a proper reference even though Landlord or Tenant may be an individual, a corporation, or a group of two or more individuals or corporations. The necessary grammatical changes required to make the provisions of this Lease apply in the plural sense where there is more than one Landlord or Tenant and to either corporations, associations, partnerships, or individuals, males or females, shall in all instances be assumed as though in each case fully expressed.

SECTION 17.09. Broker's Commission.
Tenant warrants that it has had no dealings with any broker or agent in connection with this Lease, except as designated in Section 1.01, and covenants to pay, hold harmless, and indemnify Landlord from and against any and all cost, expense, or liability for any compensation, commissions, and charges claimed by any broker or agent with respect to this Lease or the negotiation thereof.

SECTION 17.10. Partial Invalidity.
If any term, covenant, or condition of this Lease or the application thereof to any person or circumstance shall, to any extent, be invalid or unenforceable, the remainder of this Lease, or the application of such term, covenant, or condition to persons or circumstances other than those as to which it is held invalid or unenforceable, shall not be affected thereby, and each term, covenant, or condition of this Lease shall be valid and be enforced to the fullest extent permitted by law.

SECTION 17.11. Execution of Lease.
The submission of this Lease for examination does not constitute a reservation of or option for the Premises, and this Lease becomes effective as a Lease only upon execution and delivery thereof by Landlord and Tenant. If Tenant is a corporation, Tenant shall furnish Landlord

with such evidence as Landlord reasonably requires to evidence the binding effect on Tenant of the execution and delivery of this Lease.

SECTION 17.12. Recording.
Tenant agrees not to record this Lease. However, Tenant and Landlord, upon request of either, agree to execute and deliver a memorandum or so-called "short form" of this Lease in recordable form for the purpose of recordation at Tenant's expense. Said memorandum or short form of this Lease shall describe the parties, the Premises, and the Lease Term and shall incorporate this Lease by reference.

SECTION 17.13. Applicable Law.
The Laws of the State of _____ shall govern the validity, performance, and enforcement of this Lease.

SECTION 17.14. Rider.
A rider consisting of _____ pages, with sections numbered consecutively _____ through _____, is attached hereto and made a part hereof.

SECTION 17.15. Time Is of the Essence.
Time is of the essence of this Agreement.

SECTION 17.16. Successors and Assigns.
Except as otherwise provided herein, this Lease shall be binding upon and inure to the benefit of the parties hereto and their respective heirs, personal representatives, executors, successors, and assigns.

SECTION 17.17. Survival of Obligations.
The provisions of this Lease with respect to any obligation of Tenant to pay any sum owing in order to perform any act after the expiration or other termination of this Lease shall survive the expiration or other termination of this Lease.

SECTION 17.18. Counterclaim and Jury Trial.
In the event that the Landlord commences any summary proceedings or action for nonpayment of rent or other charges provided for in this Lease, Tenant shall not interpose any counterclaim of any nature or description in any such proceeding or action. Tenant and Landlord both waive a trial by jury of any or all issues arising in any action or proceeding between the parties hereto or their successors, under or connected with this Lease, or any of its provisions.

SECTION 17.19. Representations.
Tenant acknowledges that neither Landlord nor Landlord's agents, employees, or contractors have made any representations or promises with respect to the Premises, the Shopping Center, or this Lease except as expressly set forth herein.

SECTION 17.20. Landlord's Liability.
Except for warranties of Landlord under Sections 2.01 and 7.06, in the event of any alleged default of Landlord, Tenant shall not seek to secure any claim for damages or indemnification by any attachment, levy, judgment, garnishment, or other security proceedings against any property of the Landlord other than Landlord's equity in the Shopping Center. Landlord, as used herein, shall include any assignee or other successor of the original Landlord or its successors or assigns.

IN WITNESS WHEREOF, the parties hereto have executed this Lease this day and year first above written.

LANDLORD:

_____

_____ By: _____
Witness

TENANT:

_____

_____ By: _____
Witness

AGENT:

_____

_____ By: _____
Witness

International Council of Shopping Centers
Publications
665 Fifth Avenue
New York, NY 10022-5370
ISBN: 0-927547-36-8

This form is not to be construed as an ICSC-recommended form for use in a shopping center.

Source: *Shopping Center Study Lease* (New York: International Council of Shopping Centers, 1994). Reprinted with permission.

Appendix 2
Sample Bylaws of Merchants' Association

This form is a sample of typical bylaws of a shopping center merchants' association that can be used when incorporating a new association. It must be adapted to the laws of the state of incorporation.

Bylaws of
XYZ Shopping Center
Merchants' Association, Inc.

ARTICLE I. Membership

SECTION 1. Election.
There shall be two (2) classes of membership in this Corporation, as follows: Active Members and Associate Members.

(a) Only an individual, partnership, company, or corporation operating a business or practicing a profession in _____ and the owners or lessees of real property therein shall be eligible to be Active Members.

(b) Any individual, partnership, company, or corporation making application to be an Associate Member in this Corporation, and who or which in the opinion of the majority of the Board of Directors shall have a legitimate interest in the purposes and objectives of this Corporation, as set forth in the Articles of Incorporation, and who or which shall be otherwise worthy of membership, shall be elected an Associate Member if such application shall be approved by a majority of the Board of Directors. Associate Members shall be entitled only to such notices, if any, of meetings or otherwise, as these Bylaws shall from time to time prescribe that such members shall receive, and shall at no time have any right to vote at any meetings of this Corporation.

SECTION 2. Annual Meeting.
The annual meeting of the members of the Corporation shall be held at such date, hour, and place as may be designated by the Board of Directors for the election of Directors and for the transaction of any and all business authorized or required to be transacted by the members.

SECTION 3. Special Meetings.
Except as otherwise specifically provided by statute, special meetings of the members of the Corporation may be called at any time by the President or by a majority of the Board of Directors. Upon request in writing by members holding a majority of the votes of the Active Members entitled to vote at such meeting, delivered to the President, or Secretary, it shall be the duty of the President or Secretary to call forthwith a meeting of the members. if the person to whom such request in writing shall have been delivered shall fail to issue a call for such meeting within thirty (30) days after the receipt of such request, then Active Members constituting a majority of the votes of the Active Members entitled to vote at such meeting may do so by giving the notice prescribed in Section 5 of this Article I.

SECTION 4. Notice of Annual Meeting.
Notice of the annual meeting shall be given by mailing the same, not less than ten (10) and not more than fifty (50) days prior to the date of the meeting, to each person, firm, or corporation shown by the books of the Corporation, on the record date for determining membership, to be a member entitled to vote at such meeting, at his or its address as shown by the books of the Corporation, or by any other mode prescribed or authorized by statute law. At any annual meeting action may be taken upon any subject which is not by law required to be stated in the notice of meeting, and in addition thereto, upon any special subject which might be acted upon at a special meeting called for the purpose, when, in the last mentioned case, the purpose to consider and act upon such special subject is stated in the notice of such annual meeting; and if the meeting is to act on an amendment of the articles of incorporation or on a plan of merger or consolidation, notice shall be given not less than twenty-five (25) nor more than fifty (50) days before the date of the meeting, and such notice shall be accompanied by a copy of the proposed amendment or plan of merger or consolidation or a summary thereof, and any such notice which is published shall state that copies of the proposed articles of amendment or plan of merger or consolidation will be supplied to members on request.

SECTION 5. Notice of Special Meeting.
Notice of all special meetings of the members shall be given by mailing the same, not less than ten (10) and not more than thirty (30) days prior to the date of the meeting, to each person, firm, or corporation shown by the books of the Corporation, on the record date for determining membership, to be a member entitled to vote at such meeting, at his or its address as shown by the books of the Corporation, or by any other mode prescribed or authorized by statute law. Such notice shall state the time, place, and purposes of the meeting. If the special meeting shall be called to act on an amendment of the articles of incorporation or on a plan of merger or consolidation, notice shall be given not less than twenty-five (25) nor more than fifty (50) days before the date of the meeting, and such notice shall be accompanied by a copy of the proposed amendment or plan of merger or consolidation or a summary thereof, and any such notice which is published shall state that copies of the proposed articles of amendment or plan of merger or consolidation will be supplied to members on request.

SECTION 6. Quorum.
At any meeting of the members, a quorum necessary to conduct the business thereof shall be Lessor, and representatives of at least 40% of the Active Members. In the absence of a quorum, the members present in person or by proxy at any meeting (or adjournment thereof) may by vote of a majority of the Active Members so present adjourn the meeting from time to time without further notice until a quorum shall attend. At any such adjourned meeting at which a quorum shall be present, any business may be transacted which might have been transacted at the meeting as originally notified.

SECTION 7. Order of Business.
The order of business at all meetings of the members, unless changed by the Chairman of the meeting, shall be as follows:

(1) Reading of Call (if any) and Proof of Notice.
(2) Ascertainment of Quorum and voting privileges of meeting attendees.
(3) Reading of Minutes of last meeting and action thereon (may be waived by majority vote).
(4) Reports of Officers.
(5) Reports of Committees.
(6) Election of Directors (at annual meetings only).
(7) Unfinished Business.
(8) New Business.

SECTION 8. Unanimous Consent in Lieu of Meeting.
Any action required or permitted to be taken at a meeting of the members may be taken without a meeting, if a consent in writing, setting

forth the action so taken, shall be signed by all of the members entitled to vote with respect thereto.

SECTION 9. Resignation and Removal.

No member of the Corporation may resign without a compelling cause except in the manner provided for in a written contract or lease between the Lessor and such resigning member. Said resignation, if permitted, shall be in writing addressed to the Board of Directors, but shall not relieve such resigning member from any past, current, and/or future obligations as the same may be provided for in the written contract or lease between Lessor and said resigning member. Any member of the Corporation may be removed by the affirmative vote of at least three-fourths (3/4) of the Board of Directors of the Corporation, with or without cause, and such action shall be conclusive on the member so removed; such removal, however, shall not relieve the party removed from any current or future indebtedness to the Corporation. Neither Lessor nor any other permanent member of the Board of Directors, as named in Article II, Section 1, of these Bylaws may be removed from membership in the Corporation as an Active Member possessing the voting rights and privileges set forth in these Bylaws, so long as the Lessor or such other permanent member continues to make all payments of dues in the amount or manner required in contracts between Lessor and such other permanent member, and fulfills other obligations promulgated by lease or prior agreement.

ARTICLE II. Board of Directors

SECTION 1. Duties and Election.

The business and affairs of the Corporation, except as otherwise provided by statute, by the articles of incorporation, or by these Bylaws shall be conducted and managed by its Board of Directors, the members of which shall be Active Members or representatives of Active Members in good standing and not delinquent in the payment of dues and assessments and the elected members of which shall be determined at each annual meeting of the members of the Corporation. The Board of Directors shall be composed in the following manner:

(a) Permanent Directors: one Director representing each anchor department store adjoining the Shopping Center, one Director representing the Lessor, and in the event any additional anchor or department stores shall be erected within the Shopping Center complex, one Director representing each of such additional anchor stores;

(b) Elected Directors: six additional Directors elected by the Active Membership at each annual meeting, and each Director so elected shall hold office until the annual meeting held next after his or her election and until his successor has been duly chosen and qualified, or until he or she shall resign or shall have been removed. Regardless of any other provision of these Bylaws, this Section 1 of Article II may be amended only by three-fourths (3/4) of all votes of the Active Members of the Association together with unanimous consent of all Active Members entitled to designate Permanent Directors. The total number of directors shall remain at 13, including Permanent Directors. As anchors are added or subtracted from the shopping center, an elected director position shall be subtracted or added to maintain 13 directors. The Board of Directors shall keep minutes of its meetings and a full account of its transactions. The term of office of any Director who shall either resign or be removed from Active Membership in the Association shall automatically terminate upon such resignation or removal and the vacancy thereby created shall be filled in accordance with Section 13 of this Article II. All Board Members except for Lessor shall be regularly employed or occupied in subject Shopping Center.

SECTION 2. Regular Meetings.

Regular meetings of the Board of Directors shall be held as soon as practicable after every annual meeting of the members of the Corporation, and thereafter on such dates as may be fixed from time to time by resolution of the Board.

SECTION 3. Special Meetings.

Special meetings of the Board of Directors shall be held whenever called by the President or by a majority of the Board, either in writing or by vote.

SECTION 4. Place of Meetings.

The Board of Directors may hold its regular and special meetings at such place or places as it may from time to time determine. In the absence of any such determination, regular and special meetings of the Board shall be held at the principal office of the Corporation.

SECTION 5. Notice of Meetings.

Notice of the place, day, and hour of every regular and special or adjourned meeting shall be given to each Director at least three (3) business days before the meeting by delivering the same to him or her personally or by sending the same to him or her by using commercial or facsimile telephone delivery service, or by leaving the same at his or her residence or usual place of business, or by mailing such notice, postage prepaid, to be delivered at least four (4) days prior to the meeting, addressed to him to his last known post office address, as shown by the records of the Corporation. It shall not be requisite to the validity of any meeting of the Board of Directors that notice thereof shall have been given to any Director who attends such meeting, or who, if absent, waives notice thereof, in writing, filed with the records of the meeting either before or after the holding thereof.

SECTION 6. Quorum.

A majority of the number of Directors in office, including a majority of the Permanent Directors, one of whom must be the Lessor, shall constitute a quorum for the transaction of business at any meeting of the Board of Directors, but if at any meeting there be less than a quorum present, a majority of those present may adjourn the meeting from time to time, without further notice until a quorum shall attend. At any meeting at which a quorum shall be present, the act of the majority of the Directors present shall be the act of the Board of Directors.

SECTION 7. Order of Business.

The Board of Directors may from time to time determine the order of business at their meetings. The usual order of business at such meetings shall be as follows:

(1) Roll Call, and determination that a quorum is present.

(2) Reading of Minutes of preceding meeting and action thereon (may be waived by majority vote).

(3) Reports of Officers.

(4) Reports of Committees.

(5) Unfinished Business.

(6) New Business.

SECTION 8. Chairman.

The President shall preside at all meetings of the Board of Directors; in his or her absence, the Board of Directors shall designate a Director to serve.

SECTION 9. Unanimous Consent in Lieu of Meeting.

Any action required by law or which may be taken at a meeting of the Directors may be taken without a meeting, if a consent in writing, setting forth the action so to be taken, shall be signed before such action by all of the Directors.

SECTION 10. Rules and Regulations.

The Board shall have power from time to time to make and enforce such rules and regulations not inconsistent with contractual agreements or leases between Lessor and other members in order to carry out the objectives of the Association. The stated objectives of the Association shall be limited to marketing and promoting the Shopping Center and its tenants in order to enhance business and encourage patronage of the merchants within the Shopping Center.

SECTION 11. Compensation.

Directors and members of any committee of the Corporation contemplated by these Bylaws or otherwise provided for by resolution of the

Board of Directors shall not receive any compensation for services rendered as such Directors.

SECTION 12. Delinquency and Suspension.

Any elected member of the Board of Directors who is absent from three (3) consecutive Directors' meetings or whose principal is delinquent in the payment of dues or assessments to the Association may be removed by the Board of Directors. If an elected Director is removed, his or her position shall be filled for the remainder of the term in accordance with Section 13 of this Article II. Any permanent member which is delinquent in the payment of dues or assessments to the Association for thirty (30) days after written notice thereof shall be suspended until all delinquencies in the payment of dues and assessments have been cured. The Secretary of the Corporation shall give notice by registered or certified mail to any elected Board member who has missed two (2) consecutive meetings that he or she will be subject to removal by Board action as a Director if he or she is not present at the next meeting, and a copy of such notice shall be filed with the minutes of the Directors' meeting next following such mailing.

SECTION 13. Vacancies.

In the event a vacancy in the Board of Directors (not involving the Permanent Directors) occurs by reason of death, resignation, or removal, or increase of not more than two (2) in the number of Directors, or any other cause, such vacancy shall be filled by the majority vote of the Board of Directors voting thereon at a special or regular meeting. The successor Director so elected shall hold office for the unexpired term until the next succeeding annual meeting of members of the Corporation, and until the successors to the Directors are duly elected and qualified. Vacancies of any Permanent Director shall be filled by appointment of the member such Director represents.

ARTICLE III. Officers

SECTION 1. Executive Officers.

The executive officers of the Corporation shall be a President, Vice President, Secretary, and Treasurer, and such other officer or subordinate officers that shall, from time to time, be designated and appointed by the Board of Directors. The Executive Officers shall be selected from among the membership of the Board of Directors. Officers shall be elected by the Directors at their first regular meeting after the annual meeting of members, and each shall hold office until the regular meeting of Directors following the next annual meeting of the members and until his or her successor is duly elected and qualified or until his or her death, resignation, or removal. The Board of Directors may prescribe the duties of all officers and employees of the Corporation, subject to the provisions of law and of these Bylaws, and may delegate to the President or to other officers authority to appoint and dismiss clerks, agents, and employees and to prescribe their duties. Any two (2) or more offices may be held by the same person, except the offices of President and Secretary, President and Vice President, or President and Treasurer. The Directors shall have the power at any regular or special meeting to remove any officer, and such action shall be conclusive on the officer so removed.

SECTION 2. Duties.

(a) President: The President shall preside over all meetings of the Association and the Board of Directors.

(b) Vice President: In the absence or disability of the President, the Vice President selected for the purpose by the Board of Directors shall perform all the duties of the President, and when so acting, shall have all the powers of the President. The Vice President shall have such additional powers and duties as from time to time may be assigned by the Board of Directors.

(c) Secretary: The Secretary shall keep the minutes of the meetings of members and the Board of Directors and shall record same in books kept for that purpose; he or she shall see that all notices are fully given in accordance with provisions of the Bylaws or as required by law; shall be the custodian of the corporate records and of the seal of the Corporation; shall see that the corporate seal is affixed to all documents, the execution of which on behalf of the Corporation under its seal is duly authorized, and when so affixed, may attest the same; shall prepare and keep on file at the principal office of the Corporation a record of the names and addresses of its members entitled to vote; shall in general perform all duties ordinarily incident to the office of secretary subject to the directions and control of the Board of Directors; and such other duties as from time to time may be assigned to him or her by the Board of Directors or by the President.

(d) Treasurer: The Treasurer shall perform all of the duties ordinarily incident to that office. He or she shall be responsible for all monies, funds, and securities of the Corporation, and shall be charged with the duty of keeping accurate records of all financial transactions of the Corporation and of corporate investments. He or she shall report to the Board of Directors, at least quarterly and at such other times as requested by the Board of Directors, the financial condition of the Corporation. He or she shall be charged with the duty of filing all corporate tax returns and reports to supervisory governmental agencies and shall, in general, be the officer primarily charged with the administration of the financial affairs of the Corporation.

SECTION 3. Vacancies.

A vacancy occurring in any office shall be filled by the Board of Directors for the unexpired portion of the term.

ARTICLE IV. Sundry Provisions

SECTION 1. Seal.

The seal of the Corporation shall be circular in form with the name of the Corporation inscribed around the outer edge, and in the center shall be inscribed the words "Corporate Seal of _____" and the year of incorporation, and the President, the Vice President, and the Secretary shall have the authority to affix the corporate seal to instruments and documents requiring such seal and attest the same.

SECTION 2. Bonds.

The Board of Directors may require any officer, agent, or employee of the Corporation to give a bond to the Corporation for the faithful discharge of his or her duties, in such amount, on such condition, and with such sureties as may be required by the Board.

SECTION 3. Amendments.

(a) The power to alter, amend, or repeal the Bylaws or adopt new Bylaws shall be vested in the Members of the Corporation by two-thirds (2/3) vote and the recommendation of the Board of Directors.

(b) Members may adopt Bylaws and may alter, amend, or repeal Bylaws made by the Board of Directors and by the members.

(c) No amendment of these Bylaws or additions thereto may, however, alter or affect the provisions of these Bylaws relating to the Lessor and any department stores now or hereafter at the Shopping Center, or any additional department stores, and the rights and privileges granted them, without the express written consent of each of such parties so long as each such party is an Active Member in good standing of the Association. Except as otherwise provided herein, all amendments to the Bylaws adopted by the members shall require a vote of two-thirds (2/3) of the number of votes entitled to be cast.

SECTION 4. Notice.

Any notice required to be given by these Bylaws may be given by mailing the same addressed to each person, firm, or corporation entitled thereto at his or its address as shown on the Corporation's books, and such notice shall be deemed to be given at the time of such mailing.

SECTION 5. Waiver of Notice.

Whenever any notice is required to be given to any member or Director of this Corporation of any meeting for any purpose for which a meeting may be called, a waiver thereof in writing signed by the person, firm, or corporation entitled to such notice, whether signed before or after such meeting, shall be equivalent to the giving of such notice. A member or Director who attends a meeting shall be deemed to have had timely and proper notice of the meeting, unless he or she attends for the express purpose of objecting to the transaction of any business because the meeting is not lawfully called or convened.

ARTICLE V. Dues

SECTION 1. Dues.
The Board shall have power to charge dues and assessments to its members for the cost of its activities, including reasonable overhead charges, provided, however, that the amount of such dues and assessments shall be consistent with existing contractual agreements or leases between Lessor and other members of the Corporation, and the provisions of such contractual agreements for payment of dues and assessments to the Corporation shall be construed as third-party beneficiary contracts for the benefit of the Corporation. No action may be taken by the Corporation to adopt a schedule of dues and assessments less than that provided by the contracts or leases between Lessor and the other members, but action may be taken to increase same as provided by such contracts or leases, and any increase must be approved by a majority vote of members and must be in accordance with procedures stipulated in leases or contracts between Lessor and tenants.

ARTICLE VI. Merchants' Association–Sponsored Programs

SECTION 1. Advertising.
A schedule of merchandising, sales promotion, special events, advertising, and/or any other marketing program will be prepared by the designated marketing representative of the Association to be approved or modified by a majority vote of the Board of Directors. All tenants are obligated to participate actively in merchandising events by advertising in center-sponsored merchant participatory advertising, which publicizes the promotion using the amount of space or broadcast time specified in their respective leases. Failure to do so will cause the Association to bill for the cost of such advertising, which shall be due by the tenant as monetary obligation and be subject to any provision in these Bylaws pertaining to arrearage of dues.

SECTION 2. Special Events.
The Board shall encourage members to support and when possible participate in Association events intended to increase traffic into the shopping center.

SECTION 3. Limitation.
Certificates of Membership are evidence of membership in _____ and do not confer or otherwise grant any rights or privileges not otherwise provided for in the articles of incorporation or these Bylaws.

Source: *Library of Shopping Center Marketing Forms* (New York: International Council of Shopping Centers, 1992). Reprinted with permission.

Bibliography

Books

Alexander, Alan A., and Richard F. Muhlebach. *Shopping Center Management.* Chicago: Institute of Real Estate Management, 1992.

Benjamin, John D., ed. *Megatrends in Retail Real Estate.* Norwell, MA: Kluwer Academic Publishers, 1996.

International Council of Shopping Centers. *Entertainment and Retail.* New York: ICSC, 1998.

——. *Entertainment in Shopping Centers: A Compendium of ICSC Information Sources.* New York: ICSC, 1996.

——. *Essential Factors in Shopping Center Leasing.* New York: ICSC, 1992.

——. *Food Court Handbook.* New York: ICSC, 1995.

——. *Guide to Operating Shopping Centers the Smart Way.* New York: ICSC, 1996.

——. *Guide to Renovating and Expanding Shopping Centers the Smart Way.* New York: ICSC, 1996.

——. *Security & Safety: Issues and Ideas for Shopping Center Professionals.* New York: ICSC, 1995.

——. *Shopping Center Niche Marketing.* New York: ICSC, 1994.

——. *Temporary Tenant Handbook.* New York: ICSC, 1994.

ULI–the Urban Land Institute. *Developing Power Centers.* Washington, DC: ULI–the Urban Land Institute, 1996.

——. *Developing Urban Entertainment Centers.* Washington, DC: ULI–the Urban Land Institute, 1998.

——. *Parking Requirements for Shopping Centers: Summary Recommendations and Research Study Report.* Washington, DC: ULI–the Urban Land Institute, 1999.

——. *Remaking the Shopping Center.* Washington, DC: ULI–the Urban Land Institute, 1994.

——. *The Retailing Revolution: Impact of Nonstore Retailing on Shopping Centers.* Washington, DC: ULI–the Urban Land Institute, 1997.

——. *Standard Manual of Accounting for Shopping Center Operations.* Washington, DC: ULI–the Urban Land Institute, 1971.

Value Retail News. *The Art and Science of Outlet and Off-Price Retailing and Development.* St. Petersburg, FL: Off-Price Specialists, 1992.

Vernor, James D., and Joseph Rabianski. *Shopping Center Appraisal and Analysis.* Chicago: Appraisal Institute, 1993.

White, John R., and Kevin D. Gray, eds. *Shopping Centers and Other Retail Properties.* Somerset, NJ: John Wiley & Sons, 1996.

Zimmerman, Bruce G. *Shopping Center DealMaker's Handbook.* Laguna Beach, CA: Business Source Publishing Co., 1993.

Periodic Surveys/Directories

Canadian Directory of Shopping Centres. Maclean Hunter Ltd., 777 Bay Street, 5th Floor, Toronto, Ontario, Canada M5W 1A7; Phone: (416) 596-5000; Fax: (416) 593-3166.

Census of Retail Trade. Customer Services, Bureau of the Census, Washington, DC 20233; Phone: (202) 763-4100; Fax: (202) 763-4794.

Combined Financial, Merchandising, and Operating Results of Retail Stores: 1998 Edition. National Retail Federation, 325 7th Street, N.W., Suite 1100, Washington, DC 20004; Phone: (202) 783-7971; Fax (202) 737-2849.

Directory of Leading Chain Stores in the United States. Business Guides, Inc., 3922 Coconut Palm Drive, Tampa, FL 33619-8321; Phone: (813) 664-6700; Fax: (813) 664-6888.

Directory of Major Malls. MJJTM Publishing Corporation, P.O. Box 1708, Spring Valley, NY 10977; Phone; (914) 426-0040; Fax: (914) 426-0802.

Directory of Shopping Centers. National Research Bureau, Inc., 45 Danbury Road, Wilton, CT 06897; Phone: (800) 456-4555; Fax: (203) 563-3131.

Dollars & Cents of Convenience Centers: 1997. Special Report. ULI–the Urban Land Institute, 1025 Thomas Jefferson Street, N.W., Suite 500W, Washington, DC 20007-5201; Phone: (202) 624-7000 or (800) 321-5011; Fax: (202) 624-7140.

Dollars & Cents of Downtown/Intown Shopping Centers: 1997. Special Report. ULI–the Urban Land Institute, 1025 Thomas Jefferson Street, N.W., Suite 500W, Washington, DC 20007-5201; Phone: (202) 624-7000 or (800) 321-5011; Fax: (202) 624-7140.

Dollars & Cents of Power Centers: 1997. Special Report. ULI–the Urban Land Institute, 1025 Thomas Jefferson Street, N.W., Suite 500W, Washington, DC 20007-5201; Phone: (202) 624-7000 or (800) 321-5011; Fax: (202) 624-7140.

Dollars & Cents of Renovated/Expanded Shopping Centers: 1997. Special Report. ULI–the Urban Land Institute, 1025 Thomas Jefferson Street, N.W., Suite 500W, Washington, DC 20007-5201; Phone: (202) 624-7000 or (800) 321-5011; Fax: (202) 624-7140.

Dollars & Cents of Shopping Centers in the Top 20 Metropolitan Areas: 1997. ULI–the Urban Land Institute, 1025 Thomas Jefferson Street, N.W., Suite 500W, Washington, DC 20007-5201; Phone: (202) 624-7000 or (800) 321-5011; Fax: (202) 624-7140.

Dollars & Cents of Small Town/Nonmetropolitan Shopping Centers: 1997. ULI–the Urban Land Institute, 1025 Thomas Jefferson Street, N.W., Suite 500W, Washington, DC 20007-5201; Phone: (202) 624-7000 or (800) 321-5011; Fax: (202) 624-7140.

ICSC Membership Directory, 1999. International Council of Shopping Centers, 665 Fifth Avenue, New York, NY 10022; Phone: (212) 421-8181; Fax: (212) 486-0849.

Income/Expense Analysis: Shopping Centers. 1998 Edition. Institute of Real Estate Management, 430 North Michigan Avenue, Chicago, IL 60611; Phone: (312) 329-6000; Fax: (312) 329-6039.

"National Research Bureau Shopping Center Census." *Shopping Centers Today.* International Council of Shopping Centers, 665 Fifth Avenue, New York, NY 10022; Phone: (212) 421-8181; Fax: (212) 486-0849.

Off-Price Retail Directory. Value Retail News, 29399 U.S. Highway 19 North, Suite 370, Clearwater, FL 33763; Phone: (727) 781-7557; Fax: (727) 781-9717.

Outlet Project Directory. Value Retail News, 29399 U.S. Highway 19 North, Suite 370, Clearwater, FL 33763; Phone: (727) 781-7557; Fax: (727) 781-9717.

Outlet Retail Directory. International Council of Shopping Centers, 665 Fifth Avenue, New York, NY 10022; Phone: (212) 421-8181; Fax: (212) 421-6464.

SCORE: ICSC's Handbook on Shopping Center Operations, Revenues & Expenses. 1999. International Council of Shopping Centers, 665 Fifth Avenue, New York, NY 10022; Phone: (212) 421-8181; Fax: (212) 421-6464.

"Survey of Buying Power." *Sales & Marketing Management,* 355 Park Avenue South, New York, NY 10010; Phone: (212) 592-6300; Fax: (212) 592-6309.

ULI InfoPackets. ULI–the Urban Land Institute, 1025 Thomas Jefferson Street, N.W., Suite 500W, Washington, DC 20007-5201; Phone: (202) 624-7000 or (800) 321-5011; Fax: (202) 624-7140.

ULI Market Profiles. ULI–the Urban Land Institute, 1025 Thomas Jefferson Street, N.W., Suite 500W, Washington, DC 20007-5201; Phone: (202) 624-7000 or (800) 321-5011; Fax: (202) 624-7140.

Periodicals

The Appraisal Journal. Appraisal Institute, 875 North Michigan Avenue, Suite 2400, Chicago, IL 60611-1980; Phone: (312) 335-4100; Fax: (312) 335-4400.

Carlsonreport. Carlsonreport Inc., P.O. Box 502830, Indianapolis, IN 46250-7830; Phone: (317) 576-9889 or (800) 546-9889; Fax: (317) 546-0441.

Chain Store Age Executive. Lebhar-Friedman, Inc., 425 Park Avenue, New York, NY 10022; Phone; (212) 756-5252; Fax: (212) 756-5270.

Convenience Store News. 355 Park Avenue South, New York, NY 10010; Phone: (212) 979-4860; Fax: (212) 979-7431.

Discount Merchandiser. Schwartz Publications, 355 Park Avenue South, New York, NY 10010; Phone: (212) 592-6200; Fax: (212) 592-6616.

Discount Store News. Lebhar-Friedman, Inc., 425 Park Avenue, New York, NY 10022; Phone: (212) 756-5100; Fax: (212) 756-5125.

ICSC Research Bulletin. International Council of Shopping Centers, 665 Fifth Avenue, New York, NY 10022; Phone: (212) 421-8181; Fax: (212) 486-0849.

Insider. Trade Dimensions, 45 Danbury Road, Wilton, CT 06897; Phone: (203) 563-3045 or (800) 456-4555.

Jonesreport. Jones Report for Shopping, P.O. Box 502830, Indianapolis, IN 46250-7830; Phone: (800) 546-9889; Fax: (317) 576-0441.

Journal of Retailing. JAI Press, P.O. Box 811, Greenwich, CT 06830; Phone: (203) 323-9606; Fax: (203) 357-8446.

National Real Estate Investor. Communication Channels, Inc., 6151 Powers Ferry Road, N.W., Atlanta, GA 30339-2914; Phone: (770) 955-2500.

Project Reference File. ULI–the Urban Land Institute, 1025 Thomas Jefferson Street, N.W., Suite 500W, Washington, DC 20007-5201; Phone: (202) 624-7000 or (800) 321-5011; Fax: (202) 624-7140.

Shopping Center Business. France Publications, Inc., Two Securities Center, 3500 Piedmont Road, Suite 415, Atlanta, GA 30305; Phone: (770) 952-4300; Fax: (770) 952-2010.

Shopping Center Digest. Jomurpa Publishing Inc., 20 North Broadway, P.O. Box 837, Nyack, NY 10960; Phone: (914) 348-7000 or (800) 211-6858; Fax: (914) 348-7011.

Shopping Center Directions. National Research Bureau, 150 North Wacker Drive, Suite 2222, Chicago, IL 60606; Phone: (312) 541-0100; Fax: (312) 541-1492.

Shopping Center World. Communication Channels, Inc., 6151 Powers Ferry Road, Atlanta, GA 30339-2914; Phone: (770) 955-2500; Fax: (770) 955-0400.

Shopping Centers Today. International Council of Shopping Centers, 665 Fifth Avenue, New York, NY 10022; (212) 421-8181; Fax: (212) 486-0849.

Stores. National Retail Federation, 325 Seventh Street, N.W., Suite 1000, Washington, DC 20004; Phone: (202) 626-8101; Fax: (202) 626-8191.

Urban Land. ULI–the Urban Land Institute, 1025 Thomas Jefferson Street, N.W., Suite 500W, Washington, DC 20007-5201; Phone: (202) 624-7000 or (800) 321-5011; Fax: (202) 624-7140.

Value Retail News. 29399 U.S. Highway 19 North, Suite 370, Clearwater, FL 33763; Phone: (727) 781-7557; Fax: (727) 781-9717.

Organizations

Food Marketing Institute
800 Connecticut Avenue, N.W., Suite 400
Washington, DC 20006-2701
Phone: (202) 452-8444; Fax: (202) 429-4519
www.fmi.org

Institute of Real Estate Management
430 North Michigan Avenue
Chicago, IL 60611
Phone: (312) 329-6000; Fax: (312) 329-6039
www.irem.org

International Council of Shopping Centers
665 Fifth Avenue
New York, NY 10022
Phone: (212) 421-8181; Fax: (212) 421-6464
www.icsc.org

International Mass Retail Association
1700 North Moore Street, Suite 2250
Arlington, VA 22209
Phone: (703) 841-2300; Fax: (703) 841-1184
www.imra.org

National Association of Convenience Stores
1605 King Street
Alexandria, VA 22314-2792
Phone: (703) 684-3600; Fax (703) 836-4564
www.cstorecentral.com

National Research Bureau
150 North Wacker Drive, Suite 2222
Chicago, IL 60606
Phone: (312) 541-0100; Fax: (312) 541-1492

National Restaurant Association
1200 17th Street, N.W.
Washington, DC 20036
Phone: (202) 331-5900; Fax: (202) 331-2429
www.restaurant.org

National Retail Federation
325 7th Street, N.W., Suite 1000
Washington, DC 20004
Phone: (202) 626-8101; Fax: (202) 626-8191
www.nrf.com

ULI–the Urban Land Institute
1025 Thomas Jefferson Street, N.W., Suite 500W
Washington, DC 20007-5201
Phone: (202) 624-7000 or (800) 321-5011; Fax: (202) 624-7140
www.uli.org

Value Retail News
29399 U.S. Highway 19 North, Suite 370
Clearwater, FL 33763
Phone: (727) 781-7557; Fax: (727) 781-9717

Index

Minimalls, 28, 353
Miniperms, 80, 89
Mission District (San Francisco, California), 157
Mitsubishi Estates real estate company, 216
Mitsui (developer), 216
Mitsuoshi stores, 217
Mixed-use projects: in Asia, 215, *215;* and downtown retailing, 19–20; evolution of, 32; and feasibility studies, *56;* and future trends, 343, *350,* 351; leases for, 201, *201,* 203; and parking, 107–8, 109; and planning and design, 107–8, 109, 123; and redevelopment, *151;* and type of center, 17, 19–20; and type of tenants, 192–93. *See also specific project or topic*
Mizner Park (Boca Raton, Florida), *38,* 198
Mobil Land Development Corporation, *21*
Montgomery Ward, 25, 296, 299
Mortgages, 80, 89, 90, 149–50
Moscone Convention Center (San Francisco, California), 352, *352*
Movie theaters. *See* Cinema complexes; *specific theater*
Muji stores, 217
Multilevel centers, 64, 102, 131–33, *132*
Munkacy, Kenneth, 217
Myanmar stores, 214

■

NASCAR Cafe, 345
NASCAR Silicon Motor Speedway, 276
Nashville, Tennssee, 346
Nathan's, 288, *290*
Natick Mall (Framingham, Massachusetts), *185*
National Association of Real Estate Investment Trusts (NAREIT), 79
National Car Rental Center Arena (Sunrise, Florida), 358
National Check Cashers Associations, 191
National Environmental Policy Act, 89
National Hockey League, 18
National Place (Washington, D.C.), 344
National Realty & Development Corp., 191
National Research Bureau, 3, 8, 79
National Retail Federation (NRF), 162
National Skills Standards Board, 162
National Trust for Historic Preservations, 157
Naturally Untamed, 369
Nature Company, 23
Nautica, 267
NC Print & Copy Shop, 288, 294
NCS/London House, 162
Neely, Esme, 125
Negligence, 206
Neighborhood shopping centers: design in, 24; evolution of, 28; and future trends, 348, *350,* 354, 360; leases for, *197,* 199; location of, 61–62; number of, 348; operation and management of, 218, 219; ownership of, 3, 4; as type of center, 8, 12–13. *See also specific center or topic*
Neiman Marcus, 70, 174, 180, 296, 332, 333, 334, 340
Nelson, Richard L., 43
Neonopolis (Las Vegas, Nevada), *70, 218*
New Community Corporation (NCC), 288–95
New Community Extended-Care Facility, 289
New Community Neighborhood Bakery, 288, *290,* 291
New Community Neighborhood Shopping Center (Newark, New Jersey), **229, 288–95,** *289, 290, 291, 292, 293,* 357

New England Development Group, *82*
New Jersey Attorney General, 290
New Jersey Department of Community Affairs, 291
New Jersey Department of Transportation, 290
New Jersey Housing Mortgage Finance Agency, 290, 291
New Large-Scale Store Law (Japan, 1998), 214
New Plan Realty Trust, 79
New York Life Insurance Company, 246
New York, Westchester & Boston Railroad terminal (White Plains, New York), 335
Newhall Land and Farming Company, *190*
News Cafe, *146*
Niche markets, 4, 34, 343, 353–54, 366
Nichols, J.C., 26
Night lighting, 127, *127*
Nighttime entertainment centers, 346
Nike/NikeTown, 15, *81,* 135, 202, 252, *255,* 267, 302, 309, 345, 370
Nomura real estate company, 216
Nondisturbance agreements, 211
Nonresponsibility notices, 205
Nonretail tenants, 101–2, 146, 196, 224. *See also* Outparcels; *type of tenant*
Nordstrom, 15, 22, 26, *161,* 162, 172, *172,* 180, 232, 296, *99,* 332, 333, 340, 352, 358, 366
Norm Thompson, 302, 304, *304,* 309
North Michigan Avenue (Chicago, Illinois), 19–20
North Point Market Center (Alpharetta: Georgia), *134*
Northgate (Seattle, Washington), 26
Northshore Mall (Boston, Massachusetts), *82*
Northwestern Mutual Life, 242
Notices: and leases, 212

■

Oak Park Mall (Overland Park: Kansas), *161*
Oasis (Sawgrass Mills, Sunrise, Florida), 358
The O'Connor Group, 333, 335–36, 341
Off Fifth, 15, 267
Off-price retailing: design of, 24; and future trends, 348, 351, 353, 354, 361, 368; number of centers for, 348; as tenants, 181; as type of center, 14, 15. *See also* Discount retailing; *specific center or topic*
Office Depot, 135
Office Max, 135, 184
Office of Thrift Supervision (OTS), 76, 77
Offices: in mixed-use projects, 192–93; and parking, 107–8, *109;* and planning and design, 107–8, *109;* as type of tenant, 188–89, 192–93
Ogden Corporation, 369
Oglethorpe Mall (Savannah, Georgia), *26*
O'Hara, Donald, 113
Oilily, 335
Old Navy clothing store, 282, 320, 356, 370
Old Orchard Center (Skokie, Illinois), 151, **229, 296–301,** *297, 298, 299, 300,* 354
Oldenburg, Ray, 237
O'My Sole, 276
One Colorado (Pasadena, California), *49, 159*
Ontario Mills (Los Angeles, California), 15, *187*
Operating costs: and landscapeing, 121; and planning and design, 96–97, 138; and redevelopment, 143, 149, 163; tenant contributions to, 143, 201–4
Operating records, 144–45
Operating statements, 56, **58,** 86

Operation and management: in Asia, **214–17;** and leases, 195–213, 218–19; and management contracts, 218; and marketing and promotions, 221–27, *222;* most important responsibility of, 213; ongoing, 213–21; and planning and design, 139; steps in, 213; of successful center, 213–21; and type of tenants, 179. *See also* Marketing and promotion
Oral agreements, 212
Orange County, California, 272, 276
Oregon Market, 302, *303,* 304, 305
Oshman's Sporting Goods, 135, 217
Outcalt, Richard, 364
Outlet shopping centers: in Asia, 214; in Europe, **181;** and future trends, 345, 351, 353, 365, 368, 370; in Japan, 216; RVs at, *183;* as type of center, 14, *15. See also specific center or topic*
Outparcels, 105, *158*
Overnighters Association (OA) (Punta Gorda, Florida), 183
Owens, J'Amy, 357–58
Ownership, 3, 34, 67–68, 78, 141, 181. *See also specific center or owner*

■

Pacific Bell Park (San Francisco, California), 347
Pacific Development Partners, 104
Pacific Linen, 239
Pacific Place (Seattle, Washington), *96, 129, 355*
Palliser, Sarah, 154
Palm restaurant, 30
Parisian store, 232, *233*
Park Meadows (Denver, Colorado), 22, **22**
Parking: and accessibility, 112, *112;* in Canada, 108–9; and car size, 110; and cinema complexes, 98, 109, *109;* commuter, 115; construction of, 113–14, 116; and definition of center, 6, 7; for employees, 114–15, *114,* 212, *212;* and entrances, *114,* 116; expenses for, *201;* and feasibility studies, 54, 64–65; and future trends, 368; garage, *107,* 116, *120;* handicapped, 113; and landscaping, 105, 113–14, *113,* 120, *120;* layout for, 111; and leases, 114, 212, *212;* and lighting, 108, *113,* 127, 154; maintenance of, 114; and operation and management, 218, 219–20; patterns for, 112–13; and planning and design, 00, 97, 98, 100, 101, *101,* 105–17, *106,* 127; and redevelopment, 107, **108,** 145, 146, 147, *148,* 150, 154, 155–58; and safety, 108, 117, 158; shared, 109–10; and site planning, 105; stalls for, 113; standards and demands for, 7, 106–9; structures, 108, 116–17, 158; and taxes, 115–16; and tenant mix, 106, 110–11; and transit, 115; and type of center, 16; and type of tenants, 108, *170,* 188, 193; underground, 158. *See also type of center or specific center*
Parking area ratio, 106
Parking index, 54, 106
Paskewitz, Don, 105
Pathmark Stores, Inc., 288, 289, *289,* 290–91, *291,* 292, 294, 356
Pattaya Central Festival Center (Bangkok, Thailand), *2*
Pavilions (Denver, Colorado), 344
Pedestrian flow. *See* Circulation
El Pedregal (Scottsdale, Arizona), *17*
Penn Station (New York City), 305
Pennsylvania: commonwealth of, 162